P9-CAP-794

PSYCHOLOGY 95/96

Twenty-Fifth Edition

Editor

Karen G. Duffy
SUNY College, Geneseo

Karen G. Duffy holds a doctorate in psychology from Michigan State University and is currently a professor of psychology at SUNY at Geneseo. She sits on the executive board of the New York State Employees Assistance Program and is a certified community and family mediator. She is a member of the American Psychological Society and the Eastern Psychological Association.

A Library of Information from the Public Press

Cover illustration by Mike Eagle

The Dushkin Publishing Group, Inc.
Sluice Dock, Guilford, Connecticut 06437

The Annual Editions Series

Annual Editions is a series of over 65 volumes designed to provide the reader with convenient, low-cost access to a wide range of current, carefully selected articles from some of the most important magazines, newspapers, and journals published today. Annual Editions are updated on an annual basis through a continuous monitoring of over 300 periodical sources. All Annual Editions have a number of features designed to make them particularly useful, including topic guides, annotated tables of contents, unit overviews, and indexes. For the teacher using Annual Editions in the classroom, an Instructor's Resource Guide with test questions is available for each volume.

VOLUMES AVAILABLE

Africa
Aging
American Foreign Policy
American Government
American History, Pre-Civil War
American History, Post-Civil War
Anthropology
Archaeology
Biology
Biopsychology
Business Ethics
Canadian Politics
Child Growth and Development
China
Comparative Politics
Computers in Education
Computers in Business
Computers in Society
Criminal Justice
Developing World
Drugs, Society, and Behavior
Dying, Death, and Bereavement
Early Childhood Education
Economics
Educating Exceptional Children
Education
Educational Psychology
Environment
Geography
Global Issues
Health
Human Development
Human Resources
Human Sexuality
India and South Asia

International Business
Japan and the Pacific Rim
Latin America
Life Management
Macroeconomics
Management
Marketing
Marriage and Family
Mass Media
Microeconomics
Middle East and the Islamic World
Money and Banking
Multicultural Education
Nutrition
Personal Growth and Behavior
Physical Anthropology
Psychology
Public Administration
Race and Ethnic Relations
Russia, the Eurasian Republics, and Central/Eastern Europe
Social Problems
Sociology
State and Local Government
Urban Society
Violence and Terrorism
Western Civilization, Pre-Reformation
Western Civilization, Post-Reformation
Western Europe
World History, Pre-Modern
World History, Modern
World Politics

Cataloging in Publication Data
Main entry under title: Annual Editions: Psychology. 1995/96.
    1. Psychology—Periodicals. I. Duffy, Karen G., comp. II. Title: Psychology.
ISBN 1–56134–368–4   150′.5   79–180263
BF 149.A58

Twenty-Fifth Edition

Manufactured in the United States of America

Printed on Recycled Paper

To the Reader

In publishing ANNUAL EDITIONS we recognize the enormous role played by the magazines, newspapers, and journals of the *public press* in providing current, first-rate educational information in a broad spectrum of interest areas. Within the articles, the best scientists, practitioners, researchers, and commentators draw issues into new perspective as accepted theories and viewpoints are called into account by new events, recent discoveries change old facts, and fresh debate breaks out over important controversies.

Many of the articles resulting from this enormous editorial effort are appropriate for students, researchers, and professionals seeking accurate, current material to help bridge the gap between principles and theories and the real world. These articles, however, become more useful for study when those of lasting value are carefully *collected, organized, indexed,* and *reproduced* in a *low-cost format,* which provides easy and permanent access when the material is needed. That is the role played by *Annual Editions.* Under the direction of each volume's *Editor,* who is an expert in the subject area, and with the guidance of an *Advisory Board,* we seek each year to provide in each *ANNUAL EDITION* a current, well-balanced, carefully selected collection of the best of the public press for your study and enjoyment. We think you'll find this volume useful, and we hope you'll take a moment to let us know what you think.

Ronnie's parents could not understand why he did not want to be picked up and cuddled as did his older sister when she was a baby. As an infant, Ronnie did not respond to his parents' smiles, words, or attempts to amuse him. By the age of two, Ronnie's parents knew that he was not like other children. He spoke no English, was very temperamental, and often rocked himself for hours. Ronnie is autistic. His parents feel that some of Ronnie's behavior may be their fault; they both work long hours as young professionals and leave both children with an older woman during weekdays. Ronnie's pediatrician assures his parents that their reasoning, while logical, probably holds no merit because the causes of autism are little understood. What can we do about children like Ronnie? From where does autism come? Can autism be treated or reversed? Can autism be prevented?

Psychologists attempt to answer these and other questions in a specific way, with scientific methods. Researchers, using carefully planned methods, try to discover the answers to the complexities of human behavior, normal or not. The scientific results of most psychological research are published in professional journals and therefore may be difficult for the lay person to understand.

Annual Editions: Psychology 95/96 is designed to meet the needs of lay people and introductory level students who are curious about psychology. This annual edition provides a vast selection of readable and informative articles from popular magazines and newspapers. These articles are written primarily by journalists, but a few are written by psychologists with writing styles that are clear yet retain the excitement of the discovery of scientific knowledge.

The particular articles selected for this volume were chosen to be representative of current work in psychology. They were selected because they are accurate in their reporting and provide examples of the types of psychological research discussed in most introductory psychology classes. As in any science, some of the findings discussed in this collection are startling, while others will confirm what we already suspect. Some will invite speculation about social and personal ramifications; others will demand careful thought about potential misuse of the applications of research findings. You will be expected to make the investment of effort and critical judgment needed to answer such questions and concerns.

I assume that you will find this collection of articles readable and useful. I suggest that you look at the organization of this book and compare it to the organization of your textbook and course syllabus. By examining the *topic guide* provided after the *table of contents,* you can identify those articles most appropriate for any particular unit of study in your course. Your instructor may provide some help in this effort. As you read the articles, try to connect their contents with the principles you are learning from your text and classroom lectures. Some of the articles will help you better understand a specific area of research, while others are designed to help you connect and integrate information from various research areas. Both of these strategies are important in learning about psychology or any other science; it is only through intensive investigation and subsequent integration of the findings of many scientists that we are able to discover and apply new knowledge.

Please take time to provide us with some feedback to guide the annual revision of this anthology by completing and returning the article rating form in the back of the book. With your help, this collection will be even better next year. Thank you.

Karen Grover Duffy
Editor

Contents

Unit 1

The Science of Psychology

Three articles examine psychology as the science of behavior.

Unit 2

Biological Bases of Behavior

Five selections discuss the biological bases of behavior. Topics include brain functions and the brain's control over the body.

The concepts in bold italics are developed in the article. For further expansion please refer to the Topic Guide, the Index, and the Glossary.

Unit 3

Perceptual Processes

Five articles discuss the impact of the senses on
human perceptual processes.

The concepts in bold italics are developed in the article. For further expansion please refer to the Topic Guide, the Index, and the Glossary.

Unit 4

Learning and Remembering

Three selections examine how operant conditioning, positive reinforcement, and memory interact during the learning process.

Unit 5

Cognitive Processes

Five articles examine how social skills, common sense, and intelligence affect human cognitive processes.

The concepts in bold italics are developed in the article. For further expansion please refer to the Topic Guide, the Index, and the Glossary.

Unit 6

Emotion and Motivation

Five articles discuss the influences of stress, mental states, and emotion on the mental and physical health of the individual.

Unit 7

Development

Six articles consider the importance of experience, discipline, familial support, and physiological aging during the normal human development process.

The concepts in bold italics are developed in the article. For further expansion please refer to the Topic Guide, the Index, and the Glossary.

Unit 8

Personality Processes

Four selections discuss a few of the processes by which personalities are developed. Topics include sex differences, state of mind, and cynicism.

Social Processes

Three selections discuss how the individual's social development is affected by genes, stereotypes, prejudice, and self-help.

Psychological Disorders

Five articles examine several psychological disorders. Topics include unexpected behavior, the impact of depression on a person's well-being, and schizophrenia.

The concepts in bold italics are developed in the article. For further expansion please refer to the Topic Guide, the Index, and the Glossary.

Unit 11

Psychological Treatments

Three selections discuss a few psychological treatments, including psychoanalysis, psychotherapy to alleviate depression, and self-care.

The concepts in bold italics are developed in the article. For further expansion please refer to the Topic Guide, the Index, and the Glossary.

Topic Guide

This topic guide suggests how the selections in this book relate to topics of traditional concern to psychology students and professionals. It is useful for locating articles that relate to each other for reading and research. The guide is arranged alphabetically according to topic. Articles may, of course, treat topics that do not appear in the topic guide. In turn, entries in the topic guide do not necessarily constitute a comprehensive listing of all the contents of each selection.

TOPIC AREA	TREATED IN:	TOPIC AREA	TREATED IN:
Audition	10. Good Vibrations	**ESP (Extrasensory Perception)**	13. Does ESP Exist?
Behaviorism	14. Measured Learning	**Families**	31. Current Perspectives on Dual-Career Families
Brain	7. Human Mind 8. Mind and Brain 18. Visualizing the Mind 20. Return of Phineas Gage	**Freud, Sigmund**	33. Assault on Freud
Child Abuse	16. Memories Lost and Found 28. Child Injury and Abuse-Neglect	**Genes/Genetics**	4. Nature or Nurture? 5. Born Gay? 6. Eugenics Revisited 41. Divided Selves
Children	17. Child's Theory of Mind 27. How Kids Benefit from Child Care 28. Child Injury and Abuse-Neglect 29. Schools Must Tell Girls: 'You're Smart' 30. Teaching Young Children to Resist Bias	**History of Psychology**	1. Scientific and Professional Psychology 2. Has Psychology a Future?
Cognition	17. Child's Theory of Mind 19. Rethinking the Mind	**Homosexuality**	5. Born Gay?
Competition	26. How Competitive Are You?	**Hostility**	36. Is Hostility Killing You?
Conditioning	14. Measured Learning	**Language**	21. Silence, Signs, and Wonder
Culture/Society	37. Dynamics of Social Dilemmas	**Learning**	14. Measured Learning 15. How Kids Learn
Depression	42. Defeating Depression	**Love**	39. Lessons of Love
Disease/Illness	44. Immune System vs. Stress 47. Critical Life Events	**Memory**	16. Memories Lost and Found
Domestic Violence	43. Patterns of Abuse	**Mental Disorder/ Mental Illness**	40. Is Mental Illness a Myth? 41. Divided Selves 42. Defeating Depression
Eating	25. Chemistry and Craving	**Middle Age**	32. Midlife Myths
Education	15. How Kids Learn 29. Schools Must Tell Girls: 'You're Smart'	**Mind**	7. Human Mind 8. Mind and Brain 18. Visualizing the Mind
		Moods	24. How to Master Your Moods
Emotions	22. Where Emotions Come From	**Nature/Nurture**	4. Nature or Nurture? 5. Born Gay?

TOPIC AREA	TREATED IN:	TOPIC AREA	TREATED IN:
Noise	10. Good Vibrations	**Sensation/ Perception**	9. Vision Thing 10. Good Vibrations 11. Sniff of Legend 12. Touching the Phantom
Odor/Olfaction	11. Sniff of Legend		
Optimism	35. On the Power of Positive Thinking	**Sex Roles/Sex Differences**	4. Nature or Nurture? 29. Schools Must Tell Girls: 'You're Smart'
Personality	34. Piecing Together Personality		
Phantom Limbs	12. Touching the Phantom	**Stress**	44. Immune System vs. Stress 46. Outsmarting Stress 47. Critical Life Events
Polygraph	23. Doubtful Device		
Prejudice	30. Teaching Young Children to Resist Bias	**Television**	38. Media, Violence, Youth, and Society
Reinforcement	14. Measured Learning	**Therapy**	45. What You Can Change
Research Design	3. Pollsters Enlist Psychologists	**Violence**	38. Media, Violence, Youth, and Society
Schizophrenia	41. Divided Selves	**Vision**	9. Vision Thing
Self-Control	47. Critical Life Events		

The Science of Psychology

Little did Wilhelm Wundt realize his monumental contribution to science when in 1879 in Germany, he opened the first psychological laboratory to examine consciousness. Today Wundt would barely recognize the science of psychology as he knew it.

Contemporary psychology is defined as the science or study of individual mental activity and behavior. This definition reflects the two parent disciplines from which psychology emerged: philosophy and biology.

Compared to its parents, psychology is very much a new discipline. Some aspects of modern psychology are particularly biological, such as neuroscience, sensation and perception, and behavioral genetics. Other aspects are more philosophical, such as the study of personality.

Today's psychologists work in a variety of settings. Many psychologists are academics, teaching and researching psychology on university campuses. Others work in applied settings such as hospitals, mental health clinics, industry, and schools. Most psychologists also specialize in psychology after some graduate training. Industrial psychologists specialize in human performance in organizational settings, while clinical psychologists are concerned about the assessment, diagnosis, and treatment of individuals with a variety of mental disorders.

Some psychologists think that psychology is still in its adolescence and that the field seems to be experiencing some growing pains. Since its establishment, the field has expanded to many different areas. As already noted, some areas are very applied. Other areas appear to emphasize theory and research. The growing pains have resulted in some conflict over what the agenda of the first national psychological association, the American Psychological Association, should be. Because academics perceived this association as mainly serving practitioners, the academics established their own competing association, the American Psychological Society. Despite its varied nature and the so-called growing pains, psychology remains a viable and exciting field. The first unit of the book is designed to introduce you to the nature and history of psychology.

In the first article, "Scientific and Professional Psychology," Nathaniel Pallone provides an excellent overview of the discipline, both its scientific aspects and its practice. He also provides some discussion of the problems with the field, such as the split between academics and practitioners and the development of two national parallel organizations.

In the next article, noted psychologist Eleanor Gibson examines the present and future of psychology. Psychologists have long been in search of a single overarching theory that explains all human thought and behavior. Gibson encourages psychologists not to give up but to begin examining psychological processes from a systems perspective.

In our final unit selection, a few of the research aspects of psychology are explored. Surveys are one form of data collection utilized by psychologists. By means of surveys, experiments and other research techniques, psychologists come to better understand human behavior. "Pollsters Enlist Psychologists in Quest for Unbiased Results" elaborates upon how psychologists share their vast research knowledge to facilitate the design of better surveys.

Looking Ahead: Challenge Questions

Do you think that the emergence of applied areas in psychology (such as clinical psychology) has hurt or advanced scientific psychology?

Which area of psychology do you think is the most valuable and why? About which area of psychology is the public most aware? About which other areas of psychology do you think the public ought to be informed? What trends shaped psychology as we know it today? How might psychology be related to other disciplines on your campus?

Do you think psychologists will ever be able to piece together a single grand theory of human behavior? Why might an organism-environment systems explanation of behavior be good? Why does Eleanor Gibson think the nature-nurture controversy is outmoded?

Why is research important to psychology? What kinds of information can be gleaned from surveys? What types of problems are inherent in poorly designed surveys? How can psychology improve surveys?

Scientific and Professional Psychology

Nathaniel J. Pallone

Nathaniel J. Pallone is University Distinguished Professor of Psychology and Criminal Justice at Rutgers—The State University of New Jersey. He is editor of the highly specialized Journal of Offender Rehabilitation *and senior editor of the generalist* Current Psychology *(Transaction Periodicals Consortium). His latest book (with James J. Hennessy) is* Criminal Behavior: A Process Psychology Analysis, *published by Transaction.*

Over the course of *Society's* three decades of life, the number of psychologists in the nation has approximately quadrupled. By 1990, membership in the American Psychological Association, the discipline's principal national organization, reached 120,000. By way of contrast, in the same year the membership of the American Dental Association stood at 130,000. Some wags suggested that the nation had reached the point at which it considered its mental health very nearly as important as its dental health.

The numbers alone might suggest a thriving and healthy enterprise. But the numbers mislead, for American psychology is perhaps more fractionated today than at any time in its 125 year history as an independent discipline. That fractionation, which may be related to the sheer size of the enterprise, cuts the discipline along two axes: vertically, separating the scientist from the practitioner, and, horizontally, separating scientists from each other and practitioners from each other. A common core of knowledge and body of interests are so difficult to discern in 1992 that psychology may not be recognizable as a unitary discipline by the time *Society* celebrates its sixtieth birthday.

Scientists versus Practitioners

Fragmentation along the "vertical" axis is more obvious and has occurred in a more public arena. For example, five years ago a rival national organization, the American Psychological Society, was formed by disaffected members of APA. The new society's heroic slogan well recapitulates the sources of the rift: "To develop scientific knowledge in psychology and to give it away in the public interest."

The two phrases tell the story. First, the founders of APS confessed themselves disaffected because, in their view, the central thrust in APA had congealed around the practice of psychology as a profession rather than around the development of psychology as a science. Second, it followed as night follows day that the interests of practitioners lie in "selling" their products (whether knowledge or service), rather than in giving anything away.

The rift reveals deep divisions between what might be called the "academic" psychologists, those who hold university appointments (and who, some will argue, can therefore afford high-minded principles, like *scientia gratia scientiae* and "the public interest" and can commit themselves to what appears to be the "giving away" of the products of their labor), and the practitioner whose livelihood depends upon collecting fees-for-service. Those variant emphases are reflected in the contents of the principal publications of the two organizations, with APA's *American Psychologist* increasingly concerned with the "business" of psychological practice and with APS's *Psychological Science* (published for the Society by no less than the Cambridge University Press) pursuing (more or less) a holier-than-thou high road.

Horizontal Fragmentation

In some quite large degree, that rather public rift masks the loosening of bonds between members of the scientific community and between members of the professional community that are equally threatening to psychology's sense of itself as a unitary discipline. Consider, as a case in point, the scientific interests that drive the research activity of three of my close colleagues, all members of the same department. Each

 From *Society*, November/December 1992, pp. 64-69.

would identify himself with the "scientist" rather than the "practitioner" camp, with respect to the variables and the subjects they study, and the investigative techniques they employ.

One is a distinguished psychopharmacologist concerned with the metabolism of certain neuro-transmitting fluids in the brains of laboratory animals and the effects of these substances on their behavior. When last I saw him, he was wearing the typical long, white lab coat (long an emblem that distinguishes "hard" from "soft" scientists), splattered with blood. He and his assistants had just finished decapitating a colony of rats and were about to autopsy their brains to determine at what sites the substances they were investigating had "bound." His focal interests and methods of inquiry have considerably more in common with those of biological and biomedical scientists than with many of his departmental colleagues.

The second is equally distinguished in the study of patterns of psychosocial development among adults whose marriages have remained intact vs. those whose marriages have dissolved. His research "laboratory" is the living room or the den of the subjects in his studies, and the emblems of his "soft" science are a clipboard and an interview schedule. His interests and methods of inquiry have considerably more in common with those of sociologists than with those of his departmental colleagues who are concerned with animal behavior or with the neurophysiology of human behavior.

The third, also quite distinguished in research on the sources and consequences of stress, is presently investigating the behavior of professional golfers. His research apparatus includes devices that measure such physiological correlates of stress as electrodermal activity and peripheral skin temperature and the arc and force of a player's swing, along with videotape equipment capable of recording finely discriminated movements. His laboratory had earlier been an on-campus analogue to a tee-ing green. Thanks to electronic miniaturization that has yielded remote transmitting devices, his laboratory has become portable, so that he can study his subjects *in vivo*. His interests and methods of inquiry have much in common with those of investigators in orthopedic medicine and applied physics.

Among professional psychologists, the lines of demarcation include both subjects and methods, but it is important to add purpose as a differentiating dimension. By far the largest cadre, clinicians are typically engaged in assessing and evaluating adults and children (in schools, hospitals, community mental health centers, and in private practice), with discernible mental or emotional problems. Their goal (though perhaps expressed in varying and sometimes wistful terms, like "self-actualization"), is the betterment of the individual. In contrast, personnel and organizational psychologists employ many of the same techniques, that is, largely variants of measurement and interviewing, but their goal is the betterment of the organization, whether a business, manufacturing, or industrial enterprise.

At another extreme in their methodology are the human factors engineers who study the sequential steps through which an individual worker progresses in order to accomplish a particular task, with the intent of altering those steps (often by redesigning machinery, work environments, or, in today's world, computer systems) in the direction of greater efficiency and productivity. But the purpose again is the welfare of the organization rather than that of the individual.

Such remarkable diversity might seem to indicate a thriving and healthy enterprise. But when we consider the varying frames of reference that guide such diverse activity, the unifying skeins that ought to mark a unitary discipline are difficult to discern.

The lines of demarcarcation among professional psychologists include method and subjects as well as purpose.

Academic programs for advanced degrees in personnel, industrial, and organizational psychology are increasingly offered in graduate schools of management rather than in departments of psychology. Clinical and school psychology programs are offered in "professional schools" independent of graduate departments of psychology. The day-to-day experience of practitioners, or of the academics who train them, might inevitably make for stronger identification with those who share the same "intellectual space."

Among personnel, organizational, and human factors psychologists, promotion pathways are likely to lead to problems of management and into the management function itself. For the academic who trains clinicians, the community of interests may be stronger with faculty in psychiatry and in social work than with departmental colleagues who study planaria. The psychopharmacologist of our sample might identify with other psychopharmacologists and with toxicologists and neurologists rather than with social psychologists who study the antecedents to divorce versus longevity in marriage or the clinicians who intervene in interpersonal conflicts between spouses.

1. THE SCIENCE OF PSYCHOLOGY

"Professional School" Phenomenon

The net result appears to be growing insularity in psychology. Both the scientist and the professional tend to adopt not the discipline but their sub-specialty as a frame of reference. Barely a dozen of the nearly 500 psychological journals published in this country are aimed at the generalist while the others appeal frankly to the specialist and the sub-specialist, often within quite a constricted range (for example, publications with titles such as the *Journal of Post-Adlerian Psychology* or of *Phenomenological Psychology* or *Psychosocial Oncology* or *Offender Rehabilitation* or *BioBehavioral Research*).

More than half the doctorates in psychology were earned outside graduate psychology programs.

As disquieting as all these developments may be, however, the chief index to fragmentation along the scientist versus professional axis without question is the development during the past twenty-five years of professional schools of applied psychology that are independent of universities. These institutions award a degree of Doctor of Psychology (PsyD), frankly labeled a "practitioner's degree." They customarily operate in rented space, have no or inadequate library or computer facilities, rely heavily on part-time instruction provided after-hours by faculty who maintain full-time practices, and usually enroll primarily (or even exclusively) part-time students.

Prototypically, such institutions were born of the chagrin of activist members of state psychological associations. These are notoriously dominated by practitioners who are frequently hostile toward the academic institutions in their areas for all manner of mendacious reasons. That they came into being at the very time that once similarly independent schools of law and of medicine were voluntarily joining established universities itself speaks volumes about insularity. Some professional schools of applied psychology have followed that lead. But, as the founding dean of the Graduate School of Applied and Professional Psychology at Rutgers has observed, only one such institution is affiliated with what the National Research Council labels a "comprehensive research university."

In such institutions, of course, faculty and students operate outside an academic environment marked by a mix of disciplines with variant focal interests, methods of inquiry, and purposes and that provides the opportunity for rich intellectual cross-fertilization. They are also tend to be isolated from the scientific specialties within the discipline of psychology itself. As a result, the academic programs offered are insular and highly specialized, so that students customarily have no chance to study at the graduate level in a specialty or subspecialty other than their own.

When this writer began graduate study some thirty-five years ago, it was typically not possible for a graduate student to specify a major within the discipline until the second year of post-baccalaureate study, at the earliest. In effect, all students earned a master's degree in general, rather than in specialized, psychology, whatever their career plans. That we now award the PsyD degree to students who are innocent of formal instruction in the specialties and subspecialties of scientific psychology beyond the undergraduate level is frightening. Whatever else it may connote, a degree should signify that its recipient has mastered a body of knowledge in scientific psychology, along with the techniques, procedures, gimmicks, and bag-of-tricks through which that knowledge is "applied." Yet the curriculum in the independent school, born to be sure of its self-imposed insularity, moves precisely at cross-purpose.

But more frightening still is the fact, reported at a recent meeting of the directors of doctoral programs in professional psychology, that since 1990 more than half the doctorates granted annually in psychology were earned outside psychology programs in graduate schools of arts and sciences. Instead, they were earned in independent schools of professional psychology (inside and outside universities), in graduate schools of education, in graduate schools of management. With the burgeoning of the latter (and the addition of psychologists to the faculties of schools of social work, medicine, law, and criminal justice) and a steady-state, if not decline, in more traditional psychology departments, we may even be at the dawn of an era in which more academic psychologists will be appointed outside psychology units in universities than within them.

Knowledge and Marketplace

The knowledge explosion of the last thirty or so years that has produced what neuropsychiatrist Joseph Coyle of Johns Hopkins University has termed "a major paradigm shift" in the understanding of human behavior and its engines. By 1992, the availability of highly sophisticated devices for imaging brain activity through CAT, MRI, and BEAM scans had produced such a wealth of information about the interaction between brain functioning and behavior that the EEG readings of 1960 seem like guesswork by alchemists.

While such knowledge impinges virtually every specialty and subspecialty in psychology, the major scientific explosion has occurred principally outside the discipline. Its role has been more responsive rather than pro-active. Similarly, we have now become inured to the availability of mood-altering prescription medication. Librium and Valium were the most widely prescribed of all drugs in the United States for any physical or mental condition in 1990. It is difficult to remember that plain old lithium carbonate once constituted the state of the art in pharmacotherapy.

Related to this knowledge explosion in psychopharmacology is a wholesale shift in the operation of public mental hospitals. The "back ward" was once peopled by seriously disordered patients who might expect to spend years in such institutions constituted the prototype. Today, the typical psychiatric hospital stay can be counted in days rather than in weeks, months, or years. Its purpose is to stabilize the patient on an effective program of medication so that he or she can return to the community and be treated as an outpatient. Again, the pivotal scientific advances of this psychopharmacological revolution occurred outside the discipline of psychology.

Concomitantly, a variety of forces congealed in the marketplace. To accommodate the deinstitutionalized psychiatric patients, a network of federally sponsored community mental health centers was created from 1964 to 1974, providing a hitherto unparalleled marketplace for psychologists. At the same time, the Great Society programs of the Johnson Administration created new employment opportunities for psychologists in programs operated under the aegis of the departments of Labor and of Education.

By 1970, federal funds began to be channeled into brand-new programs and agencies designed to rehabilitate those addicted to alcohol and illicit drugs, creating yet other employment opportunities. Federal Medicaid regulations provided outpatient psychotherapy virtually on demand, allowing not only a panoply of services for a hitherto underserved population but also, a bonanza for private practitioners. In the private sector, health insurance carriers were essentially forced (indeed, by law in New Jersey and several other states under terms of "freedom of choice" legislation) to open their pocketbooks, so that the means to secure psychotherapy became widely available to the middle and upper socioeconomic classes on a scale probably not dreamed of in 1960.

Whether they saw these programs and sources of funding as opportunities, to borrow Justice David Bazelon's phrase, to do "good for others" or "well for themselves," psychologists and other mental health treatment providers were quick to respond. Psychologist William Schofield of the University of Minnesota has suggested that the incidence of emotional disorder increases during affluent periods in the national economy and that the mere availability of mental health treatment increases the "need" for mental health treatment. It is not surprising that, by 1990, no fewer than one million citizens were providing such treatment at a ratio of one treater to every 250 prospective treatees. Of course, not all such providers are psychologists, whether of the doctoral-level variety or not. Instead, into the mix must also be factored psychiatrists, social workers, "mental health counselors," marriage and family life counselors, clinical psychiatric nurse specialists, substance abuse counselors, lay hypnotists, pastoral counselors, school psychologists, biofeedback technicians. But the press to provide ever-expanding educational opportunities to painlessly earn the PsyD degree is certainly not mysterious.

Psychotherapy became available to the upper and middle classes on an undreamed scale.

Yet the tale of the interplay between exploding knowledge and expanding marketplace does not end there, for in truth the marketplace has become a mite crowded. The response of the psychiatric community has probably been the most sophisticated. Faced with an intrusion on their turf, many psychiatrists have stopped complaining and rediscovered that they were physicians before they became psychiatrists. Physicians hold special knowledge and special prerogatives that have heretofore been inviolate. So, instead of providing psychotherapeutic treatment at, say, $150 per hour to a single patient, they "monitor medication" for five patients during the same hour, charging for each the $50 fee standard for a medical office visit and optimizing this income by a factor of 167 percent.

For their part, psychologists in private clinical practice have been pressed by legislation that provides licensure for social workers, substance abuse counselors, and marriage and family counselors, with the lot regarded by health insurance carriers as new mouths lined up at the trough. Most health insurance carriers prefer to reimburse a portion of the $60 fee charged by licensed social workers for mental health treatment rather than the same proportion of the $100 fee charged by licensed psychologists. Consequently, several states have licensed social workers despite the cries of alarm from physicians, psychiatrists, and psychologists. In considerable testimony before legislative committees, one witness after another equated verbal psychotherapy provided by psychologists and by social workers. Since social workers, they reasoned, are willing to listen to a person's troubles for fewer dollars per session, why should they not also be licensed? Similar arguments were advanced in hearings bearing upon the licensure of marriage and family, mental health, and substance abuse counselors.

The opportunities for mayhem and massive escalation of malpractice premiums boggle the mind.

The claim was made repeatedly that the clinical procedures used were similar or identical. Rarely was it asserted, even by witnesses on the side of psychologists, that the knowledge base from which psychologists derive their procedures is quite different, in other words, that the mental health treatment provided by the practicing psychologist derives from the science of psychology. And indeed the perception that the twain rarely meet is quite pervasive among psychological practitioners, especially those who have been trained in the independent schools.

In the face of increased competition and mindful of the characteristic that distinguishes the psychiatrist from all the other mouths waiting at the trough, some psychologists have set up a clamor demanding that they be permitted to write their own prescriptions. Now, there is a solution that neatly encapsulates the exploding knowledge, the expanding marketplace, and the increased competition. This clamor has been successful enough that a federally funded "experiment" is now underway. The opportunities for mayhem, not to say massive escalation in premiums for malpractice insurance, boggle the mind. Substantial evidence from a series of studies at Albert Einstein College of Medicine clearly demonstrates misprescription even on the part even of seasoned psychiatrists with four years of medical training, an internship, and a residency.

Where Have All the Giants Gone?

Thirty years ago, if asked to name the towering figures in psychology, virtually any scientist or practitioner would have included Donald Hebb, B.F. Skinner, and Raymond Cattell, with full knowledge that Albert Bandura's star was still in the ascendance and would reach its zenith shortly. If one restricted the

question to clinicians, the name Carl Rogers would have sprung quickly to the lips. Some would have known that Arnold Lazarus was on the rise and would reach his zenith at about the same juncture. If we were to ask the same question today, virtually the same set of names would be recited in response, although a growing coterie might add Ralph Reitan and G. Terence Wilson to the list. Such remarkable constancy speaks well for the enduring contributions each has made, but it also reveals that their intellectual heirs are not apparent. Where, then, have all the giants gone?

It is certainly not the case that the well has gone dry, for a dry well could not sustain 500 actively publishing psychological journals. Instead, it seems to be the case that the capacity to grow to giant status has fallen victim to fragmentation and specialization. No doubt, our respondents of today could rattle off half a dozen names of towering figures within their specialty or sub-specialty, but not within psychology as a unitary discipline. Is it that no one today is producing the paradigm-shifting insights of a Hebb, a Skinner, a Cattell, a Bandura? Or is it that those insights are produced in narrower and narrower arenas, communicated largely in journals that strive for narrow specialization, and thus accessible only to specialists but unknown to, and perhaps (as a result of sharply demarked methods of investigation) unknowable by, the non-specialist? That, in fact, if one's frame of reference is lodged within a specialty rather than in the unitary discipline, one is not even inclined toward those intellectual breakthroughs that remake a discipline? If the latter surmise is not woefully off the mark, what is left of psychology as a unitary discipline?

A Downsized Future?

One of the topics with which I belabor and berate my students is the notorious inaccuracy of prediction. Plainly and simply, I tell them, predictions are dangerous, so silence is surely golden. I should heed my own injunction. Yet, when I contemplate the possible and probable alternate futures for psychology as science and as profession thirty years hence, I think I discern two rather clear trends.

First, it seems likely that we shall see the eclipse of current imprecise, indistinct, profession-by-profession licensure laws. These permit largely overlapping areas of practice by members of the several mental health professions, while continuing the fiction of separateness. This occurs even though each profession claims to have more in common with other mental health professions than any claims with a "parent" discipline from which it sees itself as uniquely derived. Instead, we are likely to see legislation enacted that speaks to a single standard of licensure for all non-psychiatric mental health service providers.

Such unified licensure will surely signal the demise of clinically oriented specialties as presently constituted under the aegis of psychology. These specialties will merge with other mental health professions in some as-yet unimagined configuration in universities—perhaps in schools or departments of mental health or psychosocial rehabilitation. Whatever their formal academic configuration, such units will, without doubt, be dominated by psychiatry and neuropsychiatry. Given the knowledge explosion of the past thirty years, that may well be desirable. Such a development would likely meet the needs of the marketplace better than current configurations, for it would instill cooperation rather than competition in the delivery of mental health services.

Not incidentally, it will also represent the fulfillment of a sort of prophecy made by Carl Rogers in 1956 when he observed that although earning a doctorate in psychology doubtless has many benefits, becoming an effective psychotherapist is not one of them. Similarly, for not very different reasons, the professional specialties that are congruent with the central thrusts of graduate schools of management (personnel, industrial, and organizational psychology, market research, consumer behavior studies) will probably find more hospitable homes there than they have heretofore enjoyed in unitary departments.

Second, it seems likely that the biologically anchored specialties in scientific psychology, especially neuropsychology and psychopharmacology, will voluntarily detach themselves from departments representing the unitary discipline of psychology. They will be reincarnated in academic units that represent the broad spectrum of biomedical sciences. Creditable work in these specialties is rarely achievable without active cooperation with medical faculties and/or medical facilities. Market factors would also play a role, including continuing, broad-gauged research support for schools of medicine and the differential salary scales that prevail there. Since we can expect greater research productivity to result from a stronger base of support, such a move will yield scientific progress and simultaneously constitute a substantial loss for psychology as a unitary discipline.

What, then, will be left in 2020 of what are today called departments of psychology? The various specialties and subspecialties that remain in unitary academic departments will represent some variant of focal concern with cognition, learning, human development, and/or interpersonal interaction. These are, probably not by chance, the very roots from which the unitary discipline grew, the very arenas in which psychology made its unique and independent contribution. They are also the areas on which other disciplines rely for psychology's expertise, in which Hebb, Skinner, Cattell, Bandura became intellectual giants (joining a firmament already inhabited by Guthrie, Tolman, Hull, Lewin) and in which Lazarus' and Wilson's stars gained ascendance. Those of us who remain behind will need to maintain intimate contact with our former colleagues in their new academic and intellectual homes, both to inform our own work by assimilating their advances and retreats and to better understand our own limitations and our own uniqueness. Downsizing may thus compel us to return to our roots; and smaller may turn out to be rather beautiful after all.

HAS PSYCHOLOGY A FUTURE?

Eleanor J. Gibson

I consider that psychologists have a duty to explore their own field, to create hypotheses about the behavior of animals, especially human, and to test these and look for possible causal relationships at the level of acting, thinking, perceiving humans in their environmental context. Our agenda should be at this level, not one that depends on waiting for reductionist theories at some other level, be it neural, genetic, nuclear, or especially artificial. To go about this work, a developmental approach, in a systems setting—the organism-environment system—holds great promise and has the dignity of successful precedents in other sciences.

All of behavior—perceiving, acting, problem solving, communicating with others—should be our province. The hallmarks of human behavior can and should be studied in all of these areas. It is their development that offers a road to understanding.

We should continue to look for theories of considerable generality, however elegant a model may be in a tiny realm. If we cannot find universal laws, we may still come up with unifying principles.

Not so long ago, in another keynote address, George Miller told us that it was time to "give psychology away" (Miller, 1969). I am afraid that that is exactly what we are doing, though not in the sense that Miller intended. Let us keep psychology, and recapture the old excitement, looking for the causes in behavior itself, and not giving up on the grand unified theory.

Over the last 5 or 6 years we have been celebrating, one university after another, the founding of laboratories of psychology. There have even been quarrels about which was the first. Presumably, the theme for rejoicing that motivated these celebrations was the separation of our own discipline from philosophy. We accepted an agenda that entailed the use of scientific methods of research in the service of investigating the predictable relationships in human (and animal) behavior, both cognition and action. At the time of psychology's birth as a science, I believe it was accepted, too, that humans and animals live and behave in a world, so the processes that concern us should be studied in their environment, both physical and social.

Despite the fact that early German psychologists took physics as their model, rather than biology, a kind of

psychology known as functionalism soon flourished in this country. The adaptiveness of behavior was emphasized; both comparative and applied psychology were established; and especially, from Thorndike on, the topic of learning was a focus of theoretical development.

I suppose very few of you remember the excitement in the air about the future of psychology in the 1930s. Young apprentices envisioned unlimited possibilities for new discoveries; it was unthinkable for a student not to be well schooled in earlier theories that foreshadowed a new science of psychology; and the grand theory, a truly psychological one, was eagerly awaited, certain to make its appearance during our lives as scientists. There were some visible portents, the great men of the day; Hull and Tolman are the ones I remember best, of course. There was Piaget, too. Although I never had any special reverence for him, I think now that his design for psychology was the boldest and his intentions the most ambitious. In any case, being a graduate student in a psychology laboratory then was a highly sought after privilege, and a great future lay ahead.

WHAT'S WRONG?

Something went wrong with this youthful dream, about halfway into the century. Enthusiasm waned, and wariness about the grand general theories grew. It was supposed by a fair number of psychologists, remembering perhaps the ecumenism of William James's *Principles,* that breaking the shackles of radical behaviorism would set things right. Just let us use words like *thinking, perceiving, imagining,* and *reasoning,* and a new day would dawn. That happened. We had the so-called cognitive revolution. It was spurred by events outside the mainstream of psychology, partly the hiatus caused by World War II, but principally by computers and artificial intelligence, and by architectural discoveries in neuroscience. Information processing came into its own. So did "modeling," composing very precise formulations ("minitheories") about limited problem areas. It cannot be denied that progress resulted from the work that was thereby inspired. But, as time went on, some very bright psychologists felt a little uneasy about what was happening, perhaps because of the narrowness of the lines that

Address correspondence to Eleanor J. Gibson, RR1, Box 265A, Middlebury, VT 05753.

From *Psychological Science,* March 1994, pp. 69-76. © 1994 by the American Psychological Society. Reprinted by permission of Cambridge University Press.

began to be drawn. They made a mighty intellectual thrust, and a new discipline resulted, called cognitive science. I believe the hope was that bringing together cognitive psychologists, philosophers, linguists, computer scientists, and neuroscientists would bring back the life, broaden the thinning stream, resuscitate the flagging science, and regenerate the excitement that every young psychologist felt 60 years earlier.

First-rate minds have gathered in many seminars seeking to meld the ideas from these quarters so as to generate something new and all-encompassing. The individual contributions are generally praiseworthy, but I cannot find any emergent principle rising from the meld, at least any emergent theory that sounds to me like the view of psychology for which I have waited so long. The new combination is not more than the sum of its parts, nor does it represent psychology. It will not be surprising to you that I am disappointed. But so are some of the people who were the most hopeful. A recent review of *An Invitation to Cognitive Science* (Osherson & Lasnick, 1990) proclaimed the individual chapters exceptional and even exciting, but lacking in broader implications, and concluded that "this volume as a whole does not fully convey why cognitive science is indeed a coherent and vibrant discipline" (Keil, 1991, p. 292). Another reviewer remarked that the book is dominated by the view that behavior relies "largely or entirely on language," and that the book has a "remarkably narrow biological base" (J.A. Anderson, 1991, p. 287).

I interpret the combination of praise and uneasiness as reflecting that, although there is nothing wrong with the book itself (everyone says "buy it"), this interdisciplinary approach does not, and perhaps cannot, lead to an "integrated and coherent discipline" that exposes and clarifies "deep underlying issues." I think that Keil (1991) scored a direct hit in diagnosing some of the trouble when he pointed out that a developmental view of any of the systems under discussion might well have revealed connections with one or more of the areas examined in other chapters; and that restricting discussion of cognition to humans overlooks totally the importance of an animal's encounters with its environment and the niche it occupies.

Perhaps there is danger in "big science," danger that one can be spread all over the map, without ever reaching an encompassing theory, or the heart of the whole body. There is certainly real danger in giant federal subsidies that concentrate on a single domain, enlisting hundreds of technicians, discouraging individual creativity, and bypassing other needy domains. One politician of science even suggested that universities might be requested to cut research programs that are not "world class," while pursuing increased collaboration. But ideas are generated in the small laboratories, and scientists are trained there.

If we do not endorse the grand-scale-program approach, must we give up hope for the grand idea, the universal laws? That is big science, but in a different way. It is a search for encompassing principles, ones that make sense of all the underlying relationships. I think many psychologists have given up on this, a hope we still shared 60 years ago.

AN AGENDA FOR PSYCHOLOGY

After listening to me play Cassandra, you may well ask: "If you are woeful about the plight of (or the flight from) psychology today, what do you suggest?" I do have suggestions for a brighter future. They contain some general strictures that apply to the whole field. And then, of course, I have my own agenda, an agenda inspired by attributes of living beings that are of concern to no other science, but are our responsibility as psychologists.

First, my general strictures begin with some negatives. I think we must rid ourselves of three ancient traps that we have been caught in, dichotomies that have plagued us over and over.

The first is *dualism.* Is not the uncertainty of dualism the reason why there was rejoicing when psychology was freed from philosophy? The endless argument left psychology outside the arena of natural science, threw doubt on the nature of our subject matter, and confused the young people who were trying to identify the field. In 1940, I did not give dualism a thought, but in recent years I have watched it creep back, the ghost in the machine. We do not need it.

The concept of mechanism is one of the consequences of dualistic thinking. Descartes concluded that animal behavior could be explained in terms of mechanisms; mechanisms also controlled human bodily functions, but humans were gifted in addition with a mind—a superordinate controlling force. The behaviorists accepted the mechanism notion without buying the mind. But that led in the end to dissatisfaction because of the dismissal of mental (cognitive) functions. When someone asks me (as they quite often do), "But what is the mechanism?" my answer is that I am not a mechanist and I do not believe in separation of mental processes and action. Accepting the notion of mechanism implies dualism, that there is a mind separate from the mechanism. This pernicious distinction leads subtly to reductionism, in the search for the so-called mechanism.

The second thing we do not need is *reductionism.* Meaningful explanations should be at their own level of function. Causal relations do not exist between levels, only at their own. To look for correspondences between levels is most certainly a major interest of scientists; but to be meaningful, a correspondence must exist between appropriate units of each of two levels. Correspondence as such does not in itself indicate a causal relationship, but in the final analysis we may discover more general laws that cover both levels. However impressed I am by recent progress in neuroscience (and I am—who would not be excited by the imaging techniques that now exist?), we must not let our own science be driven by that field. It is not true, as someone said to me at a recent conference, that perhaps psychology has no subject matter of its own. We are badly needed as the scientists who know how to study behavior, who can describe the intricate intertwining of perceiving and acting in the adaptive life of a human animal, and who can observe the development of this activity with insight into the constraints, opportunities, and environmental offerings that underlie the dynamics of change.

13

1. THE SCIENCE OF PSYCHOLOGY

Understanding the dynamics of change is the goal that requires us to relinquish the third hobgoblin that has haunted us—the *nature–nurture dichotomy.* Everyone ostensibly agrees with the proposition that nature and nurture are not separable, that we cannot attribute causality to one or the other alone, that the gene itself requires interaction with supportive and dynamic media in order to influence development—and yet, my sophisticated colleagues can ask (and have asked), "Where do you stand on the nature–nurture dimension?" There is no such dimension; there is always interaction of many factors in development. I have been deeply distressed in recent years by people who refer to certain achievements of infancy as "innate," and then drop the problem as if it were solved. This is a futile, evasive tactic.

What is the positive side then? We must study behavior at its own level, looking for causes, predictions, and laws (may we be so lucky!) at that level. I quote a physicist who wrote recently, "The problem with these micro levels is that one is not able to describe the process as a whole, but only piece wise, in very, very small chunks at a time. These pieces are devoid of meaning. Because the meaning of behavior is to be found on the scale of the body of the agent, one has to pick a level of abstraction that allows one to express causal connections on that scale" (Koenderink, 1992, p. 124). It is the functioning (both cognitive and active) of the whole animal in the environment in which it evolved that has to concern us.

To be more specific, I offer you my agenda. It deals with the whole creature functioning adaptively in a dynamic exchange with a world of events and places and people. I go for the big picture, and I have not given up hope on big principles.

THE HALLMARKS OF HUMAN BEHAVIOR

I think there is just one way to understand behavior, and that is to take a developmental approach. There is no typical or standard moment of maturity; besides, we gain our understanding from change and becoming. (That seems to be true of all science, from cell biology to cosmic physics.) The study of behavior should begin before birth, and we are beginning to be able to do that, even for a cognitive activity like remembering. I am not talking about the ends of development, nor an ideal or norm, nor traditional subdivisions that have been domains of specialization.

My program is organized around what I call the hallmarks of human behavior. These fundamental properties of human behavior are the ones that we, as psychologists, need to account for. They are our subject matter. All of them are present, in at least primitive form, at birth, but they also develop, differentiating and elaborating, giving us, as they shift gears or change, a way of studying the factors that interact in making them what they are (and we are), early or late.

I present each of the hallmarks very briefly, show that it is present in rudimentary form early in life, and indicate the kind of change that we may observe in the course of development. Accounting for fundamental hallmarks of

behavior is not new—in a way, that is what Tolman was challenging Hull to do years ago. But we now have new technologies and a continuity of naturalistic observation to spur the task. Certainly, the flourishing of research on infancy over the past 20 years has made this approach a more viable one, though our study only starts there.

I began with four hallmarks and have now added a fifth, urged on me by my longtime friend Ulric Neisser:

- Agency (the self in control)
- Prospectivity (the forward-looking character of behavior)
- Flexibility (transferability of means)
- Communicative creativity (multiplication of means of communicating)
- Retrospectivity (the backward-looking character of behavior)

I begin with *agency,* or control, the property that James (1879) had in mind when he wrote his famous paper "Are We Automata?" What is our answer to this question now? We can answer that activity is not reflex even in an infant. Babies can act spontaneously, observe the consequences of their actions, and show some selectivity with regard to further action. Actions have environmental consequences that can be observed. At the same time, an action provides information about oneself. This combination of intermodal information, about both oneself and a change in the external world, is perceived by the infant, and is a perfect source of knowledge for the self as a causal agent. Piaget made observations of this process on his own son at 2+ months, but we now have research galore to attest to it. High-amplitude, nonnutritive sucking has been used for years to investigate speech perception in infants. Whether or not this procedure was thought of as instrumental conditioning by its early users, it is clear now that the baby can use the action to control what it wants to hear or see. Kalnins and Bruner (1973) used sucking at high amplitude to produce clearing of focus of a movie presented to infants. When sucking reduced blur, amplitude rose to a peak; when the experimenter altered the arrangement, sucking was discontinued. Infants learned to control the rate of sucking and breathing to maintain the picture in constant focus.

In other well-known experiments, strings have been tied to a baby's wrist (as Piaget did) or to an ankle to be yanked so as to produce interesting spectacles, such as a mobile twirling (Rovee-Collier & Gekoski, 1979). Infants learn to control the mobile's motion, literally provided with a tool that controls an external event. If the event is made noncontingent on the baby's pulls, action ceases abruptly. So do expressions of enjoyment, such as smiling and vocalization. Emotional expressions accompanying learning about control and loss of it through the experimenter's manipulation are convincing evidence of the baby's discovery of causal efficacy, of itself as an agent (Lewis, Alessandri, & Sullivan, 1990). The earliest age I have heard cited in a relevant experiment was 10 days to

4 weeks (Meer, Weel, & Lee, 1993). Weights put on a baby's wrists allowed the experimenter to determine that the baby's apparently random waving of an arm was not so much random as exploratory. When a movement brought one of the baby's hands within its sight, the arm was dragged into view despite the weight, but not so the nonviewable hand. The event ceased when the erstwhile viewable hand was screened off. Infant behavior is more than mechanical responses to stimuli; it includes events initiated by the perceiver-actor that inform the perceiver about action capabilities and their outcome.

Two-year-olds have come a long way in discovering agency and seeking to exercise control over objects and people, sometimes frustrating themselves and frequently exasperating their caretakers. They are learning what they can do with a vengeance. Control of an observable event by one's own action is the essence of agency, eventually exercised in elaborate and strategic ways by skilled planners. The detection of oneself as a potential agent and controller of observable external consequences foreshadows and leads to knowledge of causal relations and a concept of oneself as agent, as Mandler (1992) has so persuasively argued in her article on "conceptual primitives."

My second hallmark of behavior is *prospectivity*. I owe the word to David Lee and Claes von Hofsten, both of whom have written about it. But the concept is very old indeed. Tolman wrote about "purposive behavior"; Hull wrote about "goal attraction and directing ideas" (as habit mechanisms, to be sure). My Psychology 101 professor spoke of the directedness of behavior. We could even take the notion back to Aristotle. Are we any wiser about it now?

All of these terms refer to the forward-looking character of behavior. And I believe all of them must take for granted the notion of control that I began with (though I certainly never heard Hull use the term control nor mention intention or agency). In any case, activity is prospective; it must be prepared for any affordance of the environment to be realized, or any task to be completed.

Affordance, a term coined by J.J. Gibson (1979), refers to a reciprocal relationship between an animal and its environment. The environment provides opportunities, and the animal provides (or does not provide) an action system that can utilize what the environment offers. Perceiving the relationship is perceiving an affordance, an animal–environment fit. To perceive an affordance implies prospectivity. It requires detection of both the opportunity offered by the environment (e.g., an object, its size, its distance from the observer) and the dimensional and dynamic properties of the observer (e.g., how far the arm can be stretched, how heavy a load can be lifted). Spontaneous exploratory activity of an animal gives rise to perceptible consequences that are utilized in ongoing activities, leading to predictable and economical utilization of affordances. Information about the environment, the actor's bodily effectiveness, and the fit between the two is constantly coming in; as changes in the information are observed, better and earlier detection of affordances is possible.

Consider a baby reaching for something. An action like reaching is always effected upon a background of postural stability. The posture must be prepared before the explicit action can be performed. Postural preparedness for reaching is demonstrably prospective from early infancy, showing intentionality in postural readiness for actions. Hofsten (1993) showed, by means of electromyographic (EMG) recordings, that preparations for the reach occur earliest in the back muscles and then in the abdominal muscles, all predating the arm extension itself. This example may be a far cry from the long jumper setting himself to clear a pit (Lee, Lishman, & Thomson, 1982), but the organization of behavior over time extending ahead is no less present.

Exploratory activity of all kinds is characteristic of early development, as new actions and new powers become available and as the actor's dimensions change (E.J. Gibson, 1988). Exploratory actions inform young perceiver-actors about their own effective properties in relation to present (and potential future) conditions to make possible, prospectively, ensuing consummatory actions.

Detection of predictable, prospective relationships may also be the result of observation of sequences of external events that are not necessarily the consequence of an action of one's own. Haith (1993) and his colleagues have conducted numerous experiments on what he terms "future-oriented processes in infancy." Experiments with infants as young as 2 months have demonstrated that visual expectations are formed for pictorial displays that appear discretely and successively in predictable places in the infant's field of view. Expectation of a presentation was demonstrated by anticipatory eye movements. Haith interpreted the anticipations as more than mere classical conditioning because the character of the pictures (their familiarity, e.g.) influenced the occurrence of anticipation; the babies apparently extracted content information in the course of detecting predictability. Haith's finding that transfer occurred when different actions were implicated is further evidence of the nonreflex character of the expectant behavior. Infants were presented first with sequences that required horizontal eye movements to observe the extended events. That procedure was followed with presentations requiring vertical movements, implicating a quite different musculature. Predictable alternative presentation in both cases resulted in facilitation of expectant behavior in the second set of presentations. As infants learn more about "what leads to what," about predictable relations within events both self-perpetrated and external, the prospective, forward-looking character of behavior increases.

Finding transfer in this primitive case brings me to my third hallmark, the *flexibility* of human behavior. I have described flexibility as the transfer of means and strategies, but typically more modest generalization occurs in early development, especially before behavior and events in the world are differentiated by a young perceiver into the embedded sequences that characterize most event relations. Events are typically nested, small ones within larger ones. Predecessor events may have different relations to later events and to encompassing ones, such as a task that involves some means to reach a goal. The ability to select from varied means to realize an affordance is a mark of flexible behavior. A need to account for such flexibility probably motivated Hull (60 years ago) to write his papers on the habit-family hierarchy (1934a, 1934b) and on "the assembly of behavior segments in novel combinations suitable for problem solution" (1935). There is a conspicuous interest today in problem solving at an adult level—for example, J.R. Anderson's (1993) work on problem solving and what he calls "means-end operators" in a problem space, during search for and selection of means. But that analysis involves very high level cognition.

There is little research in progress on transfer of any kind in children of 2 or 3 years (but see Brown & Campione, 1984), and so far as we know, transfer seems to be rather limited in neonates. Piaget (1954) observed some flexibility in 2-month-old Laurent, who was tweaking a toy with the aid of a ribbon tied to his right wrist. After Laurent succeeded in tugging the arm reliably, making the toy dance, Piaget tied the ribbon to Laurent's left wrist. Laurent then tugged with the left arm, to the exclusion of the right one.

Rovee-Collier and her colleagues have used a similar task (only with an ankle instead of a wrist) and observed the effect of changing the context in which the action occurred, for instance, substituting a different crib lining or a different mobile to be tweaked. Performance at 3 months seemed to be quite specific to the context. But if the context was changed during training, the action was resumed under a still different context several days later (Rovee-Collier & DuFault, 1991). Changing the context during learning may increase attention to an invariant property of the events, reminiscent of the old "learning to learn" research (Harlow, 1959; Stevenson, 1972).

Babies learn to use simple tools that involve separate actions as means in a task during the second half of the 1st year (Willatts, 1989). Exploratory activity in the transfer of means seems to play an essential role in tasks for which several means might be possible. An example is new research by Adolph (1993) on locomotion of novice crawlers and novice walkers presented with sloping surfaces to maneuver themselves over. The babies faced a parent, with a slope of 0° to 40° intervening. Both novice crawlers and novice walkers, given slopes to go up, would have a try on all the slopes. There is little risk in a failed attempt when attempting an upgrade, so that finding is not very surprising. But downgrades are a different matter. Novice crawlers frequently set off attempting to crawl down slopes that were too steep for safety, and had to be rescued. As they gained skill in crawling, they learned new approaches to the steeper downhill slopes, such as sliding, prone or sitting, or simply refusing to go, seemingly recognizing the risk. Surprisingly, a few months later, when the same babies shifted their mode of locomotion to walking, many plunged downward at first and went through exploratory trials a second time before the strategies learned as crawlers were adopted. Flexibility in transferring means apparently requires some learning itself.

We expect a high level of transferability and flexibility in selecting means to a goal from adult experts in a field. But there may be a long road leading to strategic behavior, including learning to differentiate tasks into subevents, acquiring a repertory of potential variations, and developing selectivity with reference to goals and affordances. Transfer of means from task to task with changing context of surroundings and affordances may also be the road to the use of analogy—using applicability of means to detect some deep similarity of process or basic dynamics, a kind of creative insight.

Flexibility, which we have traditionally measured by generalization and transfer in the laboratory, changes developmentally as exploratory activities, observation of outcomes, contextual changes, task differentiation, and the dawning of potential new affordances bring greater variation of behavioral strategies and more differentiated selection, with recognition of invariant aspects of different tasks. Learning in development need not lead to automaticity and "habit," but rather to potentially greater variability and selectivity. I think only developmental research will tell us how this happens.

My fourth hallmark has to do with *communication,* but not just communication per se. All animals communicate in some way, to some extent, the means ranging from pheromones to bird song and body language, but humans have the potential to extend the means of communication to an amazing degree. From gesture to vocalization to language to reading print to mathematical symbols and computerized codes, there seems to be no end.

Infants communicate with caretakers from day one. Eye contact and mimicking of grimaces and tongue extension soon after birth prepare us (and them) for quick development of more elaborate means via alerting parents through their cries. By 2 months, a real interaction is beginning. A wealth of research has shown that infants and their mothers have facial and vocal interchanges that are truly reciprocal, a kind of turn taking sometimes referred to as "protocommunication" (Trevarthen, 1979). The adult smiles and speaks to the baby, then stops, maintaining eye contact so the baby can detect an opportunity to make facial and other gestures and vocalize. Experiments in which the exchange is interrupted make clear that the baby anticipates its turn and expects a response that is appropriately timed and controlled—another example of prospectivity (Murray & Trevarthen, 1987).

Progress in our knowledge of how infants learn language has been rapid and intensive in recent years. Infants discriminate phonemic differences of all languages, apparently, to begin with; but by the second half of the 1st year, they are shaping their repertoire of expected sounds to the language they hear. Parents do attempt to teach children language in bouts of so-called joint attention, but language learning comes easily and naturally to most children. Our literature is now rich in observations of how this happens. Speech in quite young children indicates intentionality, prospectivity, and flexibility of usage. They do not just repeat what they hear or are taught. Speech also paves the way for reading, a further mode of communication.

My own years of research on reading (I regret to report) led to no grand theories, but they gave me a chance to observe its development. Children vary enormously in ease of learning to read. Many children, if books are put in their way, learn quickly and spontaneously, before we even realize it. When demonstrating a form of the Stroop test once, I gave it to my 4-year-old grandson as a comparison with adults to show how a preschool child would rapidly name the color of the ink whatever word was inscribed. To my total surprise, he did not say "blue," but read the word "green," which had been printed in blue. But sometimes children find the task of reading hard and need a lot of help. However it happens, children learn to read only by reading themselves. Flexibility of approach and eventual transferability of subskills mark progress, as does anticipation of the embedded structure of text.

Codes of other kinds seem to come quite easily to older children and can even serve as a kind of play, something we might investigate further. Most interesting, however, is the ability of speakers to recode linguistic expressions of events. If what we are trying to communicate is not understood, or we do not like the way a sentence turns out, we can try it other ways, using other words or other means. Communicating, by language or other means, is potentially very flexible, again illustrating the organized interaction of these prime characteristics of human behavior.

What gets recoded, in an effort to communicate about a particular event, is apt to be information about an event that has already happened. I am now warily approaching my fifth hallmark, *retrospectivity*. Young children do not usually talk about past events—they talk about what is going on here and now and what will happen, or what they want to happen, soon. Perhaps retrospectivity is achieved only as we grow old enough to weave some kind of story of our past lives. Yet babies remember things from as early a beginning as technology has allowed psychologists to probe. Newborns differentiate the voices of their mothers from those of other persons on the basis of events that took place before birth (DeCasper & Fifer, 1980). Newborns also remember a specific sound (a word) and differentiate it from another word after a 24-hr period, when the word is again presented (Swain, Zelazo, & Clifton, 1993). Evidence is plentiful that remembering, in some form, is going on.

"Memory" is one of the oldest topics in psychology. I remember a speaker being told by his host after a colloquium years ago, "Well, Ebbinghaus said it all!" But what a change we have seen in the way memory is treated! It was once thought of as a kind of bank from which we drew items (images?), the ease of doing this depending on the amount of repetition, so that one item provoked the next in a kind of list. Nowadays many kinds of memory are differentiated, and no one would think of confusing generic or generalized knowledge of the world and what to do about it with remembering specific events; nor would they confuse "implicit" memory with "explicit." I wonder if the many distinctions that have been made are telling us that the term memory was a categorical mistake in the first place. It is too static a concept, and it fails to conjure up the functional quality of remembering, its intentionality and flexibility.

Remembering has one thing in common with my other four hallmarks: The way that we remember changes developmentally. Yes, babies can remember a face, a gesture, a word, at least in the sense of responding to it differentially (implicit or procedural memory, I suppose). But it is only after considerable time that little children appear to mark particular, individual events and are able to recall them later at will. Generic recall of common happenings at a birthday party or at the pediatrician's or lunch at McDonald's is known to occur for a 3-year-old, but remembering a particular birthday party or luncheon is unlikely until later (Nelson, 1986). It is equally unlikely that any of us remembers a particular event that occurred when we were only 3 years old—so-called infant amnesia.

Retrospectivity certainly seems to demand language, an ability to recode past events, and to relate them to future anticipated ones. It implies a developing sophistication in all the other hallmarks, even flexibility in the sense of considering what might have happened, not just what did. Nelson (1993) has suggested that autobiographical memory—a kind of putting together the story of one's own life—begins as "infant amnesia" ends. The change, she thinks, has to do with communicating with other people about shared events, detecting that the same event can be perceived from both points of view, and discussed from one's own. But even autobiographical memories, however freighted with episodes they may be, can change and be recoded as development proceeds and new affordances are offered by changes in a person's environment, means of acting, and way of living. Remembering is a dynamic process, and we should look for its development to be adaptive. Retrospectivity is as loaded with developmental change as prospectivity, and thus is as potentially informative about the factors that interact in creating a never-finished, perceiving, acting, thinking human being.

I will only add that I hold these truths to be self-evident: that agency, prospectivity, flexibility, communicative creativity, and retrospectivity are, and always have been recognized as, qualities that mark human behavior, however often the names given them have been altered over history. They still give us our agenda, and because they are continuously developing, they offer us a strategy for research, a way to investigate the factors, both environmental and internal, that interact to drive the change. If we observe the ontogeny of these properties with all the new research methods at hand, are we at all likely to find any general laws or trends? We might. Biology recognizes that evolution requires variation and selection. So does ontogenetic development. Both are essential for learning to occur, as Siegler and Munukata (1993) have pointed out. Differentiation of species, organs, and cells is characteristic of evolution and of individual biological development as environmental and genetic factors interact. These thought-provoking analogies may help us understand development of the properties that mark human behavior.

1. THE SCIENCE OF PSYCHOLOGY

Acknowledgments—This article is in substance the author's keynote address to the Fifth Annual Convention of the American Psychological Society, Chicago, June 1993.

REFERENCES

Adolph, K.E. (1993). *Perceptual-motor development in infants' locomotion over slopes*. Unpublished doctoral dissertation, Emory University, Atlanta.

Anderson, J.A. (1991). Comments on foundations of cognitive science. *Psychological Science, 2,* 283, 285–287.

Anderson, J.R. (1993). Problem solving and learning. *American Psychologist, 48,* 35–44.

Brown, A.L., & Campione, J.C. (1984). Three faces of transfer: Implications for early competence, individual differences, and instruction. In M.E. Lamb, A.L. Brown, & B. Rogoff (Eds.), *Advances in developmental psychology* (pp. 143–192). Hillsdale, NJ: Erlbaum.

DeCasper, A.J., & Fifer, W.P. (1980). Of human bonding: Newborns prefer their mothers' voices. *Science, 208,* 1174–1176.

Gibson, E.J. (1988). Exploratory behavior in the development of perceiving, acting, and the acquiring of knowledge. *Annual Review of Psychology, 39,* 1–44.

Gibson, J.J. (1979). *The ecological approach to visual perception*. Boston: Houghton-Mifflin.

Haith, M.M. (1993). Future-oriented processes in infancy: The case of visual expectations. In C.E. Granrud (Ed.), *Visual perception and cognition in infancy* (pp. 235–264). Hillsdale, NJ: Erlbaum.

Harlow, H.F. (1959). Learning set and error factor theory. In M.S. Koch (Ed.), *Psychology: A study of a science* (Vol. 2). New York: McGraw-Hill.

Hofsten, C. von. (1993). Prospective control: A basic aspect of action development. *Human Development, 36,* 253–270.

Hull, C. (1934a). The concept of the habit-family hierarchy and maze learning: Part I. *Psychological Review, 41,* 33–52.

Hull, C. (1934b). The concept of the habit-family hierarchy and maze learning: Part II. *Psychological Review, 41,* 134–152.

Hull, C.L. (1935). The mechanism of the assembly of behavior segments in novel combinations suitable for problem solution. *Psychological Review, 42,* 219–245.

James, W. (1879). Are we automata? *Mind, 4,* 1–22.

Kalnins, I.V., & Bruner, J.S. (1973). The coordination of visual observation and instrumental behavior in early infancy. *Perception, 2,* 307–314.

Keil, F.C. (1991). On being more than the sum of its parts: The conceptual coherence of cognitive science. *Psychological Science, 2,* 283, 287–293.

Koenderink, J.J. (1992). Wechsler's vision: An essay review of "Computational Vision" by Harry Wechsler. *Ecological Psychology, 4,* 121–128.

Lee, D.N., Lishman, J.R., & Thomson, J.A. (1982). Regulation of gait in long jumping. *Journal of Experimental Psychology: Human Perception and Performance, 8,* 448–459.

Lewis, M., Alessandri, S.M., & Sullivan, M.W. (1990). Violation of expectancy, loss of control, and anger expressions in young infants. *Developmental Psychology, 26,* 745–751.

Mandler, J.M. (1992). How to build a baby: II. Conceptual primitives. *Psychological Review, 99,* 587–604.

Meer, A.L.H. van der, Weel, F.R. van der, & Lee, D.N. (1993). *Gravitational know-how in neonates*. Unpublished manuscript, Department of Psychology, University of Edinburgh, Edinburgh, Scotland.

Miller, G.A. (1969). Psychology as a means of promoting human welfare. *American Psychologist, 24,* 1063–1075.

Murray, L., & Trevarthen, C. (1987). Emotional regulation of interactions between two-month-olds and their mothers. In T.M. Field & N.A. Fox (Eds.), *Social perception in infants* (pp. 177–197). Norwood, NJ: Ablex.

Nelson, K. (1986). *Event knowledge: Structure and function in development*. Hillsdale, NJ: Erlbaum.

Nelson, K. (1993). The psychological and social origins of autobiographical memory. *Psychological Science, 4,* 7–14.

Osherson, D.H., & Lasnick, H. (Eds.). (1990). *An invitation to cognitive science*. Cambridge, MA: MIT Press.

Piaget, J. (1954). *The construction of reality in the child*. New York: Basic Books.

Rovee-Collier, C.K., & DuFault, D. (1991). Multiple contexts and memory retrieval at three months. *Developmental Psychobiology, 24,* 39–49.

Rovee-Collier, C.K., & Gekoski, M. (1979). The economics of infancy: A review of conjugate reinforcement. In W.H. Reese & L.P. Lipsitt (Eds.), *Advances in child development and behavior* (Vol. 13, pp. 195–255). New York: Academic Press.

Siegler, R.S., & Munukata, Y. (1993, Winter). Beyond the immaculate transition: Advances in the understanding of change. *SRCD Newsletter.*

Stevenson, H.W. (1972). *Children's learning*. New York: Appleton-Century-Crofts.

Swain, I.U., Zelazo, P.R., & Clifton, R.K. (1993). Newborn infants' memory for speech sounds retained over 24 hours. *Developmental Psychology, 29,* 312–323.

Trevarthen, C. (1979). Communication and cooperation in early infancy: A description of primary intersubjectivity. In M. Bullowa (Ed.), *Before speech: The beginning of interpersonal communication* (pp. 321–347). Cambridge, England: Cambridge University Press.

Willatts, P. (1989). Development of problem-solving in infancy. In A. Slater & G. Bremner (Eds.), *Infant development* (pp. 143–182). Hillsdale, NJ: Erlbaum.

Pollsters Enlist Psychologists In Quest for Unbiased Results

Daniel Goleman

Should laws be passed to eliminate all possibilities of special interests giving huge sums of money to candidates? Or do groups have a right to contribute to the candidate they support?

The first question comes from a survey by Ross Perot last March; the second is part of a more neutral rephrasing of that question as asked by an independent polling concern. When Mr. Perot put the question his way, 99 percent of those responding answered "yes." But in the alternate form, 40 percent favored limits on contributions.

The Perot poll has become a textbook case of how readily results of a survey can be manipulated by the pollster, a point too easily forgotten in a day when polls have become a fixture of the information landscape as a quick pulse reading of the body politic.

But survey researchers, seeking to minimize such biases in their results, are continuing to raise questions about the way they ask questions. In pursuit of greater methodological sophistication and accuracy in surveys, one of the main tools of social science, they have formed a research alliance with cognitive psychologists.

Those at the forefront of the science of polling confront longstanding challenges in asking questions that are free of bias:

• Words can mean different things to the people who devise a survey and to those who answer it. For instance, in a 1981 poll about television, respondents said the meaning of the questions was clear to them. Yet when 51 respondents were queried further about one phrase, "over the last few years," 7 said "few" meant "no more than 2 years," 19 said it meant "7 years or more," and 19 took it to mean "10 years or more."

• Respondents can offer opinions on issues they know nothing about. In a 1981 study in which respondents were asked their views of a fictitious law, 30 percent said they opposed or favored it. And in a classic study done in the 1940's, college students willingly gave their opinions when surveyed about three nationalities that do not exist: Danireans, Pireneans and Wallonians.

• The options presented as answers can strongly affect the response. In one survey, for example, people were asked if they felt "the courts deal too harshly or not harshly enough with criminals." When offered just the two options, 6 percent said "too harshly" and 78 percent answered "not harshly enough." But when a third alternative was added—"don't have enough information about the courts to say"—29 percent took that option, and 60 percent answered "not harshly enough."

• One question can influence the next. In a classic example, during the height of the Red scare in the 1950's,

only 36 percent of respondents answered "yes" to the question, "Do you think the United States should let Communist reporters from other countries come in here and send back to their papers the news as they see it?" But "yes" answers jumped to 73 percent when the same question was preceded by one asking if Russia should let American reporters in.

Much of the current interest by survey researchers in cognitive science stemmed from the wish among agencies for greater accuracy in several Federal surveys that are used to guide policy, like the Current Population Survey, done monthly to estimate the national unemployment rate.

"I'm hopeful that the cognitive sciences can help with many of the perennial problems of survey research," said Dr. Judith Tanur, a sociologist at the State University of New York at Stony Brook and editor of the book "Questions About Questions: Inquiries Into the Cognitive Bases of Surveys" (Russell Sage Foundation).

In 1980, the first of a series of meetings intended to address these problems brought together two professions that had rarely talked: survey researchers and cognitive scientists, whose expertise is in perception, memory and the nuances of comprehension.

In recent years that collaboration has begun to bear fruit in suggesting new ways to design surveys to get more accurate answers. One innovative method, for example, is a "think-aloud" protocol in which pollsters have people tell them what they are thinking as they answer questions.

"The think-aloud method allows you to see if a question is too difficult to understand or answer, and if you are getting at the concepts you want to," Dr. Tanur said.

A similar method, in which a group of people talk over the questions in a survey, has recently led to a change in a standard question in the Current Population Survey. The question, asked of those who say they are currently not working, has been, "Is there a job from which you are on lay off?"

Inaccurate Answers

To those at the Department of Labor who composed the survey, "lay off" has a specific meaning: being temporarily suspended from a job to which a person expects to be called back. Such people are tallied differently than those out of work but not laid off from a specific job.

But the research showed that many people took "lay off" to be a euphemism for having been fired. A new version of the question adding the phrase "and expect to be called back" is now being used.

"During the past 12 months, about how many times did you see or talk to a medical doctor?" is one of the questions posed to the 50,000 people queried in the National Health Survey, the results of which are used to formulate government health programs.

But research by Dr. Elizabeth Loftus, a psychologist at the University of Washington, found that when people's health records were checked, their answer to this question was highly inaccurate; people failed to remember 60 percent of their doctor visits in the preceding 12 months.

Drawing on other studies of memory, Dr. Loftus found that asking a question in ways that offered more cues for recall improved the accuracy. One method asks people to recall specific visits, starting with the most recent ones. This improved the accuracy of the responses by about 15 percent, Dr. Loftus said.

One problem that has defied cognitive psychologists is that people give incorrect answers to pollsters.

For example, experts on surveys say that when people are asked if they voted in the last election, about 10 to 15 percent of all adults will say they did when they did not. The experts say the percentages for misleading answers is about the same when people are asked if they plan to vote in a forthcoming election.

Accounting for False Answers

A research team led by Dr. Robert Abelson, a psychologist at Yale University, has tried several approaches to reduce the rate of false voting responses. One assumed that because many people view voting as socially desirable, some people gave false answers because they wanted to appear virtuous in the eyes of the pollster.

But when researchers reworded the question to offer people ready-made excuses for not voting—suggesting, for instance, that circumstance had prevented them from voting—there was no drop in the numbers who made false claims.

Testing whether faulty memory could be an explanation for the mis-

---

The Question of Questions: An Experiment in Polling

Results of H. Ross Perot's mail-in survey in the 1992 Presidential campaign are compared with those for the same question given to a national sample by Yankelovich & Partners, a more neutrally worded version of the question submitted to a national sample and still another version given to another national sample by the Gordon Black Corporation.

Question 1. / mail-in sample: *Do you believe that for every dollar of tax increase there should be $2 in spending cuts with the savings earmarked for deficit and debt reduction?*
97% Yes

Perot question / Yankelovich sample: Same wording.
67% Yes   18% No   15% Don't know

Yankelovich question/ Yankelovich sample: *Would you favor or oppose a proposal to cut spending by $2 for every dollar in new taxes, with the savings earmarked for deficit reduction, even if that meant cuts in domestic programs like Medicare and education?*
33% Favor   61% Oppose   6% Don't know

Black's redo of Perot question/Black Sample: *Which of the following deficit reduction approaches would you prefer? a) A program that relies entirely on tax increases, with no spending cuts, b) a program that requires $1 of spending cuts for every $1 of tax increases, or c) a program that requires at least $2 of more spending cuts for every $1 of tax increases.*
5% Tax increase/ no cuts   27% $1 to $1   60% $2 to $1   4% No preference

Question 2. / mail-in sample: *Should laws be passed to eliminate all possibilities of special interests giving huge sums of money to candidates?*
99% Yes

Perot question / Yankelovich sample: Same wording.
80% Yes   17% No

Yankelovich question / Yankelovich sample: *Should laws be passed to prohibit interest groups from contributing to campaigns, or do groups have a right to contribute to the candidate they support?*
40% Prohibit contrib.   55% Groups have right

Black's redo of Perot question/Black sample: *Please tell me whether you favor or oppose the proposal: The passage of new laws that would eliminate all possibility of special interests giving large sums of money to candidates.*
70% Favor   28% Oppose

Source: The Public Perspective

The New York Times

leading answers, the researchers tried another technique that asked specific questions about past elections. But they still found no drop in the numbers who gave inaccurate answers on whether they voted in the most recent election.

The cognitive psychologists did discover, however, that part of the problem was a tendency to overgeneralize from past events to current ones. For example, people who usually vote were more likely to say they had voted in the most recent election, even when voting records showed they had not. And those who usually did not vote were more likely to make the opposite error, saying they had not voted in a recent election, even when records showed that they had.

As members of the survey profession struggle to solve such problems, they also face a battle against shoddy polling methods by special-interest groups trying to advance their causes. There are about 1,500 members of the American Association for Public Opinion Research, about half academics and half independent polling companies.

"Our members agree to abide by an ethical code that requires that you disclose details of how you did a survey," said Dr. Stanley Presser, a sociologist at the University of Maryland who is president of the association. "But there's less agreement on how you should ask questions, so the code is largely silent on particulars of how to conduct a survey."

Still, said Dr. Tom Smith, director of the General Social Survey at the University of Chicago and a past chairman of the ethics committee, "there is an elaborate procedure for bringing charges of violating ethics like biasing your survey to support a vested interest."

Critiques of Surveys

The profession polices itself through peer review and open critiques of surveys, Dr. Smith said. The main journal in the field, Public Opinion Quarterly, features a column called "Poll Reviews" pointing out defects in methodology, especially those that have received wide publicity.

One critique was of a poll conducted on the night of Jan. 9, 1991, which seemed to show that 39 percent of Americans favored going to war against Iraq immediately. Because that poll was conducted overnight, no effort was made to reach people who did not answer their phones the first time. Such a poll, survey experts say, may include disproportionate numbers of retired people and fewer young men, who are less often home than other groups.

Another poll on the same topic, which was conducted over a four-day period and thus had more time to reach more people, found that 30 percent of the respondents favored going to war immediately.

The Perot poll was the topic of a similar critique in the June issue of The Public Perspective. Professional pollsters said the Perot poll had two major flaws: a skewed sample and biased questions. The questionnaire was published in TV Guide and asked the magazine's readers to reply. Thus the poll was not a random sample of Americans. Critics also said the Perot poll consisted of questions that were apparently composed by Mr. Perot's own political organization, rather than by an independent survey researcher.

"A lot of us in the survey profession were bothered by the Perot poll," Dr. Presser said. "But the practice is getting more and more common, with special-interest groups wording questions their way and letting anyone respond who wants, rather than gathering a random sample."

Efforts to reach the Perot organization by telephone were unavailing.

Dr. Presser points to call-in surveys using "900" telephone numbers as another example of a poor polling practice. "A 1990 poll in USA Today used '900' numbers to ask if Donald Trump represented what was best in America or what was wrong with this country," Dr. Presser said. "Of 7,802 calls, 5,646 came from two phone numbers at a firm controlled by one of his friends. Trump won in a landslide."

Biological Bases of Behavior

As a child, Nancy vowed she did not want to turn out like either of her parents. Nancy's mother was very passive and acquiescent about her father's drinking. When Dad was drunk, Mom always called his boss to report that Dad was "sick" and then acted as if there was nothing wrong at home. Nancy's childhood was a nightmare. Her father's behavior was unpredictable. If he drank just a little bit, most often he was happy. If he drank a lot, which was usually the case, he became belligerent.

Despite vowing not to become her father, as an adult Nancy found herself in the alcohol rehabilitation unit of a large hospital. Nancy's employer could no longer tolerate her on-the-job mistakes nor her unexplained absences from work and referred her to the clinic for help. As Nancy pondered her fate, she wondered whether her genes preordained her to follow in her father's inebriated footsteps or whether the stress of her childhood had brought her to this point in her life. After all, being the child of an alcoholic is not easy.

Just as Nancy is, psychologists are concerned with discovering the causes of human behavior. Once the cause is known, treatments for problematic behaviors can be developed. In fact, certain behaviors might even be prevented when the cause is known. But for Nancy, prevention was too late.

One of the paths to understanding humans is to understand the biological underpinnings of their behavior. Genes and chromosomes, the body's chemistry (as found in hormones, neurotransmitters, and enzymes), and the central nervous system (the brain, spinal cord, and nerves) are all implicated in human behavior. All represent the biological aspects of behavior and ought, therefore, to be worthy of study by psychologists.

Physiological psychologists and psychobiologists are the ones who often examine the role of biology in behavior. The neuroscientist is especially interested in brain functioning; the psychopharmacologist is interested in the effects of various psychopharmacologic agents or psychoactive drugs on behavior.

These psychologists often utilize one of two techniques to understand the biology-behavior connection. Animal studies involving manipulation, stimulation, or destruction of certain parts of the brain offer one method of study. However, of late, animal rights activists have questioned the validity and ethical correctness of maiming animals to advance the human condition. Therefore, for scientists there is a second available technique that includes the examination of unfortunate individuals whose brains are defective at birth or damaged later by accidents or disease. We can also use animal models to understand genetics; with animal models we can control reproduction and develop various strains of animals if necessary. Such tactics with humans would be considered extremely unethical. However, by studying an individual's behavior in comparison to natural and adoptive parents we can begin to understand the role of genetics in human behavior.

The articles in this unit are designed to familiarize you with the knowledge psychologists have gleaned by using these two techniques as well as others to study physiological processes and mechanisms in human behavior. Each article will interest you and make you more curious about the role of biology in human endeavors.

The first unit article, "Nature or Nurture? Old Chestnut, New Thoughts," provides an overview of one of the major controversies in psychology, the nature versus nurture controversy. Psychologists interested in this issue search for evidence to ascertain if a given behavior is determined by learning and experience or by genes and body chemistry. The companion article, "Born Gay?" pertains to the issue of whether homosexuality is learned or physiological. Interestingly, recent research seems to point to biological bases for homosexuality.

The role of genes in human behavior cannot be underestimated nor ignored. The next unit article addresses the topic of genetics. In "Eugenics Revisited," John Horgan describes research where the genetic basis for alcoholism and other individual differences is being explored.

In this section, we also need to examine the role of the central nervous system and, specifically, the brain. In "The Human Mind: Touching the Intangible," modern technological advances for investigating the brain, such as positron emission tomography (PET), are described. These methods have allowed researchers to better understand the role of brain functioning in vision, memory, and other processes important to human life. In the companion article, "Mind and Brain," Gerald Fischbach debates whether the mind and the brain are one and the same. Fischbach also provides us with an overview of the intricacies of the brain and the neurons that comprise the brain.

Looking Ahead: Challenge Questions

What do you think plays the most vital role in the development of human behavior—biology or environment? Do you think that the two interact in some complex fashion to determine behavior? If both biology and environment are responsible for some or many human behaviors, can you give some examples of the behaviors?

From where do you think homosexuality originates? If homosexuality is indeed inherited, does that make homosexuality seem more "natural" to you?

How is research on the genetics of behaviors such as schizophrenia, alcoholism, and homosexuality conducted? What are the controversies related to twin studies in psychology?

Do you think the brain is the consummate computer? Why, or why not? Catalog all of the myriad functions of the human brain. What modern techniques exist that allow us to examine the brain?

Are the mind and the brain the same? Defend your answer. Describe the structures of the brain and their functions. Can you do the same for neurons and neuronal transmission?

NATURE OR NURTURE?

■

Old chestnut, new thoughts

Few questions of human behaviour are more controversial than this: are people programmed by their genes, or by their upbringing? There is no simple answer, but the academic world is starting to hear a lot more from the genes brigade—on both sides of the political spectrum

ARE criminals born or made? Is homosexuality a preference or a predisposition? Do IQ tests measure innate abilities or acquired skills?

For the past 50 years, respectable academic opinion, whenever it has deigned to deal with such layman's questions, has come down firmly for nurture over nature. Nazism discredited even the mildest attempts to produce genetic explanations of human affairs. And economic growth after the second world war encouraged most western governments to imagine that they could eliminate social problems by a mixture of enlightened planning and generous spending—that, in effect, they could steer (even change) human nature.

In this atmosphere, the social sciences flourished as never before. Sociologists made lucrative careers producing "nurture" explanations of everything from school failure to schizophrenia. Geneticists stuck to safe subjects such as fruit flies and honey bees, rather than risk being accused of a fondness for jackboots and martial music.

The fashion is beginning to change. The failure of liberal reforms to deliver the Great Society has cast doubt on the proposition that better nurture can deliver better nature. The failure of sociologists to find even a few of the purported (Freudian or social) causes of schizophrenia, homosexuality, sex differences in criminal tendencies and the like has undermined their credibility. And a better understanding of how genes work has made it possible for liberals who still believe in the perfectibility

of man to accept genetic explanations. In at least one case—homosexuality—it is now the liberals who espouse nature and their opponents who point to nurture.

The pro-nature people are still a minority in universities. But they are a productive and increasingly vocal minority—and one which is beginning to increase its influence in the media. Open the American newspapers and you can read left-inclined pundits like Micky Kaus arguing that income inequality is partly the result of genetic differences. Turn on the television and you can see intelligent, unbigoted people claiming that male homosexuals have a different brain structure from heterosexual men.

This is only the beginning. Richard Herrnstein, a professor of psychology at Harvard University, and Charles Murray, a controversial critic of the welfare state, are collaborating on a study of the implications of biological differences for public policy. The book will highlight the tension between America's egalitarian philosophy and the unequal distribution of innate abilities.

The reaction of orthodox opinion has been scathing. America's National Institutes of Health provoked such an angry response to its decision to finance a conference on genetics and crime that it decided to withdraw the money. Mr Murray lost the patronage of the Manhattan Institute, a New York-based think-tank, when he decided to study individual differences and social policy.

Even in these days of politically correct fetishes, on no other subject is the gulf be-

tween academics and ordinary people so wide. Even the most hopeful of parents know that the sentiment "all men are created equal" is a pious dream rather than a statement of fact. They know full well that, say, one of their sons is brighter, or more musical or more athletic than another; they see, despite their best attentions, that girls turn every toy into a doll and boys turn every toy into a weapon; they rarely persist in believing that each and all of these differences is the result of early encouragement or training. They know that even if full equality of opportunity could be guaranteed, equality of outcome could not. Ability is not evenly distributed.

But parents' opinions are unscientific. Not until 1979 did a few academics begin to catch up. In that year the Minnesota Centre for Twin and Adoption Research began to contact more than 100 sets of twins and triplets who had been separated at birth and reared apart, mostly in the United States and Britain.

The centre subjected each pair to thorough psychological and physiological tests. If two twins are identical (or "monozygotic"), any differences between them are due to the environment they were reared in; so a measure of heritability can be attached to various mental features. The study concluded that about 70% of the variance in IQ was explained by genetic factors. It also found that on a large number of measures of personality and temperament—notably personal interests and social attitudes—identical twins reared apart are about as similar as identical twins reared together.

The Minnesota study represents the respectable end of an academic spectrum that stretches all the way through to outright racists. If IQ is 70% inherited, then perhaps much of the IQ difference between

From *The Economist,* December 26, 1992–January 8, 1993, pp. 33-34, 36. © 1993 by The Economist, Ltd. Distributed by The New York Times Special Features.

races is also inherited. The logic does not necessarily follow, since the differences could all lie in the 30% that is nurture; but still it is a hypothesis worth testing—at least for those prepared to risk being called politically incorrect.

Unfortunately, because there are no black-white pairs of identical twins, nobody has yet found a way to test whether racial differences in IQ are genetic. It would require getting 100 pairs of black parents and 100 pairs of white parents to rear their children on identical incomes in an identical suburb and send the children of 50 of each to the same good school and 50 of each to a bad one. Impossible.

This means that racial differences in IQ tend to attract scientists with dubious motives and methods. With increasing enthusiasm over the past decade, some psychologists have disinterred a technique already consigned to the attic by their Victorian predecessors: using physiological data to measure intellectual skill.

Arthur Jensen, a professor of educational psychology at the University of California, Berkeley, has assembled a large body of results purportedly demonstrating that IQ is closely correlated with speed of reaction, a theory abandoned around 1900. He claims that intelligence is correlated with the rate at which glucose is consumed in the brain, the speed of neural transmission and a large number of anatomical variables such as height, brain size and even head size.

Jean Philippe Rushton, a professor of psychology at the University of Western Ontario, Canada, has revived craniometry, the Victorian attempt to correlate head size with brain power. (In "The Adventure of the Blue Carbuncle", one of Arthur Conan Doyle's most ingenious Christmas stories, Sherlock Holmes deduces that a man is an intellectual from the size of his hat: "It is a question of cubic capacity . . . a man with so large a brain must have something in it.")

Mr Rushton has studied data on the head sizes of thousands of American servicemen, gathered to make sure that army helmets fit. Adjusting the raw data for variables such as body size, he argues that men have bigger craniums than women, that the well-educated have bigger craniums than the less educated, and that orientals have bigger craniums than whites, who have bigger craniums than blacks.

Mr Rushton has done wonders for the protest industry. David Peterson, a former premier of Ontario, called for his dismissal. Protesters likened him to the Nazis and the Ku Klux Klan. The Ontario Provincial police even launched an investigation into his work. An embarrassed university establishment required Mr Rushton to give his lectures on videotape.

Even if you could conclude that blacks have lower IQs than whites after the same education, it is not clear what the policy prescription would be. Presumably, it would only add weight to the argument for positive discrimination in favour of blacks, so as to redress an innate inferiority with a better education. The "entitlement liberalism" that prevails in American social policy and finds its expression in employment quotas and affirmative-action programmes already assumes that blacks need preferential rather than equal treatment. Indeed, to this way of thinking, merit is less important than eliminating group differences and promoting social integration.

The gene of Cain

Compared with the study of racial differences, the study of the genetics of criminality is only slightly more respectable. Harvard's Mr Herrnstein teamed up in the early 1980s with James Wilson, a political scientist, to teach a class on crime. The result was "Crime and Human Nature" (1985), a bulky book which argues that the best explanation for a lot of predatory criminal behaviour—particularly assault and arson—may be biological rather than sociological.

Certainly, a Danish study of the children of criminals adopted into normal households lends some support to the idea that a recidivist criminal's son is more likely to be a criminal than other sons brought up in the same household. But Mr Herrnstein and Mr Wilson then spoil their case with another Victorian throwback to "criminal types"—people with low verbal intelligence and "mesomorphic" (short and muscular) bodies who, they believe, are more likely to be criminal.

One reason such work strikes horror into sociologists is that it suggests an obvious remedy: selective breeding. Mr Herrnstein has suggested that the greater fertility of stupid people means that the wrong kind of selective breeding is already at work and may be responsible for falling academic standards. "We ought to bear in mind", Mr Herrnstein ruminates gloomily about America, "that in not too many generations differential fertility could swamp the effects of anything else we may do about our economic standing in the world." Luckily for Mr Herrnstein, studies reveal that, despite teenage parents in the inner cities, people of high social status are still outbreeding those of low social status. Rich men have more surviving children—not least because they tend to have more wives—than poor men.

In one sense, it is plain that criminality is innate: men resort to it far more than women. Martin Daly and Margo Wilson, of McMaster University in Canada, have compared the homicide statistics of England and Wales with those of Chicago. In both cases, the graphs are identical in shape, with young men 30 times as likely as women of all ages to commit homicide. It is perverse to deny the connection between testosterone and innate male aggressiveness. But it is equally perverse to ignore the fact that the scales of the two graphs are utterly different: young men in Chicago are 30 times as likely to kill as young men in England and Wales—which has nothing to do with nature and much to do with nurture. The sexual difference is nature; the national difference is nurture.

The most successful assault on the nurturist orthodoxy, however, has come not over race, or intelligence, or crime, but over sex. In the 1970s the nurturists vigorously repulsed an attack on their cherished beliefs by the then fledgling discipline of sociobiology. Sociobiology is the study of how animal behaviour evolves to fit function in the same way that anatomy does.

When sociobiologists started to apply the same ideas to human beings, principally through Edward Wilson of Harvard University, a furore broke out. Most of them retreated, as geneticists had done, to study animals again. Anthropologists insisted that their subject, mankind, was basically different from animals because it was not born with its behaviour but learnt it.

In the past few years, however, a new assault from scientists calling themselves Darwinian psychologists has largely refuted that argument. Through a series of experiments and analyses, they have asserted that (a) much sophisticated behaviour is not taught, but develops autonomously; and (b) learning is not the opposite of instinct, but is itself a highly directed instinct.

The best example of this is language. In 1957 Noam Chomsky of the Massachusetts Institute of Technology (MIT) argued that all human languages bear a striking underlying similarity. He called this "deep structure", and argued it was innate and not learnt. In recent years Steven Pinker of MIT and Paul Bloom of the University of Arizona have taken this idea further. They argue that human beings have a "language organ", specially designed for learning grammatical language. It includes a series of highly specific inbuilt assumptions that enable them to learn grammar from examples, without ever being taught it.

Hence the tendency to learn grammatical language is human nature. But a child reared in isolation does not start to speak Hebrew unaided. Vocabulary, and accent, are obviously 100% nurture. In this combination of nature and nurture, argue the Darwinian psychologists, language is typical of most human traits. Learning is not the opposite of instinct; people have innate instincts to learn certain things and not others.

This is heresy to sociologists and anthropologists, who have been reared since Emile Durkheim to believe the human mind is a *tabula rasa*—a blank slate upon which any culture can be written. To this, John Tooby and Leda Cosmides of the University of California at Santa Barbara, two leading thinkers on the subject, have replied: "The assertion that 'culture' explains human variation will be taken seriously when there are reports of women war parties raiding villages to capture men as husbands."

Nor will the Darwinian psychologists concede that to believe in nature is to be a Hobbesian fatalist and that to believe in nurture is to be a Rousseau-ist believer in the perfectibility of man. Many totalitarians are actually nurturists: they believe that rearing people to worship Stalin works. History suggests otherwise.

The making of macho

Physiologists have also begun to add weight to the nature side of the scale with their discovery of how the brain develops. The brain of a fetus is altered by the child's genes, by its and its mother's hormones and, after birth, by its learning. Many of the changes are permanent; so as far as the adult is concerned, they are all "nature", though many are not genetic. For example, the human brain is feminine unless acted upon by male hormones during two bursts—one in the womb and another at puberty. The hormone is nurture, in the sense that it can be altered by injections or drugs taken by the mother. But it is nature in the sense that it is a product of the body's biology.

This discovery has gradually altered the views of many psychologists about sex and education. An increasing number recognise that the competitiveness, roughness, mathematical ability and spatial skills of boys are the product of their biology (genes and hormones) not their family, and that the character-reading, verbal, linguistic and emotional interest and skills of girls are also biological. Hence girls get a better early education when kept away from boys. This conclusion, anathema to most practising educational psychologists, is increasingly common among those who actually do research on it.

Indeed, radical feminism is increasingly having to recognize the biological theme that underlies its claims. Feminists demand equality of opportunity, but they also routinely argue that women bring different qualities to the world: consensus-seeking, uncompetitive, caring, gentle qualities that inherently domineering men lack. Women, they argue, should be in Parliament or Congress in representative numbers to "represent the woman's point of view", which assumes that men cannot.

Many homosexuals have already crossed the bridge to nature. When sociobiologists first suggested that homosexuality might be biological, they were called Nazis and worse. But in the past few years things have turned around completely. The discovery that the identical twin of a homosexual man has an odds-on chance of being homosexual too, whereas a non-identical twin has only a one-in-five chance, implies that there are some influential genes involved. And the discovery that those parts of the brain that are measurably different in women and men are also different in heterosexuals and homosexuals adds further weight to the idea that homosexuality is as natural as left-handedness. That is anathema to pro-family-value conservatives, who believe that homosexuality is a (misguided) personal choice.

Assuming that the new hereditarians are right and that many human features can be related to genes (or, more likely, groups of genes), it might one day be possible to equip each member of the species with a compact disc telling him which version of each of the 50,000-100,000 human genes he has. He might then read whether he was likely to have a weight problem, or be any good at music, whether there was a risk of schizophrenia or a chance of genius, whether he might go manic-depressive or be devoutly religious. But he could never be sure. For beside every gene would be an asterisk referring to a footnote that read thus: "This prediction is only valid if you are brought up by two Protestant, middle-class, white parents in Peoria, Illinois."

BORN GAY?

**Studies of family trees
and DNA make the case
that male homosexuality
is in the genes**

WILLIAM A. HENRY III

WHAT MAKES PEOPLE GAY? TO conservative moralists, homosexuality is a sin, a willful choice of godless evil. To many orthodox behaviorists, homosexuality is a result of a misguided upbringing, a detour from a straight path to marital adulthood; indeed, until 1974 the American Psychiatric Association listed it as a mental disorder. To gays themselves, homosexuality is neither a choice nor a disease but an identity, deeply felt for as far back as their memory can reach. To them, it is not just behavior, not merely what they do in lovemaking, but who they are as people, pervading every moment of their perception, every aspect of their character.

The origins of homosexuality may never be fully understood, and the phenomenon is so complex and varied—as is every other kind of love—that no single neat explanation is likely to suffice to explain any one man or woman, let alone multitudes. But the search for understanding advanced considerably last week with the release of new studies that make the most compelling case yet that homosexual orientation is at least partly genetic.

A team at the National Cancer Institute's Laboratory of Biochemistry reported in the journal *Science* that families of 76 gay men included a much higher proportion of homosexual male relatives than found in the general population. Intriguingly, almost all the disproportion was on the mother's side of the family. That prompted the researchers to look at the chromosomes that determine gender, known as X and Y. Men get an X from

their mother and a Y from their father; women get two X's, one from each parent. Inasmuch as the family trees suggested that male homosexuality may be inherited from mothers, the scientists zeroed in on the X chromosome.

Sure enough, a separate study of the DNA from 40 pairs of homosexual brothers found that 33 pairs shared five different patches of genetic material grouped around a particular area on the X chromosome. Why is that unusual? Because the genes on a son's X chromosome are a highly variable combination of the genes on the mother's two X's, and thus the sequence of genes varies greatly from one brother to another. Statistically, so much overlap between brothers who also share a sexual orientation is unlikely to be just coincidence. The fact that 33 out of 40 pairs of gay brothers were found to share the same sequences of DNA in a particular part of the chromosome suggests that at least one gene related to homosexuality is located in that region. Homosexuality was the only trait that all 33 pairs shared; the brothers didn't all share the same eye color or shoe size or any other obvious characteristic. Nor, according to the study's principal author, Dean Hamer, were they all identifiably effeminate or, for that matter, all macho. They were diverse except for sexual orientation. Says Hamer: "This is by far the strongest evidence to date that there is a genetic component to sexual orientation. We've identified a portion of the genome associated with it."

The link to mothers may help explain a conundrum: If homosexuality is hereditary, why doesn't the trait gradually disappear, as

gays and lesbians are probably less likely than others to have children? The answer suggested by the new research is that genes for male homosexuality can be carried and passed to children by heterosexual women, and those genes do not cause the women to be homosexual. A similar study of lesbians by Hamer's team is taking longer to complete because the existence and chromosomal location of responsible genes is not as obvious as it is in men. But preliminary results from the lesbian study do suggest that female sexual orientation is genetically influenced.

In a related, unpublished study, Hamer added to growing evidence that male homosexuality may be rarer than was long thought—about 2% of the population, vs. the 4% to 10% found by Kinsey and others. Hamer notes, however, that he defined homosexuality very narrowly. "People had to be exclusively or predominantly gay, and had to be out to family members and an outside investigator like me. If we had used a less stringent definition, we would probably have found more gay men."

BEFORE THE NCI, RESEARCH IS ACcepted as definitive, it will have to be validated by repetition. Moreover, the tight focus on pairs of openly homosexual brothers, who are only a subset of the total gay population, leaves many questions about other categories of gay men, lesbians and bisexuals. The NCI researchers concede that their discovery cannot account for all male homosexuality and may be just associated with gayness rather than be a direct cause.

But authors of other studies indicating a biological basis for homosexuality saluted it as a major advance.

Simon LeVay, who won wide publicity for an analysis of differences in brain anatomies between straight and gay men, acknowledges that the brains he studied were of AIDS victims, and thus he cannot be sure that what he saw was genetic rather than the result of disease or some aspect of gay life. Says LeVay: "This new work and the studies of twins are two lines of evidence pointing in the same direction. But the DNA evidence is much stronger than the twin studies." Dr. Richard Pillard, professor of psychiatry at Boston University School of Medicine and co-author of some twin studies—showing that identical twins of gay men have a 50% chance of being gay—is almost as laudatory. Says he: "If the new study holds up, it would be the first example of a higher-order behavior that has been found to be linked to a particular gene."

Whatever its ultimate scientific significance, however, the study's social and political impact is potentially even greater. If homosexuals are deemed to have a foreordained nature, many of the arguments now used to block equal rights would lose force. Opponents of such changes as ending the ban on gays in uniform argue that homosexuality is voluntary behavior, legitimately subject to regulation. Gays counter that they are acting as God or nature—in other words, their genes—intended. Says spokesman Gregory J. King of the Human Rights Campaign Fund, one of the largest gay-rights lobbying groups: "This is a landmark study that can be very helpful in increasing public support for civil rights for lesbian and gay Americans." Some legal scholars think that if gays can establish a genetic basis for sexual preference, like skin color or gender, they may persuade judges that discrimination is unconstitutional.

In addition, genetic evidence would probably affect many private relationships. Parents might be more relaxed about allowing children to have gay teachers, Boy Scout leaders and other role models, on the assumption that the child's future is written in his or her genetic makeup. Those parents whose offspring do turn out gay might be less apt to condemn themselves. Says Cherie Garland of Ashland, Oregon, mother of a 41-year-old gay son: "The first thing any parent of a gay child goes through is guilt. If homosexuality is shown to be genetic, maybe parents and children can get on with learning to accept it." Catherine Tuerk, a nurse psychotherapist who is Washington chapter president of Parents and Friends of Lesbians and Gays, regrets sending her son Joshua into therapy from ages eight to 12 for an "aggression problem"—preference for games involving

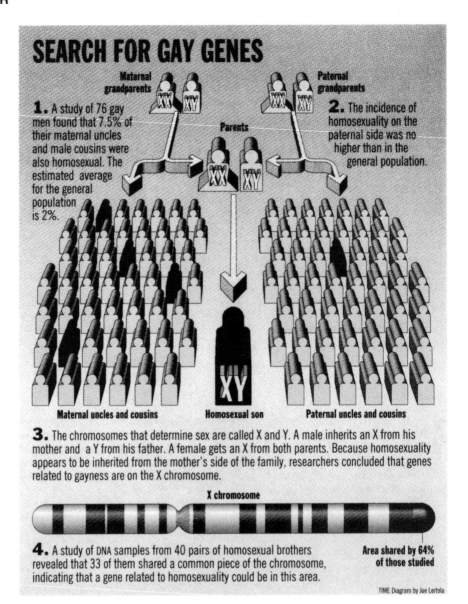

SEARCH FOR GAY GENES

1. A study of 76 gay men found that 7.5% of their maternal uncles and male cousins were also homosexual. The estimated average for the general population is 2%.

Maternal grandparents

Paternal grandparents

Parents

2. The incidence of homosexuality on the paternal side was no higher than in the general population.

Maternal uncles and cousins   Homosexual son   Paternal uncles and cousins

3. The chromosomes that determine sex are called X and Y. A male inherits an X from his mother and a Y from his father. A female gets an X from both parents. Because homosexuality appears to be inherited from the mother's side of the family, researchers concluded that genes related to gayness are on the X chromosome.

X chromosome

4. A study of DNA samples from 40 pairs of homosexual brothers revealed that 33 of them shared a common piece of the chromosome, indicating that a gene related to homosexuality could be in this area.

Area shared by 64% of those studied

TIME Diagram by Joe Lertola

relationships instead of macho play with, say, toy trucks. Says she: "We were trying to cure him of something that doesn't need to be cured. There was nothing wrong with him." On the other hand, mothers who used to blame themselves for faulty upbringing may start blaming themselves for passing on the wrong genes.

Gay brothers surveyed for the study welcome its findings. Rick and Randy Gordon, twins from Orlando, Florida, never felt being gay was a matter of free will. Rick, who works in a law firm, says, "I don't honestly think I chose to be gay." Randy, a supervisor at a bed-and-breakfast, agrees: "I always believed that homosexuality was something I was born with. If homosexuality is genetic, there is nothing you can do about it. If there is more research like this in years to come, hopefully homosexuality will be accepted rather than treated as an abnormality."

Ralph White, 36, an attorney with the General Accounting Office, says he was fired from a senatorial staff in 1982 after admitting he was gay. He foresees abiding significance in the study: "I don't expect people to suddenly change their minds. But the long-term impact will be profound. I can't imagine that rational people, presented with evidence that homosexuality is biological and not a choice, would continue to discriminate." His brother David, 32, a public relations officer, wishes he had had a basis for believing in a genetic cause during his turbulent adolescence: "I was defiant, and to this day I'm probably still that way, because when you're gay in this society you almost have to be."

While many gay leaders welcomed the study, some are queasy. Its very existence, they fret, implies that homosexuality is wrong and defective. Says Donald Suggs of the New York chapter of the Gay & Lesbian Alliance Against Defamation: "Homosexuality is not something to justify and explain, but something that should be accepted. Until people accept us, all the scientific evidence in the world will not do anything to change homophobia." Moreover, gays are worried that precise identification of a "gayness gene" might prompt efforts to tinker with the genetic code of gay adults or to test during pregnancy and abort potentially gay fetuses. Says Thomas Stoddard, director of the Campaign for Military Service: "One can imagine the science of the future manipulating information of this kind to reduce the number of gay people being born."

WARNS ERIC JUENGST OF THE National Center for Human Genome Research: "This is a two-edged sword. It can be used to benefit gays by allowing them to make the case that the trait for which they're being discriminated against is no worse than skin color. On the other hand, it could get interpreted to mean that different is pathological."

Anti-gay activists took up that cry immediately, saying that a genetic basis for homosexuality does not make it any more acceptable. They noted that genetic links are known or suspected for other traits that society judges "undesirable," such as mental and physical illness. Said the Rev. Louis Sheldon, chairman of the Traditional Values Coalition: "The fact that homosexuality may be genetically based will not make much difference for us from a public policy perspective." Reed Irvine, whose watchdog group, Accuracy in Media, increasingly criticizes favorable reportage about gays and gay rights, called for more coverage of studies that he claims show homosexuality can be "cured"—an assertion that both gays and health professionals widely dispute. Says Irvine: "It's a little more complicated than just saying you can prove there's a hereditary factor. The media have given zero attention to the many, many homosexuals who have gone straight. I think it's sending gays the wrong message to say you cannot change because it's something your genes have determined."

Even gays admit that Irvine is partly right. Homosexuality is not simply programmed but is a complex expression of values and personality. As researcher Hamer says, "Genes are part of the story, and this gene region is a part of the genetic story, but it's not all of the story." We may never know all of the story. But to have even part of it can bring light where of late there has been mostly a searing heat. —*Reported by Ellen Germain/Washington and Alice Park/New York*

Trends in Behavioral Genetics

EUGENICS REVISITED

Scientists are linking genes to a host of complex human disorders and traits, but just how valid—and useful—are these findings?

John Horgan, *senior writer*

"How to Tell If Your Child's a Serial Killer!" That was the sound bite with which the television show *Donahue* sought to entice listeners February 25. On the program, a psychiatrist from the Rochester, N.Y., area noted that some men are born with not one Y chromosome but two. Double-Y men, the psychiatrist said, are "at special risk for antisocial, violent behavior." In fact, the psychiatrist had recently studied such a man. Although he had grown up in a "Norman Rockwell" setting, as an adult he had strangled at least 11 women and two children.

"It is not hysterical or overstating it," Phil Donahue told his horrified audience, "to say that we are moving toward the time when, quite literally, just as we can anticipate . . . genetic predispositions toward various physical diseases, we will also be able to pinpoint mental disorders which include aggression, antisocial behavior and the possibility of very serious criminal activity later on."

Eugenics is back in fashion. The message that genetics can explain, predict and even modify human behavior for the betterment of society is promulgated not just on sensationalistic talk shows but by our most prominent scientists. James D. Watson, co-discoverer of the double-helix structure of DNA and former head of the Human Genome Project, the massive effort to map our entire genetic endowment, said recently, "We used to think that our fate was in our stars. Now we know, in large part, that our fate is in our genes."

Daniel E. Koshland, Jr., a biologist at the University of California at Berkeley and editor of *Science*, the most influential peer-reviewed journal in the U.S., has declared in an editorial that the nature/nurture debate is "basically over," since scientists have shown that genes influence many aspects of human behavior. He has also contended that genetic research may help eliminate society's most intractable problems, including drug abuse, homelessness and, yes, violent crime.

Some studies cited to back this claim are remarkably similar to those conducted over a century ago by scientists such as Francis Galton, known as the father of eugenics. Just as the British polymath studied identical twins in order to show that "nature prevails enormously over nurture," so do modern researchers. But the primary reason behind the revival of eugenics is the astonishing successes of biologists in mapping and manipulating the human genome. Over the past decade, investigators have identified genes underlying such crippling diseases as cystic fibrosis, muscular dystrophy and, this past spring, Huntington's disease. Given these advances, researchers say, it is only a matter of time before they can lay bare the genetic foundation of much more complex traits and disorders.

The political base for eugenics has also become considerably broader in recent years. Spokespersons for the mentally ill believe demonstrating the genetic basis of disorders such as schizophrenia and manic depression—and even alcoholism and drug addiction—will lead not only to better diagnoses and

treatments but also to more compassion toward sufferers and their families. Some homosexuals believe society will become more tolerant toward them if it can be shown that sexual orientation is an innate, biological condition and not a matter of choice.

But critics contend that no good can come of bad science. Far from moving inexorably closer to its goals, they point out, the field of behavioral genetics is mired in the same problems that have always plagued it. Behavioral traits are extraordinarily difficult to define, and practically every claim of a genetic basis can also be explained as an environmental effect. "This has been a huge enterprise, and for the most part the work has been done shoddily. Even careful people get sucked into misinterpreting data," says Jonathan Beckwith, a geneticist at Harvard University. He adds, "There are social consequences to this."

The skeptics also accuse the media of having created an unrealistically optimistic view of the field. Richard C. Lewontin, a biologist at Harvard and a prominent critic of behavioral genetics, contends that the media generally give much more prominent coverage to dramatic reports—such as the discovery of an "alcoholism gene"—than to contradictory results or retractions. "Skepticism doesn't make the news," Lewontin says. "It only makes the news when you find a gene." The result is that spurious findings often become accepted by the public and even by so-called experts.

The claim that men with an extra Y chromosome are predisposed toward violence is a case in point. It stems from a survey in the 1960s that found more extra-Y men in prison than in the general population. Some researchers hypothesized that since the Y chromo-

some confers male attributes, men with an extra Y become hyperaggressive "supermales." Follow-up studies indicated that while extra-Y men tend to be taller than other men and score slightly lower on intelligence tests, they are otherwise normal. The National Academy of Sciences concluded in a report published this year that there is no evidence to support the link between the extra Y chromosome and violent behavior.

Minnesota Twins

No research in behavioral genetics has been more eagerly embraced by the press than the identical-twin studies done at the University of Minnesota. Thomas J. Bouchard, Jr., a psychologist, initiated them in the late 1970s, and since then they have been featured in the *Washington Post, Newsweek,* the *New York Times* and other publications worldwide as well as on television. *Science* has favorably described the Minnesota team's work in several news stories and in 1990 published a major article by the group.

The workers have studied more than 50 pairs of identical twins who were separated shortly after birth and raised in different households. The assump-

tion is that any differences between identical twins, who share all each other's genes, are caused by the environment; similarities are attributed to their shared genes. The group estimates the relative contribution of genes to a given trait in a term called "heritability." A trait that stems entirely from genes, such as eye color, is defined as 100 percent heritable. Height is 90 percent heritable; that is, 90 percent of the variation in height is accounted for by genetic variation, and the other 10 percent is accounted for by diet and other environmental factors.

The Minnesota group has reported finding a strong genetic contribution to practically all the traits it has examined. Whereas most previous studies have estimated the heritability of intelligence (as defined by performance on intelligence tests) as roughly 50 percent, Bouchard and his colleagues arrived at a figure of 70 percent. They have also found a genetic component underlying such culturally defined traits as religiosity, political orientation (conservative versus liberal), job satisfaction, leisure-time interests and proneness to divorce. In fact, the group concluded in *Science,* "On multiple measures of personality and temperament...monozy-

gotic twins reared apart are about as similar as are monozygotic twins reared together." (Identical twins are called monozygotic because they stem from a single fertilized egg, or zygote.)

The researchers have buttressed their statistical findings with anecdotes about "eerie," "bewitching" and "remarkable" parallels between reunited twins. One case involved Oskar, who was raised as a Nazi in Czechoslovakia, and Jack, who was raised as a Jew in Trinidad. Both were reportedly wearing shirts with epaulets when they were reunited by the Minnesota group in 1979. They also both flushed the toilet before as well as after using it and enjoyed deliberately sneezing to startle people in elevators.

Some other celebrated cases involved two British women who wore seven rings and named their firstborn sons Richard Andrew and Andrew Richard; two men who both had been named Jim, named their pet dogs Toy, married women named Linda, divorced them and remarried women named Betty; and two men who had become firefighters and drank Budweiser beer.

Other twin researchers say the significance of these coincidences has been greatly exaggerated. Richard J. Rose of Indiana University, who is collaborating on a study of 16,000 pairs of twins in Finland, points out that "if you bring together strangers who were born on the same day in the same country and ask them to find similarities between them, you may find a lot of seemingly astounding coincidences."

Rose's collaborator, Jaakko Kaprio of the University of Helsinki, notes that the Minnesota twin studies may also be biased by their selection method. Whereas he and Rose gather data by combing birth registries and sending questionnaires to those identified as twins, the Minnesota group relies heavily on media coverage to recruit new twins. The twins then come to Minnesota for a week of study—and, often, further publicity. Twins who are "interested in publicity and willing to support it," Kaprio says, may be atypical. This self-selection effect, he adds, may explain why the Bouchard group's estimates of heritability tend to be higher than those of other studies.

One of the most outspoken critics of

the Minnesota twin studies—and indeed all twin studies indicating high heritability of behavioral traits—is Leon J. Kamin, a psychologist at Northeastern University. In the 1970s Kamin helped to expose inconsistencies and possible fraud in studies of separated identical twins conducted by the British psychologist Cyril Burt during the previous two decades. Burt's conclusion that intelligence was mostly inherited had inspired various observers, notably Arthur R. Jensen, a psychologist at the University of California at Berkeley, to argue that socioeconomic stratification in the U.S. is largely a genetic phenomenon.

In his investigations of other twin studies, Kamin has shown that identical twins supposedly raised apart are often raised by members of their family or by unrelated families in the same neighborhood; some twins had extensive contact with each other while growing up. Kamin suspects the same may be true of some Minnesota twins. He notes, for example, that some news accounts suggested Oskar and Jack (the Nazi and the Jew) and the two British women wearing seven rings were reunited for the first time when they arrived in Minnesota to be studied by Bouchard. Actually, both pairs of twins had met previously. Kamin has repeatedly asked the Minnesota group for detailed case histories of its twins to determine whether it has underestimated contact and similarities in upbringing. "They've never responded," he says.

Kamin proposes that the Minnesota twins have particularly strong motives to downplay previous contacts and to exaggerate their similarities. They might want to please researchers, to attract more attention from the media or even to make money. In fact, some twins acquired agents and were paid for appearances on television. Jack and Oskar recently sold their life story to a film producer in Los Angeles (who says Robert Duvall is interested in the roles).

Even the Minnesota researchers caution against overinterpretation of their work. They agree with their critics that high heritability should not be equated with inevitability, since the environment can still drastically affect the expression of a gene. For example, the genetic disease phenylketonuria, which causes profound retardation, has a heritability of 100 percent. Yet eliminating the amino acid phenylalanine from the diet of affected persons prevents retardation from occurring.

Such warnings tend to be minimized in media coverage, however. Writers often make the same inference that Koshland did in an editorial in *Science:* "Bet-

ter schools, a better environment, better counseling and better rehabilitation will help some individuals but not all." The prime minister of Singapore apparently reached the same conclusion. A decade ago he cited popular accounts of the Minnesota research in defending policies that encouraged middle-class Singaporeans to bear children and discouraged childbearing by the poor.

Smart Genes

Twin studies, of course, do not indicate which specific genes contribute to a trait. Early in the 1980s scientists began developing powerful ways to unearth that information. The techniques stem from the fact that certain stretches of human DNA, called polymorphisms, vary in a predictable way. If a polymorphism is consistently inherited together with a given trait—blue eyes, for example—then geneticists assume it either lies near a gene for that trait or actually is the gene. A polymorphism that merely lies near a gene is known as a marker.

In so-called linkage studies, investigators search for polymorphisms co-inherited with a trait in families unusually prone to the trait. In 1983 researchers used this method to find a marker linked to Huntington's disease, a crippling neurological disorder that usually strikes carriers in middle age and kills them within 10 years. Since then, the same technique has pinpointed genes for cystic fibrosis, muscular dystrophy and other diseases. In association studies, researchers compare the relative frequency of polymorphisms in two unrelated populations, one with the trait and one lacking it.

Workers are already using both methods to search for polymorphisms associated with intelligence, defined as the ability to score well on standardized intelligence tests. In 1991 Shelley D. Smith of the Boys Town National Institute for Communication Disorders in Children, in Omaha, and David W. Fulker of the University of Colorado identified polymorphisms associated with dyslexia in a linkage study of 19 families exhibiting high incidence of the reading disorder.

Behavioral Genetics: A Lack-of-Progress Report

CRIME: Family, twin and adoption studies have suggested a heritability of 0 to more than 50 percent for predisposition to crime. (Heritability represents the degree to which a trait stems from genetic factors.) In the 1960s researchers reported an association between an extra Y chromosome and violent crime in males. Follow-up studies found that association to be spurious.

MANIC DEPRESSION: Twin and family studies indicate heritability of 60 to 80 percent for susceptibility to manic depression. In 1987 two groups reported locating different genes linked to manic depression, one in Amish families and the other in Israeli families. Both reports have been retracted.

SCHIZOPHRENIA: Twin studies show heritability of 40 to 90 percent. In 1988 a group reported finding a gene linked to schizophrenia in British and Icelandic families. Other studies documented no linkage, and the initial claim has now been retracted.

ALCOHOLISM: Twin and adoption studies suggest heritability ranging from 0 to 60 percent. In 1990 a group claimed to link a gene—one that produces a receptor for the neurotransmitter dopamine—with alcoholism. A recent review of the evidence concluded it does not support a link.

INTELLIGENCE: Twin and adoption studies show a heritability of performance on intelligence tests of 20 to 80 percent. One group recently unveiled preliminary evidence for genetic markers for high intelligence (an IQ of 130 or higher). The study is unpublished.

HOMOSEXUALITY: In 1991 a researcher cited anatomic differences between the brains of heterosexual and homosexual males. Two recent twin studies have found a heritability of roughly 50 percent for predisposition to male or female homosexuality. These reports have been disputed. Another group claims to have preliminary evidence of genes linked to male homosexuality. The data have not been published.

Two years ago Robert Plomin, a psychologist at Pennsylvania State University who has long been active in behavioral genetics, received a $600,000 grant from the National Institute of Child Health and Human Development to search for genes linked to high intelligence. Plomin is using the association method, which he says is more suited than the linkage technique to identifying genes whose contribution to a trait is relatively small. Plomin is studying a group of 64 schoolchildren 12 to 13 years old who fall into three groups: those who score approximately 130, 100 and 80 on intelligence tests.

Plomin has examined some 25 polymorphisms in each of these three groups, trying to determine whether any occur with greater frequency in the "bright" children. The polymorphisms have been linked to genes thought to have neurological effects. He has uncovered several markers that seem to occur more often in the highest-scoring children. He is now seeking to replicate his results in another group of 60 children; half score above 142 on intelligence tests, and half score less than 74 (yet have no obvious organic deficiencies). Plomin presented his preliminary findings at a meeting, titled "Origins and Development of High Ability," held in London in January.

At the same meeting, however, other workers offered evidence that intelligence tests are actually poor predictors of success in business, the arts or even advanced academic programs. Indeed, even Plomin seems ambivalent about the value of his research. He suggests that someday genetic information on the cognitive abilities of children might help teachers design lessons that are more suited to students' innate strengths and weaknesses.

But he also calls his approach "a fishing expedition," given that a large number of genes may contribute to intelligence. He thinks the heritability of intelligence is not 70 percent, as the Minnesota twin researchers have claimed, but 50 percent, which is the average finding of other studies, and at best he can only find a gene that accounts for a tiny part of variance in intelligence. "If you wanted to select on the basis of this, it would be of no use whatsoever," he remarks. These cautions did not prevent the *Sunday Telegraph*, a London newspaper, from announcing that Plomin had found "evidence that geniuses are born not made."

Evan S. Balaban, a biologist at Harvard, thinks Plomin's fishing expedition is doomed to fail. He grants that there may well be a significant genetic component to intelligence (while insisting that studies by Bouchard and others have not demonstrated one). But he doubts whether investigators will ever uncover any specific genes related to high intelligence or "genius." "It is very rare to find genes that have a specific effect," he says. "For evolutionary reasons, this just doesn't happen very often."

The history of the search for markers associated with mental illness supports Balaban's view. Over the past few decades, studies of twins, families and adoptees have convinced most investigators that schizophrenia and manic depression are not caused by psychosocial factors—such as the notorious "schizophrenogenic mother" postulated by some Freudian psychiatrists—but by biological and genetic factors. After observing the dramatic success of linkage studies in the early 1980s, researchers immediately began using the technique to isolate polymorphic markers for mental illness. The potential value of such research was enormous, given that schizophrenia and manic depression each affect roughly one percent of the global population.

They seemed to have achieved their first great success in 1987. A group led by Janice A. Egeland of the University of Miami School of Medicine claimed it had linked a genetic marker on chromosome 11 to manic depression in an Amish population. That same year another team, led by Miron Baron of Columbia University, linked a marker on the X chromosome to manic depression in three Israeli families.

The media hailed these announcements as major breakthroughs. Far less attention was paid to the retractions that followed. A more extensive analysis of the Amish in 1989 by a group from the National Institute of Mental Health turned up no link between chromosome 11 and manic depression. This year Baron's team retracted its claim of linkage with the X chromosome after doing a new study of its Israeli families with more sophisticated markers and more extensive diagnoses.

Schizophrenic Results

Studies of schizophrenia have followed a remarkably similar course. In 1988 a group headed by Hugh M. D. Gurling of the University College, London, Medical School announced in *Nature* that it had found linkage in Icelandic and British families between genetic markers on chromosome 5 and schizophrenia. In the same issue, however, researchers led by Kenneth K. Kidd of Yale University reported seeing no such linkage in a Swedish family. Although Gurling defended his result as legitimate for several years, additional research has convinced him that it was probably a false positive. "The new families showed no linkage at all," he says.

These disappointments have highlighted the problems involved in using linkage to study mental illness. Neil Risch, a geneticist at Yale, points out that linkage analysis is ideal for studying diseases, such as Huntington's, that have distinct symptoms and are caused by a single dominant gene. Some researchers had hoped that at least certain subtypes of schizophrenia or manic depression might be single-gene disorders. Single-gene mutations are thought to cause variants of breast cancer and of Alzheimer's disease that run in families and are manifested much earlier than usual. But such diseases are rare, Risch says, because natural selection quickly winnows them out of the population, and no evidence exists for distinct subtypes of manic depression or schizophrenia.

Indeed, all the available evidence suggests that schizophrenia and manic depression are caused by at least several genes—each of which may exert only a tiny influence—acting in concert with environmental influences. Finding such genes with linkage analysis may not be impossible, Risch says, but it will be considerably more difficult than identifying genes that have a one-to-one correspondence to a trait. The difficulty is compounded by the fact that the diagnosis of mental illness is often subjective—all the more so when researchers are relying on family records or recollections.

Some experts now question whether genes play a significant role in mental illness. "Personally, I think we have overestimated the genetic component of schizophrenia," says E. Fuller Torrey, a psychiatrist at St. Elizabeth's Hospital in Washington, D.C. He argues that the evidence supporting genetic models can be explained by other biological factors, such as a virus that strikes in utero. The pattern of incidence of schizophrenia in families often resembles that of other viral diseases, such as polio. "Genes may just create a susceptibility to the virus," Torrey explains.

The Drink Link

Even Kidd, the Yale geneticist who has devoted his career to searching for genes linked to mental illness, acknowledges that "in a rigorous, technical, scientific sense, there is very little proof that schizophrenia, manic depression" and other psychiatric disorders have a genetic origin. "Virtually all the evidence supports a genetic explanation, but there are always other explanations, even if they are convoluted."

The evidence for a genetic basis for alcoholism is even more tentative than that for manic depression and schizophrenia. Although some studies discern a genetic component, especially in males, others have reached the opposite conclusion. Gurling, the University College investigator, found a decade ago that identical twins were slightly *more* likely to be discordant for alcoholism than fraternal twins. The drinking habits of some identical twins were strikingly different. "In some cases, one drank a few bottles a day, and the other didn't drink at all," Gurling says.

Nevertheless, in 1990 a group led by Kenneth Blum of the University of Texas Health Science Center at San Antonio announced it had discovered a genetic marker for alcoholism in an association study comparing 35 alcoholics with a control group of 35 nonalcoholics. A page-one story in the *New York Times* portrayed the research as a potential watershed in the diagnosis and treatment of alcoholism without mentioning the considerable skepticism aroused among other researchers.

The Blum group claimed that its marker, called the A1 allele, was associated with a gene, called the D2 gene, that codes for a receptor for the neurotransmitter dopamine. Skeptics noted that the A1 allele was actually some 10,000 base pairs from the dopamine-receptor gene and was not linked to any detectable variation in its expression.

Since the initial announcement by Blum, three papers, including an additional one by Blum's group, have presented more evidence of an association between the A1 allele and alcoholism. Six groups have found no such evidence (and received virtually no mention in the popular media).

In April, Risch and Joel Gelernter of Yale and David Goldman of the National Institute on Alcohol Abuse and Alcoholism analyzed all these studies on the A1 allele in a paper in the *Journal of the American Medical Association.* They noted that if Blum's two studies are cast aside, the balance of the results shows

BRAIN OF SCHIZOPHRENIC (*right*) appears different from the brain of his identical twin in these magnetic resonance images. Such findings suggest that factors that are biological but not genetic—such as viruses—may play a significant role in mental illness.

The Huntington's Disease Saga: A Cautionary Tale

The identification of the gene for Huntington's disease, which was announced in March, was hailed as one of the great success stories of modern genetics. Yet it provides some rather sobering lessons for researchers seeking genes linked to more complex human disorders and traits.

The story begins in the late 1970s, when workers developed novel techniques for identifying polymorphisms, sections of the human genome that come in two or more forms. Investigators realized that by finding polymorphisms linked—always and exclusively—to diseases, they could determine which chromosome the gene resides in. Researchers decided to test the polymorphism technique on Huntington's disease, a devastating neurological disorder that affects roughly one in 10,000 people. Scientists had known for more than a century that Huntington's was caused by a mutant, dominant gene. If one parent has the disease, his or her offspring have a 50 percent chance of inheriting it.

One of the leaders of the Huntington's effort was Nancy Wexler, a neuropsychologist at Columbia University whose mother had died of the disease and who therefore has a 50 percent chance of developing it herself. She and other researchers focused on a poor Venezuelan village whose inhabitants had an unusually high incidence of the disease. In 1983, through what has now become a legendary stroke of good fortune, they found a linkage with one of the first polymorphisms they tested. The linkage indicated that the gene for Huntington's disease was somewhere on chromosome 4.

The finding led quickly to a test for determining whether offspring of carriers—either in utero or already born—have inherited the gene itself. The test requires an analysis of blood samples from several members of a family known to carry the disease. Wexler herself has declined to say whether she has taken the test.

Researchers assumed that they would quickly identify the actual gene in chromosome 4 that causes Huntington's disease. Yet it took 10 years for six teams of workers from 10 institutions to find the gene. It is a so-called expanding gene, which for unknown reasons gains base pairs (the chemical "rungs" binding two strands of DNA) every time it is transmitted. The greater the expansion of the gene, researchers say, the earlier the onset of the disease. The search was complicated by the fact that workers had no physical clues about the course of the disease to guide them. Indeed, Wexler and others emphasize that they still have no idea how the gene actually causes the disease; treatments or cures may be years or decades away.

The most immediate impact of the new discovery will be the development of a better test for Huntington's, one that requires blood only from the person at risk

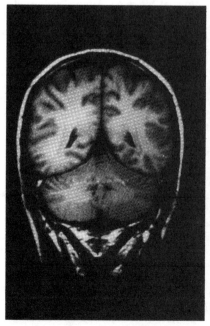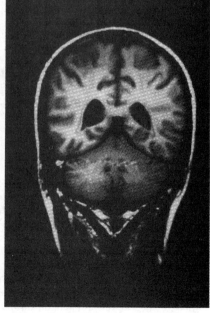

NANCY WEXLER helped to find the gene responsible for Huntington's disease by studying a population in Venezuela that has been ravaged by the disorder.

and not other family members. By measuring the length of the mutant gene, the test might also predict more accurately when carriers will show symptoms.

As difficult as it was to pinpoint the gene for Huntington's, it will be almost infinitely harder to discover genes for behavioral disorders, says Evan S. Balaban, a biologist at Harvard University. Unlike Huntington's disease, he notes, disorders such as schizophrenia and alcoholism cannot be unambiguously diagnosed. Furthermore, they stem not from a single dominant gene but from many genes acting in concert with environmental effects. If researchers do find a statistical association between certain genes and a trait, Balaban says, that knowledge may never be translated into useful therapies or tests. "What does it mean to have a 10 percent increased risk of alcoholism?" he asks.

---

no association between the D2 receptor and alcoholism, either in the disorder's milder or most severe forms. "We therefore conclude that no physiologically significant association" between the A1 allele and alcoholism has been proved, the group stated. "It's a dead issue," Risch says.

Gelernter and his colleagues point out that association studies are prone to spurious results if not properly controlled. They suggest that the positive findings of Blum and his colleagues may have derived from a failure to control for ethnic variation. The limited surveys done so far have shown that the incidence of the A1 allele varies wildly in different ethnic groups, ranging from 10 percent in certain Jewish groups to about 50 percent in Japanese.

Blum insists that the ethnic data, far from undermining his case, support it,

since those groups with the highest prevalence of the A1 allele also exhibit the highest rates of "addictive behavior." He contends that the only reason the Japanese do not display higher rates of alcoholism is that many also carry a gene that prevents them from metabolizing alcohol. "They're pretty compulsive," explains Blum, who recently obtained a patent for a genetic test for alcoholism.

These arguments have been rejected even by Irving I. Gottesman of the University of Virginia, who is a strong defender of genetic models of human behavior. He considers the papers cited by Blum to support his case to be ambiguous and even contradictory. Some see an association only with alcoholism that leads to medical complications or even death; others discern no association with alcoholism but only with "polysubstance abuse," including cigarette smoking. "I think it is by and large

garbage," Gottesman says of the alleged A1-alcoholism link.

By far the most controversial area of behavioral genetics is research on crime. Last fall complaints by civil-rights leaders and others led the National Institutes of Health to withdraw its funding from a meeting entitled "Genetic Factors in Crime: Findings, Uses and Implications." The conference brochure had noted the "apparent failure of environmental approaches to crime" and suggested that genetic research might yield methods for identifying and treating potential criminals—and particularly those prone to violence—at an early age.

Critics contend that such investigations inevitably suggest that blacks are predisposed to crime, given that blacks in the U.S. are six times more likely than whites to be arrested for a violent crime. In fact, some prominent scientists, notably Richard J. Herrnstein, a psychologist at Harvard, have made this assertion. Others reject this view but insist biological research on attributes linked to violent crime, such as aggression, may still have some value. "People who are unwilling to address genetic and biochemical factors are just putting their heads in the sand," says Goldman, the alcoholism expert. "It is not fair to say that just because there have been geneticists who have had a very narrow view of this in the past, we shouldn't explore this now."

In fact, investigations of the biology of violent crime continue, albeit quietly. Workers at City of Hope Hospital in Duarte, Calif., claim to have found an association between the A1 allele—the alleged alcoholism marker—and "criminal aggression." Last year a group led by Markus J. P. Kruesi of the University of Illinois at Chicago presented evidence of an association between low levels of the neurotransmitter serotonin and disruptive-behavior disorders in children. Kruesi concedes there is no way to determine whether the serotonin levels are genetically influenced. In fact, the serotonin levels might be an effect—a reaction to an environmental trauma—rather than a cause. "This might be a scar marker," he says.

One reason such research persists is that studies of families, twins and adoptees have suggested a genetic component to crime. Glenn D. Walters, a psychologist at the Federal Correctional Institution in Schuylkill, Pa., recently reviewed 38 of these studies, conducted from the 1930s to the present, in the journal *Criminology*. His meta-analysis turned up a small genetic effect, "but nothing to get excited about." He

"Better Breeding"

Fairly or not, modern genetics research is still haunted by the history of eugenics. "It offers a lot of cautionary lessons," says Daniel J. Kevles, a historian at the California Institute of Technology, who wrote the 1985 book *In the Name of Eugenics*. The British scientist Francis Galton, cousin to Charles Darwin, first proposed that human society could be improved "through better breeding" in 1865 in an article entitled "Hereditary Talent and Character." He coined the term "eugenics," from the Greek for "good birth," in 1883.

Galton's proposal had broad appeal. The American sexual libertarian John Humphrey Noyes bent eugenics into an ingenious argument for polygamy. "While the good man will be limited by his conscience to what the law allows," Noyes said, "the bad man, free from moral check, will distribute his seed beyond the legal limit."

A more serious advocate was the biologist Charles B. Davenport, founder of Cold Spring Harbor Laboratory and of the Eugenics Record Office, which gathered information on thousands of American families for genetic research. After demonstrating the heritability of eye, skin and hair color, Davenport went on to "prove" the heritability of traits such as "pauperism," criminality and "feeble-mindedness." In one monograph, published in 1919, he asserted that the ability to be a naval officer is an inherited trait, composed of subtraits for thalassophilia, or love of the sea, and hyperkineticism, or wanderlust. Noting the paucity of female naval officers, Davenport concluded that the trait is unique to males.

Beginning in the 1920s the American Eugenics Society, founded by Davenport and others, sponsored "Fitter Families Contests" at state fairs around the U.S. Just as cows and sheep were appraised by judges at the fairs, so were human entrants (such as the family shown above at the 1925 Texas State Fair). Less amusingly, eugenicists helped to persuade more than 20 U.S. states to authorize sterilization of men and women in prisons and mental hospitals, and they urged the federal government to restrict the immigration of "undesirable" races.

No nation, of course, practiced eugenics as enthusiastically as Nazi Germany, whose program culminated in "euthanasia" ("good death") of the mentally and physically disabled as well as Jews, Gypsies, Catholics and others. As revelations of these atrocities spread after World War II, popular support for eugenics programs waned in the U.S. and elsewhere.

observes that "a lot of the research has not been very good" and that the more recent, better-designed studies tended to turn up less evidence. "I don't think we will find any biological markers for crime," he says. "We should put our resources elsewhere."

Gay Genes

The ostensible purpose of investigations of mental illness, alcoholism and even crime is to reduce their incidence. Scientists studying homosexuality have a different goal: simply to test whether homosexuality is innate, as many homosexuals have long professed. That claim was advanced by a report in *Science* in 1991 by Simon LeVay of the Salk Institute for Biological Studies in San Diego. LeVay has acknowledged both that he is gay and that he believes evidence of biological differences between homosexuals and heterosexuals will encourage tolerance toward gays.

LeVay, who recently left the Salk Institute to found the Institute of Gay and Lesbian Education, focused on a tiny neural structure in the hypothalamus, a region of the brain known to control sexual response. He measured this structure, called the interstitial nucleus, in autopsies of the brains of 19 homosexual males, 16 heterosexual males and six heterosexual women. LeVay found that the interstitial nucleus was almost twice as large in the heterosexual males as in the homosexual males or in the women. He postulated that the interstitial nucleus "is large in individuals oriented toward women"—whether male or female.

Of course, LeVay's finding only addresses anatomic differences, not necessarily genetic ones. Various other researchers have tried to establish that homosexuality is not just biological in its origin—caused, perhaps, by hormonal influences in utero—but also genetic. Some have sought evidence in experiments with rats and other animals. A group headed by Angela Pattatucci of the National Cancer Institute is studying a strain of male fruit flies—which wags have dubbed either "fruity" or "fruitless"—that court other males.

In December 1991 J. Michael Bailey of Northwestern University and Richard C. Pillard of Boston University announced they had uncovered evidence of a genetic basis for male homosexuality in humans. They studied 161 gay men, each of whom had at least one identical or fraternal twin or adopted brother. The researchers determined that 52 percent of the identical twins were both homosexual, as compared with 22 percent of the fraternal twins and 11 percent of the adopted brothers.

Bailey and Pillard derived similar results in a study of lesbians published this year in the *Archives of General Psychiatry*. They compared 147 gay women with identical or fraternal twins or adopted sisters: 48 percent of the identical twins were both gay, versus 16 percent of the fraternal twins (who share only half each other's genes) and 6 percent of the adopted sisters. "Both male and female sexual orientation appeared to be influenced by genetic factors," Bailey and Pillard concluded.

This conclusion has disturbed some of Bailey and Pillard's own subjects. "I have major questions about the validity of some of the assumptions they are making," says Nina Sossen, a gay woman living in Madison, Wis., whose identical twin is heterosexual. Her doubts are shared by William Byne, a psychiatrist at Columbia University. He notes that in their study of male homosexuality Bailey and Pillard found more concordance between unrelated, adopted brothers than related (but non-twin) brothers. The high concordance of the male and female identical twins, moreover, may stem from the fact that such twins are often dressed alike and treated alike—indeed, they are often mistaken for each other—by family members as well as by others.

"The increased concordance for homosexuality among the identical twins could be entirely accounted for by the increased similarity of their developmental experiences," Byne says. "In my opinion, the major finding of that study is that 48 percent of identical twins who were reared together were discordant for sexual orientation."

Byne also criticizes LeVay's conclusion that homosexuality must be biological—although not necessarily genetic—because the brains of male homosexuals resemble the brains of women. That assumption, Byne points out, rests on still another assumption, that there are significant anatomic differences between heterosexual male and female brains. But to date, there have been no replicable studies showing such sexual dimorphism.

Byne notes that he has been suspected of having an antigay motive. Two reviewers of an article he recently wrote criticizing homosexuality research accused him of having a "right-wing agenda," he says. He has also been contacted by conservative groups hoping he will speak out against the admittance of homosexuals to the military. He emphasizes that he supports gay rights and thinks homosexuality, whatever its

cause, is not a "choice." He adds that genetic models of behavior are just as likely to foment bigotry as to quell it.

"Hierarchy of Worthlessness"

Despite the skepticism of Byne and others, at least one group, led by Dean Hamer of the National Cancer Institute, is searching not merely for anatomic or biochemical differences in homosexuals but for genetic markers. Hamer has done a linkage study of numerous small families, each of which has at least two gay brothers. He says his study has turned up some tentative findings, and he plans to submit his results soon. Hamer's colleague Pattatucci is planning a similar study of lesbians.

What purpose will be served by pinpointing genes linked to homosexuality? In an information sheet for prospective participants in his study, Hamer expresses the hope that his research may "improve understanding between people with different sexual orientations." He adds, "This study is not aimed at developing methods to alter either heterosexual or homosexual orientation, and the results of the study will not allow sexual orientation to be determined by a blood test or amniocentesis."

Yet even Pillard, who is gay and applauds Hamer's work, admits to some concern over the potential uses of a genetic marker for homosexuality. He notes that some parents might choose to abort embryos carrying such a marker. Male and female homosexuals might then retaliate, he says, by conceiving children and aborting fetuses that lacked such a gene.

Balaban, the Harvard biologist, thinks the possible dangers of such research—assuming it is successful—outweigh any benefits. Indeed, he sees behavioral genetics as a "hierarchy of worthlessness," with twin studies at the bottom and linkage studies of mental illness at the top. The best researchers can hope

for is to find, say, a gene associated with a slightly elevated risk of schizophrenia. Such information is more likely to lead to discrimination by insurance companies and employers than to therapeutic benefits, Balaban warns.

His colleague Lewontin agrees. In the 1970s, he recalls, insurance companies began requiring black customers to take tests for sickle cell anemia, a genetic disease that primarily affects blacks. Those who refused to take the test or who tested positive were denied coverage. "I feel that this research is a substitute for what is really hard—finding out how to change social conditions," Lewontin remarks. "I think it's the wrong direction for research, given that we have a finite amount of resources."

Paul R. Billings, a geneticist at the California Pacific Medical Center, shares some of these concerns. He agrees that twin studies seem to be inherently ambiguous, and he urges researchers seeking markers for homosexuality to consider what a conservative government—led by Patrick Buchanan, for example—might allow to be done with such information. But he believes some aspects of behavioral genetics, particularly searches for genes underlying mental illness, are worth pursuing.

In an article published in the British journal *Social Science and Medicine* last year, Billings and two other scientists offered some constructive criticism for the field. Researchers engaged in association and linkage studies should establish "strict criteria as to what would constitute meaningful data." Both scientists and the press should emphasize the limitations of such studies, "especially when the mechanism of how a gene acts on a behavior is not known." Billings and his colleagues strive to end their article on a positive note. "Despite the shortcomings of other studies," they say, "there is relatively good evidence for a site on the X chromosome which is associated with [manic depression] in some families." This finding was retracted earlier this year.

The Human Mind
Touching the intangible

The human brain is the most complex object in the known universe. But out of that complexity emerges a stranger structure still—the human mind

Only connect. Forster's injunction is the crux of modern thinking on the mechanisms of the mind. As neurologists have taken the brain apart, they have been astonished at how bitty it is. Outwardly coherent behaviour, like talking and listening, is subcontracted all over the place. Nouns are stored here, adjectives there, syntax elsewhere. Verbs spelled with regular endings are learned using one sort of memory, those spelt with irregular endings are learnt by another; for memory, too, has been atomised into so many pieces that psychologists cannot agree on their number. And the senses, the brain's link with wider reality, do not simply imprint an image of the world upon it; they decompose that image, and shuttle the pieces around like the squares in a Chinese puzzle.

Yet that intangible organ, the conscious mind, seems oblivious to all this. The connections are perfect, the garment apparently seamless. The mental sewing-machine connects nerve cell to nerve cell, senses to memory, memory to language, and consciousness to them all. At every level, the mind is a connection machine.

To understand brains (the traditional task of neurologists), and therefore minds (which psychologists have laboured to do), first remember that they have evolved to do a specific job. Each is there to run a body, keep it out of trouble and see that it passes its genes on to the next generation. Abilities to do things irrelevant to these tasks are likely to get short shrift from natural selection. Computers, with which brains are often compared, can turn their circuits to almost anything—pop in a new program and your computerised accountant is transformed into a chess grandmaster. Brains are not like this. Flexibility, except in a few, limited areas, is not at a premium. Neural "programs" are wired in during development. Circuits which deal with vision cannot be switched over to hear-

ing or taste. And such changes as do occur—for instance, when a new word or face is learnt—take place by modifying the wiring.

The nerve cells, known as neurons, which make up this wiring are rather unusual affairs. Most living cells measure a few millionths of a metre across, but neurons have filamentous projections which often go on for centimetres and occasionally for metres. These projections—called axons if they transmit messages, and dendrites if

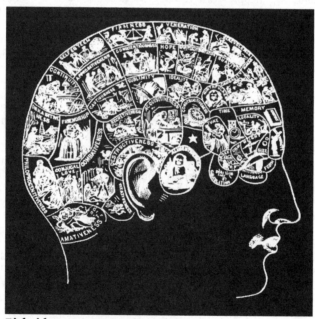

Right idea, wrong compartments

they receive them—enable neurons to talk to each other over long distances, to gather information, to pass it on, and to give and take orders.

The messages themselves are trains of electrical waves called action potentials. Unlike the current in a metal wire, which is caused by things (in this case electrons) moving along the wire, action potentials happen when electrically charged atoms (known as ions) of sodium and potassium move in and out of a filament. An action potential is like a bore in a river: the wave moves on even though the water merely

goes up and down.

Messages pass from neuron to neuron at junctions called synapses, where the tip of an axon touches the surface of a dendrite. Synapses act as the diodes of neurology, allowing the signal to go in only one direction. Action potentials cannot cross them; instead, a synapse passes the signal on via a chemical messenger known as a neurotransmitter. These neurotransmitters can leap the gap to the next cell, where special proteins are ready to greet them. Each sort of receptor protein fits hand-in-glove with a particular neurotransmitter (about 50 of which have been identified so far). If enough receptors are stimulated, one of two things may happen. The cell on the far side of the synapse may become excited and start firing pulses of its own, or it may be inhibited, damping down any pulse-firing that is already going on.

Neurons are thus devices that monitor the exciting and inhibiting signals arriving at their dendrites, weigh up the balance between them, and then decide whether or not to send out pulses of their own. This rather prosaic process is the basis for the activity of the brain. The magic lies in the way the neurons are wired together. But with around 100 billion neurons in a healthy human brain, and 60 trillion synapses, there is plenty of scope for sleight of hand.

Human conjurors have shown that the trick can work. Artificial neural networks, made by wiring lots of microprocessors together and programming them to behave like neurons, can do the same sorts of tricks as real ones. Give them senses, for example, and they can learn to recognise things. And the way they do so is instructive.

A common design for an artificial neural network is to arrange the "neurons" in a three-layered sandwich: an input layer connected to a sense organ such as a television camera; an output layer, which passes the result on to the human operator; and an intermediate, or "hidden" layer, connected to both. The network learns by changing the strengths (or "weights") of the connections between neurons in the three layers. With the correct pattern of weights, simple sensory data (such as handwritten numbers, or faces presented from different angles) can be distinguished and identified.

Real brains, of course, are much more

complicated. The main information-processing part of the brain, the cerebral cortex, has six layers of neurons, rather than three. It is, nevertheless, a layered structure. And the way an artificial network learns by varying the strength of the connections between its silicon neurons is, as will be seen later, reminiscent of the way neurologists think that learning happens in what their computing colleagues disparagingly refer to as "wetware".

Sense and sensibility

Look at the triangle below. Now look closely. There is no triangle. So why did you see it? This may sound a trivial question,

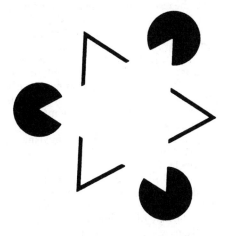

but it isn't. Imposing order on the world is not a two-stage process of first creating an image of outside events, and then interpreting it. The two things happen simultaneously as the sensory information is dismantled and re-assembled in ways which, given the coherence of the result, seem bizarre. Only occasionally, when a sensory illusion or a specific piece of damage to the brain produces some strange result, is it clear that sense and sensibility are inextricably linked.

Vision, the best-understood sense, illustrates the point. For visual information to be processed by the brain, it must first be converted into a form that neurons can deal with—action potentials. This is done by cells in the retina, the place where the image formed by the eye's lens ends up. Some retinal cells have catholic tastes, and respond to many wavelengths. Others are tuned in to specific parts of the spectrum. But each connects to a neuron, and via this to the optic nerves. These nerves carry the signals to the back of the brain, where they are processed.

The connections between the eyes and the primary visual cortex, as the receiving area is called, have been known about for decades. They are orderly. Adjacent parts of the retinal image seemed to end up next to each other. The primary visual cortex appeared, in effect, to be a map of the retina—the mind's eye. Whatever happened next—action, learning or thought—was assumed

to involve the whole image.

It all looked very neat. But it was wrong. The map is not passed around as a whole. It is broken up into different sorts of information—edges, movement, colour—which are then processed in different parts of the visual cortex. This can be seen by watching brains in action. Positron emission tomography (PET) enables researchers to watch people think. It uses a radioactive form of oxygen, mixed into the blood via a catheter in the wrist, to find out which parts of the brain are working hardest from moment to moment. Active areas need more oxygen, and the local blood supply increases to provide it. Positrons emitted by the oxygen annihilate nearby electrons—of which they are the anti-matter equivalent—producing detectable gamma rays.

PET, combined with studies of the electrical signals from single neurons in monkeys and the examination of people with localised brain damage, has revealed the true fate of the image. It does, indeed, pass first to the primary visual cortex (known to neurologists as v1). But this area is just a clearing-house. It contains two sorts of neuron. One sort, organised into columns which penetrate all six layers of the cortex, responds to colour. The other sort, between the columns, responds to form.

Area v1 is surrounded by area v2 (as medieval anatomists preferred Greek and Latin, so modern ones prefer letters and numbers). Here, instead of columns, there are stripes. Thin stripes respond to colour again, thick ones to motion. But the information in v1 and v2 is local: their cells get excited only about signals from their particular patch of the retina. From then on, the information is passed on to areas imaginatively named v3, v4 and v5. v3 and v4 both deal with shape, but v4 also deals with colour, while v3 is colourblind. v5 specialises in detecting motion. It is from these specialised areas, not from the more general-purpose image of v1, that visual information is passed on to the other areas of the brain that need it.

This parcelling-out of tasks explains some of the predicaments of people whose visual cortices have been damaged. Those who have lost v4 can no longer conceive of colour. Those with damage to v5 can see things only when they are stationary—the reverse of the case of Dr P, described in Oliver Sacks's book, "The Man Who Mistook His Wife For A Hat", who could not distinguish stationary objects, and was probably suffering from damage to area v2.

There is also a strange phenomenon called blindsight which, like the loss of the concept of colour in people with damaged v4, touches directly on the issue of consciousness. Lose area v1, and you will believe yourself blind. But you might not be. There are some direct connections from the retina to the other vision-processing areas.

People with v1 damage can often track the movement of objects through space, or tell you the colour of things they truly believe that they cannot see.

And the triangle? The illusion seems to be caused by a conflict between the cells of v1 and those of v2. v1 cells handle only smalls parts of the visual field. Some see bits of the design, some see space. v2 cells, which deal with larger areas, use the bites out of the circles and the ends of the arrows to infer a line, rather as rows of lights on an advertising hoarding are mentally connected into letters. The conflicting interpretations leave the viewer with the uncomfortable feeling of seeing a border where he knows that none exists. Neurology and a psychological test have combined to show specialisation in the brain.

Memory and learning

Another area where psychology and neurology have combined to demonstrate these specialisations is memory. On the face of it, memory seemed, like visual perception, to be a single entity. In fact, it is also highly compartmentalised, with different functions carried out in different parts of the brain.

The first evidence for this specialisation came from neuroanatomy. In the 1950s, surgeons found that, as a last resort, they could control severe epilepsy by destroying parts of the brain. One target for this surgery was the temporal lobe. Some patients suffered a strange form of amnesia after such surgery. They were able to recall things that had happened to them until a few weeks before the operation, and they were also able to remember the very recent past, a matter of a few minutes. But they could not form permanent memories any more—they could no longer learn. All these people had suffered damage to the hippocampus, a structure inside the temporal lobe. Since then, experiments done on monkeys have confirmed that the hippocampus and its neighbours in the limbic system are way-stations to the formation of permanent memories.

The actual information is stored in the cortex; but, for several weeks after it is first learnt, it is passed around via the hippocampus. If it is recalled and used, more direct connections develop in the cortex, and the hippocampus is gradually excluded. If not recalled, it may be forgotten. But if the hippocampal nexus is broken, it is always forgotten. Without a hippocampus, learning is impossible.

Or, rather, some sorts of learning are impossible. For, partly as a consequence of observations on patients with damaged hippocampuses, it has become clear that learning comes in two broad forms: the explicit, or "declarative", sort which remembers objects and events; and the implicit sort, which remembers how to do things.

Implicit learning is part of unconscious

behaviour, and is encapsulated in the phrase "practice makes perfect". It is the sort of incremental improvement which allows people to acquire skills almost incidentally and it does not require an intact hippocampus. One hippocampally damaged patient, for instance, learnt how to read mirror writing, an extraordinary feat for a man who could not remember the faces of his nurses.

Psychologists argue endlessly over how many types of implicit learning there are, and neurology has not yet come to their rescue. But another phenomenon exposed by hippocampal damage has been neatly dissected by psychology.

Patients with such damage are still able to hold the events of the very recent past in their heads, and to synthesise them with knowledge they already have. This enables them to do crosswords, for example. This short-term, or "working", memory is very amenable to psychological testing.

Such tests suggest that working memory has at least three subcomponents. They are known as the "central executive" (which controls attention), the "visuospatial sketchpad" (which manipulates visual information) and the "phonological loop" (which deals with speech). Teasing out these components was done by making people do more than one thing at a time and seeing how well they performed.

Broadly speaking, people can hold about seven pieces of information in their minds at once. But if some of that information is visual, and some linguistic, the total increases. And if an experimenter disrupts a verbal task, a parallel visual one is usually unaffected. The systems which deal with the data are independent of one another.

So how are memories actually stored? PET scanning shows that working memory is located in the pre-frontal cortex. When something is being "kept in mind", that is where it is. Working memories are retained by the continuous activity of particular neurons. These neurons stimulate themselves, either directly or via a loop involving others. When they stop firing, the memory is lost unless it has been passed on to the hippocampus for more permanent storage.

The process by which the hippocampus begins the laying down of permanent memories is different, and intriguingly like the one used to train artificial neural nets—the weights of the connections between nerve cells are altered. This process, called long-term potentiation (LTP), happens when a particular neurotransmitter called glutamate is released by the axon side of a synapse and picked up on the dendrite side by a particular sort of receptor, the N-methyl-D-aspartate (NMDA) receptor. The reaction between glutamate and NMDA stimulates two things. First, the production of proteins called kinases, which enhance the passage of action potentials by opening up passages

that pass ions through the cell membrane. Second, the manufacture in the dendrite of a messenger molecule (believed to be nitric oxide) which flows back to the axon and, in turn, stimulates more glutamate production, thus keeping the whole process going.

However, NMDA is receptive to glutamate only if enough action potentials are already passing along the dendrite it is in. This means that the strengthening of one synaptic connection depends on what is happening to generate action potentials at others. This is the key to neural networks, whether wet or dry, because it enables activity in one part of the net to affect another part indirectly. The pattern of input-signals acts in unison to produce a particular output.

LTP can preserve memories for hours or days. The final stage of the process, permanent storage, seems to involve the formation of new synapses in active areas, and the withering of those which remain unstimulated. Recent research suggests that this happens during sleep. In particular, it seems to happen during the type of sleep known as rapid eye movement (REM) sleep. During REM sleep, people dream, and one of the many explanations suggested for dreams is that they are like the film on a cutting-room floor—the bits left over when experiences that have been waiting in hippocampal limbo are edited into permanent memories. Now there is some evidence to back this up. It has been shown that disrupting REM sleep also disrupts the formation of long-term declarative memories.

Other recent work has shed some light on how memories become tinged with emotion. Fear, at least, seems to be injected by the hippocampus's limbic-system neighbour the amygdala. Drugs which block LTP (and therefore learning) if injected into the hippocampus merely block the learning of

fear if applied to the amygdala. Rats whose amygdalas have been treated in this way behave as if they do not know the meaning of fear. And it seems likely that at least some people who suffer from anxiety attacks have over-active amygdalas.

Speaking in tongues

Despite the claims made for chimpanzees, dolphins, sea-lions and even parrots, it is the use of language which distinguishes man from his fellow creatures. Language—which allows knowledge and ideas to be shared within a community and passed from generation to generation—is the basis of civilisation and of human dominion over the rest of nature. It is also bound up in consciousness; the "inner dialogue" that people often have with themselves is one example of conscious introspection.

Language, unlike memory and sensation, is not even-handed. It generally inhabits the left-hand side of the brain, a fact discovered over a century ago by studying people with localised brain-damage, and dramatically shown up in PET scans. The reason for this geographical imbalance is unclear, but it is associated with another uniquely human phenomenon: "handedness". Right-handed people almost always do their language-processing in their left cerebral hemispheres. Left-handers tend to favour the right hemisphere, although the distinction is not so clear. Indeed, there is evidence associating dyslexia with a failure of the asymmetry, an observation which helps explain why left-handers are more often dyslexic than right-handers.

Within whichever hemisphere commands the process, the component parts of language, like those of sensibility and memory, appear to be parcelled out over the cortex. Broca and Wernicke, two nineteenth-century neurologists who studied failures of

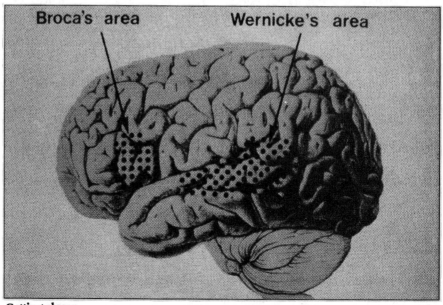

Getting closer

speech and comprehension, mapped areas of the brain where damage seemed to cause specific problems. PET shows up a broadly similar pattern. When words are heard, part of the temporal lobe lights up. Speaking provokes activity in the frontal lobe. There also seems to be a distinction between the handling of nouns (done in the temporal lobe) and verbs (where the frontal lobe seems to predominate).

The meaning of these distinctions is not clear. Some see a specific language function, separately evolved, which deals with all aspects of the phenomenon including the formation of abstract concepts. Others believe that speech developed merely because changes to the muscles of the mouth and throat (which came about when people began to walk upright) allowed it to. According to this view, speaking and listening are merely matters of training. The concepts are already there (which is why other animals can also be trained into language-like abilities); what has to be learnt is a way of attaching words to them, and this is done by the normal mechanisms of memory. Regular verbs, for instance, are learnt implicitly, but declarative memory kicks in for the irregular ones.

In any case, the concepts associated with words are also to be found in widely scattered parts of the brain, and not necessarily on its left-hand side. Colours, for instance, live in region v4 of the visual cortex. And some people with serious damage to the language-control areas can still swear like troopers. Other specific bits of damage can cause problems akin to losing colour-conception—an inability to remember the names of otherwise-familiar people, for instance. Though the connections are not so well understood as those in vision and learning (perhaps because they impinge on more mental functions), they are being thoroughly studied.

The elusive whole

Sensibility, working memory and language are all aspects of mind, but they are not the whole thing. What binds them together? What is the conscious mind? It is certainly not the be-all and end-all of complex behaviour. Anyone who has driven along a motorway and suddenly realised he cannot remember the past few miles will realise this. Nor does partial loss of faculty make a person mindless—although dementias which attack the pre-frontal cortex might.

Whatever the conscious mind is, though, it is no longer regarded by students of the brain as the proper province of philosophers and divines. The problem is under experimental attack.

Hypotheses of how the mind evolved are still vague and contradictory, but they fall into two groups. One interpretation is that consciousness is an epi-phenomenon—a side-effect of increased complexity in the brains of higher primates and particularly of people. Such side-effects, known as emergent properties, are just starting to be explored. Some theories of the origin of life see life itself as an emergent property. They think it suddenly "switched on" when a network of chemical reactions grew so big that each reaction was able to assist the progress of another. On this theory, brains, and particularly cerebral cortices, passed some threshold of size and complexity during their evolution which allowed the system to feed upon itself and generate the phenomenon now labelled consciousness.

Others believe that consciousness has evolved specifically. In their view consciousness is an evolutionary advantage which has dictated the brain's complexity rather than the other way round. One widely held theory is that consciousness is a way of dealing with the diplomatic niceties of group living. It is there mainly to answer the question, "what would I do if I were in the other person's shoes?" Armed with the answer, arrived at by conscious introspection, you can make a better guess at what the other person will actually do next, and modify your behaviour accordingly. Some evidence to support this idea comes from experiments on self-awareness. Among primates, at least, the ability to recognise oneself in a mirror is restricted to man and a few of the great apes. Even monkeys see the reflection as a stranger.

As to the question of mechanism, most neurologists agree that it is the continuity of the process—how the connections produce the stream of consciousness—that most needs to be explained. Occasionally this stream breaks down. Some people who suffer from schizophrenia report seeing the world in freeze-frame, a phenomenon which healthy people can also experience if they are very tired but are forced to concentrate on some task. Among schizophrenics, freeze-framing is associated with problems in the working memory, another piece of evidence that this structure has a key role in maintaining consciousness. But this does not explain how the information is co-ordinated.

One of the most promising lines of inquiry in the co-ordination problem is known as the 40 hertz binding frequency. Particular stimuli will set neurons all over a brain firing together at between 40 and 70 action potentials per second. Different stimuli excite different networks. This network of simultaneous firing serves to illuminate the fragmented information scattered around the brain. Change the input and, like a simple neural network switching from recognising one face to another, you change the output. Change fast enough and the result appears, like a cinema film, to be continuous. In nature, the change seems to come every tenth of a second.

Of course, there is no reason why such integration necessarily implies consciousness; but a refinement of the model looks promising. This is based on a hierarchy of the sort found in the visual system. Each level of the hierarchy is a "convergence zone", gathering information from lower levels and passing it on to a higher one if the processing task cannot be completed at that level. The system can oscillate because some axons from each level reach back into the lower ones, feeding information back to them. If the task is so difficult that it is necessary to recruit the central executive of the working memory, then it enters the stream of consciousness. Your executive normally has better things to do than drive your car, but if someone cuts you up, it connects.

Mind and Brain

The biological foundations of consciousness, memory and other attributes of mind have begun to emerge; an overview of this most profound of all research efforts

Gerald D. Fischbach

Gerald D. Fischbach is Nathan Marsh Pusey Professor of Neurobiology and chairman of the department of neurobiology at Harvard Medical School and Massachusetts General Hospital. After graduating from Colgate University in 1960, he earned his medical degree at Cornell University Medical School in 1965 and received an honorary M.A. from Harvard University in 1978. Fischbach is also a member of the National Academy of Sciences, the National Institute of Medicine and the American Academy of Arts and Sciences. He is a past-president of the Society for Neuroscience and serves on several foundation boards and university advisory panels.

Ruth gave me a piece of her mind this morning. I am grateful, of course, but I don't know where to put it or, for that matter, what it is. I suppose that the imperatives belong in the limbic system and the geographic information in the hippocampus, but I am not sure. My problem also troubled René Descartes. Three centuries ago he described the mind as an extracorporeal entity that was expressed through the pineal gland. Descartes was wrong about the pineal, but the debate he stimulated regarding the relation between mind and brain rages on. How does the nonmaterial mind influence the brain, and vice versa?

In addressing this issue, Descartes was at a disadvantage. He did not realize the human brain was the most complex structure in the known universe, complex enough to coordinate the fingers of a concert pianist or to create a three-dimensional landscape from light that falls on a two-dimensional retina. He did not know that the machinery of the brain is constructed and maintained jointly by genes and by experience. And he certainly did not know that the current version is the result of millions of years of evolution. It is difficult to understand the brain because, unlike a computer, it was not built with specific purposes or principles of design in mind. Natural

[Ed. note: Refer to *Scientific American*, Sept. 1992 for additional data referenced in this article.]

selection, the engine of evolution, is responsible.

If Descartes had known these things, he might have wondered, along with modern neurobiologists, whether the brain is complex enough to account for the mystery of human imagination, of memory and mood. Philosophical inquiry must be supplemented by experiments that now are among the most urgent, challenging and exciting in all of science. Our survival and probably the survival of this planet depend on a more complete understanding of the human mind. If we agree to think of the mind as a collection of mental processes rather than as a substance or spirit, it becomes easier to get on with the necessary empirical studies. In this context the adjective is less provocative than the noun.

The authors of the articles in this special issue of *Scientific American* and their colleagues have been pressing the search for the neural basis of mental phenomena. They assume that mental events can be correlated with patterns of nerve impulses in the brain. To appreciate the meaning of this assumption fully, one must consider how nerve cells, or neurons, work; how they communicate with one another; how they are organized into local or distributed networks, and how the connections between neurons change with experience. It is also important to define clearly the mental phenomena that need to be explained. Remarkable advances have been made at each level of analysis. Intriguing correlations have in fact begun to emerge between mental attributes and the patterns of nerve impulses that flare and fade in time and space, somewhere inside the brain.

The most striking features of the human brain are the large, seemingly symmetric cerebral hemispheres that sit astride the central core, which extends down to the spinal cord. The corrugated hemispheres are covered by a cell-rich, laminated cortex two millimeters in thickness. The cerebral cortex can be subdivided by morphological and functional criteria

into numerous sensory receiving areas, motor-control areas and less well-defined areas in which associative events take place. Many observers assume that here, in the interface between input and output, the grand syntheses of mental life must occur.

It may not be that simple. Mind is often equated with consciousness, a subjective sense of self-awareness. A vigilant inner core that does the sensing and moving is a powerful metaphor, but there is no a priori reason to assign a particular locus to consciousness or even to assume that such global awareness exists as a physiologically unified entity. Moreover, there is more to mind than consciousness or the cerebral cortex. Urges, moods, desires and subconscious forms of learning are mental phenomena in the broad view. We are not zombies. Affect depends on the function of neurons in the same manner as does conscious thought.

And so we return to the organ itself. The brain immediately confronts us with its great complexity. The human brain weighs only three to four pounds but contains about 100 billion neurons. Although that extraordinary number is of the same order of magnitude as the number of stars in the Milky Way, it cannot account for the complexity of the brain. The liver probably contains 100 million cells, but 1,000 livers do not add up to a rich inner life.

Part of the complexity lies in the diversity of nerve cells, which Santiago Ramón y Cajal, the father of modern brain science, described as "the mysterious butterflies of the soul, the beating of whose wings may some day—who knows?—clarify the secret of mental life." Cajal began his monumental studies of adult and embryonic neurons about 100 years ago, when he came across Camillo Golgi's method of staining neurons with silver salts. The great advantage of this technique, which led Cajal to his neuron doctrine, is that silver impregnates some cells in their entirety but leaves the majority untouched. Individuals thus emerged from the forest. Seeing them, Cajal

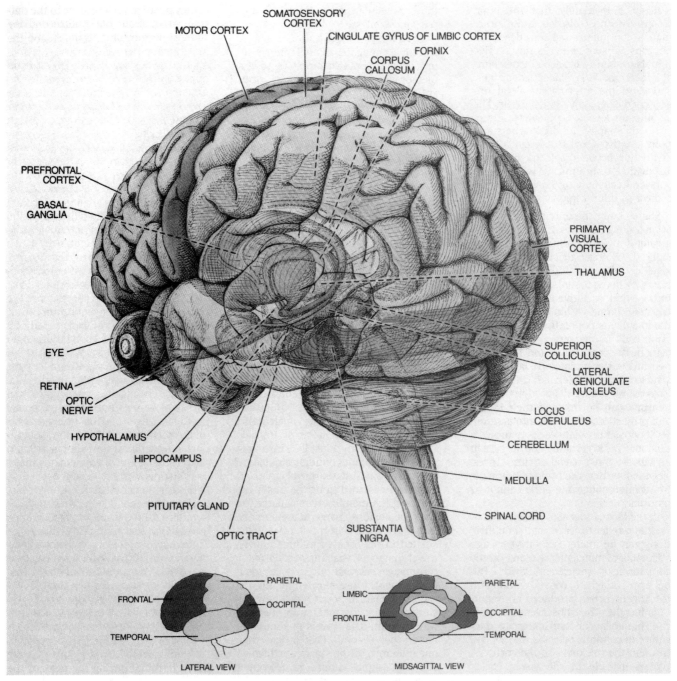

MOTOR CORTEX
SOMATOSENSORY CORTEX
CINGULATE GYRUS OF LIMBIC CORTEX
FORNIX
CORPUS CALLOSUM
PREFRONTAL CORTEX
BASAL GANGLIA
PRIMARY VISUAL CORTEX
THALAMUS
EYE
SUPERIOR COLLICULUS
RETINA
LATERAL GENICULATE NUCLEUS
OPTIC NERVE
LOCUS COERULEUS
HYPOTHALAMUS
CEREBELLUM
HIPPOCAMPUS
MEDULLA
PITUITARY GLAND
SPINAL CORD
OPTIC TRACT
SUBSTANTIA NIGRA

PARIETAL
FRONTAL
OCCIPITAL
TEMPORAL
LATERAL VIEW

LIMBIC
PARIETAL
FRONTAL
OCCIPITAL
TEMPORAL
MIDSAGITTAL VIEW

The Brain: Organ of the Mind

For good reason, the human brain is sometimes hailed as the most complex object in the universe. It comprises a trillion cells, 100 billion of them neurons linked in networks that give rise to intelligence, creativity, emotion, consciousness and memory. Large anatomic subdivisions in the brain offer a rough map of its capabilities. At a very gross level, the brain is bilaterally symmetric, its left and right hemispheres connected by the corpus callosum and other axonal bridges. Its base consists of structures such as the medulla, which regulates the autonomic functions (including respiration, circulation and digestion), and the cerebellum, which coordinates movement. Within lies the limbic system, a collection of structures involved in emotional behavior, long-term memory and other functions.

The highly convoluted surface of the cerebral hemispheres—the cortex (from the Latin word for bark)—is about two millimeters thick and has a total surface area of about 1.5 meters, approximately that of an office desk. The most evolutionarily ancient part of the cortex is part of the limbic system. The larger, younger neocortex is divided into frontal, temporal, parietal and occipital lobes that are separated by particularly deep sulci, or folds. Most thought and perception take place as nerve impulses, called action potentials, move across and through the cortex. Some brain regions with specialized functions have been studied in detail, such as the motor cortex, the somatosensory cortex and the visual pathway. From the collective activity of all the brain regions emerges the most fascinating neurological phenomenon of all: the mind.

realized immediately that the brain was made up of discrete units rather than a continuous net. He described neurons as polarized cells that receive signals on highly branched extensions of their bodies, called dendrites, and send the information along unbranched extensions, called axons. The Golgi stain revealed a great variety of cell-body shapes, dendritic arbors and axon lengths. Cajal discerned a basic distinction between cells having short axons that communicate with neighbors and cells having long axons that project to other regions.

Shape is not the only source of variation among neurons. Diversity is even greater if molecular differences are considered. Whereas all cells contain the same set of genes, individual cells express, or activate, only a small subset. In the brain, selective gene expression has been found within such seemingly homogeneous populations as the amacrine cells in the retina, the Purkinje cells in the cerebellum and the motor neurons in the spinal cord. Beyond the structural and molecular differences, even more refined distinctions among neurons can be made if their inputs and projections are taken into account. Is it possible that each neuron is unique? This is certainly not the case in all but the most trivial circumstances. Yet the fact that the brain is not made up of interchangeable parts cannot be ignored.

In the face of this astounding diversity, it is a relief to learn that simplifications can be made. Several years ago Vernon B. Mountcastle, working on the somatosensory cortex, and David H. Hubel and Torsten N. Wiesel, working on the visual cortex, produced an important insight. They observed that neurons of similar function are grouped together in columns or slabs that extend through the thickness of the cortex. A typical module in the visual cortex whose component cells respond to a line of a particular orientation measures approximately one tenth of a millimeter across. The module could include more than 100,000 cells, the great majority of which participate in local circuits devoted to a particular function.

Another simplification is that all neurons conduct information in much the same way. Information travels along axons in the form of brief electrical impulses called action potentials, the beating wings of Cajal's butterflies. Action potentials, which measure about 100 millivolts in amplitude and one millisecond in duration, result from the movement of positively charged sodium ions across the surface membrane from the extracellular fluid into the cell interior, or cytoplasm.

The sodium concentration in the extracellular space is about 10 times the intracellular concentration. The resting membrane maintains a voltage gradient of -70 millivolts; the cytoplasm is negatively charged with respect to the outside. But sodium does not enter rapidly because the resting membrane does not allow these ions easy access. Physical or chemical stimuli that decrease the voltage gradient, or depolarize the membrane, increase sodium permeability. Sodium influx further depolarizes the membrane, thus increasing sodium permeability even more.

At a critical potential called the threshold, the positive feedback produces a regenerative event that forces the membrane potential to reverse in sign. That is, the inside of the cell becomes positive with respect to the outside. After about one millisecond the sodium permeability declines, and the membrane potential returns to -70 millivolts, its resting value. The sodium permeability mechanism remains refractory for a few milliseconds after each explosion. This limits to 200 per second or less the rate at which action potentials can be generated.

Although axons look like insulated wires, they do not conduct impulses in the same way. They are not good cables: the resistance along the axis is too high and the membrane resistance too low. The positive charge that enters the axon during the action potential is dissipated in one or two millimeters. To travel distances that may reach many centimeters, the action potential must be frequently regenerated along the way. The need to boost repeatedly the current limits the maximum speed at which an impulse travels to about 100 meters per second. That is less than one millionth of the speed at which an electrical signal moves in a copper wire. Thus, action potentials are relatively low frequency, stereotypical signals that are conducted at a snail's pace. Fleeting thoughts must depend on the relative timing of impulses conducted over many axons in parallel and on the thousands of connections made by each one.

The brain is not a syncytium, at least not a simple one. Action potentials cannot jump from one cell to another. Most often, communication between neurons is mediated by chemical transmitters that are released at specialized contacts called synapses. When an action potential arrives at the axon terminal, transmitters are released from small vesicles in which they are packaged into a cleft 20 nanometers in width that separates presynaptic and postsynaptic membranes. Calcium ions enter the nerve terminal during the peak of the action potential. Their movement provides the cue for synchronized exocytosis, the coordinated release of the neurotransmitter molecules.

Once released, transmitters bind to postsynaptic receptors, triggering a change in membrane permeability. The effect is excitatory when the movement of charge brings the membrane closer to the threshold for action-potential generation. It is inhibitory when the membrane is stabilized near its resting value. Each synapse produces only a small effect. To set the intensity (action-potential frequency) of its output, each neuron must continually integrate up to 1,000 synaptic inputs, which do not add up in a simple linear manner. Each neuron is a sophisticated computer.

Many different kinds of transmitters have been identified in the brain, and this variety has enormous implications for brain function. Since the first neurotransmitter was identified in 1921, the list of candidates has grown at an increasing pace. Fifty is close to the mark. We have learned a great deal about how transmitters are synthesized, how they are released and how they activate receptors in the postsynaptic membrane.

This level of analysis is particularly relevant for psychiatric and neurological disorders that shed light on the workings of the mind. For example, drugs that alleviate anxiety, such as Valium, augment the action of gamma-aminobutyric acid (GABA), an important inhibitory transmitter. Antidepressants, such as Prozac, enhance the action of serotonin, an indoleamine with a wide variety of functions. Cocaine facilitates the action of dopamine, whereas certain antipsychotics antagonize this catecholamine. Nicotine activates acetylcholine receptors, which are distributed throughout the cerebral cortex. Further insight into the chemical bases of thinking and behavior depends on obtaining more precise data regarding the sites of action of these potent agents and on the discovery of more selective ligands, molecules that bind to receptors.

The power of the molecule-to-mind approach can be illustrated by recent advances in the pharmacologic treatment of schizophrenia, the most common and the most devastating of all thought disorders. The classic antipsychotic drugs include the phenothiazines (for example, Thorazine) and the butyrophenones (for example, Haldol). These agents ameliorate hallucinations, delusions, disorganized thinking and inappropriate af-

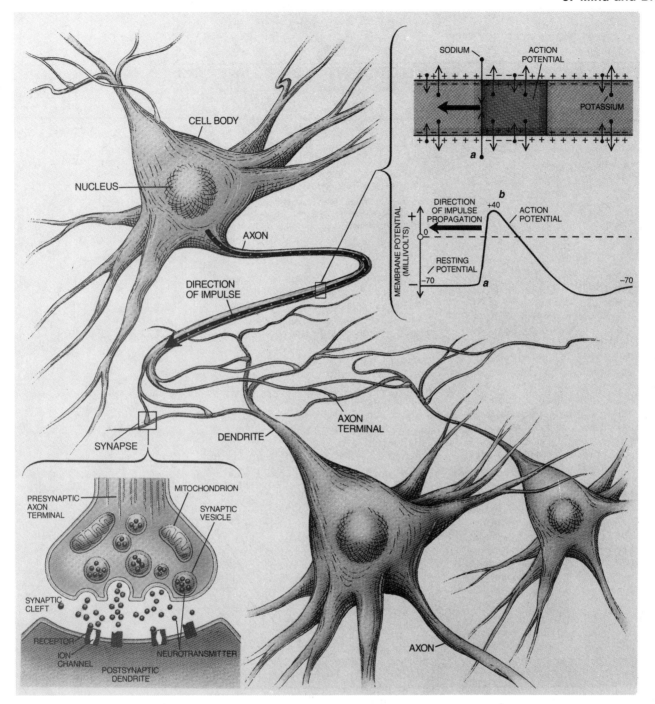

How Neurons Communicate

A neuron that has been excited conveys information to other neurons by generating impulses known as action potentials. These signals propagate like waves down the length of the cell's single axon and are converted to chemical signals at synapses, the contact points between neurons.

When a neuron is at rest, its external membrane maintains an electrical potential difference of about −70 millivolts (the inner surface is negative relative to the outer surface). At rest, the membrane is more permeable to potassium ions than to sodium ions, as indicated by the lengths of the dark arrows in the inset at the top right. When the cell is stimulated, the permeability to sodium in-

creases, leading to an inrush of positive charges (a). This inrush triggers an impulse—a momentary reversal (b) of the membrane potential. The impulse is initiated at the junction of the cell body and the axon and is conducted away from the cell body (bold arrows).

When the impulse reaches the axon terminals of the presynaptic neuron, it induces the release of neurotransmitter molecules (inset at bottom left). Transmitters diffuse across a narrow cleft and bind to receptors in the postsynaptic membrane. Such binding leads to the opening of ion channels and often, in turn, to the generation of action potentials in the postsynaptic neuron. For the sake of clarity, several elements are drawn larger than scale.

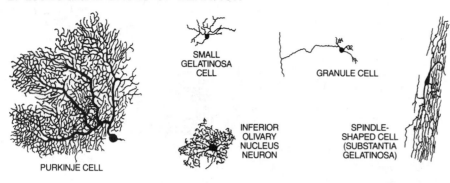

STRUCTURAL VARIETY OF NEURONS (*shown as tracings from Golgi stains*) contributes to the vast capacity of the brain to store, retrieve, use and express information, as well as to experience emotion and control movement.

fect—the "positive" symptoms of schizophrenia that are most evident during acute psychotic episodes. They are not as effective in treating autism and paucity of speech—"negative" symptoms that are prominent during interpsychotic intervals. Moreover, they all produce subtle, abnormal movements when administered to treat acute episodes of illness (hence the name "neuroleptics"). When administered for a long time, they often cause a devastating disorder called tardive dyskinesia. Involuntary and at times incessant writhing movements of the limbs and trunk characterize the disorder, which can persist long after the drug is discontinued.

Why would an agent that affects mental function also produce motor symptoms? The answer lies in the fact that conventional antipsychotics prevent the binding of dopamine to its receptors. To appreciate the importance of this insight, one must know that dopamine-containing nerve cell bodies, gathered deep in the midbrain in a region known as the ventral tegmentum, project their axons widely to the prefrontal cortex as well as to subcortical structures, including the basal ganglia, which are involved in many aspects of motor control. The prefrontal cortex is particularly relevant to schizophrenia because it contains circuits that are active during manipulation of symbolic information and in a type of short-term memory called working memory. Neurons in this region may form a central processing unit of sorts.

A new drug, clozapine, affects the negative as well as the positive symptoms of schizophrenia. Most important, clozapine does not lead to tardive dyskinesia. The discovery of additional members of the dopamine receptor family may provide the explanation for the unique efficacy and selectivity of this antipsychotic.

Transmitter receptors can be grouped into two large (and growing) superfamilies based on their amino acid sequence and on presumptions about the shape that the molecules assume as part of the cell membrane in which they are embedded. A more detailed receptor classification scheme has emerged. It incorporates molecular architecture as well as the more traditional criteria of ligand binding and function. Based on the added molecular information, one receptor superfamily consists of ion channels, proteins that can form aqueous pores through which ions cross the membrane. They underlie the changes in permeability discussed above. The other superfamily, which includes the dopamine receptors, does not form channels. Instead its members interact with a neighboring membrane protein that cleaves a high-energy phosphate bond from guanosine triphosphate. This process initiates a cascade of biochemical reactions. Such G protein–mediated effects are slow in onset, and they last longer than directly gated receptor responses. It is therefore unlikely that they mediate rapid, point-to-point synaptic transmission in the brain. Rather they modulate the way ion channels respond to stimuli. They set the gain of the system much as the pedals on a piano modulate the action of the keys.

The first dopamine receptor gene was isolated four years ago. The search was based on the presumption that the receptor would resemble other receptors that were known to couple to G proteins. This powerful "homology" screening strategy led in short order to the identification of four more dopamine receptors. One of the recent additions, imaginatively named D_4, has attracted considerable attention. The receptor binds dopamine and clozapine with extraordinarily high affinity. Of equal importance, the D_4 gene is apparently not expressed in the basal ganglia, a finding that may explain the absence of tardive dyskinesia. Precise localization of the D_4 receptor within the prefrontal cortex may reveal the origin of hallucinations or at least a component of the neural machinery that has gone awry in schizophrenia.

The slow rate at which psychoactive drugs work presents a puzzle. Drug receptor interactions are immediate, yet symptoms of schizophrenia, depression and other disorders do not resolve for several weeks. The first consequences of drug binding cannot be the sole explanation for their efficacy. This issue leads to a more general consideration of mechanisms by which the environment might change the brain.

Investigation of dopamine synapses has also provided information about the curse of drug addiction. Cocaine, which binds to and inhibits a protein that transports dopamine away from its site of action, is one of the most powerful reinforcing drugs known. Recent studies point to a neural pathway that may be a target of all addictive substances—amphetamines, nicotine, alcohol and opiates. Within this pathway, the nucleus accumbens, a small subdivision of the basal ganglia, appears to be particularly important. Further studies of neurons in this region will certainly sharpen understanding of drug-seeking behavior. They may reveal mechanisms of motivation in general.

The structural, functional and molecular variety that has been described so far would seem to provide a sufficiently complete basis for mental function. Yet another dimension must be considered: plasticity, the tendency of synapses and neuronal circuits to change as a result of activity. Plasticity weaves the tapestry on which the continuity of mental life depends. Action potentials not only encode information, their metabolic aftereffects alter the circuits over which they are transmitted.

Synaptic plasticity is the basis for the informative connectionist neural models that Geoffrey E. Hinton describes. More generally, plasticity multiplies the complexity provided by any fixed cast of molecular characters or cellular functions. Hence, it provides an even richer substrate for mental phenomena.

From the brief tour of synaptic biology presented above, you can imagine many ways that synaptic efficacy might be altered. For example, transmitter release can be enhanced by a small increase in the amount of calcium that enters a nerve terminal with each action potential. The probability of postsynaptic receptor activation can be changed, and on a longer time scale, variations in activity can alter the number of functional receptors. Increases or decreases in the number of receptors, which take time to occur, may account for the delayed effect of psychotherapeutic agents. Beyond changes in the function of synapses, activity may alter the number or location of synapses themselves. Axons sprout new endings when their neighbors become silent, and the terminal branches of dendritic arbors are constantly remodeled.

In their discussion of plasticity and learning, Eric R. Kandel and Robert D. Hawkins review evidence that short-term synaptic changes associated with simple forms of learning are accompanied by molecular modification of proteins. One such modification is phosphorylation, the addition or attachment of a phosphate group. Phosphorylation has a profound effect on the function of proteins. It is commonly stimulated by transmitters and drugs that act via G protein-coupled receptors. But proteins are degraded on a time scale that ranges from minutes to days. Maintenance of memories that may last a lifetime requires more stable alterations, such as those associated with persistent changes in gene expression. A recently discovered family of genes called immediate early genes (IEGs), which are activated rapidly by brief bursts of action potentials, may provide a crucial link. As expected of master switches that initiate long-term changes in the brain, IEGs encode transcription factors, proteins that regulate the expression of other genes.

Some evidence has been obtained that impulse activity increases the expression of genes that encode trophic factors, proteins that promote the survival of neurons. The adage "use it or lose it" may soon have a specific biochemical correlate. The actions of each transcription factor and their relevance remain to be determined, however.

Another focus of inquiry into the basis of memory is the phenomenon of long-term potentiation (LTP), a persistent increase in synaptic efficacy that follows brief periods of stimulation. Attention has focused on synapses in the hippocampus because clinical and experimental data have implicated this region of the cortex in forms of memory that require conscious deliberation. At certain synapses in the hippocampus, LTP may last for weeks. At the same junctions, LTP meets the "Hebbian" criterion for learning in that it

requires coincident presynaptic and postsynaptic activity. LTP does not occur if the postsynaptic neuron is rendered inactive during the priming, presynaptic stimulation. Donald O. Hebb suggested this relation in his 1949 book *The Organization of Behavior* as a basis for the formation of new neural ensembles during learning. It has been repeated often enough to have achieved the force of law.

Synaptic transmission in the hippocampus is mediated by glutamate, the most common excitatory transmitter in the brain, and LTP of the Hebbian type is blocked by aminophosphonovaleric acid (APV), a selective antagonist of one type of glutamate receptor. APV also diminishes the ability of rats to learn tasks that require spatial cues. This is probably not a coincidence, but it remains to be shown that these observations are causally related. The gene that encodes the APV-sensitive glutamate receptor has been cloned in recent months. We can therefore expect tests in transgenic mice bearing mutated receptors to be conducted in the near future. The work will not be straightforward. The plasticity of the brain and the likelihood that natural selection has provided alternative routes to such an important end may complicate matters.

Although the forces leading to plastic changes in the mature brain are ubiquitous and unrelenting, it is important to emphasize the precision and overall stability of the wiring diagram. We could not sense the environment or move in a coordinated manner, let alone think, if it were otherwise. All studies of higher brain function must take into account the precise way in which neurons are connected to one another.

Pathways in the brain have been traced by means of a variety of molecules that are transported along axons. Such reporter molecules can be visualized once the tissue is properly prepared. Connections have also been traced by fine-tipped microelectrodes positioned close enough to a nerve cell body or an axon to detect the small currents generated as an action potential passes by. Each technique has revealed ordered, topographic maps in the cerebral cortex. The body surface is represented in the postcentral gyrus of the cerebral cortex even though the cortical neurons are three synapses away from sensory receptors in the skin. Likewise, a point-to-point map of the visual world is evident in the primary visual cortex at the occipital pole at the back of the brain. Order is evident at each of the early relays on route to the cortex, and topographic order has also been found in projections from the primary cortices to higher centers.

To appreciate just how precise the wiring diagram can be, we need only consider a fundamental discovery made about 30 years ago by Hubel and Wiesel. They determined that neurons in the primary visual cortex (V1) respond to line segments or edges of a particular orientation rather than to the small spots of light that activate the input neurons in the retina and lateral geniculate nucleus of the thalamus. The response implies that neurons in V1 are connected, via the lateral geniculate nucleus, to retinal ganglion cells that lie along a line of the preferred orientation.

We know the anatomy of the major sensory and motor systems in some detail. In contrast, the pattern of connections within the intervening association cortices and the large subcortical nuclei of the cerebral hemispheres is not clearly defined. Goldman-Rakic's experiments are designed to decipher the wiring diagram of the monkey's prefrontal cortex in order to provide a more complete anatomy of memory. Our lack of information about similar connections in the human brain is glaring. Unlike the molecular building blocks and the functions of individual neurons, it cannot be assumed that the intricacies of cortical connectivity will be conserved in different species. The intricacy of this network, after all, is what distinguishes *Homo sapiens* from all other forms of life. An effort akin to the genome project may be called for.

How does the specificity of synaptic connections come about during development? Carla J. Shatz reviews mechanisms by which axons are guided to their appropriate targets in the visual and other systems. The initial stages of axon outgrowth and pathway selection are thought to occur independently of activity. The genetically determined part of the program is evident in the remarkably complete wiring diagram that forms during embryonic life. But once the advancing tips of the axons arrive in the appropriate region, the choices of particular targets are influenced by nerve impulses originating within the brain or stimulated by events in the world itself. Synapse formation during a critical period of development may depend on a type of competition between axons in which those that are activated appropriately are favored.

Steroid hormones also influence the formation of synapses during early development at least in certain regions of the brain. Anatomic, physiological and behavioral data indicate that the brains of males and females are not identical.

The pattern of information flow in the brain during the performance of mental tasks cannot easily be determined by anatomic studies of the circuit diagram or by studies of plasticity. Neural correlates of higher mental functions are being sought directly in awake primates trained to perform tasks that require judgment, planning or memory, or all three capacities. This demanding approach requires sophisticated instrumentation, sophisticated experimental design and months of training until the monkey thinks the same thoughts as the investigator. All-night sessions spent listening to amplified action potentials generated by one or a few neurons followed by days of data analysis are the rule. Progress is slow, but important generalizations have emerged.

One of the most important principles is that sensory systems are arranged in a hierarchical manner. That is, neurons respond to increasingly abstract aspects of complex stimuli as the distance—measured in numbers of synapses from the source—grows. The fact that neurons in V1 respond to lines rather than spots makes the case. Another important principle, discussed by Semir Zeki, is that information does not travel along a single pathway. Rather, different features of a single percept are processed in parallel pathways. A tennis player who wanders to the net from time to time will be alarmed to learn that the movement, color and shape of a tennis ball are processed in different cortical visual centers. Separation of these information streams begins in the retina; they remain segregated in the lateral geniculate nucleus and the primary visual cortex en route to the higher visual centers.

An analogous situation has been found in the auditory system. Mark Konishi and his colleagues at the California Institute of Technology have shown that the localization of sound sources by the barn owl depends on interaural phase and amplitude differences. Phase differences indicate location along the azimuth, whereas amplitude differences signal elevation. Phase and amplitude signals are processed in different pathways through three synaptic relays in the brain. It seems likely that this type of parallel processing characterizes other sensory systems, association cortices and motor pathways as well.

Where is the information reassembled? When does the subject become aware of the approaching ball? The receptive fields of neurons in higher centers are larger than those found in earlier relay stations, so they monitor a larger fraction of the external world. Zeki describes a model that depends on feedback connections from cells with large receptive fields to the cells in the primary visual cortex that have high spatial resolution. Such feedback circuits might coordinate the activity of cells in the primary cortex that have high spatial resolution and cells that respond to more abstract features of the stimulus no matter where it is located. Francis Crick and Christof Koch address the role in visual awareness of a 40-cycle-per-second oscillation in firing rate that is observed throughout the cortex. The oscillations, discovered by Wolf J. Singer and his colleagues at the Max Planck Institute for Brain Research in Frankfurt, may synchronize the firing of neurons that respond to different components of a perceptual scene and hence may be a direct neural correlate of awareness.

Konishi has identified the first neurons in the owl's brain that respond to a combination of interaural phase and amplitude differences but not to either parameter presented alone. These neurons, located deep in the animal's brain in a region called the inferior colliculus, activate a motor program that results in the owl's turning toward the sound source.

In the monkey's visual system, "face cells" located in the inferior temporal sulcus represent perhaps the highest level of abstraction yet identified. These neurons respond to faces but not to other visual stimuli. Similar cells may be present in our own brains. Lesions in the corresponding area of the temporal lobe result in prosopagnosia, a remarkably selective deficit in which the ability to recognize faces is lost. In the zebra finch's auditory system (birds again), a high level of abstraction is evident in neurons found in each male's brain that respond to the complex song of his father but not to pure tones or to the songs of other males of the same species.

How many neurons must change their firing rate to signal a coherent percept or gestalt? The most extreme view holds that one cell may do the job. Is there one face cell per face? Such a supposition seems unlikely on first principles: we lose thousands of neurons every day, so overcommitment to one would be unwise. A more compelling argument comes from recent experiments that have shown face cells to be broadly tuned, responding to faces with similar features rather than to one face alone. The number of neurons that must be activated before recognition emerges is not known, but the data are consistent with a sparse coding rather than global or diffuse activation.

Face cells have their counterparts on the motor side. "Command" neurons have been identified in certain invertebrates that trigger all-or-none, fixed-action patterns, such as stereotypical escape behaviors. Apostolos P. Georgopoulos of Johns Hopkins University has found command neurons of a kind in the monkey's motor cortex (precentral gyrus) that encode the direction of forelimb movement. The firing of these neurons is not associated with the contraction of a particular muscle or with the force of the coordinated movement. Like face cells in the temporal lobe, individual motor cortex neurons are broadly tuned.

The vector obtained by summing the firing frequencies of many neurons is better correlated with the direction of movement than is the activity of any individual cell. The vector becomes evident several milliseconds *before* the appropriate muscles contract and the arm actually moves. It must be a sign of motor planning. The vector is usually derived from less than 100 neurons, so sparse coding may be the rule in the motor cortex as it is in the temporal sulcus.

An important next step at this level of analysis is to produce mental phenomena by focal electrical stimulation. A beginning has been made by William Newsome and his colleagues at Stanford University. They trained monkeys to decide on the direction of movement of dots displayed in random positions on a screen. When the number of dots that showed net movement was set near the threshold for a consistent judgment about the population as a whole, focal stimulation of the V5 region in the cortex influenced the monkey's perceptual judgments.

Strokes and other unfortunate "experiments of nature" have also provided important insights regarding neural correlates of mental phenomena. Antonio R. and Hanna Damasio continue a long tradition of research in their studies of language disorders among neurological patients. This work requires careful examination with a battery of tests designed to elicit the most subtle deficits. Here is an example of the pressing need to define the mental phenomena that need to be explained. The Damasios propose the view that language can be considered a three-part system: word formation, concept representation and mediation between the two. If, as they suggest, language has evolved as a tool to compress concepts and communicate them in an efficient manner, a clear view of its functional anatomy brings us to the crux of the mind matter.

The very real experience of phantom limbs cautions against quick acceptance of sparse coding or even of localization as a universal mechanism. Amputated limbs, experiments of nature of another sort, may be experienced as **an integral part of the body or "self." A deep and burning pain is a distressing** component of the syndrome. It is impossible to find a local area in which such sensations are experienced. Attempts have been made to abolish phantom pain by cutting peripheral nerves, by destroying ascending pathways and by removing sensory regions of the brain. All attempts have failed to eliminate the perception of pain. It may be that the emotional response we call pain requires activation of neurons in widely dispersed regions of the brain.

The future of cognitive neuroscience depends on our ability to study the living human brain. Positron emission tomography (PET) and functional magnetic resonance imaging (MRI) hold great promise in this regard. These noninvasive imaging techniques depend on tight coupling between neuronal activity, energy consumption and regional blood flow. These relations were pointed out by Sir Charles Scott Sherrington in 1890 and later placed on a quantitative basis by Seymour S. Kety and Louis Sokoloff of the National Institute of Mental Health. The brain is never completely at rest. Furthermore, the increases in regional blood flow that MRI and PET detect are not large (they are on the order of 20 to 50 percent). So PET and MRI measurements depend on sophisticated subtraction algorithms that allow one to distinguish the pattern of blood flow during the mental task from the resting, or control, pattern. Assignment of the changes in blood flow to specific structures depends on accurately superimposing the computed images on precise anatomic maps.

At present, neither technique provides the spatial resolution to visualize single cortical columns. Moreover, the slow temporal resolution of both imaging techniques demands that mental tasks be repeated over and over again during the recording session. Technical advances, especially related to rapid MRI scanning, are sure to follow. Even with the current limitations, the advantages of working with humans, who can think on command, are overwhelming.

In sum, we can expect advances at an increasing rate on all levels of investigation relevant to the mind. We will soon know exactly how many transmitters and transmitter receptors there are in the brain and where each one is concentrated. We will also have a more complete picture of neurotransmitter actions, including multiple interactions of jointly released modulators. And we will learn much more about molecules that affect neuronal differentiation and degeneration. Molecules of the mind are not unique. Many of the neurotransmitters are common amino acids found throughout the body. Likewise, no new principles or molecules specific to the brain have emerged in studies of hormone regulation or of trophic factors that influence the survival and differentiation of neurons. The great challenge, then, is to determine how these molecules modulate the functional wiring diagram of the brain and how this functional nerve net gives rise to mental phenomena.

Ultimately, it will be essential to specify what exactly it means to say that mental events are correlated with electrical signals. Certainly, there is a need for theory at this level of analysis, and as emphasized by Crick and Koch, this effort has become one of the most exciting aspects of cognitive neuroscience.

Is the mind an emergent property of the brain's electrical and metabolic activity? An emergent property is one that cannot be accounted for solely by considering the component parts one at a time. For example, the heart beats because its pacemaker depends on the influx and efflux of certain ions. But the automaticity cannot be understood without considering the magnitude and kinetics of all the fluxes together. Once that is accomplished, what is left to explain in physiological terms? In an analogous manner, biological explanations of mental events may become evident once the component neural functions are more clearly defined. We will then have a more appropriate vocabulary for describing the emergent mind.

Perceptual Processes

Susan and her roommate have been friends since freshmen year. Because they share so much in common, they decided to become roommates in their sophomore year. They both want to travel abroad one day, both date men from the same fraternity, are education majors, and want to work with young children after graduation from college. Today they are at the local art museum. As they walk around the galleries, Susan is astonished at her roommate's taste in art. Whatever her roommate likes, Susan hates. The paintings and sculptures that Susan admires are the very ones her roommate dislikes. "How can their tastes in art be so different?" Susan wonders.

What Susan and her roommate are experiencing is a difference in perception, or the interpretation of the sensory stimulation provided by the artwork. Perception and its sister area of psychology, sensation, are the focus of this unit.

For many years in psychology, it was popular to consider sensation and perception as two distinct processes. Sensation was defined in passive terms as the simple event of some stimulus energy (i.e., a sound wave) impinging on the body or on a specific sense organ, which then reflexively transmitted appropriate information to the central nervous system. Both passivity and simple reflexes were stressed. Perception, on the other hand, was defined as an integrative and interpretive process that the higher centers of the brain supposedly accomplished based on the sensory information and available memories for similar events.

The Gestalt psychologists, early German researchers, were convinced that perception was a higher order function compared to sensation. They believed that the whole stimulus was more than the sum of its individual sensory parts. Gestalt psychologists believed this statement was made true by the process of perception. For example, some of you listen to a song and hear the words, the loudness, and the harmony as well as the main melody. However, you do not really hear each of these units; what you hear is a whole song. If the song is pleasant to you, you may declare that you like the song. If the song is raucous to you, you may believe that you do not like it. However, even the songs you first hear and do not like may become liked after repeated exposure to those songs. Hence perception, according to these early Gestalt psychologists, was a more advanced and complicated process than sensation.

This dichotomy of sensation and perception is no longer widely accepted. The revolution came in the mid-1960s when psychologist James Gibson published a then-radical treatise (*The Senses Considered as Perceptual Systems*, Boston, Houghton Mifflin, 1966) in which he reasoned that perceptual processes included all sensory events which were seen as directed by a searching central nervous system. Also, this view provided that certain perceptual patterns, such as recognition of a piece of artwork, may be species-specific. That is, all humans, independent of learning history, share some of the same perceptual repertoires.

The articles in this unit were selected to help us understand perceptual processes better. The first article, "The Vision Thing: Mainly in the Brain" by Denise Grady, discusses the dominant sense in humans. Vision is more than a simple sensory process; it is actually a complex form of sensory reasoning because of the complex role the brain plays in vision.

The next article, "Good Vibrations," examines another important sense, audition or hearing. In this article, JoAnn Gutin reveals once again that the brain is an ever-important mechanism in interpreting sounds that we hear.

The third unit article pertains to yet another sensation, smell or olfaction. In "The Sniff of Legend," Karen Wright convinces us that smell is psychologically important. Various odors have been linked to important psychological effects, one of which is attraction. Research on animals has discovered pheromones or chemical signals for attraction and other processes that one animal transmits and another decodes. Research is currently suggesting that pheromones also exist in humans.

The last two articles explore less conventional aspects of sensation and perception. "Touching the Phantom" is about amputees who often report that they still experience the presence of a missing limb. The article reviews recent research and thought about why this phenomenon occurs.

In the final selection of this unit, Daryl Bem, a renowned psychologist, questions if extrasensory perception (ESP) exists. His review of current literature suggests that trying to research and interpret results related to such concepts is very difficult at best.

Looking Ahead: Challenge Questions

Rank-order the senses (place them in a hierarchy of importance). Justify your rankings.

What role does the brain play in sensation and perception? More specifically, what role does the brain play in vision? In audition?

Do you think the remaining senses (other than vision and audition) such as olfaction are important? Give some examples of the ways odors affect us. What are pheromones? Do you think humans respond to pheromones? If so, for what purposes?

What are phantom limbs? What strange experience do people with phantom limbs report? What seems to be the cause of the phantom limb phenomenon?

What does ESP mean? How is research on parapsychological phenomena conducted? Has research supported the existence of ESP? What are the problems of ESP research?

THE VISION THING: MAINLY IN THE BRAIN

The eye and brain work in a partnership to interpret conflicting signals from the outside world. Ultimately, we see whatever our brains think we should.

Denise Grady

Denise Grady, a former staff writer for DISCOVER *and* Time, *has a degree in biology and always liked writing.*

Stuart Anstis sat in his living room in the dark, wearing a pink visor that held up a hood made of thick black paper with eye holes cut out. He couldn't see anything but the flickering images on the TV set, which he had rigged to play everything in negative. He'd been watching a movie for some time—"There was this fellow dancing and miming and flirting," he recalls—when a friend, who happened to know the film, stopped by. "Oh, Bob Hope," the friend said. "And I said, 'Bob Hope! Good Lord!' I'd been looking at him all that time and didn't know who it was."

Vision researchers like Anstis—along with photographers—have known for decades that faces are nearly impossible to identify when light and dark are reversed. But why that's so is not well understood.

Curious about the difficulty of interpreting negative images, Anstis, a perceptual psychologist at the University of California at San Diego, decided last year to plunge into a negative world. He connected a set of goggles to a video camera that reversed black and white and converted colors to their complements—green to purple, yellow to blue, and so on—then put them over his eyes. For three days Anstis saw nothing in positive. He removed the goggles only at night, and then he slept blindfolded; he

showered in the dark. The experiment was a variation on earlier studies by researchers who had worn glasses designed to turn the world upside down or shift it sideways. They had found that a surprising degree of adaptation occurred; somehow the visual system compensated, put things right, and allowed a person to function. Anstis wanted to find out if the same thing would happen when he traded black for white.

Through the goggles, faces of his friends and colleagues took on a black-toothed, menacing quality. Their pupils became white; the light glinting off their eyes appeared black. "I went on falsely seeing the highlight as the pupil," Anstis says, "so I constantly misread people's eye movements." He could never be quite sure when they were looking at him. Their blinking became a "peculiar flicker" that he found depersonalizing. "Emotional expressions were hard to read," he says. Pictures of celebrities were unrecognizable. By daylight—when the sky was a very dark yellow, almost black—a woman's sharply etched shadow, now rendered in white, looked like a paper cutout or even another person. Fuzzier shadows—cast by a hand held over a table, for instance—translated into a vague, eerie glow.

Objects were no easier to deal with than people. Meals in complementary colors—blue scrambled eggs, for instance—became so unappetizing that Anstis puckishly recommends negative goggles to dieters. Outdoors, sunlight converted to shadow made a flight of stairs a frightening experience. The risers became confused with the treads. "I lost my sense of reality, as if I'd been up

too late," he recalls. "At the curb, cars whizzing by didn't look real. They looked like toys coasting along on white platforms, which were actually their shadows. I would have been quite happy to walk in front of them if it hadn't been for the roaring sound of the traffic." He felt as if his other senses were taking over his consciousness, to compensate for the lack of meaningful visual input. The scent of a laundry room, for instance, became remarkably intense.

Over the course of three days, he says, there was very little adaptation. He did begin reinterpreting sharp shadows, but the fuzzy, glowing ones continued to trick him. A postdoctoral student who wore the goggles for eight days reacted the same way. "I was amazed at how difficult it is to deal with," Anstis says. "All the information is still there, just like reversing the signs in an equation, so we're really surprised that the brain has so much trouble."

Vision, of course, is more than recording what meets the eye: it's the ability to understand, almost instantaneously, what we see. And that happens in the brain. The brain, explains neurobiologist Semir Zeki of the University of London, has to "actively construct" or invent our visual world. Confronted with an overwhelming barrage of visual information, it must sort out relevant features and make snap judgments about what they mean. It has to guess at the true nature of reality by interpreting a series of clues written in visual shorthand; these clues help distinguish near from far, objects from background, motion in the outside world from motion created by the turn of the head. Assumptions are built into the clues—for example, that near things loom larger, or that lighting comes from above.

"The brain must process an immense amount of information as fast as it can, using any shortcuts it can," says Anstis. "It has to find a minimum hypothesis to cover a maximum amount of data. So it's got to use any trick it can." His experiment reveals one of those tricks: "We think the brain is programmed to use brightness the way it is in the world. That means shadows are always darker, and light comes from above."

A negative world, with light pouring down from the sky like black paint, shatters those basic assumptions. And when we violate the assumptions, confusion reigns. Reverse brightness, as Anstis did, and critical clues about the world, such as facial features and expressions, and shape and depth, are subverted. The result is illusion.

SEEING, IN SHORT, is a form of sensory reasoning. When the assumptions on which that reasoning is based are destroyed, seeing becomes senseless. Even though all the necessary visual information is there, we are reduced to groping around.

Everyday vision encompasses an extraordinary range of abilities. We see color, detect motion, identify shapes, gauge distance and speed, and judge the size of faraway objects. We see in three dimensions even though images fall on the retina in two. We fill in blind spots, automatically correct distorted information, and erase extraneous images that cloud our view (our noses, the eyes' blood vessels).

The machinery that accomplishes these tasks is by far the most powerful and complex of the sensory systems. The retina, which contains 150 million light-sensitive rod and cone cells, is actually an outgrowth of the brain. In the brain itself, neurons devoted to visual processing number in the hundreds of millions and take up about 30 percent of the cortex, as compared with 8 percent for touch and just 3 percent for hearing. Each of the two optic nerves, which carry signals from the retina to the brain, consists of a million fibers; each auditory nerve carries a mere 30,000.

The optic nerves convey signals from the retinas first to two structures called the lateral geniculate bodies, which reside in the thalamus, a part of the brain

THE BRAIN HAS TO INVENT OUR VISUAL WORLD. IT HAS TO GUESS AT THE TRUE NATURE OF REALITY BY INTERPRETING CLUES WRITTEN IN VISUAL SHORTHAND.

that functions as a relay station for sensory messages arriving from all parts of the body. From there the signals proceed to a region of the brain at the back of the skull, the primary visual cortex, also known as V1. They then feed into a second processing area, called V2, and branch out to a series of other, higher centers—dozens, perhaps—with each one carrying out a specialized function, such as detecting color, detail, depth, movement, or shape or recognizing faces.

The goal of much current research is to find out not only how those individual centers function but also how they interact with one another. For now, no one even knows where the higher centers ultimately relay their information. "There's no little green man up there looking at this stuff," says Harvard neurobiologist Margaret Livingstone. "In a sense, your perception *is* what's going on in those areas." Researchers would like to know just where and how the "rules" for seeing are stored, how they're acquired, which assumptions are built up from experience and which are hardwired. Anstis thinks his failure to adapt to his negative world might be evidence that brightness clues are built in, but there's not enough evidence to say for sure. "I don't know what would have happened," he says, "if we'd gone on in negative for ages and ages."

There are several approaches to ana-

lyzing the visual system. Anatomical studies look at neural wiring to learn what's connected to what. Physiological studies determine how individual cells and groups of cells react when a particular segment of the visual field is presented with a certain type of stimulus. Perceptual psychologists like Anstis start at the behavior end: they show subjects doctored, tricky images, including optical illusions, and use the responses to figure out just what elements of the environment the brain is responding to and how it's sorting out those elements for processing.

DURING THE PAST two decades the separate avenues of visual research have come together in a striking way. All point to a fundamental division of labor in the visual system: color, motion, and form appear to be processed independently, though simultaneously, through different pathways in the brain. Physicians and researchers have long suspected that the visual system broke down certain tasks, because strokes and head injuries can leave people with highly specific deficits: loss of color vision, motion perception, or the ability to recognize faces, for instance. It thus seems likely that there are a number of separate systems involved in analyzing visual information, but what's not clear is just how many exist. "Everybody will give you a different answer," Livingstone says. She suspects two or three, but Zeki suggests four.

One thing researchers do agree on is that motion is processed separately from form and color. The system that picks up motion also registers direction and detects borders as defined by differences in brightness. It reacts quickly but briefly when stimulated, and so it doesn't register sharp detail. Another system sees color, but whether it also recognizes shape is not clear. "There may be a pure color system," says Livingstone, "but it's not known." In addition, there may be a second color system, one sensitive to both shape and color but not concerned with movement. It would react slowly but be capable of scrutinizing an object for a relatively long time, thus picking up detail. Zeki believes there's still another system, which perceives the shape of moving objects but not their color.

These systems usually work in concert to give us a more or less accurate rendition of the visual world. But because they process information differently, they can sometimes lead to conflict in the eye-brain system about what's really going on. Clues can be misread or misinterpreted. At the same time, the joining of different kinds of clues in the same pathway—say, brightness, motion, and depth—can mean that depth is impossible to read correctly when brightness is absent, or vice versa. By manipulating the way the eye-brain receives information from these pathways, vision researchers have revealed a variety of interesting and instructive phenomena. We might call them illusions. But to the eye-brain system, they're merely the result of following sensory reasoning to its logical conclusion.

For example, proof that motion and color are processed separately can be derived from a clever experiment conducted several years ago at the University of Montreal by psychologist Patrick Cavanagh (now at Harvard) and his colleagues. He found that when a moving pattern of red and green stripes was adjusted so that the red and green were equally bright, or equiluminant, the motion became almost undetectable. In other words, when brightness differences between the stripes were eliminated, color alone was not enough to carry information about movement. The motion system, unable to perceive enough contrast between the stripes, had nothing to "see" move.

That experiment led Cavanagh and Anstis to devise a new test for color blindness, based on the knowledge that, depending on the type of color blindness, either red or green will appear brighter to a subject. By measuring the amount of brightness the subjects had to add to the red stripes to make the pattern stop moving—that is, to achieve equiluminance—the researchers were able to detect some forms of color blindness.

Similarly, it's relatively easy to prove that shading and depth are processed together by altering or eliminating brightness information and watching what happens to depth. In a portrait of President Eisenhower created by Margaret Livingstone, the shadows and highlights on his face have been replaced with patches of color; the brightness of the colors doesn't correspond to the relative brightness of shadows and highlights, however. Since shadows cast by the eyebrows, nose, and lips help define

> TO THE EYE-BRAIN, ILLUSIONS ARE MERELY THE RESULT OF FOLLOWING SENSORY REASONING TO ITS LOGICAL CONCLUSION.

a person's face, putting bright color in the shadow regions effectively erases and even inverts all three-dimensional information. "The features become unrecognizable," says Livingstone. "You can barely even tell it's a person."

Perspective drawings lose their depth if rendered in colors of equal brightness, as do drawings of geometric figures. The color scale used on the Eisenhower portrait is the one commonly used to produce contour maps and CAT scans; it's based on the visible spectrum, which has red at one end. The color scale therefore also uses red at one end, to code for the brightest regions; it uses yellow for comparatively darker ones. This irritates Livingstone no end. "People who read these color-coded CAT scans think they can interpret them," she says. "They think they know red is highest. But really, yellow is brighter." What the brain does is see the red areas as darker and less prominent than the yellow ones; the result can be an image whose depth is difficult to interpret. "This is a hardwired system, and no matter how much you try to override it intellectually, tell it what it should see, it will tell you what it really does see."

Recently, Livingstone has begun to suspect that artists have unique ways of exploiting the fact that motion, depth, and brightness are processed by the same pathway. "If you stare at something for a while, something three-dimensional, it goes sort of flat," Livingstone says. That occurs, she suspects, because the pathway is geared to detect changes in the environment, such as movement, and to

respond quickly and briefly. Fixed on one image, its response dies out, and the impression of depth disappears.

"I think some artists might be stereoblind," Livingstone says, meaning that they lack binocular depth perception. "I've talked to several who are. Everything looks somewhat flatter to them already." That makes it easier, she says, to translate a three-dimensional object into a flat drawing that nonetheless conveys depth. Artists with normal vision have told her that they've trained themselves to stare at their subject, wait for it to go flat, and then draw it flat, or to close one eye and eliminate stereovision automatically. "A normal person gets totally screwed up trying to draw 3-D," she says. "There are so many perspective, stereo, and occlusion cues. You need to get rid of that level of processing or you can't draw a flat picture."

Cavanagh has also been studying paintings, but for insight into how the eye-brain creates richly embroidered visual images from sparse clues. "Flat art is a treasure trove of information about how vision works," he says. "When we look at a flat picture, we recover the depth, the spatial arrangements of the objects depicted. We could easily make a 3-D model of what we're seeing in the picture."

That ability to translate between 2-D and 3-D suggests something about the way we process images. "We look around and see things that look reassuringly solid and three-dimensional, a nice euclidean world," Cavanagh says. "But it's likely that our internal representation is nowhere near that complete." What we store, he suspects, is more like a set of two-dimensional images of what we're looking at, seen from many different angles. "It's a more intelligent representation," he says, "because it's sparse, an abstraction of the real, solid world, and yet it can still give us the impression that it is real and solid. It's like getting CD-quality music from a handcranked phonograph."

Cavanagh thinks that even the most primitive art forms, such as the line drawings found in the Lascaux caves, have much to tell about how information is encoded—for example, by the use of lines. "You have to ask why lines would ever be sufficient to see the depth structure of an object that's being drawn," he says. "Even if you see a line drawing of something you've never seen before, you get it instantly. Infants get it. Why do

Close your left eye and stare at the star with your right eye while holding the page about ten inches away; slowly bring the page toward you until the dot disappears; the missing image is "filled in" with the striped background by your brain.

BLIND SPOT

Ian Worpole

lines work at all if they don't exist in the real world? No objects in the real world have lines drawn around them."

Somewhere in the visual system, he says, there must be a code for contours that separate objects from their backgrounds. The boundary could be a difference in texture or color or even motion. Sure enough, an area has been found in the brain that responds to contours. Cavanagh describes it as contour-specific and attribute-independent. "It ended up, maybe by chance, responding to lines," he says. "Which is lucky for artists, or otherwise all drawings would have to be filled in." Instead, the brain fills in for them.

Actually, filling in is a well-known strategy that the brain uses to see more than meets the eye. It's a form of shortcutting that deals not with the information that is present but with the information that is lacking. The best-known example occurs at the natural blind spot in each eye. At the point where the optic nerve is connected in a normal eye, there's a patch in the retina that doesn't respond to light. A blind spot results in the part of the visual field that would normally be monitored by that patch. The blind spot is off center, toward the side of the visual field, and it's big enough to swallow up a golf ball held at arm's length, or even, at a bit more distance, a person's head. But we're unaware of it. For one thing, when both eyes are open, they cancel out each other's blind spots. For another, the constant motion of the eye prevents the spot from lingering at any one place. The blind spot doesn't become apparent until we close one eye and stare; even then, we've got to resort to tricks to detect it.

The interesting thing about the blind spot isn't so much what we don't see as what we do. The fact that there's no visual information there doesn't lead the brain to leave a blank in your visual field; instead, it points in whatever background is likely to be there. If the blind spot falls on a dragonfly resting on a sandy beach, your brain doesn't blot it out with a dark smudge; it fills it in with sand.

But how? It's long been a subject of argument among psychologists and philosophers. Some argue that the process is a cognitive one carried out by some brain region at a higher level than the visual cortex. That process might be called logical inference: since we know the background is sandy and textured, we assume the blank spot must be, too, just

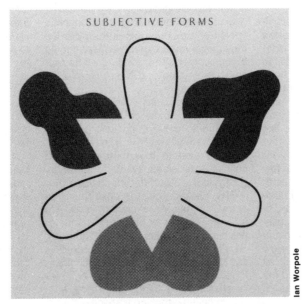

SUBJECTIVE FORMS

Ian Worpole

A white triangle appears to overlie an assortment of shapes, cutting pieces out of them. A closer look reveals that the triangle is not really there; it's created out of nothing, a consequence of the eye-brain's tendency to focus on familiar contours.

as we might assume that if there's flowered wallpaper in front of us, the wallpaper behind us will have the same flowered pattern.

But filling in is different from assuming, says neuroscientist Vilayanur Ramachandran of the University of California at San Diego. It's most likely carried out in the visual cortex, by cells near the ones that the blind spot is depriving of input. It is, he says, an active, physical process: "There's neural machinery, and when it's confronted with an absence of input, it fills it in." The brain, in other words, somehow creates a representation of the background and sticks it into the blind spot.

"We think there's a separate system in the brain for edges and contours, and then one for surface features," Ramachandran says, "and this is the one doing completion of texture. It says, 'If there's a certain texture on the edge, it must be everywhere.'" He refers to the process as surface interpolation.

Curiously, there's a visual phenomenon that's almost the converse of filling in. It's called blindsight, and it occurs in some patients who have gaps in their visual fields because of brain injuries. Whereas many of the people Ramachandran studies have blind spots they don't notice, these people have vision they don't notice. They are somehow able to identify objects presented to their blind areas—without being consciously aware that they are seeing. Blindsight suggests not only that aspects of vision are processed separately, but that vision is processed separately from awareness. Seeing, and knowing that we see, appear to be handled differently.

Blindsight has been most extensively studied by Lawrence Weiskrantz, a psychologist at Oxford University. Twenty years ago Weiskrantz and his colleagues found that a young patient who had lost the left half of his vision because of damage to his visual cortex could nonetheless identify things in the blind field: he could distinguish between an X and an O and tell whether a line of light was vertical or horizontal; he could locate objects even though he couldn't identify them.

But the odd thing was that the patient didn't think he was seeing. He would guess at what was being presented only when the researchers urged him to, and then be astonished when shown how many of his answers were correct. In subsequent years Weiskrantz studied more patients with blindsight, as did

CELLS THAT REACH OUT FOR THE LIGHT

An animal begins life as a glob of undifferentiated cells. For an embryo to emerge from this amorphous clump, millions of cells must migrate around, find their places, and line up in neat order, forming one bit of specialized tissue here, another there. But how do they know where to go? According to Guenter Albrecht-Buehler, a cell, just like a kid on the first day of school, finds out where to go by watching all the other cells. Cells, Albrecht-Buehler contends, can "see" where to go because they have a primitive form of vision. And that, he says, may mean they have some kind of "brain."

Recently, Albrecht-Buehler, a physicist-turned-biologist at Northwestern University Medical School, found that mammalian cells looked to other cells to decide how to line themselves up—other cells with which they had no physical contact. He streaked hamster fibroblasts—long, thin cells that eventually give rise to connective tissue, like cartilage—on one side of a very thin glass film. After letting them grow for two days, he randomly placed a few more fibroblasts on the opposite face of the glass. Those cells consistently positioned themselves perpendicularly to the cells on the other side. Such crosshatching, with cells on the same plane lined up and cells above and below arranged at right angles, occurs in all manner of tissue, from the cornea to the intestines. It may be nature's way of strengthening the tissue.

"The question is," says Albrecht-Buehler, "how did they manage to do this when separated by glass? There's no contact—no chemical exchange, no charge, no current. The only possible answer is that light is carrying some signal." In fact, when the glass is coated with light-reflecting metal, cells on opposite sides ignore each other. Replace the metal with silicone, which reflects visible light but transmits longer-wavelength infrared, and the order returns. That, says Albrecht-Buehler, means the signal must be infrared. Thanks to some previous work, he thinks he knows the particular wavelength.

Many cells have a front and a back, a "polarity," that determines the direction they move. In an experiment conducted a year earlier, Albrecht-Buehler had focused a tiny, pulsing beam of infrared light on a minute latex particle that sat in a field of fibroblasts. When the light hit the speck, it scattered out toward the surrounding cells. Even cells traveling on a path away from the infrared spot reached over to it with newly formed cellular extensions, without hesitation, going against their natural inclinations.

The infrared light the cells found so appealing had a wavelength of 800 to 900 nanometers, or billionths of a meter (visible light ranges from 400 to 700). Significantly, this range of infrared is radiated normally by the bonds holding together molecules integral to cell metabolism. Living things, therefore, emit this radiation—making it an ideal choice for cells seeking out other cells. The two experiments imply that cells see each other by homing in on infrared light in the 800 to 900 nanometer range.

If cells can see, what are they seeing with? Ten years ago Albrecht-Buehler proposed that the eyes of a cell would resemble centrioles, pairs of tiny, cylinder-shaped structures that are found just outside a cell's nucleus. But eyes alone would not allow a cell to "see." Something in the cell has to draw a conclusion based on the information received by the centriole. "You need more than an eye," Albrecht-Buehler insists. "You need some kind of brain—a data-integration system."

Albrecht-Buehler is not embarrassed to admit that few, if any, scientists share his unconventional views. "It's a very lonely effort," says the scientist who in the mid-1970s pioneered the study of cell movements. "In 1976, when I first showed that cells know where they are going when they migrate, no one believed me. Today this is established.

"The majority of biologists today think that cells just have very complicated molecules that bind specifically with each other to make things happen. But I think we are being sidetracked by the brilliance of the molecular design. The molecules are the carriers, the doers; they are not the content of the text, just the letters. We can study *a* and *m* as much as we want, but we'll never understand *Hamlet*."

—*Kathy Svitil*

other researchers. Again and again the patients appeared to have a primitive sort of vision in their blind fields but denied any awareness of it. "I couldn't see anything, not a darn thing," Weiskrantz's patient insisted.

How can a person see and not know it? The phenomenon of blindsight has raised as many questions about the nature of consciousness as it has about visual processing. Weiskrantz suggests that blindsight is produced in parts of the brain other than the primary visual cortex. He points out that fat bundles of fibers from each optic nerve never reach the visual cortex but instead travel to the midbrain, which controls involuntary, unconscious actions. Still other fibers bypass the primary visual cortex and enter different cortical regions. These regions may produce the unconscious vision that characterizes blindsight; if they do, it means that the visual cortex is essential not only for normal vision but also for

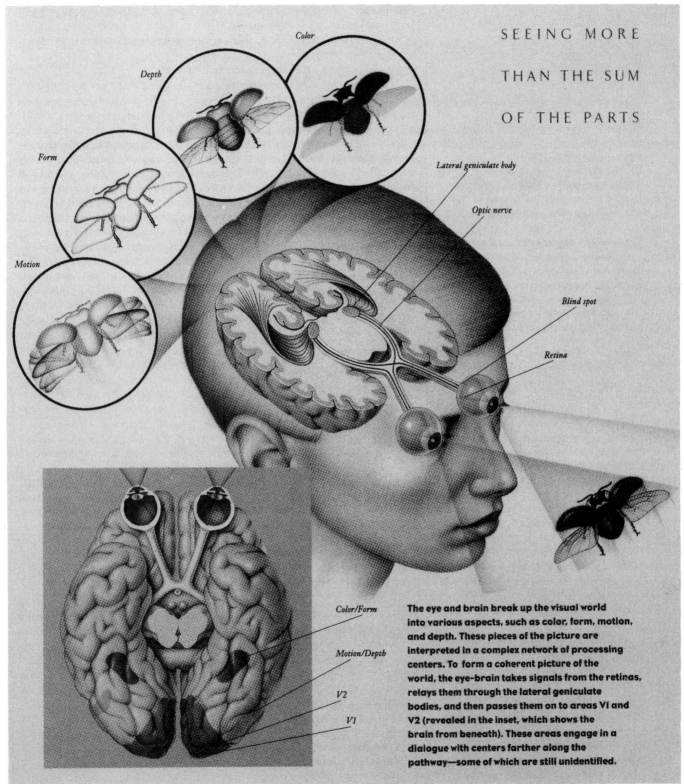

SEEING MORE
THAN THE SUM
OF THE PARTS

Color

Depth

Form

Motion

Lateral geniculate body

Optic nerve

Blind spot

Retina

Color/Form

Motion/Depth

V2

V1

The eye and brain break up the visual world into various aspects, such as color, form, motion, and depth. These pieces of the picture are interpreted in a complex network of processing centers. To form a coherent picture of the world, the eye-brain takes signals from the retinas, relays them through the lateral geniculate bodies, and then passes them on to areas V1 and V2 (revealed in the inset, which shows the brain from beneath). These areas engage in a dialogue with centers farther along the pathway—some of which are still unidentified.

John Karapelou

awareness of what's being seen. If "seeing" takes place outside the visual cortex, it apparently doesn't register in our consciousness.

LATE LAST YEAR, however, a respected neuroscientist challenged the idea that blindsight is derived from visual pathways that are diverted to the midbrain. Michael Gazzaniga, of the University of California at Davis, reported that he and his colleagues had discovered that a patient with blindsight actually had live, functioning neurons in the portion of his visual cortex that supposedly had been destroyed. Those islands of healthy tissue produce blindsight, Gazzaniga argues.

Asked why patients would remain unconscious of their vision if the processing is going on in the visual cortex, Gazzaniga suggests that because the preserved areas are so small, the signals patients get may just be too small to trigger a conscious reaction. Moreover, he doesn't find it surprising that we might be unaware of things going on in the cortex. "Lots of studies suggest that things we're not consciously aware of go on in the cortex, probably a good deal of our psychological life."

The debate over blindsight is simple, Gazzaniga says: "Weiskrantz thinks it's an alternative pathway, and we think it's the original one. More studies will be done. I have three people working around the clock on it, and it will be worked out."

An extreme form of filling in that has eerie echoes of blindsight may have afflicted American writer James Thurber, known for his humorous essays, drawings, and stories, including "The Secret Life of Walter Mitty." Thurber's experience illustrates the lengths the visual system will go to in order to "see," vision or no. Thurber lost one eye as a boy when his brother accidentally shot him with an arrow; the remaining eye began gradually to fail. By the time Thurber turned 40, his world had become a blur—something he made light of in his work. Once he wrote about how he frightened a woman off a city bus by mistaking the purse in her lap for a chicken. As his eyesight worsened, the images he saw progressed from the slapstick to the surreal. Ordinary things underwent wild transformations. Dirt on his windshield looked like "admirals in uniform" or

WHAT MAKES YOU SEE RED? For most people, it's light with a wavelength just a shade over 550 nanometers (billionths of a meter). But what you call red and what I call red may be horses (or apples) of a different hue. The color you perceive, researchers have discovered, may differ subtly, but significantly, from the color someone else sees. What's more, they've traced the mechanism for this color mismatch right down to a single amino acid sequence in our genes.

Color perception begins when light strikes specialized cone-shaped receptor cells in the retina. The cones are called red, blue, and green because proteins embedded in them respond selectively to different wavelengths of light. But the terms are misleading; in fact, each protein responds to a wide range of colors. "Color perception is a comparative system," explains molecular biologist Jeremy Nathans of Johns Hopkins. "A red apple illuminated by the afternoon sunlight is giving off all wavelengths of light. But it mostly reflects red wavelengths while absorbing blue and green and, to a lesser extent, yellow wavelengths. That distribution of light will excite the eye's red pigment most, the green somewhat less, and the blue least of all. That distribution is what your brain gets, and it says, 'That ratio means red.'"

But figuring out just how colors appear to people has always been a problem. "We couldn't get inside people's heads," says Nathans. "All we could do is design a test and ask, 'Do these two colors look identical or do they look different?'" Along with colleague Shannath Merbs, Nathans figured out a way to determine at least which colors a person was capable of perceiving. Nathans first analyzed DNA from a number of people and then genetically engineered

SEEING RED: IT'S WRITTEN IN YOUR GENES.

the proteins found in their red, green, and blue cone cells. Using a spectrometer, he measured the precise wavelengths of light absorbed by the so-called pigment proteins. He then plotted the results and came up with a bell curve representing the absorption spectrum—or range of responses—for each pigment. In effect, he found a way of seeing the same colors other people saw, using their own color receptors.

It was in the course of sequencing the DNA that Nathans found a surprising natural variation. The string of amino acids on the chromosome that codes for the red pigment protein came in two slightly different forms. "It happened to be position number 180," says Nathans. "Some people have an alanine there, some people have a serine." Color receptors with the amino acid serine at site 180, he found, respond most strongly to light with a wavelength of 557 nanometers; those with alanine prefer a wavelength of 552.

To determine the effect of this difference in the actual eyes of beholders, Samir Deeb and colleagues at the University of Washington put people from both the serine and alanine groups through standard color-matching tests. "Those with serine would be more sensitive to red light," says Nathans. "When asked to mix ingredients to form a standard color, they would require less red." Further studies then determined how frequently each variation appeared in a population of normally sighted men: approximately 60 percent had serine at site 180, and 40 percent had alanine.

It may come as no surprise that we each color our world somewhat differently, that even normally sighted people don't always see eye to eye. What is remarkable, however, is the ability to trace this difference right down to a single amino acid, making a direct link between gene and brain.—*Beth Ann Meehan* "crippled apple women"; he would whirl out of their way.

Thurber's fantastic visions, though not diagnosed at the time, fit the description of a disorder called Charles Bonnet syndrome, in which people who are blind or partly so—because of eye diseases or certain types of brain damage—see vivid, intensely realistic images of things that aren't there. Ramachandran and his colleague Leah Levi have taken a special interest in the syndrome. One of Ramachandran's patients, a 32-year-old San Diego man who sustained brain damage in a car accident several years ago, has lost the lower half of his visual field. He doesn't see a black band or sense a border between the sighted field and the blind one, any more than the rest of us detect boundaries at the periphery of our vision. The extraordinary thing about this patient, Ramachandran says, "is that he hallucinates constantly. These hallucinations occur only in the blind field. He sees little children, and zoo animals and domestic ones, creeping up from below. He might say to me, 'As I'm talking to you, I see a monkey sitting on my lap.'"

CHARLES BONNET SYNDROME, Ramachandran says, "is a more sophisticated type of filling in. It's the next level up. It's a response to visual deprivation. These hallucinations are phantom visual images, analogous to phantom limbs." He believes they originate in portions of the brain that store visual memories and generate visual imagery. In other words, they are yet another example of the puzzling array of phenomena that emerge from the complex entanglement of eye and brain.

"Let me try to give you a sense of where we are," says Margaret Livingstone, in an effort to assess the status of visual research today. "Take form perception. Human beings are very good at it. We recognize contours, faces, words, a lot of really complicated things. What we understand is that in the retinas, the lateral geniculate bodies, and the first layer of the visual cortex, we code for changes in brightness or color. In the next stage, cells become selective for the orientation of the change—that is, they code for contours, or edges. In some places cells select for the length of the contour. Then, if you go up very high, you find cells selective for certain faces." Livingstone pauses. "We know remarkably little about what happens in between. It's frightening how big a gap there is. But we do think we understand a lot about visual processing in spite of that gap."

GOOD VIBRATIONS

WE'RE UNDER SIEGE *from age, drugs, and rock and roll, and all that stands between us and utter silence is 32,000 dancing hearing receptors.*

JoAnn C. Gutin

JoAnn C. Gutin is an anthropologist living in Berkeley, California.

The lank-haired teenager in the black T-shirt was stunned. We were both standing in the damp twilight outside San Francisco's Cow Palace, waiting for the doors to the Megadeth concert to open, and I asked him a patently insane question. "Wear earplugs during the concert?" he echoed, blankly. "Why would I do that? Earplugs are, like, *condoms* for your ears."

His nonchalance about strafing his ears with 115 decibels of heavy metal is sad but understandable: hearing has always been the Cinderella of the senses. Helen Keller thought its absence was more painful and isolating than blindness, yet most people say they'd rather lose hearing than sight. Such second-class status has had a predictable effect on research funding (low), the number of scientists attracted to the field (few), and the rate of progress (slow). As recently as the early 1980s auditory researchers were still laying the foundations for the microscopic and biochemical basis of hearing while their counterparts in vision research were, so to speak, putting up the drywall. As for the numbers, sniffed one biophysicist, "Go to the vision meetings and it's like the Super Bowl or something." He estimates that serious auditory researchers might, worldwide, number 200.

But Cinderella had her moments in the limelight, and it looks as though the Cinderella sense is about to do the same. Technological advances in laboratory techniques, coupled with an aging population—and perhaps a few influential government boomers who put in some hours listening to "Stairway to Heaven" at top volume—portend a bright future for the field. There is already a whisper of a hint, in fact, that scientists may someday be able to restore some of the hearing receptors my young friend was so casually sacrificing.

Those hearing receptors are called hair cells, specialized sensory cells that are among the most remarkable structures in the body. Only 32,000 strong (compared with, say, the eyes' 300 million light-sensitive cells), under constant siege from age, drugs, and a world that includes snowmobiles and jet planes as well as Megadeth, they are all that stand between us and silence. Like princesses turning straw into gold, the inner hair cells transform the mechanical forces of sound into the electrical impulses of hearing.

The neurological phenomenon called hearing begins when the ear collects wavelike air-pressure disturbances—sound—produced by any physical force: a vibrating A string, a tree falling in the forest. The outer ear, which includes the fleshy pinna and the auditory canal, picks up and funnels these waves toward the tympanic membrane, or eardrum. The eardrum vibrates and jiggles the three articulated bones of the middle ear; in turn, the last of these three bones, the stapes (or "stirrup"), flexes the membrane of a small oval "window" in the fluid-filled, coiled cochlea.

Evolution has been called the great tinkerer, assembling new structures from bits and pieces of old ones, and the ear is certainly one of its most protracted projects. Natural selection has been remodeling and redecorating the ear for hundreds of millions of years, as the latest model of vertebrate moved from the ocean to the shore to dry land. Yet the hair cells at its core have hardly been touched; their structure is virtually identical in the hearing and balance systems of all animals with backbones. As it happens, this is a very good thing, since the cochlea has made mammalian hair cells nearly impossible to study.

The cochlea is one of those structures, like black holes or the Hoover Dam, that tend to provoke awe in observers. "It's a jewel box of an organ, isn't it?" sighed one smitten researcher, interrupting himself in midequation. Said another, "It's such an incredible structure! When I finish a session on the microscope, I feel disoriented, like I've been cave diving." The cochlea is indeed amazing: a pea-size, spiral-shaped bony fortress buried in the thickest part of the skull, containing a mechanism of mind-boggling complexity. But like most fortresses, it imprisons as much as it protects. There's no way to get to the hair cells when an organism is alive, since all the works are barricaded in bone, and the inner ear stops functioning seconds after death. And until recently it was impossible to keep hair cells alive outside the body.

Ironically, though the security system fashioned for the inner ear has discouraged invasions by armies of researchers, it hasn't worked particularly well at preserving its inhabitants: we begin losing hair cells as soon as we're born. They simply wear out from use, particularly the cells that process high-frequency sounds. Over time, exposure to loud noise makes them stiffen. No one understands the sequence of cellular events causing the stiffness, but it is known that when hair cells hold this rigid pose too long they just keel over and die.

So it goes: a firecracker too close to the ear here, a jackhammer outside the window there, perhaps even a couple of football seasons in the high-school marching band alongside the tuba and we damage a few or a hundred. By middle age the attrition has become an avalanche: studies have shown that at 65, the average male has lost more than 40 percent of his hair-cell birthright. And, in a phenomenon that might on a bad day strike you as evidence of a malign force in the universe, our hair cells are not able to regrow. Reptiles and amphibians, who have very modest hearing abilities and nonsocial life-styles, replenish their store of hair cells throughout life. We mammals, on the other hand, with our high-fidelity ears, are organisms that depend on hearing to survive both physically and—in the case of humans and other primates—emotionally. Yet we're the group stuck with a relatively paltry and nonrenewable allotment.

WITHIN THE cochlea, the architecture of the hair cells is supremely functional. The 16,000 cells are arranged in four parallel rows, one inner and three outer rows (relative to their distance from the cochlea's central pole); they are sandwiched between two membranes, the basilar below and the tectorial above. Together these two membranes form a partition that spirals down the length of the cochlea. When the stapes pushes on the cochlea's oval window, it sends a wave of pressure through the perilymph, a fluid in the inner ear, which begins a chain of events: the wave sets the basilar membrane vibrating, which vibrates the hair cells, which cause a set of bristles atop the hair cells to brush against the tectorial membrane. There are about 100 of these bristles, or stereocilia, on each human hair cell, and they are arranged in rows according to their height, as if posing for a class photo. When inactive, they lean together in a bundle in the shape of a cone. But when

they are active, their movement against the tectorial membrane ultimately results in a signal being sent along the auditory nerve. Thus the hair cells as a whole act as tiny transducers, converting the mechanical impulses they pick up from the cochlear fluid into the electrical energy that the brain interprets as sound.

There's an undeniably Rube Goldbergian aspect to this chain of events, and elucidating the final mechanical link in the chain (the place where, if the ear were one of Goldberg's fanciful contraptions for, say, making doughnuts, the dough would hit the fat) has occupied neuroscientist Jim Hudspeth for most of his career. Hudspeth, who is now director of the Center for Basic Neuroscience Research at the University of Texas Southwestern Medical Center, recalls his initial aim: "What I saw as important was getting from a macroscopic system—the whole cochlea—to a microscopic and cellular system." That involved ignoring some tantalizing questions; it forced him, he says, to "throw away the complicated and interesting mechanics and hydrodynamics of the ear." He also resigned himself to ignoring "the complicated and interesting stuff" that happens on the way to the brain. "I just wanted to deal with one step on an intimate basis." That step was the mechanical input to the hair cells.

THE QUESTION he and his group of researchers set out to answer was, How do a hair cell's stereocilia move, and what happens when you move them? In the late 1970s, using a frog as their experimental animal, they found that prodding a stereociliary bundle with an extremely fine quartz fiber—which, given the mere millionths-of-an-inch size of the stereocilia, became known as "the telephone pole approach"—sent a current through the cells. (This current produces the chemical that excites the nerve going to the brain.) They discovered two surprising things: the direction of this nudge was critical, and the magnitude of the nudge needed to get the stereocilia to respond was infinitesimal.

Hudspeth found that only a push from front or back produced the current; side-to-side nudging did nothing, for reasons that didn't become clear to the researchers until later. Furthermore, Hudspeth calculated that if the cells were deflected by an amount of prodding equivalent to that

produced by a sound at the threshold of hearing, the cilia would move the hair bundle about three-thousandths of a degree. (Just for scale, several atoms in a row add up to a full degree.) In essence, then, the whole jury-rigged mechanism—eardrum to middle-ear bones, middle-ear bones to oval window, oval window to pressure wave in the perilymph, pressure wave in the perilymph to basilar membrane vibration—is distilled to this: a movement measured in fractions of atomic diameters. Observes Hudspeth, "It's as if the Eiffel Tower were to move a thumb's breadth."

At the time Hudspeth was doing his first work, biologists understood the basic mechanism of cell signaling: a stimulus caused tiny pores—ion channels—to open in the cell membrane, and the movement of charged particles from outside to inside the cell registered as a tiny current change. Vision, for example, had been established as a process in which light hitting the eye's photoreceptors caused chemical reactions that opened ion channels and excited nerve fibers.

Hudspeth and his group assumed, then, that ion channels must be opening and closing in the hair cells when they prodded the stereocilia. What troubled them was how these relatively sluggish biochemical events could occur in the ear, which is built for speed. You can, after all, trick the eye into believing it has seen movement at 30 images a second, a phenomenon the first animators understood intuitively. But that speed is glacial to the ear: 30 cycles per second (or 30 hertz) is so low in frequency we can barely hear it. A young human ear can, however, process the highest overtone on a violin, a frequency of 20,000 vibrations a second. And our ears can discern the delay when a sound is presented to one ear six to ten millionths of a second after it's presented to the other. A biochemical cascade takes thousandths of a second—three orders of magnitude slower—and couldn't possibly do the trick.

To get around the time problem, Hudspeth's group hypothesized that there might be some kind of mechanical gate to the ion channels in the ear, a device that could open them as briskly—near instantaneously, actually—as the ear's acuity demanded. Such a device, if it existed, would be unique to the auditory system, but it would at least have the virtue of fitting the ear's design specs.

There were, Hudspeth makes clear,

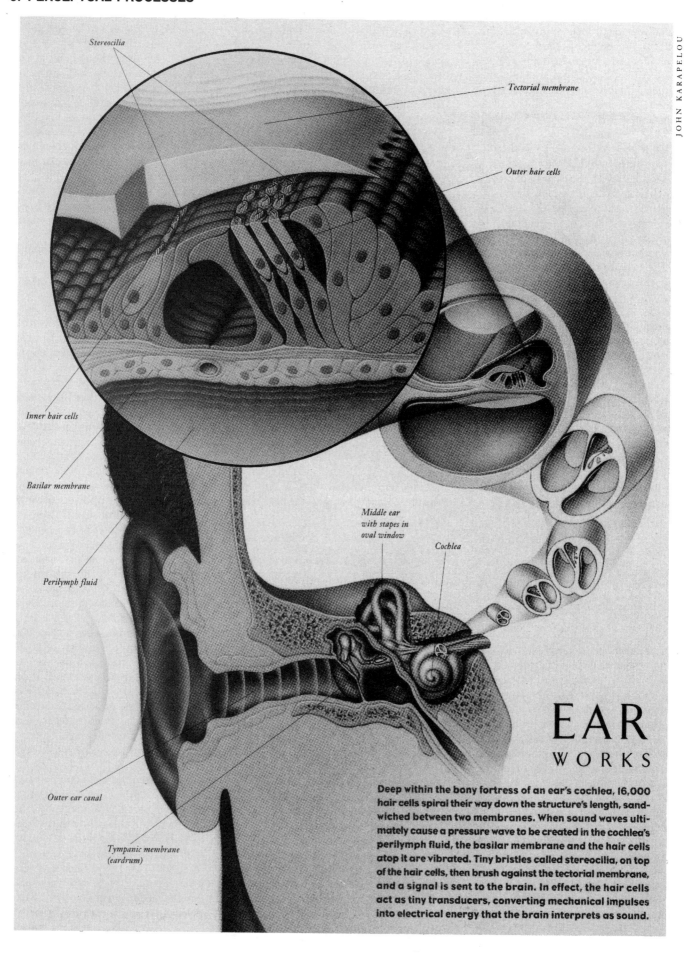

JOHN KARAPELOU

Stereocilia

Tectorial membrane

Outer hair cells

Inner hair cells

Basilar membrane

Perilymph fluid

Middle ear
with stapes in
oval window

Cochlea

Outer ear canal

Tympanic membrane
(eardrum)

EAR
WORKS

Deep within the bony fortress of an ear's cochlea, 16,000 hair cells spiral their way down the structure's length, sandwiched between two membranes. When sound waves ultimately cause a pressure wave to be created in the cochlea's perilymph fluid, the basilar membrane and the hair cells atop it are vibrated. Tiny bristles called stereocilia, on top of the hair cells, then brush against the tectorial membrane, and a signal is sent to the brain. In effect, the hair cells act as tiny transducers, converting mechanical impulses into electrical energy that the brain interprets as sound.

theoretical reasons and indirect evidence for a mechanical gate. All the same, he says, "it was kind of miraculous" when the structures began to appear in scanning electron micrographs. They were first recognized for what they were by a British lab, which, recalls Hudspeth, "was slightly embarrassing. We'd seen some of them ourselves, but we didn't know what to make of them." The strandlike structures, dubbed tip links, joined each stereocilium to its tallest neighbor, rather like wires connecting a regiment of telephone poles running over a mountain.

The front-to-back route of the tip links was the reason a side-to-side prodding of the stereocilia did not produce a current. Hudspeth likens the links to pieces of elastic tied to the handle of a door that's kept shut by one of those "noisemaking door-closers at the top of it. That's the intrinsic elasticity of the transduction channel; it keeps the door closed unless you do something about it. If you pull on the elastic—that's deflection of the hair bundle—that tension is communicated to the door. As the hair bundle moves, you're literally pulling the channels ajar." When the door closes, silence reigns.

The micron-size gadgetry sported by the hair-cell bristles is only part of the unfolding story of how the ear hears. What goes on inside the cell bodies—particularly the bodies of the three outer rows of hair cells—is equally intriguing.

Auditory physiologist Joseph Santos-Sacchi of the Yale University School of Medicine is one of those intrigued. He shares with many of his colleagues an almost paternal affection for the outer hair cells and their antics: "This is a fun system to work with," he says. To show how hair cells move and to illustrate just how much fun it is, he made a videotape of a hair cell bopping along to rap star Hammer's "Can't Touch This."

The outer hair cells that captivate

A LITTLE NIGHT MUSIC

Each night, under cover of darkness, a life-and-death struggle is played out.

Night is when the bats take wing—after their avian competitors have returned to their nests, and after the nocturnal insects, their prey, have begun to show themselves. Bats glide through the night, emitting ultrasonic clicks and cries that bounce off the insects (as well as off branches and houses and trees) and return to tell the bats where to swoop down for their dinner (or where to turn left to avoid bumping into a mighty oak). But the bats are not the only ones listening to the echoes in the night. Many insects have developed the ability to eavesdrop on the sonar signals, to give themselves a fighting chance to evade their onrushing enemy.

Researchers have known since the late 1950s that some insects can hear ultrasound. That was discovered by physiologist Kenneth Roeder of Tufts University and entomologist Asher Treat of the City University of New York when they put electrodes on the auditory nerves of moths and played sounds at different frequencies; only at ultrasound levels did the auditory nerves fire. Later experiments, in which some moths with ears and some without were thrown into a chamber with bats, showed that moths without the ability to hear ultrasound were captured almost 100 percent of the time while ultrasound-hearing moths had a 90 percent chance of getting away. Obviously, for moths, ultrasound detection is a good thing.

It's good for lots of other insects too. The ability to hear ultrasound has since been uncovered in green lacewings, tiger beetles, praying mantises, katydids, crickets, and locusts. With the moths, these keen-eared insects represent five different insect orders: the Lepidoptera, Neuroptera, Coleoptera, Dictyoptera, and Orthoptera. "We really expect this to be a pattern," says Ron Hoy, a Cornell neuroethologist who has been studying the different ways animals hear for some 20 years. "I would not be surprised if many insects that fly at night can hear ultrasound."

Indeed, Hoy thinks he has just uncovered the sixth order of ultrasound-hearing insects: the Diptera, or flies. He and his colleagues were studying a type of parasitic fly that flits through the night listening for the chirping of crickets and then lays its larvae on them. But when the researchers analyzed the fly's hearing ability, they found that not only could it pick up the cricket's song, it could pick up ultrasound as well. "Since they fly around at night," Hoy speculates, "they probably have a bat problem. And while we haven't proved that that's what their ultrasonic hearing is for, it sure is circumstantial evidence."

That many insects have developed ultrasonic hearing is in itself an intriguing finding—in fact, for moths, green lacewings, tiger beetles, and most species of praying mantis, ultrasound is all they can hear. But researchers are now focusing their attention on the organs they developed to do it. "They all have a common structural plan," Hoy explains. "If you're going to hear bats, you need certain things. You need a sensory organ contained within an air-filled chamber, where one wall of the chamber is a tympanic membrane that, when set into vibration, is going to set the whole organ into vibration. And you need receptor cells to pick up those vibrations."

Interestingly, this complex solution to the bat problem, he notes, was arrived at not once but a number of times. "Insects have ears all over the place," Hoy says. "Some stick them on their waist, some on their abdomen, some on their thorax. And what that says is there was independent evolution of the ear. In other words, not all insect ears, not even all moth ears, came from one ancestral source. Independently, in each group, there's been pressure to evolve ears."

So which came first, the bat or the insect ear? Hoy says it depends on which insect you're talking about. For the moths, probably the bats came first; for crickets and grasshoppers, it was the ears. "Insects like crickets have wings that look as if they were capable of producing sounds way before bats came on the scene. And you don't sing unless somebody's around to hear. So when bats came along, the crickets just extended their hearing range."

But he admits it's all just a matter of opinion. "It would be nice if there were a fossil record to tell us. Unfortunately, though, insect ears are very small and probably don't fossilize very well. And not an awful lot of fossil hunters give a damn about insect ears, so they don't look very hard."

—Lori Oliwenstein

Santos-Sacchi are a mammalian refinement of the more primitive hair cells found in lower animals. Though the outer hair cells are differentiated from the inner hair cells by their position in the cochlea, much more than geography marks their distinction—the real difference lies in the realm of neuroanatomy.

A nerve is a one-way street: it goes either toward the brain or away from it. Most of the nerves between the inner hair cells and the brain go from the outside in, just as you might expect; after all, our ears are supposed to get information about external events to our brains. Oddly, though, most of the nerves between the outer hair cells and the brain go the other way, from brain to ear. What could the brain be telling the outer hair cells?

In the early 1980s the outer hair cell story got stranger still. Researchers found that the outer hair cells were not only wired oddly, they behaved oddly. Rather than passively vibrating in sync with the basilar membrane, which is more or less what the inner hair cells do, they were bouncing up and down like manic kids on a trampoline. Indeed, they stretched and contracted at a speed that was orders of magnitude greater than any other cell in the body could muster.

This unexpected display of personality by the outer hair cells—called fast motility—is now one of the hottest areas of auditory research. (Santos-Sacchi has graphed the number of publications since 1985 on a time axis and says that the resulting curve can be described as "exponential, going to infinity.") Whatever its research trajectory, fast motility is hot because it poses two intriguing questions: How are the outer cells doing this? And why?

"Why" may turn out to be the easier question to answer. It's beginning to look as though one reason the outer hair cells boogie is to accelerate the motion of the basilar membrane.

The 3.2-centimeter-long membrane (about 1.25 inches) spiraling inside the cochlea is essentially an acoustical decoder. It processes the tangled mass of auditory frequencies that make up a sound like speech, sorting them into individual frequency bands. For example, in response to high-frequency sounds, the basilar membrane will vibrate more strongly at the base of the cochlea's spiral than it will at its apex. Conversely, low-frequency sounds vibrate the membrane more strongly at the apex than at the base. (Like a tiny helical keyboard up-

ended on its highest note, the basilar membrane processes about one-third of an octave per millimeter.)

But—and here's the mystery—the basilar membrane vibrates at frequencies a hundred times faster than any movement it could conceivably pick up merely by riding the sound wave that travels through the perilymph fluid in the inner ear. Might the outer hair cells be dancing in order to modify the movement of the basilar membrane? Might the connections between brain and outer hair cells be there so the brain can tell the hair cells how fast to dance?

Santos-Sacchi frames the problem thus: "Can outer hair cell motility function in the living animal as we all hope it might? That is, can the cells wiggle and modify the mechanics of the inner ear" at the high frequencies at which the ear works? There are reasons to think they can; after all, they must be moving for a reason. And drugs that were used experimentally to knock out the hair cells definitely altered the mechanics of the basilar membrane.

That's the why; the how of fast motility may be a little trickier to answer. In the laboratory, hair cells can't be coaxed to move any faster than a few thousand cycles a second, not nearly the frequencies that must be attained in living animals. Santos-Sacchi suspects his laboratory apparatus may be preventing the cells from really cutting loose, wigglewise. He thinks the limiting factor is the electrical resistance of the electrode he's using to deliver stimulus to the cell: "It's as if I were trying to measure how fast a car could actually go, but my broken ankle prevented me from pushing down on the accelerator."

However, another problem is not so easily explained away. At the base of the basilar membrane, where high-frequency sounds are decoded, hair cells don't seem to have the juice to alter the basilar membrane vibration. What researchers are left with, then, is two remarkable phenomena—the highly tuned basilar membrane and the rapidly moving cells—and no obvious bridge to connect them. "There is something missing here," Santos-Sacchi admits. "Things don't quite jibe yet." But he's sure the connection is there. "Think about it," he asks rhetorically. "Would evolution go to all this trouble for nothing?"

Of course, the average heavy-metal fan could argue that evolution didn't go to quite enough trouble. The auditory system is elaborate, sensitive, and ingenious, but it does break down before its owners do, particularly if they're partial

to noisy environments. Yet even this flaw may eventually yield to research.

IN THE MID-1980s researchers made a remarkable discovery about birds that may have important implications for us. Everyone had assumed that our feathered friends, who have relatively acute hearing, were in the same boat as mammals vis-à-vis hair cells: when you abuse 'em you lose 'em. But in 1985 both Doug Cotanche, then at the University of South Carolina, and Ed Rubel, at the University of Washington, found that in young chicks hair cells could regrow.

In Rubel's case, it was a classic story of scientific serendipity. His lab was using the chicks as their experimental animal to study the ototoxic properties of a class of antibiotics—that is, they wanted to see to what degree the drugs damaged hearing organs. "Raul Cruz, the medical resident running the study, found that the number of damaged hair cells was greatest just after we administered the drug," recalls Rubel. But when a little time had passed, there seemed to be more and more healthy cells. "He brought me the results and I, like anybody who has completely bought into the dogma of his field, said, 'Raul, you must have counted the hair cells wrong. Go back and do it again.'"

Well, as anyone familiar with Hollywood movies or checkout-stand science fiction could have told Rubel, the counting was fine but the dogma was wrong. There really *were* more hair cells because new ones were growing. Meanwhile, in South Carolina, Cotanche and his colleagues were seeing what looked like embryonic hair cells on the noise-damaged cochleas of adult birds, leading them also to suspect that the hearing organ might be repairing itself. A collective "Aha!" ensued, followed by experiments designed to isolate hair cell regeneration. These have confirmed that hair cells in birds do grow back.

And the new hair cells work. The researchers have trained starlings to peck at a key in response to a given tone by rewarding the maneuver with a food pellet. Immediately after they're dosed with ototoxic drugs, trained birds will fail the tone test, but they gradually regain the skill as hair cells regrow.

Furthermore, the birds' ears *sound* as if they're up and running. Although no one yet understands why, it turns out that a click or other soft tone made in a functioning ear will echo microseconds later. If the hair cells are damaged, the echo is absent. These "otoacoustic emissions" are the best tool yet for diagnosing deafness in infants, which is what Susan Norton, a researcher-clinician who works with Rubel, usually does. Recently, however, she has been using the emissions to track the recovery of hearing in Rubel's avian subjects. Norton finds no emission right after the hair cells are damaged; with time, as the hair cells regenerate, the emissions return, first to high-intensity sounds and then to low.

The big question, of course, is what this work means for human hearing. "Very little work has been done on mammals," Rubel cautions. His group has looked at the cochleas of gerbils and seen a small increase in cell growth, although they saw no new hair cells developing. Other labs have found small rates of hair-cell regeneration, but only in the segment of the inner ear that controls equilibrium. In March, Andrew Forge of University College in London and Jeffrey Corwin and his colleagues at the University of Virginia School of Medicine announced that they had observed hair-cell regeneration in guinea pigs. The Virginia researchers also found, in culture, signs of human hair-cell regeneration by using human tissue taken from the area of the cochlea (called the utricle) responsible for balance. Even though these are balance hair cells, the researchers are excited about the implications this raises for regenerating hearing hair cells.

But first things first: the current task is to isolate the molecule that stimulates hair-cell proliferation in birds. (Or, if a molecule inhibits proliferation in mammals, to find that.) Several labs are now working on the problem, aided by biotech companies eager to be part of research that might, over the long haul, produce a drug useful to some of the 28 million Americans with hearing loss.

Rubel is expansive about the possibilities: "We're at an absolutely wonderful time in the history of biology to have discovered this," he says happily. "We are learning so much, and we have so many powerful techniques we couldn't imagine when we were in grad school." It's early yet, he takes pains to point out. "You've got to remember, this whole field of hair-cell regeneration is only four years old. But we're doing great! And in my opinion," he adds, "when you talk about actually restoring hearing, hair-cell regeneration is the only game in town."

PINNA TO THE FORE

Forget the eardrum and those weird-shaped bones; forget the cochlea with its showy hair cells and fancy frequency sorting. Focus instead on the most visible part of our ear, the pinna—that long-ignored fleshy appendage that hugs closely (or not so closely) to the side of our head. With a few flicks of his quill pen, Darwin shrugged off the pinna in *The Descent of Man,* citing a study of a sailor who'd had one pinna cut off in a scuffle but could still hear just as well with that ear. "Darwin noted that our pinnae are small and we can't move them about as many animals can," explains psychologist Robert Butler of the University of Chicago. "He argued that our pinnae may have had a function earlier on in our evolutionary history, but that now they're vestiges. That thinking simply carried the day."

Not that the pinna's been *totally* ignored over the years; flip through the right medical text and you'll see plenty of squirm-inducing pictures of deformed ears labeled "cut ear," "lop ear," and so on. And each swirl and swivel of the pinna has its distinguished Latin title: Rufus of Ephesus, first-century Roman anatomist, named them all one rainy day, so we have *concha, meatus, antitragus, scaphoid fossa,* and more. But none of this descriptive stuff answers the central, burning question: Why do we have an outer ear at all? The answer, thanks to scientists like Butler, a pinna veteran of 25 years' standing, is now known: we need the pinna to locate precisely the origin of a sound.

A few pioneering experiments led the way to our deeper pinna knowledge. In the 1950s, for example, when glass tubes were stuck into people's ear canals so that sound bypassed the pinna entirely, researchers found that the subjects couldn't tell whether sounds were coming from front or behind—until, that is, a fake ear was added to the end of the tube. Other experiments have since shown that the pinna provides not only front-back clues but clues to the horizontal and vertical position of a sound's source as well. The horizontal contribution of the pinna isn't crucial as long as we can hear through both ears—since a sound coming from the right, for example, will reach the right ear before the left ear and will also be louder in the right ear. Combined, these time and intensity differences give us enough horizontal information to make do. But with a pair of pinnae we do a better job.

For height information, however, the pinna stands alone. "Think about a sound to your right, maybe at 45 degrees and a little above eye level," says Butler. "Make it a complex sound, like that of snapping fingers—one that's a whole mix of frequencies. If you record from a microphone in your ear canal"—that is, from somewhere past the pinna—"you'll discover that a certain frequency band is amplified. Snap your fingers from another position and a *different* frequency band gets amplified. Well, that's what the pinna does; it somehow amplifies different frequencies depending on where the sound is coming from."

It's not magic, says Butler, just physics. Sound travels through the air as waves of air compression—the higher the frequency, the closer the waves are to each other. When those waves hit the pinna, they pile up on each other like ocean waves against a rock, interacting in complicated ways that diminish some of the frequencies while amplifying others. Since the contours of the ear determine which sounds are amplified and which diminished, and since the contours encountered depend on the angle at which the waves hit the ear, it's reasonable to suppose that noises from one place will be tweaked differently from those from another.

The mysterious next step is how our brains change "enrichment at 6,000 hertz" into "Oh, it came from in front of me," and "a tad more than 8,000 hertz" into "Gee, it came from above." "The sound has to be complex so you can compare frequencies," says Butler. "If the sound is pure, then we're unable to localize that pure tone. When the frequency's high, we'll point up. If it's low, we'll point below—no matter where that sound is coming from."

—Rosie Mestel

THE SNIFF OF LEGEND

HUMAN PHEROMONES? CHEMICAL SEX ATTRACTANTS? AND A SIXTH SENSE ORGAN IN THE NOSE? WHAT ARE WE, ANIMALS?

Karen Wright

Karen Wright is a former visiting senior editor at Discover *and the recipient of the 1991 Evert Clark young science journalist award. Wright is at work on her first novel, about a naturalist's struggle to save an endangered species of desert fish.*

IT'S MONDAY MORNING, AND ONCE again Brad Murray finds himself in the position of research subject: lying flat on his back on a lab bench, flaring his nostrils for science.

Luis Monti-Bloch bends over the supine graduate student and, murmuring apologetically, sticks a stork-bill-shaped instrument called a nasal speculum into the left chamber of Murray's nose. The subject flinches but hangs tough as Monti-Bloch spreads the bifurcated beak of the speculum, thereby enlarging the aperture of Murray's own beak. The researcher trains the light from his headlamp into the orifice. He peers through his binocular loupes.

"I can see it right . . . there," says Monti-Bloch, pointing with a cotton swab. He adjusts the loupes, his gaze never straying from Murray's mucosa. He sighs. "It's really beautiful."

Monti-Bloch is one of half a dozen distinguished scientists who believe they've discovered a new sense organ half an inch or so inside the human nose. It's called the vomeronasal organ, or VNO, and if the hunches of these researchers are correct, it detects chemical signals passed unconsciously among human beings—signals that might be about identity, arousal, or sexual receptivity and that go by the name of pheromones. Such chemical communication, common among other animals, was heretofore thought to be nonexistent in humans.

Using stalwart volunteers like Murray and equipment he designed himself, Monti-Bloch has been testing the effects of putative human pheromones on cells in the VNO. To do so, he has to locate the organ's opening, a pale, tiny pit near the bottom of the septal wall dividing the nose. Assuming that Murray is bilaterally symmetrical like the rest of us, a matching inlet lies on the other side of the septum, too. It's not the kind of thing you'd notice on casual inspection.

In fact, it's the kind of thing that anatomists have overlooked for centuries. Though the human vomeronasal organ was first described almost 300 years ago, the few investigators who bothered to look for it thereafter had trouble finding it. Consequently, even as pheromones and their corresponding sensory systems gained renown for their role in the social and mating behavior of other animals, researchers concluded that people got by (and down) without them. Modern medicine had declared the VNO to be mostly absent in humans, and where present, vestigial.

Still, several late-twentieth-century scientists were captivated by the notion that human beings might have a sixth sense. One was an electron microscopist in Boulder, Colorado, who scavenged the septal tissue of nose-job patients for VNO specimens. Another was a neuroanatomist in Salt Lake City who insisted on including a VNO primer in his lectures to medical students. And then there was the physician-cum–venture capitalist in Menlo Park, California, who suspected he'd accidentally isolated human pheromones from extracts of sloughed-off skin.

Five years ago, united by the enthusiasm and lucre of David Berliner, the venture capitalist, these researchers and a few colleagues began to compare notes. With the help of Monti-Bloch, a physiologist at the University of Utah, they've now presented the first strong evidence that human beings do indeed possess a functioning vomeronasal organ. Even skeptical observers admit that the team's findings seem solid; Berliner, who is not so skeptical, has already spun off a pharmaceutical company to synthesize drugs that could be delivered via the VNO, and he's bottled his alleged human pheromones in a perfume called Realm, 50 milliliters of which retails for $79.99.

But all parties concerned stress that the evidence is as preliminary as it is provocative. Although recent surveys show that almost everybody has a VNO after all, researchers still aren't absolutely sure the organ works. Until he received patents for his pheromones last December, Berliner had refused to divulge their makeup, so investigators outside his sphere of influence—that is, those not vested in his company—are only now attempting to replicate his group's findings. For now, no one inside or outside the Berliner camp has

INSTEAD OF DISCRETE PERCEPTIONS, PHEROMONES COULD BE SAID TO MEDIATE IMPRESSIONS: BAD VIBES, WARM FUZZIES, INSTANT DISLIKES, IRRESISTIBLE ATTRACTIONS.

come close to answering the most provocative question of all: How might pheromones influence human beings?

Until recently, medical science claimed that they *don't*, period. Historical reports of the human VNO were as erratic and improbable as UFO sightings and were accorded as much credibility. A Dutch military surgeon first described the structure in 1703 in a soldier with a facial wound. In 1891 a French doctor reported seeing it in a quarter of the 200 people he examined. In 1934 one researcher wrote that the VNO "is almost constantly found in the human embryo and with diligence may occasionally be found in the adult." During the course of human development, this researcher noted, the VNO—like many a UFO—just seemed to disappear.

Finally, in the late 1930s, a widely respected neuroanatomist named Elizabeth Crosby dealt a seemingly decisive blow to the recurring rumors of the human VNO. The so-called sixth sense couldn't exist, she explained, because the place in the brain where other animals process neural impulses from the VNO—a structure known as the accessory olfactory bulb—doesn't persist past the first trimester of fetal development in humans. Even if the "end organ" was there, Crosby argued, it couldn't be functional.

UNLIKE HER PREDECESSORS, CROSBY never stooped to the level of actually searching for the VNO in embryos or adults. Instead she based her conclusion on her formidable knowledge of the olfactory processing center in the brain. Few medical researchers were qualified to challenge her; most took her word as gospel. And if the human VNO was kaput, they figured, there was no use looking for human pheromones either.

In the decades that followed, though, research amply demonstrated the importance of chemical signals to the sex lives of other animals. The vomeronasal organ was found in amphibians, reptiles,

and most mammals, and it was implicated in the most intimate details of vertebrate physiology. For example, researchers discovered that pheromones in the urine of male prairie voles make a female vole's hormones go haywire. Her ovaries swell, her uterus triples in size, and she ovulates within two days.

Pheromones were also found to exert profound effects on reproductive behavior. When a female pig gets a whiff of the pheromones in a male pig's breath, she humps her back, steels her haunches, and submits her posterior to the inevitable. Behaviorists call this a fixed-action response because free will doesn't enter into it: one blast of boar breath and she's gotta have it. Similarly, male mice whose VNOs are surgically removed lose all interest in the procreative act. They won't mount a female nor even sniff at her nether regions.

"If you want to lead a life that is dictated by chemistry, then have a vomeronasal organ," says Charles Wysocki, a neuroscientist at the Monell Chemical Senses Center in Philadelphia who's studied the rodent VNO for 15 years. To be a rodent, Wysocki says, is to live from one pheromonal fix to the next. In addition to their orchestration of sex, pheromones help animals identify relatives, mark territories, and communicate bad intentions.

The discovery of pheromones' potent effects on other animals seemed to confirm the prevailing assumption that the chemicals aren't acting on human beings: if they were, scientists reasoned, we'd know it—wouldn't we? Maybe not, says Wysocki. It's true that in humans socialization is shaped more by experience than it is in other animals, so our responses to chemical signals probably aren't as inflexible. But if they occurred, pheromonal exchanges among human beings couldn't be seen, felt, tasted, or heard—and probably not smelled, either. Unlike those conscious sensations, the messages conveyed via the VNO would bypass mental awareness and make a beeline for the primitive brain. Instead of distinct, discrete perceptions, like the taste of a cherry or the sight of a sunset, pheromones could be said to mediate impressions: bad vibes, warm fuzzies, instant dislikes, irresistible attractions.

It was a sudden change in vibes at his laboratory that led David Berliner to wonder whether such experiences could be ascribed, literally, to chemistry. Working at the University of Utah in the early 1960s, Berliner was trying to characterize the chemical components of human skin when, one

day, he and his co-workers were overcome with an inexplicable bonhomie.

Someone suggested that they learn bridge over lunch. It was an unprecedented notion.

"We all looked at her and said, 'Uh-oh. Either she's having an affair or she's going to get married,'" says Berliner. "And then we all said, 'Sure!' So now over lunch we're playing bridge. The ambience of the group became much friendlier, and I was feeling very good."

"Until we closed those flasks," he says—the flasks containing his skin extracts. "I put them away, and bridge stopped automatically. No more bridge." When Berliner brought out the extracts again several months later, camaraderie revived, as did the card game.

Berliner noticed the connection, but he was a busy man with a surfeit of good ideas. A chance investment in an oral-contraceptive manufacturer would soon land him a pile of money with which he would launch biotech companies marketing technology he himself often helped pioneer. Cetus, Alza, Advance Polymer Systems, and Biosource Genetics are among the corporations Berliner has had a hand in; his more notable (and lucrative) involvements include the development of the skin-patch technique for drug delivery. The skin patch has been used to administer estrogen to menopausal women, nitroglycerin to people at risk of a heart attack, and nicotine to smokers trying to kick the habit.

Berliner never lacked inspiration but was always short of time. Not until the mid-1980s—several decades, several millions, and several companies later—would he again thaw "those flasks" to find the secret ingredients that could compel earnest scientists to squander their lunch hour on frivolous pursuits.

At about the same time Berliner began thinking about thawing his flasks, David Moran and Bruce Jafek were conferring in a University of Colorado clinic in Denver. Moran, an electron microscopist in the university's medical school, had recently tired of studying balance sensors in the giant African cockroach and had become intrigued with the processing of sensory information in higher animals. He was particularly interested in describing the microscopic structure of human olfactory tissue, a feat that had never been achieved, owing in part to the tissue's inconvenient location in a cleft just a few hundredths of an inch wide and roughly three inches up the human nostril. One of Moran's graduate students had designed an evil-looking wire device that could collect material from the olfactory cleft, and Moran had begun taking specimens for electron microscope preparations.

Jafek, who'd recently been appointed chairman of the otolaryngology department, heard about Moran's research and asked to collaborate with him on the biopsy work. During a rambling discussion of things olfactory, Jafek happened to mention that one of his graduate students was doing some research on the VNO of the human fetus. The question arose: Whatever happened to the *adult* VNO?

"Bruce said, 'I'm going to start looking for this thing, and see what I can see,'" says Moran. As a practicing surgeon specializing in nose jobs, Jafek had access to plenty of proboscises. His grad student's work on the fetal VNO gave him an idea of where the organ's inlets might be located in the adult. "And once he learned the right place to look, he saw the VNO in everybody," says Moran. "He used a long-working-distance dissecting microscope, and he'd lay people on their backs, shine a light in there looking for this thing, and—there it was.

"So we took everyone in the lab and did an I'll-show-you-mine-if-you-show-me-yours thing. And sure enough, I had one on each side; a friend of mine had one on each side; everyone we looked at in the lab had a pair of vomeronasal pits. That," says Moran, "bent the nail over for me," confirming his belief in the existence of an adult VNO.

Moran and Jafek examined more than 200 people and found the pits in every last one of them. Eventually, surveys done by other investigators would confirm that the structures are present in more than 90 percent of noses. That these other surveys did not find the VNO in all subjects can be explained, says Moran, by the fact that the noses in question were about to undergo surgical procedures and probably had higher-than-average proportions of nasal anomalies that could obscure the organ's opening. Also, he points out, many surveyors didn't realize that the size range of vomeronasal pits straddles the line between the visible and the invisible.

"Sometimes you can see them with the naked eye and sometimes you can't," he says. "The big ones you see right away—the largest I've seen is almost a tenth of an inch across, which is a big hole. But some are as small as a hundredth of an inch. That's the human eye's limit of resolution, so you can't see the

IS THE HUMAN VOMERONASAL ORGAN OPERATIONAL? IS IT SENDING SIGNALS TO THE BRAIN? OR IS IT SIMPLY A BURNT-OUT VESTIGE OF A SCRATCH-AND-SNIFF PAST?

small ones without magnification." Moran says that other surveyors, having seen the largest cavities, assumed they didn't need a microscope to find the pits and wound up missing the smallest ones.

For Moran, the electron microscopist, seeing the VNO at 40X wasn't entirely gratifying either. Moran asked Jafek to call him into the operating room when patients were having the part of the septum near the pits surgically removed; he then took biopsies from those patients for viewing at magnifications hundreds of times higher.

His preparations showed that each pit led into a tiny duct a few tenths of an inch long and that some of the cells lining the duct looked like neurons, or nerve cells—to be exact, like receptor cells, which pick up sensory information and pass it on to the brain. But they did not look like olfactory receptors. And they did not look like nociceptors, cells that react to painful stimuli. "They didn't look like any other nerve cells I'd ever seen before in the human body," says Moran.

In 1985 he presented his micrographs in a poster session at the annual meeting of the Association for Chemoreception Sciences. "People just sort of walked by and went, 'Huh,' and walked away," says Moran. "The work was met with apathy of exciting proportions." Moran's peers wanted to know what, if anything, the neurons were doing. He didn't claim to know the answer—but several years later David Berliner would.

IT WAS 1989 WHEN BERLINER DECIDed to let his genies out of their bottles. "Let me ask you a question," he'd said to his friend Larry Stensaas, a neuroanatomist at the University of Utah. "If you thought you had some human pheromones, how would you go about finding out whether they worked?"

Stensaas had just finished debriefing Berliner on a research project he'd conducted for one of Berliner's biotech companies. He had been working with

Berliner for years, but the subject of pheromones had never come up before.

"I told him, 'In all other mammals, pheromones have to have a vomeronasal organ to work on,'" says Stensaas. "And nobody's seen the human vomeronasal organ for a long time. Berliner then said, 'Well, has anybody looked?'"

Stensaas didn't know the answer to that question, even though he himself was something of a fan of the organ. Year after year, over the protests of colleagues, he'd delivered to his medical students a detailed VNO lecture in which he candidly admitted that most experts believe the adult human version doesn't exist. He'd never had the time or the funding to pursue his interest, but it had persisted nonetheless.

"I found it fascinating that this stupid little organ could control sexual behavior in animals," Stensaas says. "And I liked the idea of the human vomeronasal organ, even if no one had seen one."

Actually, someone *had* seen the human VNO not long before. When Stensaas turned to the sensory literature, he found that in 1985 a group of Canadian investigators, working without magnification, had located at least one pit in 39 of the 100 people they examined. Discouraged by the numbers, the Canadians had abandoned their search; Stensaas took up the quest. His training as a neuroanatomist had taught him to look beyond surface phenomena, so he began to collect the brains and septal tissue from cadavers and aborted fetuses and dissect them. Unlike Elizabeth Crosby, Stensaas looked for the VNO as well as the nerve fibers associated with it, and he found the organ in most of his specimens. He also found that Crosby was right about the accessory olfactory bulb: it wasn't evident past the first trimester of fetal development. But Stensaas thought he knew why.

"Because the frontal lobes of the brain grow so big in human beings, the olfactory bulb is pulled away from its location near the brain stem," says Stensaas. As the cortex develops, the bulb becomes flattened, its nerve fibers stretched in order to maintain its connection with the frontal lobes and the brain stem; the result is that it becomes difficult to see. "Elizabeth Crosby couldn't find the accessory olfactory bulb, because it had been smeared out by this process. It isn't recognizable." But, Stensaas maintains, it's there.

The next step was to test whether or not the human VNO was operational. Is the organ sending signals to the brain? Or is it simply a burnt-out vestige of a scratch-and-sniff past? To help answer that question, Stensaas recommended Monti-Bloch, a longtime friend who'd spent decades studying the function of chemoreceptors. When the physiologist met Berliner early in 1990 he voiced some skepticism.

"I was not sure what could come out of this," says Monti-Bloch. "What I read was that in humans the organ was atrophic. And there wasn't any work we could refer to on studying the physiology of the VNO in mammals, let alone humans." He told Berliner he'd give the project six months. "'If it doesn't work by then,' I said, 'it doesn't work, period,'" says Monti-Bloch.

In the next few months Monti-Bloch designed a system for delivering chemical substances to the VNO and measuring any electrical impulses that might be generated at the organ's entrance. The trick was to contain the dispersal of the test substances so they would trigger only the cells in the VNO pits and not the smell sensors in the olfactory cleft or other nerve receptors in the nose. Monti-Bloch found that he could get the desired effect using a thin wire electrode surrounded by two concentric plastic shafts—the inner one to administer chemicals in a puff of air, and the outer one to suck away the puff like a vacuum cleaner. Placed in the VNO pit of a cooperative human subject, the rounded tip of the electrode, protruding slightly from the plastic sheaths, could detect any electrical activity that followed the chemical pulse.

Monti-Bloch connected the instrument with wires and tubes to a device that would both control the puffs of air and receive electric signals. He could inject one-second blasts of test chemicals into the airstream by depressing a pedal. A computer monitored the entire procedure, recording the chemical and electrical impulses on a chart called—what else?—an electrovomeronasogram (aka EVG).

Building the electrovomeronasometer itself required the machining of several novel parts and the extensive modification of off-the-shelf equipment. When Monti-Bloch had the system together, he tested it by positioning the electrode in some poor unfortunate's olfactory cleft and recording the responses of olfactory receptors to smelly substances such as mint and clove oil. The apparatus worked for olfactants, but the six months were nearly up.

"I am going to send you a little package with some things for you to try on the VNO," Berliner told Monti-Bloch when the physiologist phoned in from Utah.

"I asked him, 'What are these things?'" says Monti-Bloch. "And he said, 'I can't tell you that.' But the first thing I noticed when I got them was that they didn't smell. So I grabbed one of my collaborators and tried the substances in his olfactory cleft, and indeed, they didn't have any effect.

"Then I placed the electrode in the vomeronasal organ, put a puff of the substance into the airstream, and all of a sudden—" Monti-Bloch raises his eyebrows and becomes speechless. In short, the substances Berliner had shipped put spikes all over the EVG of Monti-Bloch's volunteer, suggesting that neurons in the VNO were discharging in response to those substances.

Monti-Bloch has now tested several dozen of the putative pheromones, all of which are derived from the 20 natural isolates Berliner discovered in his skin extracts. The tests have shown that the substances can evoke other physiological reactions, including changes in heart rate, respiration, pupil size, and skin temperature. Responses vary from person to person, and some of the compounds affect only men or only women—as would be expected, given the role of pheromones in the rest of the animal kingdom.

The possible behavioral effects of Berliner's compounds are still unproved. Though Monti-Bloch has yet to conduct a systematic appraisal of subjective reactions (that is, vibes), some volunteers have mentioned feeling less nervous and more confident during their exposure to Berliner's elixirs. Brad Murray, for example, claims to have experienced "a little bit of a relaxing effect from one or two of the substances." But he admits to being distracted by procedural details. "Mostly it just feels like somebody stuck a wire up my nose," he says.

In 1991 Stensaas heard about David Moran's work through a colleague and passed his phone number on to Berliner. Moran's micrographs of the human VNO provided visual support for the physiological evidence Monti-Bloch had been collecting. In Moran's pictures the cells lining the vomeronasal pits look like receptor cells; Monti-Bloch's work suggests they act like receptor cells too. In 1992 Berliner asked olfaction experts at the University of Kentucky to identify the cell types; the Kentucky team treated VNO tissue with chemical markers that bind to nerve cells. The markers indicate that the apparent receptors in the VNO are indeed neurons and "probably some kind of receptor cells," says Kentucky neuroscientist Marilyn Getchell. "But the question we still haven't answered is, are there nerve fibers coming out of this organ to the brain?"

That's what everyone in VNO research would like to know. From Moran's and Getchell's work, it's clear that the surface of the VNO is chockablock with receptor cells. From Stensaas's exploration of fetal and cadaver tissue, it's clear that the region surrounding the VNO is laden with neurons that make all kinds of interesting connections to the brain. Monti-Bloch's experiments demonstrate that stimulating the VNO receptors can effect significant changes in physiology. For most people, this assembly of evidence would be proof enough that the VNO is sending signals to the brain.

But neuroscientists are not most people. And so far no one has demonstrated exactly how VNO receptor cells hook up with their neighboring nerve complex.

"The wiring diagram hasn't been worked out yet," says Moran. "And that's because not many people are willing to have dyes that trace nerve cells injected into their brains, then have their heads cut off so you can take sections and look to see where the dyes went."

STENSAAS AND HIS COLLEAGUES, believers in a functioning human accessory olfactory bulb, already suspect the general direction. They think nerve fibers emanating from the vicinity of the vomeronasal organ head straight through the bulb to the hypothalamus, the command center for basic body functions such as sleeping, eating, and mating. Nerves from the VNO may also rendezvous with the limbic system, where emotions are thought to originate.

To the researchers, these neural pathways suggest that the human vomeronasal organ is linked inextricably, albeit subconsciously, with psyche and soma alike. If true, the organ would be an ideal target for pharmaceutical intervention—a point that has not been lost on Berliner. Drugs delivered via the VNO could in theory remedy both psychological and somatic disturbances without the side effects, such as nausea, that can be common with oral and intravenous medications. Berliner's team claims it has already identified certain substances that may decrease anxiety, diminish hunger, and relieve PMS.

But what about, you know, the boar-breath effect.

3. PERCEPTUAL PROCESSES

If Berliner has discovered an aphrodisiac, he isn't saying. The substances in his perfume, for example, are meant to enhance only the wearer's "positive feelings of romance, confidence, attractiveness, and self-assurance," according to Realm's infomercial. True, the perfume comes in male and female versions, reflecting the fact that each has a sex-specific formula. But Berliner says his women's scent contains a pheromone only women can detect, while the men's will only boost the "positive feelings" of men. He claims to have an ethical aversion to substances that would act on other people rather than the user. Of course, there's nothing to stop a scheming man from liberally dousing himself with the female scent, or a designing woman with the male. Berliner's stance may have less to do with ethics than with the Food and Drug Administration's requirement that any product calling itself an aphrodisiac be sold as a prescription drug.

Whether or not Realm is *l'eau de lust*, the idea that chemicals can stimulate arousal in human beings is not farfetched. The presence of a vomeronasal organ could account for menstrual synchrony in women who are in frequent and close contact with one another, says Monell's Wysocki. It may also explain how mothers and infants can identify each other by what was thought to be smell alone. As for chemical communication between genders, Wysocki's colleague George Preti has shown that the timing of a woman's menstruation can be altered by smearing her upper lip with an extract of male underarm sweat.

Fortunately, there is a more palatable way to swap pheromones with your loved ones. "The kiss might play a very important role in the transference of chemical signals," says Wysocki. "In other species, physical contact is often necessary for the exchange of the substances that activate the vomeronasal organ.

"On the other hand, one could argue that in the course of evolution human beings are shedding control by pheromones and leading more of an independent life. If one takes that view, then the kiss is nothing more than a vestigial behavior for transmitting pheromones."

Of course, a kiss is nothing less, either. And for now, a sigh *is* still a sigh. But no doubt its role too will be clarified—as time goes by.

Amputees can feel missing hands grab a cup of coffee, missing feet itch, and missing legs ache.

Behind these ghostly sensations lies the secret of touch.

TOUCHING THE PHANTOM

JAMES SHREEVE

James Shreeve is the coauthor, with anthropologist Donald Johanson, of Lucy's Child: The Discovery of a Human Ancestor *and the author of* Nature: The Other Earthlings.

Ten years ago, Fred Aryee almost lost his life in a storm at sea. When an enormous swell hit the tuna boat on which he served as engineer, a falling beam crushed his right arm. The boat was five days from land. His crew mates managed to stem the loss of blood and keep him alive until they reached shore, but it was too late to save the limb.

A decade later Aryee sits in a chair, stripped to the waist. The physical flesh of his right arm below the elbow has long since ceased to exist. The physical flesh of Aryee's brain, however, has yet to be convinced of that fact.

"See if you can reach out and grab this cup in your right hand," says neuroscientist Vilayanur Ramachandran, head of the Brain and Perception Laboratory at the University of California at San Diego. Aryee gestures with his stump toward a cup on a table, a couple of feet away.

"What are you feeling now?" asks Ramachandran.

"I feel my fingers clasping the cup," says Aryee.

"Okay, try it again," says Ramachandran. This time, as Aryee begins his motion, Ramachandran quickly moves the cup farther away, to see if Aryee's imagined arm has the limitation of real flesh or can stretch out as long as needed to complete a task. The result astonishes him.

"Ouch!" says his patient, grimacing in pain. "Why did you *do* that?"

"Do what?"

"It felt like you ripped the cup out of my fingers."

Fred Aryee's eerily stubborn grip on that cup is a compelling example of "phantom limb," the perception of vivid feeling arising from the airy appendages of amputees and the nerve-dead limbs of accident victims. A legless veteran complains of an irrepressible itch on an instep floating in space. A double arm amputee reports phantom arms that swing normally with his stride as he walks. Aryee, an avid tennis player, has managed to switch his game to his left hand, but he has trouble with his serving motion when his ghostly right arm insists on holding the racket, too. Another of Ramachandran's patients, a young woman missing both arms since birth, feels her arms gesticulate in tempo with the points she is making in a heated discussion. Virtually all amputees experience such sensations.

More disconcerting is the pain. Patients complain of burning or prickling, horrible muscle cramps, or the feeling that their fingers are being twisted out of shape or pushed through their palms. Sometimes a tender bunion or a splinter that afflicted a real foot will harass the phantom too, in precisely the same spot. Arm amputees have said that they sometimes feel as if their fingernails are being pulled off.

"The other night, it hurt so bad I was literally screaming," says 80-year-old Brian Sheehan, who has lost the lower portion of both of his legs as a result of diabetes. "You just learn to live with it."

Some patients apparently do not, taking their own lives to escape from torments felt in purely phantom flesh.

"Opiates and other drugs that address the pain system are useless, because that's not what's causing the pain anymore," says neurobiologist Jon Kaas of Vanderbilt University. "It's some other system, inadvertently signaling pain."

SINCE PHANTOM LIMB PAIN was first described in the nineteenth century, researchers have been trying to figure out where in the tactile system the mysterious sensations originate. When a limb is removed, the severed nerves in the remaining stump—nerves that formerly carried messages of touch, temperature, and pain from the skin—form nodules

By James Shreeve. Reprinted with permission from *Discover* magazine, June 1993, pp. 35-42. © 1993 by the Walt Disney Company.

"WE'RE LOOKING AT A NEW ROUTE TO THE HOLY GRAIL OF NEUROBIOLOGY, THE PHYSICAL BASIS OF LEARNING AND MEMORY."

called neuromas on their cut ends. The classic explanation for phantom limb pain is that these truncated nerve endings continue to send impulses up the spinal cord to the brain. Cutting the nerves just above the neuromas or where they enter the spinal cord does seem to bring some relief, but only temporarily. Applying the scalpel inside the spinal cord works no better. Within a few months or years the affliction of the ghost limb returns, painful proof that the true seat of the sensation must lie even farther up the touch pathway, within the brain itself.

While chasing the phantom, neurobiologists have thus been led to a solid revelation: the sense of touch, and the physical world it ushers into existence, has much more to do with what is going on in our heads than at our fingertips. The illusory sensations may even be on the verge of revealing one of the brain's most powerfully guarded secrets. If neuroscientists like Ramachandran and Kaas are correct, the exotic phenomenon of phantom limb offers one keenly magnified perspective on what routinely happens in the brain as we engage the world around us and learn from the experience.

"We're looking at a new route to the Holy Grail of neurobiology," says Ramachandran. "An understanding of the physical basis of learning and memory."

When nerve endings in the skin, known as receptors, receive a stimulus—a brush of silk or the prick of a needle, an icy stream of water or the grip of a warm hand—the bioelectrical impulse generated by the receptors travels through the spinal cord to connections called synapses in the brain stem. Further synapses send the signal to a critical relay station in the brain called the thalamus. From there the impulses are routed up to the "somatosensory cortex." This projection screen for sensation is as neatly laid out as a French garden. Nerve impulses originating in the thumb stimulate a region of the cortex

devoted only to the thumb, a region that lies immediately adjacent to one responding to nerves from the index finger, and so on down the digits. Arm cortex lies next to shoulder cortex, shoulder next to trunk, with just a few topographically necessary odd pairings. (The toes, for instance, plunk their signals down next to impulses zinging in from the genitals.) The more receptors active in an area of skin, the bigger its allotment of sensory cortex. (In us humans, nearly a quarter of the skin cortex is dedicated to our highly sensitive hands.) It is as if there exists a tiny, orderly, though distorted version of oneself—a homunculus—outlined on the pleated surface of the brain.

In their search to find the source of phantom limb, researchers came up against this fastidiously arranged little person. It was waving a fundamental credo of neuroscience in their faces. Since the early 1960s, neuroscientists have generally accepted the notion that except for a critical period of flexible growth in infancy, the brain's neuronal circuitry is "hardwired," its connections as fixed in place as the electrical system of a house. The "critical-period theory" derived largely from experiments such as those of David Hubel and Torsten Wiesel, who shared a Nobel Prize in 1981. Hubel and Wiesel found that a patch placed over one eye of a kitten during its critical period of neural growth would lead to permanent blindness in that eye. While the eye was patched, inputs arriving from the functioning eye would take over the deprived eye's allotment of visual cortex. The blind eye was unable to recover once the patch was removed because it was too late for the inputs to be redirected—they had become fixed in place. Other studies on eye, ear, and touch reception supported the idea that the adult brain was rigidly organized.

The sensory homunculus in the cortex is, of course, a part of that hardwired brain. How then can it possibly be the source of phantom limb? What is dead in a hard-wired system is simply dead; once nerve impulses from an amputated or paralyzed limb are no longer received by the cortex, the portion of its map allotted to the limb should forever after be as silent as a telephone whose line has been cut. Thus, after chasing phantom limb up into the brain itself, most clinical neurobiologists have lost sight of it in a fog of semi-explanations and begged questions. As two researchers recently concluded in the *Canadian Medical Association Journal*, the

feelings are "probably psychic," the evidence suggesting "some form of obsession neurosis" having to do with the ghastly trauma of losing a piece of one's body.

"We suggest that general measures of a psychotherapeutic nature are likely to be of benefit," they wrote. Headshrinking, in other words.

A possible tunnel through this impasse—with perhaps a glimpse of the Holy Grail shining in its recesses—was first approached in the mid-1980s by Michael Merzenich of the University of California at San Francisco, working with Jon Kaas of Vanderbilt, among others. Merzenich and his colleagues wanted to see what would happen to the skin map in the cortex when it was deprived of normal input. In one experiment, they amputated a finger of an adult monkey, waited a few weeks, and then took recordings of signals reaching the associated part of the monkey's cortical map. According to the critical-period theory, this region of cortex, lacking input from touch receptors, would be as lifeless as an office building abandoned by its tenants. Instead, the researchers discovered, neurons within the region fired whenever the two fingers *adjacent* to the missing one were touched. Apparently nerve impulses from neighboring sections were being "remapped" into the vacated zone—suggesting that the adult brain was a much more flexible commodity than most scientists thought.

"There had always been a countercurrent to the mainstream that suspected the brain could make such adjustments," says Merzenich. "We witnessed them happening."

Nevertheless, the amount of remapping Merzenich and his colleagues had seen might still be explained with no threat to the dogma of a hardwired brain. The nerve impulses from the neighboring regions of the monkey's sensory cortex had encroached only one or two millimeters. This just happens to be the length of an individual nerve axon, the "business end" of nerve cells, which makes connections with other nerves running from the thalamus to the sensory cortex. When Merzenich and his colleagues amputated *two* of the monkey's fingers, the cortical remapping was not as extensive. The most likely explanation, therefore, was that existing, unused branches of the axons were already in contact across the borders of the cortical regions. When normal input from one amputated finger ceased, these dormant connections were unmasked, and new impulses were sent into the vacated region—but only so far as an individual axon could reach. In other words, you *could* teach an old brain new tricks, as long as you used preexisting hardwired circuits to do the learning.

IN 1991 NEUROSCIENTIST Timothy Pons of the National Institute of Mental Health announced new evidence that both supported Merzenich's observations and utterly confounded any such tidy explanation for them. Pons's study made serendipitous use of the infamous Silver Spring monkeys, a group of macaques that, in an unrelated experiment 12 years earlier, had had the sensory nerves from one arm cut where they entered the spinal cord. The monkeys had become the focal point of a celebrated animal rights trial (see DISCOVER, January 1992). While the ethical issue raged in the courts, the monkeys languished in limbo, off-limits to research but deteriorating to the extent that the courts agreed four of them would be better off put to sleep. Before they were killed, however, Pons was permitted to plant electrodes in their cortex to see what 12 years of dormancy had done to the portion of brain map once devoted to impulses from the unplugged limbs. He expected to find confirmation of Merzenich's results: a couple of millimeters of encroachment from the two adjacent sensory regions—in this case, from the face and the trunk. Certainly the encroachment should be no more than the length an individual nerve axon could reach.

"We were astounded," says Pons. "Instead of a little bit of trespassing from both sides, we discovered that the face region had completely invaded the neighboring cortex. In each of the four animals, the entire hand and arm zone responded when we stimulated the face."

In effect, fully a third of the entire touch map—over half an inch of cortex—had switched its allegiance. With no orders coming in from the numbed limb, it had married its fortunes to those of the face instead. This is neural reorganization on a massive scale, unimaginable in a hardwired brain. Input from dormant branches of neighboring axons could not be the answer, since they are not nearly long enough to make connections over such a vast swath of gray matter.

"It's really a mystery how this can occur," says Pons. "We don't have the mechanism yet to explain it."

IN NEUROLOGICAL TERMS, THE HAND WAS NOT MISSING AT ALL— INDEED, IT WAS NOW A *PAIR* OF LEFT HANDS.

Given that years had elapsed since the monkeys' nerves had been severed, one possible explanation was that new connections between neurons had actually sprouted up, forging links from the facial cortex right across the whole vacated zone. Such fecund growth of tissue in the cortex seems unlikely, however, given that adult brains have never been known to grow *any* new neuronal connections—they only lose them. On the other hand, experiments on monkeys have shown that new axons can sprout from already existing cells in the spinal cord. Pons speculates that the enormous changes witnessed in the monkeys' skin maps might be the consequence of relatively modest growth occurring in more constricted places farther down the touch pathway, before the nerve impulses ever reach the cortex itself.

One obvious point of constriction is the thalamus. Within this relay station, nerve impulses traveling from the face to the cortex must pass through the region that is simultaneously receiving input from the hand and arm. Normally the facial pathway crosses through the hand-and-arm portion of thalamus without making any connections, like a road crossing a highway without an interchange. Over time, however, even a little local sprouting where these facial nerves pass through the limb's portion of thalamus could create new synapses—and throw the whole facial input up onto the hand and arm region of the cortical map. Pons prefers the analogy of hooking up your telephone line to the neighbors' house. At this constricted, local level, it doesn't take much wire to send your calls spinning out over their entire long-distance network.

Whatever its ultimate explanation, the flagrant remapping Pons had witnessed in the Silver Spring monkeys sent a surge of excitement through the growing coterie of neuroscientists who believe in brain plasticity. Among the inspired was Ramachandran. For several years he had been probing the mystery of "blind spots" in the visual system. Everyone has a small natural blind area on each retina, about

15 degrees off center. None of us walks around with a corresponding black hole in our visual field, however, because the brain fills in the missing portion with information from the surrounding background. Victims of stroke or head wounds may have much larger blind spots—yet in most circumstances, they too automatically fill in the gap with details from the background. Ramachandran and others strongly suspected that this neural sleight of hand is achieved by the remapping of impulses normally delivered to adjacent parts of the visual cortex.

When Ramachandran saw Pons's paper, he began to wonder whether much the same sort of filling in was taking place in the tactile system of phantom limb sufferers. He recruited some amputees to help test his hypothesis. One volunteer was a teenager named Victor Quinterro, who had lost his left arm in an auto accident only four weeks earlier. As Victor sat blindfolded in a chair, Ramachandran gently touched his face with a Q-tip.

"Where do you feel that?" he asked.

"You are touching my face," said the teenager. "But I also feel my left thumb tingling."

"And here?" asked Ramachandran, stroking the skin above Victor's upper lip.

"You are touching my index finger."

"Now?" The Q-tip moved to Victor's chin.

"My pinkie."

Ramachandran continued his probing, touching his patient's chest, abdomen, and various points on his good arm, without any reaction from the phantom. Only when he touched the cotton-tipped wand to an area just above Victor's stump did the magic return.

"There, my thumb tingled again . . . now my index finger . . . the ball of the thumb . . ."

In effect, Ramachandran's Q-tip had ferreted out the physical, fleshly substance of Victor's illusory hand. Neurologically speaking, at least, the hand was not missing at all—indeed, it was now a *pair* of left hands, one meticulously laid out across his lower face, the other wiggling its digits just below his shoulder. In the version of Victor mapped into his somatosensory cortex, these two regions happen to border the area that formerly received messages from the amputated arm. This suggests that much the same kind of complete, orderly takeover as Pons had witnessed in his monkeys was indeed occurring in phantom-limb patients too. In this

PHANTOM IN THE BRAIN

In an uninjured person (left), nerve signals from all over the body are sent to the thalamus, a relay station in the middle of
the brain. This structure has sections made up of neurons assigned to each body area—arm and chin, for instance.
From here the signals are passed on to neurons in the somatosensory cortex, which contains the brain's own map
of the body. One theory about phantom limb is that signals get mixed up in the thalamus (right).
When a limb is amputated, the "arm" neurons in the thalamus don't get their usual signals. Those neurons are available
for other input, and they get it if their neighbors, the "chin" neurons, sprout connections to them. So a touch on
the chin sends signals into the thalamus, where they are now thrown to two areas on the brain's body map: the chin and the arm.

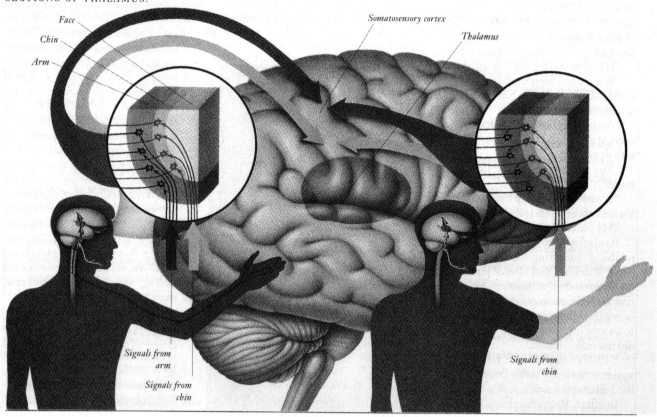

SECTIONS OF THALAMUS:

Face
Chin
Arm
Somatosensory cortex
Thalamus
Signals from arm
Signals from chin
Signals from chin

case, however, the invasion was a flank attack from *both* adjacent regions, rather than from the face alone.

Ramachandran performed similar experiments on half a dozen other patients. All possessed at least one remapped edition of the lost piece of themselves, the transference achieved with uncanny orderliness and vivid clarity. Another patient, who had had both his right arm and part of his shoulder removed, was amazed to feel Ramachandran's Q-tip tracing out his complete missing forequarter across his face—the shoulder tucked into the jaw joint, the elbow etched across the elbow-like bend of the lower jaw, the hand and fingers reaching toward his chin. Another version of the amputated region was mapped onto his torso, which was so sensitive that nudging a single body hair at one point keenly tickled his phantom

elbow. Working with another patient, a man who had lost all feeling in his left arm when its nerves were yanked from his spinal cord in an auto accident, Ramachandran accidentally dribbled a little warm water from his Q-tip. It ran down the patient's face and under his collar.

"Hey, that was really weird," said the patient. "It felt like you were literally pouring water down my arm."

Perhaps the most astonishing observation was the shortness of time it had apparently taken for the remapping to be completed—in Victor Quinterro's case, only four weeks. To Ramachandran, such a rapid remapping of inputs makes Pons's "sprouting" hypothesis unlikely, because there simply isn't enough time for even a modest amount of new nerve tissue to grow. Instead, he believes, hidden circuits must already exist in the neural wiring that

allow for the expansion of one cortical area into an adjacent one. As long as the normal, stronger inputs are being received from the touch receptors, these circuits lie dormant. But when the receptors suddenly shut down—for example, when a limb is amputated or paralyzed—the latent circuits are unmasked and the whole limb cortex begins to sing its neighbor's tune.

"It is as if there is a competition going on between different circuits," says Ramachandran, "with the strongest one laying claim to the whole contested territory."

If he is right, the unmasking hypothesis might hold some therapeutic wisdom. Normally, stroke victims who have lost the use of a hand are encouraged to exercise their arms as much as possible to encourage feeling in the adjoining hand to return. But if unmasking is the secret to cortical remapping, then logically the arm should

A TOUCH OF PAIN

Smashing your thumb with a hammer elicits quite a different sensation than does, say, brushing your fingertips across satin sheets. One action signals pain; the other is a touch of pleasure. Somehow the body knows which is which.

More than 2,000 years ago Aristotle proposed that pain and touch were opposite ends of the same spectrum—just the right amount of stimulation was a pleasurable touch, too, too much was a hurt. Today we know that recognizing pain is not that simple. The intense nerve signals emitted from damaged tissue are not the only elements that come into play when we experience pain. Tissue damage activates an entire network of specialized fibers, and the signals course through the body—and the brain—differently from the way other sensory messages do.

The distinctions begin at the farthest reaches of our nervous system. The force of a hammer blow, as well as extreme temperatures and chemicals released by injured cells, activates two types of nerve fibers, called C and A deltas. A third type of fiber, called A beta, carries nonpain signals. All three fibers converge in the spinal cord, where neurons relay the incoming information to the brain.

At the gateway to the brain, the signals enter the area known as the thalamus. From its position atop the brain stem, the thalamus fields sensations from all over the body, including the eyes, ears, and tongue, and directs them to various regions of the cortex, the convoluted outer

part of the brain where learning takes place and memories are stored. The thalamus also picks out pain signals for special treatment.

"We found a definite difference in the manner in which the thalamus processes non-noxious information, such as touch and vibration, and noxious stimulation," says Diane Daly Ralston, a neuroanatomist at the University of California at San Francisco. The difference involves GABA, a brain chemical that inhibits or mutes nerve signals. By staining different types of neurons entering the thalamus of macaque monkeys, Ralston and her husband, Henry Ralston, found that a neuron relaying touch signals meets up with two other, different types of neurons—an exiting neuron, which carries the signal into the cortex, and an interneuron, which produces GABA. As a touch signal passes through the junction between the three neurons, the interneuron is turned on, and it immediately releases GABA into the gap, muting the signal.

Neurons transmitting messages of pain, however, have a less mediated exchange. Few GABA-producing interneurons hook up with pain-carrying neurons, so the signal travels to the cortex at full strength. The Ralstons speculate that the difference between the strong and GABA-weakened messages is what distinguishes pain from anything else inside the cortex.

After slipping through the thalamus unmuted, pain signals head for the cortex.

One destination is the narrow strip across the surface of the cortex that houses the brain's map of the body. The signals home in on the spot on the map that coincides with the injured body part.

Another destination is the cingulate gyrus, a region in the limbic system, which is the brain's emotional headquarters. Recently neurobiologists Gary Duncan and Catherine Bushnell of the University of Montreal used PET (positron emission tomography) scans—which measure levels of cellular activity—together with magnetic resonance images of human brains to pinpoint areas activated by pain. They found that along with the thalamus and the body map in the cortex, the front portion of the cingulate gyrus is very active during painful stimulation.

The finding underscores the complexity of pain perception and how it's affected by memories and emotions. Soldiers in the heat of battle can be oblivious to severe wounds, while cancer patients may dread even the faintest twinges. "Pain is a perception colored by experience and particularly by emotions," says pain researcher Allan Basbaum of the University of California at San Francisco. "In some respects pain is like beauty—it's a stimulus plus emotion. Different observers of a particular painting receive identical visual input. But each person's perception can be completely different."

—Charlene Crabb

be immobilized instead, its input muted as much as possible to allow the hand's weakened circuits a chance to reestablish their former hegemony over their parcel of cortex.

Pons insists, however, that there is no evidence for latent circuits capable of invading whole cortical regions, waiting to be unmasked. "It's like saying that when your electricity blacks out, your backup generator will kick in," he says. "Only in this case, there isn't any backup generator."

Like Pons, Ramachandran admits that at this point his favored explanation for how remapping occurs is little more than speculation. But he is confident nonetheless. "We know now that the source of phantom

limb is in the brain itself," he says. "Far from being deadweight in the brain, the cortex associated with the lost limb is alive and well, passing messages further on up the system. The messages may not be originating in the limb anymore, but the rest of the brain doesn't know that."

IS "THE REST OF THE BRAIN," then, just an innocent dupe, taken in by a switch play of inputs in the cortex? What is happening in phantom limb "further on up the system"? The precise region where Tim Pons witnessed massive remapping in his monkeys—called the primary somatosensory cortex, or S1 for short—is in fact only the initial receiving

station in a chain of a dozen or so increasingly complex skin maps in the cortex. Each presents an opportunity for shaping and refining the sensations arriving from farther down—and another opportunity for inputs to be remapped. This touch pathway runs parallel to another series of cortical maps—which respond to receptors in the muscles and joints—governing proprioception, the sense that allows you to know the position of your limbs and other body parts. Both the touch system and the body-position system communicate with cortical regions controlling muscle movements, and they jointly feed another area of the brain, in the parietal lobe, that is responsible for body image and recognition. A brain lesion in this region can lead to a condition called unilateral neglect—a sort of bizarre mirror image of phantom limb. Rather than feeling sensations from a nonexistent appendage, the sufferer denies that a perfectly functional part of his body belongs to him; he may stubbornly shave only one side of his face, or thrust away the "stranger's" leg that is inexplicably attached to his own body.

Ramachandran suspects that regions along this proprioceptive pathway must also remap for the phantom limb phenomenon to occur. But would this explain why Fred Aryee feels a shock of pain as a cup is wrenched out of a hand that exists only in his mind? According to the neuroscientist, Aryee's discomfort might be explained by the involvement of motor command centers in the brain, which are sending a signal to the missing limb, telling it to grab the cup. In the absence of proprioceptive feedback from the hand itself, the motor command virtually swamps the pathway, barking its imperative—GRAB THE CUP!—much more forcefully than normal. The same phenomenon might explain why the young woman missing both arms since birth is hyper-aware of the animated gestures her arms make during an argument. Or maybe it doesn't.

"The surprising thing about her is that after 22 years of never receiving feedback from her arms, she still feels the phantom," says Ramachandran. "We can't explain everything yet."

Ronald Melzack, a neuropsychologist at McGill University in Montreal, believes that such an encompassing explanation will only come from the understanding of an extensive "neuromatrix" of circuits, extending beyond the sensory pathways and into the brain's limbic system, which is critical to emotion and motivation. "Remapping sits just fine with me," he says. "But you can't just focus on the primary somatosensory cortex alone, as if that's the place where all the bells are ringing. It's only part of the picture."

Nevertheless, from a research point of

"AFTER 22 YEARS OF NEVER RECEIVING FEEDBACK FROM HER ARMS, SHE STILL FEELS THE PHANTOM."

view, it is the part of burning interest. Talk about vast networks of interacting neurons is notoriously cheap; a glimpse of a piece of such a network physically reorganizing itself is a priceless novelty. The major question, of course, is why.

"I doubt that it does anybody any good to have their missing arm mapped out across their face, or to suffer from extreme phantom pain," says Kaas. "But these things demonstrate that the adult brain has far greater flexibility than we thought. They are a result of brain plasticity that works against the person."

In normal circumstances, Kaas believes, the ability of the brain to restructure itself may be what allows people to recover from head injuries that snap axons in the brain and sever critical connections. After a period of confusion, normal functioning returns—presumably because other, adjacent areas of the brain are able to take over the chores of the dead nerves. Neuronal loss is in fact a natural process that continues through adult life, whether you are clobbered on the head or not. Up to a certain age, perhaps our brains cope with their own steady deterioration by recommitting still-lively regions of the cortex to the tasks formerly handled by the defunct circuits. Much would depend on keeping the alternative circuits strong by *using* them. This may explain why people who remain mentally engaged as they grow older seem to hold on to their acuity longer.

"There's been folklore that says 'Use it or lose it,'" says Kaas. "This work gives a theoretical justification for that belief."

The boldest hope of all is that the understanding of brain plasticity will eventually solve the mystery of learning and memory. When a tennis player practices a

new backhand or a pianist masters a sonata, *something* must physically change in their brains to allow them to perform effortlessly a task that was initially difficult. Remapping in and among higher levels of the brain may be that something. Recently, Merzenich and his colleagues trained monkeys to recognize different vibrations using their middle fingers. As the monkeys became more adept at discriminating different frequencies of vibration, neuronal connections within the cortical maps of their middle fingers grew stronger, and the map itself expanded into adjacent areas. Neurobiologist Alvaro Pasqual-Leone of the National Institutes of Health has shown that training blind people to read braille similarly swells the cortical maps devoted to their newly literate fingers.

"The idea that training actually modifies the microstructure of the brain has terrific implications for the future," says brain researcher Vernon Mountcastle of Johns Hopkins. "If structure can be modified at low-level ranges like these, why not at higher levels too? You might eventually be able to train for specific skills in better ways."

Much remains to be understood, however, before we can send our children to neurology labs to have their math aptitude puffed. The first step would be a resolution to the nagging mystery of the mechanism of remapping—is it the sprouting of new axons, as Pons suspects, or the unmasking of latent circuits, as Ramachandran believes? The two investigators may soon be collaborating on new experiments, testing amputees with a powerful new brain scanning technique called functional magnetic resonance imaging. With no harm to the patient, the technique produces "snapshots" of the brain clear enough to determine where in the touch pathways inputs from missing limbs first go astray. Knowing that could tip the balance toward one explanation or the other. At the outset, however, each scientist concedes that his own favorite hypothesis seems barely more possible than its rival.

"That's the real excitement of all this," says Pons. "We are forced to consider the impossible."

Does ESP Exist?

Daryl J. Bem

Daryl J. Bem is professor of psychology at Cornell University. He became involved in the world of psi research in 1983, when he was asked to critically examine the experimental procedures for the autoganzfeld studies from the perspective of an experimental psychologist and mentalist (a magician who specializes in the simulation of psi).

Recent laboratory research suggests that parapsychologists might finally have cornered their elusive quarry: reproducible evidence for psychic functioning.

Reports of psychic phenomena are as old as human history. Experimental tests of psychic phenomena are almost as old. According to Herodotus, the ancient Greek historian, King Croesus of Lydia dispatched several of his men to test seven oracles to see if any of them could divine what he, the king, was doing on the day of the test. Only Pythia, priestess of Apollo at Delphi, was able to divine correctly that the king was making a lamb and tortoise stew in a bronze kettle.

Convinced of her powers, Croesus then posed the question that really interested him: If he attacked the rival kingdom of Persia, would he be able to defeat its army? Pythia replied, "When Croesus has the Halys crossed, a mighty empire will be lost." Insufficiently alert to the ambiguity of this prediction, Croesus crossed the river, attacked, and lost his mighty empire. Evaluating "psychic" data is a risky business.

The contemporary technical term for psychic phenomena is psi. More precisely, psi denotes anomalous processes of information or energy transfer, processes that are currently unexplained in terms of known physical or biological mechanisms. These processes include *extrasensory perception* (ESP), the acquisition of information without using the known senses, and *psychokinesis*, the ability to affect physical objects or events without the intervention of any known physical force.

In turn, ESP comprises the following:

● *Telepathy.* The transfer of information from one person to another without the mediation of any known channel of sensory communication.

● *Clairvoyance.* The acquisition of information about places, objects, or events without the mediation of any of the known senses (for example, Pythia's knowledge that the king was making stew).

● *Precognition.* The acquisition of information about a future event that could not be anticipated through any known inferential process. (Pythia's prediction about the loss of an empire, although dubious, is an example.)

Serious scholarly investigation of psi began in 1892, when a group of scholars in London founded the Society for Psychical Research (SPR) to

investigate that large body of debatable phenomena designated by such terms as mesmeric, psychical and spiritualistic . . . without prejudice or prepossession of any kind, and in the same spirit of exact and unimpassioned inquiry which has enabled Science to solve so many problems, once not less obscure nor less hotly debated.

The SPR was active until the early years of the twentieth century, when many of the original founders had died and enthusiasm declined.

Contemporary psi research is usually considered to have begun in 1927, when Joseph Banks Rhine and his wife/collaborator, Louisa, arrived in the psychology department at Duke University in Durham, North Carolina. Rhine's experiments, which tested for ESP with decks of cards containing geometric symbols, became well known to the general public in 1937 when he published *New Frontiers of the Mind*. The book received widespread press coverage and became a Book of the Month Club selection. Even today, many Americans know of Rhine's work.

Since Rhine, many parapsychologists have reported positive psi results using a wide variety of experimental procedures. Yet most academic psychologists are not yet persuaded that the existence of psi has been established.

Searching for a repeatable experiment

In science generally, a phenomenon is not considered established until it has been observed repeatedly by several researchers. This criterion has been the source of the most serious criticism of parapsychology: that it has failed to yield a single reliable demonstration of psi that can be replicated by other investigators. In 1974, an experimental procedure was introduced that holds out the promise of supplying that repeatable demonstration: the ganzfeld procedure.

By the late 1960s, several parapsychologists had become dissatisfied with the repetitive forced-choice procedures pioneered by Rhine, believing that they failed to capture the kinds of psi experiences that people report in everyday life. Both historically and cross-culturally, psi has usually been associated with dreaming, meditation, trances of various kinds, and other altered states of consciousness. This suggested that psi information may

function like a weak signal normally masked by the sensory "noise" of everyday life. Thus, altered states of consciousness may enhance a person's ability to detect psi information simply because they reduce interfering sensory input. Psi researchers first sought to test this hypothesis by adapting the ganzfeld procedure, a mild sensory isolation technique introduced into experimental psychology during the 1930s.

In a ganzfeld telepathy experiment, one subject (the receiver) rests in a reclining chair in a soundproof chamber. Translucent Ping-Pong ball halves are taped over the eyes,

> *By the late 1960s, several parapsychologists had become dissatisfied with the repetitive forced-choice procedures pioneered by Rhine.*

and headphones are placed over the ears. A red floodlight is directed toward the receiver's eyes, and white noise is played through the headphones. (White noise is a random mixture of sound frequencies similar to the hiss made by a radio tuned between stations.) This homogeneous visual and auditory environment is called the Ganzfeld, a German word meaning "total field." To quiet "noise" produced by internal bodily tension, the receiver is also led through a set of relaxation exercises at the beginning of the ganzfeld period.

While the receiver is in the ganzfeld, a second subject (the sender) sits in a separate soundproof room and concentrates on the "target," a randomly selected picture or videotaped sequence. For about 30 minutes, the receiver thinks aloud, providing a continuous report of all the thoughts, feelings, and images that pass through his or her mind. At the end of the ganzfeld period, the

receiver is presented with several stimuli (usually four) and, without knowing which one was the target, is asked to rate the degree to which each matches the thoughts and images experienced during the ganzfeld period. If the receiver assigns the highest rating to the target, it is scored as a "hit." Thus, if the experiment uses judging sets containing four stimuli (the target and three control stimuli), the hit rate expected by chance is one out of four, or 25 percent.

In 1985 and 1986, the *Journal of Parapsychology* devoted two entire issues to a critical examination of the ganzfeld studies, featuring a debate between Ray Hyman, a cognitive psychologist and a knowledgeable, skeptical critic of parapsychological research, and the late Charles Honorton, a prominent parapsychologist and major ganzfeld researcher. At that time, there had been 42 reported ganzfeld studies conducted by investigators in 10 laboratories.

Across these studies, receivers achieved an average hit rate of about 35 percent. (This might seem like a small margin of success over the 25 percent hit rate expected by chance, but a person with this margin of advantage in a gambling casino would get rich very quickly.) Statistically, this result is highly significant: The odds against getting a 35 percent hit rate across that many studies by chance are greater than a billion to one.

Correcting the flaws

If the most frequent criticism of parapsychology is that it has not produced a repeatable psi effect, the second most frequent criticism is that many, if not most, psi experiments have inadequate controls and safeguards. A frequent charge is that positive results emerge primarily from initial, poorly controlled studies and then vanish as better controls and safeguards are introduced.

The potentially most fatal flaws in a psi study are those that would allow a receiver to obtain the target information in normal sensory fashion, either inadvertently or through deliberate cheating. This is called the problem of sensory leakage. Critic Hyman and parapsychologist Honorton agreed that the studies with

the experimental procedures, including the random selection and presentation of the targets and the recording of the receiver's ratings. These studies were published by Honorton in the *Journal of Parapsychology* in 1990, and the complete history of ganzfeld research was resummarized by Bem (the author of this article) and Honorton in the January 1994 issue of the *Psychological Bulletin* of the American Psychological Association.

The autoganzfeld studies confirmed the results of the earlier, less sophisticated studies, obtaining virtually the same hit rate: about 35 percent. These studies also reconfirmed several

themselves, satisfy the further requirement that ganzfeld experiments be conducted by a broader range of investigators. In that sense, then, the jury is still out; the verdict awaits the outcome of future experiments. This state of affairs is not likely to change soon.

The history of science demonstrates that resolving disagreements over the existence of a disputed phenomenon has never been a matter of simply gathering more evidence until it reaches some objective, a priori threshold of quality and quantity. The amount of evidence required to persuade any given scientist that a phenomenon exists depends on his or her belief as to how likely it is that the phenomenon exists in the first place.

Most scientists require more and better evidence for an anomalous phenomenon—one unexplained by known physical and biological mechanisms— than for other phenomena. This is usually expressed by the dictum that "extraordinary claims require extraordinary evidence." But in any given instance, there is no agreement on or objective measure of what constitutes "extraordinary."

> *Resolving disagreements over the existence of a disputed phenomenon has never been a matter of simply gathering more evidence.*

good safeguards against sensory leakage obtained results that were just as strong as studies that had less good safeguards.

But because Hyman and Honorton disagreed on other aspects of the studies, they issued a joint communiqué in 1986, in which they agreed that the final verdict awaited the outcome of future experiments conducted by a broader range of investigators and according to more stringent standards. They then spelled out in detail the more stringent methodological and statistical standards they believed should govern all future ganzfeld experiments.

In 1983, Honorton and colleagues had initiated a new set of 11 ganzfeld studies that complied with all the guidelines he and Hyman later published in their joint communiqué. They are called autoganzfeld studies because a computer controlled

findings from other research. For example, it has often been reported that creative or artistically gifted persons show high psi ability. The autoganzfeld studies tested this by recruiting twenty students from the Juilliard School in New York City to serve as receivers. Overall, these students achieved a hit rate of 50 percent, one of the highest rates ever reported for a single sample in a ganzfeld study. The autoganzfeld studies also found that significantly higher hit rates were obtained when the targets were videotaped film sequences rather than still pictures.

Belief and skepticism

Even if skeptical critics can agree that the autoganzfeld studies satisfy the strict methodological and statistical criteria set forth in Hyman and Honorton's joint communiqué, the studies cannot, by

Moreover, scientists' diverse reactions to evidence in disputed areas of research are strongly determined by their attitudes toward many other issues, not all of them strictly scientific. For example, scientists differ in the kinds of intellectual risks they are willing to take. For many scientists, it is far more sinful to conclude that an effect exists when it does not than to conclude that an effect does not exist when it does. The choice of which kind of error is more tolerable is not a matter of good science versus bad science but a matter of taste.

As Croesus learned the hard way, evaluating "psychic" data is inherently a risky business.

Learning and Remembering

Do you remember your first week of classes at college? There were so many new buildings and new people's names to remember. And you had to recall accurately where all your classes were as well as your professors' names. Just remembering your class schedule was problematic enough. For those of you who lived in dormitories, the difficulties multiplied. You had to remember where your residence was, recall the names of individuals living on your floor, and learn how to navigate from your dormitory to other places on campus, such as the dining halls and library. Then came examination time. Did you ever think you would survive college exams? The material in terms of difficulty level and amount was perhaps more than you thought you could handle. What a stressful time you experienced when you first came to campus! Much of what created the stress was the strain on your learning and memory systems, two complicated processes unto themselves. Indeed, most of you survived just fine and with your memories, learning strategies, and mental health intact.

Learning and memory are two of the oldest processes studied by psychologists. Today, with their sophisticated experimental techniques, psychologists have detected several types of memory processes, and they have discovered what makes learning more complete so that subsequent memory is more accurate. Psychologists also discovered that humans are not the only organisms capable of these processes; all types of animals can learn, even if the organism is as simple as an earthworm or an amoeba.

Psychologists know, too, that rote learning and practice are not the only forms of learning. For instance, at this point in time in your introductory psychology class, you might be studying operant and classical conditioning, two very simple but nonetheless important forms of learning by both human and simple organisms. Both types of conditioning can occur without our awareness or active participation in them. The articles in this unit examine the processes of learning and remembering (or its reciprocal, forgetting).

This unit begins with a look at two simple forms of learning, operant and classical conditioning. In "Measured Learning," we commence with B. F. Skinner and Ivan Pavlov and their work on conditioning. Because of the magnitude of Skinner's contributions to American psychology, though, the emphasis is on his work and the Skinner box.

We next examine more complicated forms of learning such as the learning that you accomplish when you study in school. What kind of instructional environment is most beneficial for learning? The "back-to-basics" approach to instruction emphasizes repetition, drill, and sustained attention in a highly structured classroom setting. Another approach, "open education," emphasizes self-pacing and exploration in an unstructured setting. In "How Kids Learn," Barbara Kantrowitz and Pat Wingert review evidence suggesting that children learn best when the learning environment is based on the concept of "developmentally appropriate practice." This approach, firmly grounded in the knowledge gained from scientific studies of child development, stresses matching educational programs to the child's developmental level. Implementing "developmentally appropriate practice" in American schools, however, will require extensive retraining of teachers and actively involving more parents in the education of children.

There are perhaps times when we would rather not remember something or simply cannot learn or remember something despite concerted efforts. One such occasion might occur when an individual is abused as a child and then is motivated to forget the experience only to have it rise into consciousness later in adulthood. Whether this actually happens or whether adulthood memories of abuse are fictional is the point of "Memories Lost and Found."

Looking Ahead: Challenge Questions

What are the differences between operant and classical conditioning? What is a Skinner box, and what has it taught us about principles of learning? What are the contributions of B. F. Skinner to psychology? What are the basic tenets of Skinnerian psychology? How can Skinnerian principles be practiced or put into effect in everyday life?

What was your schooling in early childhood like? Do you think that the processes and environment experienced by you could have been improved? How so? What are the differences between back-to-basics education and open education? How will schools, teachers, and parents have to change if we adopt open education?

What forms does child abuse take? Do most abused children remember being abused? Do most adults remember abuse from their childhoods? Why is there such a furor between psychology and law about remembered abuse?

Measured Learning

The fourth [in a series] of briefs on scientific experiments looks at the "Skinner box". Through simple gadgetry, the box measures animal behavior; it led psychologists to review their ideas about learning.

IN THE 1930s Frederic Skinner invented the Skinner box: or so his colleagues would have said. Skinner did not relish the eponymy. He preferred to call the box an operant conditioning apparatus. Whatever it was called, though, the box appeared at a time when psychologists were eager to put their work on a more "scientific" footing. It provided them with a tool easily turned to the measured and repeatable study of all sorts of learnt behaviour.

Until the early part of the 20th century, psychologists spent most of their time analysing people's feelings—often their own, introspectively. But Skinner's attempt to make their investigations more objective was not without antecedents.

In a series of lectures published in 1913 John Watson, an American psychologist, advanced the view that introspection does not lend itself to rigorous scientific appraisal, because an introspective account of feeling cannot be measured in any way that will allow comparison. More discipline and objectivity would be needed before psychology could join the ranks of the natural sciences.

Moreover, Watson did not want psychology to content itself with understanding the mind. Its goal, he said, ought to be the "control and prediction of behaviour". Only through prediction could psychology show itself to be a science in the same sense that physics was. And control of behaviour offered the possibility of improving behaviour.

Watson's ideas, with their emphasis on behaviour rather than consciousness, came as a shock to a discipline then as close to philosophy as to physiology. Few were prepared to accept that human beings should be observed like dumb animals, their capacity for self-awareness left unused for the sake of scientific purity. Over time, though, Watson's views gained in popularity; the behaviourist movement he had spawned came into its own in the 1930s, and was still strong three decades later.

Skinner helped to ensure the behaviourist success by providing a method for achieving Watson's goals. From the 1920s, the behaviourists searched for precise laboratory measurements of behaviour. Skinner, a postgraduate at Harvard University, turned his skill with gadgets to the challenge of developing a scientific procedure which would enable behaviour to be measured in a continuous, consistent way. The result was the Skinner box. It was not the first system that could do such measurement; but the box's sheer simplicity, and the enormous number of ways conditions within it could be changed, made it by far the most popular.

The simplest form of the box is a bare, sound-proofed chamber with a dish on one side, below a protruding lever. To this, you add a hungry rat. Left alone, the rat explores its surroundings; eventually, it will inspect the lever and in so doing press on it. When the lever is pressed, food is delivered to the dish. The rat eats the food, and eventually presses the bar again; more food. The food "reinforces" the pressing.

Meanwhile, outside the box, a pen records each lever press on a rotating roll of paper. Skinner was particularly proud of this. From it, a curve showing the rate of pressing is easily constructed. In the simplest case, the rate increases exponentially as the rat in the box learns the effect of pressing the lever.

Simple lever-pressing is not the only trick the boxes can be used to impart. Different behaviours can be reinforced: a rat in a box can be trained to raise its head or to press its nose against a disc, rather than to press a lever. Nor are rats the only subjects. Pigeons, which live longer than rats and have colour vision (rats do not), were also used a lot—they were given discs to peck at rather than levers to press. Using this method, Skinner was able to teach pigeons some surprisingly "advanced" behaviour. His most notorious success was in teaching a pair of pigeons to play ping-pong with each other.

Skinner was not primarily interested in the behaviour the animals developed, though; he wanted to study the ways in which behaviours were acquired and maintained. The crucial variable in Skinner's experiments was the schedule of rewards—the reinforcement. If, for example, food is available only every 15 seconds, regardless of how often the lever is pressed—a "fixed interval" reinforcement—an appropriate pattern of pressing is learnt (see box).

One of Skinner's most discussed findings, also illustrated in the box, was that if rats are rewarded only sporadically, they will continue to press a lever for a long time after the experimenter has stopped rewarding them altogether. If they are used to a regular pattern of rewards, they learn to anticipate, and they stop

From *The Economist*, December 5, 1992, pp. 90-91. © 1992 by The Economist, Ltd. Distributed by the New York Times Special Features.

responding much more quickly when they no longer get results.

Against Pavlov

Skinner's first major work was "The Behaviour of Organisms: an Experimental Analysis" (1938). To communicate the novelty of his approach, he coined the phrase "free operant conditioning" to describe the type of behaviour the box measured. "Free", because the animal is uninterrupted and free to press the lever whenever it likes. "Operant" because the animal is having to do things to get its reward—pressing the lever.

In making these points, Skinner was trying to distinguish his research from that of his famous Russian predecessor, Ivan Pavlov. In the early 1900s Pavlov did experiments on learnt-reflex responses. Skinner was keen to show that free operant behaviour was not based on reflexes, and was thus more representative of the learning processes that people employ in everyday life. The distinction had to be made clearly, because Skinner was using a number of technical terms derived from and reminiscent of the ones Pavlov used.

The difference in approach is demonstrated by the famous experiment on Pavlov's dog. Pavlov's dog—or, indeed, any dog—will salivate when presented with food. This is known as an unconditional stimulus; it is not learnt, it just comes with being a dog. People have similar unconscious reflexes; they will salivate when a drop of lemon juice is put on their tongues. Pavlov's discovery was that, if a bell is rung just before the dog is presented with food, the dog will eventually salivate at the sound of the bell, even when no food is present. The bell, the conditional stimulus, is automatically associated with food. Learnt associations like these are the stuff of classical conditioning.

Pavlov's experiments differ from those of Skinner in several ways:

• Pavlov's dog has no impact on its environment. The food will always be given, whether the dog salivates or not.
• Pavlov's dog cannot help salivating. The rat does not have to press the lever.
• Pavlov's dog has a specific and unalterable response: drooling. The rats can be trained to do all

sorts of things, and to respond to all sorts of stimuli (thirsty rats are as trainable as hungry ones).

The point that Skinner was most eager to stress was the difference in the nature of the link between stimulus and response. In classical conditioning, the link was a direct causal one: the bell caused the salivation. In free operant conditioning, Skinner saw a subtler process that he likened to Darwinian natural selection. There is no real reason why a rat presses the lever a first time; but once it does, the reinforcement leads to that behaviour being selected in preference to others. That, at least, was Skinner's view.

Another difference was that, although Skinner was keen to

haviour that Skinner wanted to understand, though it was not what he studied in the box. He thought that human behaviour was moulded by the environment just as the rat's lever-pressing was. If manipulating the environment changes rats' behaviour, it can change people's behaviour, too.

Black boxes

The Skinner box is still much used today, by drug researchers among others. They train animals to behave differently under the effects of different known drugs—to do one thing when given a stimulant, another when given a tranquilliser, for example. Then when an animal is

of psychology at the University of Cardiff and an admirer of Skinner's work, has used a Skinnerian system to measure "self-control" in pigeons. A pigeon is presented with two discs, each of which can be illuminated with different-coloured lights. Both discs, when pecked, can prompt the release of grain into a hopper. The pigeon is made to take tough choices: if one disc is pecked, the bird gets a little food quickly; when the other is pecked it has to wait longer—but gets double the amount of food.

Skinner's ideas have also been widely adopted in everyday life. His finding that rewards for "correct" behaviour gave much better results than punishments for "incorrect" behaviour had great influence on the methods used to encourage inmates in prisons and psychiatric institutions to behave well. Child psychologists have praised the use of reward rather than punishment.

For all his influence, though, the obituaries which appeared for Skinner in August 1990 were surprisingly critical. It is now the feeling in psychological circles that the behavioural model set up in the Skinner box is too simplified to provide the ground for sweeping inferences about human behaviour. The learning processes involved in Skinner's box are now seen by most as automatic, "unconscious", and only a trivial part of human learning; for all his protests, Skinner is seen as studying something little more profound than Pavlov's classical conditioning.

The fundamental criticism of Skinner was that he ignored internal mental processes in his interpretation of behaviour. That, of course, was the point. Skinner and the behaviourists were deliberately trying to get away from unverifiable talk of mental states. The rat in the box was, in psychological jargon, a "black box" itself. Its interior workings did not matter: all that mattered was the way in which its output—behaviour—varied when its input—the environment around it—was changed.

By the 1970s other approaches were reopening that black box. Physiologists were beginning to make some rudimentary sense of how the brain worked, and what went on where. Computers were providing new models for the work of "cognitive scientists" trying to see how the work of the

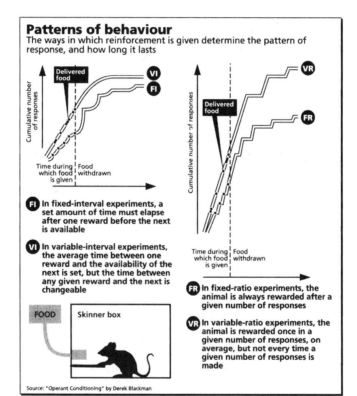

Patterns of behaviour

The ways in which reinforcement is given determine the pattern of response, and how long it lasts

(Graph axis labels) Cumulative number of responses — Delivered food — VI — FI — Time during which food is given | Food withdrawn

(Right graph) Cumulative number of responses — Delivered food — VR — FR — Time during which food is given | Food withdrawn

FI In fixed-interval experiments, a set amount of time must elapse after one reward before the next is available

VI In variable-interval experiments, the average time between one reward and the availability of the next is set, but the time between any given reward and the next is changeable

FR In fixed-ratio experiments, the animal is always rewarded after a given number of responses

VR In variable-ratio experiments, the animal is rewarded once in a given number of responses, on average, but not every time a given number of responses is made

FOOD | Skinner box

Source: "Operant Conditioning" by Derek Blackman

avoid dealing with mental states, he knew that he had to allow room for them in the theory. The effect of environment on behaviour is normally not as straightforward as it is in classical conditioning. By insisting that, during free operant conditioning, the animal was working in an "if/then" mode, Skinner made it more reasonable that free operant conditioning be considered a model for the learning that people do.

It was, after all, human be-

given a drug of unknown effect, its behaviour enables the scientists to determine the class of pharmaceutical to which the new compound might belong.

Over the years, though, the box has been refined. Rats are no longer made to press levers: in their natural environments it is something they never do. Pigeons are preferred because they are more "biologically prepared" to peck discs. And the experiments have become far more complex.

Derek Blackman, a professor

mind was organised. The analysis of mental process was no longer shunned, and a technique designed to avoid it thus lost its *raison d'être*.

The modern practitioners of cognitive psychology have no room for Skinner or his box. They tend to dismiss him as a fanatic—a task made easier by his fictionalised account of a Utopian society, "Walden II" (1948). Published the same year "1984" was written, this description of a society "engineered" to perfection through a system of rewards became an international best-seller. It did little in the long run for the scientific claims of behaviourism.

That view of Skinner, though, was not entirely fair. In a 1980 meeting of the American Psychological Association in Montreal, Skinner was acknowledged as one of the world's most misunderstood scientists. Skinner never denied the existence of private thought; he merely said it is unknowable, and thus not a proper subject for experimental scientific study. The focus of experiments should therefore lie in analysing the results of private thought: behaviour.

Skinner certainly never saw cause to recant. Asked what he would have done differently, he could think of "just one thing . . . I've been laughed at by enemies and kidded by my friends. If I could do it all over again, I'd never teach those pigeons to play ping-pong."

Further reading

OPERANT CONDITIONING.
Derek Blackman.
Methuen.
A textbook description of the uses of the Skinner box and the conclusions that can be drawn from them.

ABOUT BEHAVIOURISM.
B. F. Skinner.
Jonathan Cape.
A explanation of his work and its applications to people and animals.

WALDEN TWO.
B. F. Skinner.
Macmillan.
The second edition (1976) includes a foreward by Skinner justifying his behaviourist Utopia against its critics.

How Kids Learn

BARBARA KANTROWITZ & PAT WINGERT

Ages 5 through 8 are wonder years. That's when children begin learning to study, to reason, to cooperate. We can put them in desks and drill them all day. Or we can keep them moving, touching, exploring. The experts favor a hands-on approach, but changing the way schools teach isn't easy. The stakes are high and parents can help.

With Howard Manly in Atlanta and bureau reports

It's time for number games in Janet Gill's kindergarten class at the Greenbrook School in South Brunswick, N.J. With hardly any prodding from their teacher, 23 five- and six-year-olds pull out geometric puzzles, playing cards and counting equipment from the shelves lining the room. At one round table, a group of youngsters fits together brightly colored wooden shapes. One little girl forms a hexagon out of triangles. The others, obviously impressed, gather round to count up how many parts are needed to make the whole.

After about half an hour, the children get ready for story time. They pack up their counting equipment and settle in a circle around Gill. She holds up a giant book about a zany character called Mrs. Wishy-washy who insists on giving farm animals a bath. The children recite the whimsical lines along with Gill, obviously enjoying one of their favorite tales. (The hallway is lined with drawings depicting the children's own interpretation of the book; they've taken a few literary liberties, like substituting unicorns and dinosaurs for cows and pigs.) After the first reading, Gill asks for volunteers to act out the various parts in the book. Lots of hands shoot up. Gill picks out four children and

they play their parts enthusiastically. There isn't a bored face in the room.

This isn't reading, writing and arithmetic the way most people remember it. Like a growing number of public- and private-school educators, the principals and teachers in South Brunswick believe that children between the ages of 5 and 8 have to be taught differently from older children. They recognize that young children learn best through active, hands-on teaching methods like games and dramatic play. They know that children in this age group develop at varying rates and schools have to allow for these differences. They also believe that youngsters' social growth is as essential as their academic achievement. Says Joan Warren, a teacher consultant in South Brunswick: "Our programs are designed to fit the child instead of making the child fit the school."

Educators call this kind of teaching "developmentally appropriate practice"—a curriculum based on what scientists know about how young children learn. These ideas have been slowly emerging through research conducted over the last century, particularly in the past 30 years. Some of the tenets have appeared

The Lives and Times of Children

Each youngster proceeds at his own pace, but the learning curve of a child is fairly predictable. Their drive to learn is awesome, and careful adults can nourish it. The biggest mistake is pushing a child too hard, too soon.

● Infants and Toddlers

They're born to learn. The first important lesson is trust, and they learn that from their relationships with their parents or other caring adults. Later, babies will begin to explore the world around them and experiment with independence. As they mature, infants slowly develop gross motor (sitting, crawling, walking) and fine motor (picking up tiny objects) skills. Generally, they remain egocentric and are unable to share or wait their turn. New skills are perfected through repetition, such as the babbling that leads to speaking.

■ 18 months to 3 years

Usually toilet training becomes the prime learning activity. Children tend to concentrate on language development and large-muscle control through activities like climbing on jungle gyms. Attention spans lengthen enough to listen to uncomplicated stories and carry on conversations. Vocabulary expands to about 200 words. They enjoy playing with one other child, or a small group, for short periods, and learn that others have feelings too. They continue to look to parents for encouragement and protection, while beginning to accept limits on their behavior.

▲ 3-year-olds

Generally, they're interested in doing things for themselves and trying to keep up with older children. Their ability to quietly listen to stories and music remains limited. They begin telling stories and jokes. Physical growth slows, but large-muscle development continues as children run, jump and ride tricycles. They begin to deal with cause and effect; it's time to plant seeds and watch them grow.

● 4-year-olds

They develop better small motor skills, such as cutting with scissors, painting, working with puzzles and building things. They can master colors, sizes and shapes. They should be read to and should be encouraged to watch others write; let them scribble on paper but try to keep them away from walls.

■ 5-year-olds

They begin to understand counting as a one-to-one correlation. Improved memories make it easier for them to recognize meaningful words, and with sharper fine motor skills, some children will be able to write their own names.

▲ Both 4s and 5s

Both groups learn best by interacting with people and concrete objects and by trying to solve real problems. They can learn from stories and books, but only in ways that relate to their own experience. Socially, these children are increasingly interested in activities outside their immediate family. They can play in groups for longer periods, learning lessons in cooperation and negotiation. Physically, large-muscle development continues, and skills such as balancing emerge.

● 6-year-olds

Interest in their peers continues to increase, and they become acutely aware of comparisons between themselves and others. It's a taste of adolescence: does the group accept them? Speech is usually well developed, and children are able to joke and tease. They have a strong sense of true and false and are eager for clear rules and definitions. However, they have a difficult time differentiating between minor and major infractions. Generally, children this age are more mature mentally than physically and unable to sit still for long periods. They learn better by firsthand experiences. Learning by doing also encourages children's "disposition" to use the knowledge and skills they're acquiring.

■ 7- to 8-year-olds

During this period, children begin developing the ability to think about and solve problems in their heads, but some will continue to rely on fingers and toes to help them find the right answer. Not until they're 11 are most kids capable of thinking purely symbolically; they still use real objects to give the symbols— such as numbers—meaning. At this stage they listen better and engage in give and take. Generally, physical growth continues to slow, while athletic abilities improve—children are able to hit a softball, skip rope or balance on a beam. Sitting for long periods is still more tiring than running and jumping.

under other names—progressivism in the 1920s, open education in the 1970s. But they've never been the norm. Now, educators say that may be about to change. "The entire early-childhood profession has amassed itself in unison behind these principles," says Yale education professor Sharon Lynn Kagan. In the last few years, many of the major education organizations in the country—including the National Association for the Education of Young Children and the National Association of State Boards of Education—have endorsed remarkably similar plans for revamping kindergarten through third grade.

Bolstered by opinions from the experts, individual states are beginning to take action. Both California and New York have appointed task forces to recommend changes for the earliest grades. And scores of individual school districts like South Brunswick, figuring that young minds are a terrible thing to waste, are pushing ahead on their own.

The evidence gathered from research in child development is so compelling that even groups like the Council for Basic Education, for years a major supporter of the traditional format, have revised their thinking. "The idea of putting small children in front of workbooks and asking them to sit at their desks all day is a nightmare vision," says Patte Barth, associate editor of Basic Education, the council's newsletter.

At this point, there's no way of knowing how soon change will come or how widespread it will be. However, there's a growing recognition of the importance of the early grades. For the past few years, most of the public's attention has focused on older children, especially teenagers. "That's a Band-Aid kind of approach," says Anne Dillman, a member of the New Jersey State Board of Education. "When the product doesn't come out right, you try and fix it at the end. But we really have to start at the beginning." Demographics have contributed to the sense of urgency. The baby boomlet has replaced the baby-bust generation of the 1970s. More kids in elementary school means more parents asking if there's a better way to teach. And researchers say there is a better way. "We've made remarkable breakthroughs in understanding the development of children, the development of learning and the climate that enhances that," says Ernest Boyer of The Carnegie Foundation for the Advancement of Teaching. But, he adds, too often, "what we know in theory and what we're doing in the classroom are very different."

The early grades pose special challenges because that's when children's attitudes toward school and learning are shaped, says Tufts University psychologist David Elkind. As youngsters move from home or preschool into the larger, more competitive world of elementary school, they begin to make judgments about their own abilities. If they feel inadequate, they may give up. Intellectually, they're also in transition, moving from the intensely physical exploration habits of infancy and toddlerhood to more abstract reasoning. Children are born wanting to learn. A baby can spend hours studying his hands; a toddler is fascinated by watching sand pour through a sieve. What looks like play to an adult is actually the work of childhood, developing an understanding of the world. Studies show that the most effective way to teach young kids is to capitalize on their natural inclination to learn through play.

But in the 1980s, many schools have tried to do just the opposite, pressure instead of challenge. The "back to basics" movement meant that teaching methods intended for high school students were imposed on first graders. The lesson of the day was more: more homework, more tests, more discipline. Children should be behind their desks, not roaming around the room. Teachers should be at the head of the classrooms, drilling knowledge into their charges. Much of this was a reaction against the trend toward open education in the '70s. Based on the British system, it allowed children to develop at their own pace within a highly structured classroom. But too many teachers and principals who tried open education thought that it meant simply tearing down classroom walls and letting children do whatever they wanted. The results were often disastrous. "Because it was done wrong, there was a backlash against it," says Sue Bredekamp of the National Association for the Education of Young Children.

At the same time, parents, too, were demanding more from their elementary schools. By the mid-1980s, the majority of 3- and 4-year-olds were attending some form of pre-school. And their parents expected these classroom veterans to be reading by the second semester of kindergarten. But the truth is that many 5-year-olds aren't ready for reading—or most of the other academic tasks that come easily to older children—no matter how many years of school they've completed. "We're confusing the numbers of years children have been in school with brain development," says Martha Denckla, a professor of neurology and pediatrics at Johns Hopkins University. "Just because a child goes to day care at age 3 doesn't mean the human brain mutates into an older brain. A 5-year-old's brain is still a 5-year-old's brain."

As part of the return to basics, parents and districts demanded hard evidence that their children were learning. And some communities took extreme measures. In 1985 Georgia became the first state to require 6-year-olds to pass a standardized test before entering first grade. More than two dozen other states proposed similar legislation. In the beginning Georgia's move was hailed as a "pioneering" effort to get kids off to a good start. Instead, concedes state school superintendent Werner Rogers, "We got off on the wrong foot." Five-year-olds who used to spend their days finger-painting or singing were hunched over ditto sheets, preparing for the big exam. "We would have to spend a month just teaching kids how to take the test," says Beth Hunnings, a kindergarten teacher in suburban Atlanta. This year Georgia altered the tests in favor of a more flexible evaluation; other states have changed their minds as well.

The intense, early pressure has taken an early toll. Kindergartners are struggling with homework. First graders are taking spelling tests before they even understand how to read. Second graders feel like failures. "During this critical period," says David Elkind in his book "Miseducation," "the child's bud-

In Japan, First Grade Isn't a Boot Camp

Japanese students have the highest math and science test scores in the world. More than 90 percent graduate from high school. Illiteracy is virtually nonexistent in Japan. Most Americans attribute this success to a rigid system that sets youngsters on a lock-step march from cradle to college. In fact, the early years of Japanese schooling are anything but a boot camp; the atmosphere is warm and nurturing. From kindergarten through third grade, the goal is not only academic but also social—teaching kids to be part of a group so they can be good citizens as well as good students. "Getting along with others is not just a means for keeping the peace in the classroom but something which is a valued end in itself," says American researcher Merry White, author of "The Japanese Educational Challenge."

Lessons in living and working together grow naturally out of the Japanese culture. Starting in kindergarten, youngsters learn to work in teams, with brighter students often helping slower ones. All children are told they can succeed if they persist and work hard. Japanese teachers are expected to be extremely patient with young children. They go over lessons step by step and repeat instructions as often as necessary. "The key is not to scold [children] for small mistakes," says Yukio Ueda, princi-pal of Mita Elementary School in Tokyo. Instead, he says, teachers concentrate on praising and encouraging their young charges.

As a result, the classrooms are relaxed and cheerful, even when they're filled with rows of desks. On one recent afternoon a class of second graders at Ueda's school was working on an art project. Their assignment was to build a roof with poles made of rolled-up newspapers. The children worked in small groups, occasionally asking their teacher for help. The room was filled with the sound of eager youngsters chatting about how to get the job done. In another second-grade class, the subject was math. Maniko Inoue, the teacher, suggested a number game to practice multiplication. After a few minutes of playing it, one boy stood up and proposed changing the rules just a bit to make it more fun. Inoue listened carefully and then asked if the other students agreed. They cheered, "Yes, yes," and the game continued according to the new rules.

Academics are far from neglected in the early grades. The Education Ministry sets curriculum standards and goals for each school year. For example, third graders by the end of the year are supposed to be able to read and write 508 characters (out of some 2,000 considered essential to basic literacy). Teachers have time for play and lessons: Japanese children attend school for 240 days, compared with about 180 in the United States.

Mothers' role: Not all the teaching goes on in the classroom. Parents, especially mothers, play a key role in education. Although most kindergartens do not teach writing or numbers in any systematic way, more than 80 percent of Japanese children learn to read or write to some extent before they enter school. "It is as if mothers had their own built-in curriculum," says Shigefumi Nagano, a director of the National Institute for Educational Research. "The first game they teach is to count numbers up to 10."

For all their success in the early grades, the Japanese are worried they're not doing well enough. After a recent national curriculum review, officials were alarmed by what Education Minister Takeo Nishioka described as excessive "bullying and misconduct" among children—the result, according to some Japanese, of too much emphasis on material values. So three years from now, first and second graders will no longer be studying social studies and science. Instead, children will spend more time learning how to be good citizens. That's "back to basics"—Japanese style.

BARBARA KANTROWITZ *with*
HIDEKO TAKAYAMA *in Tokyo*

ding sense of competence is frequently under attack, not only from inappropriate instructional practices . . . but also from the hundred and one feelings of hurt, frustration and rejection that mark a child's entrance into the world of schooling, competition and peer-group involvement." Adults under similar stress can rationalize setbacks or put them in perspective based on previous experiences; young children have none of these defenses. Schools that demand too much too soon are setting kids off on the road to failure.

It doesn't have to be this way. Most experts on child development and early-childhood education believe that young children learn much more readily if the teaching methods meet their special needs:

Differences in thinking: The most important ingredient of the nontraditional approach is hands-on learning. Research begun by Swiss psychologist Jean Piaget indicates that somewhere between the ages of 6 and 9, children begin to think abstractly instead of concretely. Younger children learn much more by touching and seeing and smelling and tasting than by just listening. In other words, 6-year-olds can easily understand addition and subtraction if they have actual objects to count instead of a series of numbers written on a blackboard. Lectures don't help. Kids learn to reason and communicate by engaging in conversation. Yet most teachers still talk at, not with, their pupils.

Physical activity: When they get to be 10 or 11, children can sit still for sustained periods. But until they are physically ready for long periods of inactivity, they need to be active in the classroom. "A young child has to make a conscious effort to sit still," says Denckla. "A large chunk of children can't do it for very long. It's a very energy-consuming activity for them." Small children actually get more tired if they have to sit still and listen to a teacher talk than if they're allowed to move around in the classroom. The frontal lobe, the part of the brain that applies the brakes to children's natural energy and curiosity, is still immature in 6- to 9-year-olds, Denckla says. As the lobe develops, so does what Denckla describes as "boredom tolerance." Simply put, learning by doing is much less boring to young children.

Language development: In this age group, experts say language development should not be broken down into isolated skills—reading, writing and speaking. Children first learn to reason and to express themselves by talking. They can dictate stories to a teacher before they actually read or write. Later, their first attempts at composition do not need to be letter perfect; the important thing is that they learn to communicate ideas. But in many classrooms, grammar and spelling have become more important than content. While mastering the technical aspects of writing is essential as a child gets older, educators warn against emphasizing form over content in the early grades. Books should also be interesting to kids—not just words strung together solely for the purpose of pedag-

ogy. Psychologist Katherine Nelson of the City University of New York says that her extensive laboratory and observational work indicates that kids can learn language—speaking, writing or reading—only if it is presented in a way that makes sense to them. But many teachers still use texts that are so boring they'd put anybody to sleep.

Socialization: A youngster's social development has a profound effect on his academic progress. Kids who have trouble getting along with their classmates can end up behind academically as well and have a higher incidence of dropping out. In the early grades especially, experts say youngsters should be encouraged to work in groups rather than individually so that teachers can spot children who may be having problems making friends. "When children work on a project," says University of Illinois education professor Lillian Katz, "they learn to work together, to disagree, to speculate,

The early years of a child's education are indeed wonder years. They begin learning to socialize, to study, and to reason. More and more education experts are favoring a hands-on approach to introducing young children to the mysteries of their surroundings.

to take turns and de-escalate tensions. These skills can't be learned through lecture. We all know people who have wonderful technical skills but don't have any social skills. Relationships should be the first 'R'."

Feelings of competence and self-esteem: At this age, children are also learning to judge themselves in relation to others. For most children, school marks the first time that their goals are not set by an internal clock but by the outside world. Just as the 1-year-old struggles to walk, 6-year-olds are struggling to meet adult expectations. Young kids don't know how to distinguish between effort and ability, says Tynette Hills, coordinator of early-childhood education for the state of New Jersey. If they try hard to do something and fail, they may conclude that they will never be able to accomplish a particular task. The effects of obvious methods of comparison, such as posting grades, can be serious. Says Hills: "A child who has had his confidence really damaged needs a rescue operation."

Rates of growth: Between the ages of 5 and 9, there's a wide range of development for children of normal intelligence. "What's appropriate for one child may not be appropriate for another," says Dr. Perry Dyke, a member of the California State Board of Education. "We've got to have the teachers and the staff reach children at whatever level they may be at . . . That takes very sophisticated teaching." A child's pace is almost impossible to predict beforehand. Some kids learn to read on their own by kindergarten; others are still struggling to decode words two or three years later. But by the beginning of the fourth grade, children with very different histories often read on the same level. Sometimes, there's a sudden "spurt" of learning, much like a growth spurt, and a child who has been behind all year will catch up in just a few weeks. Ernest Boyer and others think that multigrade classrooms, where two or three grades are mixed, are a good solution to this problem—and a way to avoid the "tracking" that can hurt a child's self-esteem. In an ungraded classroom, for example, an older child who is having problems in a particular area can practice by tutoring younger kids.

Putting these principles into practice has never been easy. Forty years ago Milwaukee abolished report cards and started sending home ungraded evaluations for kindergarten through third grade. "If anything was developmentally appropriate, those ungraded classes were," says Millie Hoffman, a curriculum specialist with the Milwaukee schools. When the back-to-basics movement geared up nationally in the early 1980s, the city bowed to pressure. Parents started demanding letter grades on report cards. A traditional, direct-teaching approach was introduced into the school system after some students began getting low scores on standardized tests. The school board ordered basal readers with controlled vocabularies and contrived stories. Milwaukee kindergarten teachers were so up-

A Primer for Parents

When visiting a school, trust your eyes. What you see is what your child is going to get.

● Teachers should talk to small groups of children or individual youngsters; they shouldn't just lecture.

■ Children should be working on projects, active experiments and play; they shouldn't be at their desks all day filling in workbooks.

▲ Children should be dictating and writing their own stories or reading real books.

● The classroom layout should have reading and art areas and space for children to work in groups.

■ Children should create freehand artwork, not just color or paste together adult drawings.

▲ Most importantly, watch the children's faces. Are they intellectually engaged, eager and happy? If they look bored or scared, they probably are.

set by these changes that they convinced the board that their students didn't need most of the standardized tests and the workbooks that go along with the readers.

Some schools have been able to keep the progressive format. Olive School in Arlington Heights, Ill., has had a nontraditional curriculum for 22 years. "We've been able to do it because parents are involved, the teachers really care and the children do well," says principal Mary Stitt. "We feel confident that we know what's best for kids." Teachers say they spend a lot of time educating parents about the teaching methods. "Parents always think school should be the way it was for them," says first-grade teacher Cathy Sauer. "As if everything else can change and progress but education is supposed to stay the same. I find that parents want their children to like school, to get along with other children and to be good thinkers. When they see that happening, they become convinced."

Parental involvement is especially important when schools switch from a traditional to a new format. Four years ago, Anne Norford, principal of the Brownsville Elementary School in Albemarle County, Va., began to convert her school. Parents volunteer regularly and that helps. But the transition has not been completely smooth. Several teachers refused to switch over to the more active format. Most of them have since left the school, Norford says. There's no question that some teachers have trouble implementing the developmentally appropriate approach. "Our teachers are not all trained for it," says Yale's Kagan. "It takes a lot of savvy and skill." A successful child-centered classroom seems to function effortlessly as youngsters move from activity to activity. But there's a lot of planning behind it—and that's the responsibility of the individual teacher. "One of the biggest problems," says Norford, "is trying to come up with a program that every teacher can do—not just the cadre of single people who are willing to work 90 hours a week." Teachers also have to participate actively in classroom activities and give up the automatic mantle of authority that comes from standing at the blackboard.

Teachers do better when they're involved in the planning and decision making. When the South Brunswick, N.J., schools decided in the early 1980s to change to a new format, the district spent several years studying a variety of curricula. Teachers participated in that research. A laboratory school was set up in the summer so that teachers could test materials. "We had the support of the teachers because teachers were part of the process," says teacher consultant Joan Warren.

One residue of the back-to-basics movement is the demand for accountability. Children who are taught in nontraditional classrooms can score slightly lower on commonly used standardized tests. That's because most current tests are geared to the old ways. Children are usually quizzed on specific skills, such as vocabulary or addition, not on the concepts behind those skills. "The standardized tests usually call for one-word answers," says Carolyn Topping, principal of Mesa Elementary School in Boulder, Colo. "There may be three words in a row, two of which are misspelled and the child is asked to circle the correctly spelled word. But the tests never ask, 'Does the child know how to write a paragraph?'"

Even if the tests were revised to reflect different kinds of knowledge, there are serious questions about the reliability of tests on young children. The results can vary widely, depending on many factors—a child's mood, his ability to manipulate a pencil (a difficult skill for many kids), his reaction to the person administering the test. "I'm appalled at all the testing we're doing of small children," says Vanderbilt University professor Chester Finn, a former assistant secretary of education under the Reagan administration. He favors regular informal reviews and teacher evaluations to make sure a student understands an idea before moving on to the next level of difficulty.

Tests are the simplest method of judging the effectiveness of a classroom—if not always the most accurate. But there are other ways to tell if children are learning. If youngsters are excited by what they are doing, they're probably laughing and talking to one another and to their teacher. That communication is part of the learning process. "People think that school has to be either free play or all worksheets," says Illinois professor Katz. "The truth is that neither is enough. There has to be a balance between spontaneous play and teacher-directed work." And, she adds, "you have to have the other component. Your class has to have intellectual life."

Katz, author of "Engaging Children's Minds," describes two different elementary-school classes she visited recently. In one, children spent the entire morning making identical pictures of traffic lights. There was no attempt to relate the pictures to anything else the class was doing. In the other class, youngsters were investigating a school bus. They wrote to the district and asked if they could have a bus parked in their lot for a few days. They studied it, figured out what all the parts were for and talked about traffic rules. Then, in the classroom, they built their own bus out of cardboard. They had fun, but they also practiced writing, problem solving, even a little arithmetic. Says Katz: "When the class had their parents' night, the teacher was ready with reports on how each child was doing. But all the parents wanted to see was the bus because their children had been coming home and talking about it for weeks." That's the kind of education kids deserve. Anything less should get an "F."

MEMORIES LOST AND FOUND

One man's account of his painful past raises complex questions about child abuse, human psychology, ethics and American law

For Ross Cheit, it began with a phone call in the spring of 1992. "I have happy news," his sister promised, speaking from her California home. "Your nephew is joining a boys' chorus. Aren't you pleased he wants to follow in the footsteps of his Uncle Ross?"

Though he could not yet name the reason, Cheit felt sickened by the news—and gradually began sinking into a bewildering depression. He didn't link it to the phone call; indeed, he blamed anything and everything else for what his wife Kathy Odean now calls "the months Ross lost his mind." It must be professional pressures that had thrown his life into such turmoil, thought the 38-year-old Brown University ethics professor. Or perhaps it was his marriage, which had been happy for 10 years but now seemed dried up, built of sand. He told his wife he thought their marriage was failing. He entered therapy. Then on August 23 while on vacation, he had something like a dream.

He woke with the baffling sense that a man he had not seen or thought of in 25 years was powerfully present in the room. William Farmer had been the administrator of the San Francisco Boys Chorus summer camp, which Cheit had attended in the late '60s between the ages of 10 and 13. Cheit could picture him clearly—the big stomach and bent shoulders, the round head, wispy hair. Over the course of the day, he recalled still more. How Farmer would enter his cabin night after night, just as the boys were

The narrative in this story is based on Ross Cheit's account of his recovered-memory experience, as described in interviews and legal documents. Cheit and Miriam Horn, the author, have been acquainted since junior high school.

going to sleep. How he would sit on Cheit's bed, stroking the boy's chest and stomach while he urged him in a whisper to relax, relax. "I was frozen," says Cheit. "My stomach clenched against his touch. And then he would slowly bring his hand into my pants."

For Cheit, the memory was embarrassing and disgusting. There was no spectacular epiphany.

Fifteen months later, Cheit is engaged in a lawsuit that may have far-reaching implications for one of the most divisive questions ever to emerge in human psychology: whether it is possible for an adult to recover a lost memory of childhood sexual abuse. The charge two weeks ago by 34-year-old Steven Cook that 17 years earlier he had been sodomized by Roman Catholic Cardinal Joseph Bernardin—an event Cook claims he remembered in therapy—heightens an already bitter controversy whose stakes are inordinately high. In 1990, George Franklin became the first person in history convicted on the basis of a recovered memory—his daughter Eileen's recollection of witnessing, 20 years earlier, his rape and murder of her 8-year-old friend. Nineteen states have recently revised their statutes of limitations, making it possible for adults to bring civil suits against sexual abusers, even if decades have passed; several hundred such cases are now in the courts. Juries have made awards as high as $5 million to adult victims of childhood incest. No institution has been more affected than the Catholic church, which since 1982

has paid close to $500 million in legal fees and compensation to men and women molested as children by priests.

Equally dramatic countersuits are being filed. Adult children now recanting their "memories" of sexual abuse and parents who say they have been wrongly accused are suing therapists for inducing false memories through methods they charge are akin to brainwashing. In a trial set to begin in March, a California man is suing a medical center and two therapists who, he claims, helped his bulimic adult daughter manufacture memories of his sexually abusing her as a child; on the basis of the charges against him, his wife has divorced him and sought custody of their two minor daughters. Two years ago in Ohio, an appeals court upheld a malpractice award to a woman whose psychiatrist injected her with "truth serum" more than 140 times to help her uncover buried memories of alleged childhood sexual abuse by her mother. The backlash has even spawned its own organization. Since 1992, when the False Memory Syndrome Foundation was founded in Philadelphia to assist those claiming to be wrongly charged with abuse, the organization has received more than 6,500 calls.

While the debate grows increasingly virulent, most psychologists and psychiatrists are convinced that memories of external trauma can be placed out of reach of consciousness and later retrieved—though many now avoid the Freudian term "repression" (see box) in favor of a more purely descriptive vocabulary. Judith Herman, a clinical professor of psychiatry at Harvard Medical School and author of *Trauma and Recovery,* refers simply to "amnesia and delayed recall," which, she says, are beyond dispute." Others refer to dissociation, which describes the mind's protective detachment from a

From *U.S. News & World Report,* November 29, 1993, pp. 52-56, 60, 62-63. © 1993 by U.S. News & World Report. Reprinted by permission.

traumatic experience as it is happening, effectively fragmenting consciousness. Researchers who study dissociative disorders maintain that memories of traumatic events formed while a person is in the altered state of mind induced by terror are frequently inaccessible to ordinary consciousness.

Although unconscious, experts say, dissociated memories remain indelible and can be triggered decades later by a related sensation or event. Eileen Franklin's memory returned, she told the court, when an innocuous gesture by her 5-year-old daughter brought back a similar gesture by Eileen's childhood friend as she tried to ward off George Franklin's murderous blows. Frank Fitzpatrick, a 38-year-old insurance adjuster in Rhode Island, was lying in bed, trapped in an anguish he could not explain, when he remembered being molested as a child. "I began to remember the sound of heavy breathing," he said, "and realized I had been sexually abused by someone I loved." When Fitzpatrick went public with his suit against Father James Porter, several of the nearly 100 Porter victims who came forward said they remembered only when they heard about the case on the news.

The physiology of such memory loss and recovery is only beginning to be understood. Memories are stored, scientists believe, as electrical patterns in neurons deep in the brain's hippocampal region. Over time, these patterns are translated into new neural circuitry in different brain areas, creating a permanent record of the events. Intensely traumatic events, says Yale University psychiatry Prof. Michael Davis, "produce unusually strong nerve connections that serve as long-lasting memories." Years later the right stimulus can set those nerve circuits firing and trigger the fear, with no immediate understanding of its source.

"My God, that's me."
For Cheit, there was no spectacular epiphany. The memory of Farmer was embarrassing and disgusting but hardly momentous. It was not until October, when at his therapist's suggestion Cheit went to a bookstore to buy Mic Hunter's *Abused Boys,* that he felt the full impact of what he had remembered. "As soon as I pulled the book off the shelf, I began to shake all over. I thought I was going to collapse. I looked at the title and thought, 'My God, that's me.' "

Compelled now to know more, Cheit began to dredge his past. From his parents, he recovered the letters he had written from camp, and reading them brought the most painful revelation yet. "He broke down and cried with his whole body, as if he would never stop," says his wife. "He came into the bedroom where I was half asleep, saying over and over, 'But he was such a great guy.' He was so hurt that someone he loved did this to him." It was only then, says Cheit, that he fully understood the damage that had been done. "These were not just perverse sexual acts," he says, "but the most profound betrayal possible for a kid."

While many scientists accept the idea that a memory can be lost for years and then accurately recovered, a growing number do not. "Sixty years of experiments have failed to produce any empirical evidence that repression exists," says University of California at Berkeley sociologist Richard Ofshe. "People forget things, of course, or intentionally avoid painful subjects. They may even have selective traumatic amnesia, if the terror of an experience is so great that the normal biological process underlying information storage is disrupted—as in an alcohol-induced blackout. But no one has ever shown that the memory of repeated abuses can be uncontrollably and completely stripped from a person's consciousness." In fact, says psychiatry Prof. Paul McHugh of Johns Hopkins University, "most severe traumas are not blocked out by children but remembered all too well." In one study of children ages 5 to 10 who saw a parent's murder, not one repressed the memory.

COURTESY OF ROSS CHEIT

Ross Cheit (in front with glasses), shown here with other campers in 1968, spent four summers at the choral camp in the Sierras.

Psychologists also dispute the possibility of any kind of reliable retrieval. "What's being claimed," says Elizabeth Loftus, a memory researcher at the University of Washington, "is that traumatic memory is driven into a corner of the unconscious where it sits like Rip van Winkle and doesn't age and wakes up 20 years later. But memory is not a computer or videotape recording. We don't just pop in a tape or call it up in perfect condition. Memory is not objective fact but subjective, suggestible and malleable." In experimental situations, Loftus has firmly implanted in adults false memories of unhappy childhood incidents simply by having the event recounted by an authoritative older sibling.

The possibility of retrieving pristine memories is made all the more unlikely, say skeptics, by the use of such methods of "memory retrieval" as age regression, hypnosis and injections of sodium amytal ("truth serum"), all of which are known to promote confabulation of extraordinarily vivid memories and to cement in the patient's mind the certainty of their truth. The American Medical Association has twice warned against the use of such techniques.

The current "tabloid and talk show" culture of abuse, experts believe, is an equally effective creator of false memories. The bestselling self-help book *The Courage to Heal* advises that "even if you are unable to remember any specific instances but still have a feeling that something happened to you, it probably did." E. Sue Blume's *Secret Survivors* offers an all-embracing list of symptoms of unremembered abuse, ranging from eating disorders and intestinal problems to substance abuse and suicidal tendencies. Group therapy and survivor support groups add to the pressures. New members may feel the need to match the drama of the other members' stories and may even internalize them as their own. Troubled patients, debunkers believe, may embrace a "discovery" of past abuse because it offers a single, unambiguous explanation for complex problems and a special identity as "survivors."

Therapists may be eager to dig up evidence of abuse, says University of Minnesota law Prof. Christopher Barden, "to turn a $2,000 eating-disorder patient into a $200,000 multiple-personality disorder." Or they may be politically motivated; since most charges are brought by women against male relatives, some critics perceive a radical feminist agenda, another avenue for women to voice rage against sexual violence. Due process is sometimes thrown to the wind: For $10 and the name of an alleged perpetrator, one organization will inform neighbors, the police and local employers without the accuser having ever to be named.

When the charges become most extreme—involving alleged "satanic cults" engaged in baby breeding for human sacrifice and cannibalism—critics see a misguided form of fundamentalism at work. In the most notorious case, in 1988 in Olympia, Wash., allegations of sexual abuse against Paul Ingram by his two daughters—based on memories "recovered" at a Pentecostal retreat, assisted by the visions of a charismatic Christian who claimed to be filled with the Holy Spirit—quickly spun into accounts of witch covens and ceremonial weddings to Satan. Under pressure of zealous investigators, Ingram confessed to crimes more horrible than those charged; his wife, her eyes rolling, described a book spilling blood. "We now have hundreds of victims alleging that thousands of offenders are abusing and even murdering tens of thousands of people as part of organized satanic cults," says Kenneth Lanning of the FBI's Behavioral Science Unit, "and there is little or no corroborative evidence." The epidemic of allegations, contends Ofshe, who testified for the Ingram defense, is a "way of reasserting the authority of fundamentalist perspectives on society."

In the discussion of recovered memory, the distinction between satanic rituals and sexual abuse is often obscured. But if the prosecution of the former is indeed a "witch hunt," the latter is all too real. More than 200,000 cases of sexual abuse are documented annually, according to the National Committee to Prevent Child Abuse, and evidence suggests that the majority of cases go unreported.

Of all traumas, many researchers say, sexual abuse may be the most likely to result in memory disturbances, surrounded as it is by secrecy and treachery. To fix a childhood memory so that it lasts into adulthood requires shaping those events into a story, says Emory psychologist Ulric Neisser, and then rehearsing the narrative, telling the tale. Yet in cases of child sexual abuse, the events are rarely confronted, shared, ratified, even adequately described. Psychologist John Daignault, who teaches at Harvard Med-

The San Francisco Boys Chorus is one of the city's most revered cultural institutions. The "Singing Angels" have performed for U.S. presidents, the queen of England and the pope.

ical School and evaluated more than 40 of Father Porter's victims, says children "lack the perspective to place the trauma in the overall course of life's events." When the abuser is in a position of power or veneration, the child's ability to make sense of the event is more compromised still.

It is perhaps not surprising, then, that studies show that from 18 to 59 percent of sexual-abuse victims repress memories for a period of time. In one follow-up study of 200 children who had been treated for sexual abuse, Linda Williams of the Family Violence Research Laboratory at the University of New Hampshire found that 1 in 3 did not recall the experiences that had been documented in

---

Intent on finding Farmer, Cheit hired private investigator Frank Leontieff.

---

their hospital records 20 years before. A study by Judith Herman of women in group therapy found a majority reporting delayed recall of abuse; approximately 75 percent of those were able to obtain corroborating evidence. "False claims of childhood sexual abuse are demonstrably rare," says Herman (in the range of 2 to 8 percent of reported cases), "and false memories of childhood trauma are no doubt equally so. To fasten upon false memory as the main event is far-fetched and bizarre."

The debate over the credibility of some memories, researchers worry, is being used to discredit people making legitimate assertions. Some question the motives of the False Memory Syndrome Foundation, which gathers data on denials of abuse charges but concedes it has no way of knowing the truth or falsity of any report it receives. "Denial signifies little," says Herman. "Research with known pedophiles has illustrated that they often exhibit a cognitive distortion, minimizing or rationalizing their behavior." In fact, the FMSF recently asked one of its board members, Ralph Underwager, to resign after he gave an interview to a Dutch journal in which he seemed permissive and sympathetic toward pedophilia.

"The strongest compulsion in my life"
Intent on finding William Farmer, Cheit hired private investigator Frank Leontieff—a man he had known from his own previous career as a lawyer—and in January went to visit the 87-year-old founder of the chorus, Madi Bacon, in Berkeley. It was under Bacon's guidance in the '60s that the chorus became one of San Francisco's most revered arts institutions. Nicknamed "the Singing Angels," it regularly performed with the San Francisco Opera and sang for U.S. presidents, the pope and the queen of England. Much to his surprise, says Cheit, at the mention of Farmer's name, Bacon launched into how she'd once almost had to fire the man for what she called "hob-nobbing" with one of the boys. When Cheit told her he had been one of those boys, he says, Bacon said that if he'd been a strong kid he would have shaken it off. And why didn't he tell his friends,

she wanted to know. Didn't he want to protect them? (Asked about the conversation, Bacon told *U.S. News* she "may well have said those things, but I don't remember." Elsewhere, Bacon said that had she known of the abuse, she would have done something.)

Until that moment, Cheit had been embarked on a private search for private solace.

Until that moment, Cheit had been on a private search for private solace. Now, he had not only his first external evidence of the authenticity of his memory but a recognition that there might be more at stake. He was not, it seemed, the only one. Worse, it appeared chorus officials had known. It was at that moment, says Cheit, that the investigation became "the strongest compulsion in my life."

The history of responses by organizations confronted with accusations of child sexual abuse has not been particularly noble. A recent report by the Boy Scouts of America revealed that between 1971 and 1991, 1,800 scoutmasters suspected of molesting boys were removed from their positions—but "quietly," so that many simply went elsewhere and continued to abuse scouts. The Catholic Church, concerned to protect its reputation, has similarly relied on what child advocates call "the geographic cure." In the course of the Father Porter trial, church officials admitted that they had witnessed the priest's assaults or were told of them but permitted him to continue supervising altar boys and youth activities. When parents complained, documents uncovered in the lawsuits revealed, Porter was simply transferred from parish to parish. Porter's was not an isolated case. In *Lead Us Not into Temptation,* Jason Berry chronicles the decade-long nationwide effort by the Catholic Church to protect itself from its flock. Kids who made accusations were asked what the state of their soul was that they could cast such judgment and were forced to face the accused; defamation suits were often filed in the secular courts. At one point, Milwaukee Archbishop Rembert Weakland went so

---

FREUDIAN ORIGINS
Is it abuse or fantasy?

The battle over the nature of memory has its origins in Freud, who was the first to propose that painful or dangerous memories are "repressed"—buried beyond reach in the unconscious. The goal of psychoanalysis, as Freud conceived it, was to bring repressed material into consciousness where it could be disarmed.

Over the course of the 1890s, Freud's beliefs shifted, an evolution critical to the present battle. In 1893, he believed that many of his adult patients had been sexually abused as children by adults, and that it was the repressed memory of those "seductions" that caused their "hysteria." Four years later, he was insisting that most such memories were actually the child's repressed incestuous fantasies and desires. Freud critic Jeffrey Masson deems that shift a cowardly and destructive lie, an attempt to avoid professional ostracism. But others dismiss Masson as politically fashionable, contending that Freud feared his patients' stories were being suggested or distorted by his own analytic probings and deemed them fantasies in order to dodge that conclusion.

Freud's focus on childhood fantasies as opposed to real trauma has dominated psychotherapeutic thought for most of the century. Only in the '70s did the return of damaged Vietnam vets rekindle interest in post-traumatic stress reactions. Today, that interest has once again expanded to include the effects of childhood trauma.

---

far as to suggest that "not all adolescent victims are so innocent."

To conceal the criminal behavior of child molesters is exceedingly dangerous. Most experts consider pedophilia an incurable disease, and studies of known sex offenders have found that men who target male children will, over a career, assault on average more than 100 boys. Still, in conversations with *U.S. News,*

Madi Bacon expressed dismay that Cheit had broken the code of silence. "I don't see what good it's going to do for a young man with a family to be known publicly as having been abused. I mean it's such bad taste. And for Ross to involve other boys is serious. The boys would say that's snitching, wouldn't they?"

He managed to track down dozens of the 118 boys who had been at camp with him 25 years earlier.

"This is your one chance, Bill"
After his visit to Bacon, Cheit accelerated the investigation. Using chorus records from the time, he tracked down dozens of the 118 boys who had been at camp with him in the Sierra foothills 25 years earlier. The conversations usually began with warm reminiscences of greased watermelon races and idyllic afternoons floating in inner tubes in the warm sun. Soon, however, the recollections turned dark. For a professor at a Michigan university, Cheit's phone call brought back his own lost memory of a time Farmer invited him to his cabin, unzipped the child's pants and began to fondle him. He began to cry, he now recalls, and ran away. A librarian in the Midwest told Cheit on the phone that Farmer had invited the boy into his sleeping bag, but that he had refused; he wrote in a troubled letter the next day that he had been deceiving himself for years and now realized he had in fact climbed in. "I remember feeling something warm and hard pressed up against my lower abdomen. My T-shirt must have been pushed up and it was sticky. . . . Then I saw his penis. . . . I'm glad you called me, but I've been feeling sick about it all day." The camp nurse from the time, Lidia Ahumada, told the investigator and *U.S. News* of an event at the end of the summer of 1968, when she walked into the infirmary and caught Farmer in bed with a sick boy. Bacon recalled for *U.S. News* the nurse's angry report, adding: "I think Farmer's somewhat sick. To me it's an illness. But the man apologized, said to the chairman of the board that he would never do it again.

What do you do when camp's over? The chairman certainly wanted to play a thing like that down from a public standpoint because he didn't want to embarrass anybody." The investigator subsequently tracked down the child identified by the nurse. He has spent the past 15 years in San Francisco flophouses and has no memory of a man named Bill Farmer.

In letters and phone calls, former campers alleged what Cheit's first conversation with Bacon had implied, that at least two other men on the staff had been molesting boys and that on at least four occasions both children and adult staff

COURTESY OF ROSS CHEIT

Bill Farmer was the administrator of the chorus's summer camp, which Cheit attended from age 10 to 13. Farmer is circled in this staff photograph from the summer of 1968.

Cheit began to dial Farmer's number. After 34 attempts, he answered.

had told the chorus director of the abuses, with no result. One alleged report came in 1967, when a whole cabin full of boys ran to Bacon to tell her of molestations by a staff member who is now dead. A second allegedly came at the beginning of the summer of 1968, when a counselor, 21 years old at the time, twice witnessed Farmer's molestations of a boy and went with the child to report it to the director. Bacon doesn't recall the incident. Farmer remained.

Cheit's investigator, meanwhile, had tracked Farmer's movements over the years. Farmer had been a student minister from 1966–68 at the Point Richmond, Calif., Methodist Church, the investigator learned from church historian Mildred Dornan (who confirmed the account for *U.S. News*), but had abruptly left after parents overheard children discussing the "massages" he had given them. Farmer then secured a ministerial position in Georgetown, near Sacramento, Calif. He hadn't been there three weeks, the church's district supervisor from the time told the investigator (and confirmed for *U.S. News*), when a former El Dorado County Municipal Court judge complained that Farmer had molested his son. If Farmer would leave the ministry and seek help, said the judge, he would not press charges. Farmer signed a statement withdrawing from his position and surrendered his ministerial credentials, according to the supervisor. He then moved to Oregon, where he held teaching credentials for several years and for a time ran a ministry out of his home.

Having located Farmer, now 55, in the tiny town of Scio, Ore., Cheit began to dial his phone. After 34 attempts, Farmer answered. "What can I do for you?" Farmer asked his former charge, whom he had quickly recalled. "You can tell me whether you have any remorse," responded Cheit, his breath rapid and fierce. "Give me your number so I can call you back at another time." "This is your chance, Bill. This is your one chance." For nearly an hour, Cheit held Farmer on the phone, a tape recorder running all the while. Farmer admitted molesting Cheit in his cabin at night, confessed he had lost jobs and fled California because of "it," acknowledged that Bacon knew what happened at the end of the summer but allowed him to remain camp administrator because "no act had been consummated." Though Farmer conceded knowing that the acts he committed were criminal, he balked at Cheit's suggestion that he register as a sex offender. "It's 25 years, Ross," he said, his voice weary. "It's nine months, Bill, [since I remembered]. And I have to live with it for the rest of my life."

The chorus's attempt to disconnect from its past, says Cheit, is a luxury I don't have.

Six months earlier, says Cheit, he had been terrified of anyone finding out what had happened; now, he says, "I realized that is the problem." On July 2, Cheit's lawyers sent a letter to the chorus offering to settle without litigation if the organization would publicly acknowledge what had happened, investigate evidence that the problem had persisted over many years, install safeguards to ensure it would never happen again and provide $450,000 to Cheit "for injuries beyond compensation." On August 6, the chorus responded. "The SFBC sees no purpose at this point in even attempting to challenge the charges," stated the letter from Pillsbury, Madison & Sutro, the esteemed law firm handling pro bono the chorus's defense. It went on to raise doubts as to the chorus's liability, pointed out its meager financial resources and concluded "it is hard to imagine how bankrupting or ruining the reputation of an organization that has done so much to serve the Bay Area community would serve any good purpose."

The response infuriated Cheit. "The chorus's attempt to disconnect from their past is a luxury I don't have. To claim their reputation is to cash in on their past, but selectively; they don't want those parts of their history that might be shameful. And if this is how they handle a corroborated claim from an adult, how would they respond if a 10-year-old came to them right now? Would they value their reputation over their moral responsibility to children?" On August 19, Cheit and his parents filed suit, charging that the chorus "negligently or intentionally" permitted molestation of boys in its care. The chorus denied all the allegations.

The entanglement of psychology and the law is not an entirely easy marriage. The clinic and the courtroom have different criteria for establishing truth. Those who dispute the possibility of recovering memories insist the courts should not be admitting what Barden calls "pseudoscience" into testimony. Ofshe questions the wisdom of extending statutes of limitations designed to protect the accused, who after decades may find it impossible to gather the necessary evidence and witnesses to mount an effective defense. Of the 19 states that have extended their civil statutes on child sexual abuse, 16 have done so on the basis of the "delayed discovery doctrine." Just as a patient can sue who discovers 20 years later that a doctor had left a surgical instrument in his abdomen, so too, the theory goes, should a victim of child abuse be permitted to sue when he or she discovers the injury through recovering a memory. "If that's the premise, then how you characterize the forgetting is critical," says Ofshe. "If the plaintiff just avoided thinking about it, or later forgot how as a young adult he'd agonized over it, that's different than if the memory was put wholly out of reach by some imagined trick of the mind." Three states have simply extended statutes for civil prosecution of sexual abuse a set number of years beyond the victim's age of majority; nine states have no statutes of limitations on criminal prosecution of such crimes. "That's a straightforward social choice," says Ofshe, "not predicated on some mythic mental mechanism."

"Let a jury decide"

Addressing the three demands made in the suit—for open accounting, protective procedures and financial compensation—chorus lawyer Kim Zeldin told *U.S. News* that efforts are being made to investigate the allegations, though "it is difficult because so many years have passed." She has not been able to evaluate the validity of the Farmer tape, she says, because she has not been provided with a copy. But Farmer has called her firm to deny Cheit's charges, she added, and to deny ever telling Cheit otherwise. (Farmer's lawyer, Carleton Briggs, con-

firms that his client, who now lives in Corpus Christi, Texas, says he has never admitted to any of the charges. Farmer himself would not talk to *U.S. News.*) As for protecting the boys in the chorus's charge, Zeldin listed unwritten procedures she says have been in place for 10 years, including careful screening of staff, involvement of parents in many camp activities and policies to ensure boys are never alone with any staff member. In response to Cheit's letter, she says, the chorus also retained over the summer an outside consultant to instruct the boys on how to avoid unwanted contact. As for money demands, she questioned Cheit's motivations, saying "he's trying to reach into a deep pocket that doesn't exist." Cheit responds that the demand for money was made to ensure that his suit be taken seriously, but remains his last priority. "If they offered me a million dollars tomorrow, with the condition that they admit no liability and that I keep silent, the answer would be no. We are now in a suit requesting unspecified damages. I'm perfectly content to let a jury decide." In one last odd twist to the suit—signifying just how important the cultural climate now surrounding memory has become to the resolution of these cases—Pillsbury Madison & Sutro submitted to the court a two-part *New Yorker* story on Ingram's apparently false recovered memories of satanic abuse.

If there is one area of consensus among warring psychologists, it is that the sexual abuse of children does enduring damage. A summary of major studies published this year in the bulletin of the American Psychological Association concluded that, while no one set of symptoms characterized all victims, abuse tends to produce an inappropriate conditioning of sexual responsiveness, the shattering of a child's trust and an enduring sense of stigmatization and powerlessness. The report further hypothesized that for some, traumatization may occur later. Studies of adults who were sexually abused in childhood have consistently found them to be more prone to depression, substance abuse, sexual problems and thoughts of suicide.

"Forever, my childhood"

The boy who was allegedly molested by Farmer at the beginning of that summer of 1968—now a professor in New York—

Bill Farmer, now 55, was photographed earlier this year in Scio, Ore. He now lives in Corpus Christi, Texas.

lives with an injury of a different kind. When he and his counselor reported Farmer to Bacon, he says, she assured him that she would fire Farmer and tell the boy's parents the whole thing, but did neither. For 24 years, until Cheit's call, he was left believing that his parents knew about Farmer's actions but had left him to cope on his own. 'Even more than the molestation, it is the lie that changed my life."

The past remains a persistent presence for Cheit as well. In the past year, he has often wondered whether he could go on teaching ethics. "They're such moral relativists," he says of his students. "In the midst of this whole thing, one of my seniors asked, 'Aren't these moral taboos just cultural constructions? Isn't incest bad just because we think it is?' I wanted to shake her and say, "There is evil in the world. I just got off the phone with it.' "

The loss he suffered, Cheit says, can never be redeemed. "Forever, this is going to be my childhood." And he knows that more painful disclosures may yet come. "I think they thought all along I couldn't stomach the publicity. But if I have to divulge in a courtroom the most private consequences of this, I will. It's not me who should be ashamed of this, but them. And I can't be upset with people who did nothing then if I do nothing now, for the same reasons. I have so much support. If I don't do this, who ever will?"

MIRIAM HORN

Cognitive Processes

As Howard watches his four-month-old baby, he is convinced that the child possesses a degree of understanding of the world around her. In fact, Howard is sure he has one of the smartest babies in the neighborhood. Although he is indeed a proud father, he keeps these thoughts to himself so as not to alienate his neighbors whom he perceives to have less intelligent babies.

Jack lives in the same neighborhood as Howard. However, Jack does not have any children, but he does own two fox terriers. Despite Jack's most concerted efforts, the dogs never come to him when he calls them. In fact, the dogs have been known to run the opposite way on occasion. Instead of being furious, Jack accepts his dogs' disobedience because he is sure the dogs are just dumb beasts and do not know any better.

Both of these vignettes illustrate important and interesting ideas about cognition or thought processes. In the first vignette, Howard ascribes cognitive abilities and high intelligence to his child; in fact, Howard perhaps ascribes too much cognitive ability to his baby. On the other hand, Jack assumes that his dogs are incapable of thought, more specifically, that they are incapable of premeditated disobedience, and therefore he forgives the dogs.

Few adults would deny the existence of their cognitive abilities. Cognition is critical to our survival as adults. But are there differences in mentation in adults? And what about other organisms? Can children think like adults? And what about animals; can they think and solve problems? These and other questions are related to cognitive psychology and cognitive science that we showcase in this unit.

Cognitive psychology has grown faster than most other specialties in psychology in the past 20 years in response to new computer technology as well as to the growth of psycholinguistics. Computer technology has prompted an interest in artificial intelligence, the mimicking of human intelligence by machines. Similarly, the study of psycholinguistics has prompted the examination of the influence of language on thought and vice versa.

While interest in these two developments has eclipsed interest in more traditional areas of cognition, such as intelligence, we cannot ignore these traditional areas in this anthology. With regard to intelligence, one persistent problem has been the difficulty of defining intelligence. David Wechsler, author of several of the most popular intelligence tests in current clinical use, defines intelligence as the global capacity of the individual to act purposefully, to think rationally, and to deal effectively with the environment. Other psychologists have proposed more complex definitions. The definitional problem arises when we try to develop tests that validly and reliably measure such concepts. Edward Boring once suggested that we define intelligence as whatever it is that an intelligence test measures!

In the first unit article, "A Child's Theory of Mind," Bruce Bower reviews developmental aspects of cognition. The revered theory in psychology has been Jean Piaget's. Today, however, developmental and cognitive psychologists realize that much more goes on in a child's head than what Piaget attributed to children. Bower shares with the reader a newer approach to children's cognitive understanding of the world.

Two companion pieces appear next. In "Visualizing the Mind" by Marcus Raichle, modern brain imaging techniques are described. What we have discovered about the brain using these techniques, particularly about the role of language, is also showcased. Some philosophers and scientists have challenged the traditional view of the adult mind, too. Cognitive scientists have typically regarded the mind as a collection of relatively independent modules that contain rules for language, perception, and other cognitive processes. Some philosophers and scientists

have challenged this view of the adult mind. Their challenges are discussed in "Rethinking the Mind."

The next unit article is especially fascinating. It examines the case of Phineas Gage, a man whose brain was impaled by a steel rod as he worked on a railroad in the 1800s. Gage recovered physically from the accident but his cognitions were never the same. While Gage's intellect remained intact, his social behavior became deplorable. He seemed unable to tell right from wrong in a social context.

Sign language is the topic of the last unit article in which Peter Radetsky profiles neuroscientist Ursula Bellugi. Her discoveries about sign language and its use in other countries enable us to understand the human capacity for language.

Looking Ahead: Challenge Questions

What were Jean Piaget's views of cognitive development? Has research upheld his theory? What are some of the newer ideas about cognitive development? Which view do you subscribe to?

How is adult cognition different from children's? What are the more traditional views of the human mind, i.e., how is the mind described by cognitive scientists? Who challenges this view? Why? What techniques are available for studying the brain? Why study the brain in relationship to cognition? What role does the brain play in cognitive abilities, for example language processing? How does the brain produce a unified cognitive experience?

What area of Phineas Gage's brain was damaged? How did the injury alter his life? What abilities did he maintain after the accident? What does his accident tell us about the link between brain and behavior?

How does sign language work? Is it merely broken English? What does the study of sign language tell us about the human capacity for language?

A Child's Theory of Mind

Mental life may change radically around age 4

BRUCE BOWER

If you think kids say the darnedest things, get a load of what they think.

Consider a group of preschoolers shown a box that they all agree appears to contain candy. Each child gets a chance to fling open the receptacle, but only a stash of crayons greets their hungry glares. If asked by an experimenter what someone else will think the box contains upon first seeing it, 4- and 5-year-olds typically grin at the trick and exclaim "Candy!"

They realize, in their devilish way, that the shape and design of the box at first create a false belief.

Yet most 3-year-olds react entirely differently to the trick box. After falling for the sweet deception, they insist that a newcomer will assume crayons lie within the container. If an adult enters the room, peers into the box, and does an obvious double take, 3-year-olds still maintain that the grown-up expected to find crayons. What's more, the same youngsters confidently assert that they, too, initially thought the box held crayons.

Of course, 3-year-olds cherish cantankerous and contrary remarks, but further experiments indicate that a deeper process orchestrates their explanations of the world.

Observe, for instance, preschoolers given some toys purchased at a novelty store: a large sponge shaped and painted to look like a rock, a "sucker" egg made of chalk, and a green cardboard cat covered by a removable red filter that makes it appear black. Give them plenty of time to examine the objects. Most 4- and 5-year-olds separate each object's real qualities from its apparent attributes; they note, for instance, that the sponge only looks like a rock.

But those obstinate 3-year-olds find such subtleties about as appealing as going to bed early. In their minds, an object possesses either real or apparent characteristics, but not both at the same time. For instance, some assert that the phony rock looks like a sponge and really is a sponge, while the cat looks black and really is black.

These findings emerge from research conducted over the past decade to examine how children reach an understanding of the mind's trappings, such as beliefs, desires, intentions, and emotions. Some investigators contend that this hybrid of developmental and cognitive psychology explores the ways in which children construct "theories of mind." Others argue that the research illuminates the origins of "folk psychology," or people's shared assumptions about how the mind works.

Whatever terminology they use, scientists generally agree that knowledge about mental states and attitudes changes substantially throughout childhood. Debate revolves around a number of clashing explanations of how and why that change takes place.

"There's a genuine argument now over whether a fundamental shift occurs in children's understanding of their own and others' minds between ages 3 and 5," says John H. Flavell, a psychologist at Stanford University and an early explorer of how preschoolers understand thinking.

The March BEHAVIORAL AND BRAIN SCIENCES contains two opposing reviews of research on children's understanding of the mind, as well as 60 written comments from an international group of investigators.

Swiss psychologist Jean Piaget launched the study of how youngsters conceptualize mental life more than 50 years ago. He argued that infants use a few basic reflexes, such as sucking objects that enter their mouths and following moving objects with their eyes, but extract no other meaning from the environment. Preschoolers make themselves the center of the universe, in Piaget's theory; they fail to grasp that other people have different viewpoints and different sources of knowledge. A full appreciation of mental states as experienced by oneself and others blooms in later childhood and adolescence, Piaget held.

Today, researchers contend that more goes on in the heads of babies and young children than Piaget imagined. "Theory of mind" advocates argue that infants possess a primitive sense of being like others; soon thereafter, children assemble a succession of progressively more sophisticated predictions about the types of thought that coordinate behavior in particular situations. This process resembles the accumulation of knowledge through theory testing in science, they propose.

In 1978, investigations into children's theories of mind got a major boost from a controversial article in which two researchers suggested that chimpanzees theorize about mental states. To test this assertion, scientists began to look at whether chimps and children attribute false beliefs to others. Chimps showed little talent for viewing the world from another's misleading perspective, but children at different ages yielded intriguing results that spurred continued research.

Some investigators now suggest that an

innate brain mechanism allows even very young children to begin theorizing about mental states. Others view the child's emerging understanding of the mind as a by-product of a maturing brain that manipulates many types of information in increasingly complex ways.

Another school of thought regards commonsense notions about mental life as socially and culturally learned tools for dealing with others rather than as theories for making predictions about people.

And a final account emphasizes intuition as the driving force behind children's take on the mind. In this view, preschoolers first imagine having the desires or beliefs of another person and then mentally simulate what that person would do and feel.

Alison Gopnik, a psychologist at the University of California, Berkeley, champions an influential version of the theory of mind approach known as the "theory theory." Individuals gradually construct commonsense psychological beliefs as a way of explaining themselves and others, according to Gopnik. On the basis of their experience, children theorize that invisible mental entities, such as beliefs and desires, exist and operate in lawful ways, she contends. Youngsters modify or discard a favored theory if it encounters too many difficulties or continually leads them astray in social situations, just as scientists drop or modify a theory that cannot account for or predict key phenomena, the Berkeley psychologist posits.

"The same mental capacities that children use to understand the mind have been applied to science by adults. It's not that children are little scientists, but scientists are big children," she says, chuckling at the implication.

However, the nature of these proposed psychological launching pads for abstract thought remains hazy. Gopnik presents a rough outline of what researchers know about the development of an understanding of the mind.

Even infants display a vague notion of internal psychological states, she asserts. For example, studies find that babies deftly mimic adult facial expressions and gaze in the direction they see others looking.

From around 18 months to 3 years, children learn to distinguish between mental and physical events, Gopnik notes. They know the difference between, say, an imagined dog and a real dog, and begin to engage in pretense and make-believe games. Their talk includes words for perceptions, such as "see," "look," and "taste," and emotions, such as "happy,"

"love," and "want." By age 3, most also use words such as "know," "think," and "remember."

In Gopnik's opinion, 3-year-olds retain a fascination with "silly" states that stand apart from the real world, such as dreams and make-believe. They also assume that beliefs and other mental states apprehend the world directly, just as their eyes see whatever lies in front of them. They do not assume that a person holds a belief about the contents of a box; in the 3-year-old's theory, the person's belief corresponds to what the box holds. Thus, the typical youngster says the box contains candy when assessing its appearance. But the same child sheds that assumption upon seeing its contents and acquires a belief that the box has always held crayons and other people share that knowledge.

A theory of mental states as direct conduits to reality, rather than as representations of what may or may not exist, also sometimes causes children to confuse appearance with reality, as in encounters with spongy rocks and chalky eggs.

Further evidence suggests that 3-year-olds assign either total knowledge or absolute ignorance to mental states, Gopnik says. In other words, they fail to appreciate that belief comes in degrees. For instance, in contrast to 4-year-olds, 3-year-olds show no preference for information offered by people who express certainty about what a box contains versus people citing doubts about what the box holds.

Some investigators argue that 3-year-olds know enough about false beliefs to attempt to deceive others. A child at that age who breaks an expensive lamp may, when asked by his mother if he touched the lamp, quickly utter "No." But Gopnik maintains that

◆◆◆◆◆◆◆◆◆◆◆◆◆◆◆◆◆◆◆◆◆◆◆◆◆◆◆◆◆◆◆◆

Don't just sit there, think something

Children know much about the mind by age 4, but their conception of how people think still diverges sharply from that of older children and adults, according to a report in the April CHILD DEVELOPMENT. Beginning around age 7, youngsters tend to conclude that mental activity goes on continuously in a waking mind. Younger children, in contrast, assume that the mind switches on when it has a job to do and switches off at the conclusion of a task, leaving the mental landscape blank.

A 4-year-old who attributes complex meaning to beliefs and other mental states, as proposed by "theory of mind" researchers, at the same time fails to realize that people lead continuous inner lives and experience a "stream of consciousness," contend John H. Flavell, a psychologist at Stanford University, and his colleagues.

In one trial conducted by Flavell's team, groups of 20 children at ages 3, 4, and 6 to 7 years, as well as 20 adults, stated whether they believed a female experimenter entertained any thoughts or ideas in three situations: waiting quietly in a chair facing a blank wall, looking at pictures on the wall, and attempting to explain how someone got a big pear into a small glass bottle. Participants indicated the absence of thought by selecting a drawing of a woman's head underneath an empty "thought bubble" (commonly used to indicate the thoughts of cartoon characters) and signaled the presence of

thought by choosing a portrayal of a woman's head under a thought bubble containing three asterisks.

Warm-up tests established that all of the participants viewed the asterisks as representing ongoing thoughts or ideas.

Only one of the 3-year-olds attributed mental activity to a waiting person. That number increased to four in the 4-year-olds, 11 in the 6- to 7-year-olds, and 19 in the adults. In contrast, at least 13 members of each age group granted thoughts to a person looking at pictures or trying to explain the pear-bearing bottle.

In further trials with 4-year-olds, most of these youngsters contended that people can voluntarily empty their minds of all thoughts and ideas for a few minutes and that the mind of a waiting person "was not doing anything."

And in unpublished results, Flavell's group finds that not until about age 7 do children consistently recall thoughts they just had while contemplating a problem.

Preschoolers may seldom reflect on their own and others' thoughts and probably experience problems when they try, Flavell suggests. Prior studies directed by Flavell suggest that at around age 7 kids realize that one thought triggers another in a chain reaction, a person's facial expression may contradict inner thoughts, and some psychological states linger indefinitely, such as worries that a monster will emerge from the dark at night.

— B. Bower

◆◆◆◆◆◆◆◆◆◆◆◆◆◆◆◆◆◆◆◆◆◆◆◆◆◆◆◆◆◆◆◆

researchers cannot yet say whether the denial signals a conscious attempt to manipulate mother's beliefs or a learned strategy for avoiding punishment, devoid of any deeper understanding of why it might work.

By age 4 or 5, at least in Western cultures, children come to the conclusion that people form beliefs and other mental states *about* the world, Gopnik holds. These youngsters entertain notions of false belief, distinguish between real and apparent qualities of the same object, and recognize changes in their own beliefs, she says.

Moreover, 5-year-olds usually understand that individuals may perceive an object in different ways depending on their line of sight. They also recognize that beliefs dictate a person's emotional reactions to particular situations, such as an adult's expression of surprise at discovering crayons in a candy box.

"By 5 years of age, children have acquired a remarkable understanding of the mind, in many ways quite like that of adults, and certainly very different from that of 2- or even 3-year-olds," Gopnik contends.

Although adults generally believe that each person uses direct knowledge of his or her own mental states to make educated guesses about how others think, research with children suggests otherwise, she adds. At any given stage of development, children make the same inferences about their own minds and those of other people, Gopnik argues.

When confronting false beliefs, she points out, 3-year-olds make errors about their own immediately past beliefs, such as saying they thought the box contained crayons all along, and commit a similar blunder in claiming that a newcomer believes the box holds crayons.

In contrast, 3-year-olds perform much better when dealing with "silly" mental states that bear no relation to the real world. For example, in one study directed by Gopnik, 3-year-olds knew they had first pretended that an imaginary glass contained hot chocolate and then had imagined that the same glass was full of lemonade. Children at this age also realize that other people may engage in pretense and change the details of an imagined situation.

Arriving at an adult-like, abstract account of thought requires a child to continually tinker with and sometimes replace theories about how the mind works, Gopnik says. Other psychologists, including Henry M. Wellman of the University of Michigan in Ann Arbor and Josef Perner of the University of Sussex in Brighton, England, currently direct investigations aimed at shedding further light on these theories.

In an ironic twist, relatively stable theories of mind rapidly become second nature after age 5 and foster the false impression that we directly experience our own mental states rather than making well-practiced inferences about what we believe, want, and feel, Gopnik asserts. Master chess players experience a similar warping of perception, she says. After years of practice, their consideration of numerous potential moves during a match occurs so quickly and effortlessly that they report only a sensation of reacting to the competing forces and powers on the chessboard rather than making a step-by-step analysis of the proper move.

Other researchers argue that a child's ability to theorize about mental life depends on a specialized brain mechanism that exerts its influence by around age 2, when children begin to use pretense. Contrary to Gopnik's proposal, 4-year-olds probably do not overhaul their assumptions about mental states, argues Alan M. Leslie, a psychologist at the University of London in England. Instead, he says, their new treatment of false belief and other psychological concepts reflects a maturing capacity to parcel out different sources of information in their minds.

For instance, unlike many 3-year-olds, 4-year-olds also realize that an out-of-date photograph — say, a picture of candy in a cupboard that is now bare — represents a past state of affairs that has changed.

Leslie and his colleagues propose that young children easily slip into and out of pretend play because the brain's "theory-of-mind mechanism" allows them to grasp that people hold invisible attitudes about the veracity of a fictional state of affairs. Hence, even 2-year-olds understand that if mother pretends a banana is a telephone, she won't serve the telephone for lunch and call up father on the banana.

The same brain mechanism allows 3- to 4-year-olds to understand that a person behaves according to potentially misleading beliefs, hopes, or other attitudes held about people and objects, Leslie asserts.

Autistic children provide an example of what happens when apparent brain damage destroys the theory-of-mind mechanism, he contends. Studies conducted by Leslie and University of London coworkers Uta Frith and Simon Baron-Cohen indicate that autistic youngsters fail to develop any rules of thumb for understanding how mental states cause behavior. Autistic children cannot conceive that they or others hold false beliefs, and they find it difficult to understand deception, according to the British investigators.

As a result, symptoms of autism revolve around the absence of imagination, an inability to communicate with others, and a poverty of social skills, Leslie suggests.

Philip D. Zelazo of the University of Toronto and Douglas Frye of New York University, both psychologists, take a different approach. They hold that a 4-year-old's altered conception of mental states depends on the emergence of a general ability to reason first from one perspective and then from another, incompatible perspective.

One experiment conducted by Zelazo and Frye required children to place cards in various locations according to their colors and then sort the same cards according to their shapes. Three-year-olds succeeded at the first set of rules but could not immediately switch to the alternate rules; 4- and 5-year-olds performed well at sorting cards both by color and by shape.

Other investigators doubt that commonsense notions of the mind spring either from specific theories or a more general versatility at manipulating information.

Instead, children possess a powerful innate tendency to make sense of their own and other's actions by telling stories about those deeds, argues Jerome Bruner, a psychologist at New York University. Myths, oral stories, books, and other cultural influences on family and social life shape the ways in which children arrive at a personal understanding of belief, deception, and the rest of mental life, he asserts. Bruner expands on this notion in his book *Acts of Meaning* (1990, Harvard University Press).

If Bruner's argument is correct, children in the United States and Sri Lanka, or in other contrasting cultures, should report striking differences in their assumptions about the mind. To date, virtually all evidence regarding children's understanding of the mind comes from Western cultures, Gopnik points out.

Another explanation of folk psychology rests on a child's powers of imagination. Three-year-olds have trouble imagining mental states that contradict their own current mental states, and thus exhibit difficulty with false-belief tests, holds Alvin I. Goldman, a philosopher at the University of Arizona in Tucson. By age 4, children can imagine having the beliefs and desires of another person; they then mentally simulate that person's resulting feelings and behaviors, Goldman argues.

Paul L. Harris, a psychologist at the University of Oxford in England, agrees. In some studies, 3-year-olds accurately report their psychological experience and understand that mental states refer to the real world, according to Harris. When asked to visualize an imaginary object, 3-year-olds understand the direction to "make a picture in your head" and describe the mind as a container which at times displays pictures of nonexistent things, he notes.

Children apparently adopt such metaphors as a way of capturing their inner psychological experiences and improving their mental simulations of how others think, Harris asserts.

In addition, he says, 3-year-olds perform much better on false-belief tasks when an experimenter presents a situation in words rather than in actions.

For instance, an experimenter may tell 3-year-olds that an object that apparently belongs in one box has been secretly transferred to another box, rather than showing them the transfer. The children then look in both boxes to verify the transfer. Compared with same-age counterparts who only observe the transfer, these youngsters are much more likely to realize that an uninformed newcomer will guess the object's location incorrectly.

A verbal description makes it easier for 3-year-olds to imagine the object in its initial location and to ignore the knowledge that they saw the object in an unexpected box, Harris holds.

Still, Gopnik argues, the presence of an underlying theory best accounts for the wide range of understanding about the mind achieved by children around age 4. What's more, considerable research already suggests that adults often remain unaware of the unconscious mental states that direct their attitudes and judgments (SN: 3/28/92, p.200), adding to the likelihood that children also lack direct access to their own mental states and must construct theories to explain mental life, she points out.

Unfortunately, much remains unclear about the origins of theories and the reasons for their change in childhood as well as in science, Gopnik acknowledges.

"The scientist's ability to learn about the world is still almost as mysterious as the child's," she maintains. "Nevertheless, reducing two mysteries to one is an important advance, and a great deal more than we usually achieve."

Visualizing the Mind

*Strategies of cognitive science and techniques
of modern brain imaging open a window
to the neural systems responsible for thought*

Marcus E. Raichle

Marcus E. Raichle is professor of neurology, radiology and neurobiology as well as a senior fellow of the McDonnel Center for Studies of Higher Brain Function at the Washington University School of Medicine in St. Louis. He received his B.S. and M.D. degrees from the University of Washington in Seattle. He began researching brain metabolism and circulation when he was a neurology resident at the New York Hospital–Cornell Medical Center. His current focus is the use of positron-emission tomography and magnetic resonance imaging to study human cognition and emotion.

What causes the pity we might feel for the melancholy Dane in *Hamlet* or the chill during a perusal of the *Raven?* Our brains have absorbed from our senses a printed sequence of letters and then converted them into vivid mental experiences and potent emotions. The "black box" description of the brain, however, fails to pinpoint the specific neural processes responsible for such mental actions. While philosophers have for centuries pondered this relation between mind and brain, investigators have only recently been able to explore the connection analytically—to peer inside the black box. The ability stems from developments in imaging technology that the past few years have seen, most notably positron-emission tomography and magnetic resonance imaging. Coupled with powerful computers, these techniques can now capture in real time images of the physiology associated with thought processes. They show how specific regions of the brain "light up" when activities such as reading are performed and how neurons and their elaborate cast of supporting cells organize and coordinate their tasks. The mapping of thought can also act as a tool for neurosurgery and elucidate the neural differences of people crippled by devastating mental illnesses, including depression and schizophrenia.

I hasten to point out that the underlying assumptions of current brain mapping are distinct from those held by early phrenologists. They posited

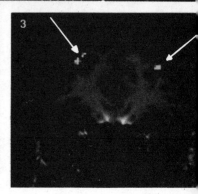

ACTIVE NEURAL AREAS from a subject remembering a sequence of letters are mapped by magnetic resonance imaging. The images below represent six slices through the frontal cortex. The slices are identified by numbers in the corners that correspond to those in the scan at the right. Arrows indicate areas of increasing activity. Jonathan D. Cohen and his colleagues at the University of Pittsburgh and Carnegie Mellon University Departments of Psychiatry formed the images.

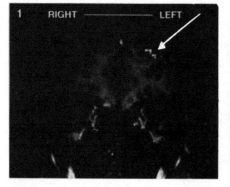

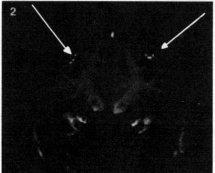

that single areas of the brain, often identified by bumps on the skull, uniquely represented specific thought processes and emotions. In contrast, modern thinking posits that networks of neurons residing in strictly localized areas perform thought processes. So just as specific members of a large orchestra perform together in a precise fashion to produce a symphony, a group of localized brain areas performing elementary operations work together to exhibit an observable human behavior. The foundation for such analyses is that complex behaviors can be broken down into a set of constituent mental operations. In order to read, for example, one must recognize that a string of letters is a word; then recognize the meaning of words, phrases or sentences; and finally create mental images.

The challenge, of course, is to determine those parts of the brain that are active and those that are dormant during the performance of tasks. In the past, cognitive neuroscientists have relied on studies of laboratory animals and patients with localized brain injuries to gain insight into the brain's functions. Imaging techniques, however, permit us to visualize safely the anatomy and the function of the normal human brain.

The modern era of medical imaging began in the early 1970s, when the world was introduced to a remarkable technique called x-ray computed tomography, now known as x-ray CT, or just CT. South African physicist Allan M. Cormack and British engineer Sir Godfrey Hounsfield independently developed its principles. Hounsfield constructed the first CT instrument in England. Both investigators received the Nobel Prize in 1979 for their contributions.

Computed tomography takes advantage of the fact that different tissues absorb varying amounts of x-ray energy. The denser the tissue, the more it absorbs. A highly focused beam of x-rays traversing through the body will exit at a reduced level depending on the tissues and organs through which it passed. A beam of x-rays passed through the body at many different angles through a plane collects sufficient information to reconstruct a picture of the body section. Crucial in the development of x-ray CT was the emergence of clever computing and mathematical techniques to process the vast amount of information necessary to create images themselves. Without the availability of sophisticated computers, the task would have been impossible to accomplish.

X-ray CT had two consequences. First, it changed forever the practice of medicine because it was much superior to standard x-rays. For the first time, investigators could safely and effectively view living human tissue such as the brain with no discomfort to the patient. Standard x-rays revealed only bone and some surrounding soft tissue. Second, it immediately stimulated scientists and engineers to consider alternative ways of creating images of the body's interior using similar mathematical and computer strategies for image reconstruction.

One of the first such groups to be intrigued by the possibilities opened by computed tomography consisted of experts in tissue autoradiography, a method used for many years in animal studies to investigate organ metabolism and blood flow. In tissue autoradiography, a radioactively labeled compound is injected into a vein. After the compound has accumulated in the organ (such as the brain) under interest, the animal is sacrificed and the organ removed for study. The organ is carefully sectioned, and the individual slices are laid on a piece of film sensitive to radioactivity. Much as the film in a camera records a scene as you originally viewed it, this x-ray film records the distribution of radioactively labeled compound in each slice of tissue.

Once the x-ray film is developed, scientists have a picture of the distribution of radioactivity within the organ and hence can deduce the organ's specific functions. The type of information is determined by the radioactive compound injected. A radioactively labeled form of glucose, for example, measures brain metabolism because glucose is the primary source of energy for neurons. Louis Sokoloff of the National Institute of Mental Health introduced this now widely used autoradiographic method in 1977.

Investigators adept with tissue autoradiography became fascinated when CT was introduced. They suddenly realized that if they could reconstruct the anatomy of an organ by passing an x-ray beam through it, they could also reconstruct the distribution of a previously administered radioisotope. One had simply to measure the emission of radioactivity from the body section. With this realization was born the idea of autoradiography of living human subjects.

A crucial element in the evolution of human autoradiography was the choice of radioisotope. Workers in the field selected a class of radioisotopes that emit positrons, which resemble electrons except that they carry a positive charge. A positron would almost immediately combine with a nearby electron. They would annihilate each other, emitting two gamma rays in the process. Because each gamma ray travels in nearly opposite directions, devices around the sample would detect the gamma rays and locate their origin. The crucial role of positrons in human autoradiography gave rise to the name positron-emission tomography, or PET [see "Positron-Emission Tomography," by Michel M. Ter-Pogossian, Marcus E. Raichle and Burton E. Sobel; SCIENTIFIC AMERICAN, October 1980].

Throughout the late 1970s and early 1980s, researchers rapidly developed PET to measure various activities in the brain, such as glu-

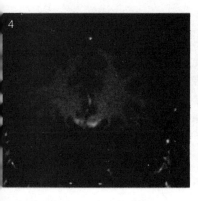
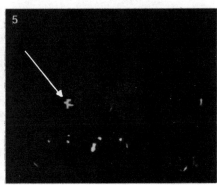
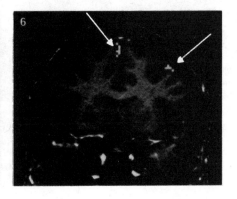

5. COGNITIVE PROCESSES

BRAIN SECTION (*a*) is compared with corresponding images of the slice taken by x-ray computed tomography (CT) (*b*), positron-emission tomography (PET) (*c*) and magnetic resonance imaging (MRI) (*d*). CT depicts the features of the brain section, whereas PET shows the amount of neuronal work (the darker the area, the greater the activity). Properly set up, MRI can do both tasks. Here it images structure.

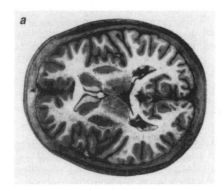

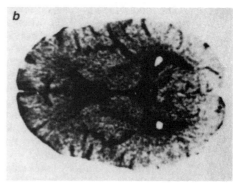

cose metabolism, oxygen consumption, blood flow and interactions with drugs. Of these variables, blood flow has proved the most reliable indicator of moment-to-moment brain function.

The idea that local blood flow is inti-

mately related to brain function is a surprisingly old one. English physiologists Charles S. Roy and Charles S. Sherrington formally presented the idea in a publication in 1890. They suggested that an "automatic mechanism" regu-

lated the blood supply to the brain. The amount of blood depended on local variations in activity. Although subsequent experiments have amply confirmed the existence of such an automatic mechanism, no one as yet is entirely certain

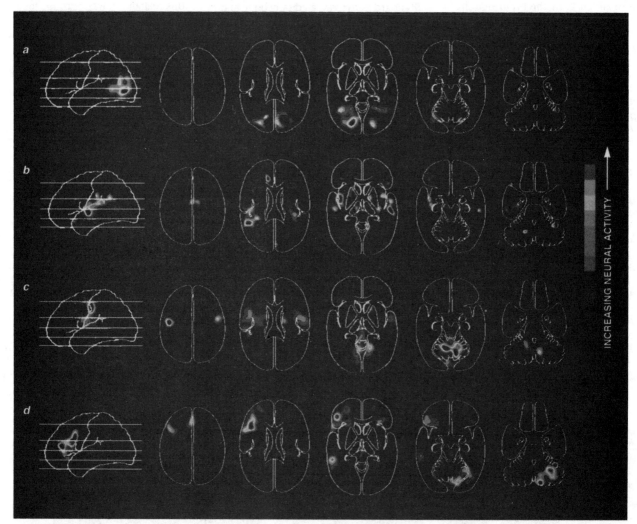

PET SCANS show active neural areas. In the far left column the left side of the brain is presented; the next columns show five horizontal layers (the right side faces to the right, with the front to the top). Each row corresponds to the difference between a specific task and the control state of gazing at a dot on a television monitor. When subjects passively view nouns (*a*), the primary visual cortex lights up. When nouns are heard (*b*), the temporal lobes take command. Spoken nouns minus viewed or heard nouns (*c*) reveal motor areas used for speech. Generating verbs (*d*) requires additional neural zones, including those in the left frontal and temporal lobes corresponding roughly to Broca's and Wernicke's areas.

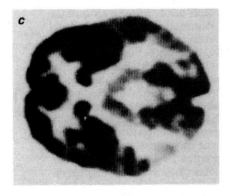

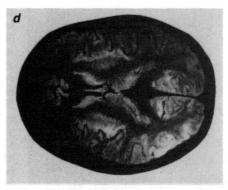

about its exact nature. It obviously remains a challenging area for research.

PET measures blood flow in the normal human brain by adapting an autoradiographic technique for laboratory animals developed in the late 1940s by Seymour S. Kety of the National Institute of Mental Health and his colleagues. PET relies on radioactively labeled water—specifically, hydrogen combined with oxygen 15, a radioactive isotope of oxygen. The labeled water emits copious numbers of positrons as it decays (hydrogen isotopes cannot be used, because none emit positrons). The labeled water is administered into a vein in the arm. In just over a minute the radioactive water accumulates in the brain, forming an image of blood flow.

The radioactivity of the water produces no deleterious effects. Oxygen 15 has a half-life of only two minutes; an entire sample decays almost completely in about 10 minutes (five half-lives) into a nonradioactive form. The rapid decay substantially reduces the exposure of subjects to the potentially harmful effects of radiation. Moreover, only low doses of the radioactive label are necessary.

The fast decay and small amounts permit many measurements of blood flow to be made in a single experiment. In this way, PET can take multiple pictures of the brain at work. Each picture serves as a snapshot capturing the momentary activity within the brain. Typical PET systems can locate changes in activity with an accuracy of a few millimeters.

A distinct strategy for the functional mapping of neuronal activity by PET has emerged during the past 10 years. This approach extends an idea first introduced to psychology in 1868 by Dutch physiologist Franciscus C. Donders. Donders proposed a general method to measure thought processes based on a simple logic. He subtracted the time needed to respond to a light (with, say, the press of a key) from the time needed to respond to a particular color of

light. He found that discriminating color required about 50 milliseconds. In this way, Donders isolated and measured a mental process for the first time.

The current PET strategy is designed to accomplish a similar subtraction but in terms of the brain areas implementing the mental process. In particular, images of blood flow taken before a task is begun are compared with those obtained when the brain is engaged in that task. Investigators refer to these two periods as the control state and the task state. Workers carefully choose each state so as to isolate as best as possible a limited number of mental operations. Subtracting blood-flow measurements made in the control state from each task state indicates those parts of the brain active during a particular task.

To achieve reliable data, workers take the average of responses across many individual subjects or of many experimental trials in the same person. Averaging enables researchers to detect changes in blood flow associated with mental activity that would otherwise be easily confused with spurious shifts resulting from noise.

One of the first assignments in which PET blood-flow mapping has proved useful is in the study of language. The manner in which language skills are acquired and organized in the human brain has been the subject of intense investigation for more than a century. Work began in earnest in 1861, when French physician Pierre Paul Broca described a patient whose damaged left frontal lobe destroyed the ability to speak. (To this day, patients who have frontal lobe damage and have trouble speaking are often referred to as having Broca's aphasia.) Broca's studies of language localization were complemented by Carl Wernicke, a German neurologist. In 1874 Wernicke told of people who had difficulty comprehending language. They harbored damage to the left temporal lobe, a region now usu-

ally referred to as Wernicke's area. From these beginnings has emerged a concept of language organization in the human brain: information flows from visual and auditory reception to areas in the left temporal lobe for comprehension and then on to frontal areas for speech production [see "Specializations of the Human Brain," by Norman Geschwind; SCIENTIFIC AMERICAN, September 1979].

All this information was gleaned from brain-damaged patients. Can investigators derive insight about language organization from a healthy brain? In 1988 my colleagues Steven E. Petersen, Michael I. Posner, Peter T. Fox and Mark A. Mintun and I at the Washington University Medical Center began a series of studies to answer just this question. The initial study was based on a PET analysis of a seemingly simple job: speaking an appropriate verb when presented with a common English noun. For example, a subject might see or hear the word "hammer," to which an appropriate response might be "hit."

We chose this assignment because it could be broken down into many components. Each component could separately be analyzed through a careful selection of tasks. The most readily apparent elements include visual and auditory word perception, the organization and execution of word output (speech), and the processes by which the brain retrieves the meanings of words. (Of course, each of these operations can be divided further into several additional subcomponents.)

To identify the areas of the brain used in a particular operation, we composed four levels of information processing. Such a hierarchy has become standard among laboratories doing this type of research [*see bottom illustration on opposite page*]. In the first level, subjects were asked to fix their gaze on a pair of small crosshairs—the arrangement looks like a small plus sign—in the middle of a television monitor. At the same time, a PET scan measured blood flow in the brain, providing a snapshot of mental activity.

In the second level, subjects continued to maintain their gaze on the crosshairs as blood flow was measured, but during this scan they were exposed to common English nouns. The nouns either appeared below the crosshairs on the television monitor or were spoken through earphones (separate scans were performed for visual and auditory presentations). In the third level, subjects were asked to recite the word they viewed or heard. Finally, in the fourth

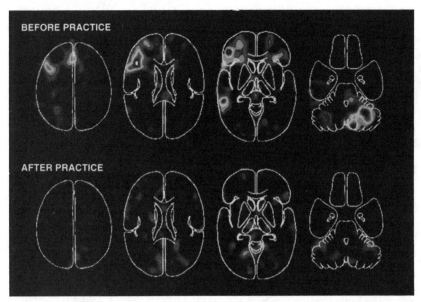

LEARNING-INDUCED CHANGES in neural activity are revealed by PET imaging. The top row shows the brain of a subject who must quickly generate verbs appropriate to visually presented nouns. The bottom row shows the result of 15 minutes of practice; the regions activated are similar to those used in simply reading out loud.

level, the subjects said out loud a verb appropriate for the noun.

Subtracting the first level from the second isolated those brain areas concerned with visual and auditory word perception. Deducting the second level from the third pinpointed those parts of the brain concerned with speech pro-

duction. Subtracting level three from level four located those regions concerned with selecting the appropriate verb to a presented noun.

The final subtraction (speaking nouns minus generating verbs) was of particular interest, because it provided a portrait of pure mental activity (perception

and speech—or input and output—having been subtracted away). This image permitted us to view what occurs in our brains as we interpret the meaning of words and, in turn, express meaning through their use. It renders visible conscious function because much of our thinking is carried out by concepts and ideas represented by words.

The results of this study clearly demonstrate how brain imaging can relate mental operations of a behavioral task to specific networks of brain areas orchestrated to perform each operation. As anticipated by cognitive scientists and neuroscientists, the apparently simple task of generating a verb for a presented noun is not accomplished by a single part of the brain but rather by many areas organized into networks. Perception of visually presented words occurs in a network of areas in the back of the brain, where many components of the brain's visual system reside. Perception of aurally presented words occurs in an entirely separate network of areas—in our temporal lobes.

Speech production (that is, simply repeating out loud the presented nouns) predictably involves motor areas of the brain. Regions thought to be Broca's and Wernicke's areas do not appear to be engaged routinely in this type of speech production, an activity that would be viewed by many as quite automatic for most fluent speakers in their native language. This finding suggests what we might have suspected: we occasionally speak without consciously thinking about the consequences.

Regions of the left frontal and temporal lobes (those corresponding in general to the respective locations of Broca's and Wernicke's areas) only become active when two tasks are added: consciously assessing word meaning and choosing an appropriate response. Moreover, two other areas come into play under these circumstances, forming a network of four brain regions. Interestingly, two areas used in the routine repetition of words were turned off. This shutdown suggests that the demands of generating a verb to a presented noun does not simply build on the task of just saying the noun. Rather the act of speaking a verb to a presented noun differs from speaking the noun, as far as the brain is concerned.

This finding caused us to pause and consider what would happen if we allowed subjects a few minutes of practice on their task of generating verbs. Although subjects initially discover that forming verbs rapidly is difficult (nouns are presented every 1.5 seconds), they become relaxed and proficient after 15

IMAGE SUBTRACTION AND AVERAGING serve as the foundation of functional brain imaging. Researchers subtract the PET blood-flow pattern of a control state from that of a task state to produce a difference image (*top row*). Data from different subjects are averaged (*bottom two rows*) to eliminate statistical fluctuations.

TASK STATE   CONTROL STATE   DIFFERENCE

INDIVIDUAL DIFFERENCE IMAGES

MEAN DIFFERENCE IMAGE

minutes of practice. An examination of the brain after training reveals that practice completely changes the neural circuits recruited [*see top illustration on opposite page*]. The circuits responsible for noun repetition now generate the verbs. Thus, practice not only makes perfect (something we have always known) but also changes the way our brain organizes itself (something we may not have fully appreciated).

As cognitive neuroscientists demonstrated the utility of PET technology, a newer method swiftly emerged that could compete with PET's abilities. Magnetic resonance imaging, or MRI, has now become a fairly common tool for diagnosing tissue damage. Recent developments have vastly increased the speed with which MRI can form images, thus making it suitable for research in cognitive neuroscience.

MRI derives from a potent laboratory technique known as nuclear magnetic resonance (NMR), which was designed to explore detailed chemical features of molecules. It garnered a Nobel Prize for its developers, Felix Bloch of Stanford University and Edward M. Purcell of Harvard University, in 1952. The method depends on the fact that many atoms behave as little compass needles in the presence of a magnetic field. By skillfully manipulating the magnetic field, scientists can align the atoms. Applying radio-wave pulses to the sample under these conditions perturbs the atoms in a precise manner. As a result, they emit detectable radio signals unique to the number and state of the particular atoms in the sample. Careful adjustments of the magnetic field and the radio-wave pulses yield particular information about the sample under study.

NMR moved from the laboratory to the clinic when Paul C. Lauterbur of the University of Illinois found that NMR can form images by detecting protons. Protons are useful because they are abundant in the human body and, by acting as little compass needles, respond sensitively to magnetic fields. Their application resulted in excellent images of the anatomy of organs that far surpassed in detail those produced by x-ray CT [see "NMR Imaging in Medicine," by Ian L. Pykett; SCIENTIFIC AMERICAN, May 1982]. Because the term "nuclear" made the procedure sound dangerous, NMR soon became known as magnetic resonance imaging.

The current excitement over MRI for brain imaging stems from the technique's ability to detect a signal inaccessible to PET scans. Specifically, it can detect an increase in oxygen that occurs in an area of heightened neuronal activity. The basis for this capacity comes from the way neurons make use of oxygen. PET scans had revealed that functionally induced increases in blood flow accompanied alterations in the amount of glucose the brain consumed but not in the amount of oxygen it used. In effect, the normal human brain during spurts of neuronal activity resorts to anaerobic metabolism. Few had suspected that the brain might rely on tactics similar to those used by sprinter's muscles. In fact, this form of metabolism occurs despite the presence of abundant oxygen in the normal brain. Why the brain acts this way is a mystery worthy of intense scientific scrutiny.

Additional blood to the brain without a concomitant increase in oxygen consumption leads to a heightened concentration of oxygen in the small veins draining the active neural centers. The reason is that supply has increased, but the demand has not. Therefore, the extra oxygen delivered to the active part of brain simply returns to the general circulation by way of the draining veins.

Why does oxygen play a crucial role in MRI studies of the brain? The answer lies in a discovery made by Nobel laureate Linus C. Pauling in 1935. He found that the amount of oxygen carried by hemoglobin (the molecule that transports oxygen and gives blood its red color) affects the magnetic properties of the hemoglobin. In 1990 Seiji Ogawa and his colleagues at AT&T Bell Laboratories demonstrated that MRI could detect these small magnetic fluctuations. Several research groups immediately realized the importance of this observation. By the middle of 1991 investigators showed that MRI can detect the functionally induced changes in blood oxygenation in the human brain. The ability of MRI machines to detect functionally induced changes in blood oxygenation leads many to refer to the technique as functional MRI, or fMRI.

Functional MRI has several advan-

FUNCTIONAL MRI

PET

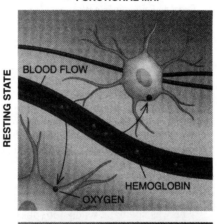
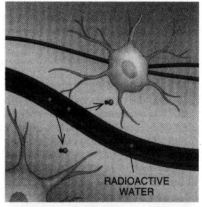
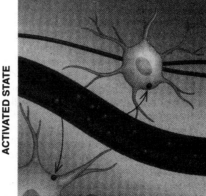
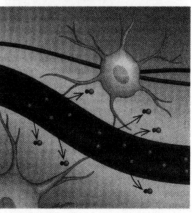

BLOOD FLOW to the brain provides the signals detected by functional MRI and PET. When resting neurons (*top*) become active (*bottom*), blood flow to them increases. MRI (*left*) detects changes in oxygen levels, which rise in the nearby blood vessels because active neurons consume no more oxygen than when they are at rest. PET (*right*) relies on the increased delivery of injected radioactive water, which diffuses out of the vessels to reach all parts of the brain.

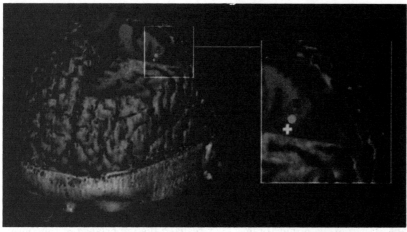

MAGNETOENCEPHALOGRAPHY, or MEG, captures neural activity too brief to be detected by PET or MRI. Above, MEG has located the areas in the normal adult somatosensory cortex associated with the digits of the right hand (*symbols*). The symbols on the MRI image of the brain correspond to those on the fingers.

tages over x-ray CT and other imaging techniques. First, the signal comes directly from functionally induced changes in the brain tissue (that is, the change in venous oxygen concentration). Nothing, radioactive or otherwise, needs to be injected to obtain a signal. Second, MRI provides both anatomical and functional information in each subject, hence permitting an accurate structural identification of the active regions. Third, the spatial resolution is quite good, distinguishing parts as small as one to two millimeters (better than PET's resolution). Fourth, when properly equipped (that is, given so-called echoplanar capability), MRI can monitor the rate of change in the blood-flow-induced oxygen signal in real time [*see illustration on preceding page*].

Finally, MRI has little, if any, known biological risk. Some workers have raised concerns about the intensity of the magnetic field to which the tissues are exposed. So far most studies have found the effects to be benign. The largest drawback is the claustrophobia some subjects may suffer. In most instrument designs the entire body must be inserted into a relatively narrow tube.

Several intriguing results with functional MRI were reported this past year. Robert G. Shulman and his colleagues at Yale University have confirmed PET findings about language organization in the brain. Using conventional, hospital-based MRI, Walter Schneider and Jonathan D. Cohen and their colleagues at the University of Pittsburgh have corroborated work in monkeys that indi-

cated the primate visual cortex is organized into topographic maps that reflect the spatial organization of the world as we see it. Other groups are actively trying to visualize other forms of mental activity, such as the way we create mental images and memories.

The ability of MRI systems to monitor the oxygen signal in real time has suggested to some the possibility of measuring the time it takes for different brain areas to exchange information. Conceptually, one might think of a network of brain areas as a group of individuals in the midst of a conference call. The temporal information sought would be equivalent to knowing who was speaking when and, possibly, who was in charge. Such information would be critical in understanding how specific brain areas coordinate as a network to produce behavior.

The stumbling block, however, is the speed of neuronal activity compared with the rate of change of oxygenation levels. Signals from one part of the brain can travel to another in 0.01 second or less. Unfortunately, changes in blood flow and blood oxygenation are much slower, occurring hundreds of milliseconds to several seconds later. MRI would not be able to keep up with the "conversations" between brain areas. The only methods that respond quickly enough are electrical recording techniques. Such approaches include electroencephalography (EEG), which detects brain electrical activity from the scalp, and magnetoencephalography

(MEG), which measures the magnetic fields generated by electrical activity within the brain.

Why don't researchers just use EEG or MEG for the whole job of mapping brain function? The limitations are spatial resolution and sensitivity. Even though great strides in resolution have been made, especially with MEG [*see illustration at left*], accurate localization of the source of brain activity remains difficult with electrical recording devices. Furthermore, the resolution becomes poorer the deeper into the brain we attempt to image.

Neither MRI nor PET suffers from this difficulty. They both can sample all parts of the brain with equal spatial resolution and sensitivity. As a result, a collaboration seems to be in the making between PET and MRI and electrical recording. PET and MRI, working in a combination yet to be determined, can define the anatomy of the circuits underlying a behavior of interest; electrical recording techniques can reveal the course of temporal events in these spatially defined circuits.

Regardless of the particular mix of technologies that will ultimately be used to image human brain function, the field demands extraordinary resources. Expensive equipment dominates this work. MRI, PET and MEG equipment costs from $2 million to $4 million and is expensive to maintain. Furthermore, success requires close collaboration within multidisciplinary teams of scientists and engineers working daily with these tools. Institutions fortunate enough to have the necessary technical and human resources need to make them available to scientists at institutions less fortunate. Although some radiology departments have such equipment, the devices are usually committed mostly for patient care.

In addition to the images of brain activity, the experiments provide a vast amount of information. Such an accumulation not only yields answers to the questions posed at the time of the experiment but also provides invaluable information for future research, as those of us in the field have repeatedly discovered to our amazement and delight. Recent efforts to create neuroscience databases could organize and quickly disseminate such a repository of information.

Wise use of these powerful new tools and the data they produce can aid our understanding and care of people who have problems ranging from developmental learning disorders to language disabilities arising from, say, stroke. Researchers have begun to use functional brain imaging to learn about the mood disturbances that afflict patients with such mental illnesses as depression. The technology could guide neurosurgeons in the excision of brain tumors, enabling them to judge how the removal of tissue will hamper the patient. Centers across the world are investigating such other mental activities as attention, memory, perception, motor control and emotion. Clearly, we are headed toward a much richer grasp of the relation between the human mind and the brain.

FURTHER READING

INTRINSIC SIGNAL CHANGES ACCOMPANYING SENSORY STIMULATION: FUNCTIONAL BRAIN MAPPING WITH MAGNETIC RESONANCE IMAGING. S. Ogawa, D. W. Tank, R. Menon, J. M. Ellermann, S.-G. Kim, H. Merkle and K. Ugurbil in *Proceedings of the National Academy of Sciences,* Vol. 89, No. 13, pages 5951–5955; July 1, 1992.

SOMATOSENSORY CORTICAL PLASTICITY IN ADULT HUMANS REVEALED BY MAGNETOENCEPHALOGRAPHY. A. Mogilner et al. in *Proceedings of the National Academy of Sciences,* Vol. 90, No. 8, pages 3593–3597; April 15, 1993.

IMAGES OF MIND. M. I. Posner and M. E. Raichle. W. H. Freeman and Company, 1994.

PRACTICE-RELATED CHANGES IN HUMAN FUNCTIONAL ANATOMY DURING NONMOTOR LEARNING. M. E. Raichle, J. A. Fiez, T. O. Videen, A.-M. K. MacLeod, J. V. Pardo, P. T. Fox and S. E. Petersen in *Cerebral Cortex,* Vol. 4, No. 1, pages 8–26; January/February 1994.

Rethinking the Mind

Cognitive science faces a philosophical challenge

BRUCE BOWER

John R. Searle sees gaping cracks in the edifice of the mind constructed by cognitive scientists. Searle, a philosopher at the University of California, Berkeley, peruses the mental rules and representations and computer programs that buttress the cognitive citadel with the eye of a skeptical contractor. Watch out for falling bricks, he warns; the structure lacks the mortar of consciousness to hold it together.

"More than anything else, it is the neglect of consciousness that accounts for so much barrenness and sterility in psychology, the philosophy of mind, and cognitive science," Searle asserts.

Although Searle's remark will win him no popularity contests among scientists of the mind, it nevertheless reflects the recently renewed interest in deciphering the nature of consciousness. From a variety of perspectives, scientists are now trying to define more clearly what they mean when they refer to "conscious" and "unconscious" mental activity.

Searle first rankled cognitive scientists in 1980 when he published his widely cited "Chinese Room" argument, an attack on the notion, promoted by advocates of "strong artificial intelligence," that the mind corresponds to a computer program implemented in the hardware of the brain.

Searle compared the computers favored by artificial intelligence enthusiasts to a person who does not speak Chinese but sits in a room with Chinese dictionaries and a filing system. If an outsider slips questions written in Chinese under the door, the person uses the reference works to compose answers in Chinese. Responses emerging from the room might prove indistinguishable from those of a native Chinese speaker, Searle contended, even though the person toiling in the Chinese Room understands neither the questions nor the answers.

The moral of this exercise: A system such as a computer can successfully employ a set of logical rules without knowing the meaning of any of the symbols it manipulates using those rules.

Supporters of strong artificial intelligence view the Chinese Room as a flimsy sanctuary from the argument that a properly programmed computer possesses a "mind." Philosopher Daniel C. Dennett of Tufts University in Medford, Mass., calls Searle's analogy simplistic and irrelevant. A computer program that could hold its own in a conversation would contain layers of complex knowledge about the world, its own responses, likely responses of a questioner, and much more, Dennett contends. Indeed, computers have displayed a growing conversational prowess in the last several years. Their increasingly deft dialogue stems from the interactions among various strands of information, each of which comprehends nothing on its own, Dennett maintains.

Put another way, proper programming transforms a bunch of unreflective parts into a thinking system, whether they reside in a mainframe or a human skull.

For Searle, the Chinese Room debate lies behind him as he aims his new assault on what he calls the "much deeper" mistake of cognitive scientists — their neglect of conscious experience. He describes his views in the December 1990 BEHAVIORAL AND BRAIN SCIENCES (with sometimes heated responses from more than 30 cognitive scientists) and in his book *The Rediscovery of the Mind* (1992, MIT Press).

Cognitive science tends to regard the mind as a collection of relatively independent faculties, or modules, that contain unconscious rules for language, perception, and other domains of thought,

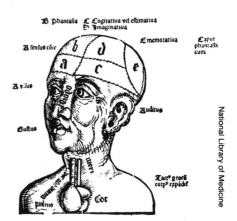

Searle argues. Consciousness, in the sense that one can pay attention to, reason about, or describe these rules, rarely gets attention in their theories. Other facets of the unconscious, such as memories and repressed conflicts, sometimes enter awareness but more often influence thought and behavior in surreptitious ways, according to cognitive researchers.

Searle spurns this approach, with its reliance on what he calls a "deep unconscious" unable to pierce the surface of awareness. Mental life consists of conscious states and those neurophysiological processes that, under the right circumstances, generate conscious states, he argues. Most brain states that participate in mental life do not reach consciousness, but they must have the capacity to do so, Searle proposes. He dubs this formulation the "Connection Principle."

For example, the unconscious intention to satiate hunger with food simply reflects some biological aspect of the brain's workings that has the capacity to produce conscious appetite and food-seeking behavior in certain situations, Searle asserts. Unconscious processes totally divorced from awareness, such as the transfer of chemical messengers from one brain cell to another, harbor no intentions and do not meet Searle's criteria for "mental."

Mental life emerges as an inherent

From *Science News*, October 17, 1992, pp. 264-266. © 1992 by Science Service, Inc. Reprinted by permission of *Science News*, the weekly newsmagazine of science.

feature of the brain, just as liquidity is a feature of water, in Searle's view.

Moreover, consciousness feeds off an individual's singular point of view, thus rendering it subjective and not reducible to traditional objective measurements of behavior, he maintains. Investigators of consciousness must strive to understand "the first-person point of view," Searle says.

His model treats consciousness as an on-off switch — one is either conscious or not. But once the switch goes on, the brain produces consciousness in a broad range of intensities. Even dreams are a mild form of consciousness, Searle asserts, though they fall far short of full-blown alertness.

The center of conscious attention contrasts with "peripheral consciousness," he adds. For example, while focused on writing an article, a person retains peripheral awareness of the shirt on his or her skin, the feel of computer keys, and numerous other thoughts and sensations.

Searle treats the unconscious mental conflicts and desires described by Sigmund Freud as cases of "repressed consciousness," because they typically bubble to the surface, although often in disguised form. Most beliefs, worries, and memories also operate outside awareness, with the potential for entering consciousness, and thus follow the Connection Principle, he notes.

But the unconscious does not consist of fully formed thoughts, Searle asserts. The brain contains "brute" biological processes that create the wide variety of conscious experiences, he says; in essence, the brain builds consciousness on the spot, rather than hauling it out of storage.

Cognitive researchers make a mistake comparable to that of scientists more than a century ago who erroneously believed that the leaves of a plant turn toward the sun because the plant wants to survive, he maintains. Biologists later learned that secretions of a specific hormone direct the movements of a plant's leaves, not a floral "decision" to catch as many rays as possible.

In the same way, the brain's neurophysiology produces certain types of conscious experience without making any inferences or following any rules, according to Searle.

Consider a visual phenomenon known as the Ponzo illusion. When two parallel, horizontal lines of equal length lie between two vertical lines that converge toward the top, the parallel line on top looks longer. Cognitive psychologists who specialize in perception suggest that the brain computes sensory information

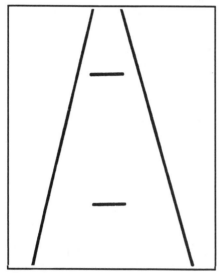

The Ponzo illusion, in which the upper of two equal and parallel lines looks slightly longer.

Cornering the unconscious

Suppose you want to find out what an acquaintance really thinks about you. Your best bet might be to ask one of your friends and one of your enemies to query the acquaintance about his or her feelings toward you. Then you can estimate the acquaintance's true attitude by comparing the rosy comments delivered to your friend — undoubtedly boosted by social pressure — with the positive comments expressed to your enemy, which likely underestimate actual friendly feelings.

This strategy guides a new approach to teasing out conscious from unconscious influences on memory and perception, described in the June AMERICAN PSYCHOLOGIST by psychologist Larry L. Jacoby of McMaster University in Hamilton, Ontario, and his co-workers. "It's an important advance," remarks psychologist John F. Kihlstrom of the University of Arizona in Tucson.

Kihlstrom and other researchers typically chart unconscious influences by contrasting explicit and implicit forms of memory and perception. Explicit tests tap conscious knowledge, as when volunteers try to identify previously studied words on a multiple-choice test; implicit tests reveal unconscious influences of memories or perceptions, as when volunteers unwittingly complete ambiguous word fragments with previously studied words.

But many investigators acknowledge that conscious recollections or perceptions at least partly boost scores on implicit tests.

"Just as gaining a true measure of friendship requires bad times as well as good times, a measure of unconscious influences requires separate conditions in which unconscious processes oppose and act in concert with the aims of conscious intention," Jacoby says.

The Canadian psychologist devised such a measure to confirm a prior study in which volunteers who were distracted while reading a list of concocted names later rated many of them as famous when shown a new list containing the same names, new nonfamous names, and famous names. Unconscious familiarity with previously read names apparently produced "false fame" judgments, Jacoby theorizes. In the new experiment, he first gave participants a conscious opportunity to reject the influence of unconscious familiarity by telling them that the earlier read names were not famous. This "opposition test" corresponds to a known enemy questioning an acquaintance, Jacoby says.

Experimenters then told the volunteers that another list of previously read names came from "obscure" famous people, thus putting conscious recollection and unconscious familiarity "in concert" — similar to an acquaintance being questioned by a known friend.

To estimate the extent of volunteers' conscious recollections for names, Jacoby subtracted the probability of making "false fame" judgments on the opposition test from that on the in-concert test. With this measure, he calculated the contribution to false fame responses made by unconscious familiarity.

The results: Dealing with distractions while reading names radically reduced conscious recollection, but false fame judgments soared. Undisturbed study of the names reversed this pattern.

Manipulations of attention apparently open the door to particularly strong unconscious influences, Jacoby asserts. For example, background music accompanied by audible lyrics pitching a commercial product probably leaves people open to far more unconscious persuasion than a "subliminal" sales message hidden in the same music, he contends. *— B. Bower* using unconscious rules that sometimes produce optical distortions. One theory holds that the Ponzo illusion may result from two unconscious inferences: first, that the top parallel line lies farther away because it's closer to the converging lines, and second, that the top line extends farther because it's farther away.

Searle offers an alternative theory: Still-unclear brain processes handle parallel and converging lines in such a way as to produce the conscious experience of the Ponzo illusion. "Nonconscious operations of the brain know nothing of inference, rule following, or size and distance judgments," he argues.

Searle also attacks the notion of unconscious rules of "universal grammar" championed by linguists such as Noam Chomsky of the Massachusetts Institute of Technology in Cambridge. Chomsky and others have theorized that the ability of healthy children to learn readily the language of their community and other natural human languages — but not logically possible "artificial" languages — shows that the brain contains an innate "language-acquisition device" consisting largely of grammatical rules that are unavailable to conscious thought.

Searle, an ardent foe of universal grammar for more than 15 years, agrees that human brains contain a biological capacity for language acquisition that limits the type of languages we can learn. But proposing language rules that lie beyond the grasp of consciousness makes as little sense as proposing a universal visual grammar that tells us, "If it is infrared, don't see it, but if it's blue, it's okay to see it," Searle holds. The brain's visual system simply limits what sort of colors humans can see.

The Berkeley philosopher says it often proves tempting to theorize about thought processes unavailable to consciousness, especially when studying complex abilities such as language learning. But "brute neurophysiology," not hidden rules, translates perceptions and language into thought and behavior, Searle contends.

Connectionist computers, also known as neural networks, work on this principle, he notes. Some connectionist models convert meaningful input into meaningful output by mathematically altering the sensitivity of connections between processing units rather than by manipulating rules or symbols. Neural networks may still fail as models of the mind, but they avoid the quicksand of "deep unconscious rules" that sucks down cognitive science, Searle says.

Searle's critique wins little favor with some cognitive scientists. His demand for conscious accessibility to all unconscious mental states "is arbitrary and pointless," contends MIT's Chomsky.

One current version of universal grammar theory, proposed by Chomsky and his colleagues, describes specific types of mental rules and representations handled automatically by a computational system in the brain. These theoretical mental guidelines help explain why people extract meaning from certain expressions (such as "John is easy to catch") but find the wording of other expressions confusing or somehow wrong (as with "John is easy to be caught"), according to Chomsky.

Searle's abandonment of unconscious rules for language understanding in favor of unknown neurophysiological properties presents a prescription for scientific confusion, Chomsky asserts.

Moreover, Searle's contention that unconscious mental states possess intentions or goals appears erroneous, holds psychologist Maria Czyzewska of Southwest Texas State University in San Marcos. Psychological researchers currently assume that the unconscious contains information that lies mainly outside conscious control but that shapes thoughts and behavior, despite lacking a preset agenda, she points out.

For example, multiple-choice or recall tests containing words on a previously studied list evoke conscious memories. However, volunteers often unintentionally use the same words on tests that do not ask for those words, such as lists of word fragments that can be completed in a number of ways (SN: 11/17/90, p.312). The latter memories receive the label "implicit," or unconscious.

Implicit responses do not spring from unconscious intentions, nor do they suggest a distinction only between consciousness and neurophysiological states that produce consciousness, Czyzewska contends.

Another critique comes from physiologists Walter J. Freeman and Christine A. Skarda, both of the University of California, Berkeley. Neurophysiological processes do not cause mental states, conscious or otherwise, as Searle proposes; they *are* mental states, Freeman and Skarda argue.

Background electrical activity in the brain reflects a chaotic process, in the mathematical sense, they theorize (SN: 1/23/88, p.58). The brain uses this flexible energy state to organize massive numbers of brain cells instantaneously in response to sensory information the scientists contend. They have reported that chaotic electrical activity appears in both the olfactory and visual cortex of rabbits.

Self-organized, unpredictable electrical activity throughout the brain incorporates past experiences and creates an unconscious "space of possibilities" for handling further experiences, Skarda maintains. As the brain takes in new stimuli, various patterns of chaotic activity assume consciousness in the form of thoughts and memories, she contends, rather than emerging from an unconscious storage bin, as in digital computer models of memory and learning.

"Brains are less like libraries than like nurseries and farms," Freeman notes.

Even if Freeman proves right, cognitive scientists have yet to develop a green thumb for cultivating true insight into the mind, Searle responds. They invoke a bevy of invisible rules and computer programs in the brain that only stoke intellectual chaos, he holds.

No simple scientific remedies will cure what ails cognitive science, Searle remarks, but researchers must remember that "the brain is the only thing in our skulls, and the brain causes consciousness."

The Return of Phineas Gage: Clues About the Brain from the Skull of a Famous Patient

When the landmark patient Phineas Gage died in 1861, no autopsy was performed, but his skull was later recovered. The brain lesion that caused the profound personality changes for which his case became famous has been presumed to have involved the left frontal region, but questions have been raised about the involvement of other regions and about the exact placement of the lesion within the vast frontal territory. Measurements from Gage's skull and modern neuroimaging techniques were used to reconstitute the accident and determine the probable location of the lesion. The damage involved both left and right prefrontal cortices in a pattern that, as confirmed by Gage's modern counterparts, causes a defect in rational decision making and the processing of emotion.

Hanna Damasio, Thomas Grabowski, Randall Frank,
Albert M. Galaburda, Antonio R. Damasio*

H. Damasio and A. R. Damasio are in the Department of Neurology, University of Iowa Hospitals & Clinics, Iowa City, IA 52242, and the Salk Institute for Biological Research, San Diego, CA 92186–5800, USA. T. Grabowski and R. Frank are in the Department of Neurology, University of Iowa Hospitals & Clinics, Iowa City, IA 52242, USA. A. M. Galaburda is in the Department of Neurology, Harvard Medical School, Beth Israel Hospital, Boston, MA 02215, USA.

*To whom correspondence should be addressed.

On 13 September 1848, Phineas P. Gage, a 25-year-old construction foreman for the Rutland and Burlington Railroad in New England, became a victim of a bizarre accident. In order to lay new rail tracks across Vermont, it was necessary to level the uneven terrain by controlled blasting. Among other tasks, Gage was in charge of the detonations, which involved drilling holes in the stone, partially filling the holes with explosive powder, covering the powder with sand, and using a fuse and a tamping iron to trigger an explosion into the rock. On the fateful day, a momentary distraction let Gage begin tamping directly over the powder before his assistant had had a chance to cover it with sand. The result was a powerful explosion away from the rock and toward Gage. The fine-pointed, 3-cm-thick, 109-cm-long tamping iron was hurled, rocket-like, through his face, skull, brain, and then into the sky. Gage was momentarily stunned but regained full consciousness immediately thereafter. He was able to talk and even walk with the help of his men. The iron landed many yards away (1).

Phineas Gage not only survived the momentous injury, in itself enough to earn him a place in the annals of medicine, but he survived as a different man, and therein lies the greater significance of this case. Gage had been a responsible, intelligent, and socially well-adapted individual, a favorite with peers and elders. He had made progress and showed promise. The signs of a profound change in personality were already evident during the convalescence under the care of his physician, John Harlow. But as the months passed it became apparent that the transformation was not only radical but difficult to comprehend. In some respects, Gage was fully recovered. He remained as able-bodied and appeared to be as intelligent as before the accident; he had no impairment of movement or speech; new learning was intact, and neither memory nor intelligence in the conventional sense had been affected. On the other hand, he had become irreverent and capricious. His respect for the social conventions by which he once abided had vanished. His abundant profanity offended those around him. Perhaps most troubling, he had taken leave of his sense of responsibility. He could not be trusted to honor his commitments. His employers had deemed him "the most efficient and capable" man in their "employ" but now had to dismiss him. In the words of his physician, "the equilibrium or balance, so to speak, between his intellectual faculty and animal propensities" had been destroyed. In the words of his friends and acquaintances, "Gage was no longer Gage" (1). Gage began a new life of wandering that ended a dozen years later, in San Francisco, under the custody of his family. Gage never returned to a fully independent existence, never again held a job comparable to the one he once had. His accident had made headlines but his death went unnoticed. No autopsy was obtained.

Twenty years after the accident, John Harlow, unaided by the tools of experimental neuropsychology available today, perceptively correlated Gage's cognitive and behavioral changes with a presumed area of focal damage in the frontal region (1). Other cases of neurological damage were then revealing the brain's foundation for language, motor function, and perception, and now Gage's case indicated something even more surprising: Perhaps there were structures in the human brain dedicated to the planning and execution of personally and socially suitable behavior, to the aspect of reasoning known as rationality.

Given the power of this insight, Harlow's observation should have made the scientific impact that the comparable suggestions based on the patients of Broca and Wernicke made (2). The suggestions, although surrounded by controversy, became the foundation for the understanding of the neural basis of language and were pursued actively, while Harlow's report on Gage did not inspire a search for the neural basis of reasoning, decision-making, or social behavior. One factor likely to have contributed to the indifferent reception accorded Harlow's work was that the intellectual atmosphere of the time made it somewhat more acceptable that there was a neural basis for processes such as movement or even language rather than for moral reasoning and social behavior (3). But the principal explanation must rest with the substance of Harlow's report. Broca and Wernicke had autopsy results, Harlow did not. Unsupported by anatomical evidence, Harlow's observation was the more easily dismissed. Because the exact position of the lesion was not known, some critics could claim that the damage actually involved Broca's so-called language "center," and

5. COGNITIVE PROCESSES

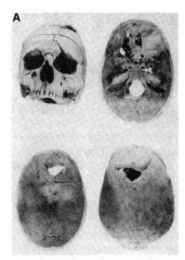

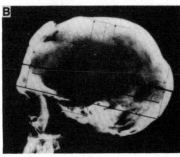

Fig. 1. Photographs of (**A**) several views of the skull of Phineas Gage and (**B**) the skull x-ray.

a particular type of cognitive and behavioral defect caused by damage to ventral and medial sectors of prefrontal cortex, rather than to the left dorsolateral sector as implicit in the traditional view. It then occurred to us that some of the image processing techniques now used to investigate Gage's counterparts could be used to test this idea by going back in time, reconstituting the accident, and determining the probable placement of his lesion. The following is the result of our neuroanthropological effort.

We began by having one of us (A.M.G.) photograph Gage's skull inside and out and obtain a skull x-ray (Fig. 1) as well as a set of precise measurements (6) relative to bone landmarks. Using these measurements, we proceeded to deform linearly the three-dimensional reconstruction of a standard human skull (7) so that its dimensions matched those of Phineas Gage's skull. We also constructed Talairach's stereotactic space for both this skull and Phineas Gage's real skull (8). On the basis of the skull photographs, the dimensions of the entry and exit holes were scaled and mapped into the deformed standard skull. Based on measurements of the iron rod and on the recorded descriptions of the accident, we determined the range of likely trajectories of the rod. Finally, we simulated those trajectories in three-

dimensional space using Brainvox (9). We modeled the rod's trajectory as a straight line connecting the center of the entry hole at orbital level to the center of the exit hole. This line was then carried downward to the level of the mandibular ramus. The skull anatomy allowed us to consider entry points within a 1.5-cm radius of this point (20 points in all) (Fig. 2).

Possible exit points were determined as follows: We decided to constrain the exit point to be at least 1.5 cm (half the diameter of the rod) from the lateral and posterior margins of the area of bone loss (Fig. 3) because there were no disruptions of the outer table of the calvarium in these directions (Fig. 1). However, we accepted that the rod might have passed up to 1.5 cm anterior to the area of bone loss because inspection of the bone in this region revealed that it must have been separated completely from the rest of the calvarium (Fig. 1). Furthermore, the wound was described as an inverted funnel (1). We tested 16 points within the rectangular-shaped exit area that we constructed (Fig. 3).

The trajectory connecting each of the entry and exit points was tested at multiple anatomical levels. The three-dimensional skull was resampled in planes perpendicular to the best a priori trajectory (C in Figs. 2 and 3). We were helped by several impor-

perhaps would also have involved the nearby "motor centers." And because the patient showed neither paralysis nor aphasia, some critics reached the conclusion that there were no specialized regions at all (4). The British physiologist David Ferrier was a rare dissenting voice. He thoughtfully ventured, in 1878, that the lesion spared both motor and language centers, that it had damaged the left prefrontal cortex, and that such damage probably explained Gage's behavioral defects, which he aptly described as a "mental degradation" (5).

Harlow only learned of Gage's death about 5 years after its occurrence. He proceeded to ask Gage's family to have the body exhumed so that the skull could be recovered and kept as a medical record. The strange request was granted, and Phineas Gage was once again the protagonist of a grim event. As a result, the skull and the tamping iron, alongside which Gage had been buried, have been part of the Warren Anatomical Medical Museum at Harvard University.

As new cases of frontal damage were described in this century, some of which did resemble that of Gage, and as the enigmas of frontal lobe function continued to resist elucidation, Gage gradually acquired landmark status. Our own interest in the case grew out of the idea that Gage exemplified

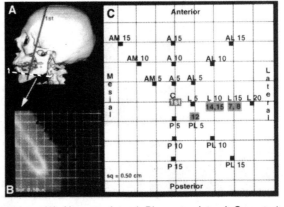

Fig. 2. View of the entry-level area with the a priori most likely first trajectory. (**A**) Skull with this first vector and the level (dotted line) at which entry points were marked. (**B**) View of a segment of section 1. On the left is the mandibular ramus, and on the right is the array of entry points. (**C**) Enlargement of the array of entry points. One additional point was added (L20) to ensure that every viable entry point was surrounded by nonviable points. Nonviable vectors are shown in black and viable vectors with labels identifying their exit points are shown in grey. Abbreviations: A, anterior; L, lateral; P, posterior; AM, anteromesial; AL, anterolateral; PL, posterolateral; C. central.

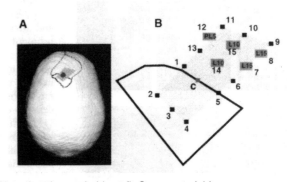

Fig. 3. (**A**) View from above the deformed skull with the exit hole and the anterior bone flap traced in black. The black circle represents the first vector tested, and the grey surface represents the area where exit points were tested. (**B**) Schematic enlargement of the exit hole and of the area tested for exit points. The letter C marks the first tested vector. The numbers 1 through 15 mark the other exit points tested. Black indicates nonviable vectors, grey indicates viable vectors, and the label identifies the entry point. Note that the a priori best fit C was not viable.

tant anatomical constraints. We knew that the left mandible was intact; that the zygomatic arch was mostly intact but had a chipped area, at its medial and superior edge, that suggested the rod had grazed it; and that the last superior molar socket was intact although the tooth was missing. Acceptable trajectories were those which, at each level, did not violate the following rules: The vectors representing the trajectories could not be closer than 1.5 cm from the mid-thickness of the zygomatic arch, 1 cm from the last superior molar, and 0.5 cm from the coronoid process of the mandible (10). Only seven trajectories satisfied these conditions (Fig. 4). Two of those seven invariably hit the anterior horn of the lateral ventricle and were therefore rejected as anatomically improbable because they would not have been compatible with survival (the resulting massive infection would not have been controllable in the preantibiotic era). When checked in our collection of normal brains, one of the remaining five trajectories behaved better than any other relative to the lower constraints and was thus chosen as the most likely trajectory. The final step was to model the five acceptable trajectories of the iron rod in a three-dimensional reconstruction of a human brain that closely fit Phineas Gage's assumed brain dimensions (11). Talairach's stereotactic warpings were used for this final step.

The modeling yielded the results shown in Fig. 5. In the left hemisphere, the lesion involved the anterior half of the orbital frontal cortex (Brodmann's cytoarchitectonic fields 11 and 12), the polar and anterior mesial frontal cortices (fields 8 to 10 and 32), and the anterior-most sector of the anterior cingulate gyrus (field 24). However, the lesion did not involve the mesial aspect of field 6 [the supplementary motor area (SMA)]. The frontal operculum, which contains Broca's area and includes fields 44, 45, and 47, was also spared, both cortically and in the underlying white matter. In the right hemisphere, the lesion involved part of the anterior and mesial orbital region (field 12), the mesial and polar frontal cortices (fields 8 to 10 and 32), and the anterior segment of the anterior cingulate gyrus (field 24). The SMA was spared. The white matter core of the frontal lobes was more extensively damaged in

the left hemisphere than in the right. There was no damage outside of the frontal lobes.

Even allowing for error and taking into consideration that additional white matter damage likely occurred in the surround of the iron's trajectory, we can conclude that the lesion did not involve Broca's area or the motor cortices and that it favored the ventromedial region of both frontal lobes while sparing the dorsolateral. Thus, Ferrier was correct, and Gage fits a neuroanatomical pattern that we have identified to date in 12 patients within a group of 28 individuals with frontal damage (12). Their ability to make rational decisions in personal and social matters is invariably compromised and so is their processing of emotion. On the contrary, their ability to tackle the logic of an abstract problem, to perform calculations, and to call up appropriate knowledge and attend to it remains intact. The establishment of such a pattern has led to the hypothesis that emotion and its underlying neural machinery participate in decision making within the social domain and has raised the possibility that the participation depends on the ventromedial frontal region (13). This region is reciprocally connected with subcortical nuclei that control basic biological regulation, emotional processing, and social cognition and behavior, for instance, in amygdala and hypothalamus (14). Moreover, this region shows a high concentration of serotonin S_2 receptors in monkeys whose behavior is socially adapted as well as a low concentration in aggressive, socially uncooperative animals (15). In contrast, structures in the dorsolateral region are involved in other domains of cognition concerning extrapersonal space, objects, language, and arithmetic (16). These structures are largely intact in Gage-like patients, thus accounting for the patients' normal performance in traditional neuropsychologic tests that are aimed at such domains.

The assignment of frontal regions to different cognitive domains is compatible with the idea that frontal neurons in any of those regions may be involved with attention, working memory, and the categorization of contingent relationships regardless of the domain (17). This assignment also agrees with the idea that in non–brain-damaged individuals the separate frontal regions are interconnected and act cooperatively to support reasoning and decision making. The mysteries of frontal lobe function are slowly being solved, and it is only fair to establish, on a more substantial footing, the roles that Gage and Harlow played in the solution.

REFERENCES AND NOTES

1. J. M. Harlow, *Pub. Mass. Med. Soc.* **2**, 327 (1868).
2. P. Broca, *Bull. Soc. Anthropol.* **6**, 337 (1865); C. Wernicke, *Der aphasische Symptomencomplex* (Cohn und Weigert, Breslau, Poland, 1874). A remarkable number of basic insights on the functional specialization of the human brain, from motor function to sensory perception and to spoken and written language, came from the description of such cases mostly during the second half of the 19th century. The cases usually acted as a springboard for further research, but on occasion their significance was overlooked, as in the case of Gage. Another such example is the description of color perception impairment (achromatopsia) caused by a ventral occipital lesion, by D. Verrey [*Arch. Ophthalmol.* (Paris) **8**, 289 (1888)]. His

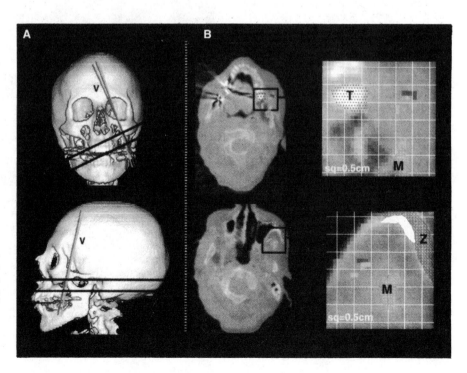

Fig. 4. (A) Front and lateral skull views with the projection of the five final vectors (V). The two black lines show the position of the two sections seen in (B). **(B)** Skull sections 2 and 3: examples of two bottleneck levels at which the viability of vectors was checked. Next to each section is an enlargement of the critical area. Abbreviations: T, missing tooth; M, intact mandible; Z, intact zygoma with a chipped area (white).

5. COGNITIVE PROCESSES

astonishing finding was first denied and then ignored until the 1970s.

3. Reasoning and social behavior were deemed inextricable from ethics and religion and not amenable to biological explanation.

4. The reaction against claims for brain specialization was in fact a reaction against phrenological doctrines, the curious and often unacknowledged inspiration for many of the early case reports. The views of E. Dupuy exemplify the attitude [*Examen de Quelques Points de la Physiologie du Cerveau* (Delahaye, Paris, 1873); M. MacMillan, *Brain Cognit.* **5**, 67 (1986)].

5. D. Ferrier, *Br. Med. J.* **1**, 399 (1878).

6. The first measurements were those necessary to construct Gage's Talairach stereotactic space and deform a three-dimensional, computerized tomography skull: the maximum length of the skull, the maximum height of the skull above the inion-glabella line, the distance from this line to the floor of the middle fossa, the maximum width of the skull, and the position of the section contour of Gage's skull relative to the inion-glabella line. The second measurements were those necessary to construct the entry and exit areas: on the top external view, the measure of edges of the triangular exit hole; on the internal view the distances from its three corners to the mid-sagittal line and to the nasion; the distance from the borders of the hole to the fracture lines seen anteriorly and posteriorly to this hole; and the dimensions of the entry hole at the level of the orbit.

7. Thin-cut standard computerized tomography image of a cadaver head obtained at North Carolina Memorial Hospital.

8. We introduced the following changes to the method described by P. Fox, J. Perlmutter, and M. Raichle [*J. Comput. Assist. Tomogr.* **9**, 141 (1985)]. We calculated the mean distance from the anterior commissure (AC) to the posterior commissure (PC) in a group of 27 normal brains and used that distance for Gage (26.0 mm). We also did not consider the AC-frontal pole and the PC-occipital pole distances as equal because our group of normals had a mean difference of 5 mm between the two measures, and Talairach himself did not give these two measurements as equal [J. Talairach and G. Szikla, *Atlas d'Anatomie Stereotaxique du Telencephale* (Masson, Paris, 1967); J. Talairach and P. Tournoux, *Co-Planar Stereotaxic Atlas of the Human Brain* (Thieme, New York, 1988)]. We introduced an anterior shift of 3% to the center of the AC-PC line and used that point as the center of the AC-PC segment. This shift meant that the anterior sector of Talairach's space was 47% of the total length and that the posterior was 53%. We had no means of calculating the difference between the right and left width of Gage's brain; therefore, we assumed them to be equal.

9. H. Damasio and R. Frank, *Arch. Neurol.* **49**, 137 (1992).

10. There were two reasons to allow the vector this close to the mandible: (i) The zygomatic arch and the coronoid process were never more than 2 cm apart; (ii) we assumed that, in reality, this distance might have been larger if the mouth were open or if the mandible, a movable structure, had been pushed by the impact of the iron rod.

11. The final dimensions of Phineas Gage's Talairach space were as follows: total length, 171.6 mm; total height, 111.1 mm; and total width, 126.5 mm. Comparing these dimensions to a group of 27 normal subjects, we found that in seven cases at least two of the dimensions were close to those of Phineas Gage [mean length, 169.9 mm (SD, 4.1); mean height, 113.6 (SD, 2.3); mean width, 125 (SD, 3.9). The seven brains were fitted with the possible trajectories to determine which brain areas were involved. There were no significant differences in the areas of damage. The modeling we present here was performed on subject 1600LL (length, 169 mm; height, 115.2 mm; width, 125.6 mm).

12. Data from the Lesion Registry of the University of Iowa's Division of Cognitive Neuroscience as of 1993.

13. P. Eslinger and A. R. Damasio, *Neurology* **35**, 1731 (1985); J. L. Saver and A. R. Damasio, *Neuropsychologia* **29**, 1241 (1991); A. R. Damasio, D. Tranel, H. Damasio, in *Frontal Lobe Function and Dysfunction*, H. S. Levin, H. M. Eisenberg, A. L. Benton, Eds. (Oxford Univ. Press, New York, 1991), pp. 217–229; S. Dehaene and J. P. Changeux, *Cereb. Cortex* **1**, 62 (1991).

14. P. S. Goldman-Rakic, in *Handbook of Physiology; The Nervous System*, F. Plum, Ed. (American Physiological Society, Bethesda, MD, 1987), vol. 5, pp. 373–401; D. N. Pandya and E. H. Yeterian, in *The Prefrontal Cortex: Its Structure, Function and Pathology*, H. B. M. Uylings, Ed. (Elsevier, Amsterdam, 1990); H. Barbas and D. N. Pandya, *J. Comp. Neurol.* **286**, 253 (1989).

15. M. J. Raleigh and G. L. Brammer, *Soc. Neurosci. Abstr.* **19**, 592 (1993).

16. M. Petrides and B. Milner, *Neuropsychologia* **20**, 249 (1982); J. M. Fuster, *The Prefrontal Cortex* (Raven, New York, ed. 2, 1989); M. I. Posner and S. E. Petersen, *Annu. Rev. Neurosci.* **13**, 25 (1990).

17. P. S. Goldman-Rakic, *Sci. Am.* **267**, 110 (September 1992); A. Bechara, A. R. Damasio, H. Damasio, S. Anderson, *Cognition* **50**, 7 (1994); A. R. Damasio, *Descartes' Error: Emotion, Reason and the Human Brain* (Putnam, New York, in press).

18. We thank A. Paul of the Warren Anatomical Museum for giving us access to Gage's skull. Supported by National Institute of Neurological Diseases and Stroke grant PO1 NS19632 and by the Mathers Foundation.

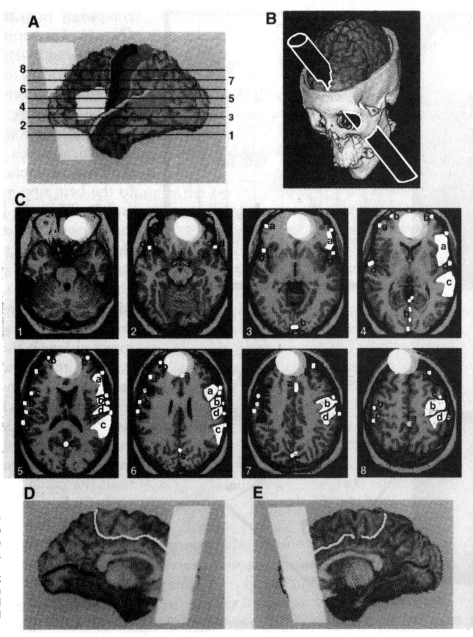

Fig. 5. Normal brain fitted with the five possible rods. The best rod is highlighted in solid white [except for (**B**), where it is shown in black]. The areas spared by the iron are highlighted: Broca (a); motor (b); somatosensory (c); Wernicke (d). (**A**) Lateral view of the brain. Numbered black lines correspond to levels of the brain section shown in (**C**). (**D** and **E**) Medical view of left and right hemispheres, respectively, with the rod shown in white.

SILENCE, SIGNS, AND WONDER

WHAT IS IT ABOUT OUR BRAIN THAT GIVES US THE CAPACITY FOR LANGUAGE? NEUROSCIENTIST URSULA BELLUGI IS LOOKING FOR THE ANSWER IN A LANGUAGE THAT EVOLVED IN THE ABSENCE OF SOUND.

Peter Radetsky

As Ursula Bellugi delivers her talk, an expert in sign language translates for her. The signer's hands hurtle furiously through the air, fingers dancing as though possessed. They swoop through the air, puncture it with staccato stabs, furl and unfurl to form shapes in space. The signer's face is equally animated. Expressions flit rapidly across it, conveying nuance, inflection, and grammatical detail unimaginable to a casual, nonsigning observer. And all at blinding speed.

Bellugi, a bustling neuroscientist, is making a point: anything she can say, the signer can "say." Sign is bona fide language. It's not mime, not a poor, pidgin derivative of spoken tongues—it's a richly endowed language in and of itself. And it is Bellugi herself who over the past two decades has convinced a doubting world of that reality.

But as director of the Laboratory for Cognitive Neuroscience at the Salk Institute for Biological Sciences in La Jolla, California, and as the world's expert in the neurobiology of American Sign Language ("She's the founder of the field, the most important person in the field, the grandmother of the field," as one researcher puts it), the 63-year-old Bellugi is interested in sign for more than its own sake. Sign offers her a window into the brain, a means of discovering the biological foundations of language. She and other investigators around the country are pinpointing areas of the brain that are uniquely suited for linguistic tasks. In fact, they are suggesting that the capacity for language may well be innate, genetically determined, one of our defining characteristics as human beings.

Bellugi's fascination with the roots of language began in 1968, soon after she received her doctorate in linguistics and psychology from Harvard. Jonas Salk invited her to start a lab at the institute that bears his name, a stark concrete complex overlooking the Pacific. At Harvard she'd investigated the ways in which children learn the dizzyingly complex underlying rules of spoken language. Now, with her husband and fellow linguist, Edward Klima, she began to think about language in a neurobiological context. How, she wondered, was language processed in the brain?

In those days language was thought to be contingent on the ability to speak, the product of humans' ability to utter sounds. So Bellugi decided to compare the way hearing children learn to speak with the way deaf children learn to sign. By comparing language with what seemed like a completely different system of communication, she hoped to tease out differences between the two. "We knew nothing about sign," recalls Bellugi. "We just thought comparing speech with sign was a theoretically interesting question, one that might move us toward the biology of language."

Little did she know what she was in for. Not only did Bellugi know nothing about sign, she soon found that virtually no one did. "There was almost nothing in the literature," she recalls, "and what there was was contradictory." Whatever sign was, however, it wasn't treated as real language. Some linguists said that sign was a "loose collection of pictorial gestures"; others that it was merely a crude communication system derived from spoken language—"broken English on the hands." Others declared that it was too vague, still others that it was too concrete, that it "dreaded and avoided the abstract." Bellugi didn't know which was right, but she did know one thing: "All of them couldn't be true—they just didn't fit together."

One concept caught her imagination, though. It was the brainchild of William Stokoe, a renegade teacher at Gallaudet University in Washington, D.C., the world's only liberal arts university for the deaf. Stokoe suspected that sign wasn't merely a collection of unrelated gestures. He perceived that signs were made up from a repertoire of distinct constituent parts: namely, the shapes signers make with their hands, where they place the shapes in space, and the manner in which they move their hands through space. Indeed, these parts reminded him of the modular bits of sound, called phonemes, that are combined to make words in spoken language. (Phonemes are roughly equivalent to the three sound units in c-a-t, or th-a-t, or ch-ea-t; each language has a finite set of these building blocks.) In 1965 Stokoe and his colleagues published a *Dictionary of American Sign*

SOME LINGUISTS SAID THAT SIGN WAS A "LOOSE COLLECTION OF PICTORIAL GESTURES"; OTHERS THAT IT WAS MERELY A CRUDE SYSTEM, "BROKEN ENGLISH ON THE HANDS."

Language, cataloging thousands of signs and their various constituent parts.

It was only a first, highly controversial step toward understanding sign, but to Bellugi it offered a clue that sign might have structure after all, just like "real" languages. Intrigued, she decided to take a closer look. "Our brains are very good at cataloging—at imposing order even where none exists," she says. "We didn't know if the dictionary was just the result of a zeal for cataloging, or if there was some reality to it." Establishing that reality was crucial if she was going to compare sign with spoken language in her investigations of the language-learning process. "After all," says Bellugi, "you can't ask questions about the way a child learns the underlying structure of something if you don't know if it even has a structure."

So, starting at ground zero, Bellugi and her lab began to find out. It wasn't

easy. First she had to master sign. "I used to go to a bowling alley frequented by deaf people," she recalls, "and I'd pester them to teach me. It was an old-fashioned way of learning. Now there are classes in the structure of sign. But in those days, remember, we were trying to find out whether sign even *had* structure." Second, she had no idea how to do the experiments to answer that question. How do you discern structure in a purely visual-spatial form of communication? ("We didn't have a toolbox," she says with a hearty laugh, recalling the challenges of those early days.) To devise her studies, she asked deaf signers' help. (To visit her lab today is to be struck by its pockets of silence. Not that nothing is going on: researchers are often conversing intently. It's just that much of the communication is in sign.)

Obviously you need an acute understanding of language to find out whether another communication system follows the same principles. For Bellugi, the essence of language is its grammar. A collection of words or signs is just a vocabulary; its use is restricted to pretty crude communiqués. But for the full flower of language—for Shakespeare, for Nabokov, or just for your everyday gossipy chitchat—you need words that relate to one another through certain rules and that lend themselves to modulation. This lets you generate all sorts of meaningful possibilities from a finite vocabulary.

CONSIDER A REALLY simple sentence: "The girl looks at the boy." In spoken English, the meaning of a sentence is determined by the order of its words. "The girl looks at the boy" has a different meaning from "The boy looks at the girl." This order relationship—subject, verb, object—is an aspect of syntax, the part of grammar that arranges words into sentences. Now zoom in on the word *looks*. In the lingo of linguists, the smallest meaningful chunks in a word are called morphemes. *Looks* contains two morphemes: the root *look* and the *-s* ending, here signifying person and tense. Logically enough, if you change morphemes, you alter meaning. So, for example, switching the *-s* for an *-ing* at the end of *look* conveys a more continuous action. "The girl is looking at the boy" has a distinctly different flavor from "The girl looks at the boy." Syntax

and morphology—these are two of the fundamental characteristics of a grammar.

American Sign Language (ASL), Bellugi found from studying signers, is also defined by a grammar, but its grammar relies on space, hand shapes, and movement. What a speaker gets across in linear sequences of sounds, a signer communicates in three dimensions. In ASL, for example, the basic sign for *look* resembles a peace sign, but instead of being raised up, the two slightly splayed fingers are bent horizontally and extended toward the looked-at thing. To say "The girl looks at the boy," a signer places the sign for *girl* at one point in space, and the sign for *boy* at another, then moves the *look* sign from one point toward the other. (For "The boy looks at the girl" the *look* sign moves between the two points in the opposite direction.)

Not only does ASL have its own spatial syntax, Bellugi found, it also has its own vivid morphology. To say "The girl is looking at the boy," the *look* sign is modified by a morphemic change in hand movement: the continuous action of *looking* is conveyed by moving the hand like a Ferris wheel from the girl toward the boy and back full circle to the girl again. What's more, the face is a fund of grammatical information. Very particular facial movements (a certain way of raising and lowering the eyebrows, of pursuing and clenching the lips) fill in information about relative clauses, questions, and adverbial nuances. These facial markers, for want of a better word, go well beyond the scope of the facial expressions universally used to show emotion.

By 1979, in their groundbreaking book *The Signs of Language*, Bellugi and Klima had come to the conclusion that sign undoubtedly *is* language. "The surface form of sign is terribly different," says Bellugi. "But the basic stuff, the underlying organization, is the same as for spoken language." As a language, they found, sign is as rich as the spoken variety, and in some ways richer; for those attuned to it, it has a dazzling visual drama unavailable to speech. "I remember one day I came home and said to my husband, 'It's as if there's a stage. There's a very distinct plane in space, right here'"—Bellugi delineates an area in front of her, from waist level to face, and from shoulder to shoulder—"'where the action is taking place.'" And the "listener," in effect the audience at the play, watches the action unfold before his or her eyes.

One of Bellugi's experiments underscored the power of this visual world. She fixed small lights to the hands of signers, then placed her subjects in a darkened room to obscure the physical details of their hands and faces: when they signed, their words were expressed purely as dancing patterns of light. What looked like firefly flashes to the uninitiated was clearly language to other signers. Even when words were hard to make out, signers recognized distinct grammatical patterns—like the Ferriswheel motion that conveys continuous action for *looking*. Bellugi also ascertained that foreign sign languages follow similar grammatical principles, though superficially they look nothing like ASL. Just as spoken Chinese has different sounds, you find different hand and movement combinations in Chinese Sign Language, she explains. "An ASL signer can't understand a Chinese signer. Even the way you close the hand is different." (A common ASL phoneme consists of a fist with the thumb placed on the index finger; its Chinese equivalent looks rather more like a hitchhiking sign.) "In fact, when a Chinese native signer comes to America and learns ASL, he usually signs with an accent." She laughs with delight. "Gives you shivers, doesn't it?"

Showing that sign was language, however, raised even more profound questions. "Obviously a great deal of human evolution has gone into creating language in the spoken mode," says Bellugi. "Spoken language is really what we were designed for." Yet here was a visual language articulated silently in space, and the human brain could clearly encompass it too. "It became a burning question. I wanted to know how sign language is organized in the brain."

By the late 1970s it was already well known that the brain's two halves are specialized for different purposes. The left side dominates when we talk and listen to speech; the right side lets us perceive spatial relationships. But here was an odd duck—a language that was visual and spatial. How did the brain handle that? "It would have been plausible," says Bellugi, "if sign were processed bilaterally, or more in the right hemisphere because of its spatial nature."

To find out, Bellugi adapted techniques classically used to study spoken language, one of which was to observe the language impairments of people who'd suffered brain damage. In this case, though, the sufferers had to be life-long deaf signers with an injury specific to one or the other hemisphere—"a rare population indeed," says Bellugi. "But by this time we had a nationwide network of some 500 deaf people. They found us deaf signers who had suffered strokes."

These experiments, begun in the eighties and still ongoing, have been full of surprises. One volunteer had been an artist before a stroke damaged part of her brain's right hemisphere. She could still draw, but she could no longer complete the left side of her pictures—a result of an injury to the part of the right brain that governs attention to the left field of vision. Thus she omitted the left side of figures like elephants, houses, and flowers. Yet when asked to sign sentences that included the words for elephants, houses, and flowers, she was as fluent as ever, "speaking" with fully

> "WHEN A CHINESE NATIVE SIGNER COMES HERE AND LEARNS AMERICAN SIGN LANGUAGE, HE USUALLY SIGNS WITH AN ACCENT. GIVES YOU SHIVERS, DOESN'T IT?"

formed gestures and using the space to the left as well as to the right of her body. "Her signing was absolutely impeccable," says Bellugi. "No difficulties whatsoever, perfectly grammatical, using space on both sides."

Other signers with right-brain damage showed similar quirks. Asked to draw the layout of her bedroom, one woman piled all the furniture to the right of her picture, leaving the left side blank. And when she signed, she described all the furniture as being on the right because her sense of what was where in space was distorted. But although her spatial perception was distorted, her signing abilities per se were intact. She could form signs as accurately as ever, even if they involved three-dimensional space on the left and right sides of her body.

The performance of deaf signers who had suffered strokes on the other side of the brain, the left side, was precisely the opposite. In contrast to right-hemisphere-damaged patients, they were able to draw pictures of their bedrooms with all the furniture in its correct location. But they could not sign effectively—their left-hemisphere damage had impaired their language ability.

The conclusion was inescapable:

"Sign language, like spoken language, is predominantly processed in the left side of the brain," says Bellugi. When it comes to sign, the supposed visual-spatial/language dichotomy between the right and left brain doesn't hold.

Now Bellugi is finding that patients' impairments vary according to precisely *where* the stroke occurred in their left brain. For example, one patient had damage to the left frontal lobe that resulted in halting, labored signing; she could not string signs together into sentences. Damage to other left-brain areas in Bellugi's subjects resulted in different problems—difficulty in forming and comprehending signs, errors in syntax and grammar. One woman with a lesion in the middle of her left hemisphere had trouble with her phonemes, the equivalent in spoken language of substituting "gine" for "fine," or "blass" for "glass."

Sometimes—but not always—the site of damage and the resulting deficit correspond to similar damage-deficit relationships in stroke patients whose use of spoken language is impaired. That suggests that some neural networks for signed and spoken language are shared, and some aren't. With luck, similarities and differences like these should allow researchers to pinpoint the systems in the brain that are essential for different aspects of language. "This is the way we're going to trace the neural systems underlying both spoken and sign language," says Bellugi.

BELLUGI'S CONCLUSION, that language—regardless of form—emanates from the left brain, flies in the face of accepted wisdom concerning the role of the brain's hemispheres. But her views are backed by other evidence from colleagues across the country. One is her Salk Institute neighbor, neuropsychologist Helen Neville (whose lab occupies the floor directly above Bellugi's).

Neville, who works with both deaf and hearing people, chronicles their brain activity while they perform linguistic tasks. During experiments, her volunteers wear a cap studded with electrodes that measure their brain waves as they read and listen to English sentences, or look at ASL sentences signed on a video screen. She, too, has found that "there's a strong biological bias for the left hemisphere to be the language hemisphere." That's not to say there aren't some interesting exceptions. For example, while nearly all right-handers rely on the left brain for language, only two-thirds of left-handers do. Of the other third, half show language activity in the right side of the brain, half on both sides. "But left-handers make up only about 10 percent of the population, so we're not talking about a lot of people," says Neville.

The dominance of one hemisphere or the other is also a function of the age at which a person learns a tongue. It's long been suspected that the earlier you learn a language, the better you learn it. Early acquisition is strongly associated with the left brain. "If you don't learn English until you're 18, you don't show left-hemisphere specialization for English," says Neville. "And if you don't learn ASL until the late teens, you don't show left-hemisphere specialization for ASL. It's dispersed throughout the brain." However, since most people learn their main language during childhood, the left-brain bias remains primary—for both spoken and signed language. "It's really amazing to think that such different forms of language are mediated by similar brain systems," notes Neville. "It suggests an al-

SPOKEN LANGUAGE IS WHAT WE WERE DESIGNED FOR. YET HERE WAS A VISUAL LANGUAGE ARTICULATED IN SPACE, AND THE BRAIN COULD ENCOMPASS IT.

most uncanny invariance, as though the capacity for language is inherent."

Bellugi agrees that language function seems to be built into the human brain. "The left hemisphere has an innate predisposition for language," she says firmly, "whatever the mode of expression."

THAT STATEMENT goes to the heart of a long-standing debate in linguistic circles. Is language more a product of nature or nurture? In one corner are the "experience" crowd, who contend that mastering a language is largely a question of mastering the skill, and then practice, practice, practice. The "innate" crowd, on the other hand, point out that children are never taught all the rudiments of lan-

guage. They are exposed to it haphazardly, in bits and pieces, yet sometime during their second year they begin to talk, displaying a grasp of grammar entirely at odds with the meager language exposure they've had. How can they arrive at so much, having received so little? Because, goes the argument, they have an inborn ability. In effect, language lives within us—it seeks only the opportunity to come out.

Much of the evidence behind the innate school of thought comes from sign. Three years ago, Laura Ann Petitto, a cognitive psychologist at McGill University in Montreal and a former student of Bellugi's, published a captivating study on babbling babies. Deaf babies whose parents sign to them babble just like hearing babies whose parents coo to them—the difference being that deaf infants do their babbling with their hands. Petitto has since shown that hearing children exposed to both speech and sign (because one of their parents is deaf) show no preference for speech. They make babbling sounds and signs, and they go on to learn both speech and sign simultaneously. As for hearing children unexposed to speech (because both their parents are deaf), they learn sign as readily as any deaf child and become fluently bilingual when they're later exposed to speech. What's so striking, says Petitto, is how these babies grasp the essential structure of language, regardless of whether it's spoken or signed. "We humans are born with a mechanism that combs the environment looking for the rhythmic patterns of language, whether these patterns are expressed with the hands or with the tongue."

Further intriguing evidence for a language instinct comes from a study of deaf children in Nicaragua. Before the revolution of 1979, these children were scattered throughout the country—isolated and silenced. Because there's virtually no hereditary deafness in Nicaragua (in contrast to the United States, where 4 to 6 percent of the deaf are children of deaf parents), no sign language tradition had passed from generation to generation. Children used gestures to communicate with hearing relatives, but one child's gestures had little in common with another's.

In 1980 schools for the deaf were established throughout Nicaragua. For the first time, deaf children were thrown together, forming the beginnings of a distinct community. And for the first time,

these children began to talk to one another. What transpired is described by Judy Kegl, a behavioral neuroscientist at Rutgers, as "the first documented case of the birth of a language."

The process unfolded like this: Soon after they were brought together, the children devised a shared set of pidgin signs based on gestures they'd used in their families. These signs allowed

CHILDREN ARE NEVER TAUGHT ALL THE RUDIMENTS OF LANGUAGE. IN EFFECT, LANGUAGE LIVES WITHIN US—IT SEEKS ONLY THE OPPORTUNITY TO COME OUT.

them to communicate in a rudimentary way but didn't display the properties of grammar that make up a real language. What happened next was magic. "Little kids about the age of three or four got exposed to that makeshift pidgin and absorbed it," says Kegl. "And then, by virtue of their own language-generation capability, they came out with a full-fledged language."

For more than a decade now these children, some 500 of them, have been creating a language out of whole cloth. It displays characteristic rules of grammar such as noun and verb agreement, subject-verb-object sentence construction, and a distinct number of hand-shape and movement building blocks. But in contrast to ASL, which has been handed down for generations, this new language has sprung from nowhere. "There is nothing that they could have used as a model," says Kegl. "It's clear evidence of an innate language capacity."

Could it be, then, that language is in our genes? McGill linguist Myrna Gopnik thinks so. "One or several genetic factors apparently affect the acquisition of language," she says. Gopnik bases her view on the study of otherwise normal, hearing families who display a very specific, inherited language impairment—in essence, the inability to construct and apply grammatical rules. Perhaps up to 3 percent of populations as diverse as Inuit, Greek, Japanese, and American have the problem. Ask these people to formulate the past tense of a simple verb and they can't—or at least not without stopping to run through the gamut of grammatical rules to come up with the appropriate construction. They can't spontaneously select the right word. Their halting speech suggests a more profound disability, when actually they are normal in every other regard.

Patrick Dunne, a geneticist at Baylor College of Medicine in Houston, is collaborating with Gopnik on a search for the gene or genes that may cause the impairment. If they find it—a large *if*—it could open the door to understanding normal grammatical processing and pos-

sibly point the way to other language genes. (That's the basis of genetics," says Dunne. "You track down the mutated gene responsible for the problem. Then you can see how it functions in a normal situation.")

All this has flowed from Bellugi's realization that the silent world of sign could let her dissect language in the brain. "She had the novel insight, the brilliant insight, that languages that

evolved in the absence of sound are an incredibly powerful avenue into our brain," says Petitto.

"Sign tells us a great deal about the human capacity for language," says Bellugi. "I can say this now after 26 years of research. I've had this drive, this curious drive, to understand language and the brain. And I've gotten deaf people curious along with me. It's just been a very exciting quest."

Emotion and Motivation

Janet's sister was a working mother and always reminded Janet about how exciting life on the road as a sales representative was. Janet was a stay-at-home mom and she loved her children, two-year-old Jennifer, four-year-old Tommy, and newborn Sara. One day, Janet was having a difficult time with the children. The baby, Sara, had been crying all day because of her colic. Jennifer and Tommy had been bickering over their toys. Janet, realizing that it was already 5:15 and her husband would be home any minute, frantically started preparing dinner. She wanted to fix a nice dinner so that she and her husband could eat after the children went to bed, then relax and enjoy each other. This was not to be. Janet sat waiting for her no-show husband. When he finally walked in the door at 10:15, Janet was furious. His excuse that his boss had invited the whole office for cocktails and dinner did not reduce Janet's ire. Janet reasoned that her husband could have called to say that he would not be home for dinner; he could have taken five minutes to do that. Janet yelled and ranted at her husband for almost an hour. Her face was taut and red with rage. Her voice wavered as she escalated her decibel level. Suddenly, bursting into tears, she ran into the living room. Her husband retreated to the safety of their bedroom and the respite that a deep sleep would bring.

Exhausted and disappointed, Janet sat alone and pondered why she was so angry with her husband. Was she just tired? Was she frustrated by negotiating with children all day and simply wanted another adult around once in a while? Was she secretly worried and jealous that her husband was seeing another woman and lied about his whereabouts? Was she combative because her husband's and her sister's lives seemed so much more fulfilling than her own? Janet was unsure just how she felt and why she exploded in such rage at her husband, someone she loved dearly.

This story, while sad and gender stereotyped, is not necessarily unrealistic. There are times when we are moved to deep emotion. On other occasions when we expect waterfalls of tears, we find that our eyes are dry or simply a little misty. What are these strange things we call emotions? What motivates us to rage at someone we love? Why do we autopsy our every mood?

These questions and others have inspired psychologists to study emotions and motivation. The above episode about Janet, besides introducing these topics, also illustrates why these two topics are usually interrelated in psychology. Some emotions are pleasant, so pleasant that we are motivated to keep them going. Pleasant emotions are exemplified by love, pride, and joy. Other emotions are terribly draining and oppressive, so negative that we hope they will be over as soon as possible. Negative emotions are exemplified by anger, grief, and jealousy. Emotions and motivation and their relationship to each other are the focus of this unit.

The first three unit articles introduce some general information about emotions. In the first unit article, "Where Emotions Come From," we are reminded that the range of human emotions is vast. Despite this, some individuals fake emotions, thereby adding more emotions to their personal repertoires. Certain genuine emotions are readily identifiable by all of us, including individuals outside of our culture. Some researchers suggest that this is because the brain is intimately involved in the perception and reproduction of facial movements that express emotion.

One way to measure emotions has been the polygraph or lie detector. The courts and prospective employers eagerly embraced this apparatus as a scientific way to detect emotionality, particularly emotions related to lying. Research, however, has demonstrated that the polygraph is a very questionable apparatus, in fact, so questionable that it is no longer admissible evidence in a court of law. A critique of the polygraph is the topic of "A Doubtful Device."

Moods differ from emotions in that emotions are typically transient states, while moods are more long-lasting. Moods are therefore also important for psychologists to understand and study. In "How to Master Your Moods," Melvin Kinder investigates four different mood styles and how each style can be managed better.

The relationship between motivation and physiology is explored with regard to eating in "Chemistry and Craving." The hypothalamus seems to be the region of the brain related to hunger. However, various neurochemicals appear to be responsible for specific cravings, cravings that can upset the best laid diet plans.

In the final article for this unit, Josh Halberstam explores personal competition. Many Americans are highly competitive. Halberstam concludes that highly competitive individuals might actually be doing themselves harm.

Looking Ahead: Challenge Questions

Do you think emotions are triggered by the brain? Or do you believe that something in our environment elicits emotions in us? Do you think that some people are more emotional than others? From where do you think these individual differences originate?

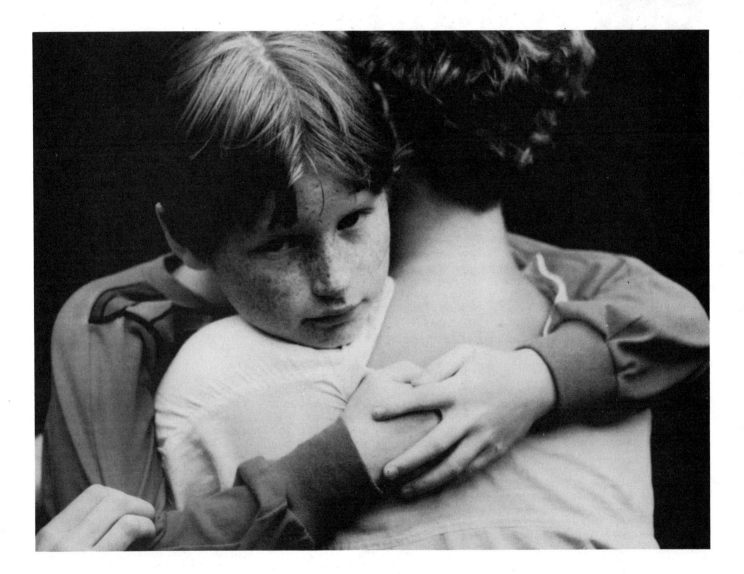

What is the polygraph? Does it measure lying? Can it detect what emotion a person is experiencing? What are the limitations of this device?

How does a mood differ from an emotion? Why do people become moody or experience bad moods? What are the four mood styles identified in the article "How to Master Your Moods"? Is there anything we can do to beat a bad mood? When is professional help recommended for bad moods?

What is happiness? Can we maintain a constantly happy state? Do some people expect too much of life; that is, do some people search for perpetual happiness? What are the different paths to happiness?

Is there a link between the immune system and negative emotions? Cite research to support your answer.

Does the brain play a role in motivation? Give an example. What region of the brain controls eating? How do neurochemicals affect eating? Why don't some diets work?

Why are people competitive? Can individuals be too competitive? What are the consequences of having a highly competitive personality?

Where emotions come from

Joy and disgust. Sorrow and shame. Science is plumbing the passions that make us human

"We humans are full of unpredictable emotions that logic cannot solve."
—Capt. James Kirk, "Star Trek"

Pop singer Morris Albert crooned about them. Wives complained that their husbands wouldn't discuss them. And by the 1970s, an entire generation of Americans had learned to "get in touch" with their feelings. Scientists, however, were preoccupied with thinking, not emotion. Rational thought, after all, was the faculty deemed by the English philosopher Francis Bacon "the last creature of God." Leagues of researchers devoted their attention to how people solved problems, made decisions, formed opinions and learned skills. Fear and joy, anger and disgust were seen as peripheral, of interest mostly when they interfered with thought or became deviant or extreme, as in mental illness.

It was, in the words of psychologist Silvan Tomkins, an "overly imperialistic cognitive theory." Tomkins, who died last week at age 80, published two thick volumes in the early 1960s arguing that emotions were a crucial component of evolutionary design, even more important than basic drives such as hunger and sex. Anxiety, he pointed out, could drive a man from the bedroom. Fear could pre-empt appetite. Despair could lead to a fatal flirtation with a razor blade.

Tomkins was a lone voice, and he was almost entirely ignored by mainstream

psychology. Yet there was a very small core of scientists who took his work seriously, and, building upon it, began to pioneer a new field of emotion research. Today, in disciplines ranging from psychology to neuroscience, from semiotics to genetics and anthropology, emotions have moved center stage. What was once a trickle of journal articles has become a publishing torrent. Researchers have developed methods for mapping the face and measuring emotional responses. They are studying the development of emotions in infants. Their work meshes with the efforts of biologists and neuroscientists who, using increasingly sophisticated technologies, were beginning to trace the "pathways" of emotion in the brain. Cognitive scientists, too, are talking about "hot" cognition, realizing that emotions and moods influence memory, judgment and learning.

It is not that there are, as yet, any solid answers. Even the most elemental question posed by turn-of-the-century psychologist William James—"What is an emotion?"—remains controversial. But researchers are beginning to untangle the first threads of an enormously complex tapestry, finding clues not only to normal emotions but also to how feelings go awry, fear turning to phobia, sadness to debilitating depression.

In the process, they are rejecting the notion of man as simply a "thinking machine," seeing human beings instead as biological organisms whose survival de-

pends upon constant interaction with the environment. In this interplay, evolved over countless centuries and through dozens of steps on the evolutionary ladder, emotions have a critical role. Far from being "trivial," they contain, as one expert put it, "the wisdom of the ages"—warning us of danger, guiding us toward what is good and satisfying, signaling our intentions and our reactions to others. Emotions are the most familiar—and the most intimate—aspect of human experience, and they are gradually yielding their secrets.

Brain researchers, like other scientists, have spent much of the 20th century engrossed in the study of thinking and memory. But earlier investigators took some first steps toward tracing the biological underpinnings of emotion. In the late 1900s, for example, physiologists discovered that surgically removing a dog's cerebral cortex—the brain's thin outer layer of gray matter—did not prevent it from displaying primitive rage responses. By the late 1950s, researchers were identifying specific brain regions that seemed to play a central role in emotion. But only in the last few years have high-tech brain scanners, new methods of staining cells, powerful computers and other developments allowed scientists to begin systematically mapping the highways and traffic patterns of the emotional brain.

Neural pathways. While earlier in-

FALSE OR GENUINE?

FALSE OR GENUINE?
Anatomy of a smile

GRIMACE & GRIN
Faces of emotion

Not all smiles are the same. Psychologist Paul Ekman describes 18 different types, including the miserable smile, the false "cocktail party" smile and the smile of relief, each marked by different movements of the facial muscles. Most striking is the disparity between the "social" smile and the smile of true enjoyment, called the "Duchenne smile" after French anatomist Duchenne de Boulogne, who first described it in 1862. Smiles of real joy draw in the *Orbicularis oculi* muscle around the eyes, as well as the *Zygomaticus major* cheek muscle (see below). But when people put on a phony expression of pleasure, they smile only with their cheeks, not their eyes. Ten-month-old infants, experts find, are more apt to display a Duchenne smile when their mother approaches, while the approach of strangers often elicits "false" smiles.

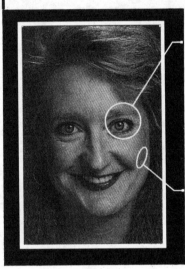

ORBICULARIS OCULI MUSCLE. This muscle "does not obey the will," wrote Duchenne de Boulogne, but "is put in play only by the sweet emotions of the soul . . ."

ZYGOMATICUS MAJOR MUSCLE. Faked smiles exercise voluntary cheek muscles; eye muscles remain unsmiling.

ANXIETY. When people are anxious, cerebral blood flow—a measure of brain cell activity—increases in an area at the tips of the brain's temporal lobes just behind the eyes, according to brain scanning studies by University of Arizona psychiatrist Eric Reiman.

DISGUST. Would you stir your coffee with a new comb? Eat a sterilized cockroach? Most Americans wouldn't, though both are perfectly safe. Psychologist Paul Rozin argues that the things we find disgusting often evoke primitive beliefs about contamination.

HAPPINESS. Moments of intense happiness are not necessarily the key to an overall sense of well-being, says psychologist Ed Diener. Long-term happiness, his studies suggest, depends more on the frequency than the vividness of happy experiences.

EMBARRASSMENT. Darwin believed blushing was like the appendix, a fluke with no purpose. But Wake Forest University psychologist Mark Leary finds that turning red may serve to repair people's social image after they have appeared stupid or incompetent.

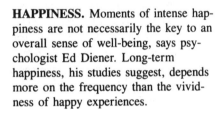

vestigators probed the emotional roles played by specific brain regions, scientists now put more emphasis upon the complex circuitry that interconnects them. Until recently, the limbic system, a loose network of brain structures beneath the cortex, was thought to do the majority of the work in coding "emotional" information and orchestrating the body's responses. But studies are now linking more and more areas of the brain—both the cortex and in subcortical regions—to the complex mix of perceptions, sensations and judgments we call emotion.

At the same time, brain centers once viewed as intimately involved in emotions are now known to be more marginal. The sea horse-shaped hippocampus, for example, one of several limbic regions, appears more involved in memory and other cognitive tasks than in emotion, as previously believed. Much more critical, scientists are finding, is a tiny almond called the amygdala, buried deep in the temporal lobe (see diagram).

Indeed, the fingernail-size amygdala, which communicates with many other brain areas, is increasingly being viewed as a kind of "Emotion Central." As far back as 1937, studies showed that damage to the amygdala region produced changes in emotional behavior in monkeys: They became tame and oblivious to normally frightening situations, copulated with other monkeys of the same sex and ate nearly anything they were offered. Recent work has refined this understanding—showing, for example, that amygdala nerve cells fire selectively in response to emotionally laden stimuli, and that some of these neurons are more sensitive to unfamiliar stimuli.

Quick and dirty. According to New York University neuroscientist Joseph LeDoux, the amygdala may make the first, crude judgment of an event's emotional significance. Consider a man walking through a forest who hears what sounds like a rifle shot at close range. Scientists previously believed that sensory information traveled first to the cerebral cortex, where the sound was consciously perceived. The cortex then sent signals to subcortical areas of the brain like the amygdala, which eval-

An emotional "shortcut"

The brain appears "programmed" to size up the emotional importance of certain stimuli, such as a flash of light, much more quickly than scientists once thought. Researchers previously knew that information taken in by the senses (1) travels to the thalamus (2), an early sensory processing station, then to the cortex (3), where it is consciously taken in and relayed to subcortical areas of the brain such as the amygdala (4). These interior regions then send messages back to the cortex, and also set in motion physiological responses (5). But neuroscientist Joseph LeDoux has found an additional and more direct pathway btween thalamus and amygdala that bypasses the cortex completely. In primitive emotions like fear, nerve impulses transmitted along this route reach the amygdala two to three times faster, allowing a "quick and dirty" judgment of whether the stimulus is something to be afraid of—probably even before it is consciously perceived. This assessment is then elaborated by thinking and memory.

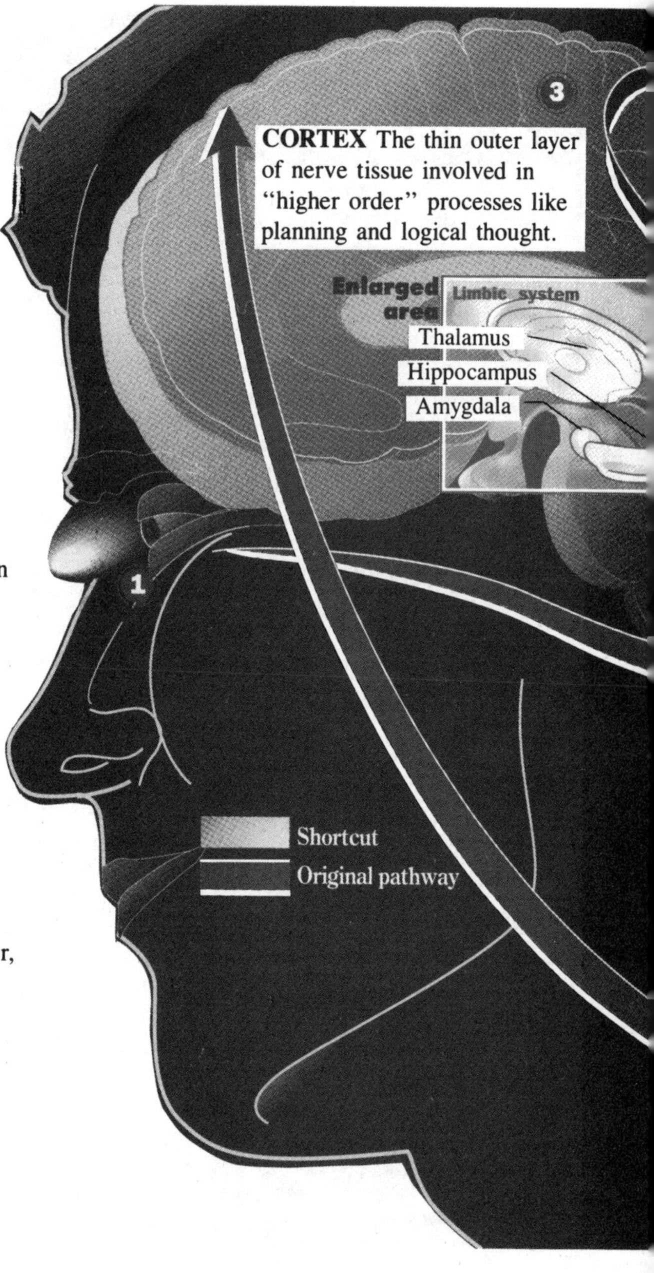

MATT ZANG—*USN&WR*

CORTEX The thin outer layer of nerve tissue involved in "higher order" processes like planning and logical thought.

Enlarged area

Limbic system

Thalamus
Hippocampus
Amygdala

Shortcut
Original pathway

uated the sound's emotional importance. These "lower" regions then sent return messages back up to the cortex and fired up the autonomic nervous system, producing the pounding heart, rapid breathing and rising blood pressure that are the familiar accompaniments of fear.

But LeDoux's research indicates that, at least for primitive emotions like fear, the brain is constructed to respond even more quickly to potentially threatening events. He and his colleagues have identified in animals an additional nerve pathway carrying impulses directly between the thalamus—an early processing station for sensory input—and the amygdala. Information sent along this "shortcut" reaches the amygdala two to three times faster than that sent

up to the cortex first. Studies also demonstrate that even when the "longer" route through the cortex is destroyed, animals still are able to learn fear of sudden noises, or, in very recent work, flashing lights.

Such high-speed transmission, LeDoux contends, may allow the amygdala to make an almost instantaneous analysis of whether the sound is something to be afraid of, probably even before it is consciously heard or identified. This "quick and dirty" assessment, he speculates, is then elaborated and refined by the neocortex and other brain regions, allowing the hunter to conclude, for example, that the sound was the crack of a tree branch, not a rifle.

LeDoux's findings support the view that at least some emotional processes

take place unconsciously, and that cognition and emotion—though they interact—are separate systems in the brain—both points that have been vigorously debated for decades. In addition, the studies imply that the brain is designed, quite sensibly from an evolutionary standpoint, to react more to some things—loudness, for instance, or abrupt movement—than to others.

No fear of mushrooms. The idea that human beings are "programmed" to be wary of particular events may help explain why some people develop irrational fears of spiders, snakes, heights or close spaces, but never of electrical outlets or daffodils. Northwestern University psychologist Susan Mineka and her coworkers have found that monkeys quickly acquire an exaggerated fear of

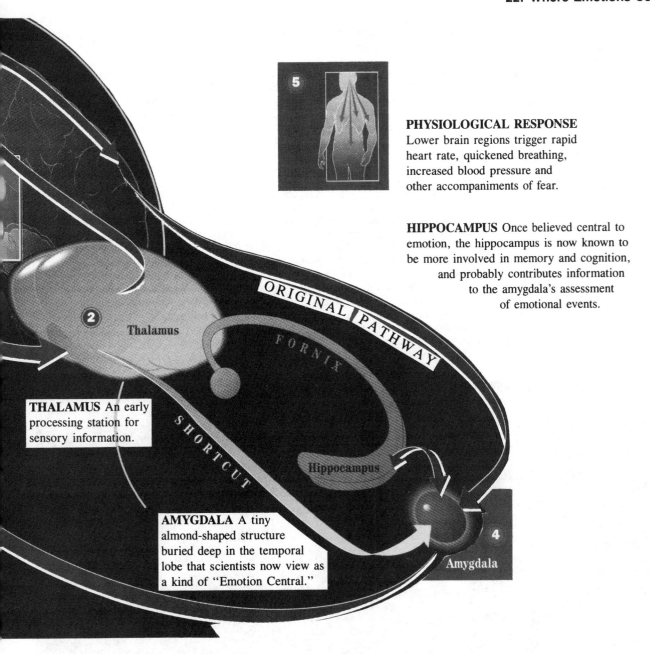

5

PHYSIOLOGICAL RESPONSE
Lower brain regions trigger rapid
heart rate, quickened breathing,
increased blood pressure and
other accompaniments of fear.

HIPPOCAMPUS Once believed central to
emotion, the hippocampus is now known to
be more involved in memory and cognition,
and probably contributes information
to the amygdala's assessment
of emotional events.

2
Thalamus

ORIGINAL PATHWAY

FORNIX

THALAMUS An early
processing station for
sensory information.

SHORTCUT

Hippocampus

AMYGDALA A tiny
almond-shaped structure
buried deep in the temporal
lobe that scientists now view as
a kind of "Emotion Central."

4

Amygdala

snakes—even toy reptiles that don't
move—when they watch videotapes of
other monkeys reacting fearfully. But if
the same monkeys watch concocted videos of monkey role models jumping in
fright at mushrooms or flowers, they
remain unswayed.

Twenty years ago, much was made of
reports that the brain's left and right
hemispheres seemed to "specialize" in
different types of thinking, though media
accounts of this "right brain/left brain"
division were often greatly oversim-
plified. Now a growing body of work
suggests that the two sides of the brain
may play distinct emotional roles, perhaps because such a division of labor is
more efficient. Neurologists have known
for many years that stroke patients whose

right hemispheres have been damaged
have trouble both expressing emotion
and perceiving the emotional signals of
others. They will understand the statement, "I am angry," for example, but fail
to detect the speaker's injured tone or the
angry expression on his face.

University of Florida neurologist Kenneth Heilman suggests that the right
hemisphere may contain a kind of "lexi-
con" of emotion-laden images, which is
impaired when the hemisphere is injured. In a series of studies, Heilman and
his colleagues found that patients with
right hemisphere damage had great difficulty imagining and describing a smiling
face, though they could easily describe
imagined objects such as pennies or
horses. Yet such patients do retain some

ability to grasp emotional concepts, the
scientists have found, perhaps relying
upon a combination of logical reasoning
and past experience. Told that a man
"drank the water and then saw the sign,"
for example, they can usually figure out
that the man is anxious about what he just
drank.

The brain's right and left hemispheres may divide negative and positive emotions as well. When subjects report feeling emotions such as fear and
disgust, their right frontal lobes show
increased electrical activity, according
to studies by psychologists Richard Davidson at the University of Wisconsin
and Donald Tucker at the University of
Oregon. Sadness seems to diminish activity in the left frontal lobe as measured

by an electroencephalogram (EEG), while certain positive emotions like happiness and amusement increase it.

Right and left brain asymmetries may even prove to be a marker of differences in overall temperament. In a series of studies, Davidson and his colleagues have found that infants more prone to distress when separated from their mothers show increased activity in the right frontal lobe, as do people with a more pessimistic outlook. People who have at some point in their lives been clinically depressed show decreased left frontal lobe activity compared with subjects who have never been depressed.

Such emotional lopsidedness, Davidson suggests, may be adaptive in a broader, evolutionary sense. Positive emotions draw people toward things that are pleasant or satisfying, engaging them with the world; negative emotions encourage withdrawal from what may be threatening or dangerous. In the hostile environment in which early man

evolved, it may have been useful to have approach and avoidance unmistakably delineated in the brain.

"Your face, my thane, is a book where men may read strange matters," Lady Macbeth warns her husband in Shakespeare's great tragedy, knowing that a furrowed brow or curled lip can be a revealing barometer of emotional life. But it remained for psychologists, inspired by Silvan Tomkins, to develop systematic ways to measure and compare the precisely tuned movements of more than 30 facial muscles, and to link the language of sneers, smiles and grimaces to other aspects of emotion.

Their work has challenged long-held assumptions about facial expression. It was widely believed, for example, that the way emotions are expressed by the face was learned after birth and differed from culture to culture. But in cross-cultural studies over the past two decades, psychologists Paul Ekman at the University of California at San

Francisco and Carroll Izard of the University of Delaware have demonstrated that facial representations of sadness, fear, anger, disgust and other emotions are remarkably constant and recognizable around the globe.

Darwin's delight. The social roles for displaying emotion *do* vary culturally. The Japanese, for example, are more likely to hold back negative expressions in public. Individuals, of course, also differ in the intensity of their emotional expressions, and to some extent in the events that trigger different emotions. But the researchers found familiar scowls and grins even in members of isolated cultures in New Guinea and Indonesia and in blind children, who cannot learn them by visual imitation.

Such findings would have pleased biologist Charles Darwin, who explored the universality of emotion in his 1872 book, "The Expression of Emotions in Man and Animals" (see box). The findings are equally sweet to modern investigators who believe that humans possess innate,

ANCIENT TRADITION

The philosophy of feeling, the biology of barks

The nature of emotion has bedeviled great thinkers ever since Cain slew Abel in a jealous rage. Plato and Aristotle argued over how sharply the "rational" and "irrational" parts of the "soul" were divided -- a question that modern scientists, with a modern vocabulary, still quarrel about. Philosophers proposed master lists of "basic" emotions, only to have the next pundit in line revise them or object that there were no such things – an avocation still popular among emotion researchers.

Enlightenment theories of emotion tended to credit mysterious fluids for emotional life, regarding emotions as "provided by God to protect us," says Colby College philosopher Cheshire Calhoun, co-author of "What is an Emotion?" Descartes, for example, explained that the approach of a "strange and frightful figure" triggers the action of "animal spirits" that "proceed thence to take their places partly in the nerves ... and dispose the legs for flight."

In the 19th century, the notion of emotional "instincts" grew stronger. But William James, writing in 1890, contended that the experience of "feeling" followed the physiological sensa-

Darwin's dogs. *Patterns for hostility (bottom) and humble affection (top)*

tions of emotion, rather than the other way around. "We feel sorry because we cry, angry because we strike, afraid because we tremble," James asserted.

But the scientist who first tried to study emotional expression systemati-

cally was not a psychologist but a biologist, Charles Darwin, who delved into emotion to gather support for his broader theory of evolution, contended that emotions were universal and not unique to human beings. He described characteristic displays of fear, rage or joy in a variety of animals, including dogs, monkeys, swans and cats. A dog, Darwin pointed out, stiffens, its tail erect, the hairs on its neck bristling when it approaches a stranger. But upon recognizing its master, its demeanor instantly changes to one of affectionate submission.

Human beings required different tactics of study. Darwin sent out questionnaires to missionaries and ambassadors around the globe, asking if emotional expressions were the same in different cultures. Among his questions: "Is astonishment expressed by the eyes and mouth being opened wide, and by the eyebrows being raised?"

Thirty-six questionnaires were returned to the biologist, allowing him to argue his case in his now classic 1872 book, "The Expression of Emotions in Man and Animals." Today, emotion theorists remain split between those who emphasize the contribution of thinking to emotional experience, and those who stress biology. But Darwin's belief that emotions are innate, adaptive mechanisms for dealing with the environment is slowly gaining ground in a field that once scorned such notions.

genetically wired templates of emotional expression and recognition, refined versions of those seen in primates and other "lower order" species.

But how does the face, with its Esperanto of feeling, fit into the larger emotional system—the rising pulse and rapid breathing of a man who has just been called a "sniveling scum bucket," for example, or the intangible experiences we label grief and joy? In an intriguing series of studies, their results still being debated, Ekman and his colleagues Robert Levenson and Wallace Friesen have shown that instructing people to produce the muscular movements of a particular emotional expression—a grimace of disgust, for example—produces changes in autonomic nervous system response, such as heart rate and skin temperature, even though the subjects are not told which emotion they are displaying. The scientists also found that these physiological patterns are, to some extent, specific for different emotional expressions, particularly negative ones such as anger, fear and disgust. The research team recently reported that distinctive heart rate and skin temperature patterns are also produced when subjects are asked to relive the memory of a particular emotional experience.

The person who communicates his feelings is, of course, only half the equation. In a complex social world, we are readers of emotion, too. Using ever more sophisticated tools, researchers are beginning to find out how the brain detects and analyzes emotional signals. Working with monkeys, for example, neuroscientist Edmund Rolls and his colleagues at Oxford University have isolated a group of nerve cells, located in part of the brain's temporal lobe that processes visual information, that respond exclusively to faces and appear capable of recognizing individual faces as well. A second set of neurons, about 2 millimeters away, apparently helps determine which emotion a face displays. Together, Rolls says, the two sets of cells allow monkeys—and probably humans as well—to determine who and what they are dealing with in the environment.

Unfamiliar faces. Just how crucial these mechanisms are is evident in the extraordinary case of a 41-year-old brain-injured patient studied over several years by Massachusetts Institute of Technology neuroscientist Nancy Etcoff. Mr. H., who suffered damage to the temporal lobes of his brain in a car accident many years ago, has no trouble conversing. He holds a responsible job and can quickly distinguish a Mercedes from a Mazda. But he has entirely lost the ability to recognize faces—even those of the people closest to him. He asks his wife to wear a ribbon

in her hair at parties, so he can tell her from the other guests. Arriving at his own house, Mr. H. will stare blankly at the two children in the driveway. "Are those your children?" Etcoff will ask him. "I guess they must be," her patient replies. "They're in my yard."

Yet Mr. H., whose condition is called prosopagnosia, still retains some ability to discern emotions, lending support to the notion that facial recognition and emotional interpretation are separate in the brain. Shown a picture of a sad face, he cannot at first name the feeling he sees. But he *is* able to mimic the downcast expression and in some way, Etcoff believes, this re-creation of sadness on his own face "teaches" his brain, which then correctly labels the emotion in the picture. Still, such maneuvering makes any sojourn into the social world difficult. Says Etcoff: "People who can't recognize facial emotions feel like they

can't read between the lines, and there's a tremendous awkwardness in relating to other people."

The snubbing of emotion in scientific theory was not confined to the study of adults. Child psychologists, too, were riveted by logical reasoning, as if infants and toddlers were, as one expert put it, "little computerized robots dealing with their environment." Even Swiss psychologist Jean Piaget—whose meticulous observations of his own children's intellectual growth serve as a primer for every student of child psychology—barely nodded at emotion, stressing instead the child's developing powers of thought and analysis. Feelings seemed irrelevant to infants, who could not even form goals or distinguish cause and effect.

In the last decade, the scientific work that has reshaped the understanding of emotion has transformed the field of

---

HORMONE OF LOVE

The chemistry of romance and nurturance

The romantic notion that love is a matter of the right chemistry may not be far off the mark. Scientists are now finding links between behavior and the brain's many chemicals; and recent animal studies of one particular hormone, oxytocin, suggest the chemical promotes the social bondings involved in choosing a mate and reproducing. Scientists speculate that the hormone may do the same for humans, fostering friendship, love and nurturance.

Oxytocin is well known for its ability to hasten childbirth and promote lactation, but it is also present in areas of the brain linked to emotions and seems to influence how animals relate to one another. For example, when the hormone is given to two prairie voles, according to zoologist Sue Carter, they immediately form a monogamous bond. In the wild, the small mammals pair up only after sex, when oxytocin floods their systems. In sociable mice, adding oxytocin boosts the instinct for cuddling to a frenzied pitch.

The hormone not only seems to ensure that animals are attracted in the first place, it also appears to promote good parenting later on. Studies by Cort Pedersen and Jack Caldwell at the University of North Carolina and Gustav Jirikowski at Scripps Research Institute show that virgin female rats,

normally nasty to babies, will respond to oxytocin by acting in a more motherly way. Parent rats will even mistreat their children if oxytocin is blocked.

In humans, oxytocin levels rise dramatically during sex, and scientists believe the chemical's presence may promote accompanying feelings of love or infatuation. Some researchers even suspect that oxytocin may play a part in most social behavior. "Human relations are influenced by the model of the parent-child relationship in that they include the notions of nurturing, care, help," says Pedersen. "The deficiency of a hormone tied to that parenting instinct may account for some of the anti-social behavior we think of as psychopathic."

Scientists emphasize that no hormone acts alone. Several dozen chemicals combine in intricate ways to influence emotions. "You will never find one specific hormone for one emotion," neurologist Marsel Mesulam notes. "Rather, it's the overall pattern that's important, just as in music it is the song that makes you feel happy or sad, not a particular instrument." Even so, scientists hope that understanding how oxytocin works may illuminate the most powerful of human emotions.

BY JOANNIE M. SCHROF

child psychology as well. A rapidly expanding body of work now makes it clear not only that infants have emotions, but that they are crucial from the very first moments of life. Nonverbal expressions of enjoyment, anger and other sentiments have been detected in children younger than 8 months old, and even a 10-week-old baby can distinguish his mother's smile of joy from her scowl of anger. "By nine months, the infant is an emotional being," writes Alan Sroufe, at the University of Minnesota.

It is not just that the infant is joyful upon seeing his mother's face or fearful at a loud noise. University of California at Berkeley developmental psychologist Joseph Campos and others argue that emotions are powerful tools for becoming a human being. Through them, children signal their needs and wants and are spurred to satisfy them. Feelings help forge—or sever—bonds with other people. By closely observing the emotional reactions of others—a mother's welcoming look when a stranger approaches, for example—a child also learns to size up uncertain situations, a process Campos and his colleagues call "social referencing."

Language adds sophistication and subtlety both to the expression of emotion and to children's ability to influence the feelings of others. By the age of 20 months, most children possess an emotional vocabulary, voicing in words their distress, pleasure or fatigue: In one study, each of six children said, "I love you" to a parent before his or her second birthday. By 28 months, discussions of feelings take place in a wide variety of contexts, from squabbles with siblings to pretend tea parties given for imaginary guests. And during their third year, children begin to refer to past and future states of emotion, and probe the reasons behind feelings, asking, for example, why an older brother is crying.

Jokes and affection. Experts in child development once devoted their attention mostly to how children learned to "damp down" emotional extremes, controlling tantrums, for example. But in groundbreaking studies, Pennsylvania State University child development expert Judith Dunn has shown that children also actively use emotional expression to obtain comfort, give affection, learn social rules, make jokes, irritate siblings, form friendships and deepen intimacy in relationships.

According to new research by Dunn's group, how much time parents devote to discussing emotions with their children may influence sensitivity to the feelings of others later in life. Studies indicate, for example, an association between the frequency of mothers' exchanges about emotions with firstborn children and the friendly behavior of those children toward their infant brothers and sisters. Dunn and her colleagues have recently suggested that the frequency and content of family conversations about feelings may affect children's ability to recognize emotions in adults six years later.

Even at birth, investigators are finding, children vary in their emotional reactions to people and events, suggesting a hereditary contribution to temperament. Studies of children over a period of time by Harvard University psychologist Jerome Kagan show marked differences between those who are "inhibited"—by which Kagan means shy, quiet and socially withdrawn—and their more talkative, outgoing and sociable peers. Kagan has found that inhibited children have higher and more stable heart rates, react more to stress and may be more prone to depression and anxiety disorders later in life.

Primatologists are now finding that similar temperamental differences are present in monkeys studied in the wild, and may play a role in evolutionary adaptation. Male rhesus monkeys who are highly reactive emotionally, for example, display differences in heart rate similar to those of Kagan's socially inhibited children, according to research by Stephen Suomi and Kathlyn Rasmussen of the National Institute of Child Health and Human Development. These heart rate patterns appear to predict how male monkeys will react at puberty, when they typically emigrate from their own troop and join another. Unusually "shy" monkeys, the scientists found, tend to hang back, working their way into the new group slowly over months or years, while more aggressive monkeys tend to fight their way into the group instead. Both strategies, says Suomi, have pros and cons: "Outgoing individuals have the opportunity to get into the gene pool earlier, but they run a greater risk of getting killed. Shy ones, slower to integrate, are at greater risk for starving to death, but their chances of being killed in a fight are lower."

Sadly, cancer stole the seven more books that Silvan Tomkins hoped to write. But before his death, he completed the final two volumes of "Affect/Imagery/Consciousness," the treatise he began 30 years ago. The books, one just published and the other soon to follow, make their appearance in a vastly changed climate. Emotion research is now everywhere, its importance no longer argued before indifferent auditors. Scientists, finally, are joining the poets in granting the "passions" their rightful place as "the elements of life."

BY ERICA E. GOODE WITH
JOANNIE M. SCHROF AND SARAH BURKE

A Doubtful Device

Lisa Davis

When Anita Hill took a polygraph test last year in the midst of the Clarence Thomas Pro-Am National Consciousness-Raising Debacle, it would have been hard to find a newspaper that didn't report the fact that she passed. A few months earlier Patricia Bowman, accuser of William Kennedy Smith, passed a lie detector test regarding her allegations—which helped the district attorney decide to file charges of rape. And last May, Virginia Governor Douglas Wilder pointed to a failed polygraph test in defending his decision to allow the execution of Roger Coleman, a convicted murderer who protested his innocence until being put to death just 12 hours after the test indicated he lied.

All of this goes on—all the tests, and all their life-changing consequences—despite the fact that for practical purposes the lie detector proves . . .

Nothing.

"An innocent person has about a fifty-fifty chance of failing a polygraph test," says David Lykken, psychologist at the University of Minnesota. "Society would be much better off if the polygraph were retired to a shelf in the Smithsonian."

To be fair, that assessment is offered by the polygraph's most vocal critic in an extremely acrimonious debate. Proponents of the lie-detector hotly dispute Lykken's claims and his statistics. But listen to one of the technique's best-known *supporters,* a researcher who says that under the proper conditions, the polygraph test has an accuracy rate of at least 90 percent.

"There's a great disparity between the potential of the polygraph and the way it's actually used," says University of Utah psychologist David C. Raskin.

"As far as I'm concerned, the whole Department of Defense polygraphy department is atrocious—and almost all the federal examiners are trained at the DOD institution. Polygraphers in law enforcement train at private schools, and most of those are terrible," says Raskin. "We're talking about a mess."

In other words, Raskin has complaints about the way the principles of the polygraph are put into practice; Lykken and other critics take on the principles themselves. So first things first. The idea behind the polygraph is a simple one, and compelling: We can lie, we can even do it convincingly—but we can't do it calmly.

If the lie detector can't tell an honest person from a practiced liar, then what good is it?

The awareness of deceit and the fear of detection inevitably produce physiological changes such as shallow breathing, surging blood pressure, and the sweaty palms familiar to every schoolchild.

Scientists began trying to assess credibility by measuring such changes as long ago as the late 1800s. The modern polygraph still retains the clumsy look of a proto-technological era: rows of knobs, scrolling paper charts, and trailing wires. The wires are connected to equipment worn by the test subject: a blood-pressure cuff, electrical sensors fitted onto two fingers to measure subtle changes in perspiration, and bands around the chest and abdomen that are sensitive to changes in breathing. As an examiner asks questions—Is your name Joe? Is today Friday? Did you take the diamond ring from the desk?—scribbling pens record the physiological responses.

There's no doubt that the polygraph measures physiological arousal. The question is what that arousal means. According to Leonard Saxe, a City University of New York psychologist who in 1983 led an analysis of the device for Congress, the polygraph simply shows whether a question makes someone anxious, and there are a thousand and one reasons that explain why a person hooked up to a polygraph might become anxious. For instance, you're worried because you're lying about a crime you committed. Or, you're afraid you're going to be convicted for a crime you didn't commit.

There are measures meant to prevent such an unhappy outcome, of course. A pre-test session is designed to reassure suspects about the test's accuracy. The examiner even goes over the questions ahead of time. In a perfect world, all this would leave only the guilty feeling nervous during the test.

As a backup measure in a manifestly imperfect world, polygraphers use what they call control questions. Interspersed with questions about the misbehavior at issue, control questions are intended to make even the innocent test-taker feel like a liar at key moments. Say Joe has been accused of theft. "I need to know whether you're the sort of person who could do this kind of thing," the examiner might say, though he or she is concerned about no such thing. "So I'm going to ask you whether before the age of 21 you ever stole something." If Joe mentions taking nickels from his mother at the age of six, the examiner prods—says, yes, but surely there was nothing *else,* was there?

The purpose of the put-on disapproval is to push Joe into lying, or at least into

By Lisa Davis. Reprinted with permission from *Hippocrates,* November/December 1992, pp. 28-29. © 1992 by Hippocrates Partners.

making a denial he's unsure of, while the polygraph measures the physiological responses during his deceit. It gives the examiner something to use for comparison as Joe answers the central questions of the polygraph test.

But what happens, asks Lykken, when an *innocent* person is more disturbed by a serious accusation than by the control questions? Lykken testified in one such case, in which a woman was eventually cleared of charges of molesting her son. "She failed the polygraph because when she was asked, 'Did you take Tommy's penis in your mouth?' it upset her more than the control question, 'Did you ever lie to stay out of trouble?'" Lykken says. "The jury, fortunately, believed her."

Unfortunately, the jury didn't believe Floyd "Buzz" Fay. Fay was arrested in 1978 for the shooting of a convenience-store clerk in Ohio. Three months later, he was in jail awaiting trial for murder when he was offered the chance to take a lie detector test, and was told that charges would be dropped if he passed. "I thought, hey, great—I can go home tomorrow," says Fay.

But the railroad worker failed the test, and failed a second one as well—results that were entered as evidence during his trial. Fay served nearly three years of a life sentence before an informant revealed the names of the real killers.

Polygraph proponent Raskin examined the test results when Fay, from his jail cell, sent them to polygraph experts. According to Raskin, while one of Fay's tests was unreadable, the other had been improperly scored. That's not a rare occurrence. Three of the four commonly used scoring systems are subjective, a matter of a polygrapher's deciding whether one response is "dramatically stronger" or merely "significantly stronger" than another.

Such judgments are prey to error, and the mistakes are more likely to be against the innocent than in favor of the guilty, according to Saxe. In Fay's case, says Raskin, the chart was full of difficult calls; and the examiner ruled every questionable response deceitful. "He probably looked at the case facts and said, 'This guy's clearly guilty,' and gave him the minimum guilty score," speculates Raskin.

> Anita Hill passed the polygraph test, which means she was either telling the truth or a practiced lie.

Polygraph tests are subject to another practical problem. They can be beaten, although it takes some training to do it well. A guilty person can boost his or her physiological response during non-threatening questions by biting the tongue, for instance, or clenching the toes. Done at the right moment, each faked response can make the reaction to crucial questions look mild by comparison. "If I set out to lead a life of crime, I could beat the test time and time again," says Fay, who has campaigned against the use of the polygraph since his release.

In 1989, Congress attempted to limit the opportunities for use *or* abuse of the polygraph, partly because the study led by psychologist Saxe found neither statistics nor other evidence to support the test's reliability. The Polygraph Protection Act made it illegal for most private businesses to use the device to try to weed out dishonest job applicants (or, as sometimes happens, applicants of unwanted sexual or political orientation).

But polygraphs are still used, and used frequently. Under certain circumstances, private employers are allowed to use the test during investigations of workplace theft. And according to psychologist Honts, the federal government administers at least 100,000 polygraph tests each year to screen potential employees, or during investigations of transgressions like leaks to the press or espionage.

Moreover, some courts still allow polygraph test results as evidence, under some circumstances. Researchers—both critics of the device and some supporters as well—are particularly worried by a related use. Women who allege that they've been raped have been pressured or even required to prove their truthfulness by passing a polygraph test. "The cards are really stacked against the victim coming across as truthful," Saxe says. "Her anxiety about anything relating to the attack may be so great that she may very easily appear deceptive."

So what does it mean if that woman passes, or if she fails? Or, to return to the well-known cases, what does it mean that Roger Coleman failed his polygraph test? According to Saxe, Raskin, and other experts, it could mean that he was lying about his innocence, or it could mean that *no one* could calmly answer a question carrying the penalty of death.

And what does it mean that Anita Hill passed a polygraph test? It could mean that she was telling the truth. Or, as Saxe points out (for the sake of argument only, since he was convinced by Hill's account), it could mean that Hill's physiological responses had been dampened by the hours of grueling cross-examination she'd already endured.

In other words, the polygraph results mean that Hill was telling either the truth or a practiced lie. Put it another way: The results prove . . . nothing.

How to Master Your Moods

Recognize your emotion style and make it work for you.

Do you often feel apprehensive but can't pinpoint any reason for your anxiety? Do you tend to experience intense feelings and think you're going to explode unless you express them immediately? Or are you the kind of person who secretly wonders why you're so restless, so quickly bored with jobs or romances?

Melvin Kinder, Ph.D.

If you're like most people, you may find that your moods are sometimes baffling. While everything we read tells us we should be able to *control* our emotions, we just can't seem to do it. The gap between what we feel and what we're told we *should* feel is a constant condemnation. What is wrong with us? The answer may be surprising.

As a therapist, I have always been intrigued by the psychological myths that give us misleading information and unrealistic expectations about ourselves. I believe that the core dilemma behind our problems in our relationships, our work, and our sense of self is that we have neglected the emotional cornerstone of who we are. Under the layers of "shoulds" and "should nots" about our feelings is the source of our true, **instinctive emotional response**—what I call the natural self.

The exciting news is that our emotions may be largely biochemical—not a product of childhood traumas, moral deficiencies, the wrong husband, the wrong job, and so forth. But we're still operating on old ideas and outdated theories about why we feel the way we do. As a result, we're left confused and disheartened by the puzzling and enigmatic nature of our emotions. The new findings point to their true source:

- **Our emotions have biological origins.**
- **Each of us is born with an emotional temperament.**
- **Who we are and how we react to the world around us is determined more by these inborn traits than by environment or our upbringing.**

The answer then to the question of "what's wrong with me" may well be a combination of false expectations and **denying your natural self.**

Indisputably, life experiences shape us in many ways, but they are not the most important determinants. Our natural temperament will give the signature, the definitive mark, to who we are, how we navigate through the world. And, when you understand this, you will find that it is *liberating* rather than imprisoning— you will know exactly why you feel the way you do and what you need to do in order to feel better.

And you'll feel more at ease with those around you.

The Four Temperament Types

As my observations crystallized over the years, I eventually identified distinct similarities and differences between my clients. Four emotional types emerged:

1. The Sensor—prone to be extra sensitive to outer stimulation; sometimes wonderfully sensitive, other times overly anxious and fearful.

2. The Seeker—craves sensation and is emotionally satisfied with its quest; can also be inclined to unhappy cravings and unsettling restlessness and boredom.

3. The Discharger—vents his or her feelings; can be spontaneous, expressive, and passionate, but is also prone to anger and easily set off by frustrations.

4. The Focuser—prone to excessive awareness of inner feelings or lack of them; can be delicately aware and inwardly focused, but is also prone to worry and sadness.

From *Psychology Digest*, Summer 1994, pp. 56-62. Excerpted from *Mastering Your Moods* by Melvin Kinder. © 1994 by Melvin Kinder. Reprinted by permission of Simon & Schuster, Inc.

The Sensor is perceptive, empathetic, even soulful and sensual. Sensors are aware of every nuance of mood in people around them but often feel too much and become overwhelmed. They are predisposed to anxiety; life can be too intense, too painful—there are far too many ups and downs. People inclined to emotional sensitivity often feel touchy, high-strung, tense, nervous. Many sensors ignore their fears and lead, risk, socialize, and compete with the most thick-skinned and outgoing of the pack. They are very likely to rush into that which they fear.

Digest Synopsis: Each of us is born with a particular emotional style that, to some extent, dictates our emotions. By working within our style, we can be less vulnerable to unpleasant moods.

These are broad groups, and there are individual differences within each group, but the similarities outweigh the differences. Each temperament type has a biochemical base that dictates emotional patterns and responses in any situation. In addition, each temperament has an emotional *comfort zone*—a range of experiences, intensity, and stimulation—that each of us finds tolerable. When we're pushed outside our comfort zone, we're vulnerable to unpleasant emotions and moods.

Our goal, therefore, is to expand our emotional comfort zone so that we are less vulnerable to bad feelings, and more comfortable with a broader range of experience. I believe it is possible to become educated about your temperament and to work within that context to achieve a more genuine sense of self as well as emotional self-confidence.

Sensors: From Anxiety to Courage

Sherry, a marketing executive, loves and hates her work at the same time. At 33, she already felt burned out, mentally exhausted, and fearful that she would fall behind and no longer be considered a player in her industry.

In childhood she had been shy, hypersensitive, and timid in new situations. Her parents had pushed her to be more outgoing; consequently, Sherry forced herself to act confident in spite of her feelings. As an adult, she still feels nervous and secretly views herself as scared rather than courageous.

Profile

• **In relationships:** Your emotional sensitivity and ability to empathize can cause serious problems in a marriage. The danger is that you can be so afraid to displease your mate that you compromise your own goals and values.

• **Friendships:** You typically establish friendships in a slower and more cautious manner than others. Wary of possible threats, you implicitly require that others prove their trustworthiness. Yet when trust is established, you may be more steadfast and loyal.

• **As a parent:** You're likely to be caring and attentive, building your life around home and family. You may, however, find that you're oversensitive to your children's needs and need to encourage autonomy and independence in them.

• **At work:** You work best in a secure atmosphere where there is little turnover. You are most comfortable with a defined work role, and with the right combination of prodding and reassurance, you work creatively and confidently.

The Sensor's Task

The key to enlarging your comfort zone is to stop avoiding and start facing threats. "Systematic desensitization" means

---

Myths About Emotions

1. The Myth of Uniformity: We are all alike in our emotional makeup. All "normal" and "healthy" people should feel and respond in the same ways.

2. The Myth of Good and Bad: Feelings are either good or bad; unpleasant feelings are bad and should be eliminated.

3. The Myth of Control: We can and should strive to control our emotions.

4. The Myth of Perfectibility: We can and should strive for psychological perfection.

5. The Myth of Emotional Illness: Emotional distress is a sign of mental illness.

6. The Myth of Positive Thinking: We create what we feel by what we think. We believe "it's all in our minds" and willpower can change our emotions.

gradual exposure to feared situations. In time, less anxiety is aroused by employing mental imagery and visualization. For example, the more you rehearse a speech in your mind, the less anxious you may feel giving it.

1. First become aware of your body and its signals of arousal, including breathing, sweating, jitters, lack of concentration, fearful thoughts. Begin looking at these as natural and commonplace. Start reminding yourself that they won't kill you. Awareness defuses the power of these signals.

2. Rehearse in your mind situations that trigger your arousal. Close your eyes and think about that scary date, the talk you have to give, or a boss criticizing you. Now focus solely, coolly, and deliberately on what you feel in your body. Some desensitization will occur. Arousal will tend to decrease as you are now raising your threshold.

3. Next, do the last step in real life. Pick out a scary situation. Maybe it's a phone call you've been avoiding. Let arousal wash over you as you deliberately face the anxiety-provoking situation. You'll find you're not overwhelmed.

4. Inventory the situations and people that overstimulated you and take them on. But don't expect to have lost your temperament entirely.

Seekers live in a perpetual state of craving. Classic extroverts—gregarious and assertive—they are driven to reach goals they set for themselves. In a society that values achievement and action, they are often held in high regard. Their relentless drive often translates into success. Yet for every entrepreneur or sportsperson or dynamo, there is probably a seeker who is a compulsive gambler, romance addict, or alcoholic. There are also seekers who have never found their niche in life—people with big ideas and too little luck or opportunity.

P A R T N E R S

Potentially Problematic Pairings

The Focuser/Sensor Couple

While the focuser tends to criticize and make demands, the sensor is predisposed to feeling anxious. And the no-win battle is engaged. As the sensor withdraws, the focuser worries and becomes more critical. The bruised sensor withdraws even more. Bad chemistry.

The Focuser/Seeker Couple

The focuser is threatened by the seeker. Focusers are biochemically "allergic" to any threat of loss. The seeker's elusiveness, noncommitment, and inevitable abandonment can throw the focuser into a depression. The focuser can be easily shattered by a love affair with a seeker.

The Sensor/Sensor Couple

The cautious sensor often marries a sensor who denies their own temperament and blindly reaches far beyond their comfort zone. They may empathize with each other's anxiety and feel understood. But they may encounter contagious anxiety. When they sense the other's apprehension, they may pull away. One reads the other's withdrawal as rejection, and apprehension doubles.

The Sensor/Seeker Couple

The sensor is easily threatened, but intimidation is often overpowered by fascination with the courageous, charismatic seeker. Chemistry pops and crackles when the timid sensor feels a contact high of boldness and confidence in connecting with the seeker.

The Discharger/Sensor Couple

It's not uncommon for the male sensor to be with a woman who seems loud, overbearing, and overcontrolling. One may cringe and think this woman will push him over the edge. But it doesn't happen. If they've been together long enough, he feels secure in her love for him, even though others may not see it. Security can override a confrontational style.

Seekers: From Craving to Contentment

Janet often wondered, "What's wrong with me that I feel so bored and empty when I'm doing everything right? I thought I had grown out of that phase." Feeling ashamed and morally defective for secretly missing the drama and excitement of her past, she was unaware that her innate emotional biochemistry had set up her craving for adventure and sensation.

Profile

• **In relationships:** You can be a challenge as a husband or wife. Your intense emotional hunger sends out powerful messages that you cannot be satisfied by one person for long. Your mate can easily fear that you will abandon him or her.

• **Friendships:** You gather friends effortlessly, looking for others who are engaging and enlivening. But if the relationship becomes dull or routine, you may easily tire of it.

• **As a parent:** You are both dynamically engaging and a bit of a burden because you have little time for quietude and patience—the hallmarks of good parenting. Yet by providing intensity and stimulation, you can also be an interesting parent.

• **At work:** You prove outstanding in career situations that are goal and results oriented. You prefer to work in situations where your energy remains unfettered; you do well in leadership roles.

The Seeker's Task

When you are not in motion, you feel underaroused—and you loathe this dead feeling. Your innate tendency to escape is to seek external stimuli. Your task therefore is to learn to tolerate periods of calm and relaxation, and to alternate these with constructive, challenging activities that will satisfy your needs.

1. Search for behaviors that will provide a counterbalance to sensation seeking. Alternate between moderate sensation and calm. Balance is the key for the seeker—not sitting on the middle ground but somewhere between calm and sensation.

2. Find calmness on a daily basis. When you are *overly* intense, your thermostat becomes conditioned to register only high-level sensations or emotions. You can gradually reset your emotional thermostat so that you feel satisfied more often.

3. Find a variety of sources for your excitement. With several diverse focuses—work, love, sports, community—you don't deplete individual parts of your life.

Dischargers: From Anger to Release

Ellen's friends describe her as vivacious, charming—and fiery: "the most loyal person I know, but at the drop of a hat, she gets hurt and angry." Ever since she was a child, Ellen had been excitable and temperamental. Secretly, she felt uncomfortable with her emotional reactivity. Whenever she had an outburst, she felt ashamed afterward.

Profile

• **In relationships:** Often, you will find a passive partner who admires you and won't challenge your authority—a classic dominant/submissive role split. You can have the satisfac-

> *Dischargers are demonstrative, quick to react to others, not afraid of interpersonal clash. Containing their emotions is foreign to them—intense feelings must be expressed. But they are also easily frustrated and likely to vent on anyone who happens to be handy, often feeling ashamed after expressing their anger.*

tion of venting your feelings without being suppressed or punished for doing so.

• **Friendships:** You often feel frustrated, disappointed, hurt, or ignored by the people around you. And you find creative ways to tell them off or put them in their place.

• **As a parent:** You may be seen as overbearing, but you are not mean or bad. You are expressive, and your children may be fearful at times, but will still feel loved. Indeed, your children will always know where they stand.

• **At work:** Often one of two people—a dynamic leader or a source of problems for yourself and those around you. When you get into emotional difficulty, it is usually because you have not harnessed your energy in adaptive and positive ways.

The Discharger's Task

Simple or brief expression of your anger will do the job, but you need to shift attention away from the target and back onto the arousal. Such catharsis has an inherent appeal for the discharger, for release is partly what is needed. Express your emotion in a way that does no harm to others or yourself: Don't hit people or things, don't insult others, and don't tell off your boss or your best friend. These are all self-defeating strategies. Venting anger briefly while you are alone is sufficient to air your arousal.

What the discharger needs to realize is that the majority of the time when they are aroused, the arousal comes from within. It often has no meaning or purpose, but is a biological phenomenon.

1. Identify the triggers in your life. Most are familiar and need no analysis: your spouse, a boss, a friend, a family feud, even a political figure. The spark may be internally generated with no apparent trigger.

2. Don't stifle your anger. It only builds up because your arousal will build, but don't just let it blow. Follow the next step.

3. Allow yourself some release or catharsis. Move away from the target—leave the room, go for a walk. As you walk, clench your muscles, breathe deeply, expel your anger with your breath, yell, walk vigorously, and swing your arms. You have to do something with the energy or it loops back into your arousal. Benign release raises your threshold and the arousal-caused anger drops.

4. Distract your thoughts from the target. You may have to analyze the situation later, but focusing on the target will typically make you angrier.

Focusers: From Moody to Alive

For years, Willis worked long hours. Both his wife and his cardiologist were concerned. His symptoms ranged from a sense of agitation, to exhaustion, to an inner "hollowness"— he felt that life was meaningless. Yet it was obvious that whenever he spoke about his work, he came alive. It was at home that he most often found himself feeling blue. "Am I exhausted and depressed because I'm a workaholic?" he asked.

> *Focusers' strengths include a heightened ability to concentrate on, analyze, and devise solutions to intricate issues or projects. Their vulnerabilities are boredom, sadness, and worry, especially when they're not busy. In times of quiet, they may work themselves into anxious, unsettled moods, imagining worst-case scenarios.*

THERAPY

How to Reset Your Emotional Thermostat

We cannot change the biological determinants of our feelings. What we can do is change the way we relate to our emotions and modify the ways we respond to them.

1. Accept the Unchangeable
Any desire to alter our psychological existence starts at the moment of acceptance, when we automatically alter how we experience our feelings.

2. Embrace Your Temperament
Acceptance is an active process. It is not passive, nor is it resignation. Enlarge your comfort zones if you choose to. But I have found that many people are satisfied by simply understanding why they feel the way they do and have no need and/or discipline to systematically modulate their emotions.

3. Be Patient
I cannot overemphasize the importance of pure understanding. So often in therapy, patients get, well, impatient. As I explain my ideas or observations, they will say, "Yeah, okay. I get it. Now what do I do?"

This happens in any therapy. What the patient is saying is, "I don't care about *theory,* I don't want to *analyze* and all that. I only want to fix things fast, and get rid of whatever it is I'm feeling." Some patients don't realize that any strategies or processes built on self-deception or self-rejection are doomed to fail—that denial is the very core of their problem.

4. Accept Your Limitations
As you assess your own ebbing and flowing of emotions and arousal, whether at work or in your personal life, it is your choice to do what you need to do. You can learn to design your own comfort zone through awareness of your response patterns.

Realize that your emotional style is innate and unchangeable. With enlightened acceptance, you can begin to carve out new goals, new strategies for feeling better—for truly *mastering* your emotional life.

6. EMOTION AND MOTIVATION

Profile

• **In relationships:** You are usually drawn to people who excite you. The quest for love and for someone who will change everything—to save you from your moodiness or boredom—is likely to be the solution to your internal lack of arousal.

• **Friendships:** You are certainly a good friend, but you may have difficulty trusting people. The fear that you are not getting enough back from your friends may trouble you.

• **As a parent:** You probably worry a lot more than other parents. The good news is you are also very conscientious and consistent in your loving and protectiveness.

• **At work:** You can be an outstanding employee—analytical, precise, and attentive to details. Yet you may also get bogged down in details, become overanalytical, and may lose time fixating on problems.

The Focuser's Task

Find an ideal balance between attentiveness and distraction. Many of us shift between the two instinctively. If we become too worried, we'll get up, take a walk, return a phone call. By using distraction, the focuser finds emotional relief.

1. First, have faith. You often end up feeling very pessimistic. You may have withdrawn from the very activities in your life that would prove to be distracters because you feel sad or worried. You are ashamed of your emotions: you feel weak, vulnerable. You shame yourself into solitary confinement, where you can work your way deeper into a rut.

2. Deliberately focus, then distract. Deal with your emotions head on, without fear, and then take action to embrace distracters. This becomes a learning chain, by which you break the linkage between arousal and reflexive self-focusing.

3. Develop a repertoire of distracters: friends, sports activities, workout videos, movies, shopping. Even when distracters are only momentary, they can be effective, for they create room to break the fixation on self-focusing behavior and direct your attention elsewhere.

4. Take action. In the case of actual losses and real worries, for example, the appropriate action is to jump right in and find substitutes. If a romance ends, don't sit home and sink into sadness. If you suffer a career setback, don't work yourself into feeling worthless. Get busy facing the problem.

Chemistry &Craving

NOT

THE SAME OLD

DIET STORY

H A R A   E S T R O F F   M A R A N O

some revolutions are waged with guns. Others are waged with words. But perhaps the major American revolt of the past two decades has been waged primarily with knife and fork. With butter banished, red meat in retreat, and humble grains advancing on our plates, we've toppled the old dietary regime on the grounds that you are what you eat.

Still, decisive victories in the battle of the bulge, the war on heart disease, and just plain healthy appetites elude us. And so we begin each year with solemn vows to tackle anew our waistlines and our arteries. But if a behavioral scientist in New York is right, a winning strategy can come only from a simple turn of the tables—we eat what we are.

In meticulous studies over the last 10 years, Sarah F. Leibowitz, Ph.D., of The Rockefeller University, has discovered that what we put in our mouths and when we do it is profoundly influenced by a brew of neurochemicals based in a specific part of our brain. They not only guide our selection of morsels at breakfast, lunch, and dinner—and even the need for high tea—they are probably the power behind individual differences in appetite and weight gain. They appear to determine whether we are sitting ducks for the eating disorders that now afflict 30 percent of Americans.

Unless we take into account the physiological function of these brain chemicals in dictating natural patterns of food intake and metabolism, we will never get closer than annual avowals in regulating our eating behavior, whatever our reason for doing so. The only plausible way to control body weight is by working *with* the neurochemical systems that control appetite—and re-tuning them.

Leibowitz' studies point far beyond our forks. They challenge the deeply held belief that we are strictly self-determining individuals acting, at least at the table, by unfettered choice—whim, if the moon is right. Sooner or later, in one context or another, we will have to overhaul our view of human behavior to acknowledge that there are a variety of physiological signals guiding what we now believe to be free will.

Leibowitz, however, has little taste for the philosophical soup. In classic meat-and-potatoes neuroscience, she has located the epicenter of eating behavior. It is a dense cluster of nerve cells, the neurochemicals they produce, and the receptors through which they act and are acted upon. They make up the paraventricular nucleus, deep in the brain's hypothalamus, a structure toward the base of the brain already known to control sexuality and reproduction.

A Matter of Energy

The neurons that affect eating are part of the body's elaborate mechanism for regulating energy balance, the power ensuring that we take in sufficient fuel, in the form of food, to meet internal and external energy demands to survive from day to day. This is

> At the table, there are a variety of physiologic signals guiding what we now believe to be free will. Two brain chemicals—neuropeptide Y and galanin—control the appetite for carbohydrate-rich and fat-rich foods.

perhaps the body's most fundamental need.

Given so crucial a need, the location of the nerve cells of appetite in the hypothalamus is no accident of nature. They are the neurons next door to those that orchestrate sexual behavior. Leibowitz has found that we have clear-cut cycles of preference for high-carbohydrate and fat-rich foods, and they are closely linked to reproductive needs—that is, the ability of humans to survive from generation to generation. After all, the power to reproduce requires that we maintain a sufficient amount of body fat. The group of cells that tangle with sex and the cells that fancy our forks are in constant communication—like the sometimes overprotective mother she is, nature is constantly seeking reassurance that we have enough body fat for the survival of the species.

There are, in truth, many other brain areas that influence appetite. But from the lower brain stem up to the thalamus, which controls sensory processes such as taste, and on up to the forebrain and the cortex, where pleasure, affect, and cognitive aspects come into play, everything converges on the hypothalamus. The hypothalamus integrates all of the information affecting appetite. Its neurochemical signals coordinate our behavior with our physiology.

Through a daunting system of chemical and neural feedback, the brain monitors the energy needs of all body systems moment to moment. And it makes very emphatic suggestions to the stomach as to what we should ingest.

On the menu are the standard nutritional war-horses: carbohydrate for immediate fuel, fat for longer-term energy reserves—it is particularly essential for reproduction—and protein for growth and muscle maintenance. Directives from the brain to the belly are issued by way of neurochemical messengers and hormones. These directives, Leibowitz finds, have their own physiological logic, their own sets of rhythms, and are highly nutri-

Taste preferences for fat and carbohydrate, dictated by brain chemicals, show up early in life and reflect differences in genetic makeup.

ent-specific. There's one thing we now know for sure—the stomach definitely has a brain.

A Taste for Carbo

In the dietary drama unfolding in Leibowitz' ground-floor laboratory, there are two star players. One is Neuropeptide Y (NPY), a neurochemical that dictates the taste for carbohydrate. Produced by neurons in the paraventricular nucleus (PVN), it literally turns on and off our desire for carbohydrate-rich foods.

In animal studies the researcher has conducted, the amount of Neuropeptide Y produced by cells in the PVN correlates directly, positively, with carbohydrate intake. The more Neuropeptide Y we produce, the more we eat carbohydrate.

"These Cells Tell Us To Eat"

"We can see these neurons and analyze the neuropeptides in them," says Leibowitz. "We know that these cells tell us to eat carbohydrate. In studies, we either give injections of a known amount of Neuropeptide Y, or measure the amount of Neuropeptide Y that's naturally there. Then we correlate it to what the animal ate in carbohydrate." Neuropeptide Y increases both the size and duration of carbohydrate-rich meals.

If production of Neuropeptide Y turns on the taste for carbohydrate, what sets production of Neuropeptide Y spinning? Probably signals from the burning of carbohydrates as fuel are the routine appetite stimulants. But Leibowitz has found that cortisol, a hormone produced by the body during stress, has a particular propensity to turn on the taste for carbohydrate by revving up production of Neuropeptide Y. High levels of Neuropeptide Y lead to weight gain by prompting overeating of carbohydrate.

Fat's Chance

The body also has a built-in appetite system for fat, the most concentrated form of energy, and it marches to a different neurochemical drumbeat, a neuropeptide called galanin, also produced in the paraventricular nucleus of the hypothalamus. Galanin is the second star player in Leibowitz' studies.

These have shown that the amount of galanin an animal produces correlates positively with what the animal eats in fat. And that correlates with what the animal's body weight will become. The more galanin produced, the heavier the animal will become later on. To add insult to injury, galanin not only turns on the taste for fat, it affects other hormones in such a way as to ensure that fat consumed is turned into stored fat.

What turns on the taste for galanin? When the body burns stored fats as fuel, the resulting metabolic byproducts signal the paraventricular nucleus for more fat—a case of nature safeguarding our energy storage. But hormones also turn galanin production on. To be specific, the sexual hormone estrogen activates galanin.

"Estrogen just increases the production of galanin and it makes us want to eat. It makes us want to deposit fat," says Leibowitz. The influence of estrogen on our taste for fat "is important in the menstrual cycle and in the developmental cycle, when we hit puberty."

Of Time and the Nibbler

The two neurohormones of nibbling are not uniformly active throughout the day. Each has its own built-in cycle of activity.

Neuropeptide Y has its greatest effect on appetite at the start of the feeding cycle—morning, when we're just waking up. It starts up the entire feeding cycle. After overnight fasting, we have an immediate need for energy intake. Neuropeptide Y is also switched on after any environmentally imposed period of food deprivation—such as dieting. And by stress. "If you have lots of Neuropeptide Y in the system at breakfast," says Leibowitz, "you're going to be doing lots of eating."

Necessary as a quick-energy start is to get going, man cannot live by carbohydrate alone. After carbohydrate turns on our engines, the desire for this nutrient begins a slow decline over the rest of the daily cycle.

Around lunchtime, we begin looking for a little more sustenance. An afternoon of sustained energy expenditure stretches before us; we can afford to take in the other major nutrients—fat to refill our fat cells and protein to rebuild muscle. Both of these are converted more slowly to fuel. Our interest in protein rises gradually toward midday, holds its own at lunch, and keeps a more or less steady course during the rest of the day.

A Clockwork Orange

After lunch, the taste for fat begins rising, supported by increasing sensitivity to galanin and increasing galanin production; it peaks with our heaviest meal, at the end of the daily cycle. That's when the body is looking to store energy in anticipation of overnight fasting.

Take a late-afternoon coffee—or tea—break and you're virtually programmed to dive for energy-rich pastry, as appetite, spearheaded by the drive for fat, is gaining. We might, however, be better off appeasing the chemicals of consumption with a banana, or an orange.

Leibowitz believes that circadian cycles of neurochemical activity play a major role in eating problems. A late-afternoon fat snack, for example, could prime us neurochemically to consume more fat later into the night. Galanin activity late in the day gives fat consumed at dinner a head start, as it were, on our thighs.

Silent Signals

What drives us from a carbohydrate-rich breakfast to a more nutrient-mixed lunch? The carbohydrate we take in at breakfast has a direct impact on more widely distributed neurotransmitters such as serotonin. Active in many systems of the brain, including learning and memory, serotonin is believed to play a general role of modulator; it is essentially an inhibitor of activity.

Eating carbohydrate leads straightaway to synthesis of serotonin. Under normal conditions, rising levels of serotonin are the feedback signals to the paraventricular nucleus to shut off production of Neuropeptide Y and put a stop to the desire for carbohydrate.

Behind the Binge

Leibowitz now thinks that this serotonin signal is directly related to the bingeing behavior that is the *sine qua non* of bulimia. "Bulimics have a deficit in brain serotonin. The mechanism for stopping carbohydrate intake doesn't seem to be there."

Every meal, then, and the appetite for it, is differently regulated and presided over by a separate cocktail of neurochemicals. The neurochemically correct breakfast is a quick blast of carbohydrate right after awakening. Say, a glass of orange juice for speedy transport of sugar into the bloodstream to restore glycogen. Then a piece or two of toast, a more complex carbohydrate to deliver a more sustained supply of glucose over the morning.

For those who don't do it regularly, a breakfast of, say, eggs benedict—rich in protein and fat as well as carbohydrate—will send your neurochemicals spinning, throw off their normal rhythm of production, and affect many other neurotransmitters in the bargain. Ever wonder why you're just not sharp enough after an unusually rich breakfast?

The Big Switch

Not only are the neurochemicals of appetite active at different times over the course of a day, they are differently active over the course of development. Before puberty, Leibowitz finds, animals have no interest in eating fat. Children, too, have little appetite for fat, preferring carbohydrates for energy and protein for tissue growth. But that, like their bodies, changes.

In girls, the arrival of the first menstrual period is a milestone for appetite as well as for sexual maturation. It stimulates the first

desire for fat in foods. And that, says Leibowitz, is when a great deal of confusion sets in for anorexics. (See box.)

"We hit puberty and that turns galanin on." The female hormone estrogen primes the neurochemical pump for galanin.

There are other sex-based differences in nutrient preference. In studies of animals, young females tend to have higher levels of Neuropeptide Y and favor carbohydrates. Their preference for carbohydrates peaks at puberty. Males favor protein to build large muscles.

When puberty strikes up the taste for fats, males are inclined to mix theirs with protein—that sizzling porterhouse steak. Women, their already high levels of Neuropeptide Y joined by galanin, are set to crave high-calorie sweets—chocolate cake, say, or ice cream. It's bread-and-butter nutritional knowledge that carbohydrate makes fat palatable in the first place.

This neurochemical combo particularly sets women up for late-afternoon snacking, possibly bingeing. Late afternoon may be the time when those who skip breakfast are particularly likely to pay for it, and there in turn with exaggerated increases in their Neuropeptide Y levels leading them into late-day gorging.

Patterns of Preference

When Leibowitz allows animals to choose what they eat, they show marked individual preferences for nutrients. These nutrient preferences, in turn, create specific differences in feeding patterns. In this animals are just like people, and fall into one of three general categories.

In about 50 percent of the population, carbohydrate is the nutrient of choice. Such people naturally choose a diet in which about 60 percent of calories are derived from carbohydrate, and up to 30 percent come from fat. They are neurochemically in line with what nutritionists today are recommending as a healthy diet. High-carbohydrate animals consume smaller and more frequent

Through a daunting system of chemical and neural feedback, the brain monitors the energy needs of all body systems moment to moment and makes very emphatic suggestions to the stomach as to what and how much we should eat.

A Radical New View of Anorexia

Anorexia nervosa is regarded as an eating disorder. But Sarah Leibowitz looks on it as an appetite disorder. Where does body image come into it? After the physiology. She believes it's a case where physiology sets the stage for the psychology, and the neurochemical switching on of fat appetite is the trigger event.

"If physiology is telling you you're going to be a little bit heavy, anyone who has a problem with body weight, body shape is going to have the stage set for a problem." Leibowitz insists that anorexia is a no-holds-barred attempt to avoid fatness in those predisposed to plumpness either because of family history or metabolism. "They are," she says, "trying to avoid the inevitable."

Explaining her neurochemical model of anorexia, Leibowitz points out that anorexia typically starts at puberty—just when the brain's eating center suddenly switches on the taste for fat in foods. "You see yourself getting fat, and the culture is telling you it's wrong. Your boyfriend is telling you not to get fat. Your mother is telling you not to get fat. Then you come to this bottleneck in development. You're asking, 'Who am I?' 'Am I going to be as fat as my mother?' Psychology plays into it, but it is also a matter of just fighting a natural tendency."

Her view contradicts conventional wisdom, and regards the failure of sexual maturity that typifies anorexia as a *consequence* of the disorder, not its raison d'être. Before puberty, appetite in girls is dominated by a physiologically based preference for carbohydrate. Production of Neuropeptide Y in the supraventricular nucleus of the hypothalamus presides over this taste preference.

At puberty, rising levels of estrogen turn on production of the neurochemical galanin, which drives an everyday appetite for fat. It's part of nature's attempt to ensure a future for the species; reproduction in women requires a substantial amount of body fat. With their energy needs so intertwined, the brain center for eating behavior and the brain center for reproduction, located just next to it in the hypothalamus, coordinate their activities through regular neurochemical cross talk.

When the switched-on taste for fat alerts young women to the possibility of getting fat, some women swing into high gear—notably those with obsessive-compulsive personality traits. Performing a behaviorally heroic feat, they shun fat altogether. They cling instead to the prepubertal pattern of food intake—very small, frequent meals based on carbohydrate. "They're trying to keep going all day on what is normally that early-morning feeling. It takes very little food." They are literally starving.

Here's the catch. Starvation pumps up abnormally high levels of Neuropeptide Y in the brain. Neuropeptide Y confines their dietary interest to foods with carbohydrate. But the high levels of Neuropeptide Y have an effect on the sex center next door as well; they turn off production of gonadal hormones, which diminishes sexual function.

"It's important for anorexics and bulimics to know that there's this chemistry of the brain that they're fighting. Then they don't feel that they're just crazy. They're fighting nature. Of course, the approach is to alter that tendency before they become anorexic."

Not surprisingly, Leibowitz' unconventional view of the disorder leads her into a new approach to treatment. She wants to temporarily shut off production of galanin at puberty, the neurochemical that turns on the appetite for fat. "Eating disorders set in very close to the onset of menstruation. We find that estrogen increases the production of galanin, and it makes us want to eat. It makes us want to deposit fat, and it makes us want to eat fat."

She has administered to animals a substance that blocks production of the appetite stimulant for fat. It is an antagonist to galanin. "It is a newly developed experimental drug, M40. The animals just stop eating fat. It doesn't affect carbohydrate or protein intake. Now, if we can work with an individual who is getting all stressed out about having to eat fat, we can help her over the hump with the drug. Then we have a fighting chance to bring on board behavioral modification, nutrition, and education, which work more gradually to control appetite."

meals, and they weigh significantly less, than other animals.

Some Like It Fat

A small number of people and animals are dedicated to protein. But 30 percent of us have a predilection for fat. And those who do take in 60 to 70 percent of their calories in straight fat, as opposed to the 30 percent considered appropriate to a lifestyle that's more sedentary than our ancestors'.

Not only is this not likely to sit well with arteries, but such preferences also correlate highly with body weight in animals. Those constituted to favor fat consume the most calories and weigh the most. And they seem to be particularly predisposed to food cravings late in the day.

Early Indicators

What is perhaps most intriguing in all of this to Leibowitz is that individual taste preferences first show themselves when animals are very young, notably at the time of weaning, even before their neurochemical profiles are fully elaborated. The same is true of people. "We know early in family life what we are going to become," she contends.

The New York researcher believes that by sampling infants' tastes, it will be possible to predict eating and weight-control problems long before they occur. And, of course, if we choose, do something to prevent them from ever occurring.

More than Metabolism

At the time of weaning—21 days in rat pups, 1½ to 2 years in human infants—taste preferences largely reflect differences in genetic makeup. And in those animals that prefer sucrose or fat—"you put it on an infant's tongue and watch how they react to it, whether they become active or not"—their appetite is strongly predictive of how much weight they will gain later on in life. And their neurochemical make-up.

"We believe there is strong appetitive component to pre-ordained weight gain," Leibowitz

says. "We think there's more to it than just metabolism. We are on the verge of linking that early taste with later eating behavior and weight gain."

The Wages of Stress

These ground-breaking studies of nutrient preferences show that inborn patterns are one way we can be set up for eating problems or weight gain we might prefer not to have. They also implicate another—stress. Stress potentially wreaks havoc with our eating patterns by altering us internally.

When we feel under stress, the body increases production of the hormone cortisol, from the adrenal gland. The purpose of this chemical messenger of alarm is to marshall forces of energy for immediate use—to prepare us, as it were, for fight or flight. It puts our whole system on alert, and makes us hyper-vigilant.

As it enters the bloodstream from the adrenal gland and circulates throughout the body, cortisol sees that carbohydrate, stored in muscles and liver as glycogen, is swiftly turned into glucose for fuel. If we are not burning up glucose, we have no energy. One reason cortisol is elevated in the morning is because the food deprivation of overnight fasting is a kind of stress to the body, destabilizing the system.

Cortisol, however, is also critical in the regulation of the neurochemicals that control eating behavior. "It up-regulates the neuropeptides when you don't want it to," says Leibowitz. Cortisol specifically stimulates production of Neuropeptide Y, which turns on the appetite—for more carbohydrate. "Stress is very much related to turning on Neuropeptide Y," reports Leibowitz. "It doesn't appear to increase galanin."

What's particularly tricky is that the effect of stress on eating is not uniform throughout the day. A bout of stress at the right time in the morning may keep Neuropeptide Y turned on all day. "We know that some people under stress get fat and others do

Skipping meals upsets the natural rhythm of neurochemicals, and that's important because the body works on routines. It affects your mood, your energy, even your sex life. And it turns your next meal into a high-carbohydrate binge.

not overeat. It depends on when the stress is occurring. Wouldn't it be nice to get your stress at a time when you are not so vulnerable?" Now if only she knew when that was.

Why We Overeat

What she does know is that if there is no muscular activity to use up the carbohydrate stress sets us up to eat, the carbohydrate is put directly into storage as fat. But wait—there are other consequences. It is an axiom of neuroscience that the same chemical messenger has different effects at different sites.

Through neurochemical cross talk in the hypothalamus, the increase in Neuropeptide Y activity affects the master switch for sexual and reproductive behavior in the cluster of cells next door. In this back-and-forth signaling between cell groups, high levels of Neuropeptide Y, hell-bent on carbohydrate intake, turn off the gonadal hormones, which are far more interested in fat. The upshot is a dampening of sexual interest and activity. This effect turns out to be critically important in anorexia.

Eating carbohydrate under stress, however, has something going for it. It chases away the stress-induced changes in neurochemistry. The hormonal alarm signals dissipate. "After we eat a carbohydrate-rich meal, the world actually seems better," explains Leibowitz. We feel less edgy. "That's why we overeat."

Dieting—Bad for the Brain

Many studies have shown that curbing body weight by food restriction—dieting—makes no sense metabolically; in fact it's counterproductive. Leibowitz finds it also makes no sense to the biochemistry of our brains, either. "All dieting does is disturb the system," she says emphatically. "It puts you in a psychological altered state. You're a different person. You respond differently."

Erratically skipping meals upsets the natural daily rhythm of neurochemicals; "that's important because the body works on routines. If you disturb the routine, you're going to be a different person at lunch than if you didn't skip breakfast." What's more, "the chemicals that regulate appetite also directly affect moods and state of mind, our physical energy, the quality of our sex lives," says Leibowitz.

Fasting—restricting, in the parlance of those who study eating behavior—is particularly counterproductive to appetite. It simply turns on the neurochemical switches. "It's got to come out somehow," says Leibowitz. It specifically drives up levels of Neuropeptide Y and cortisol. Then, when the next meal rolls around, it turns it into a high-carbohydrate binge. "Neuropeptide Y is truly the neurochemical of food deprivation." Fasting or dieting drives the body to seek more carbohydrate. Her studies show that animals that love carbohydrate have higher levels of Neuropeptide Y in the paraventricular nucleus.

The Way We Were

How, then to lose weight? Certainly not diet pills. One reason they don't work is that they don't even aspire to cope with the array of neurochemicals setting the table for appetite. Assuming such an approach to be possible or even desirable, it would, in fact, take assorted concoctions of

> We need to help people understand what they are, what their appetite is, and how to work with their body the way it is."

chemicals at different times of the day, since each meal is regulated differently.

Nevertheless, the way to control appetite and body weight, Leibowitz believes, is by working *with* the neurochemical systems—and re-tuning them. "We need to help people understand what they are and what their appetite is, and how to work with the body the way it is. Some people are more sensitive." This may be a far gentler approach than skipping lunch, but in the long run, it may be the only workable one, the only one that can possibly do away with the preoccupation with dieting that now consumes 50 to 70 percent of all women.

However deterministic biochemistry at first appears, that is not, within broad bounds, the case with behavior. We are not wholly slaves of neurochemistry. "Neurons are plastic. They change. We can therefore educate the neurons," explains Leibowitz. "You can say that God dictated this biochemical pattern. But we are here to mold ourselves and train ourselves."

The secret to modifying neurons is to introduce a very gradual shift in their sensitivity to the neurochemicals of appetite—to down-regulate them s-l-o-w-l-y.

Given the plasticity of neurons, early experience is heavily weighted in shaping the behavior of brain cells for life. Early exposure to a certain nutrient—say, a high-fat diet—will bias neurochemistry—it will up-regulate sensitivity to galanin and prompt production of greater amounts of it, aiding and abetting the appe-

tite for fat. "Your training, your habits, all have an effect," says Leibowitz. "We don't know how much is permanent and how much is reversible. It may be like the case with fat cells in the body; if you overeat when young and get fat cells, you may not be able to get rid of them." The bottom line is, we may be remarkably adaptable but not infinitely malleable.

Taste Texts for All?

The ideal, then, is to start the neurochemicals of appetite out on the right foot, "to modulate them before an eating disorder sets in, or any disturbance in dieting. It's got to be preventative. What you eat is going to affect production of these peptides." At some point in the future, it may be possible to determine the right calorie and nutrient mix even to dampen the genetically outlined production of the appetite hormones.

Leibowitz would bypass the dismal enterprise of dieting altogether with a taste test at age two. "We're aiming for the goal of trying to characterize people at a very early age, just as we can now do with animals. We can predict adult height at two years of age. We may also want to predict adult eating behavior and weight gain."

Then, with nutrition and planning and behavioral therapy she would set out to educate the appetite. "I'm not thinking drugs, but there could be drugs. If we could do this ahead of time, we could prevent the development of eating disorders," disorders that now affect, by her calculation, 30 percent of the population.

"The question is, can we find some specific dietary situation, different foods at different times, that might help us to reduce neuropeptide activity without depriving ourselves. The whole point is, we can't deprive ourselves. But if we know that what we eat and when we eat it affect the production of neuropeptides, we can modulate what we eat and work the appetite so that we can get a new routine in."

Gastronomy may never be the same again.

HOW COMPETITIVE ARE YOU?

*Considering the latest psychological research, it's time to
examine your winning ways*

Josh Halberstam

*Josh Halberstam teaches philosophy at New York University; he
[has also written] about vanity for SELF.*

Divide the players into two teams, give each side "horse-shoes" and begin. Sounds like the start of a rousing competition. But in this children's game on a South Seas island, no one ever wins. After the first side throws horseshoes and gets a certain score, the other side tries to get the same number of hits. Both sides keep tossing until they reach an exact tie. The goal of the game is not to win but to draw. No winners, no losers, just happy kids.

Surprisingly enough, cooperative endeavors like this are common in many societies around the world, including those of the Eskimo, New Guineans and the aboriginal people of South Australia. Such games are alien to most Americans, though; as children we learn combative games like dodgeball, football and hockey. Even musical chairs is a brutal competition—one player wins, and everyone else loses. Our culture inculcates the value of competition in us as toddlers; by the time we're adults, we take it for granted.

Indeed, by almost all cross-cultural measures, the United States is among the most competitive countries in the world. (We win the competition for competitiveness.) We turn practically every activity into a contest, replete with awards, trophies and rankings. The children of the Pacific islands play the games they do because their society values and celebrates cooperation; we play the games we do because we value and celebrate competition. (When soccer was introduced in New Guinea, the games always ended in a draw and it took a long time before the players learned to play to win!)

Competition is a fact of life for most of us. Many of our jobs do pit us against each other. And it is often said that our competitive spirit is precisely what has made this country the economic success that it is. Recent data show, however, that too many people just don't know when to stop, and they carry their competitiveness into everything they do.

To compete means to seek or strive for something (a position, possession or reward) for which others are also contending. Competition always involves a reference to others: If you win, someone else loses. This is a situation we find ourselves in regularly. We contend at work for promotions and status; we battle in the gym to own the most lithe body; we vie at parties for appreciative attention; we strive among our friends for the title of most charming and wise. But our truly wrenching rivalries are those closest to home. The competition between mothers and daughters is a perennial theme for a hundred modern novels. And a third of Americans describe their sibling relationships as lifelong competitions. (Brother-to-brother rivalries tend to be more severe than other sibling relationships, and identical-twin brother relationships are the most intense of all.)

Is all this competition harmful? For the most part, the answer is "yes," according to some surprising recent studies by social scientists, psychologists and philosophers. Granted, in our culture, it would be unrealistic to try to eradicate competition; it can't consistently be escaped. (For one thing, society is full of other competitive people.) But it can be controlled. It helps to examine how competition works in your life. It can be something you enjoy engaging in within a defined arena; something you manage to turn off when it's inappropriate, something you feel is constructive for you. Or it can be all consuming, pervasive, out of control—an obsession masquerading as healthy American sportsmanship.

Most of us are convinced that we play better when we want to win. We make that extra effort to look the sexiest of all at that gala, we spend that extra hour on the proposal to win that account. Competition, we assume, provides the needed edge. In fact, the much-heralded competitive spirit often inhibits us from concentrating on and pursuing our interests, and actually results in underachievement. Instead of focusing on winning, research suggests, we need to learn how to establish realistic personal goals and concentrate on individual performance. Unfortunately, it isn't easy.

The first step is often the hardest: to acknowledge your competitiveness. (Few of us admit to being competitive, although we have little problem attributing competitiveness to others.) Perhaps you're unable to walk into a room without wondering whether you are the prettiest, most engaging, smartest. Or you (secretly) take satisfaction in the fact that a colleague has been criticized by the boss. According to the stereotype, women can be especially competitive with one another—*aka* catty—and there is some hard evidence that women do judge other women in positions of power more harshly than they do men in comparable positions. But paradoxically, women are also very uncomfortable competing with each other. Laura Tracy, author of *The Secret Between Us*, a study of female rivalry, concludes that "their most intense and highly charged relationships existed in the context of competition. . . . But [competition] is a connection that must be kept secret, especially from ourselves."

The result of a life devoted to competition is perpetual uncertainty, exhaustion and not a little bitterness.

If female competitiveness is a secret, it is quickly becoming a secret all around the block. Fifty-six percent of white-collar jobs are now held by women, and those include jobs in the most so-called cutthroat, adversarial professions. The jury is still out on whether the increasing presence of women in top management positions will change the competitive atmosphere of corporate America, but this is no longer a subject women can avoid. Whether at work or at home, the chances are that you are participating in some serious competition. Recognize it.

The second hurdle is the refusal to take responsibility for your competitiveness. It is always a choice. Loretta works at a leading investment house and readily admits to her desire to win. But she doesn't believe it's something she chooses. "Look," she says, "I work in a combat zone. I compete to survive here. The truth is that we all do, everywhere. Competitiveness is a basic, natural human condition."

We hear this message repeatedly: "It's a jungle out there, a dog-eat-dog world where the only rule is the survival of the fittest. " We watch nature clips of leopards pouncing on their prey and conclude that that's the way the world works. In fact, it's only a small part of reality. Nature exhibits at least as much evidence of cooperation as competitiveness. And interestingly enough, testosterone, the hormone responsible for aggressiveness, increases at the end of a fight and not at the beginning, suggesting that competition makes us aggressive rather than that natural aggression makes us competitive. As noted naturalist Stephen Jay Gould points out, "The

equation of competition with success in natural selection is merely cultural prejudice."

It certainly isn't human nature to be competitive; anthropologists report on societies all over the world in which our style of contending is viewed as exceedingly rude and uncaring. But we aren't naturally cooperative either. Humans can and do cut it both ways. Loretta works in a fiercely competitive environment and has to struggle to succeed. But this isn't true for all our jobs, and even in Loretta's case, she *is* making a choice. So if you are competitive, you can't blame it on your genes.

A third obstacle to controlling the competition in your life is the widespread notion that competition leads to improved performance. *Competition leads to inferior performance; striving for self-mastery produces results.* It isn't really the desire to win that gets you to play extra hard at Scrabble or makes you lunge for those tough returns in your squash games. It's the desire to master a well-defined goal: You want to find a word for that triple and won't, as usual, settle for less, or you're determined to get that backhand finally working well. Internal motivation is, it turns out, a far more effective incentive than exterior motivation.

This seems to be true in all areas of human endeavor, and numerous studies indicate that it is especially true in education and artistic development. In one classic study, reported in *Personality and Social Psychology Bulletin* in 1978, seven-to-11-year-old girls were asked to make "silly" collages, some competing for prizes and some not. A panel of professional artists independently rated their work with the result that "those children who competed for prizes made collages that were significantly less creative than those made by children in the control group." Children in the competitive condition produced works judged to be less spontaneous, less complex and less varied.

The same pattern emerges with adults. In one landmark study, Robert L. Helmreich, Ph.D., professor of psychology at the University of Texas, Austin, examined the publishing records of more than one hundred Ph.D.'s in science. Those who rated high on the scale of interest in work and self-mastery produced significantly more quality work than those who ranked high on the competitive scale. He found the same results with undergraduate students, airline pilots, reservations agents and seven other professions. The most startling finding comes from recent research in business conducted by Janet Spence, Ph.D., professor of psychology, also at the University of Texas, Austin. Dr. Spence found that performance-oriented business executives earned 16 percent more money than those motivated by competition. This result makes sense when you consider that businesspeople locked into a competitive mind-set tend to have a greater fear of failure, are content with just winning and therefore take fewer creative risks and enjoy their work less.

Some of the most intriguing recent studies of competitiveness come, not surprisingly, from sports psychologists. We all grew up hearing slogans such as Vince Lombardi's "Winning isn't everything, it's the only thing" or Leo Durocher's "Show me a good loser and I'll show you a loser." But here again, this research refutes popular assumptions. Athletes who pay attention to personal performance goals—to shoot 70 percent from the free-throw line, say, or run a mile 20 seconds faster than they did the previous month—shoot better and run faster than athletes who just concentrate on beating their opponents.

Other studies indicate that athletes who focus on skill mastery tend to attribute their success more directly to their own efforts and make fewer excuses for poor performance than do athletes who are devoted to being victorious. This also happens elsewhere in our lives—people overly concerned with winning invariably make excuses for losing.

But isn't competition fun? It is, for some—not for most. It has a way of draining the *playfulness* from any activity—sports, music, even conversation. Losing isn't fun, and in most competitions, more than half of the competitors lose—think of beauty-pageant contestants, and the many applicants for a single job.

So what are we to conclude from all this research? That you should avoid all competitive "I win–you lose" interactions? Precisely, says Tufts professor Alfie Kohn in his influential book *No Contest:* " 'Healthy competition' is a contradiction in terms."

But not all experts agree. To some, it's a matter of degree and attitude. Ivan Bresgi, Ph.D., a New York City psychotherapist who is also a competitive swimmer and rugby player, cautions against undervaluing competitiveness: "The problem occurs when you focus *entirely* on winning. For one thing, that always involves an accompanying focus on losing. But the desire to win is helpful in combination with other internal motivations. Your opponent can provide you with strong, clear goals that can inspire you to do even better."

It's helpful to distinguish between constructive and destructive competition, between fair play and dirty tricks. Receiving the "salesperson of the month" prize is a reward for your hard work. But you can't justifiably feel pleased about the award if you won it by surreptitiously sabotaging the efforts of your coworkers.

The key here is to remember that competitiveness is determined by your attitude, not by the activity. For you, the morning jog is about exercise; for Sally, it's a contest to see who has greater stamina. You stay late at work because you need to get your project done; Michael stays late to prove how dedicated he is. You can avoid getting trapped in destructive competitions by keeping a few things in mind:

1. Attend to your own goals, not to beating someone else. When the very best people in any profession talk about their motivation, they always refer to the work itself, rarely about outdoing others. Whether the pursuit is running your business, running the marathon or performing your duties as a daughter or a friend, determine what you want to accomplish and then pursue that goal. Use winning only as a temporary marker to judge your progress, not as an end in itself. In other words, *stop comparing yourself with others*. The end of that road is incessant envy and frustration.

2. Don't tangle with the obsessively competitive. Sure, it's easy to cooperate with cooperative individuals, but what happens when you interact with competitive people? Invariably, you get sucked into their game.

Take Mark, for example. Mark turns every discussion into a competition. He thinks the only interesting conversation is an argument. And even though you're aware of his ploy, you always find yourself trapped in useless debates with him. Or think of your sister. You just want to get Mom a gift for her birthday, but your sister is turning the event into a contest: Who is the more devoted daughter? Somehow, your sister always manages to get you to compete with her.

Decision theorist Thomas Gilovich explains: "Because competitive behavior creates more of a demand for the other person to respond in kind than does cooperation, a competitive person's belief that the world is full of selfish opportunities will always be confirmed, whereas the less gloomy orientation of cooperative individuals will not." In other words, if someone wants to make every interaction a contest, nothing will stop him. But *you* don't have to be a victim and you don't have to engage in the contest. Avoid discussions with the likes of Mark, unless he's willing to have a real talk, not a litigation. It's trickier, of course, with the subtle competitions between family members. But even here, you can lay down the rules: Here's what you're going to do, and your sister can do what she likes. You won't compete.

3. Learn how to manage competition so that it is as cooperative and constructive as possible. The Latin root of the word competition, *competere*, provides a useful clue here. It means "to strive together." When you compete with an ally, there are no losers. Both you and your supportive tennis opponent are really on the same side—you both want to improve your game and have fun. You help pace each other instead of spending your energies calling each others' faults. This is a useful strategy for the workplace as well. Even though only one of you may get the promotion, you can help each other raise the overall quality of your output—and everyone gains in the end.

Most competitions are structured as what economists call zero-sum games—what you win the other person loses (poker is a good example). But keep in mind that much of the best stuff in life is not scarce. There's enough parental love for all children; you can share your friendships, ideas and interests without anyone losing out. The result of a life devoted to competition is perpetual uncertainty, exhaustion and not a little bitterness. So if you're competing more than you think might be good for you, ask yourself what you're trying to prove—and to whom.

Development

The Hoyers and the Szubas are parents of newborns. Both sets of parents wander down to the hospital's neonatal nursery where both babies, Joey Hoyer and Kimberly Szuba, are cared for by pediatric nurses when the babies are not in their mothers' rooms. Kimberly is alert, active, and often crying and squirming when her parents watch her. On the other hand, Joey is quiet, often asleep, and less attentive to external stimuli when his parents monitor him in the nursery.

Why are these babies so different? Are the differences gender-related? Will these differences disappear as the children develop, or will the differences become exaggerated? What does the future hold for each child? Will Kimberly excel at sports and Joey excel at English? Can Joey overcome his parents' poverty and succeed in a professional career? Will Kimberly become a doctor like her mother or a pharmacist like her father? Will both of these children escape childhood disease, abuse, and the other misfortunes visited upon some American children?

Developmental psychologists are concerned with all of the Kimberlys and Joeys of our world. Developmental psychologists study age-related changes in such behaviors as language, motor skills, cognition, physical health, and social adeptness. Developmental psychologists are interested in the common skills shared by all children as well as the differences between children and the events that create these differences.

In general, developmental psychologists are concerned with the forces that guide and direct development. Some developmental theorists argue that the forces that shape a child are found in the environment in such factors as social class, quality of available stimulation, parenting style, and so on. Other theorists insist that genetics and related physiological factors such as hormones underlie the development of humans. A third set of psychologists, in fact, many psychologists, believe that some combination or interaction of both factors, physiology and environment, or nature and nurture, is responsible for development.

In this unit, we are going to look at issues of development in a chronological fashion. We begin with young children or preschoolers. In "How Kids Benefit from Child Care," Vivian Cadden takes a close look at how working mothers feel about child care. In specific, Cadden reports results of a survey of working mothers who agree that child care benefited their children. The mothers claim that their children are more socially and intellectually advanced than children not in day care.

Lizette Peterson, in the next article, debates yet another issue for American society—child abuse. There are now more reported cases of child abuse than ever before. This article reviews the work of psychologists who study children who are injured versus children who have been abused. The article highlights how to tell the difference between the two, one of which (abuse) tragically occurs more intentionally than the other.

Differences in the way schools treat boys and girls are addressed next. Teachers, it seems, do not engage girls in the learning process as actively as boys. Myra and David Sadker, who wrote the article and scientifically investigated this issue, claim that some classroom experiences are actually detrimental to girls. The article that follows, "Teaching Young Children to Resist Bias: What Parents Can Do," also pertains to school-age children and relates to prejudice and bigotry, which some children learn from their parents. Both the victim and the bigot are harmed by these negative attitudes. Ways in which the issue of prejudice can be better managed by teachers and parents are also explored.

We next turn to adulthood. Families today are strapped for money; thus, in many families both parents work outside the home. The stresses and delights of dual-career families are detailed in Lucia Albino Gilbert's article, "Current Perspectives on Dual-Career Families."

Middle age is one of the least studied developmental eras of all. Winifred Gallagher, in "Midlife Myths," reviews research on midlife crisis and other life transitions in this era. She concludes that the midlife crisis is a myth as revealed in the title she selected for her article.

Looking Ahead: Challenge Questions

Describe how the lives of working mothers and stay-at-home mothers differ. How does family life differ for these two groups? What are the types of child care that exist? In your opinion, how does child care impact the child? What could our society do to ensure quality day care for all children?

How common is child abuse? What causes child

abuse? What are the effects of abuse to the child who is the victim? What characterizes abusive parents? How can the cycle of abuse be stopped? How can we tell childhood injuries from childhood abuse?

How are girls and boys treated differently by teachers? What are the consequences to the girls of this differential treatment? What are the consequences to the boys? How can we change our educational system so that girls are not treated less well than boys?

What is prejudice? Is only the victim of prejudice harmed by it? What effects does prejudice have on its victims? How can we raise children to be less prejudiced?

What is a dual-career family? Why would psychologists study these families? What have researchers discovered about the advantages and disadvantages of having both parents work?

Why is middle age important? Why has it received less attention than other developmental eras? Is there such a thing as a midlife crisis? What transitions does a middle-age person face?

HOW KIDS BENEFIT FROM CHILD CARE

In a breakthrough study, over 1,700 readers reveal that their children learn critical academic and social skills from being in day care

Vivian Cadden

Vivian Cadden, a WORKING MOTHER contributing editor, is a member of the board of the Child Care Action Campaign.

Attitudes among working women toward child care have changed profoundly. A solid three out of four mothers of infants, toddlers and preschoolers believe that their child is learning more in day care than he or she would staying home with Mom all day. This surprisingly positive view of the advantages of child care emerges from a survey of 1,762 readers of WORKING MOTHER.

"The recognition that a quality child care arrangement can actually be *educational* for children represents an entirely new perspective; as recently as fifteen years ago, child care was seen as just an unavoidable necessity for working families," says Barbara Reisman, executive director of the Child Care Action Campaign (CCAC), which coauthored the survey. (The results of the questionnaire will be presented at the CCAC conference, "Child Care and Education: The Critical Connection," taking place in New York City March 31st through April 2nd.)

In fact, so great is the acceptance of child care now, that working mothers are almost unanimously (97 percent) convinced that their child benefits from it because it is educational, contributes to personal development and builds social skills. The women also have decided opinions on how young children learn and why certain forms of care are more conducive to learning than others:

- Eighty-five percent say that because their youngster is in child care he or she is "more independent."
- Eighty percent believe that "children who have had good child care are readier for first grade than other children."
- Three quarters say their kids gain valuable social skills in child care.
- Signaling a new trend, a majority (56 percent) prefer center-based care as a learning environment.
- Women have a new respect for teachers as professionals who are experts on child development.
- Respondents believe that one-on-one care, whether by a nanny, a relative or the mother herself, is of lesser educational value than group care.

What Children Learn

Parents put an especially high premium on the social skills their child gains from a group experience. In answer to an open-ended question, "What is the most important thing your youngster has learned from child care?", the most frequent responses were "learning to share" and "making friends." It is these perceptions that lead mothers to believe that their child is learning more from outside care than he would staying home with Mom.

"The most important thing my daughter has learned is how to interact with other children and adults. I don't think she would have received the stimulation and encouragement at home that she has received from her center's director, teachers and classmates," writes a woman from Waverly Hall, Georgia.

A San Ramon, California, mother says, "In addition to sharing and taking turns, my two-year-old has learned a wonderful quality—empathy. If Amanda sees another child cry, she asks what's wrong and tries to cheer him up."

A majority of women say that their youngster is "more outgoing" and "happier" because of being in child care; about half believe that he or she is "smarter," "less clingy" and "more cooperative."

Mothers of three- and four-year-olds are likely to talk about academic accomplishments that they believe contribute to their youngster's readiness for first grade: the growth of vocabulary and mastery of ABCs and numbers and color.

A Norfolk, Virginia, mother, for instance, is proud that her four-year-old "can count to twenty, knows her ABCs and can recognize letters."

Many mothers have such a strong belief in the benefits of group care that they would want their child to spend part of the day or several days a week in group care even if they didn't work. A Freeport, New York, woman writes, "Our center offers so much that I'm not trained to do. . . . I have often said that even if I didn't work I would want my son to attend this center a couple of days a week!"

Good Marks for Centers

One notable finding of the survey is a new enthusiasm for center-based care and a preference for it over every other type of care. This mirrors a trend in the country at large, but the preference is greater among WORKING MOTHER readers.

Overall, 57 percent of mothers in the survey have their youngster in a child care center, while 32 percent use a family day care home; 5 percent have in-home care, and 3 percent rely on a spouse or other relative. Even mothers of infants under two use center care about as often

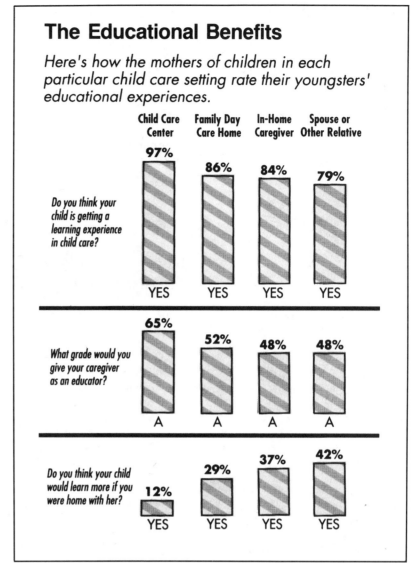

The Educational Benefits

Here's how the mothers of children in each particular child care setting rate their youngsters' educational experiences.

	Child Care Center	Family Day Care Home	In-Home Caregiver	Spouse or Other Relative
Do you think your child is getting a learning experience in child care?	97% YES	86% YES	84% YES	79% YES
What grade would you give your caregiver as an educator?	65% A	52% A	48% A	48% A
Do you think your child would learn more if you were home with her?	12% YES	29% YES	37% YES	42% YES

ILLUSTRATED CHARTS BY STANFORD KAY/PARAGRAPHICS

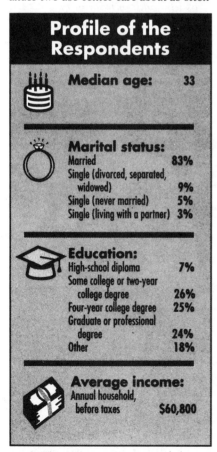

Profile of the Respondents

Median age: 33

Marital status:
Married 83%
Single (divorced, separated, widowed) 9%
Single (never married) 5%
Single (living with a partner) 3%

Education:
High-school diploma 7%
Some college or two-year college degree 26%
Four-year college degree 25%
Graduate or professional degree 24%
Other 18%

Average income:
Annual household, before taxes $60,800

as they do family day care. And a whopping 72 percent of three- and four-year-olds are cared for in centers.

Even more striking is the degree of satisfaction mothers express with center care and their faith in its educational content. On practically every question dealing with the educational value of care, the center comes out on top. Mothers were asked, for example, "What grade would you give your caregiver for the job she is doing at providing learning experiences for your child?" Sixty-five percent of those whose child attends a center answered "A," compared to only 52 percent of those with a child in family care. And barely half—48 percent—were as pleased with the learning experience a child got from a nanny or relative. (See "The Educational Benefits.")

A Lowell, Massachusetts, respondent whose six-year-old and three-year-old

have been in centers since infancy writes, "Our children have gained insight into many facets of life, which I believe they would not have experienced if they had stayed home with me: exposure to many different types of adults and children; a wide variety of toys, games, books and activities; learning about cooperation and sharing; being able to giggle and act silly with lots of friends one day and being alone in a cozy corner with a book the next day; being in a physical environment that supports children's needs instead of placing limitations on them; being in a place where children are not pushed to learn but where they learn and discover because it's fun and they want to do it."

Anne Mitchell, senior consultant to CCAC on the New York City conference, marveled at the sophistication of readers' views as expressed in their replies. "Clearly, these women know the kind of environment in which children learn and flourish," she says.

The high regard for center care is all the more remarkable because over the years such care has so often come under attack. Mothers are aware of this, and many comment on it in their letters.

The Lowell, Massachusetts, mother says of her children's center, "This is the kind of day care center that should be featured when television journalists insist on 'exposing the care that children get in the day care centers of our nation.'"

"Many of us," a Brooklyn mother adds, "are disgusted by the negative media coverage of child care centers."

Teachers Are Pros

Readers also voice great respect for the people who care for their children. Likely to be well educated themselves (see "Profile of the Respondents"), these women value the training their children's caregivers have acquired.

A mother with a graduate degree who has a one-year-old daughter in a center says, "I don't have the experience nor do I know how and what to teach a kid!" Another writes, "I feel teachers are better geared to educate a small child. After all, that's what they went to college for."

Many women feel that if they were home all day they wouldn't be concentrating on educational activities for their child as teachers are able to do. A mother from Newnan, Georgia, puts it this way: "The day care center doesn't have to worry about washing clothes, cleaning house, running errands and getting distracted."

A Bloomington, Indiana, mother writes, "I am not as focused on creative ideas for children." As an example, she describes how her four-year-old learned to lace his shoes at his center by lacing a shoe box that had been made into a mock shoe. "I was so amazed," she says, "that I brought the teacher flowers!"

After citing some of the things her toddler has learned in child care, a Newark, Delaware, mother says, "I, too, have learned from child care, observing the teachers. I have learned how to talk to Jennifer in a positive and encouraging way. I have learned how much she is capable of doing. I have learned to give her choices whenever possible, to encourage her to make decisions."

Readers also understand that teaching young children is not a matter of formal indoctrination. "Learning is not shoved down my son's throat. He learns by playing and the thoughtful direction of his teachers" is how one mother puts it.

In fact, her enlightened view that "children learn through playing" is shared almost unanimously by the respondents: Ninety-eight percent agree.

One-on-One Care

The respondents' enthusiasm about the educational value of day care does not carry over to their assessment of one-on-one care provided by nannies or relatives.

Only 12 percent of mothers who use center care believe their child would learn more if they stayed home. But a hefty 42 percent of those who rely on a spouse or other relative think so. And 37 percent of moms with a nanny feel they could give their child a better learning experience if they stayed home.

The marked confidence in group care and more tepid enthusiasm for individual care represents a real turnabout in women's opinion. An affluent Arlington, Virginia, mother with an infant in center care says, "I am particularly interested in your

What Government Should Do

One of the most remarkable findings of the survey is how strongly women feel about the need for public schools to accommodate the changing needs of society. The vast majority, for instance, want before- and after-school care for elementary-age children. In fact, at a time when most people feel enormously burdened by taxes, 85 percent of the respondents not only think public schools should provide such care, but an amazing 74 percent would be willing to pay higher taxes for it.

There is less enthusiasm for schools getting involved in child care for the very young, however. Only 29 percent of the women support public-school programs for three-to-five-year-olds and a meager 18 percent want such programs for children from birth through three.

What should public schools provide?

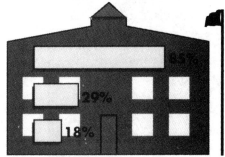

Before- and after-school programs 85%

Child care for kids three and up 29%

Child care for kids from birth onward 18%

What would you pay more taxes for?

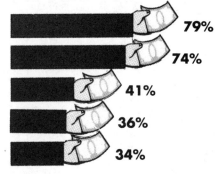

Better public schools 79%

Before- and after-school programs 74%

Child care for four-year-olds 41%

Child care for three-year-olds and up 36%

Child care for infants and toddlers 34%

survey because I have begun to believe that as social creatures, babies and children are meant to be around many more familiar people than is the norm in our culture. Many societies have a much broader, extended family network in which children are with many older children and adults throughout the day. It strikes me as odd that we see mother and child cloistered at home as the ideal."

The Income Factor

Across the board, no matter what their income, mothers believe almost unanimously that their child benefits from child care. But their answers to other questions suggest that income (with the consequent ability or inability to afford high-quality care) plays an important part in determining the learning experience the youngster receives.

■ Asked "Would you change your child's arrangement if another affordable option were available?", about 32 percent of mothers with household incomes under $20,000 replied "yes." Only 17 percent with household incomes of $100,000 and over would make a change.

■ Twenty-eight percent of those in the lowest income group believe their child would learn more if Mom stayed home; only 18 percent of those with household incomes of $100,000 and over think so.

These findings are consistent with other studies, in which respondents with family incomes above $60,000 express high levels of general satisfaction with their child care arrangement, while respondents with incomes below $20,000 are less satisfied.

The outstanding impression that has emerged from the survey results and the readers' letters is that working mothers with children in quality child care believe their youngsters are getting the best of two worlds. As an Aurora, Colorado, woman with a two-year-old and a six-year-old puts it: "My children are growing up seeing Mom and Dad as their base, but also having the ability to branch out in relationships and experiences they would not have readily received staying at home with me all day."

Editor's note: Readers who need assistance finding child care in their area can call the National Association of Child Care Resource and Referral Agencies at this number: 1-800-424-2246.

Child Injury and Abuse-Neglect:

Common Etiologies, Challenges, and Courses Toward Prevention

Lizette Peterson

Lizette Peterson is Professor of Psychology at the University of Missouri-Columbia and is the current Editor of *Behavior Therapy*. Address correspondence to Lizette Peterson, Psychology Department, 210 McAlester, University of Missouri-Columbia, Columbia, MO 65211.

Six-month-old Michael Todd Davis was admitted to Children's Hospital at 8:00 p.m. on a Monday evening, with a serious head injury. His mother reported that he had fallen from the changing table while she searched nearby for a clean diaper. He never regained consciousness and died during the night.[1]

A fall from a changing table is a prototypical injury for an infant, as it is predictable and well studied, yet very difficult to prevent because prevention must rely on changes in the caregiver's behavior rather than on a permanent environmental change. After more than three decades of study, the epidemiology of such unintentional injuries is well known. In fact, pediatrics has evolved very specific forms of anticipatory guidance

or routinized teaching of parents to avoid falls in the 1st year of life.

Unfortunately, none of these approaches would have helped Michael Todd, whose injuries were actually inflicted when his exhausted mother threw him against the rails of his crib. His injuries were unintentional in the sense that they were the product of his mother's anger and lack of information about the force an infant's head can withstand, rather than her desire to harm him. However, little of the prevention literature on unintentional injuries seems to apply to such a case. Alarmingly, recent studies have revealed that at least 80% of fatal head injuries in children less than 2 years of age are inflicted by their caregivers.[2]

FRAGMENTED APPROACHES TO THE STUDY OF CHILD INJURY

Injuries take the lives of more children in the United States than any other cause of death and require medical intervention for one third of all children each year. Two differing research areas, unintentional injury

and child abuse-neglect, have developed in the past four decades to study this phenomenon, which the National Academy of Science has termed "the neglected disease of modern society." Historically, both areas have been underfunded and understaffed, lacking a constituency of public and research support, although currently support for both areas is increasing. In this article, I argue that because of the close connections between these areas, they should join forces. Each area could learn from the other, and, more important, combined efforts toward prevention are likely to be more effective than separate efforts because they will have more support (both political and empirical) and be more comprehensive in addressing the true origins of childhood injury.

Laypersons believe the majority of childhood injuries are "accidental" and only a heinous few are due to maltreatment by parents.[3] The term "accidental" implies the event is unpredictable and that no one is culpable for the outcome. Researchers within the growing field of injury prevention accept as their subject matter the bulk of child injuries but

From *Current Directions in Psychological Science*, Vol. 3, No. 4, August 1994, pp. 116-120. © 1994 by the American Psychological Society. Reprinted by permission of Cambridge University Press.

deny the premise that such events are random and unpreventable, using the terms "unintentional" or "inadvertent," rather than "accidental." In contrast, researchers on abuse and neglect frequently term their subject matter "nonaccidental" injury. Thus, at the outset, these two literatures fail even to use the same language, documenting their lack of communication.

Despite the fact that injury poses an enormous threat to children, the scientific study of injuries began relatively recently, and with the exception of a few isolated pioneers,[4] contributions of psychologists to the area began only a decade or so ago. The epidemiological, public-health research tradition that has dominated the field of unintentional injury has focused more on isolating environmental factors in unintentional injury than on revealing person-based risk factors, and until recently has explicitly advocated intervening in the environment and source of injury itself (e.g., designing safer cribs, barriers next to highways, safer containers for medicines) over behavioral programs. In contrast, the literature on injuries due to child abuse and neglect has evolved entirely separately, dominated by what Garbarino[4] termed a "kinds-of-people" orientation from fields such as sociology and social work. Increasingly, however, closer study of unintentional injury versus injury due to neglect and abuse suggests that past classification systems are faulty and that there are more common factors in those two isolated fields of study than there are differences.

BLURRED BOUNDARIES BETWEEN INADVERTENT INJURIES AND INJURIES DUE TO NEGLECT OR ABUSE

In one of the best examples of detailed exploration of the categorization of causes of children's injuries, Ewigman, Kivlahan, and Land[5] examined all records pertaining to infants through preschoolers (birth through 4 years of age) who died because of injury in the State of Missouri between January 1, 1983, and December 31, 1986. Official records (e.g., death certificates) had labeled only 15% of these deaths as due to abuse or neglect. Each child's death was re-reviewed using all existing sources of information and was coded into one of five categories:

- *Definite maltreatment* was coded only when a local or federal agency had records substantiating the death as due to child abuse or neglect, the perpetrator was convicted of homicide, or the death was coded on the death certificate as a maltreatment fatality.

- *Probable maltreatment* was coded only when findings strongly suggested maltreatment (e.g., unexplained head injury, burns clearly inconsistent with physical history offered by the caregiver).

- *Possible maltreatment* was coded when there was evidence that lack of adequate supervision or parental action resulted in the child's death (e.g., unattended drowning, previously substantiated abuse or neglect of the same type as led later to death). In other words, possible maltreatment was coded when there was no adequate explanation suggesting inadvertent injury as the cause of death and at least one clear indicator of abuse or neglect was present.

- *Inadequate information* was coded when too little information was available to allow other categorization.

- *Nonmaltreatment* indicated there was no reason to suspect abuse.

As shown in Figure 1, of the 384 cases, one third were designated as definite maltreatment, another fourth were rated as possible maltreatment, and one fourth had inadequate information. A small number (6%) were rated as probable maltreatment, and only 11% were clearly not related to abuse or neglect. Subsequent collaboration between Ewigman and officials from the Centers for Disease Control utilized the Missouri categorizations to extend the findings to estimate national trends.[6] This extrapolation revealed that potentially more than half of cases now viewed as unintentional injury could actually be ascribed to abuse-neglect. The resulting continuum of cause-of-death categories underlines the premise that asking whether an injury is due to unintentional causes or due to abuse or neglect shows an inadequate appreciation of how children's injuries occur.

The field of unintentional injury and the field of abuse and neglect have produced different conceptualizations of injury, have arisen from different scientific disciplines (public health vs. sociology and social work), and have had different foci historically (physical and environmental factors vs. cultural factors and parental psychopathology). Yet both areas originated at about the same time, and the two research literatures have shown parallel development over the past four decades. Despite their differences, these disciplines have discovered substantially overlapping etiologies for injury.[7] For example, both areas suggest that risk of injury is increased by sociocultural factors including extreme poverty, chaotic family life, crowding, and recent change in residence. Similarly, parental factors common to both types of injuries include being young, stressed, a single parent, isolated, a substance abuser, or emotionally disturbed. Finally, fatal injuries of both types occur more often in children from birth to age 4 than in elementary-school-age children, and children who are distractible and impulsive, who have behavioral problems and poor sleep habits, are at greater than average risk according to both literatures.

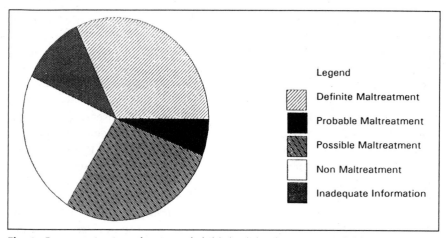

Fig. 1. Recategorization of causes of child death by the Missouri Child Fatality Study.

Legend

- Definite Maltreatment
- Probable Maltreatment
- Possible Maltreatment
- Non Maltreatment
- Inadequate Information

Thus, not only is it clear that many young children's injuries currently regarded as unintentional are actually misclassified instances of abuse or neglect (the Centers for Disease Control model derived from Ewigman's data suggests as many as 80%, in younger children ages 0 to 4), but many of the same risk factors apply both to unintentional injury and to abuse or neglect. Furthermore, the data suggest that there is no dichotomy between unintentional injury and abusive injury, or even a single continuum ranging from one to the other; rather, there is a series of discrete injury-related continua, with either extreme on any continuum posing a risk to the child.

SUPERVISION AND DISCIPLINE: TWO EXAMPLES OF INJURY-RELATED CONTINUA

The extent to which parents vigilantly oversee and process a child's activities influences injury. Failing to prevent an ambulatory small child from gaining access to water, poisons, busy streets, or open flames definitively contributes to unintentional injury and thus might be conceptualized as neglectful. Even older children rely on parental supervision to decrease risk of injury.

On the other end of the continuum, supervision that is too intrusive and intense may be a factor in establishing an abusive relationship. Descriptive research has shown that abusive parents have strong needs for control and intermittently show hypervigilant supervision, exerting both verbal and physical control that is disproportionate to the situation.[8]

A similar continuum is seen in parents' intervention to alter risky behavior in their children. My collaborators and I have studied more than 1,000 minor injuries monitored and reported by mothers and their 8-year-old children, and found that mothers reported doing nothing after more than 80% of the injuries and said they "lectured" their children 15% of the time. Children reported no action following 96% of their injuries, recalling lectures after only 2% of the injuries, despite excellent recall for other aspects of the events. Mothers and children agreed that changes in family rules or discipline in the form of loss of privileges, time-out, or other punishment occurred following only 2% of the injuries. The potential seriousness of an injury had no impact on whether it had remediative consequences, whereas maternal anger did. If these data are representative, they suggest that most opportunities to reduce risky behavior by changing the environment, rules, or the child's behavior directly after injury are lost.

There is no doubt that at the other end of the continuum, too much and too strenuous physical discipline is related to serious child injury. Abusing parents nearly always perceive their response to the child as legitimate discipline, even when the response is as extreme as burning the child with cigarettes or leaving permanent scars from beatings.

Healthy parenting is characterized by behavior toward the center of these continua. Abusive and neglectful practices, and parenting practices that lead to unintentional injury, tend to occur at one extreme or to vacillate between extremes of overcontrol and absence of appropriate supervision and control.

BASIS FOR SUPERVISION AND DISCIPLINE PRACTICES

Decisions concerning appropriate levels of both supervision and discipline must be based on the parents' own, often faulty, understanding of the child's abilities and needs, and on vague and elusive community norms for acceptable practices for a child of a given age.

Insensitivity to Age Norms

The classic unintentional injury to an infant occurs when the child exhibits an ability not anticipated by the parent, such as pulling over a container of hot liquid or crawling to and then tumbling down the stairs. Much of preventive parental instruction within pediatrics is termed anticipatory guidance, instructing parents concerning upcoming risky behaviors. However, injuries still occur because some parents underestimate their infants' motor abilities.

Somewhat ironically, research has shown repeatedly that parents of older children overestimate their children's safety knowledge and abilities. In one survey from our laboratory, both parents and 8-year-olds rated the children's knowledge of the family rules as high, yet the children knew less than 40% of the safety rules and less than 20% of general household rules. In the study just described, parents permitted their children to engage in a myriad of risky behaviors, such as cooking on top of the stove, playing in rooms with accessible, loaded guns, riding on powerful all-terrain vehicles, and crossing streets at younger ages than recommended by safety experts. The existing data thus suggest that parents' faulty knowledge of children's developmental needs for supervision and guidance often exposes the children to undesirable levels of risk.

Insensitivity to age norms is also one of the best known attributes of abusive caregivers.[9] The abusive caregiver tends to have unrealistic expectations for the child's ability to be compliant, quiet, and sensitive to the caregiver's needs. The child's failure to live up to the faulty expectations triggers abuse.

Lack of Community Norms

Finding no literature articulating acceptable norms for supervising children, my collaborators and I surveyed a variety of respondents, including randomly selected mothers, family-service workers, and primary-care physicians. We asked about five locations, which contained up to three levels of escalating risk each (e.g., the three levels within the home were the bedroom, kitchen, and garage). For each specific location, we asked the same question: How many minutes would the respondent allow a child of a given age to be in that location without auditory or visual contact from an adult? The question was repeated for children for each year from infancy to age 10.

There was substantial variability within each group; in one case, some respondents noted that a 10-year-old could not be left unsupervised in a neighborhood with hazards such as creeks, ponds, or swimming pools for even a minute, and other respondents suggested such a child could be without supervision for an entire day. Even after removal of 10 clear outliers (i.e., individuals whose data were outside the boundaries of the other subjects'), the primary finding of the study was that there was no consistent belief concerning appropriate levels of supervision, especially for children in middle childhood. When the central 50% of the respondents were considered (see Fig. 2), some consensus was seen for younger children, but suggestions still varied widely for school-age children. These recommended levels of supervision were not those necessarily practiced; they were, instead, those advocated as acceptable. The recommendations also do not represent what safety experts might suggest for these various ages; for example, safety experts recommend supervision for crossing busy streets at ages where this sample thought supervision could be discontinued.

Community norms for what constitutes appropriate discipline are equally difficult to ascertain and seem equally removed from findings on childhood injury. There appears to be a growing contingent of parents who advocate nonphysical methods of discipline. Nonetheless, in one survey, the majority of caregivers (70%) acknowledged hitting or slapping their children, a sizable minority (15% of fathers and 20% of mothers) reported hitting their children with objects, and 6.7% of fathers and 8.7% of mothers admitted that they had kicked, bitten, or punched their children.[10] Child abuse laws are written very ambiguously, so that the extent of physical damage that constitutes abuse is often unclear. The absence of clear norms of acceptability, together with greater tolerance of harsher physical discipline in populations at greater risk for abuse (e.g., low income, isolated), potentiates the problem.

FUTURE PREVENTIVE INTERVENTIONS

Although different federal funding agencies and scientific bodies control research on unintentional injury

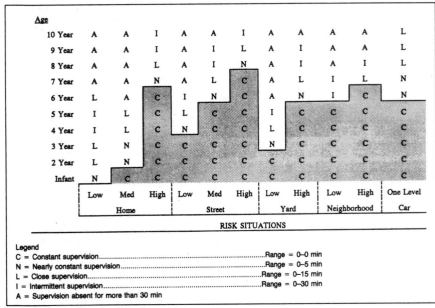

Fig. 2. Community mothers', physicians', and Division of Family Service workers' response to the request "Please indicate the number of minutes an average child of each of the following ages could, in your opinion, safely be left unsupervised (when awake and out of visual and auditory contact) in these situations. Zero indicates the child should not be left alone at all." Each letter in the figure indicates the range of responses given by the central 50% (removing extreme high and low scores) of the subjects. All time periods begin with zero because for all questions at least some respondents gave zero as a response. Shaded sections indicate areas in which these subjects showed complete agreement in level of supervision suggested.

and research on physical abuse and neglect, there seem to be few other reasons to regard these two literatures as describing differing phenomena. The two approaches have shown parallel historical development, including recent rapprochement with behavioral interventions; have identified common etiologic factors; have encountered similar challenges; and have recently moved toward multidimensional interventions.[9,11] Why do investigators in these fields continue to bifurcate their resources, efforts, and political power, as opposed to uniting to realize their common goals? People in both fields agree on a number of important points: They agree that reform at a national level, through both societal change and legislative action, is needed; they describe the importance of enlisting community systems, such as schools, health-care providers, and networks of neighbors; they underline the importance of intervening with parents, to increase skills and to improve the quality of the relationships between parents and their children; and they believe in empowering children through teaching, without making children responsible for their own safety. Integrating approaches from both fields offers enhanced promise for broad-spectrum prevention of the leading killer of children in this country, childhood injury.

Acknowledgments—Much of the research on unintentional injury and supervision reported here was supported by the National Institute of Child Health and Human Development (HD25414).

Notes

1. This vignette is representative of many cases of documented head injury in infancy. The name of the child and details mentioned here are fictitious, however.

2. See D.A. Bruce and R.A. Zimmering, Shaken impact syndrome, *Pediatric Annals, 18,* 488–494 (1989).

3. "Maltreatment" has been used as a generic label for physical, sexual, and psychological abuse, as well as neglect. All types of child maltreatment are undeniably related (e.g., child sexual abuse implies neglect by the primary caregiver charged with the child's welfare). Because this article focuses on physical injury, I do not explicitly discuss sexual abuse, emotional abuse, and other forms of neglect that do not result in physical injury. However, the prevention programs advocated here would likely be effective against these forms of child maltreatment as well.

4. These "isolated pioneers" have made definitive contributions to the direction of the field, however. The present article is a direct outgrowth of the powerful, early contributions of Garbarino, an excellent exemplar of these pioneers. See J. Garbarino, The human ecology of child maltreatment: A conceptual model for research, *Journal of Marriage and the Family, 39,* 721–735 (1977); J. Garbarino, Preventing childhood injury: Developmental and mental health issues, *American Journal of Orthopsychiatry, 58,* 25–45 (1988).

5. B. Ewigman, C. Kivlahan, and G. Land, The Missouri Child Fatality Study: Underreporting of maltreatment fatalities among children under five years of age. 1983–1986, *Pediatrics, 91,* 330–337 (1993).

6. P. McClain, J. Sachs, R. Foehlke, and B. Ewigman, A model estimating child abuse fatalities among U.S. children less than eighteen. 1979–1988, *Pediatrics* (in press).

7. The history of these two research areas and current findings on etiology are detailed by L. Peterson and D. Brown, Integrating child injury and abuse/neglect research: Common histories, etiologies, and solutions, *Psychological Bulletin* (in press).

8. See, e.g., R.C. Herrenkohl, E.C. Herrenkohl, and B.P. Egolf, Circumstances surrounding the occurrence of child maltreatment, *Journal of Consulting and Clinical Psychology, 51,* 424–431 (1983); L.D. Monroe and C.J. Schellenbach, Relationship of Child Abuse Potential Inventory scores to parental responses: A construct validity study, *Child and Family Behavior Therapy, 11,* 31–58 (1989).

9. Rather than possessing a deficit in knowledge of developmental milestones, such as walking and talking, as was previously thought, abusive parents unrealistically expect their children to engage in self-care and self-control earlier than do nonabusive or nonneglectful parents, as shown by S.T. Azar, D.R. Robinson, E. Hekiman, and C.T. Twentyman, Unrealistic expectations and problem solving ability in maltreating and comparison mothers, *Journal of Consulting and Clinical Psychology, 52,* 687–691 (1984).

10. R.J. Gelles and M.A. Straus, Is violence toward children increasing? A comparison of 1975 and 1985 national survey rates, *Journal of Interpersonal Violence, 2,* 212–222 (1987).

11. See recent programs such as those advocated by C.E. Walker, B.L. Bonner, and K.L. Kaufman, *The Physically and Sexually Abused Child: Evaluation and Treatment* (Pergamon Press, New York, 1988); D.J. Willis, W. Holden, and M. Rosenberg, Eds., *Prevention of Child Maltreatment* (Wiley, New York, 1992); D. Wolfe, *Preventing Physical and Emotional Abuse of Children,* (Guilford Press, New York, 1992). Also see Garbarino (1988), note 4.

Why schools must tell girls:
'YOU'RE SMART, YOU CAN DO IT'

Myra and David Sadker

Bias in education *is an issue that has stirred debate since 1954's Brown vs. Board of Education, the Supreme Court decision integrating public schools. In a new book,* Failing at Fairness: How America's Schools Cheat Girls *(Charles Scribner's Sons, $22), the focus is on girls. Authors Myra and David Sadker document how teachers and schools unwittingly shortchange girls up and down the educational ladder, from kindergarten through graduate school. Here the Sadkers, professors of education at The American University in Washington, D.C., and among the nation's leading experts in sex discrimination, describe the problem—and what educators and students are doing to combat it.*

Rachel Churner, 15, remembers seventh grade at her McKinney, Texas, middle school as the year she was scared silent. "You couldn't be too dumb because then you would be laughed at," she says. "But if you were too smart, you would be called a brain."

Rachel decided it was best for girls to be completely average. She stopped answering questions in class and tried to hide her intelligence. "If I got an A and people asked me how I did, I would say, 'I just got a B minus.' There were even times I wrote down the wrong answer to make a lower grade."

Reading from the same textbook, listening to the same teacher, sitting in the same classroom, girls and boys are getting very different educations. For 20 years, we've been watching girls in the classroom and studying their interactions with teachers. After thousands of hours of classroom observation, we remain amazed at the scope and stubborn persistence of gender bias.

These studies show that from grade school to grad school boys capture the lion's share of teachers' time and attention. Whether the class is science or social studies, English or math—and whether the teacher is female or male—girls are more likely to be invisible students, spectators to the educational process.

One reason that boys receive more teacher attention: They demand it. Boys call out eight times more often than girls—and get real feedback. But when girls call out, they're more likely to be reprimanded or to get the brushoff with responses like "OK."

'If you were too smart, you'd be called a brain.' —Rachel Churner

Girls not only are less visible in classrooms; they're missing from textbooks, too. Brand-new history textbooks still devote only 2 percent of their space to women. A simple test demonstrates the impact of this male curriculum. We've walked into classrooms—elementary, secondary, even college—and asked students to name 20 famous American women from history. We've given only one restriction: no athletes or entertainers. Few have met the challenge. Many couldn't name 10, or even five. One class of Maryland fifth-graders, embarrassed at coming up with so few, put "Mrs." in front of presidents' names, creating an instant list of famous-sounding women they knew nothing about. Other students wrote down names like Mrs. Fields, Betty Crocker and Aunt Jemima in a desperate attempt to find famous females.

Education is not a spectator sport. Over time, the lack of attention by teachers and the omission of women in textbooks takes its toll in lowered achievement, damaged self-esteem and limited career options. The proof:

• In the early grades, girls are equal to or even ahead of boys on almost every standardized test. By the time they leave high school or college, they have fallen behind.

• By high school, girls score lower on the SAT and ACT exams, crucial for college admission. The gender gap is greatest in math and science.

• On the College Board achievement exams, required by the most selective colleges, boys outscore girls on 11 of 14 tests by an average 30 points.

Girls are the only group who begin school scoring ahead and leave behind, a theft occurring so quietly that most people are unaware of its impact

---

Today, in small towns and large cities across the nation, parents and teachers, concerned about the future of America's daughters, have begun to take action. From college professors in Urbana, Ill., to elementary school teachers in Portland, Maine, educators are asking for help, signing up for workshops that we conduct on fighting gender bias in the classroom. Women's colleges such as Smith and Mount Holyoke have started sponsoring special summer sessions to help elementary and secondary school teachers battle bias against girls, especially in math and science.

And high on the agenda for change is renewed interest in girls-only education, until recently an endangered species.

Although not everyone agrees, most studies show that girls in single-sex schools achieve more, have higher self-esteem and are more interested in subjects like math and science.

Says Rachel Churner, now at Hockaday, a private all-girls school in Dallas: "Now I put my education first. I don't think that would have happened if I had stayed in my coed school."

Even coed schools are experimenting with single-sex classes. This includes some public schools, in one of the most surprising developments of the 1990s. After nine years of teaching coed high school math, Chris Mikles now teaches an all-girls Algebra II class at public Ventura (Calif.) High School. "The girls come in with such low self-esteem," she says. "I keep trying to get through to them: 'You're smart. You can do it.'"

This year, the Illinois Math and Science Academy in Aurora, a public coed residential school for 620 gifted students, is trying for the first time an experiment that tests a girls-only class. In the first part of the year, the school separated 13 girls for an all-girls calculus-based physics class. For the second half of the school year, the girls have rejoined coed classes. School officials will compare their performance with and without the boys, as well as against the girls and boys in coed classes.

Girls in the experimental class are feeling the results. In the girls-only class, Denab Bates, 17, says she was "more enthusiastic, more there than in my other classes"—asking and answering more questions, jumping "out of my seat to put a problem on the board. In my other classes, I sink back—'Oh, please, don't call on me.'" Kara Yokley, 15, also says she participated more, but she is not sure what will happen this semester as the class goes coed. "We need to make sure we don't lose our newfound physics freedom," she says.

Not every girl is as positive. "We took the same exams as the coed class, but the guys thought that girls weren't learning on the same level," worries 16-year-old Masum Momaya.

Legally, single-sex education in public schools is a sticky business. Laws like Title IX prohibit sex discrimination in public schools, including teaching girls and boys separately in most cases. In Illinois, educators say it works because IMSA is a laboratory school set up by the state to try innovations. In Ventura, Mikles says all-girls classes are permissible because they are open to male students, although not a single boy has yet enrolled.

Many educators have reservations that go beyond legal problems. They view single-sex education as a defeatist approach, one that gives up on girls and boys learning equally, side by side. Other critics say that the model focuses on "fixing up the girls" but leaves boys in the dust.

Where the Boys Are

It was not long ago that the focus was on boys—specifically, black boys, who some educators believed would benefit from separate schools. That movement has since lost steam. "Without a body of research to prove their effectiveness," Myra Sadker explains, boys-only schools "ran into legal problems."

AN UPDATE:

• **In Detroit,** the Malcom X Academy, an elementary and middle school with 500 students, and two other public schools were established in 1990 as all-boys schools. They were forced to admit girls after a judge ruled the same year that single-sex schools violated Title IX. Today, Malcolm X is 92 percent male.

• **The Milwaukee** school board wanted to create three boys-only schools in 1990, after evaluating the poor performance of many black males in public schools. School officials halted the project after the Detroit decision; instead, schools changed their curricula.

• **New York City's** Ujamaa Institute, intended for black and Hispanic boys, has yet to open since the proposal was challenged in court by the New York Civil Rights Coalition.

—*Myron B. Pitts*

Diane Ravitch of the Brookings Institution in Washington, D.C., is outspoken in her view that girls already are treated fairly in the educational system. Ravitch, assistant secretary of Education under President Bush, points to the fact that more women than men are enrolled in college, more women than men earn master's degrees, and the number of women graduating with law and medical degrees has increased dramatically since 1970. "The success of women in education has soared in the last 20 years," Ravitch says.

Despite such progress, women still tend to major in lower-paying fields, such as education and literature. Today, a woman with a college degree earns little more than a man with a high school diploma.

The remedy? Realistically, most schools remain committed to coeducation for philosophic, legal and economic reasons. Increasingly, though, educators are becoming convinced that changes need to be made. And when teachers change, so do their students. Our research suggests these key ways to make girls more active and assertive:

- Teachers and parents must encourage girls to speak up—both at home and in school.
- Textbooks need to be monitored to make sure that enough women are included.
- Seating arrangements in class need to be flexible, because students in the front or middle of the class get more attention.
- Comments to girls should encourage their academic progress. "You look so pretty today" and "Your handwriting is so neat"—standard comments to girls—are less helpful than "What a great test score" or "That was an insightful comment."

Parents, girls and even traditional women's organizations are beginning to join educators in making such simple but important changes. And groups nationwide are providing support and service. The National Women's History Project in California, for example, develops books and posters on multicultural women's history. The Girl Scouts has featured images of active girls in printed materials and highlighted badges in math and science. The Women's Educational Equity Act Publishing Center in Massachusetts says requests for materials have surged recently, especially in science and math. The American Association of University Women has sponsored research projects and roundtables. The Gender Equity in Education Act, currently before Congress, proposes programs to help pregnant teenagers, combat sexual harassment and provide gender-equity training for teachers.

Throughout the history of education in America, the angle of the school door has determined the direction girls travel to various adult destinies. Sometimes the door was locked and barred; at other times it was slightly ajar. Today girls face subtle inequities that have a powerful cumulative impact, chipping away at their achievement and self-esteem. But as a new generation of teachers and parents enters the school system, and an existing generation becomes increasingly open to reform, schools and educators appear ready to adapt—and girls will be the winners.

Teaching Young Children to Resist Bias

What Parents Can Do

Louise Derman-Sparks, María Gutiérrez, and Carol B. Phillips

Building self-identity and skills for social interaction are two major tasks in early childhood. Gradually, young children begin to figure out how they are the same and different from other people, and how they feel about the differences. What children learn in the pre-school years greatly influences whether they will grow up to value, accept, and comfortably interact with diverse people or whether they will succumb to the biases that result in, or help to justify, unfair treatment of an individual because of her or his identity.

Research tells us that between ages 2 and 5, children become aware of gender, race, ethnicity, and disabilities. They also become sensitive to both the positive attitudes and negative biases attached to these four key aspects of identity, by their family and by society in general. Young children develop "pre-prejudice": misconceptions, discomfort, fear, and rejection of differences that may develop into real prejudice if parents and teachers do not intervene.

"Girls aren't strong." "Boys can't play house."

"You're a baby in that wheelchair; you can't walk."

"You can't play with us, only light-skinned kids can."

Many adults find it hard to accept that 2-, 3-, and 4-year-olds actually make these comments. They would prefer to believe that young children are blissfully unaware of the differences between people upon which prejudice and discrimination are based. But young children not only recognize differences, they also absorb values about which differences are positive and which are not. How we as parents and teachers react to the ideas that young children express will greatly affect the feelings they will form. If we want children to like themselves and to value diversity, then we must learn how to help them resist the biases and prejudice that are still far too prevalent in our society.

HOW BIAS INFLUENCES CHILDREN'S DEVELOPMENT

Bias based on gender, race, handicap, or social class creates serious obstacles to all young children's healthy development. When areas of experience are gender stereotyped and closed to children simply because of their sex, neither boys nor girls are fully prepared to deal intellectually or emotionally with the realities and demands of everyday life. "Handicapism" severely harms children with disabilities by limiting access to the educational experiences necessary for well-rounded development. It also prevents non-disabled children from knowing and comfortably interacting with different types of people and teaches a false and anxiety-inducing sense of superiority based on their not being disabled.

Racism attacks the very sense of self for children of color. It creates serious obstacles to their obtaining the best education, health care, and employment. Racism also teaches White children a false identity of superiority and distorts their perceptions of reality. Thus they are not equipped to fairly and productively interact with more than half of the world's humanity.

The "isms" interfere as well with our ability as adults to effectively teach children about themselves and others. All of us have learned the negative values attached to gender, race, class, and handicapping conditions. And, to varying degrees, they make us uncomfortable as they affect our personal attitudes and behavior. At times, we hide such negative feelings from ourselves by denying the reality or significance of differences. We may hope to sidestep the impact of prejudice by saying, "people are all the same," or teaching children it is impolite to notice or ask about differences. However, avoidance doesn't give children the information they need. By selectively ignoring children's natural curiosity, we actually teach them that some differences are not acceptable. And by failing to attach positive value to certain specific differences, children are left to absorb the biases of society. The more that we face our own prejudiced and discriminatory attitudes toward diversity and, where necessary, change them, the better prepared we will be to foster children's growth.

WHAT PARENTS AND TEACHERS CAN DO

Recognize that because we live in a racist and biased society, we must actively foster children's anti-bias development. Remember that in such an environment, we are all constantly and repeatedly exposed to messages that subtly reinforce biases. If we do nothing to counteract them, then we silently support these biases by virtue of our inaction.

Create an environment at home or at school that deliberately contrasts the prevailing biased messages of the wider society.

Provide books, dolls, toys, wall decorations (paintings, drawings, photographs), TV programs, and records, that reflect diverse images that children may not likely see elsewhere in

• Gender roles (including men and women in nontraditional roles)

• Racial and cultural backgrounds (e.g., people of color in leadership positions)
• Capabilities (people with disabilities doing activities familiar to children)
• Family lifestyles (varieties of family composition and activities)

Show that you value diversity in the friends you choose and in the people and firms you choose for various services (e.g., doctor, dentist, car mechanic, teachers, stores). Remember that what you do is as important as what you say.

Make it a firm rule that a person's identity is never an acceptable reason for teasing or rejecting them. Immediately step in if you hear or see your child engage in such behavior. Make it clear that you disapprove, but do not make your child feel rejected. Support the child who has been hurt. Try to find out what underlies the biased behavior. If the reason is a conflict about another issue, help your child understand the real reason for the conflict and find a way to resolve it. If the underlying reason is discomfort with or fear or ignorance about the other child's differences, plan to initiate activities to help overcome negative feelings.

Helping children to deal with bias

Lisa, Pete, and Elana are playing hospital when Lisa's dad hears an argument break out over who will be the doctor and who will be the patient. Lisa finally says, "I don't want to be your friend anymore, you stupid Mexican!" Lisa's dad intervenes, "Lisa, what you just said is mean and it hurts Elana." Putting his arm around Elana's shoulders, he says, "I am sorry Lisa said that to you." Turning to all three children, he asks, "What is the problem?" Each child explains her side. Dad says, "Sounds like the real problem is that you both want to be the doctor. That has nothing to do with Elana being Mexican. Elana, who you are is just fine, just like who you, Lisa, and you, Peter, are is also just fine. But you all have a problem with taking turns. How can you work that out?"

Another step would need to happen if the scenario were somewhat different. For instance: Elana and her family have just moved into the neighborhood, and Lisa's parents invite them over for a visit. When they arrive, Lisa refuses to play with Elana in her room. After the family leaves, Lisa says, "I don't like them. Mexicans are stupid!" "I wonder why you think that?" her mom asks. "That's what my friend Cindy says." To which Lisa's mom replies, "Lisa, Cindy is wrong! To say that Mexicans are stupid is unfair and hurtful. Mexican people are just as smart as everyone else. Tomorrow, let's go to the library and get some books about Mexican-Americans so that we can learn more about them.

We want you to get to know Elana and her family because they are our neighbors."

One evening, after watching his favorite TV show, Mark (age 4) says, "I wish I wasn't Black." "Why?" asks his mother. "Cause I want to be a paramedic."

"You think you have to be White to be a paramedic, because that's what you saw on TV, isn't it?" Seeing Mark nod yes, his mother says "Even though you saw only White paramedics on TV, there are many Black paramedics, Black firefighters, and Black police officers. You can be anything you want when you grow up. You know, there should be more Black people on many TV shows. Some people who write the stories and own TV stations are not being fair. They are allowing racism to exist. Let's write a letter to the TV station and say that they should show paramedics, firefighters, and all kinds of people of all colors on TV." (From: Derman-Sparks et al., 1980)

"Heather wouldn't let me play house with her at school today," complains 5-year-old Miriam. "She says I act like a boy because I like boy things." "I'm sorry that happened. How did you feel?" "It hurt my feelings and made me mad." "I would feel that way too. You know, Heather is wrong. You don't act like a boy. You act like a girl who likes to play with blocks and trucks and to play ball."

7. DEVELOPMENT

Initiate activities and discussions to build positive self-identity and to teach the value of differences among people. Educate yourself about common stereotypes in our society so that you can evaluate your selection of children's materials and experiences. Whenever possible, either remove those containing biased messages, or learn to use such material to teach children about the difference between "fair" and "true" images and those that are "unfair" and "untrue" and which hurt people's feelings.

Talk positively about each child's physical characteristics and cultural heritage. Tell stories about people from your ethnic group of whom you are especially proud. Include people who have stood up against bias and injustice. Encourage children to explore different kinds of materials and activities that go beyond traditional gender behaviors.

Help children learn the differences between feelings of superiority and feelings of self-esteem and pride in their heritage.

Provide opportunities for children to interact with other children who are racially/culturally different from themselves and with people who have various disabilities. If your neighborhood does not provide these opportunities, search for them in school, after-school activities, weekend programs, places of worship, and day camps.

Visit museums, concerts, and cultural events that reflect diverse heritages as well as your own.

Respectfully listen to and answer children's questions about themselves and others. Do not ignore questions, change the subject, sidestep, or admonish the child for asking a question. These responses suggest that what a child is asking is bad. However, do not *over-respond*. Answer all questions in a direct, matter-of-fact, and brief manner. Listen carefully to what children want to know *and* what they are feeling.

Teach children how to challenge biases about who they are. By the time children are 4 years old, they become aware of biases directed against aspects of their identity. This is especially true for children of color, children with disabilities, and children who don't fit stereotypic gender norms. Be sensitive to children's feelings about themselves and immediately respond when they indicate any signs of being affected by biases. Give your children tools to confront those who act biased against them.

Teach children to recognize stereotypes and caricatures of different groups. Young children can become adept at spotting "unfair" images of themselves and others if they are helped to think critically about what they see in books, TV, movies, greeting cards, and comics.

Use accurate and fair images in contrast to stereotypic

Common questions that parents and teachers ask

Q: "My child never asks questions about race, disability, or gender. If I raise it myself, will I introduce her to ideas she wouldn't have thought of on her own?"
A: Yes, you may, thereby expanding your child's awareness and knowledge. Your child may also have had questions for which she didn't have words or didn't feel comfortable raising until you brought up the subject. Remember that children do not learn prejudice from open, honest discussion of differences and the unfairness of bias. Rather, it is through these methods that children develop anti-bias sensitivity and behavior.

Q: "I don't feel competent to deal with these issues; I don't know enough. What if I say the wrong thing?"
A: Silence "speaks" louder than we realize, sending messages that are counter to the development of anti-bias attitudes. It is far better to respond, even if, upon hindsight, you wish you had handled the incident differently. You can always go back to your child and say "Yesterday, when you asked me about why Susie uses a wheelchair, I didn't give you enough of an answer. I've thought about your question some more, and today I want to tell you . . ." If you really do not have the information to answer a question, you can say, "That's a good question, but I don't know the answer

right now. Let me think about it a little and I will tell you later." Or, "Let's go find some books to help us answer your question." Then be sure to follow through.

Examine your own feelings about the subject raised by your child's questions or behaviors. Feelings of incompetence often come from discomfort rather than a lack of knowledge. Talk over your feelings with a sympathetic family member or friend in order to be better prepared the next time.

Q: "I don't want my children to know about prejudice and discrimination until they have to. Won't it upset them to know about injustices?"
A: It is natural to want to protect our children from painful subjects and situations. Moreover, adults may mask their own pain by choosing not to address issues of bias with their children. Avoiding issues that may be painful doesn't help children. Being unprepared to deal effectively with life's realities only leaves them more vulnerable and exposed to hurt. Silence about children's misconceptions and discriminatory behavior gives them permission to inflict pain on others. It is alright for children to sometimes feel sad or upset as long as they know that you are there to comfort and support them.

Common questions children ask and ways to respond

"Why is that girl in a wheelchair?"
Inappropriate
"Shh, it's not nice to ask." (admonishing)
"I'll tell you another time." (sidestepping)
Acting as if you didn't hear the question. (avoiding)
Appropriate
"She is using a wheelchair because her legs are not strong enough to walk. The wheelchair helps her move around.

"Why is Jamal's skin so dark?"
Inappropriate
"His skin color doesn't matter. We are all the same underneath."
This response denies the child's question, changing the subject to one of similarity when the child is asking about a difference.
Appropriate
"Jamal's skin is dark brown because his mom and dad have dark brown skin."
This is enough for 2- or 3-year-olds. As children get older, you can add an explanation of melanin:
"Everyone has a special chemical in our skin called melanin. If you have a lot of melanin, your skin is dark. If you only have a little, your skin is light. How much melanin you have in your skin depends on how much your parents have in theirs."

"Why am I called Black? I'm brown!"
Inappropriate
"You are *too* Black!"
This response is not enough. It doesn't address the child's confusion between actual skin color and the name of the racial and/or ethnic group.
Appropriate
"You're right; your skin color *is* brown. We use the name 'Black' to mean the group of people of whom our family is a part. Black people can have different skin colors. We are all one people because our great-great-grandparents once came from a place called Africa. That's why many people call themselves 'Afro-Americans.' "

"Will the brown wash off in the tub?"
This is a fairly common question because children are influenced by the racist equation of dirtiness and dark skin in our society.

Inappropriate
Taking this as an example of "kids say the darndest things" and treating it as not serious.
Appropriate
"The color of Jose's skin will never wash off. When he takes a bath, the dirt on his skin washes off, just like when you take a bath. Whether they have light or dark skin, everybody gets dirty, and everyone's skin stays the same color after it is washed. Everybody's skin is clean after they wash it, no matter what color their skin is."

"Why does Miyoko speak funny?
Inappropriate
"Miyoko can't help how she speaks. Let's not say anything about it."
This response implies agreement with the child's comment that Miyoko's speech is unacceptable, while also telling the child to "not notice," and be polite.
Appropriate
"Miyoko doesn't speak funny, she speaks *differently* than you do. She speaks Japanese because that's what her mom and dad speak. You speak English like your mom and dad. It is okay to ask questions about what Miyoko is saying, but it is *not* okay to say that her speech sounds funny because that can hurt her feelings."

"Why do I have to try out that dumb wheelchair? . . ."
. . . asks Julio who refuses to sit in a child-sized wheelchair in the children's museum.
Inappropriate
"It is not dumb. All the children are trying it and I want you to."
This response does not help uncover the feelings underlying Julio's resistance and demands that he do something that is clearly uncomfortable for him.
Appropriate
Putting his arm around Julio, his dad gently asks, "Why is it dumb?" Julio: "It will hurt my feet, just like Maria's feet." Dad: "Maria's feet can't walk because she was born with a condition called cerebral palsy. The wheelchair helps her move around. Nothing will happen to your legs if you try sitting and moving around in the wheelchair. It's OK if you don't want to, but if you do try it you'll find out that your legs will still be fine."

---

ones, and encourage children to talk about the differences. For example, at Thanksgiving time, greeting cards which show animals dressed up as "Indians" and a stereotypic image of an "Indian" child with buckskins and feather headdress abound. Talk about how it is hurtful to people's feelings to show them looking like animals, or to show them portrayed inaccurately. Read good children's books to show the reality and the variety of Native American peoples. As children get older, you can also help them learn about how stereotypes are used to justify injustice, such as lower wages, poor housing and education, etc.

Let children know that unjust things can be changed. Encourage children to challenge bias and give them skills appropriate to their age level. First set an example by your own actions. Intervene when children engage in discriminatory behavior, support your children when they challenge bias directed against themselves and others, encourage children to identify and think critically about stereotypic images, and challenge adult biased remarks and jokes—all methods of modeling anti-bias behavior.

Involve children in taking action on issues relevant to their lives.

- Talk to a toy store manager or owner about adding more toys that reflect diversity, such as dolls, books, and puzzles.
- Ask your local stationery store to sell greeting cards that show children of color.
- Take your child to a rally about getting more funding for child care centers.

As you involve children in this type of activity, be sure to discuss the issues with them, and talk about the reasons for taking action.

SUMMARY

Keep in mind that developing a healthy identity and understanding of others is a long-term process. While the early years lay an essential foundation, learning continues throughout childhood and into adulthood and will take many different forms. Children will change their thinking and feelings many times.

FOR FURTHER INFORMATION

Contact the Council On Interracial Books For Children, 1841 Broadway, New York, NY 10023. 212-757-5339.

BIBLIOGRAPHY

The Children's Foundation. (1990). *Helping children love themselves and others: A professional handbook for family day care.* Washington, DC: Author.

Council On Interracial Books For Children. *Selecting bias-free textbooks and storybooks.* New York: Author.

Derman-Sparks, L., & the A.B.C. Task Force. (1989). *Anti-bias curriculum: Tools for empowering young children.* Washington, DC: National Association for the Education of Young Children. (To order NAEYC #242, send $7 [includes postage and handling] to NAEYC, 1834 Connecticut Avenue, N.W., Washington, DC 20009.)

Derman-Sparks, L., Hilga, C. T., & Sparks, B. (1980). Children, race and racism: How race develops. *Interracial Books for Children Bulletin, 11* (3 & 4), 315.

Children *can* learn to become anti-biased!

We can all take heart from examples such as the following examples of 4- and 5-year-olds challenging racism: Kiyoshi, (age 4 $\frac{1}{2}$) sees a stereotypic "Indian warrior" figure in the toy store. "That toy hurts Indians' feeling," he points to his grandmother.

* * *

Casey (age 5), and another White friend, Tommy, are playing. Casey calls two other boys to join them. "You can't play with them, they're Black," Tommy says to him. Casey replies. "That's not right. Black and White kinds should play together. My Dad tells me civil rights stories."

* * *

After hearing the story of Rosa Parks and the Montgomery bus boycott, Tiffany (age 5 $\frac{1}{2}$), whose skin is light brown, ponders whether she would have had to sit in the back of the bus. Finally, she firmly asserts, "I'm Black, and anyway all this is stupid. I would just get off the bus and tell them to keep their old bus."

* * *

Kiyoshi, Casey, and Tiffany are learning to think critically and to speak up when they believe something is unfair. They are becoming "empowered": gaining the confidence and skills that will enable them to resist and challenge bias and to participate in the creation of a more just society.

Current Perspectives on Dual-Career Families

Lucia Albino Gilbert

Lucia Albino Gilbert, Professor of Educational Psychology at the University of Texas at Austin, studies the career development of women and various aspects of dual-career family life. Address correspondence to Lucia A. Gilbert, Department of Educational Psychology, University of Texas, Austin, TX 78712.

In 1969, the Rapoports, working in England, first used the term dual-career family to describe what they considered to be an unusual and "revolutionary" type of dual-wage heterosexual family that emerged as the result of complex social changes.[1] Revolutionary from their perspective was the dual-career family's apparent inconsistency with traditional notions of gender. In such a family, the woman and man both pursued lifelong careers, relatively uninterrupted, and also established and developed a family life that often included children. Contrary to tradition, the woman viewed her employment as salient to her self-concept and life goals and pursued occupational work regardless of her

family situation. The male partner, in turn, appeared less defined (relative to other married men) by the traditional "good provider" role long associated with male privilege and power.[2]

The notion of a two-career family was met with both excitement and skepticism. It promised to preserve the best of marriage—intimacy and enduring love—but freed partners from the harness of gender roles. True equality between women and men—social, economic, and political equality—seemed highly possible, if not inevitable. Now, some 25 years later, both the excitement and the skepticism appear realistic. Although increasing numbers of couples establish dual-career relationships, the larger promise of true equality has yet to be achieved.

From a theoretical perspective, role sharing in the private lives of heterosexual partners represents the elimination of gender-based role specialization and male power associated with patriarchy. Because dual-career marriages still exist within a larger world of gender inequity, it is not yet possible for the role-sharing dual-career family to

emerge as a normative societal marital pattern. Nonetheless, the surprisingly high percentage of employed couples for whom role sharing is an interpersonal relational characteristic attests to this pattern's growing importance.

This article provides an overview of research on dual-career family life. Before summarizing this research, I review current facts on working women and men in the United States. These facts and figures describe the broad social context of dual-career families today.

FACTS AND FIGURES ON EDUCATION AND EMPLOYMENT

Currently, women and men ages 25 to 29 are equally likely to have 4 or more years of college. Women also experience fewer barriers to using their education than was the case previously, and a sizable number have entered professional fields formerly closed to them, such as medicine, law, and university teach-

From *Current Directions in Psychological Science,* Vol. 3, No. 4, August 1994, pp. 101-105. © 1994 by the American Psychological Society. Reprinted by permission of CAMBRIDGE UNIVERSITY PRESS.

ing. In 1990, women represented 25% of full-time employed physicians, 27% of lawyers, 30% of college and university teachers, and 36% of Ph.D. psychologists; overall, women now constitute about 39% of the professional labor force.[3]

A direct corollary of women's increased educational and occupational opportunities is the dramatic increase in the number of U.S. families in which both partners report full-time employment.[4] Most married women with children under 6 years old are employed; 59.2% are in the labor force, and of these, 69.6% are employed full-time. For married women with children under the age of 18, these percentages increase to 67.0% employed and 72.9% employed full-time.

The average working wife with full-time employment contributes approximately 40% of the family's annual income. Increasing numbers of women view work in professional fields as central to their self-identities, a fact that obviously increases the number of families in which both partners consider themselves to be in careers (as opposed to women moving in and out of the work force depending on their families' needs).

THE KINDS OF QUESTIONS ASKED BY RESEARCHERS

As women's and men's roles have changed, so have the kinds of questions asked by researchers. From a gender perspective,[5] research on dual-career families can be viewed as falling into three somewhat distinct phases. The first phase focused on women's changing roles. Questions centered around how women could "do it all" and continue to meet their traditional responsibilities of caring for husbands and children. Implicit in this approach was the idea that women's roles were changing but men's were not, and that women made any necessary accommodations. Close watch was kept on how women dealt with the stress of their "multiple roles," how their children fared, and how happy their husbands were. Researchers, for example, looked for harm to children and compared children reared in traditional and dual-wage homes; however, results from the many studies conducted showed preschool-aged children to be at no added risk if they received alternate child or day care instead of parental care for some portion of the day.[6]

The second phase is best characterized as gender comparative. A woman's decision to pursue occupational work was viewed as "her right" as well as "her choice." Women began to push for changes within the home and family, and hence for changes in men's behaviors. Assumptions about how to arrange occupational work and family life shifted from women doing all the accommodating to arrangements being worked out between spouses. Both women and men were viewed as having multiple roles. Much of the research in this phase centered on comparisons of women and men. How much were men doing in the home compared with women? Did women and men cope in different ways? Were there gender differences in marital, occupational, or parenting satisfaction?

One major finding was that having multiple roles benefits women and men.[7] Benefits for women include increased self-esteem, better physical and mental health, and enhanced economic independence. For men, benefits include increased emotional involvement and bonding with children, better overall health, and lowered pressure to be financial providers. A related finding was that men increased their participation in parenting.[8] Some studies indicated that when both parents of preschoolers are employed, the combined time fathers and mothers spend in direct interaction with their children is about the same as for parents in families in which only one spouse is employed. The difference is that working parents spend more time with children on weekends and plan more for their time with children overall. Census data on primary child-care arrangements used by dual-wage families indicate that 17.9% of fathers provide primary care for children under 5 years of age. Reports from the Department of Labor indicate that increasing numbers of men use vacation and sick days to tend to newborns and other children, refuse long work hours, and seek flexible schedules or family leave.[8]

This second phase, although providing valuable insights into the day-to-day life of partners, used the behavior of individual women and men as its primary focus of inquiry. Little attention was given to the larger context in which these behaviors occurred. The third, and current, phase, in contrast, broadens investigations of dual-career family life to include the context of societal norms and practices. Thus, this phase recognizes explicitly that how couples combine work and family and carry out their multiple roles depends on much more than partners' personal wishes or preferences. In the case of parenting, research paradigms now include such structural variables as the kinds of care provided, definitions of optimal care,

REALITIES OF THE DUAL-CAREER FAMILY LIFE-STYLE

and the type of employer policies available to spouses.[9-11] Maternal employment, which in itself is generally unrelated to child outcomes, is viewed through its effects on the family environment and the child-care arrangements, and these are moderated by parental attitudes, family structure, workplace policies, and other relevant variables.[10] Obviously, the more employers' policies reflect a traditional workplace culture in which women with children leave the workplace and men with children are unencumbered by family responsibilities, the more difficult it becomes for both partners to parent.

Let us turn to four crucial areas of dual-career family life and briefly consider key findings and key issues. All four areas involve some aspect of spouses' multiple roles. Investigations range from studies of spouses' actual role behaviors to studies of the support spouses need for their roles.

How Partners Combine Family Life and Occupational Work

Although women today have greater economic and legal equality with men than in the past, partners must still act out their private roles as spouses, parents, and homemakers within the larger world of "gendered" occupational and institutional structures and policies. Thus, men still earn much more than women on average and hold most of the positions of power in society. Women can more readily and explicitly use family-related employee benefits such as parental leave and flextime. Moreover, individuals, female or male, still feel they must accommodate their personal lives to the traditional occupational structures if they expect to be rewarded by employers.

Despite this situation, recent data on the division of domestic labor indicate that the inevitability of a "second shift" for wives is overstated and that although some wives do face a double day, others are in more equitable arrangements. Overall, men's participation in family work has continued to increase from 1970 to the present time, more so in the area of parenting than in the area of household work.[12] There is also important variation among couples. My studies of dual-career families indicate three general marital patterns, which I have labeled conventional, modern, and role sharing. In a conventional dual-career family, both partners are involved in careers, but the responsibility for family work (household work and parenting) is retained by the woman, who adds her career role to her traditionally held family role. Typically, both partners agree to the premise that work within the home is women's work, and men "help out" as long as doing so does not interfere with their career pursuits. Far more professionally ambitious than their spouses, the men in these families typically command much higher salaries and see the choice of whether to combine a career with family life as belonging to women.

In the modern pattern, parenting is shared by the spouses, but the wife takes more responsibility for household work than does the husband. Characteristically, the men in these families are motivated to be active fathers, a motivation that may or may not be strongly associated with egalitarian views. These men want close relationships with their children but may still see other aspects of family work as more the responsibility of women than of men.

The third pattern—the role-sharing dual-career family—is the most egalitarian and a pattern many couples, and female partners in particular, strive for. In this variation, both partners actively involve themselves in household work and family life as well as occupational pursuits. At least one third of heterosexual two-career families fit this variation,

Table 1. *Factors that influence how partners combine occupational and family roles*

Factor	Examples
Personal factors:	
Personality	How important is a partner's need to dominate? to be emotionally intimate? to be tops in her or his field?
Attitudes and values	What are a partner's views about rearing a child? about women being as successful as men professionally?
Interests and abilities	How committed is a partner to occupational work? to family relations? Are both partners satisfied with their occupations and career plans?
Stages in careers	Is one partner peaking and the other thinking about retirement?
Relationship factors:	
Equity and power	How are decisions made? What seems fair? How do partners come to agreements about household work? about parenting? about money?
Partner support	Can partners count on each other for support in most areas?
Shared values and expectations	Do partners share the same views of women's and men's roles? Do partners have similar life goals?
Environmental and societal factors:	
Work situation	Are work hours flexible? Is there evidence of sex discrimination or other kinds of gender bias? Are policies prohibiting sexual harassment in place and understood?
Employer's views	Are policies family oriented? What is the general attitude toward employees who involve themselves in family life?
Availability and quality of child care	Is child care available? Does it meet parents' criteria for high-quality care?
Support systems	Do family members live nearby? Are friends and colleagues also in dual-wage families? Is the community responsive to the needs of employed parents?

although many spouses who are not role sharing describe their situations as equitable.

Differences among dual-career families involve variables associated with individual partners, employment practices, and social norms. Table 1 summarizes the usual personal, relational, and environmental factors that influence how couples combine occupational and family roles. Satisfaction does not necessarily differ for people with different family patterns; rather, satisfaction with a particular pattern adopted depends on these factors, especially each partner's perceptions of fairness and sources of support.

Perceptions of Fairness: Equity Versus Equality

Spouses' perceptions of what constitutes equity relate directly to marital quality and personal well-being.[13] The issue is not equality of power, but rather perceptions of equity or proportional returns in the exchange of personal and economic resources. Thus, wives who define themselves as co-providers, compared with wives who view themselves as persons who generate a second income, feel more entitled to their husbands' participation in family work and feel relatively unsatisfied if they perceive their husbands as not doing their fair share of this work. Similarly, husbands typically involve themselves more in family work when wives make greater financial contributions to the family and when both partners attribute greater meaning and importance to the wife's employment.

Women who perceive themselves as co-providers but who are hesitant to ask their husbands to do more at home may inadvertently act in ways that keep husbands in the dominant position, at the cost of their own marital happiness. Wives who perceive husbands as doing too little, but whose husbands disagree, report lower marital satisfaction and happiness than wives and husbands who

agree the wife is doing more or who see themselves as equitably sharing roles. Overall, women and men who achieve desired outcomes through participation in family work are unlikely to be aware of injustice. Desired outcomes typically include family harmony, time for family activities, or care and responsiveness among family members.

Parenting and Role Conflict

Among heterosexual dual-career couples, deciding when to have a child is typically more the question than deciding whether to have a child. The timing of the transition to parenthood has important consequences for parental behaviors, divisions of household labor, and partners' well-being. Once partners decide to parent, decisions about the child's day-to-day care are made in the context of variables such as partners' values, employers' policies, flexibility of work schedules, and the availability of care.

Generally, role conflict and day-to-day stress associated with parenting and careers are lowest under the following conditions:[14]

- Employers of both partners have benefit policies that are responsive to families' needs.

- Both partners participate actively in parenting.

- Partners feel comfortable sharing the parenting with child-care personnel.

- Partners view each other's involvement in home roles as fair.

- Partners are satisfied with the child care they are using.

- Partners are happy in their occupational work.

- Partners employ cognitive-restructuring strategies in coping with stress. For example, a parent whose work is never-ending might say, "No sense worrying about what I can't get done. I'll do

what I can. Besides, I like what I'm doing."

Sources of Support

Two sources of support are particularly crucial to spouses' and families' well-being. First, significant others have a central and extensive role. The mutuality of spousal support and affirmation is particularly important. Shared values and expectations about love and work and perceptions of fairness enhance the ability of spouses to be supportive.

Second, societal and institutional support is extremely important. Effective coping and satisfaction among partners with children invariably are associated with societal support—equitable salaries for women, flexibility of work schedules, suitable child care, family-supportive employers and benefit policies. Currently, a number of companies offer flexible scheduling in the form of flextime, part-time employment, job sharing, compressed work schedules, or work at home. Companies with supportive work and family policies, good health coverage, and flexible work hours have significantly less employee burnout and turnover than companies without such policies.[11]

CLOSING REMARKS

As recent studies indicate, female and male employees hold increasingly similar attitudes toward relocation, business travel, and child care, and family obligations influence the plans and experiences of women and men.[9] It is now the norm for women and men to combine occupational work and family life across the life cycle, although this pattern is still somewhat out of step with social institutions and with how people define careers and achieve occupational advancement. Although change comes slowly, a new picture of contemporary marriage is nonetheless emerging. For women and men who live in these more egalitarian times, the variations of the dual-career family form stand among the marital patterns available.

Notes

1. The term career, although sometimes used to indicate any kind of employment, is defined in the literature more specifically: A career comprises positions requiring special education and training and undertaken or engaged in as a lifework. Typically, such positions require a high degree of commitment and provide the person with a sense of consecutive, progressive achievement, be it through promotions or other recognition of accomplishments and skills; R. Rapoport and R.N. Rapoport, The dual-career family, *Human Relations, 22*, 3–30 (1969).

2. J. Bernard, The good provider role: Its rise and fall, *American Psychologist, 36*, 1–12 (1981).

3. National Science Foundation, *Selected Data on Science and Engineering Doctorate Awards* (Author, Washington, DC, 1991).

4. S.K. Wisensale, Toward the 21st century: Family change and public policy, *Family Relations, 41*, 417–422 (1992).

5. Gender refers not only to biological sex, but also to the psychological, social, and cultural characteristics that have become strongly associated with the biological categories of female and male.

6. S. Scarr, D. Phillips, and K. McCartney, Facts, fantasies, and the future of child care in the United States, *Psychological Science, 1*, 26–35 (1990).

7. See, e.g., R.C. Barnett, N.L. Marshall, and J.D. Singer, Job experiences over time, multiple roles, and women's mental health: A longitudinal study, *Journal of Personality and Social Psychology, 62*, 634–644 (1992).

8. See, e.g., U.S. Bureau of the Census, *Who's Minding the Kids?* Series P-70, no. 20 (U.S. Government Printing Office, Washington, DC, 1990); U.S. Department of Labor, Women's Bureau, *Employers and Child Care: Benefiting Work and Family* (U.S. Government Printing Office, Washington, DC, 1989); J.H. Pleck, Are "family-supportive" employer policies relevant to men? in *Work, Family, and Masculinities*, J.C. Hood, Ed. (Sage, Beverly Hills, CA, 1994).

9. S. Zedeck and K.L. Mosier, Work in the family and employing organization, *American Psychologist, 45*, 240–251 (1990).

10. L.W. Hoffman, Effects of maternal employment in the two-parent family, *American psychologist, 44*, 283–292 (1989).

11. J. Aldous, Ed., The impact of workplace family policies, *Journal of Family Issues, 11*(4) (1990).

12. L.A. Gilbert, *Men in Dual-Career Families: Current Realities and Future Prospects* (Erlbaum, Hillsdale, NJ, 1985); M.M. Ferree, The gender division of labor in two-earner marriages, *Journal of Family Issues, 12*, 158–180 (1991).

13. J.H. Pleck, *Working Wives/Working Husbands* (Sage, Beverly Hills, CA, 1985); L. Thompson, Family work: Women's sense of fairness, *Journal of Family Issues, 12*, 181–196 (1991).

14. L.A. Gilbert, *Sharing It All: The Rewards and Struggles of Two-Career Families* (Plenum Press, New York, 1988); L. Thompson and A. J. Walker, Women and men in marriage, work, and parenthood, *Journal of Marriage and the Family, 51*, 845–872 (1989).

Recommended Reading

Ferree, M.M. (1990). Beyond separate spheres: Feminism and family research. *Journal of Marriage and the Family, 52*, 866–884.

Gilbert, L.A. (1993). *Two Careers/One Family: The Promise of Gender Equality.* Beverly Hills, CA: Sage.

Pleck, J.H. (1985). *Working Wives/Working Husbands.* Beverly Hills, CA: Sage.

*Far from being the slough of despond it is considered, middle age
may be the very best time of life, researchers say—the "it" we work toward*

MIDLIFE MYTHS

WINIFRED GALLAGHER

Winifred Gallagher ("Midlife Myths") is a senior editor of
American Health. *Her latest book [is]* The Power of Place:
How Our Surroundings Shape Our Thoughts, Emotions, and
Actions.

According to the picture of human development drawn by traditional scientific literature, after a busy childhood and adolescence young adults launch their careers and social lives and then stride into a black box, from which they hobble some forty years later to face a darkly eventful senescence. According to popular literature, what takes place inside the box is an anticlimactic, unsatisfying, and even traumatic march over the hill and toward the grave—or, worse, the nursing home. This scenario complements the anecdotes that often figure in conversations about middle age: that friend of a friend whose lifetime investment in career and family went up in the flames of a passion for the au pair, or that second cousin rumored to have gone off the deep end during the "change of life" when the kids left for college.

So entrenched is the idea that middle age is bad or boring or both that the almost 80 million members of the graying Baby Boom generation won't use the term except in referring to Ozzie and Harriet Nelson or Ward and June Cleaver. "We have a problem here, and it's called denial," the television producer Stan Rogow, whose 1992 series *Middle Ages* was a critical success, recently told *Newsweek*. He blames the show's title for its commercial failure: "'Middle age' is this horrible-sounding thing you've heard throughout your life and hated." The denial he describes frustrates the efforts of researchers who are conducting the first comprehensive, multidisciplinary studies of middle age. They are finding that it is not just an aging process but life's peak experience.

The study of development concentrates mostly on life's early stages, when behavioral and physiological growth and change are simultaneous. In the 1960s the new discipline of gerontology revealed that as people lived much further into old age, a reverse synchrony obtained toward life's end. Looking back from studies of the elderly and, to a lesser extent, forward from studies of the young, researchers began to suspect that middle age might be not simply a long interval during which things are worse than they are in youth and better than they are

in old age but a developmental process in its own right—albeit one not particularly tied to changes in the body. Common perceptions of middle age are that it occurs from roughly forty to sixty; in the future, increased longevity and better health may push back the period of middle age even further. The scientists and scholars exploring this part of life, which is probably better described experientially than chronologically—the very concept of middle age itself is something of a cultural artifact, with social and economic components—range from the medically, sociologically, and psychologically oriented John D. and Catherine T. MacArthur Foundation Research Network on Successful Midlife Development (MIDMAC), administered from Vero Beach, Florida, to the psychoanalytically and spiritually grounded C. G. Jung Foundation's Center for Midlife Development in New York City.

Although there are plenty of exceptions, "the data show that middle age is the very best time in life," says Ronald Kessler, a sociologist and MIDMAC fellow who is a program director in the survey research center of the University of Michigan's Institute for Social Research. "When looking at the total U.S. population, the best year is fifty. You don't have to deal with the aches and pains of old age or the anxieties of youth: Is anyone going to love me? Will I ever get my career off the ground? Rates of general distress are low—the incidences of depression and anxiety fall at about thirty-five and don't climb again until the late sixties. You're healthy. You're productive. You have enough money to do some of the things you like to do. You've come to terms with your relationships, and the chance of divorce is very low. Midlife is the 'it' you've been working toward. You can turn your attention toward being rather than becoming."

Whereas Kessler's picture of middle age is drawn from facts and figures, the image in most Americans' minds is based on myths, derived not from the ordinary experiences of most people but from the unusual experiences of a few. Although these make for livelier reading and conversation, they generate an unnecessarily gloomy attitude about the middle years which limits people's horizons, according to Margie Lachman, a psychologist, a MIDMAC fellow, and the director of the Life-span Developmental Psychology Laboratory at Brandeis University. When Lachman asked young adults what it means to be middle-aged, they gave such answers as "You think more

The overwhelming majority of people, surveys show, accomplish the task of coming to terms with the realities of middle age through a long, gentle process—not an acute, painful crisis.

about the past than the future" and "You worry about money for health care." They also assumed that the stress experienced in middle age came from the desire to be young again. Older subjects Lachman surveyed, who knew better, attributed stress to coping with the many demands of the busiest time in life. And whereas the older group saw their lives as generally stable, the younger expected to experience a lot of change—and a crisis—in midlife. "The images and beliefs we have about middle age are the guideposts for our planning, evaluation, and goal-setting," Lachman says. "Are they accurate? Or negative self-fulfilling prophesies?"

Gilbert Brim, a pioneer in the study of social development through the life-span and the director of MIDMAC, agrees. "Passed on from generation to generation," he says, "widely shared cultural beliefs and untested theories about middle age put forward in the media continue to be played out in society. But they're likely to be wrong. There are probably as many myths about midlife now as there were about aging thirty years ago, before the advent of gerontology. The time has come to rid ourselves of these obsolete ideas."

The Inexorable Midlife Crisis?

MOST YOUNGER ADULTS ANTICIPATE THAT BEtween their late thirties and their early fifties a day will come when they suddenly realize that they have squandered their lives and betrayed their dreams. They will collapse into a poorly defined state that used to be called a nervous breakdown. Escape from this black hole will mean either embracing an un-American philosophy of eschatological resignation or starting over—jaded stockbrokers off to help Mother Teresa, phlegmatic spouses off to the StairMaster and the singles scene. In short, they will have a midlife crisis.

If youth's theme is potential, midlife's is reality: childhood fantasies are past, the fond remembrances of age are yet to be, and the focus is on coming to terms with the finite resources of the here and now. The overwhelming majority of people, surveys show, accomplish this devel-

opmental task, as psychologists put it, through a long, gentle process—not an acute, painful crisis. Over time the college belle or the high school athlete leans less on physical assets, the middle manager's horizons broaden beyond the corner office, and men and women fortunate enough to have significant others regard the rigors of courtship with indulgent smiles. In relying on brains and skill more than beauty and brawn, diffusing competitive urges to include the tennis court or a community fundraising project, and valuing long-term friendship and domestic pleasures over iffy ecstasies, these people have not betrayed their youthful goals but traded them in for more practical ones that bring previously unsuspected satisfaction. Ronald Kessler says, "The question to ask the middle-aged person isn't just What has happened to you? but also How has your experience changed your thinking?"

The middle-aged tend to be guided not by blinding revelations associated with emotional crisis but by slowly dawning adaptive insights into the self and others, which Kessler calls "psychological turning points." Early in midlife these usually involve a recognition of limitations: the local politician realizes that she'll never make it to the U.S. Senate, and the high school English teacher accepts that he's not going to be a famous man of letters. In the middle period of middle age the transitions usually concern what Kessler calls a redirection of goals: "You say to yourself, 'I'm killing myself at work, but the thing that really satisfies me is my family. I'm not going to change jobs, but from now on I'm going to focus more on home, and career will mean something different to me.'" In later middle age, turning points, especially for women, often involve a recognition of strength—"just the opposite of what you'd suppose," Kessler says. "The shy violet, for example, finds herself chairing a committee." These soundings taken and adjustments made prompt not dramatic departures from one's life course but gentle twists and curves.

"Mastery experiences," the more robust versions of which figure in Outward Bound–type adventure vacations, can be catalysts for middle-aged people in their ordinary settings as well. One of Kessler's subjects finally got his college diploma at fifty-eight, observing that he

"Mastery experiences," the more robust versions of which figure in Outward Bound–type vacations, can be catalysts for middle-aged people in their ordinary settings as well.

had thereby "resolved a lot of things and completed something important"; in almost the same language, a man of fifty said that he had "done something important" when he became proficient enough in his hobby of electronics to tutor others. Overcoming her lifelong fear of water, one woman learned to swim at the age of forty-five. "One day her family went to the pool, and she just jumped in," Kessler says. "This was a very powerful experience for her, not because she wanted to be a lifeguard but because she had mastered her anxiety as well as a new skill."

Even an apparently negative turning point can have benefits. Quite a few of Kessler's subjects, when asked if they had realized a dream in the past year, said yes, "but quite a few said they had given up on one," he says. "When the folks who have dreamed for years about a big summer house where all the kids would flock finally accept that they don't have the money and the kids have other plans, they release a lot of tension. This kind of surrender is very productive, because dreams that run counter to reality waste a lot of energy."

Although all people make psychological transitions and adjustments in the course of middle age, relatively few experience these as catastrophic. In surveys 10 to 12 percent of respondents report that they have had a midlife crisis, Kessler says. "What they often mean is that the kind of disaster that can happen at other times in life—divorce, or being fired, or a serious illness—happened to them during their middle years." An unusual convergence of such unhappy events can push even a hardy middle-aged person into a state of emotional emergency. "First you notice that your hair is falling out," Gilbert Brim says. "Then you go to the office and learn you didn't get that raise, and when you get home, your wife says she's leaving." But most of those who have a true psychological crisis in middle age—according to MIDMAC, about five percent of the population—have in fact experienced internal upheavals throughout their lives. "They see the world in those terms," says David Featherman, a MIDMAC fellow and the president of the Social Science Research Council, in New York City. "They aren't particularly good at absorbing or rebounding from life's shocks."

People prone to midlife crisis score low on tests of introspection, or reflecting on one's self and on life, and high in denial, or coping with trouble by not thinking about it. "Take the guy who still thinks he's a great athlete," Kessler says. "Somehow he hasn't let reality intrude on his boyhood fantasy. But one day something forces him to wake up. Maybe he's at a family reunion playing ball with his twelve-year-old nephew and he can't make his shots. Suddenly he's an old man, a failure." Heading for the same kind of shock are the people banking on the big promotion that their colleagues know will never happen, along with those who believe that hair transplants and breast implants mean eternal youth. "Such individuals have to work hard to maintain their illusions," Kessler says. "They spend a lot of energy on the cogni-

tive effort of self-delusion, until reality finally intervenes." Because most middle-aged people have grown skilled at monitoring changes in reality—the jump shot isn't what it used to be, the figure has changed for good—they are spared the abrupt, traumatic run-ins with reality that result in a psychic emergency.

Midlife crises are an affliction of the relatively affluent: rosy illusions are easier to maintain when a person is already somewhat shielded from reality. Just as childhood is often constricted among the poor, who early in life face adult realities and burdens, so middle age may be eclipsed by a premature old age brought on by poverty and poor health. Among working-class people, for whom strength and stamina mean earning power, middle age may begin at thirty-five rather than the forty-five often cited in studies by respondents drawn from the sedentary middle class. Because any fanciful notions that poor and blue-collar people might have are rigorously tested by daily life, Kessler says, they rarely dwell in fantasy. "In terms of career, factory workers are likelier to be wherever they're going to be at thirty than executives," he says. "In terms of mental health, being disappointed at what *is* is a better kind of problem to have than being anxious about what will be. Once you know the reality, you can say, 'I can't afford to buy a boat, so I'll rent one for vacations.' Being up in the air is the big problem."

Despite the lurid tales of fifty-year-olds who run off with their twenty-five-year-old secretaries, such events are relatively rare in real-life midlife. Most couples who divorce break up in the first six or eight years of matrimony, and by midlife the majority report being more or less content. "The family-demography side of the midlife crisis just isn't there," says Larry Bumpass, a MIDMAC fellow and a professor of sociology at the University of Wisconsin at Madison, who directs the federally funded National Survey of Families and Households, the largest demographic study of its kind. "After ten or fifteen years together, the probability that a couple will split up is low. I've looked at the data every way possible to see if there's even a blip in the divorce rate when the children leave home, but that's just folklore too."

Even the nature of the difficulties most commonly reported suggests that the majority of the middle-aged operate from a position of strength. "The problems mentioned usually concern not the self but someone else—a child or parent," Kessler says. "Part of the reason for this outward focus is that the middle-aged person has secured his or her own situation and can afford to pay attention to others. Compared with the issues that arise in youth and old age, for most people the management-type problems that crop up in midlife aren't nearly as emotionally devastating."

Carl Jung divided life into halves—the first devoted to forming the ego and getting established in the world, the second to finding a larger meaning for all that effort. He then took the unorthodox step of paying more attention to the second. When shifting from one stage to the other, Jung observed, people experience an external loss of some kind—physical prowess or upward mobility or a relationship. When they treat this loss as a signal that it's time to develop new dimensions, Jung thought, transformation is in store. However, he predicted stagnation or even a breakdown if the loss is met with denial, fear, or a sense of defeat. Aryeh Maidenbaum, the executive director of the C. G. Jung Foundation's Center for Midlife Development, offers the Jungian rule of thumb for midlife crises: "The greater the disparity between the outer and inner person, the greater the chance for trouble. The most important inner need people have is to be seen for who they are. If that's what's happening at midlife, there's no crisis."

The Change for the Worse

IF THERE'S ONE ISSUE REGARDING WHICH MISINFORmation feeds mounting hysteria about middle age, it's menopause. After finishing any of a number of recent books and articles, a reader might conclude that for a few years a middle-aged woman might as well choose between sobbing alone and riding around on a broom. One of the few people who have gleaned their own hard data on the subject is Karen Matthews, a professor of psychiatry, epidemiology, and psychology at the University of Pittsburgh School of Medicine, who has conducted a longitudinal survey of the psychological and physical changes experienced by 500 women passing through menopause. "The fact is that most women do very well in the menopausal transition," she says, refuting the popular image of women who are invariably depressed, extremely unpleasant, or both. "There are some common physical symptoms that aren't fun, notably hot flashes, but only a minority of women—about ten percent—have a tough time psychologically."

Matthews has identified the characteristics of those who experience few problems in menopause and those who experience many. "The women who do well respond to the menopause with action," she says. "That may not be their direct intention, but they end up coping with the stressor by making positive changes. Those who, say, step up their exercise regimen don't even show the biological changes, such as the adverse shifts in lipids implicated in coronary disease, that others do. These 'active copers' say, 'Hey, I look a little different, feel a little less energetic. Why don't I . . .'"

Try hormone-replacement therapy? In evaluating its effects on physical health, women and doctors must juggle evidence suggesting that while HRT cuts the number of hot flashes by about half and reduces vulnerability to osteoporosis and perhaps coronary disease, it may raise the risk of breast cancer and, if estrogen is taken without progestin, uterine cancer. The National Institutes of Health is now conducting a badly needed controlled long-term clinical trial of large numbers of women on HRT which should provide some answers. Meanwhile, some doctors, confronted with incomplete data, tell women that the decision is up to them. Considering the threat of os-teoporosis and of coronary disease, which is the leading cause of death for women over fifty, many other doctors recommend HRT to those whose risk of breast cancer is low. Still others regard its widespread use with dismay. Their concerns range from the fact that only one in three women is vulnerable to osteoporosis to a flaw in the argument that hormones can prevent heart disease. In part because doctors are cautious about prescribing HRT for women with illnesses such as hypertension and diabetes, the population that takes it is healthier to begin with—a built-in selection bias that skews studies of the therapy's effects. Among HRT's vocal critics are the doctors Sonja and John McKinlay, epidemiologists at the New England Research Institute, in Watertown, Massachusetts. "HRT is inappropriate for the vast majority of women, who shouldn't use it," John McKinlay says. "Yet the pharmaceutical industry's goal is to have every post-menopausal woman on it until death." Having surveyed the literature on menopause and HRT, Alice Rossi, a MIDMAC fellow and an emeritus professor of sociology at the University of Massachusetts at Amherst, says, "I wish we had a better scientific foundation for deciding if it's appropriate for women to take hormones for decades. At this point there's no strong evidence for a pro or anti position."

Although the process of weighing HRT's effects on physical health continues, Matthews has determined that as far as behavioral effects are concerned, HRT is "*not* the most important factor in most women's psychological well-being during menopause." For that matter, she says, women who do and don't use HRT may report differing experiences because they are different types of people to begin with. In Matthews's study the typical user was not only better educated and healthier but also likely to be a hard-driving "Type A" person, less content with the status quo. "These women are up on the literature," Matthews says, "more aware of HRT, and more interested in seeking treatment."

If active copers, whether or not they take hormones, fare best during menopause, Matthews says, the women likely to have the worst time have two disparate things in common: HRT and a low regard for themselves. "Women who have poor self-esteem but don't use hormones don't have a hard time," she says. One hypothesis is that reproductive hormones, particularly progesterone, cause some women to become dysphoric, or moody; if a woman who has this adverse reaction to HRT also has a poor self-image, she is likely to be more upset by a stressor such as a menopausal symptom than a woman with a sturdier ego.

"The idea that most women have a hard time psychologically is the major myth our data have dispelled," Matthews says. "Eighty percent of our subjects thought they were going to become depressed and irritable at menopause, but only ten percent did. Those who had a rough time had showed signs long before of being anxious, depressed, or pessimistic. Menopause makes women with that pre-existing set of characteristics, which are not age-related, more emotionally vulnerable."

Much of the dark mythology of menopause derives not from the thing itself but from simultaneous aspects of the aging process. "It's the physical manifestation of aging—and a woman's reaction to it—that's critical in predicting whether the years from forty-five to fifty-five will be difficult or not," Alice Rossi says. "Society's image of an attractive woman is ten years younger than that of an attractive man. Graying at the temples and filling out a bit can be attractive in a man—look at Clinton and Gore. But their wives are still trying to look twenty-eight." Rossi isn't necessarily advocating the grin-and-bear-it attitude toward aging favored by Barbara Bush. Seeming ten years younger than you are can be a good thing, she says, if it means a concern for good health and well-being, rather than an obsession with youth.

Matthews considers a lot of the anxiety expressed by women about menopause to be unnecessary. In response to the often-heard complaint that there has been no good research on the subject, she points to several major long-term investigations—including hers, one by Sonja and John McKinlay, and one conducted in Sweden—that independently show that the majority of women have no serious problems making the transition.

In discussing a recent bestseller on the subject, Gail Sheehy's *The Silent Passage*, she says, "Ms. Sheehy interviewed me at length, but the experience of menopause she describes in her book is not the one that emerges as typical in the three major studies. Some women have a very difficult menopause, and Ms. Sheehy feels there's a message there. We need to figure out why some women do have problems, so that we can help. "There has been no generation of women like this one. They're better educated. They're healthier to the point that they now live half their adult lives after the menopause. For them, the menopausal transition is best characterized as a time of optimism. It's a bridge—an opportunity for women to think about what they want to do next."

Despite persistent rumors, there's probably no such thing as male menopause. Men simply don't experience a midlife biological change equivalent to the one women undergo. Whereas nature is responsible for that inequity, culture is at the bottom of a far more destructive one. For a research project, John McKinlay videotaped visits to doctors' offices made by patients matched for every variable but gender. The films showed that a man and a woman who complained of the same symptoms were often treated very differently: men were twice as likely to be referred to a medical specialist, and women were much likelier to be referred to a psychotherapist; men were urged toward health-enhancing behavior such as dieting and exercise, but women rarely were. ("This is particularly unfortunate where smoking is concerned," McKinlay says, "because the health benefits for women who give it up may be greater than those for men.") He concludes that the gender-related disparities apparent in much medical literature may reflect what doctors see more than actual physiological differences. Accordingly,

Many studies show that satisfaction with the marital relationship climbs again after couples weather the labor-intensive period of launching careers and babies.

he suspects that when middle-aged men complain of bad moods and decreased libido and energy, most doctors see a need for behavioral change. When women report the same symptoms, many doctors attribute them to menopause and prescribe hormones. "Don't forget that most women get their primary health care from a gynecologist," McKinlay says, "which would be like most men getting theirs from a urologist."

Among endocrinologists outside the United States there is more support for the notion of a male climacteric, in which older men's lower testosterone levels cause decreased fertility, increased body fat, bone loss, and skin-tone changes, along with the same behavioral symptoms that are often attributed to female menopause. While allowing that a small percentage of older men suffer from an endocrinological problem and can benefit from hormone-replacement therapy, McKinlay insists that there is no evidence that the majority would benefit. For that matter, he says, testosterone has little effect on the sexuality of those over fifty or fifty-five, and taking it as a supplement may in fact increase the risk of prostate cancer. Having conducted a study of the sex lives of 1,700 men aged forty to seventy which is considered by many to be the best information on the subject, he says, "There's no physiological, endocrinological, psychological, or clinical basis for a male menopause. Whether or not people believe in it has nothing to do with whether it exists, only with whether the pharmaceutical industry can persuade them that it does. In ten years male climacteric clinics will sprout up to treat a condition that may or may not exist—but, of course, they'll make money."

McKinlay's major reservation about most of the existing research on the effects of reproductive hormones is that it has been conducted with "small, atypical" samples of people who are seeking treatment in the health-care system. "What's talked about in the literature—both professional and popular—is the experience of *patients*," he says, "not healthy people, about whom we know very little."

The Best Years of Your Life Are Over

MANY PEOPLE HAVE A MEMORY FROM ADOLES-
cence of gazing around a gathering of adults,
no longer in the green days of their youth
yet dressed to kill and living it up, and
thinking the equivalent of "How valiant they are to make
an effort at their age." Because Hollywood and Madison
Avenue project this same juvenile notion, many of the
middle-aged are surprised and relieved to find that their
lives aren't nearly so dreary as they expected. After analyzing decades of social research for his 1992 book *Ambi-
tion*, Gilbert Brim found that a person's zest for and satisfaction with life don't depend on youth—or on status,
sexuality, health, money, or any of the other things one
might expect. "What people really want out of life are action and challenge—to be in the ballgame," he says. "To
feel satisfied, we must be able to tackle a task that's hard
enough to test us, but not so difficult that we'll repeatedly fail. We want to work hard, then succeed."

This maxim has a special resonance for today's middle-
aged, career-oriented middle class, often portrayed as be-
leaguered victims of "role strain" or burnt-out cases operating on automatic pilot. In fact, Brim says, most are
instinctively seeking the level of "just manageable difficulty"—an optimum degree of effort that taps about 80
percent of a person's capacity and generates that satisfied,
job-well-done feeling. Pushing beyond that level for prolonged periods leaves people stressed and anxious; falling
below it leaves them bored. Because what is just manageable at forty might not be at sixty, people rearrange their
lives, often unconsciously, to balance capacities and challenges. When one does well at something, one ups the
ante; when one fails, one lowers the sights a bit or even
switches arenas. Brim draws an illustration from a study
of AT&T executives: over time the most successful grew
more work-oriented; the others began to turn more to
their families and social lives—educating the children or
lowering the golf handicap—for feelings of accomplish-
ment. The key point, he says, is that neither group was
more satisfied than the other. "This intuitive process by
which we constantly reset our goals in response to our
gains and losses is one of the most overlooked aspects of
adult development."

One way in which the middle-aged are particularly
skilled in adjusting their goals is in choosing which Joneses
to keep up with. "Our mental health is very much affected by our estimation of how we're doing in terms of the
people around us," says Carol Ryff, a psychologist and a
MIDMAC fellow who is the associate director of the Institute on Aging and Adult Life, at the University of Wisconsin at Madison. "We all make these important measurements, even though we're often barely conscious of
doing so." Whereas the young person launching a career
might try to outdo Maurizio Pollini or Donna Karan, the
savvy middle-aged one knows that holding to this standard beyond a certain point ensures misery—or a genuine

midlife crisis. Particularly when faced with a difficult situation, the mature person makes a "downward comparison" that puts his own problems in a different perspective and helps him soldier on. Thus the executive who
has just been laid off compares his finances not with the
Rockefellers' but with those of the couple across the
street who are both on unemployment, and reminds himself that at least his wife's position is secure. "The better
your mental health, the less often you measure yourself
against people who make you feel crummy," Ryff says.
"In midlife you begin to say, 'Well, so I'm not in the
same category as the Nobelists. That's just not an expectation I'm going to drag around anymore.'"

By middle age most people destined for success have
achieved it, which erects some special hurdles in the just-
manageable course of life. "Winning is not simply the opposite of losing," Brim says. "It creates its own disruptions." If a person becomes psychologically trapped by
the need to do better, go higher, and make more, for example, he can end up operating at 90 to 100 percent of his
capacity—a level at which stress makes life very uncomfortable. At this level, too, Brim says, he will begin to lose
more than he wins. Burdened with more roles than he can
handle, or promoted beyond the level of just-manageable
difficulty, he may end up "held together by a thin paste
of alcohol, saunas, and antibiotics." Brim says that because our society does not supply many ways to step
down gracefully, it "pays the price in burnout and incompetence in high places."

Even those who can sustain Hollywood-style success
must do some internal retooling in order to maintain the
charge of the just-manageable mode. To keep life interesting, Brim says, the people who handle winning best
don't merely raise the challenge in the same area but go
into a new one—a sport, a hobby, a community project—
where they again find a lot of room for moving up. "Certain professional athletes are good examples," he says.
"Because they know that their peak will be short-lived, at
a certain point they diversify their aspirations to include
family, business interests, and volunteer activities."

So skilled are most people at maintaining a just-manageable life through the years that Brim finds no appre-
ciable differences in the sense of well-being reported by
different age groups. Indeed, he says, despite the insis-
tent propaganda to the contrary, "except for concerns
about health, most research shows that older people are
as happy as younger ones."

Midlife Romance:
The Bloom Is Off the Rose

IF MIDDLE AGE IS SEEN AS A DULL BUSINESS, ITS RELA-
tionships are imagined to be the dreariest part. In the
course of studying beliefs about and images of
midlife, Margie Lachman compared the experiences
of a group of Boston-area people aged eighteen to eighty-
five, and found no evidence that the middle-aged are less

loving. In fact, steady levels of intimacy and affection were two of the few constants she tracked. Largely because married people make up the majority of the middle-aged—about 75 percent—most of the data about life relationships concern them. Then too, less is known about other bonds because until the mid-seventies studies of midlife focused on the experience of white middle-class heterosexual men. Although there is still very little information about gay midlife, some data are emerging about how single people in general fare socially during middle age.

It's about time, according to Alice Rossi. "Considering the longer life-span, a person may be without a partner at many points in life," she points out. "We not only marry later today but often have intervals between relationships, and perhaps lengthy spells as widows and widowers." She thinks that the stereotype of the aging spinster who is unfulfilled without a man is heading into the realm of midlife mythology. "There's recent evidence that single women have better mental and physical health and social lives than single men," she says. "Rather than being all alone, they have friends and close family ties, not only with parents but also with young nieces and nephews, with whom they may enjoy special relationships."

As for the married, many studies show that satisfaction with the relationship is lower throughout the child-rearing years that it had been, but climbs again after couples weather the labor-intensive period of launching careers and babies. In Lachman's Boston survey, reports of stress related to marriage decreased steadily from youth through old age. Although divorce and death may account for some of that decline, she says, "people may in fact grow more skilled in handling their relationships." Observing that by midlife couples have fewer fights and more closeness, Ron Kessler says, "Once they get the little kids out of their hair, husbands and wives catch their breath, look at each other, and ask, 'What are we going to talk about now? What was it all about twenty years ago?'"

In his study of sexuality John McKinlay found that only two percent of the 1,700 middle-aged and older men reported having more than one current sexual partner. This figure, vastly lower than the usual guesstimates, challenges the stereotype of the bored middle-aged philanderer. Moreover, although McKinlay recorded steady declines in the men's sexual activity, from lusty thoughts to erections, he found no decrease in their sexual satisfaction—a phenomenon Gilbert Brim calls "a triumph of the adaptation of aspirations to realities." Equivalent data about women have not been gathered, but McKinlay's findings complement other surveys that show that aging has little impact on people's enjoyment of sex.

People and their doctors, McKinlay says, should distinguish between sexual problems caused by aging and those caused by things that often get lumped with it, such as poor health, weight gain, lack of exercise, and the use of nicotine or too much alcohol. Compared with a healthy nonsmoking peer, for example, a smoker who has heart disease has a sevenfold greater risk of impotence.

Psychological fitness, too, plays a vital role. A man may think his primary problem is impotence caused by age when in fact his sexual trouble is a symptom of a very treatable depression. "We must not resort to biological reductionism, which is what women have been struggling against," McKinlay says.

Widely publicized conclusions drawn from the sex lives of the ill—that a vigorous sex life is not a reasonable expectation in middle age, for instance—may cast their pall on the well. "When I hear a healthy fifty-year-old man say, 'That sexy stuff is for kids,' I feel sorry for him," McKinlay says. "Only five percent of the women in our institute's long-term study of menopause reported suffering from vaginal dryness, but women are told it's a very common problem after a certain age." Contrary to the stereotype of the asexual older woman, he says, some women feel liberated by menopause and the end of birth control. If older women have a problem with their sex lives, according to McKinlay, it may be that their husbands aren't in good health. His prescription for a vital midlife: "If I were feeling troubled about aging, I'd look first at the behavioral modifications I could make—diet, exercise, alcohol-monitoring, and so on. If they didn't work, then I'd think about treatments."

Having edited a book about sexuality through the course of life, Alice Rossi observes that although the mature expression of eroticism remains poorly understood by science, let alone by our youth-oriented culture, middle-aged people are likely to expand their definition of sex to include sensual, not just reproductive, acts. "If the message we get from society is that we have to keep on acting as we did at thirty," she says, "a lot of us are going to feel that we have a sexual disorder at some point." After a certain age, for example, men in particular may require physical stimulation to feel aroused. An awareness of this normal tendency, Rossi says, added to modern women's generally greater assertiveness, lays the groundwork for a new kind of relationship for older couples—one in which women have a more active role. "If the middle-aged don't feel pressured to conform to a youthful stereotype," she says, "I think we can predict some good things for their sex lives."

The Empty Nest and the Sandwich Generation

WHEN THE ROLE OF FAMILY IN THE EXPERIENCE of middle age is mentioned, one of two scenarios usually comes to mind. In the better established, the abandoned mother waves a tearful good-bye to her last chick and dully goes through the motions of life in the "empty nest." According to Larry Bumpass's demographic survey, however, the nest may be anything but empty: expensive housing and a weak economy and job market mean that the young delay their own marriages and are likelier to return home after a brief foray outside.

The more contemporary midlife family myth concerns the plight of the "sandwich generation": in a recent *Doonesbury* cartoon starring a professional couple, the forty-something husband tells his wife, busy juggling the needs of her children and their grandmother, "Don't die. Everyone's counting on you." Women's entry into the job market has focused much attention on a purported host of adults who make the circuit from the day-care center to Gramps's place to the office with nary a moment for themselves. "It's true that there's a lot going on in your life in middle age and you have little time for leisure," Margie Lachman says. "Fortunately, you're also at your peak in terms of competence, control, the ability to handle stress, and sense of responsibility. You're *equipped* for overload." According to Carol Ryff, people busy with both careers and relationships enjoy not only greater financial security and intellectual and social stimulation but also a psychological benefit. The eminent behavioral scientist Bernice Neugarten thinks that the hallmark of healthy middle age is "complexity," or a feeling of being in control of a crowded life and involved in the world at the same time. Ryff found in the course of one of her studies that this quality was most marked among the first generation to combine family and career. "It seems," she says, "that all the role-juggling that middle-aged people complain about actually makes them feel more engaged in life."

Rossi is dubious that the sandwich-generation problem is either new or widespread. "This phenomenon is a lot like the supposed midlife crisis," she says. "There are people who think that spending two hours a week with Mother is a big deal. But the fact is that very few men or women are caring both for little children and for elderly parents." One reason for this is that the "old old" who need considerable care are still a small group, and few of them are a daily drain on their children. Then, too, as Bumpass says, "over the past several decades the elderly have increasingly lived independently. They're economically more able to do so, and both sides prefer things that way." According to research conducted by Glenna Spitze, of the State University of New York at Albany, close involvement by the middle-aged with their parents—usually with a mother who has already cared for and buried her own husband—is likeliest to occur when the middle-aged person's children are older and need less attention. "For that matter," Rossi says, "rather than being a drain, the children are likely to be a comfort and help. It's important to remember that intimacy with children, which bottoms out from ages fifteen to nineteen, climbs steeply through the twenties and thirties. One of the things to look forward to in midlife is the continuity and shared interests that will come as your children in turn become parents."

To the list of underestimated family pleasures Ryff adds the satisfaction that parents take in knowing that grown-up children have turned out all right. She found that adult offspring are a vital if underrecognized element in middle-aged well-being, and that adjusting to how well or poorly they have matured is another of midlife's important developmental tasks. After studying 215 parents, Ryff found that their adult children's level of psychological adjustment was a major predictor for almost all aspects of both fathers' and mothers' mental health—although mothers took more credit for it. "The literature on parenting includes very little on what *parents* get out of it," she says, "or on how it affects their self-image, especially when the kids are older. Parenting never ends."

At Last, the Reward: Wisdom

LONG ON THE PROCESS OF BECOMING, THE LITERature of human development remains short on the business of being. That adults don't grow and change in the predictable, simultaneously physiological and behavioral fashion that children do partly explains why. So tidy is early development by comparison that it's even possible to link certain ages to certain behavioral stages, such as the "terrible twos" and the "temperamental teens." Although Gail Sheehy's bestseller *Passages* (described by Gilbert Brim as focused on "selected case studies that illustrate a theory that has no broad empirical support") advanced an adult model of such "age-stage" development, research continues to show that the ways in which adults evolve are not universal, not likely to occur in clear-cut stages, and not tied to particular ages. So poorly do the middle-aged fit into developmental patterns, in fact, that the huge National Survey of Families and Households revealed that of more than forty projected "typical midlife events," none was likely to happen at a certain, predictable age.

Biologically oriented behavioral scientists argue that at the individual level certain basic tendencies evident at birth or shortly after are the immutable building blocks of personality. The aversion to novel stimuli which becomes shyness, denoted by a low score in extroversion, is one such element. Some claim, moreover, that anyone can be defined even in early childhood in terms of how high or low he or she scores in tests that measure the "big five"

Most middle-aged adults benefit from knocking about in the world. When they go down a blind alley, they soon recognize the mistake, and save themselves much time and energy.

traits: neuroticism, extroversion, openness, agreeableness, and conscientiousness. This largely biological programming, trait theorists believe, means that personality is set in concrete around the time that physical development ceases. Afterward one may grow in terms of changing attitudes, skills, interests, and relationships, but only in ways consistent with one's big-five template.

Environment-minded researchers, including the MID-MAC team, take the influence of things like attitudes, interests, and relationships more seriously. They're working on a different, flexible model of adult development, based not on genes but on experience. Brim and his colleagues don't dispute that someone born shy or dutiful may very well stay that way, but they stress that whether he or she is raised in a sociable or a reclusive family, has a happy or an unhappy marriage, gets an exciting or a dull job, and has good or poor health will have considerable impact on identity. Bringing up reports of "aberrant outcomes"—people who early in life seem destined for success or failure yet somehow turn out the other way—Brim observes that adult change is shaped not just by the characteristics a person brings to bear on life but also by what life brings to bear on him or her, from family feuds to fatal attractions, religious experiences to traffic accidents. Accordingly, the MIDMAC group and others interested in tracking adult development focus on the ways in which, as a result of the depth and variety of their experience, their subjects' goals and values alter over time.

To illustrate experiential midlife development, Ron Kessler points to ways in which people are shaped by the influence of the workplace. "During early life you're socially segregated—all your school companions are also eight- or twelve-year-olds from the same neighborhood," he says. "Then comes adulthood, and suddenly you're working alongside different kinds of people of different ages. You can look around and say to yourself, 'In twenty years, if I act like him, I could have a heart attack, or end up divorced.' Or 'Sure, she makes a lot of money, but do I really want to work sixty hours a week?'"

Most middle-aged adults benefit from knocking about in the world, a process that greatly increases their efficiency in managing life. When they go down a blind alley, they soon recognize the mistake, and save themselves much time and energy. "Because they have all this material to plot trajectories with, the middle-aged are equipped to do an enormous amount of internal reshuffling," Kessler says. "Unlike younger people, they don't have to test everything themselves in the real world. Adults who learn from their mistakes change and grow, and those who don't, don't." Kessler describes a bright corporate lawyer who remains developmentally stalled in the "becoming" phase appropriate to youth: "He goes around saying '*This* is being a lawyer? I'd rather be a kid *wanting* to be a lawyer.'"

Perhaps the best refutation of the myths that adults don't develop and that adults do develop but only in rigid stages is a new body of research on the genesis of a psy-chological and cognitive capacity that scientists can only call wisdom. As is often the case in science, this inquiry began with the investigation of a mistaken premise. Assuming that the formalistic SAT-type process was the human norm in solving problems, those studying the effects of aging concluded that older people suffer a cognitive deficit, because they do worse than the young on such tests. The more researchers explored this apparently biological decline, however, the more they had to consider another possibility: people of different ages may perceive the same problem differently.

Any adult who has debated with a bright adolescent about, say, the likelihood that the world's nations will erase their boundaries and create a passportless global citizenry knows that there are two types of intelligence: the abstract, objective, Platonic-dualism sort that peaks early, and the practical, subjective type, born of shirtsleeves experience, which comes later. When asked the way to Rome, the young trace the most direct route very quickly, while their elders ponder: "Why Rome? Is this trip really a good idea? At what time of year? For business or pleasure? Alone or with others?"

The pre-eminent wisdom researcher is Paul Baltes, a MIDMAC fellow and a co-director of the Max Planck Institute for Human Development and Education, in Berlin. Baltes conducts studies of "whether living long can produce a higher level of mental functioning." The cognitive mechanics of the brain—the speed and accuracy with which we process information—are biological and subject to decline, he finds. But the brain's pragmatics—our knowledge and skill in using information—are not. When Baltes's subjects take the intellectual equivalent of a medical stress test, the young do in two seconds what the older do, with many more mistakes, in eight. But, Baltes says, unlike other species, ours can compensate for biological deficits. "If people have hearing problems, society develops hearing aids, and if I train an older subject in test-taking skills, he'll outperform an untutored younger person. By providing knowledge and strategies for using it, culture outwits biology. In all the areas of functioning in which age means more access to information, older people may be better off than young ones." In short, the middle-aged may be slower but they're smarter.

Beyond the commonsensical savvy acquired through daily experience lies a rarefied ability to deal with the fundamental problems of the human condition: matters ambiguous and existential, complex and conflicted, which call for the wisdom of Solomon. Using literary analysis, Baltes finds evidence in all cultures of people equipped to deal with these difficult issues, and he has devised several ways to test for the presence of this ability. In one type of study, subjects read vignettes of difficult situations—for example, a person pondering how to respond to a friend who has decided to commit suicide—and then "think aloud" through their decision-making process to a resolution of the problem. In another type, people with many contacts in the world of high achievers are asked to nominate those they consider especially wise; researchers then monitor how these candidates think about difficult problems. Both forms of testing allow Baltes to score subjects on his "wisdom criteria," which include great factual and procedural knowledge, the capacity to cope with uncertainty, and the ability to frame an event in its larger context. "Those who have these attributes are the people we call wise," he says, "and they are easily recognized. People who are said to have this quality do score higher than others."

To sense the difference between the wise and the hoi polloi, one might imagine a successful fifty-year-old urban lawyer who announces that she is going to quit her job, move to the country, and start a mail-order seed and bulb business. Most listeners will think, if not say, something like "What a crazy idea." But there might be someone who says, "Wait. What are the circumstances? Maybe this lawyer feels that her life has grown sterile. Maybe she has some solid plans for this change. Let's talk some more." According to Baltes's statistics, this wise person is probably neither young nor very old but somewhere between the ages of forty and seventy. "The highest grades we record occur somewhere around sixty," he says. "Wisdom peaks in midlife or later."

While intelligence is essential to wisdom, certain personal qualities predict with greater accuracy who will be wise. Thoreau observed, "It is a characteristic of wisdom not to do desperate things," and Baltes agrees. "Modulation and balance are crucial elements," he says, "because wisdom has no extremes. You can't be passionate or dogmatic and wise at the same time." Just as the Lao-tzus and Lincolns among us are likely to be reasonable and open-minded, they are not likely to be motivated by selfish concerns, at least not markedly so: Machiavelli was clever but not wise.

"At some point in middle age," says David Featherman, of the Social Science Research Council, "we're inclined to become more tolerant of the uncertain, the complex, and the impossible, and even to learn to dismiss some problems as unsolvable or not worth our effort. Perhaps most important, we grow more interested in how our solutions affect others. Along with being good at figuring out what to do in real-life situations themselves, the wise are skilled in advising others—in sharing their wisdom. Unfortunately, Americans' Lone Ranger mentality about solving everything on our own means we don't always profit from this resource." The concern for others that is a hallmark of wisdom seems to augur well for those who have it as well as for its beneficiaries. The evolutionary neurobiologist Paul D. MacLean once observed, "We become nicer mammals as we age." Featherman points out that the benignity integral to wisdom seems characteristic of people who enjoy a happy, healthy old age.

In a youth-obsessed culture the suggestion that at least one element of character emerges only in middle age is both appealing and iconoclastic. "Wisdom doesn't happen at the age of six, or eighteen," Featherman says. "It may take a long time for all of its components to be in place. The timing of its emergence means that in maturity we get a new start—a new way of understanding life that's more apt to benefit others. It may turn out that caring about people is the capstone of the process of living."

Personality Processes

Anna and Sadie are identical twins. When the girls were young children, their parents tried very hard to treat them equally. Whenever Anna received a present, Sadie received one. Both girls attended dance school and completed early classes in ballet and tap dance. In elementary school, the twins were both placed in the same class with the same teacher. The teacher also tried to treat them the same.

In junior high school, Sadie became a tomboy. She loved to play rough-and-tumble sports with the neighborhood boys. On the other hand, Anna remained indoors and practiced her piano and read poetry. Anna was keenly interested in the domestic arts such as sewing, needlepoint, and crochet. Sadie was more interested in reading novels, especially science fiction, and in watching adventure programs on television.

As the twins matured, they decided it would be best to attend different colleges. Anna went to a small, quiet college in a rural setting, and Sadie matriculated at a large public university. Anna majored in English, with a specialty in poetry; Sadie switched majors several times and finally decided on a communications major.

Why, when these twins were exposed to the same early childhood environment, did their interests and paths diverge in adolescence? What makes people, even identical twins, so unique, so different from one another?

The study of individual differences is the domain of personality. The psychological study of personality has included two major thrusts. The first has focused on the search for the commonalties of human life and development. Its major question would be: How are all humans affected by specific events or activities? Personality theories are based on the assumption that a given event, if it is important, will affect almost all people in a similar way, or that the processes by which events affect people are common across events and people. Most psychological research into personality variables has made this assumption. Failures to replicate a research project are often the first clues that differences in individual responses require further investigation.

While some psychologists have focused on personality-related effects that are presumed to be universal among humans, others have devoted their efforts to discovering the bases on which individuals differ in their responses to environmental events. In the beginning, this specialty was called genetic psychology, because most people assumed that individual differences resulted from differences in genetic inheritance. By the 1950s the term genetic psychology had given way to the more current term: the psychology of individual differences.

Does this mean that genetic variables are no longer the key to understanding individual differences? Not at all. For a time, psychologists took up the philosophical debate over whether genetic or environmental factors were more important in determining behaviors. Even today, behavior geneticists compute the heritability coefficients for a number of personality and behavior traits, including intelligence. This is an expression of the degree to which differences in a given trait can be attributed to differences in inherited capacity or ability. Most psychologists, however, accept the principle that both genetic and environmental determinants are important in any area of behavior. These researchers are devoting more of their efforts to discovering how the two sources of influence interact to produce the unique individual. Given the above, the focus of this unit is on personality characteristics and the differences and similarities among individuals.

What is personality? Most researchers in the area define personality as "patterns of thoughts, feelings, and behaviors that persist over time and over situations, are characteristic or typical of the individual, and usually distinguish one person from another" (Phares, 1991).

In the first two unit articles we consider three differing views or theories of personality. The first theory of interest is psychoanalysis, which was developed by Sigmund Freud. Freud viewed people as having a lurking, animalistic unconscious that played tricks on them. He also believed that individuals pass through some notable developmental stages, some of which are based on sexual urges. His views are harshly criticized today as divulged in "The Assault on Freud."

Next, another theory of personality is explored—trait theory. Trait theorists believe that psychology's main goal should be the measurement of traits that describe an individual and differentiate one individual from another. In "Piecing Together Personality," Bruce Bower discusses five major traits or dimensions that can be used to characterize each of us while also distinguishing us from one another.

We next examine two important issues in the study of personality. One issue is optimism; the other is hostility. Michael Scheier and Charles Carver are noted for their work on optimism. In their article, "On the Power of Positive Thinking: The Benefits of Being Optimistic," they review research on positive thinking and conclude that it enhances both our psychological and physical well-being. Optimism, then, not only feels good, it is good for you.

In the final unit article, hostility is the focus. Hostile people are cynical, angry, and easily provoked. Recent

research has found that hostile people tend to be prone to heart attacks. How to recognize hostile people and how to manage hostility better are showcased in this article.

Looking Ahead: Challenge Questions

Differentiate the major theories of personality. Which theory do you think is best and why?

What are some of the major tenets of Sigmund Freud's theory? Why is his theory framed the way it is? Why is Freud's theory subject to so much criticism? Is the criticism deserved?

What is a personality trait? How can we use personality

measurement or measurement of traits? What traits seem to describe everyone? Do you have any personality characteristics that you think are not included in the "big five" personality traits?

What are some of the differences between optimists and pessimists? Are optimists healthier than pessimists? Do optimists really live longer? How do children become optimists or pessimists?

Are any psychological factors related to heart disease? If so, what psychological factors can cause heart disease? What new treatments are available to assist those whose heart disease seems to be caused by hostility?

THE ASSAULT ON
FREUD

*He invented psychoanalysis and revolutionized 20th century ideas about
the life of the mind. And this is the thanks he gets?*

PAUL GRAY

MANY ARE THE WAYS OF COPING WITH THE WORLD'S vicissitudes. Some people fear and propitiate evil spirits. Others order their schedules according to the display of the planets across the zodiac. There are those who assume that they carry, somewhere inside of them, a thing called the unconscious. It is mostly invisible, although it can furtively be glimpsed in dreams and heard in slips of the tongue. But the unconscious is not a passive stowaway on the voyage of life; it has the power to make its hosts feel very sad or behave in strange, self-destructive ways. When that happens, one recourse is to go to the office of a specially trained healer, lie down on a couch and start talking.

The first two beliefs can, except by those who hold them, easily be dismissed as superstitions. The third—a tenet of the classic theory of psychoanalysis devised by Sigmund Freud—has become this troubled century's dominant model for thinking and talking about human behavior. To a remarkable degree, Freud's ideas, conjectures, pronouncements have seeped well beyond the circle of his professional followers into the public mind and discourse. People who have never read a word of his work (a voluminous 24 volumes in the standard English translation) nonetheless "know" of things that can be traced, sometimes circuitously, back to Freud: penis envy; castration anxiety; phallic symbols; the ego, id and superego; repressed memories; Oedipal itches; sexual sublimation. This rich panoply of metaphors for the mental life has become, across wide swaths of the globe, something very close to common knowledge.

But what if Freud was wrong?

This question has been around ever since the publication of Freud's first overtly psychoanalytical papers in the late 1890s. Today it is being asked with unprecedented urgency, thanks to a coincidence of developments that raise doubts not only about Freud's methods, discoveries and proofs and the vast array of therapies derived from them, but also about the lasting importance of Freud's descriptions of the mind. The collapse of Marxism, the other grand unified theory that shaped and rattled the 20th century, is unleashing monsters. What inner horrors or fresh dreams might arise should the complex Freudian monument topple as well?

That may not happen, and it assuredly will not happen all at once. But new forces are undermining the Freudian foundations. Among them:

► The problematical proliferation, particularly in the U.S., of accusations of sexual abuse, satanic rituals, infant human sacrifices and the like from people, many of them guided by therapists, who suddenly remember what they allegedly years or decades ago repressed. . . . Although Freud almost certainly would have regarded most of these charges with withering skepticism, his theory of repression and the unconscious is being used—most Freudians would say misused—to assert their authenticity.

► The continuing success of drugs in the treatment or alleviation of mental disorders ranging from depression to schizophrenia. Roughly 10 million Americans are taking such medications. To his credit, Freud foresaw this development. In 1938, a year before his death, he wrote, "The future may teach us to exercise a direct influence, by means of particular chemical substances." Still, the recognition that some neuroses and psychoses respond favorably to drugs chips away at the domain originally claimed for psychoanalytic treatment.

► The Clinton health-care reform proposals, oddly enough, which are prompting cost-benefit analyses across the whole spectrum of U.S. medicine, including treatments for mental illness. Whatever package finally winds its way through Congress, many experts concede that insurance will not be provided for Freud's talking cure. (A 50-min. hour of psychoanalysis costs an average of $125.) Says Dr. Frederick K. Goodwin, director of the National Institute of Mental Health: "It's clear that classical psychoanalysis, which is four to five times a week for a four- to five-year duration, will not be covered. It won't be covered because there is no real evidence that it works." Goodwin, for the record, professes himself an admirer of Freud the theoretician.

► A spate of new books attacking Freud and his brainchild psychoanalysis for a generous array of errors, duplicities, fudged evidence and scientific howlers.

This last phenomenon is an intensification of an ongoing story. While Freud was winning cadres of acolytes and legions of notional recruits, he and his ideas regularly attracted sharp attacks, often from influential quarters. As early as 1909, philosopher

William James observed in a letter that Freud "made on me personally the impression of a man obsessed with fixed ideas." Vladimir Nabokov, whose novels trace the untrammeled and unpredictable play of individual imaginations, regularly tossed barbs at "the witch doctor Freud" and "the Viennese quack." For similar reasons, Ludwig Wittgenstein objected to the pigeonholing effects of psychoanalytic categories, even though he paid Freud a backhanded compliment in the process: "Freud's fanciful pseudo explanations (precisely because they are so brilliant) perform a disservice. Now any ass has these pictures to use in 'explaining' symptoms of illness."

The steady rain of anti-Freud arguments did little to discourage the parade of his theories or to dampen the zeal of his followers. In fact, Freud erected an apparently invulnerable umbrella against criticisms of psychoanalytical principles. He characterized such disagreements, from patients or anyone else, as "resistance" and then asserted that instances of such resistance amounted to "actual evidence in favor of the correctness" of his assertions. For a long time, this psychoanalytic Catch-22 worked wonders: those who opposed the methods put forth to heal them and others could be banished, perhaps with a friendly handshake and a knowing smile, as nuts.

That illogical defense has largely crumbled. The recent discovery of documents relating to Freud and his circle, plus the measured release of others by the Freud estate, has provided a steadily expanding body of evidence about the man and his works. Some of the initial reassessments are unsettling.

For one example, the 10-year collaboration between Freud and Carl Gustav Jung broke off abruptly in 1914, with profound consequences for the discipline they helped create. There would henceforth be Freudians and Jungians, connected chiefly by mutual animosities. Why did a warm, fruitful cooperation end in an icy schism? In *A Most Dangerous Method* (Knopf; $30), John Kerr, a clinical psychologist who has seen new diaries, letters and journals, argues that the growing philosophical disputes between Freud and Jung were exacerbated by a cat-and-mouse game of sexual suspicion and blackmail. Freud believed an ex-patient of Jung's named Sabina Spielrein had also been Jung's mistress; Jung in turn surmised that Freud had become involved with his sister-in-law, Minna Bernays. Both antagonists in this standoff held bombshells that could blow each other's reputation from Vienna to Zurich and back; both backed off, divided up the spoils of their joint investigations and retreated into opposing tents of theory.

Was this any way to found an objective science? Freud's defenders argue that his personal life is irrelevant to his contributions to learning—a rather odd contention, given Freud's statement that his development of the analytic method began with his pioneering analysis of himself. Nevertheless, Arnold Richards, editor of the American Psychoanalytic Association newsletter, dismisses any attention paid to Freud's private conduct: "It has no scientific practical consequence. It's not relevant to Freud's theory or practice."

What, then, about attacks on Freud's theory and practice? In *Father Knows Best: The Use and Abuse of Power in Freud's Case of 'Dora'* (Teachers College Press; $36), academicians Robin Tolmach Lakoff and James C. Coyne offer a fresh view of one of Freud's most famously botched analyses. When "Dora," 18, sought Freud's help at her father's insistence in 1901, she told him the following story: her father was having an affair with the wife of Herr "K," a family friend. Herr K had been paying unwanted sexual attentions to Dora since she

> Sigmund Freud's rich panoply of metaphors for the mental life has evolved into something closely resembling common knowlege

was 14 and was now being encouraged in this pursuit by her father, presumably as a way to deflect attention from the father's alliance with Frau K. After hearing this account, Freud, as feminists say, did not get it. He decided Dora really desired Herr K sexually, plus her father to boot, and he criticized her "hysterical" refusal to follow her true inclinations, embrace her circumstances and make everyone, including herself, satisfied and fulfilled. She left Freud's care after three months.

IF THIS SOUNDS DAMNING, MORE OF the same and then some can be found in Allen Esterson's *Seductive Mirage: An Exploration of the Work of Sigmund Freud* (Open Court; $52.95). As a mathematician, Esterson is vulnerable to charges from Freud loyalists that he is an amateur, unqualified to discuss the mysteries of psychoanalysis. Maybe so, but his relentless examinations of discrepancies, doctored evidence and apparent lies within Freud's own accounts of individual cases make for disturbing reading. Esterson's argument is often most effective when it quotes the analyst directly on his therapeutic techniques. Freud regularly sounds like a detective who solves a crime before interviewing the first witness: "The principle is that I should guess the secret and tell it to the patient straight out." Once Freud had made a diagnosis, the case, as far as he was concerned, was closed, although the treatment continued: "We must not be led astray by initial denials. If we keep firmly to what we have inferred, we shall in the end conquer every resistance by emphasizing the unshakable nature of our convictions."

Noting the fact that Freud's published case histories largely record inconclusive or lamentable results, some loyalists have adopted a fall-back position: Freud may not have been very good at practicing what he preached, but that lapse in no way invalidates his overarching theories.

These defenders must now confront *Validation in the Clinical Theory of Psychoanalysis* (International Universities Press; $50) by Adolf Grünbaum, a noted philosopher of science and a professor at the University of Pittsburgh. The book, which builds on Grünbaum's 1984 critique of psychoanalytic underpinnings, is a monograph (translation: no one without a Ph.D. need apply) and a quiet, sometimes maddeningly abstruse devastation of psychoanalysis' status as a science. Grünbaum dispassionately examines a number of key psychoanalytic premises: the theory of repression (which Freud called "the cornerstone on which the whole structure of psychoanalysis rests"), the investigative capabilities offered by free association, the diagnostic significance of dreams. Grünbaum does not claim that the idea of repressed memories, for instance, is false. He simply argues that neither Freud nor any of his successors has ever proved a cause-and-effect link between a repressed memory and a later neurosis or a retrieved memory and a subsequent cure.

Off the page, Grünbaum is able to make his critique a little more accessible to lay people. Of the presumed link between childhood molestation and adult neurosis, he remarks, "Just saying the first thing happened and the second thing happened, and therefore one caused the other, is not enough. You have to show more." Grünbaum finds similar flaws in the importance Freud attached to dreams and bungled actions, such as so-called Freudian slips: "All three of these tenets—the theory of neurosis, the theory of why we dream and the theory of slips—have the same problem. All are undermined by Freud's failure to prove a causal relationship between the repression and the pathology. That's why the foundation of psychoanalysis is very wobbly."

How wobbly? Interestingly, Grünbaum himself thinks all is not lost, although his verdict is not entirely cheering: "I categorically don't believe Freud is dead. The question is, Are they trustworthy explanations? Have the hypotheses been validated by cogent, solid evidence? My answer to that is no."

FRANK SULLOWAY, A VISITING scholar of science history at M.I.T. and a longtime critic of Freud's methods, takes a somewhat more apocalyptic view: "Psychoanalysis is built on quicksand. It's like a 10-story hotel sinking into an unsound foundation. And the analysts are in this building. You tell them it's sinking, and they say, 'It's O.K.; we're on the 10th floor.' "

Sure enough, the view from this imaginary elevation remains largely untroubled. Psychoanalysts like to point out that their treatment is gaining converts in Spain, Italy and Latin America, plus parts of the former Soviet Union, where it had formerly been banned. Some 14,000 tourists a year flock to the Freud Museum in London, where they walk through the Hampstead house Freud owned during the last year of his life. His daughter Anna, who carried on her father's work with dedication and skill, remained there until her death in 1982. Freud's library and study, the latter containing a couch covered with an Oriental rug, remain largely as he left them. Some visitors last week may have come fresh from seeing a Channel 4 TV documentary put together by Peter Swales, another persistent critic of Freud, titled *Bad Ideas of the 20th Century: Freudism*. If so, their interest in Freud memorabilia seemed undiminished. Michael Molnar, the Museum's research director and an editor of Freud's diaries, acknowledges that psychoanalysis is being challenged by new drug treatments and advances in genetic research. "But," he argues, "Freud is in better shape than Marx."

Across the English Channel, a play called *The Visitor*, by the young French dramatist Eric-Emmanuel Schmitt, has opened in Paris, featuring the octogenarian Freud and his daughter Anna as principal characters. Meanwhile, the Grand Palais is staging an exhibition called "The Soul in the Body," with objects that manifest the interplay between art and science. One of the major displays is the couch on which Freud's patients in Vienna reclined. In his leather-upholstered office a few blocks away, Serge Leclaire, 69, an ex-president of the French Society for Psychoanalysis, notes all this cultural hubbub in France and contrasts it with the assaults on Freud in the U.S. "What happened to Freudian psychoanalysis in America is the fault of American psychoanalysts," he says. "They froze things into a doctrine, almost a

religion, with its own dogma, instead of changing with the times."

For their part, U.S. psychoanalysts admit that Freud has been taking some pretty hard knocks lately but deny that his impact or importance has waned as a result. Says George H. Allison, a Seattle-based analyst: "I think Freud's influence in mental health as well as the humanities is much greater than it was 40 years ago. I hear much more being written and said about Freud." Allison points to the proliferation of therapies—there are now more than 200 talking cures competing in the U.S. mental health marketplace, and 10 to 15 million Americans doing some kind of talking—and he argues that "they really are based on Freudian principals, even though a lot of people who head these movements are anti-Freudian officially. But they are standing on the shoulders of a genius."

This image raises anew the quicksand question. If Freud's theories are truly as oozy as his critics maintain, then what is to

> In the ultimate accounting, psychoanalysis and all its offshoots may turn out to be no more reliable than phrenology or mesmerism

keep all the therapies indebted to them from slowly sinking into oblivion as well? Hypothetically, nothing, though few expect or want that event to occur. Surprisingly, Peter Kramer, author of the current best seller *Listening to Prozac*, comes to the defense of talking cures and their founder: "Even Freudian analysts don't hold themselves 100% to Freud. Psychotherapy is like one of those branching trees, where each of the branches legitimately claims a common ancestry, namely Freud, but none of the branches are sitting at the root. We'd be very mistaken to jettison psychotherapy or Freud."

Frederick Crews, a professor of English at the University of California, Berkeley, and a well-known reviewer and critic, once enthusiastically applied Freudian concepts to literary works and taught his students to do likewise. Then he grew disillusioned and now ranks as one of Freud's harshest American debunkers. Even while arguing that Freud was a liar and that some of his ideas did not arise from clinical observa-

tions but instead were lifted from "folklore," Crews grows cautious about the prospect of a world suddenly without Freud or his methods: "Those of us who are concerned about pointing out Freud's intellectual failings are not, by and large, experts in the entire range of psychotherapy. I take no position on whether psychotherapy is a good thing or not."

Such prudence may be well advised. Freud was not the first to postulate the unconscious; the concept has a long intellectual ancestry. Nor did Freud ever prove, in empirical terms that scientists would accept, the existence of the unconscious. But Jonathan Winson, professor emeritus of neurosciences at Rockefeller University in New York City, who has done extensive research on the physiology of sleep and dreams, now claims Freud's intuition of its existence was correct, even if his conclusions were off the mark: "He's right that there is a coherent psychological structure beneath the level of the conscious. That's a marvelous insight for which he deserves credit. And he deserves credit too for sensing that dreams are the 'royal road' to the unconscious."

That, finally, may be the central problem with declaring Freud finished. For all of his log rolling and influence peddling, his running roughshod over colleagues and patients alike, for all the sins of omission and commission that critics past and present correctly lay on his couch, he still managed to create an intellectual edifice that *feels* closer to the experience of living, and therefore hurting, than any other system currently in play. What he bequeathed was not (despite his arguments to the contrary), nor has yet proved itself to be, a science. Psychoanalysis and all its offshoots may in the final analysis turn out to be no more reliable than phrenology or mesmerism or any of the countless other pseudosciences that once offered unsubstantiated answers or false solace. Still, the reassurances provided by Freud that our inner lives are rich with drama and hidden meanings would be missed if it disappeared, leaving nothing in its place.

Shortly after Freud actually died in 1939, W.H. Auden, one of the many 20th century writers who mined psychoanalysis for its ample supply of symbols and imagery, wrote an elegy that concluded:

> *. . . sad is Eros, builder of cities,*
> *and weeping anarchic Aphrodite.*

Auden's choice of figures from Greek mythology was intentional and appropriate. Perhaps Homer and Sophocles and the rest will prove, when all is said and done, better guides to the human condition than Freud. But he did not shy away from such competition.   —**Reported by Ann Blackman/ Washington, Barry Hillenbrand/London, Janice M. Horowitz/ New York and Benjamin Ivry/Paris**

Piecing Together Personality

BRUCE BOWER

Psychological research presents a challenge to psychiatric diagnosis

A lice exhibited a bewildering array of problems when she entered psychotherapy. At least three separate conditions in the *Diagnostic and Statistical Manual of Mental Disorders* (DSM) — the bible of psychiatry — applied to the 24-year-old woman. Unfortunately, each diagnosis held different implications for how best to help her.

Frequent eating binges followed by induced vomiting qualified Alice for a diagnosis of bulimia. But she also heeded destructive urges to abuse a wide variety of drugs and to seek anonymous sexual encounters, felt intensely self-conscious, careened between anxiety and depression, and showed other signs of what DSM labels borderline personality disorder. And to complete the triple whammy, her extreme inhibition and timidity supported a diagnosis of avoidant personality disorder.

Faced with this morass of distress, Alice's therapist, psychologist Cynthia G. Ellis of the University of Kentucky in Lexington, took a heretical step: She abandoned DSM's guiding principles and instead evaluated her client's behavior, feelings, and motivations along five broad dimensions. This allowed the psychologist to characterize Alice as displaying a single personality disorder marked by introversion and excessive neuroticism — in Alice's case, primarily impulsive acts, emotional vulnerability, and depression.

Ellis then composed a treatment plan.

First, she dealt with Alice's immediate symptoms of bulimia. Then, over the next 2½ years, therapy sessions began carefully to explore Alice's longstanding fears of emotional intimacy and their reverberations in her life.

A minority of psychotherapists would take this dimensional approach to treating Alice or anyone else whose personality somehow goes seriously awry. But an increasingly vocal group of scientists is pushing for official recognition of dimensional techniques — particularly the five-factor model employed by Ellis.

"There may never be a consensus on how to define and measure personality," asserts University of Kentucky psychologist Thomas A. Widiger. "But there's enough support for the five-factor model to indicate that it provides a useful point of departure for understanding personality disorders."

I n 1980, the DSM's authors elevated personality disorders to a status alongside so-called symptom disorders, such as depression and schizophrenia. In a single stroke, certain personality traits — enduring ways of behaving, perceiving, and thinking about oneself and others — coalesced into medical disorders that lay across a theoretical Rubicon from "normal" personalities.

Clinicians diagnose personality disorders alone or in combination with symptom disorders. However, the frequency with which personality disorders occur in the general population is unknown.

Widiger served on the task force that developed definitions of the 11 personality disorders in the current DSM and of the 10 that will be retained in the fourth edition, or DSM-IV, slated for publication

by the American Psychiatric Association later this year. An appendix in DSM-IV will list two additional personality disorders deemed worthy of further study.

Although many DSM diagnoses have sparked debate, personality disorders quickly achieved the dubious distinction of arousing the most intense controversy. Psychiatrists and other mental health workers disagreed over which personality defects truly belonged in DSM, and tempers flared over proposed diagnoses that carried social and political overtones, such as the self-defeating and sadistic disorders (SN: 2/25/89, p.120).

Studies also found that clinicians often disagreed about which personality disorder to assign to a given individual. Some reports noted that people displaying severely disturbed personalities met DSM criteria for an average of four different personality disorders, a sure recipe for clinical confusion.

As psychiatrists grappled with these issues, psychologists undertook intensive studies of individual differences in personality traits for the first time in more than 20 years. This work had fallen out of favor during the 1960s and 1970s, which featured behaviorists' examinations of conditioned responses to various rewards and punishments and social psychologists' emphasis on how specific situations mold thoughts and behaviors.

Amid the current resurgence of personality research, some psychologists contend that attempts to chart unchanging traits fail to illuminate the ways in which the same personality changes from one social situation to another. Others argue that individuals construct multiple selves, a theory that questions the entire notion of stable, measurable personalities.

8. PERSONALITY PROCESSES

Nevertheless, trait theories of personality — exemplified by the five-factor model — enjoy considerable prominence. Their proponents treat personality disorders as instances in which traits that are present to some degree in all people reach inflexible and harmful extremes. DSM's partitioning of personality disturbances into medical conditions ignores the underlying links between well-functioning and disrupted personalities, these researchers hold.

The five-factor model focuses on the extent to which personality traits vary across five broad dimensions: neuroticism, or proneness to various forms of psychological distress and impulsive behavior; extroversion, the tendency to seek interactions with others and feel joy and optimism; openness to experience, a measure of curiosity, receptivity to new ideas, and the ability to experience emotions; agreeableness, which indicates the extent to which someone shows both compassion and antagonism toward others; and conscientiousness, the degree of organization and stick-to-itiveness regarding personal goals.

One set of questionnaires to measure these traits comes from studies of adjectives used to describe personality. Factor analyses, which mathematically divvy up such adjectives into as few coherent groups as possible, identified five independent personality dimensions as early as 1934. In the January 1993 AMERICAN PSYCHOLOGIST, Lewis R. Goldberg, a psychologist at the University of Oregon in Eugene, describes attempts to develop ratings scales for the five factors based on factor analysis.

Perhaps the bulk of research now focuses on one particular questionnaire inspired by the five-factor model. Paul T. Costa Jr. and Robert R. McCrae, both psychologists at the National Institute on Aging's Gerontology Research Center in Baltimore, devised this instrument to elicit self-reports as well as observations by spouses, peers, and clinicians. It consists of 181 statements that describe personality attributes; those who complete the questionnaire rate their level of agreement with each statement on a scale of 0 to 4.

Costa and McCrae's questionnaire breaks down each of the five factors into a number of component parts, or facets. An overall neuroticism score, for instance, consists of items that provide separate measures for anxiety, hostility, depression, self-consciousness, impulsiveness, and emotional vulnerability.

Studies of large groups administered this questionnaire indicate that numerous personality traits and factors proposed by other scientists — which have often created a sense of disarray in personality research — fall within the bounds of the five-factor model, Costa and McCrae argue.

On the heels of these findings comes a book in which researchers and clinicians apply the five-factor model to personality disorders. Costa and Widiger edited the volume, titled *Personality Disorders and the Five-Factor Model of Personality* (1994, American Psychological Association).

One chapter describes research supporting the view that the five-factor model accounts for both broken-down and finely tuned personalities. Directed by Lee Anna Clark, a psychologist at the University of Iowa in Iowa City, this work finds that people diagnosed with various personality disorders stretch one or more of the five basic traits to maladaptive extremes.

Clark's group administered trait questionnaires developed by Goldberg, Costa and McCrae, and her own scales derived from DSM criteria for personality disorders to groups of college students and psychiatric patients. All three inventories, particularly the one informed by DSM symptoms, accurately identified people in each population who suffered from personality disorders, Clark contends.

More specifically, in cases of borderline personality disorder, data on the five factors gleaned from Costa and McCrae's questionnaire offer valuable insight to clinicians, according to Cynthia Sanderson and John F. Clarkin, both of Cornell University Medical College in New York City. In a study of 64 women assigned this diagnosis, Sanderson and Clarkin find extremely high levels of neuroticism, as evidenced by anxiety, depression, self-consciousness, and a wide range of impulsive behaviors.

The same women also display low conscientiousness, reflected in aimlessness and a lack of clear goals, and low agreeableness, marked by cynicism, vengefulness, and constant attempts to manipulate others. Not surprisingly, psychotherapists encounter many difficulties in treating borderline personalities and need to monitor their problem traits from the start, the researchers maintain.

Widiger, Costa, and their colleagues propose five-factor profiles of each DSM personality disorder. Their profile of paranoid personality disorder, for instance, stresses excessively low agreeableness, characterized most strongly by suspiciousness and antagonism. Hostility, one facet of neuroticism, also shows up consistently in people diagnosed with this disorder, they contend.

Agreeableness also plummets in both narcissistic and antisocial personality disorders, the researchers note. The exorbitant self-importance and arrogance typical of the former condition translate into low scores on the agreeableness facets of modesty, altruism, and empathy, they assert. The latter disorder, marked by repeated criminal, aggressive, and irresponsible acts, features low altruism and a copious supply of extroversion, particularly as measured by items that signal a constant need for excitement and sensory stimulation.

Five-factor descriptions of paranoid personality disorder and other diagnoses that involve odd or eccentric behavior may be improved by rewording the openness-to-experience items to address such peculiarities directly, Widiger says. Auke Tellegen, a psychologist at the University of Minnesota in Minneapolis, has completed such a revision and changed the name of the dimension from "openness-to-experience" to "unconventionality."

Unlike its predecessor, Tellegen's unconventionality scale assesses, for instance, the tendency to read hidden and threatening meanings into others' remarks, one symptom of a paranoid personality. This scale also considers the magical thinking and perceptual illusions that often characterize schizotypal personality disorder.

Tellegen also proposes adding two new factors to the five-factor model; these tap into highly negative and positive qualities attributed to the self, such as a propensity for evil, treachery, excellence, and superiority.

A more far-reaching challenge to the five-factor model comes from research directed by C. Robert Cloninger, a psychiatrist at Washington University School of Medicine in St. Louis. In the December 1993 ARCHIVES OF GENERAL PSYCHIATRY, Cloninger and his coworkers describe the seven dimensions that they deem crucial to understanding healthy and disordered personalities.

Four dimensions account for temperament: novelty seeking, harm avoidance, reward dependence, and persistence. Individuals largely inherit their temperamental styles, which are triggered by perceptions of their surroundings, Cloninger's group theorizes. Temperament orchestrates the habitual behaviors that a person carries out unthinkingly throughout the day, they suggest.

The St. Louis scientists also devised three character dimensions: self-directedness (a measure of commitment to goals and purposes), cooperativeness, and self-transcendence (associated with deeply held spiritual beliefs and feelings of connection with nature or the universe). Character development leans heavily on a conscious sorting out of one's memories and experiences, the investigators argue. This process picks up steam during adulthood as misfortunes and death more frequently intrude on people's lives, they note.

Cloninger and his colleagues administered a true-false questionnaire consisting of 107 temperament items and 119 character items to 300 psychologically healthy adults. Volunteers ranged in age from 18 to 91. The seven personality dimensions clearly emerged in the sample, they contend. Character dimensions assumed increasing importance and complexity in older age groups.

The researchers also obtained questionnaire responses from 66 psychiatric patients who ran the gamut of DSM personality disorders. Low self-directedness and low cooperativeness emerge as core features of all personality disorders, they report. Moreover, each personality disorder displays a unique pattern of temperament and character scores, the investigators contend.

Most clinicians, and particularly psychiatrists, who deal with people suffering from personality disorders remain skeptical of the five-factor model and other dimensional measures of personality.

Theodore Millon, a psychiatrist at Harvard Medical School in Boston, considers it best to view the symptoms that make up each DSM category as a prototype, or most typical example, of that personality disorder. Individuals assigned the same diagnosis usually differ to some degree from the prototype, Millon asserts.

So, for example, a diagnosis of borderline personality disorder may apply to someone exhibiting five of the eight required symptoms listed in the current DSM. Other cases of borderline personality disorder may include more than five symptoms and may feature shifting mixes and different intensities of the various symptoms.

In this approach, the personality disorders shade into one another as they veer farther away from their prototypes. Clinicians must determine the degree to which a person's symptoms match prototypes of relevant personality disorders in order to come up with a primary diagnosis, Millon argues.

Dimensional models deal with surface characteristics that may only illuminate the few personality disorders that create moderate problems, adds John G. Gunderson, a psychiatrist at McLean Hospital in Belmont, Mass. Severe personality disorders, including borderline and antisocial disorders, occur most frequently and involve complex underlying problems that elude trait questionnaires, Gunderson asserts.

Other psychiatrists harbor more practical concerns. Although the dimensional approach holds much promise for analyzing personality disturbances, its acceptance and sophisticated use by clinicians "will require a monumental educational effort," according to Allen J. Frances of Duke University Medical Center in Durham, N.C. Frances directed work on DSM-IV.

What's more, notes five-factor proponent Thomas Widiger, many clinicians fear that discarding DSM categories for a dimensional focus on normal traits gone bad will result in denial of insurance coverage for treatment of serious personality disturbances.

Ongoing research aims to establish cutoff points at which scores on five-factor questionnaires signify major personality problems, Widiger says. Some psychologists have proposed that the American Psychological Association issue a rival DSM that takes this approach. Widiger, however, hopes that the next edition of DSM will include the five-factor model as a supplement to traditional personality disorder categories.

DSM-IV includes a statement acknowledging the existence of several dimensional models of personality but fails to recommend any of them for clinical use, Widiger says.

Michael H. Stone, a psychiatrist at Columbia University, would welcome a hybrid approach to treating personality disturbances.

"Sophisticated clinicians use both categories and dimensions all the time in thinking about their patients," Stone asserts. "But psychiatrists have largely ignored the research of personality psychologists."

In a book titled *Abnormalities of Personality* (1993, W.W. Norton), Stone lists 500 negative and 100 positive personality adjectives that he considers components of the five-factor model. He often administers to his patients questionnaires that inquire about these qualities; the results greatly assist in diagnosis and treatment planning, he says.

For the most part, though, psychiatrists prefer that personality dimensions take a backseat to DSM's personality disorders. "The general psychiatric public may not be ready for a sea change in diagnostic practice," Stone contends.

But true to form, personality disturbances continue to make waves.

On the Power of Positive Thinking: The Benefits of Being Optimistic

Michael F. Scheier and Charles S. Carver

Michael F. Scheier is Professor of Psychology at Carnegie Mellon University. **Charles S. Carver** is Professor of Psychology at the University of Miami. Address correspondence to Michael F. Scheier, Department of Psychology, Carnegie Mellon University, Pittsburgh, PA 15213; e-mail: ms0a@andrew.cmu.edu.

If believing in something can make it so, then there really would be power in positive thinking. From the little train in the children's tale who said, "I think I can," to popular writers such as Norman Cousins and Norman Vincent Peale, to wise grandmothers everywhere—many people have espoused the benefits of positive thinking. But are these benefits real? Do people who think positively really fare better when facing challenge or adversity? Do they recover from illness more readily? If so, how and why do these things happen?

We and a number of other psychologists who are interested in issues surrounding stress, coping, and health have for several years focused our research attention on questions such as these. The primary purpose of this brief review is to provide a taste of the research conducted on this topic. We first document that positive thinking can be beneficial. We then consider why an optimistic orientation to life might confer benefits. After considering how individual differences in optimism might arise, we take up the question of whether optimism is always good and pessimism always bad. We close by discussing the similarities between our own approach and other related approaches.

CHARACTERIZING POSITIVE THINKING

Psychologists have approached the notion of positive thinking from a variety of perspectives. Common to most views, though, is the idea that positive thinking in some way involves holding positive expectancies for one's future. Such expectancies are thought to have built-in implications for behavior. That is, the actions that people take are thought to be greatly influenced by their expectations about the likely consequences of those actions. People who see desired outcomes as attainable continue to strive for those outcomes, even when progress is slow or difficult. When outcomes seem sufficiently unattainable, people withdraw their effort and disengage themselves from their goals. Thus, people's expectancies provide a basis for engaging in one of two very different classes of behavior: continued striving versus giving up.

People can hold expectancies at many levels of generality. Some theoretical views focus on expectancies that pertain to particular situations, or even to particular actions.[1] Such an approach allows for considerable variation in the positivity of one's thinking from one context to the next. Thus, a person who is quite optimistic about recovering successfully from a car accident may be far less optimistic about landing the big promotion that is up for grabs at work.

Our own research on positive and negative thinking began with a focus on situation-specific expectancies, but over the years we began to consider expectancies that are more general and diffuse. We believe that generalized expectancies constitute an important dimension of personality, that they are relatively stable across time and context. We refer to this dimension as optimism and construe it in terms of the belief that good, as opposed to bad, things will generally occur in one's life. We focus on this dimension for the rest of this article.

MEASURING OPTIMISM

We measure individual differences in optimism with the Life Orientation Test, or LOT.[2] The LOT consists of a series of items that assess the person's expectations regarding the favorability of future outcomes (e.g., "I hardly ever expect things to go my way," "In uncertain times, I usually expect the best"). LOT scores correlate positively with measures of internal control and self-esteem, correlate negatively with measures of depression and hopelessness, and are relatively unrelated to measures of social desirability.[2]

If dispositional optimism is in fact a personality characteristic, it should be relatively stable across time. We have reported a test–retest correlation of .79 across a 4-week period.[2] More recently, Karen Matthews has found a correlation of .69 between LOT scores assessed 3 years apart in a sample of 460 healthy, middle-aged women. Indeed, LOT scores seem to remain relatively stable even in the face of catastrophes. For example, Schulz, Tompkins, and

From *Current Directions in Psychological Science*, Vol. 2, No. 1, February 1993, pp. 26-30. © 1993 by the American Psychological Society. Reprinted by permission of Cambridge University Press.

Rau[3] tracked LOT scores in a group of stroke patients and their primary caregivers across a 6-month period. Although the LOT scores of both the patients and the support persons dropped over time (significantly so for the latter), the absolute magnitude of the drop was exceedingly small (less than 1 point on a 32-point scale). Thus, optimism as measured by the LOT seems to be a relatively enduring characteristic that changes little with the vagaries of life.

Factor analyses of the LOT routinely yield two separate factors,[2,4] comprised of positively worded (optimistic) items and negatively worded (pessimistic) items, respectively. Identification of two factors raises the question of whether it is better to view optimism and pessimism as opposite poles of a single dimension or as constituting two separate but correlated dimensions.[4] Though this is an interesting question, we have thus far taken the former view.

PSYCHOLOGICAL WELL-BEING

A growing number of studies have examined the effects of dispositional optimism on psychological well-being.[5] These studies have produced a remarkably consistent pattern of findings: Optimists routinely maintain higher levels of subjective well-being during times of stress than do people who are less optimistic. Let us briefly describe two illustrative cases.

One study[6] examined the development of postpartum depression in a group of women having their first children. Women in this study completed the LOT and a standard measure of depression in the third trimester of pregnancy. They completed the same depression measure again 3 weeks postpartum. Initial optimism was inversely associated with depression 3 weeks postpartum, even when the initial level of depression was controlled statisti-

cally. In other words, optimism predicted changes in depression over time. Optimistic women were less likely to become depressed following childbirth.

Conceptually similar findings have recently been reported in a study of undergraduate students' adjustment to their first semester of college.[7] A variety of factors were assessed when the students first arrived on campus, including dispositional optimism. Several measures of psychological well-being were obtained 3 months later. Optimism had a substantial effect on future psychological well-being: Higher levels of optimism upon entering college were associated with lower distress levels 3 months later. Notably, the effects of optimism in this study were distinct from those of the other personality factors measured, including self-esteem, locus of control, and desire for control. Thus, an optimistic orientation to life seemed to provide a benefit over and above that provided by these other personality characteristics.

PHYSICAL WELL-BEING

If the effects of optimism were limited to making people feel better, perhaps such findings would not be very surprising. The effects of optimism seem to go beyond this, however. There is at least some evidence that optimism also confers benefits on physical well-being.

Consider, for example, a study conducted on a group of men undergoing coronary artery bypass graft surgery.[8] Each patient was interviewed on the day prior to surgery, 6 to 8 days postsurgery, and again 6 months later. Optimism was assessed on the day prior to surgery by the LOT. A variety of medical and recovery variables were measured at several times, beginning before surgery and continuing through surgery and several months thereafter.

The data showed a number of effects for dispositional optimism.

One notable finding concerns reactions to the surgery itself. Optimism was negatively related to physiological changes reflected in the patient's electrocardiogram and to the release of certain kinds of enzymes into the bloodstream. Both of these changes are widely taken as markers for myocardial infarction. The data thus suggest that optimists were less likely than pessimists to suffer heart attack during surgery.

Optimism was also a significant predictor of the rate of recovery during the immediate postoperative period. Optimists were faster to achieve selected behavioral milestones of recovery (e.g., sitting up in bed, walking around the room), and they were rated by medical staff as showing better physical recovery.

The advantages of an optimistic orientation were also apparent at the 6-month follow-up. Optimistic patients were more likely than pessimistic patients to have resumed vigorous physical exercise and to have returned to work full-time. Moreover, optimists returned to their activities more quickly than did pessimists. In sum, optimists were able to normalize their lifestyles more fully and more quickly than were pessimists. It is important to note that all of the findings just described were independent of the person's medical status at the outset of the study. Thus, it was not the case that optimists did better simply because they were less sick at the time of surgery.

HOW DOES OPTIMISM HELP?

If an understanding can be gained of why optimists do better than pessimists, then perhaps psychologists can begin to devise ways to help pessimists do better. One promising line of inquiry concerns differences between optimists and pessimists in how they cope with stress. Research from a variety of sources is beginning to suggest that optimists cope in more adaptive ways than do pessimists.[5] Optimists are more likely than pessimists to take direct action to solve their problems, are more planful in dealing with the adversity they confront, and are more focused in their coping efforts. Optimists are more likely to accept the reality of the stressful situations they encounter, and they also seem intent on growing personally from negative experiences and trying to make the best of bad situations. In contrast to these positive coping reactions, pessimists are more likely than optimists to react to stressful events by trying to deny that they exist or by trying to avoid dealing with problems. Pessimists are also more likely to quit trying when difficulties arise.

We now know that these coping differences are at least partly responsible for the differences in distress that optimists and pessimists experience in times of stress. When Aspinwall and Taylor[7] studied adjustment to college life, they collected information about the coping tactics the students were using to help themselves adjust to college, as well as measuring their optimism and eventual adjustment. Optimists were more likely than pessimists to rely on active coping techniques and less likely to engage in avoidance. These two general coping orientations were both related to later adjustment, in opposite directions. Avoidance coping was associated with poorer adjustment, whereas active coping was associated with better adjustment. Further analysis revealed that these two coping tendencies mediated the link between optimism and adjustment. Thus, optimists did better than pessimists at least partly because optimists used more effective ways of coping with problems.

A similar conclusion is suggested by a study of breast cancer patients that we and our colleagues recently completed. The women in this study reported on their distress and coping reactions before surgery, 10 days after surgery, and at 3-month, 6-month, and 12-month follow-ups. Throughout this period, optimism was associated with a coping pattern that involved accepting the reality of the situation, along with efforts to make the best of it. Optimism was inversely associated with attempts to act as though the problem was not real and with the tendency to give up on the life goals that were being threatened by the diagnosis of cancer. Further analyses suggested that these differences in coping served as paths by which the optimistic women remained less vulnerable to distress than the pessimistic women throughout the year.

ANTECEDENTS OF OPTIMISM

Where does optimism come from? Why do some people have it and others not? At present, not much is known about the origins of individual differences on this dimension. The determinants must necessarily fall in two broad categories, however: nature and nurture.

On the nature side, the available evidence suggests that individual differences in optimism-pessimism may be partly inherited. A translated version of the LOT was given to a sample of more than 500 same-sex pairs of middle-aged Swedish twins, and the heritability of optimism and pessimism was estimated to be about 25% using several different estimation procedures.[9] Thus, at least part of the variation in optimism and pessimism in the general population seems due to genetic influence.

On the environmental side, less is known. It is certainly reasonable to argue that optimism and pessimism are partly learned from prior experiences with success and failure. To the extent that one has been successful in the past, one should expect success in the future. Analogously, prior failure might breed the expectation of future failure. Children might also acquire a sense of optimism (or pessimism) from their parents, for example, through modeling. That is, parents who meet difficulties with positive expecta-tions and who use adaptive coping strategies are explicitly or implicitly modeling those qualities for their children. Pessimistic parents also provide models for their children, although the qualities modeled are very different. Thus, children might become optimistic or pessimistic by thinking and acting in ways their parents do.

Parents might also influence children more directly by instructing them in problem solving. Parents who teach adaptive coping skills will produce children who are better problem solvers than children of parents who do not. To the extent that acquiring adaptive coping skills leads to coping success, the basis for an optimistic orientation is provided. We have recently begun a program of research designed to examine how coping strategies are transmitted from parent to child, with particular emphasis on the manner in which parental characteristics affect the kinds of coping strategies that are taught.

IS OPTIMISM ALWAYS GOOD? IS PESSIMISM ALWAYS BAD?

Implicit in our discussion thus far is the view that optimism is good for people. Is this always true? There are at least two ways in which an optimistic orientation might lead to poorer outcomes. First, it may be possible to be too optimistic, or to be optimistic in unproductive ways. For example, unbridled optimism may cause people to sit and wait for good things to happen, thereby decreasing the chance of success. We have seen no evidence of such a tendency among people defined as optimistic on the basis of the LOT, however. Instead, optimistic people seem to view positive outcomes as partially contingent on their continued effort.

Second, optimism might also prove detrimental in situations that are not amenable to constructive action. Optimists are prone to face problems with efforts to resolve them, but perhaps this head-on approach is maladaptive in situations that are uncontrollable or that involve major loss or a violation of one's world view. Data on this question are lacking, yet it is worth noting that the coping arsenal of optimists is not limited to the problem-focused domain. Optimists also use a host of emotion-focused coping responses, including tendencies to accept the reality of the situation, to put the situation in the best possible light, and to grow personally from their hardships. Given these coping options, optimists may prove to have a coping advantage even in the most distressing situations.

What about the reverse question? Can pessimism ever work in one's favor? Cantor and Norem[10] recently coined the term *defensive pessimism* to reflect a coping style in which people expect outcomes that are more negative than their prior reward histories in a given domain would suggest. Defensive pessimism may be useful because it helps to buffer the person against future failure, should failure occur. In addition, defensive pessimism may help the person perform better because the worry over anticipated failure prompts remedial action in preparation for the event.

Defensive pessimism does seem to work. That is, the performance of defensive pessimists tends to be better than the performance of real pessimists, whose negative expectations are anchored in prior failure. On the other hand, defensive pessimism never works better than optimism. Moreover, this style apparently has some hidden costs: People who use defensive pessimism in the short run report more psychological symptoms and a lower quality of life in the long run than do optimists.[10] Such findings call into serious question the adaptive value of defensive pessimism.

RELATIONSHIP TO OTHER APPROACHES

The concept of optimism, as discussed here, does not stand apart from the rest of personality psychology. There are easily noted family resemblances to several other personality constructs and approaches that have arisen in response to the same questions that prompted our line of theorizing. Two well-known examples are attributional style[11] and self-efficacy.[1] It may be useful to briefly note some similarities and differences between our conceptualization and these other approaches.

Attributional Style

Work on attributional style derives from the cognitive model[11] that was proposed to account for the phenomenon of learned helplessness[12] in humans. In this model, people's causal explanations for past events influence their expectations for controlling future events. The explanations thus influence subsequent feelings and behavior. As the attributional theory developed, it evolved toward a consideration of individual differences and began to focus on the possibility that an individual may have a stable tendency toward using one or another type of attribution. A tendency to attribute negative outcomes to causes that are stable, global, and internal has come to be known as pessimistic. A tendency to attribute negative events to causes that are unstable, specific, and external has come to be known as optimistic.

There is a clear conceptual link between this theory and the approach that we have taken. Both theories rely on the assumption that the consequences of optimism versus pessimism derive from differences in people's expectancies (at least in part). This assumption has been focal in our theory, and it is also important—albeit less focal—in the attributional approach. More-

over, despite differences in the types of measures used to assess optimism and attributional style, research findings relating attributional style to psychological and physical well-being have tended to parallel findings obtained for dispositional optimism.[13] Thus, the data converge on the conclusion that optimism is beneficial for mental and physical functioning.

Self-Efficacy

Self-efficacy expectancies are people's expectations of being either able or unable to execute desired behaviors successfully. Although there are obvious similarities between self-efficacy and optimism-pessimism, there are also two salient differences. One difference involves the extent to which the sense of personal agency is seen as the critical variable underlying behavior. Our approach to dispositional optimism intentionally deemphasizes the role of personal efficacy. Statements on self-efficacy make personal agency paramount.[1]

The second difference concerns the breadth of the expectancy on which the theory focuses. Efficacy theory holds that people's behavior is best predicted by focalized, domain-specific (or even act-specific) expectancies. Dispositional optimism, in contrast, is thought to be a very generalized tendency that has an influence in a wide variety of settings. Interestingly, relevant research[8] suggests that both types of expectancies (specific and general) are useful in predicting behavior.

CONCLUDING COMMENT

Our purpose in writing this article (perhaps in line with its subject matter) was to put a positive foot forward in presenting work on the benefits of optimism. In so doing, we may have created a false sense that the important questions about positive thinking have all been answered. Such is not the case. Understanding of the nature and effects of optimism is still in its infancy, and there is much more to learn. For example, although the effects of optimism seem attributable in part to differences in the ways optimists and pessimists cope with stress, this cannot be the complete answer. It is impossible to account fully for differences between optimists and pessimists on the basis of this factor alone.

Similarly, more work is needed to tease apart the effects of optimism from the effects of related variables. As noted earlier, a number of personality dimensions bear a conceptual resemblance to optimism-pessimism. Some of these dimensions, such as personal coherence, hardiness, and learned resourcefulness, have appeared in the literature only recently. Other dimensions, such as neuroticism, self-esteem, and self-mastery, have a longer scientific past. Given the existence of these related constructs, it is reasonable to ask whether their effects are distinguishable. This question cannot be resolved easily on the basis of one or two studies alone. An answer must await the gradual accumulation of evidence from many studies using different methodologies and assessing different outcomes.

There does seem to be a power to positive thinking. It surely is not as simple and direct a process as believing in something making it so. But believing that the future holds good things in store clearly has an effect on the way people relate to many aspects of life.

Acknowledgments—Preparation of this article was facilitated by National Science Foundation Grants BNS-9010425 and BNS-9011653, by National Institutes of Health Grant 1R01HL44432-01A1, and by American Cancer Society Grant PBR-56.

Notes

1. A. Bandura, *Social Foundations of Thought and Action: A Social Cognitive Theory* (Prentice-Hall, Englewood Cliffs, NJ, 1986).

2. M.F. Scheier and C.S. Carver, Optimism, coping, and health: Assessment and implications of generalized outcome expectancies, *Health Psychology, 4,* 219–247 (1985).

3. R. Schulz, C.A. Tompkins, and M.T. Rau, A longitudinal study of the psychosocial impact of stroke on primary support persons, *Psychology and Aging, 3,* 131–141 (1988).

4. G.N. Marshall, C.B. Wortman, J.W. Kusulas, L.K. Hervig, and R.R. Vickers, Jr., Distinguishing optimism from pessimism: Relations to fundamental dimensions of mood and personality, *Journal of Personality and Social Psychology, 62,* 1067–1074 (1992).

5. See M.F. Scheier and C.S. Carver, Effects of optimism on psychological and physical well-being: Theoretical overview and empirical update, *Cognitive Therapy and Research, 16,* 201–228 (1992).

6. C.S. Carver and J.G. Gaines, Optimism, pessimism, and postpartum depression, *Cognitive Therapy and Research, 11,* 449–462 (1987).

7. L.G. Aspinwall and S.E. Taylor, Modeling cognitive adaptation: A longitudinal investigation of the impact of individual differences and coping on college adjustment and performance, *Journal of Personality and Social Psychology* (in press).

8. M.F. Scheier, K.A. Matthews, J.F. Owens, G.J. Magovern, Sr., R. Lefebvre, R.C. Abbott, and C.S. Carver, Dispositional optimism and recovery from coronary artery bypass surgery: The beneficial effects of optimism on physical and psychological well-being, *Journal of Personality and Social Psychology, 57,* 1024–1040 (1989).

9. R. Plomin, M.F. Scheier, C.S. Bergeman, N.L. Pedersen, J.R. Nesselroade, and G.E. McClearn, Optimism, pessimism and mental health: A twin/adoption analysis, *Personality and Individual Differences* (in press).

10. N. Cantor and J.K. Norem, Defensive pessimism and stress and coping, *Social Cognition, 7,* 92–112 (1989).

11. L.Y. Abramson, M.E.P. Seligman, and J.D. Teasdale, Learned helplessness in humans: Critique and reformulation, *Journal of Abnormal Psychology, 87,* 49–74 (1978).

12. M.E.P. Seligman, *Helplessness: On Depression, Development, and Death* (Freeman, San Francisco, 1975).

13. For a review, see C. Peterson and L.M. Bossio, *Health and Optimism: New Research on the Relationship Between Positive Thinking and Physical Well-Being* (Free Press, New York, 1991).

Recommended Reading

Scheier, M.F., and Carver, C.S. (1992). Effects of optimism on psychological and physical well-being: Theoretical overview and empirical update. *Cognitive Therapy and Research, 16,* 201–228.

Seligman, M.E.P. (1991). *Learned Optimism* (Knopf, New York).

Taylor, S.E. (1989). *Positive Illusions: Creative Self-Deception and the Healthy Mind* (Basic Books, New York).

Is HOSTILITY KILLING YOU?

To protect your heart, try not to simmer or boil over.

Back in the 1950's, researchers first proposed that "Type A" behavior harms the heart. Since then, numerous studies have shown that the danger lies not in the full package of hard-driving, competitive, aggressive behavior that characterizes that classic personality type, but mostly in just one facet: hostility.

Today, the evidence linking hostility to an increased risk of coronary heart disease makes the most compelling case so far in the search for a connection between personality and disease. Recent research has shed new light on the nature of that link, suggesting that people prone to angry outbursts are not the only ones endangered by hostility.

A hostile takeover

Some people seem to go through life with a bad attitude. They're cynical, angry, and easily provoked. Whereas most people let minor aggravations slide, hostile people shift into emotional overdrive. In experiments using deliberate provocations such as frustrating math problems and rude assistants, researchers have identified a potentially catastrophic chain reaction in hostile people:

■ The brain signals the adrenal glands to dump an extra dose of stress hormones, including adrenaline, into the bloodstream.

■ Spurred on by adrenaline, the heart races and blood pressure rises.

■ The strain of hormone-laden blood raging unchecked through the arteries appears to injure the artery walls and make them more susceptible to blood clots and plaque deposits that can eventually choke off the heart.

■ In people with coronary damage, hostile reactions further constrict the narrowed arteries and hamper the heart's pumping capacity.

That exaggerated response to everyday stress apparently takes its toll. Tests of blood flow to the heart and of plaque deposits in the arteries show that hostile people have greater arterial blockage than more even-tempered people. As a result, hostile people have more than their share of angina (chest pain) and heart attacks. Over the past decade, several reports—including, most recently, a Harvard study presented at an American Heart Association meeting in March—have implicated chronic hostility or even a bout of anger as a risk factor for heart attack.

Some researchers have charted that downward spiral by assessing hostility in healthy volunteers and then following them for a period of years. Most of those prospective studies, including the landmark Multiple Risk Factor Intervention Trial, have found that hostility tends to at least double the risk of developing coronary disease.

To isolate hostility as an independent risk factor for coronary disease, researchers have carefully controlled for the influence of three known risky behaviors: smoking, overeating, and excessive drinking. Hostile people are more likely than others to indulge in those bad habits, compounding their risk.

Does gender matter?

The latest research on hostility and the heart has turned up some interesting differences between men and women. All of the prospective studies that provided the most damning evidence against hostility involved only men. The one prospective study to include women found no link between hostility and coronary disease among either men or women. But that study, published last year by Mayo Institute researchers, failed to control adequately for other risk factors. And well over half the original participants dropped out—perhaps including hostile people who might have developed coronary disease.

At least one retrospective study has also failed to find any evidence of an increased risk of coronary disease among hostile women. But that may be because, in our culture at least, women have traditionally been less likely than men to express hostility openly in the first place. So studies looking for harm among outwardly hostile women may have missed most of the hostility experienced by women. Indeed, new research among women suggests that suppressing hostile feelings can be just as harmful as expressing them.

In one study presented at a meeting of the American Psychosomatic Society last month, University of Maryland researchers used a standard interview to gauge levels of hostility in some 150 people undergoing tests for impaired blood flow to the heart. Among the men, those who expressed hostility during the interview—for example, by getting angry at the interviewer—had less blood flow than those who didn't express hostility. Among women, expressed hostility was only weakly linked to blood flow; but those who showed signs of suppressed hostility—such as evading any questions that dealt with anger-provoking topics—had markedly less blood flow to the heart.

That finding among women is supported by data from the ongoing Framingham Heart Study and a similar study in Sweden. A follow-up of heart-attack survivors published last year offers further support. Researchers tracked more than 80 women for at least eight years after their first heart attack. Those who suppressed anger and other emotions were more likely to have a second heart attack.

But all that doesn't mean that women should let loose their hostility and that men can safely bottle up theirs. "I think it will eventually turn out that both expressing and suppressing hostility are dangerous in both men *and* women," says University of Maryland researcher Aron Siegman, Ph.D. "The most important finding is that one's risk of coronary disease is increased by a 'hostile style'—whether that hostility is expressed or suppressed."

Handling hostility

Is it really possible for a hostile person to mellow out more than superficially—enough to change harmful physical responses to stress?

While no study has directly tested whether changing hostile responses can lower the risk of developing coronary disease, there's some encouraging evidence. One study published 10 years ago found that curbing Type A behavior cut the chance of having a second heart attack. Researchers now believe that the key may have been lessened hostility.

Preliminary research by Siegman's team suggests that controlling how you express hostile feelings may modulate your body's response: When college students freely described incidents that had made them angry, their blood pressure and heart rate increased sharply—but not at all when they were told to use a calm, measured voice while recounting the events.

In addition to any direct benefit to the heart, resolving hostility could also help indirectly. Some re-

---

ARE YOU TOO HOSTILE?

To help answer that question, Duke University researcher Redford Williams, M.D., has devised a short self-test. While it's not a scientific evaluation, it does offer a rough measure of hostility.

True or false?

___ I often get annoyed at checkout cashiers or the people in front of me when I'm waiting in line.
___ I usually keep an eye on the people I work or live with to make sure they do what they should.
___ I often wonder how extremely fat people can have so little respect for themselves.
___ I believe that most people will take advantage of you if you let them.
___ The habits of friends or family members often annoy me.
___ When I'm stuck in traffic, I often start breathing faster and my heart pounds.
___ When I'm annoyed with people, I really want to let them know it.
___ If someone does me wrong, I want to get even.
___ I'd like to have the last word in any argument.
___ At least once a week, I have the urge to yell at, or even hit, someone.

According to Williams, five or more "true" statements suggest that you're excessively hostile and should consider taking steps to mellow out.

---

searchers speculate that a less hostile outlook could make it easier to reform other bad health habits.

At the very least, however, a person who recognizes the hostility he or she harbors should pay special attention to other known, controllable risk factors for coronary disease—quit smoking, eat less fat, control weight, and exercise more.

How to mellow out

The best way to curb hostility involves a "cognitive-behavioral" approach. Similar strategies for changing destructive patterns of thinking and behaving are often used to overcome anxiety, depression, obsessive behavior, panic, and phobias. In his book "Anger Kills," Duke University researcher Redford Williams, M.D., suggests the following techniques:

Reason with yourself. Each time you feel your temper rise, ask yourself three important questions:
■ Is my anger justified?
■ Does the situation deserve continued attention?
■ Do I have a constructive response?

For example, say someone cuts you off in heavy traffic. Are you justified in your anger? Certainly. Is it worth attending to? Well, the other driver could have caused an accident. But there's no constructive response to the aggravation: It won't help to lean on the horn, shout obscenities, or sit and stew.

Call a halt. When there's really no constructive response, rationalizing the situation still may not dissolve your anger. Try to sweep it out of your mind:

■ Practice meditation to take a "time out."

■ Distract yourself—for example, by picking up a magazine in a slow-moving checkout line.

■ Try "thought stopping," a technique that involves saying "stop" to yourself—aloud or under your breath—whenever you feel your anger rising.

Practice assertiveness. When an aggravating situation does call for a response, you need to find a positive one. If someone's behavior is causing the aggravation, the most constructive response is often a simple request—delivered with empathy.

Many people may be able to reduce their hostility by practicing those strategies on their own; others may prefer to work with a psychotherapist. Either way, supportive friends and family can help. Such emotional support may reinforce efforts to reduce hostility. And mounting evidence indicates that close personal relationships help protect against damage from psychological stressors like hostility.

Social Processes

Everywhere we look there are groups of people. Your general psychology class is a group. It is what social psychologists would call a secondary group, a group that comes together for a particular, somewhat contractual reason and then disbands after its goals have been met. Other secondary groups include athletic teams, church associations, juries, committees, and so forth.

There are other types of groups, too. One other type is a primary group. A primary group has much face-to-face contact, and there is often a sense of we-ness in the group (cohesiveness as social psychologists would call it). Examples of primary groups include sets of roommates, families, sororities, fraternities, etc.

Collectives or very large groups are loosely knit, large groups of people. A bleacher full of football fans would be a collective. A line of people waiting to get into a rock concert would also be a collective. As you might guess, collectives' behavior is different from primary and secondary groups.

Mainstream American society and any other large group sharing common rules and norms are also a group, albeit an extremely large group. While we might not always think about our society and how it shapes our behavior and our attitudes, society and culture nonetheless have a vast influence on us. Psychologists, anthropologists, and sociologists alike are all interested in studying the effects of a culture on its members.

Any process in interpersonal relations is eligible for study by social psychologists. Interpersonal space or social distance is one aspect of behavior that fascinates many a layperson as well as social psychologists. Another interesting process is how people make decisions about whether they will change or give up some valued object or service so that others might benefit. Psychologists have developed scenarios or dilemmas that pit individual interests against collective interests. The results of research on social dilemmas is the focus of "The Dynamics of Social Dilemmas" by Natalie Glance and Bernardo Huberman.

We next look at our own society and an issue that does not seem to want to go away—television violence. In "Media, Violence, Youth, and Society," Ray Surette examines research about television and its effects on us. Not only does television desensitize us to violence, it has other deleterious effects for viewers.

"The Lessons of Love" explores a more positive issue, love. Beth Livermore captures scientifically this often poetic state, and she carefully reviews psychologists' research on love: who loves whom, types of love, why people love, and other fascinating topics.

Looking Ahead: Challenge Questions

What is a social dilemma? Why is it important to study social dilemmas? What has research shown us about the average American's welfare when it is pitted against societal gain?

What are some of the negative consequences of television viewing? Is there a link between televised violence and violence on our streets? Do you think we will ever eliminate some of the problematic themes of television programs and commercials? Describe how television can or does promote positive social change.

What is love? Why do people fall in love? Are there differences between men and women in why they fall in love? Is love always a positive emotion?

Unit 9

The Dynamics of Social Dilemmas

Individuals in groups must often choose between acting selfishly or cooperating for the common good. Social models explain how group cooperation arises—and why that behavior can suddenly change

Natalie S. Glance
Bernardo A. Huberman

Imagine that you and a group of friends are dining at a fine restaurant with an unspoken agreement to divide the check evenly. What do you order? Do you choose the modest chicken entrée or the pricey lamb chops? The house wine or the Cabernet Sauvignon 1983? If you are extravagant, you could enjoy a superlative dinner at a bargain price. But if everyone in the party reasons as you do, the group will end up with a hefty bill to pay. And why should others settle for pasta primavera when someone is having grilled pheasant at their expense?

This lighthearted situation, which we call the Unscrupulous Diner's Dilemma, typifies a class of serious, difficult problems that pervade society. Sociologists, economists and political scientists find that this class of social dilemma is central to a wide range of issues,

such as protecting the environment, conserving natural resources, eliciting donations to charity, slowing military arms races and containing the population explosion. All these issues involve goals that demand collective effort and cooperation. The challenge is to induce individuals to contribute to common causes when selfish actions would be more immediately and personally beneficial. Studies of these problems cast light on the nature of interactions among individuals and the emergence of social compacts. Moreover, they explain how personal choices give rise to social phenomena.

Social dilemmas have often been studied using groups of people who are given choices that present a conflict between the general good and the costs to an individual. Such experiments confirmed the hypothesis, first made by the economist Mancur L. Olson in the 1950s, that small groups are more likely to secure voluntary cooperation than are larger ones. They also revealed that repeated iterations of a situation tend to promote cooperative attitudes. The amount of cooperation further increases when communication among the participants is permitted.

More recently, powerful computers have been drafted for simulations of the social behavior of groups. The computer experiments gloss over the complexities of human nature, but we believe they can help elucidate some of the principles that govern interactions involving many participants. For the past three years, we have investigated social cooperation using both analytical techniques and computer simulations. We have tried to look not just at

the outcomes of the dilemmas but also at the dynamics of the interactions and the ways in which those outcomes evolve in various groups.

Our mathematical theory of social dilemmas indicates that overall cooperation cannot generally be sustained in groups that exceed a critical size. That size depends on how long individuals expect to remain part of the group as well as on the amount of information available to them. Moreover, both general cooperation and defection can appear suddenly and unexpectedly. These results can serve as aids for interpreting historical trends and as guidelines for constructively reorganizing corporations, trade unions, governments and other group enterprises.

Mathematical theories of social dilemmas have traditionally been formulated within the framework of game theory. The mathematician John von Neumann and the economist Oskar Morgenstern developed that discipline in the mid-1940s to model the behavior of individuals in economic and adversarial situations. An individual's choices are ranked according to some payoff function, which assigns a numerical worth—in dollars or apples or some other commodity—to the consequences of each choice. Within game theory, individuals behave rationally: they choose the action that yields the highest payoff. (Real people may not be consistently rational, but they do behave that way when presented with simple choices and straightforward situations.)

Social dilemmas can readily be mapped into game settings. In general

NATALIE S. GLANCE and BERNARDO A. HUBERMAN explore their joint interest in the dynamics of social systems at the Xerox Palo Alto Research Center. For several years, Glance has studied the role of expectations and beliefs in systems of intentional agents. She received her Ph.D. in physics from Stanford University. Huberman is a Xerox Research Fellow and has been a visiting professor at the University of Paris and the University of Copenhagen. He received his physics degree from the University of Pennsylvania and has worked in condensed matter physics, statistical mechanics and chaotic dynamics. He is a co-recipient of the 1990 Prize of the Conference on Economics and Artificial Intelligence.

terms, a social dilemma involves a group of people attempting to provide themselves with a common good in the absence of central authority. In the Unscrupulous Diner scenario, for instance, the common good is achieved by minimizing the amount of the check. The individuals are said to cooperate if they choose a less expensive meal; they defect if they spare no expense (for the group, that is!). Of course, the game is only an idealized mathematical model—how well can one quantify intangibles such as the enjoyment of the meal or guilt over saddling friends with a large bill? Nevertheless, the dynamics of the game are still instructive.

Each individual can choose either to contribute to the common good or to shirk and "free ride" on the sacrifices of others. All individuals share equally in the common good, regardless of their actions. Each person who cooperates therefore increases the common good by a fixed amount but receives back only some fraction of that added value. (The return is diminished by free riders who benefit without contributing.)

When an individual realizes that the costs of cooperating exceed her share of the added benefit, she will rationally choose to defect and become a free rider. Because every individual faces the same choice, all the members of a group will defect. Thus, the individually rational strategy of weighing costs against benefits has an inferior outcome: no common good is produced, and all the members of the group are less well off than they could be.

The situation changes, however, if the players know they will repeat the game with the same group. Each individual must consider the repercussions of a decision to cooperate or defect. The issue of expectations then comes to the fore. Individuals do not simply react to their perceptions of the world; they choose among alternatives based on their plans, goals and beliefs.

O f what do these expectations and beliefs consist? First, an individual has a sense of how long a particular social interaction will last, and that estimate affects her decision. A diner who goes out with a group once is more likely to splurge at the expense of others than is one who goes out with the same friends frequently. We call the expected duration of a game the horizon length. A short horizon reflects a player's belief that the game will end soon, whereas a long one means the player believes the game will repeat far into the future.

Second, each player has beliefs about how her actions will influence the rest of the group's future behavior. A diner may reject the option of an expensive meal out of fear that it would prompt others to order lavishly at the next gathering. The size of the group bears directly on this thinking. In a large crowd, a player can reasonably expect that the effect of her action, cooperative or not, will be diluted. (Ten dollars more or less on the group's bill matters less when it is divided among 30 diners rather than five.) The player will reason that her actions become less influential as the size of the group increases.

For groups beyond some size, overall cooperation becomes unsustainable. The likelihood of bad consequences from an individual's defection becomes so small, whereas the potential gain stays so large, that the disincentive to defect vanishes. As our experiments have determined, this critical size depends on the horizon length: the longer that players expect the game to continue, the more likely they are to cooperate. That conclusion reinforces the commonsense notion that cooperation is most likely in small groups with lengthy interactions.

The smallest possible social group, consisting of only two players, raises the special limiting case widely known as the Prisoner's Dilemma. It is so named because of one common way in which it is framed: a prisoner is given the choice of betraying a fellow prisoner (defecting) and going free or keeping silent (cooperating) and thereby risking a harsh punishment if the other prisoner betrays him. Because the psychology of the interactions is unique, certain strategies that work well for individuals in the Prisoner's Dilemma fail in larger groups. The highly successful one known as tit-for-tat depends on retaliation and forgiveness. A player initially cooperates and thereafter does whatever the other player last did. Tit-for-tat works because it allows each player to recognize that the other's actions are in direct response to her own. In groups of more than two, however, it is impossible for one player to punish or reward another specifically because any modification of her own actions affects the entire group.

In larger groups, an individual caught in a social dilemma forms a strategy for conditional cooperation from a calculation of the expected payoffs: she will cooperate if at least some critical fraction of the group is also cooperating. When enough of the others are cooperating, she expects that her future gains will compensate for present losses. If the number of cooperating individuals falls below that threshold, then her expected losses rule out cooperation, and she will defect. The strategies, expectations and thresholds of the individuals

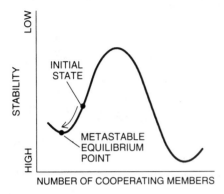

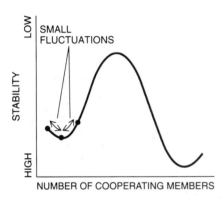

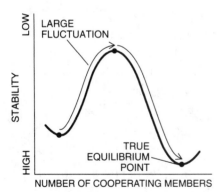

STABILITY FUNCTION explains the dynamics of groups confronting social dilemmas. No matter what a group's initial state may be, it quickly shifts into a state of relative equilibrium, in which either many or few people are cooperating (*top*). Small fluctuations around this equilibrium point are routine (*middle*). Large fluctuations, however, which are rare, can carry the group over a stability barrier. The group will then very rapidly advance to a lower true equilibrium state (*bottom*). In the long run, a group will always settle into the lowest equilibrium state.

determine whether cooperation within a group is sustainable.

Quite aside from the question of whether a group can achieve cooperation is the equally important matter of how cooperation or defection emerges in a social setting. Imagine that the hypothetical diners, after many consecutive budget-busting meals, decide to split into smaller groups, hoping that the limited size of the resulting tables will aid cooperation. How long does it take for the small groups of defectors to switch? Is the process smoothly evolutionary or sudden?

To study the evolution of social cooperation, we borrowed methods from statistical thermodynamics. This branch of physics attempts to derive the macroscopic properties of matter from the interactions of its constituent molecules. We adapted the approach to study the aggregate behavior of individuals confronted with social choices.

Our method relies on the mathematical construction of a curve called a stability function. This curve describes the relative stability of a group's behavior in terms of the amount of cooperation present. The values of the curve derive from a knowledge of the costs, benefits and individual expectations associated with a given social dilemma. The stability function generally has two minima, or troughs, which represent the most stable states of the group: widespread defection and widespread cooperation. They are separated by a high barrier, which is the least stable state. The relative heights of these features depend on the size of the group and the amount of information available to its members. From this function, one can predict the possible outcomes of the dilemma and how long the group will stay in a particular state.

Like a ball rolling downhill, the group's behavior will always gravitate from its initial state toward the closest trough. Once in a trough, however, the system does not become static. Instead it jiggles back and forth randomly, just as a small ball would be moved by vibrations. These random perturbations are caused by the uncertainty that individuals have about the behavior of others. If an individual misperceives the level of cooperation in the group, she may erroneously defect and thereby briefly move the system away from equilibrium. The more uncertainty there is in the system, the more likely there will be fluctuations around an equilibrium state.

These perturbations are usually small, so in the short run the system

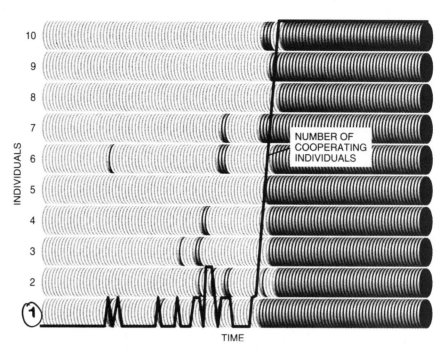

OUTBREAKS OF COOPERATION can be simulated using computer agents that act like individuals. In a homogeneous group of agents that are all initially defectors (*light gray*), the shift to widespread cooperation (*dark gray*) is sudden and rapid.

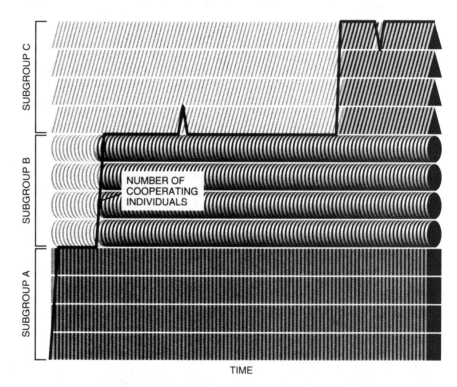

HETEROGENEOUS GROUPS evolve stepwise toward overall cooperation, with each subgroup experiencing a distinct transition on its own.

stays near one minimum. Over the long run, however, large fluctuations become important. Such fluctuations, caused by many individuals switching from defection to cooperation, or vice versa, can push the group over the barrier between the minima. Consequently, given

sufficient time, a group will always end up in the more stable of the two equilibrium states, even if it initially moves into the other, metastable one.

Huge random fluctuations are extremely rare—on average, they occur over periods proportional to the exponential of the size of the group. Once the transition from the local minimum to the maximum of the function takes place, however, the system slides down to the global minimum very quickly— in a period proportional to the logarithm of the group size. Thus, the theory predicts that although the general behavior of a group in a dilemma stays the same for long periods, when it does change, it does so very fast.

Computer experiments demonstrate those predictions. A society of computational agents, or programs acting like individuals, can be presented with a social dilemma. The agents intermittently and asynchronously reevaluate their options and decide whether to cooperate or to defect. They base their decisions on information, which may be imperfect and delayed, about how many of the others are cooperating. The sum of all the agents' actions reveals the degree of cooperation or defection in the group. The experimenter can compile statistics on the level of cooperation over time.

One typical experiment features a group of 10 agents, all of which are initially defecting. If one agent misjudges how many others are cooperating and switches its behavior, that change might lead the rest of the group to make a similar shift. The group therefore stays at or near its initial metastable state of mutual defection for a long time, until a sudden and abrupt transition carries the group to mutual cooperation.

That abrupt appearance of cooperation in a computer simulation well describes certain real social phenomena, such as the recent upsurge in environmental awareness and activism. In many parts of the U.S. and Europe, voluntary recycling has become a normal part of daily life. A decade ago that was not the case. Recycling poses a social dilemma for the consumer: the environmental benefits are great if most of the population recycles but marginal if only a few do, and the individual's invested effort in bringing bottles and newspapers to the recycling center is the same in either case. Our theory may help explain why the population, after a long period of relative apathy, has so quickly embraced recycling, emissions controls and other environmental protection measures.

In the hypothetical social dilemmas we have described so far, all the individuals evaluate their payoffs the same way and share the same expectations about the outcomes of their actions. In any real group of humans, however, individuals have largely disparate beliefs. We have therefore looked at how diversity affects the dynamics of social dilemmas.

A heterogeneous group can display two different types of diversity: variation around a common average or segregation into factions. The first involves a simple spread in opinion or concern among individuals who are fundamentally the same. For example, some unscrupulous diners may anticipate and value more future meals than others. If the typical diner looks about 10 meals into the future, then individuals will have horizons that vary but cluster around that average.

Although models of social dilemmas that include this type of diversity are more complicated than ones for homogeneous groups, their dynamics still follow a clear pattern. Basically the diversity acts as an additional form of uncertainty, instigating fluctuations in the state of the group. If most individuals are defecting, the first to decide to cooperate will probably be the one who has the longest horizon. That decision might then convince others who have longer-than-average horizons to cooperate, too. Those transitions can trigger a cascade of further cooperation, until the whole group is cooperating.

The events that led to the mass protests in Leipzig and Berlin and to the subsequent downfall of the East German government in November 1989 vividly illustrate the impact of such diversity on the resolution of social dilemmas. Earlier that year Mikhail S. Gorbachev, then president of the Soviet Union, stopped backing the Eastern European governments with the force of the Soviet military. His new policy reopened the issue of whether the Eastern European population would still subscribe to the existing social compact. The citizens of Leipzig who desired a change of government faced a dilemma. They could stay home in safety or demonstrate against the government and risk arrest—knowing that as the number of demonstrators rose, the risk declined and the potential for overthrowing the regime increased.

A conservative person would demonstrate against the government only if thousands were already committed; a revolutionary might join at the slightest sign of unrest. That variation in threshold is one form of diversity. People also differed in their estimates of the duration of a demonstration as well as in the amount of risk they were willing to take. Bernhard Prosch and Martin Abraham, two sociologists from Erlangen University who studied the Leipzig demonstrations, claim that the diversity in thresholds was important in triggering the mass demonstrations. They also documented that over just six weeks the number of demonstrators grew from a handful of individuals to more than 500,000.

A second type of diversity within a social group describes differences that do not range around an average value. It is found in groups composed of several distinct factions, each characterized by a distinct set of beliefs. Among the diners, for example, might be a mix of students and professionals. Students on a tight budget have concerns different from those of well-off professionals. On the whole, the variation among the students' preferences would be small as compared with the average differences between the two subgroups.

When a large group containing several factions changes from overall defection to cooperation, it does so through progressive transitions. The subgroup with the greatest tendency to cooperate (for example, the one with the longest horizon in its average expectations or the one with the lowest average costs for cooperation) will usually be the first to cross over. The other groups will then follow in turn, probably in the order of their willingness to cooperate.

Relationships among subgroups may powerfully influence the evolution of cooperation, a fact that is notably important in large hierarchical organizations. The weight that an individual in one division gives to the actions of others depends on those persons' placement in the hierarchy. Hierarchies are therefore very different from level groups.

Functional hierarchies often hide in informal settings. Air pollution is a problem that the whole world faces and must solve collectively. Yet each person is usually bothered more by a neighbor burning a compost pile than by someone across town doing the same. The dilution of environmental impact with distance can be represented as a hierarchy of layered interactions between neighborhoods, towns, counties, states, countries and continents. The effect of someone else's actions on your own choices will depend on how many layers distant she is from you.

The effective size of the hierarchy is therefore much smaller than the number of its constituents. Suppose that in its effect on your decisions, the action of your nearby neighbor counts as much as the summed actions of an entire distant neighborhood. Then the effective number of people influencing your decision is much smaller than the total population of your town. We can say that the hierarchy has been re-scaled, because the whole is smaller than the sum of its parts.

Computer experiments show how cooperation can spread in large hierarchical organizations. Transitions from defection to cooperation (or the other way around) tend to originate within the smallest units, which usually occupy the lowest level of the hierarchy. Cooperation can then progressively spread to higher levels. The switching trend can even terminate if the cooperative influence of distant units is too attenuated to be felt. In such a case, the organization may contain some branches that cooperate and others that defect for long periods.

These results suggest practical ways to restructure organizations to secure cooperation among members faced with a social dilemma. Corporations benefit, for example, when managers share their knowledge with one another. Yet managers may withhold information they fear their colleagues can use for their own advancement. To volunteer information, a person needs to feel secure that others will, too. Setting up a network of smaller groups of managers could overcome the dilemma by promoting that sense of security. Moreover, restructuring a large corporation into smaller units may encourage the appearance of pockets of collaboration that might spread rapidly.

Conversely, when organizations grow without a major reorganization, the tendency to ride for free grows and lowers efficiency. The act of reorganizing does not guarantee instant improvement: the switch to collective cooperation may still take a long time. That time can be shortened by increasing the benefits for individuals who cooperate and by dispersing the most cooperative managers among small core groups throughout the organization.

The study of social dilemmas provides insight into a central issue of behavior: how global cooperation among individuals confronted with conflicting choices can be secured. These recent advances show that cooperative behavior can indeed arise spontaneously in social settings, provided that the groups are small and diverse in composition and that their constituents have long outlooks. Even more significantly, when cooperation does appear, it does so suddenly and unpredictably after a long period of stasis.

The world still echoes with the thunderous political and social events marking the past few years. The fall of the Berlin Wall, leading to a unified Germany, and the breakdown of the centralized Soviet Union into many autonomous republics are examples of abrupt global defections from prevailing social compacts. The member coun-

tries of the European Union currently face their own social dilemma as they try to secure supranational cooperation. The pressing issue is whether or not those countries can build a beneficial cooperative superstructure while each one remains autonomous. If our predictions are accurate, these restructurings will not proceed smoothly. Rather they will always be punctuated by unexpected outbreaks of cooperation.

FURTHER READING

THE LOGIC OF COLLECTIVE ACTION: PUBLIC GOODS AND THE THEORY OF GROUP. Mancur Olson, Jr. Harvard University Press, 1965.
THE TRAGEDY OF THE COMMONS. Garrett Hardin in *Science,* Vol. 162, pages 1243-1248; December 13, 1968.
COLLECTIVE ACTION. Russell Hardin. Johns Hopkins University Press, 1982.
INSTITUTIONAL STRUCTURE AND THE LOGIC OF ONGOING COLLECTIVE ACTION. Jonathan Bendor and Dilip Mookherjee in *American Political Science Review,* Vol. 81, No. 1, pages 129-154; March 1987.
THE OUTBREAK OF COOPERATION. N. S. Glance and B. A. Huberman in *Journal of Mathematical Sociology,* Vol. 17, Issue 4, pages 281-302; April 1993.
SOCIAL DILEMMAS AND FLUID ORGANIZATIONS. N. S. Glance and B. A. Huberman in *Computational Organization Theory.* Edited by K. M. Carley and M. J. Prietula. Lawrence Erlbaum Associates (in press).

MEDIA, VIOLENCE, YOUTH, AND SOCIETY

Ray Surette

Ray Surette is professor of criminal justice in the School of Public Affairs and Services, Florida International University, North Miami, and author of Media, Crime and Criminal Justice: Images and Realities.

It is guns, it is poverty, it is overcrowding, and it is the uniquely American problem of a culture that is infatuated with violence. We love it, we glamorize it, we teach it to our children.[1]

The above testimony by Dr. Deborah Prothrow-Stith on gangs and youth violence presented before the U.S. Senate contains two important points concerning the mass media and youth violence. First, it does not mention the media as a factor in violence, lending support to the view that the media are not crucial agents in youth violence. Second, it does cite an American culture that is infatuated with violence, and the glamorization and teaching of violence to our children, as problems. Culture, glamorization, and instruction, however, are areas where the media have been shown to play important social roles. The above statement simultaneously provides support for the position that the media are indeed important players in the production of youth violence and yet paradoxically also supports the position that they are not contributors. The relative validity of these two dichotomous positions, the media as unimportant and the media as central in fostering youth violence, has dominated the public discussion, resulting in much confusion about this issue and public posturing by various groups and individuals. The actual relationship of the media to youth violence lies somewhere between these two extremes.

Research interest in the relationship of the mass media to social violence has been elevated for most of this century. Over the twentieth century, the issue of the media as a source of violence has moved into and out of the public consciousness in predictable ten-to twenty-year cycles. If a consensus has emerged from the research and public interest, it is that the sources of violence are complex and tied to our most basic nature as well as the social world we have created and that the media's particular relationship to social violence is extremely complicated. (See the discussion in this author's *Media, Crime, and Criminal Justice* [1992] and in *Crime and Human Nature* [1985] by J. Wilson and R. Herrnstein.)

Therefore, when discussing the nature of the relationship between the media and violence, it is important not to be myopic. Social violence is embedded in historical, social forces and phenomena, while the media are components of a larger information system that creates and distributes knowledge about the world. The media and social violence must both be approached as parts of phenomena that have numerous interconnections and paths of influence between them. Too narrow a perspective on youth violence or the media's role in its generation oversimplifies both the problem and the solutions we pursue. Nowhere is this more apparent than in the current concern about media, youth, and violence.

STATISTICS ON YOUTH VIOLENCE

The source of this concern is revealed by a brief review of the statistics of youth violence.[2] Youth violence, and particularly violent crime committed by youth, has recently increased dramatically. Today about 5 out of

every 20 robbery arrests and 3 of every 20 murder, rape, and aggravated assault arrests are of juveniles. In raw numbers, this translates into 3,000 murder, 6,000 forcible rape, 41,000 robbery, and 65,000 aggravated assault arrests of youths annually.

The surge in youth criminal violence is concentrated within the past five years. During the first part of the 1980s, there was a general decline in youth arrests for both violent and property crimes. In the latter half of the 1980s, however, youth arrests increased at a pace greater than that of adults for violent crimes. Youth arrests increased substantially between 1981 and 1990 for nonaggravated assault (72 percent), murder and nonnegligent manslaughter (60 percent), aggravated assault (57 percent), weapons violations (41 percent), and forcible rape (28 percent). Looking over a generational time span from 1965 to 1989, the arrest rate for violent crimes by youths grew between the mid-1960s and the mid-1970s but then leveled off and remained relatively constant until the late 1980s. At that time, the rate again began to increase, reaching its highest recorded level in the most recent years.

Thus, while the proportion of youth in the general population has declined as the baby-boom generation has aged, the rate of violence from our youth has increased significantly. We have fewer youth proportionately, but they are more violent and account for increased proportions of our violent crime. Attempts to comprehend and explain this change have led invariably to the mass media as prime suspects, but deciphering the media's role has not been a simple or straightforward task.

This difficulty in deciphering the media's role is due to the fact that the relationship of media to violence is complex, and the media's influence can be both

■ The Trojan priest Laocoon and his twin sons, Antiphas and Thymbraeus, being attacked by Apollo's sea serpents. A Roman copy, c. 100 B.C.

direct and indirect. Research on their relationship (reported, for example, in George Comstock's 1980 study *Television in America*) has revealed that media effects that appear when large groups are examined are not predictable at the individual subject level. The media are also related to social violence in ways not usually considered in the public debate, such as their effects on public policies and general social attitudes toward violence.

Adding to the complexity of the media's relationship, there are many other sources of violence that either interact with the media or work alone to produce violence. These sources range from individual biology to characteristics of our history and culture. The importance of nonmedia factors such as neighborhood and family conditions, individual psychological and genetic traits, and our social structure, race relations, and economic conditions for the generation of violence are commonly acknowledged and analyzed, as in Jeffrey Goldstein's 1986 study *Aggression and Crimes of Violence*. The role of the mass media is confounded with these other sources, and its significance is often either lost or exaggerated. One task of this essay is thus to dispel the two popular but polarizing notions that have dominated the public debate. The first is that the media

are the primary cause of violence in society. The second is that the media have no, or a very limited, effect on social violence.

The former view of the media as the source of primary effects is often advanced along with draconian policy demands such as extensive government intervention or direct censorship of the media. The counterargument to this position is supported by a number of points. The most basic is that we were a violent nation before we had mass media, and there is no evidence that the removal of violent media would make us nonviolent.[3] Some research into copy-cat crime additionally provides no evidence of a criminalization effect from the media as a cause.[4] The media alone cannot turn a law-abiding individual into a criminal one nor a nonviolent youth into a violent one. In sum, individual and national violence cannot be blamed primarily on the media, and violence-reducing policies directed only at the media will have little effect.

The latter argument, that the media have limited to no effect on levels of social violence, is structured both in posture and approach to the tobacco industry's response to research linking smoking to lung cancer and it rings just as hollow. The argument's basic approach is to ex-

pound inherent weaknesses in the various methodologies of the media-violence research and to trumpet the lack of evidence of strong, direct effects, while ignoring the persistent pattern of positive findings. Proponents of the nil effect point out that laboratory experiments are biased toward finding an effect. To isolate the effect of a single factor, in this case the media, and observe a rare social behavior, namely violence, experiments must exaggerate the link between media and aggression and create a setting that will elicit violent behavior. They therefore argue that all laboratory research on the issue is irrelevant. They continue, however, to dismiss the nonlaboratory research because of a lack of strict variable controls and designs that leave open noncausal interpretations of the results. "No effects" proponents lastly argue that while society reinforces some behaviors shown in the media such as that found in commercials, it does not condone or reinforce violence and, therefore, a violence-enhancing effect should not be expected (a view discussed in "Smoking Out the Critics," a 1984 *Society* article [21:36–40] by A. Wurtzel and G. Lometti).

In reality, the research shows persistent behavioral effects from violent media under diverse situations for differing groups.[5] Regarding the strong behavioral effects apparent in fashion and fad, effects that Madison Avenue touts, the argument of a behavioral effect only on sanctioned behavior but not on unsanctioned violence is specious. The media industry claim of

If a consensus has emerged from the research and public interest, it is that the media's particular relationship to social violence is extremely complicated.

having only positive behavioral effects is as valid as the tobacco industry claiming that their ads do not encourage new smokers but only persuade brand switching among established smokers. First, violence is sometimes socially sanctioned, particularly within the U.S. youth and hypermasculine culture that is the target audience of the most prominently violent media. And although the media cannot criminalize someone not having criminal predispositions, media-generated, copy-cat crime is a significant criminal phenomenon with ample anecdotal and case evidence providing a form for criminality to take.[6] The recurring mimicking of dangerous film stunts belies the argument of the media having only positive behavioral effects. It is apparent that while the media alone cannot make someone a criminal, it can change the criminal behavior of a predisposed offender.

CONFLICTING CAUSAL CLAIMS

The two arguments of primary cause and negligible cause compete for public support. These models not only posit differing causal relations between the media and violence but imply vastly different public policies regarding the media as well. The primary-cause model (fig. 1) is that of a significant, direct linear relationship between violent media and violent behavior. In this model, violent media, independent of other factors, directly cause violent behavior. If valid, it indicates that strong intervention is necessary in the content, distribution, and creation of violent media.

Figure 1

Primary Cause Model

Violent Media ⟶ Violent Behavior

The negligible-cause model (fig. 2) concedes a statistical association between the media and violent behavior but poses the connection as due not to a causal relationship but to persons predisposed to violence simultaneously seeking out violent media and more often behaving violently. As the relationship is associative and not causal in this model, policies targeted at the media will have no effects on violent behavior and the media can be safely ignored.

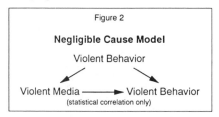

Figure 2

Negligible Cause Model

Violent Behavior

Violent Media ⟶ Violent Behavior
(statistical correlation only)

Both models inaccurately describe the media-violence relationship. The actual relationship between the factors is felt to be bidirectional and cyclical (fig. 3). In addition to violently predisposed people seeking out violent media and violent media causing violent behavior, violent media play a role in the generation of violently predisposed people through their effects on attitudes. And as the made-for-

The view of the media as the source of primary effects is often advanced along with draconian policy demands such as extensive government intervention or direct censorship of the media.

TV movie industry reflects, violent behavior sometimes results in the creation of more violent media. Finally, by providing live models of violence and creating community and home environments that are more inured to and tolerant of violence, violent behavior helps to create more violently predisposed youth in society. Therefore, while the direct effect of media on violence may not be initially large, its influence cycles through the model and accumulates.

An area of research that provides an example of the bidirectional model is the relationship of pornography to sexual violence; a recent (1993) overview of such research can be found in *Pornography,* by D. Linz and N. Malamuth. On one hand, the research establishes that depictions of sexual violence, specifically those that link sex with physical violence toward women, foster antisocial attitudes toward women and lenient perceptions of the

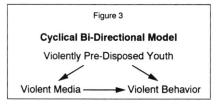

Figure 3

Cyclical Bi-Directional Model

Violently Pre-Disposed Youth

Violent Media ⟶ Violent Behavior

---

crime of rape. Aberrant perceptions, such as increased belief in the "rape myth" (that women unconsciously want to be raped or somehow enjoy being raped), have been reported. Virtually none of the research, however, reveals strong direct effects from pornography, and even sexually violent media do not appear to negatively affect all male viewers. Many cultural and individual factors appear to mediate the effects and to foster the predisposition to sexually violent media and sexual violence. Researchers in this area have concluded that the media are one of many social forces that affect the development of intervening variables, such as thought patterns, sexual arousal patterns, motivations, and personality characteristics that are associated with tolerance for

sexual violence and perhaps an increase in sexually violent behavior in society.[7] As in other areas of media-violence research, sexually violent media emerge as neither a primary engine nor an innocuous social factor.

THE KEY TO MEDIA EFFECTS

The key to media effects occurring in any particular instance, then, are the intermediate, interactive factors. In terms of the media, there are numerous interactive factors that have been identified as conducive to generating aggressive effects. Among the many delineated in the research, a sample includes: reward or lack of punishment for the perpetrator, portrayal of violence as justified, portrayal of the consequences of violence in a way that does not stir distaste, portrayal of violence without critical commentary, the presence of live peer models of violence, and the presence of sanctioning adults (all discussed in Comstock's *Television in America*). Only unambiguous linking of violent behavior with undesirable consequences or motives by the media appears capable of inhibiting subsequent aggression in groups of viewers.

A list of nonmedia factors deemed significant in the development of crime and the number of violently predisposed individuals can be culled from *Crime and Human Nature* by J. Wilson and R. Herrnstein. The authors list constitutional, developmental, and social-context factors including gender, age, intelligence, personality, psychopathology, broken and abusive families, schools, community, labor markets, alcohol and heroin, and finally history and culture. As can be seen, most aspects of modern life are implicated, and only tangential factors like diet and climate (which other researchers would have included) are left out. With such a large number of factors coming into play, the levels of interactions and complexity of relationships are obviously enormous.

The research on violence suggests that certain factors are basic to violent crime, as detailed by Wilson and Herrnstein. None of these factors dominates, but none are without significant effects.

Accordingly, the research (contained in this author's 1992 study *Media, Crime and Criminal Justice*) clearly signifies the media as only some of many factors in the generation of youth violence and that media depictions of violence do not affect all

A Brief History of Television and Youth Violence Research

The logic of science requires that in order to establish the causal effect of a variable, one must be able to examine a situation without the variable's effect. In terms of television and violence, this requirement means that a group of subjects (a control group) who have not been exposed to violent television is necessary for comparison with a violent television-exposed group. Television, however, is ubiquitous and an integral part of a modern matrix of influences on social behaviors. Therefore, when the interest is in the effects of television on mainstream citizens in Western industrialized and urbanized nations, finding nontelevision-exposed controls is essentially impossible. In response, artificial laboratory situations are created, or statistical controls and large data sets are employed. Thus, while social sciences abound with research reporting variables that are correlated with one another, research firmly establishing causal relationships is rare. Unlike the content of television, there are few smoking guns in social science. Rather than conclusively proven, cause is more often inferred in a trial-like decision from the predominance of evidence. Such is the case with television and violence.

In a traditional laboratory experiment, two sets of matched, usually randomly assigned, subjects are placed in identical situations except for a single factor of interest. Early research in the television-violence quest were in this vein, with the seminal ones conducted in the 1960s by researchers Bandura, Ross, and Ross.[1] These laboratory studies basically consisted of exposing groups of young children to either a short film containing violence (frequently an adult beating up an inflated Bobo doll) or a similar but nonviolent film. The two groups of children were then placed in playrooms and observed. Children who watched the film where a doll was attacked would significantly more often attack a similar doll if given the opportunity shortly after viewing their film than children who had observed a nonviolent film. These and other studies established the existence of an "observational imitation" effect from visual violence; in short, children will imitate violence they see in the media. It was concluded by many that television violence must therefore be a cause of youth violence.

However, critics of this conclusion argued that because laboratory situations are purposely artificial and contrived to isolate the influence of a single variable, the social processes producing aggression in the laboratory are not equal to those found in the real world. In summary, one cannot assume that behavior and variable relationships observed in the lab are occurring in the home or street.

In addition to the laboratory studies, at about the same time a number of survey studies were reporting positive correlations between youth aggression and viewing violent television.[2] Efforts to extend the laboratory findings and determine if the correlational studies reflected real-world causal relationships led to two types of research: natural field experiments[3] and longitudinal panel studies.

The better known and most discussed research efforts came from longitudinal panel studies conducted in the 1970s and early '80s. Expensive and time consuming, in panel studies a large number of subjects are selected and followed for a number of years. Three such studies are particularly important due to their renown, similarities in approach, and differences in conclusions.

The first study (called the Rip van Winkle study) by L. Rowell Huesmann, Leonard Eron, and their colleagues used a cross-lag panel design (that is, comparison over time and with different populations) in which television habits at grade three (approximately age eight) were correlated with aggression in grade three and with television viewing and aggression ten years later for a sample of 211 boys.[4] The researchers collected their data in rural New York State from students in the third, eighth, and "thirteenth" grades (one year after graduation). Favorite television programs were rated based on their violent content, and frequency of viewing was obtained from the children's mothers in grade three and from the subjects in grades eight and thirteen. The measure of aggression was a peer-nominated rating obtained from responses to questions such as, "Who starts fights over nothing?" The most significant finding

1. See, for example, A. Bandura, D. Ross, and S. A. Ross, "Transmission of Aggression through Imitation of Aggressive Models," *Journal of Abnormal and Social Psychology* 63 (1961), 575–82; and "Imitation of film-mediated aggressive models" *Journal of Abnormal and Social Psychology* 66 (1963), 3–11.

2. See G. Comstock, et al., *Television and Human Behavior* (New York: Columbia University Press, 1978) for a review.

3. Natural field experiments typically take advantage of a planned introduction of television to a previously unexposed population. This allows both a pretelevision and posttelevision comparison of the new television group and comparisons with similar but still unexposed other groups. Although rare because of the unique circumstances necessary and by definition confined to non-mainstream populations, these studies report significant increases in aggressive behavior for children who watched a lot of television in the new-television populations. See, for example, G. Granzberg, "The Introduction of Television into a Northern Manitoba Cree Community" in G. Granzberg and J. Steinberg, eds. *Television and the Canadian Indian* (Winnipeg, Manitoba; University of Winnipeg Press, 1980); and T. Williams, ed., *The Impact of Television: A Natural Experiment in Three Communities* (New York: Academic Press, 1985).

4. M. Lefkowitz, et al., "Television Violence and Child Aggression: A Follow-up Study" in G. A. Comstock and E. A. Rubinstein, eds. *Television and Social Behavior*, vol 3 *Television and Adolescent Aggressiveness* (Washington, D.C.: U.S. Government Printing Office, 1971).

reported was a strong, positive association between violent television viewing at grade three and aggression at grade thirteen. However, this study was criticized for a number of reasons. For example, the measure of aggression used in grade thirteen was poorly worded and phrased in the past tense (i.e., "Who started fights over nothing?") and thus the answers were ambiguous in that the grade thirteen subjects may have been referring to general reputations rather than current behaviors. In addition, cross-lagged correlation analysis has a built-in bias toward finding relationships where none exist. Despite the study's weaknesses, Huesmann and Eron concluded that a causal relationship between television violence and aggression existed. This study had a strong public impact.

A second longitudinal panel study was conducted by Ronald Milavsky and his colleagues in the early 1970s that had an opposite conclusion. This study was based on surveys of about 2,400 elementary students age seven to twelve, and 403 male teenagers age twelve to sixteen in Minneapolis, Minnesota, and Fort Worth, Texas.[5] The subjects were surveyed five to six times over nineteen months. This study also used peer-nominated aggression measures for the younger group and four self-reported measures of aggression for the teenagers.[6] Unlike the "van Winkle" study, which used the children's mothers' selection of favorite programs, this study measured exposure to violent programming based on the subjects' own reports. Their analysis further controlled for earlier levels of aggression and exposure to television violence, in effect searching for evidence of significant incremental increases in youth aggression that could be attributed to past exposure to television violence after taking into account past levels of aggressive behavior.

Huesmann and Eron report meaningful lagged associations between later aggression and a number of prior conditions such as earlier aggression in a child's classroom, father's use of physical punishment, family conflict, and violent environments—but not for prior exposure to violent television. Although some significant positive relationships were found between exposure to television violence and later aggression, the overall pattern and number of findings regarding television were interpreted as inconsistent. These researchers conclude that chance, not cause, is the best explanation for their findings regarding television and aggression.

Partly in response to the Milavsky study and criticisms of their earlier methodology, Huesmann, Eron, and their colleagues conducted a third panel study (the Chicago Circle study) in the late 1970s using first and third graders in Chicago public and parochial schools as subjects.[7] Six hundred seventy-two students were initially sampled and tested for three consecutive years in two groups. One group was followed from first through third grades, the second from third through fifth grades. Aggression was measured once more by a peer-generated scale in which each child designated other children on fifteen descriptive statements, ten of which dealt with aggression. (An example is, "Who pushes and shoves other children?") Exposure to violent television was measured by asking each child to select the show most often watched and frequency of watching from eight different ten-program lists. Each list contained a mix of violent and nonviolent programs.

The study was simultaneously conducted in the United States, Australia, Finland, Israel, the Netherlands, and Poland. Their analysis of the U.S. data showed a significant general effect for television violence on girls but not for boys. However, the interaction of viewing violent television and identification with aggressive television characters was a significant predictor of male aggression. Huesmann and Eron conclude that the relationship between television violence and viewer aggression is causal and significant but bidirectional.

At this time, most reviewers of these studies and the subsequent research that followed conclude that a modest but genuine causal association does exist between media violence and aggression.[8] The fact is that, once introduced, the effect of television on a society or an individual can never be fully extricated from all the other forces that may contribute to violence. Television's influence is so intertwined with these parallel forces that searches for strong direct causal effects are not likely to be fruitful. But similar to smoking/lung cancer research, evidence of a real causal connection of some sort has been established beyond a reasonable doubt for most people.

—*R.S.*

5. J. Milavsky, et al., *Television and Aggression: A Panel Study* (New York: Academic Press, 1982).

6. Personal aggression toward others, aggression against a teacher (rudeness or unruliness), property aggression (theft and vandalism), and delinquency (serious or criminal behaviors).

7. See Rowell Huesmann and Leonard Eron, "Television Violence and Aggressive Behavior" in D. Pearl, L. Bouthilet, and J. Lazar, eds. *Television and Behavior: Ten Years of Scientific Progress and Implications for the 80's* (Washington, D.C., 1982); and "Factors Influencing the Effect of Television Violence on Children" in Michael Howe, ed., *Learning from Television: Psychological and Educational Research* (New York: Academic Press, 1983).

8. See, for example, L. Heath, L. Bresolin, and R. Rinaldi, "Effects of Media Violence on Children: A Review of the Literature," *Archives of General Psychiatry* 46 (1989), 376–79.

persons in the same way. The media contribute to violence in combination with other social and psychological factors. Whether or not a particular media depiction will cause a particular viewer to act more aggressively is not a straightforward issue. The emergence of an effect depends on the interaction between each individual viewer, the content of the portrayal, and the setting in which exposure to the media occurs. This gives the media significant aggregate effects but makes these effects difficult to predict for individuals. There is no doubt, however, that violent children, including those who come to have significant criminal records, spend more time exposed to violent media than do less violent children. The issue is not the existence of a media effect but the magnitude or importance of the effect.

Media violence correlates as strongly with and is as causally related to the magnitude of violent behavior as any other social behavioral variable that has been studied. This reflects both the media's impact and our lack of knowledge about the etiology of violence. Because of the many individual and social factors that come into play in producing any social behavior, one should not expect to find more than a modest direct relationship between the media and violence. Following their review of the research, Thomas Cook and his colleagues conclude:

> No effects emerge that are so large as to hit one between the eyes, but early measure of viewing violence adds to the predictability of later aggression over and above the predictability afforded by earlier measures of aggression. These lagged effects are consistently positive, but not large, and they are rarely statistically significant, although no reliable lagged negative effects have been reported. . . . But is the association causal? If we were forced to render a judgment, probably yes. . . . There is strong evidence of causation in the wrong setting (the lab) with the right population (normal children) and in the right setting (outside the lab) with the wrong population (abnormal adults).[8]

MEDIA AMONG MANY FACTORS

In summation, despite the fact that the media are among many factors, they should not be ignored, regardless of the level of their direct impact. Because social violence is a pressing problem, even those factors that only modestly contribute to it are important. Small effects of the media accumulate and appear to have significant long-term social effects.[9] The

research strongly indicates that we are a more violent society because of our mass media. Exactly how and to what extent the media cause long-term changes in violent behavior remains unknown, but the fact that it plays an important, but not independent, role is generally conceded.

What public policies are suggested by the knowledge we now possess about media and violence? Not all of the factors discussed above are good candidates for public intervention strategies, but there are three sources of youth violence that government policy can influence. In order of importance, they are: extreme differences in economic conditions and the concentration of wealth in America; the American gun culture; and, exacerbating the problems created by the first two, the media's violence-enhancing messages. Family, neighborhood, and personality factors may be more important for generating violence in absolute magnitude, but they are not easily influenced by public actions.

The magnitude of economic disparity and the concentration of wealth in the United States is greater than in comparable (and, not surprisingly, less violent) societies. Our richest citizens not only earn vastly more than our poorest, but, more important, the wealth in the country is increasingly concentrated in fewer and fewer hands. The trend during this century, which accelerated during the 1980s, is for an ever-shrinking percentage of the richest Americans to control greater proportions of the country's wealth, while the poorest have access to increasingly smaller proportions. The burden of this economic disenfranchisement, both psychologically and fiscally, falls heavily on the young, and especially on the young who are urban poor minorities, as is shown in Elliott Currie's 1985 study *Confronting Crime*. In a consumerism-saturated society like the United States, hopelessness, bitterness, and disregard for moral values and law are heightened by this growing economic disparity.

And as the economic polarization and violent crime have grown, we also became nationally fixated on heightening and extending our punishment capacities in an attempt to suppress violent behavior, evidenced by Diana Gordon's 1991 study *The Justice Juggernaut*. Since 1975, we have increased the rate of juvenile incarceration steadily. Today we hold in custody approximately one hundred thousand juveniles every year. Despite our strengthened capacity to punish, however, youth violence has not abated.

■ Marsyas being flayed alive by Apollo after losing a musical contest to him, c. 200 B.C.

This result should have been expected because two social mechanisms are needed to reduce violence—punishing violent criminal behavior and rewarding law-abiding, nonviolent behavior. Societies that are more successful in balancing the two mechanisms are less violent, as shown in *Crime and Control in Comparative Perspective*, by H. Heiland and L. Shelley (1992). While punishment of violent behavior is certainly necessary and justified, its emphasis, coupled with the concentration of wealth in America, has resulted in the degrading of the equally important social capacity to reward law-abiding behavior. By emphasizing one, we have lamed and discredited the other. Nonmaterial rewards like social status, an esteemed reputation, and a clear conscience have been losing their legitimacy

The fear and loathing we feel toward criminals—youthful, violent, or not—is tied to our media-generated image of criminality.

with the young, while material rewards for law-abiding life-styles such as careers, comfortable incomes and affordable goods are less generally available to our poorest and, not surprisingly most crime-prone and violent citizens.

We have chosen to emphasize the mechanism, punishment, that is actually the weaker of the two in actually influencing behavior. As operant conditioning theory would predict, punishment, if severe enough, can suppress one type of violent crime. But the suppression of one behavior gives no push toward a desirable replacement activity, and a substitute violent crime will likely emerge. So "smash and grab" robberies give way to "bump and rob" holdups. Shaping behavior requires a credible reward system. In social terms, youth must see law-abiding behavior as credible and potentially rewarding as well as seeing violent behavior as potentially resulting in punishment.

The second area that government policy can immediately address is the gun culture in America. Our culture of violence, referred to in the opening quote, is made immeasurably more deadly by the enfolded gun culture. The availability of guns as cheap killing mechanisms is simply a national insanity. The mass production of these killing "toys" and the easy access to them must be addressed. The most recent statistics show that one out of every ten high school students report that they carry a handgun. Gun buy-back programs should be supported, and production and availability must be reduced if a positive net effect is to be expected. Irrespective of the difficulty of controlling the sources of individual violent behavior, the implements of fatal violence should not be ignored.

The third area of policy concern, the mass media, exacerbates the gun culture by portraying guns as glamorous, effective, omnipotent devices. The mass media also heighten the negative effects of economic disparities through their consumer messages in advertising and entertainment. Although both of these effects that add to the problem of youth violence are

sometimes discussed, the debate about the media remains tightly focused on measuring and reviewing violent media content. Within this focus, the emphasis has been on counting violent acts rather than on exploring the context of its portrayal. Deciphering the media's moral and value messages about violence has been mostly ignored.

EFFECTS ON CRIMINAL JUSTICE

A closer examination of the context of violence in the media would tell us that we should not try to purge the media of violence, for violent media can be good when programs teach that violence is bad. Our goal should be to reduce graphic, gratuitous, and glorified violence; to portray it not as a problem solver but as a reluctant, distasteful, last resort with tragic, unanticipated consequences. Violence shown consistently as a generator of pain and suffering, not as a personal or social panacea, would be positive media violence. Too often, violence in the media is shown as an effective solution, and, too often, it is simply met by increased counterviolence. But, despite the recurring interest and current debate about media violence, there is little direction for the media industry regarding the context of violence and its effects. A goal should be to provide better information to the industry that details the various contexts and messages of violence and their effects.

Perhaps the most significant social effect of media violence is, however, not the direct generation of social violence but its impact on our criminal justice policy. The fear and loathing we feel toward crimi-

nals—youthful, violent, or not—is tied to our media-generated image of criminality. The media portray criminals as typically animalistic, vicious predators. This media image translates into a more violent society by influencing the way we react to all crime in America. We imprison at a much greater rate and make reentry into law-abiding society, even for our nonviolent offenders, more difficult than other advanced (and, not coincidentally, less violent) nations. The predator-criminal image results in policy based on the worst-case criminal and a constant ratcheting up of punishments for all offenders. In its cumulative effect, the media both provide violent models for our youth to emulate and justify a myopic, harshly punitive public reaction to all offenders.

Currently, the debate concerning both the media and youth violence has evolved into "circles of blame" in which one group ascribes blame for the problem to someone else in the circle. Thus, in the media circle, the public blames the networks and studios, which blame the producers and writers, who blame the advertisers, who blame the public. In the violence circle, the government blames the youth, who blame the community, which blames the schools, which blame the parents, who blame the government. A more sensible, productive process would be a shift to a "ring of responsibility," with the groups addressing their individual contributions to the problem and arriving at cooperative policies. We can't selectively reduce one aspect of violence in a violent society and expect real results. Youth violence will not be seriously reduced without violence in other aspects of our culture being addressed. In the same vein, modifying media violence alone will

■ A Lapith woman fighting the brutal grip of a centaur. From the west pediment of the temple at Olympia, c. 460 B.C.

not have much effect but to ignore it will make efforts on other fronts less successful. Ironically, despite the fact that the media have limited independent effects on youth violence, we need to expand the

> *Youth violence will not be seriously reduced without violence in other aspects of our culture being addressed.*

focus on them. This should incorporate other social institutions, such as the media industry itself, and the social norms and values reflected in the media. We could then derive more general models of media effects and social violence.

Violence is a cultural product. The media are reflections of the culture and engines in the production process. Although they are not the only or even the most powerful causes, they are tied into the other violence-generating engines, and youth pay particular attention to them. The aggregate result of all of these forces in the United States is a national character that is individualistic, materialistic, and violence prone. If we wish to change our national character regarding violence, we cannot take on only some aspects of its genesis. We must address everything we can, such as economic inequities, the gun culture, and the glamorization of violence. And, by a slow, painful, generational process of moral leadership and example, we must work to modify the individual, family, and neighborhood factors that violently predispose youth.

In conclusion, our youth will be violent as long as our culture is violent. The local social conditions in which they are raised and the larger cultural and economic environments that they will enter generate great numbers of violently predisposed individuals. As we have experienced, violently predisposed youth, particularly among our poor, will fully develop their potential and come to prey upon us. Faced with frightful predators, we subsequently and justly punish them, but the use of punishment alone will not solve the problem. The role that the media play in the above scenario versus their potential role in deglorifying violence and showing our youth that armed aggression is not an American cultural right, will determine the media's ultimate relationship to youthful violence in society.

NOTES

1. Dr. Deborah Prothrow-Stith testifying before the Senate Subcommittee on Juvenile Justice, November 26, 1991.

2. Sources of the statistics cited in this essay are drawn from "Arrests of Youth 1990," January 1992, *Office of Juvenile Justice and Delinquency Prevention Update on Statistics; and Sourcebook of Criminal Justice Statistics—1992,* Bureau of Justice Statistics, U.S. Department of Justice, 1993.

3. Hugh Davis Graham and Ted Robert Gurr, eds., *Violence in America* (Beverly Hills, CA: Sage, 1979).

4. See S. Milgram and R. Shotland, *Television and Antisocial Behavior: Field Experiments* (New York: Academic Press, 1973) and A.

Schmid and J. de Graaf, *Violence as Communication* (Newbury Park, CA: Sage, 1982).

5. T. Cook, D. Kendzierski, and S. Thomas, "The Implicit Assumptions of Television Research," *Public Opinion Quarterly* 47: 161–201.

6. For a listing of examples see S. Pease and C. Love, "The Copy-Cat Crime Phenomenon," in *Justice and the Media* by R. Surette (Springfield IL: Charles C. Thomas, 1984), 199–211; and A. Schmid and J. de Graaf, *Violence as Communication* (Newbury Park, CA: Sage, 1982).

7. N. Malamuth and J. Briere (1986), Sexual Violence in the Media: Indirect Effects on Aggression against Women," *Journal of Social Issues 42,* 89.

8. T. Cook, D. Kendzierski, and S. Thomas (1993), "The Implicit Assumptions of Television Research," *Public Opinion Quarterly* 47: 191–92.

9. R. Rosenthal (1986), "Media Violence, Anti-Social Behavior, and the Social Consequences of Small Effects," *Journal of Social Issues* 42: 141–54.

ADDITIONAL READING

George Comstock, *Television in America,* Sage, Newbury Park, Calif., 1980.

Elliott Currie, *Confronting Crime,* Pantheon, New York, 1985.

Jeffrey Goldstein, *Aggression and Crimes of Violence,* Oxford University Press, New York, 1986.

Diana Gordon, *The Justice Juggernaut,* Rutgers University Press, New Brunswick, N.J., 1991.

Joshua Meyrowitz, *No Sense of Place,* Oxford University Press, New York, 1985.

Ray Surette, *Media, Crime, and Criminal Justice,* Brooks/Cole, Pacific Grove, Calif., 1992.

James Q. Wilson and Richard Herrnstein, *Crime and Human Nature,* Simon & Schuster, New York, 1985.

THE LESSONS OF LOVE

Yes, we've learned a few things. We now know that it is the insecure rather than the confident who fall in love most readily. And men fall faster than women. And who ever said sex had anything to do with it?

Beth Livermore

As winter thaws, so too do icicles on cold hearts. For with spring, the sap rises—and resistance to love wanes. And though the flame will burn more of us than it warms, we will return to the fire—over and over again.

Indeed, love holds central in everybody's everyday. We spend years, sometimes lifetimes pursuing it, preparing for it, longing for it. Some of us even die for love. Still, only poets and songwriters, philosophers and playwrights have traditionally been granted license to sift this hallowed preserve. Until recently. Over the last decade and a half, scientists have finally taken on this most elusive entity. They have begun to parse out the intangibles, the *je ne sais quoi* of love. The word so far is—little we were sure of is proving to be true.

OUT OF THE LAB,
INTO THE FIRE

True early greats, like Sigmund Freud and Carl Rogers, acknowledged love as important to the human experience. But not till the 1970s did anyone attempt to define it—and only now is it considered a respectable topic of study.

One reason for this hesitation has been public resistance. "Some people are afraid that if they look too close they will lose the mask," says Arthur Aron, Ph.D., professor of psychology at the University of California, Santa Cruz. "Others believe we know all that we need to know." But mostly, to systematically study love has been thought impossible, and therefore a waste of time and money.

No one did more to propagate this false notion than former United States Senator William Proxmire of Wisconsin, who in 1974 launched a very public campaign against the study of love. As a member of the Senate Finance Committee, he took it upon himself to ferret out waste in government spending. One of the first places he looked was the National Science Foundation, a federal body that both funds research and promotes scientific progress.

Upon inspection, Proxmire found that Ellen Berscheid, Ph.D., a psychologist at the University of Minnesota who had already broken new ground scrutinizing the social power of physical attractiveness, had secured an $84,000 federal grant to study relationships. The proposal mentioned romantic love. Proxmire loudly denounced such work as frivolous—tax dollars ill spent.

The publicity that was given Proxmire's pronouncements not only cast a pall over all behavioral science research, it set off an international firestorm around Berscheid that lasted the next two years. Colleagues were fired. Her office was swamped with hate mail. She even received death threats. But in the long run, the strategy backfired, much to Proxmire's chagrin. It generated increased scientific interest in the study of love, propelling it forward, and identified Berscheid as the keeper of the flame. Scholars and individuals from Alaska to then-darkest Cold War Albania sent her requests for information, along with letters of support.

Berscheid jettisoned her plans for very early retirement, buttoned up the country house, and, as she says, "became a clearinghouse" for North American love research. "It became eminently clear that there were people who really did want to learn more about love. And I had tenure."

PUTTING THE SOCIAL INTO PSYCHOLOGY

This incident was perfectly timed. For during the early 1970s, the field of social psychology was undergoing a revolution of sorts—a revolution that made the study of love newly possible.

For decades behaviorism, the school of psychology founded by John B. Watson, dominated the field. Watson argued that only overt actions capable of direct observation and measurement were worthy of study. However, by the early seventies, dissenters were openly calling this approach far too narrow. It excluded unobservable mental events such as ideas and emotions. Thus rose cognitive science, the study of the mind, or perception, thought, and memory.

Now psychologists were encouraged to ask human subjects what they thought and how they felt about things. Self-report questionnaires emerged as a legitimate research tool. Psychologists were encouraged to escape laboratory confines—to study real people in the real world. Once out there, they discovered that there was plenty to mine.

Throughout the seventies, soaring divorce rates, loneliness, and isolation began to dominate the emotional landscape of America. By the end of that decade, love had become a pathology. No longer was the question "What is love?" thought to be trivial. "People in our culture dissolve unions when love disappears, which has a lasting effect on society," says Berscheid. Besides, "we already understood the mating habits of the stickleback fish." It was time to turn to a new species.

Today there are hundreds of research papers on love. Topics range from romantic ideals to attachment styles of the young and unmarried. "There were maybe a half dozen when I wrote my dissertation on romantic attraction in 1969," reports Aron. These days, a national association and an international society bring "close relationship" researchers close together annually. Together or apart they are busy producing and sharing new theories, new questionnaires to use as research instruments, and new findings. Their unabashed aim: to improve the human condition by helping us to understand, to repair, and to perfect our love relationships.

SO WHAT *IS* LOVE?

"If there is anything that we have learned about love it is its variegated nature," says Clyde Hendrick, Ph.D., of Texas Tech University in Lubbock. "No one volume or theory or research program can capture love and transform it into a controlled bit of knowledge."

Instead, scholars are tackling specific questions about love in the hopes of nailing down a few facets at a time. The expectation is that every finding will be a building block in the base of knowledge, elevating understanding.

Elaine Hatfield, Ph.D., now of the University of Hawaii, has carved out the territory of passionate love. Along with Berscheid, Hatfield was at the University of Minnesota in 1964 when Stanley Schacter, formerly a professor there and still a great presence, proposed a new theory of emotion. It said that any emotional state requires two conditions: both physiological arousal and relevant situational cues. Already studying close relationships, Hatfield and Berscheid were intrigued. Could the theory help to explain the turbulent, all-consuming experience of passionate love?

Hatfield has spent a good chunk of her professional life examining passionate love, "a state of intense longing for union with another." In 1986, along with sociologist Susan Sprecher, she devised the Passionate Love Scale (PLS), a questionnaire that measures thoughts and feelings she previously identified as distinctive of this "emotional" state.

Lovers rate the applicability of a variety of descriptive statements. To be passionately in love is to be preoccupied with thoughts of your partner much of the time. Also, you likely idealize your partner. So those of you who are passionately in love would, for example,

give "I yearn to know all about—" a score somewhere between "moderately true" and "definitely true" on the PLS.

True erotic love is intense and involves taking risks. It seems to demand a strong sense of self.

The quiz also asks subjects if they find themselves trying to determine the other's feelings, trying to please their lover, or making up excuses to be close to him or her—all hallmarks of passionate, erotic love. It canvasses for both positive and negative feelings. "Passionate lovers," explains Hatfield, "experience a roller coaster of feelings: euphoria, happiness, calm, tranquility, vulnerability, anxiety, panic, despair."

For a full 10 percent of lovers, previous romantic relationships proved so painful that they hope they will never love again.

Passionate love, she maintains, is kindled by "a sprinkle of hope and a large dollop of loneliness, mourning, jealousy, and terror." It is, in other words, fueled by a juxtaposition of pain and pleasure. According to psychologist Dorothy Tennov, who interviewed some 500 lovers, most of them expect their romantic experiences to be bittersweet. For a full 10 percent of them, previous romantic relationships proved so painful that they hope never to love again.

Contrary to myths that hold women responsible for romance, Hatfield finds that both males and females love with equal passion. But men fall in love faster. They are, thus, more romantic. Women are more apt to mix pragmatic concerns with their passion.

And people of all ages, even four-year-old children, are capable of "falling passionately in love." So are people of any ethnic group and socioeconomic stratum capable of passionate love.

Hatfield's most recent study, of love in three very different cultures, shows that

romantic love is not simply a product of the Western mind. It exists among diverse cultures worldwide.

Taken together, Hatfield's findings support the idea that passionate love is an evolutionary adaptation. In this scheme, passionate love works as a bonding mechanism, a necessary kind of interpersonal glue that has existed since the start of the human race. It assures that procreation will take place, that the human species will be perpetuated.

UP FROM THE SWAMP

Recent anthropological work also supports this notion. In 1991, William Jankowiak, Ph.D., of the University of Nevada in Las Vegas, and Edward Fischer, Ph.D., of Tulane University published the first study systematically comparing romantic love across 166 cultures.

They looked at folklore, indigenous advice about love, tales about lovers, love potion recipes—anything related. They found "clear evidence" that romantic love is known in 147, or 89 percent, of cultures. Further, Jankowiak suspects that the lack of proof in the remaining 19 cultures is due more to field workers' oversights than to the absence of romance.

Unless prompted, few anthropologists recognize romantic love in the populations that they study, explains Jankowiak. Mostly because romance takes different shapes in different cultures, they do not know what to look for. They tend to recognize romance only in the form it takes in American culture—a progressive phenomenon leading from flirtation to marriage. Elsewhere, it may be a more fleeting fancy. Still, reports Jankowiak, "when I ask them specific questions about behavior, like 'Did couples run away from camp together?', almost all of them have a positive response."

For all that, there is a sizable claque of scholars who insist that romantic love is a cultural invention of the last 200 years or so. They point out that few cultures outside the West embrace romantic love with the vigor that we do. Fewer still build marriage, traditionally a social and economic institution, on the individualistic pillar of romance.

Romantic love, this thinking holds, consists of a learned set of behaviors; the phenomenon is culturally transmitted from one generation to the next by example, stories, imitation, and direct instruc-

LOVE ME TENDER

How To Make Love to a Man (what men like, in order of importance)	**How To Make Love to a Woman** (what women like, in order of importance)
taking walks together	taking walks together
kissing	flowers
candle-lit dinners	kissing
cuddling	candle-lit dinners
hugging	cuddling
flowers	declaring "I love you"
holding hands	love letters
making love	slow dancing
love letters	hugging
sitting by the fireplace	giving surprise gifts

tion. Therefore, it did not rise from the swamps with us, but rather evolved with culture.

THE ANXIOUS ARE ITS PREY

Regardless whether passionate, romantic love is universal or unique to us, there is considerable evidence that what renders people particularly vulnerable to it is anxiety. It whips up the wherewithal to love. And anxiety is not alone; in fact, there are a number of predictable precursors to love.

To test the idea that emotions such as fear, which produces anxiety, can amplify attraction, Santa Cruz's Arthur Aron recorded the responses of two sets of men to an attractive woman. But one group first had to cross a narrow 450-foot-long bridge that swayed in the wind over a 230-foot drop—a pure prescription for anxiety. The other group tromped confidently across a seemingly safe bridge. Both groups encountered Miss Lovely, a decoy, as they stepped back onto terra firm.

Aron's attractive confederate stopped each young man to explain that she was doing a class project and asked if he would complete a questionnaire. Once he finished, she handed him her telephone number, saying that she would be happy to explain her project in greater detail.

Who called? Nine of the 33 men on the suspension bridge telephoned, while only two of the men on the safe bridge called. It is not impossible that the callers simply wanted details on the project, but Aron suspects instead that a combustible mix of excitement and anxiety prompted the men to become interested in their attractive interviewee.

Along similar if less treacherous lines, Aron has most recently looked at eleven possible precursors to love. He compiled the list by conducting a comprehensive literature search for candidate items. If you have a lot in common with or live and work close to someone you find attractive, your chances of falling in love are good, the literature suggests.

Other general factors proposed at one time or another as good predictors include being liked by the other, a partner's positive social status, a partner's ability to fill your needs, your readiness for entering a relationship, your isolation from others, mystery, and exciting surroundings or circumstances. Then there are specific cues, like hair color, eye expression, and face shape.

Love depends as much on the perception of being liked as on the presence of a desirable partner. Love isn't possible without it.

To test the viability and relative importance of these eleven putative factors, Aron asked three different groups of people to give real-life accounts of falling in love. Predictably, desirable characteristics, such as good looks and personality, made the top of the list. But proximity, readiness to develop a relationship, and exciting surroundings and circumstances ranked close behind.

The big surprise: reciprocity. Love is at heart a two-way event. The perception of being liked ranked just as high as the presence of desirable characteristics in the partner. "The combination of the two appears to be very important," says Aron. In fact, love just may not be possible without it.

Sprecher and his colleagues got much the same results in a very recent cross-cultural survey. They and their colleagues interviewed 1,667 men and women in the U.S., Russia, and Japan. They asked the people to think about the last time they had fallen in love or been infatuated. Then they asked about the circumstance that surrounded the love experience.

Surprisingly, the rank ordering of the factors was quite similar in all three cultures. In all three, men and women consider reciprocal liking, personality, and physical appearance to be especially important. A partner's social status and the approval of family and friends are way down the list. The cross-cultural validation of predisposing influences suggests that reciprocal liking, desirable personality and physical features may be universal elements of love, among the *sine qua non* of love, part of its heart and soul.

FRIENDSHIP OVER PASSION

Another tack to the intangible of love is the "prototype" approach. This is the study of our conceptions of love, what we "think" love is.

In 1988, Beverly Fehr, Ph.D., of the University of Winnipeg in Canada conducted a series of six studies designed to determine what "love" and "commitment" have in common. Assorted theories suggested they could be anything from mutually inclusive to completely separate. Fehr asked subjects to list characteristics of love and to list features of commitment. Then she asked them to determine which qualities were central and which more peripheral to each.

People's concepts of the two were to some degree overlapping. Such elements as trust, caring, respect, honesty, devotion, sacrifice, and contentment were deemed attributes of both love and commitment. But such other factors as intimacy, happiness, and a desire to be with the other proved unique to love (while commitment alone demanded perseverance, mutual agreement, obligation, and even a feeling of being trapped).

The findings of Fehr's set of studies, as well as others', defy many expectations. Most subjects said they consider caring, trust, respect, and honesty central to love—while passion-related events like touching, sexual passion, and physical attraction are only peripheral. "They are not very central to our concept of love," Fehr shrugs.

Recently, Fehr explored gender differences in views of love—and found remarkably few. Both men and women put forth friendship as primary to love. Only in a second study, which asked subjects to match their personal ideal of love to various descriptions, did any differences show up. More so than women, men tended to rate erotic, romantic love closer to their personal conception of love.

Both men and women deem romance and passion far less important than support and warm fuzzies . . .

Still, Fehr is fair. On the whole, she says, "the essence, the core meaning of love differs little." Both genders deem romance and passion far less important than support and warm fuzzies. As even Nadine Crenshaw, creator of steamy romance novels, has remarked, "love gets you to the bathroom when you're sick."

LOVE ME TENDER

Since the intangible essence of love cannot be measured directly, many researchers settle for its reflection in what people do. They examine the behavior of lovers.

Clifford Swensen, Ph.D., professor of psychology at Purdue University, pioneered this approach by developing a scale with which to measure lovers' behavior. He produced it from statements people made when asked what they did for, said to, or felt about people they loved . . . and how these people behaved towards them.

Being supportive and providing encouragement are important behaviors to all love relationships—whether with a friend or mate, Swensen and colleagues found. Subjects also gave high ratings to self-disclosure, or talking about personal matters, and a sense of agreement on important topics.

But two categories of behaviors stood out as unique to romantic relationships.

Lovers said that they expressed feelings of love verbally; they talked about how they enjoyed being together, how they missed one another when apart, and other such murmurings. They also showed their affection through physical acts like hugging and kissing.

Elaborating on the verbal and physical demonstrations of love, psychologist Raymond Tucker, Ph.D., of Bowling Green State University in Ohio probed 149 women and 48 men to determine "What constitutes a romantic act?" He asked subjects, average age of 21, to name common examples. There was little disagreement between the genders.

Both men and women most often cited "taking walks" together. For women, "sending or receiving flowers" and "kissing" followed close on its heels, then "candle-lit dinners" and "cuddling." Outright declarations of "I love you came in a distant sixth. (Advisory to men: The florists were right all along. Say it with flowers instead.)

. . . as one romance novelist confides, "love gets you to the bathroom when you're sick."

For men, kissing and "candle-lit dinners" came in second and third. If women preferred demonstrations of love to outright declarations of it, men did even more so; "hearing and saying 'I love you didn't even show up among their top ten preferences. Nor did "slow dancing or giving or receiving surprise gifts," although all three were on the women's top-ten list. Men likewise listed three kinds of activity women didn't even mention: "holding hands," "making love"—and "sitting by the fireplace." For both sexes, love is more tender than most of us imagined.

All in all, says Tucker, lovers consistently engage in a specific array of actions. "I see these items show up over and over and over again." They may very well be the bedrock behaviors of romantic love.

SIX COLORS OF LOVE

That is not to say that once in love we all behave alike. We do not. Each of us

has a set of attitudes toward love that colors what we do. While yours need not match your mate's, you best understand your partner's approach. It underlies how your partner is likely to treat you.

There are six basic orientations toward love, Canadian sociologist John Allen Lee first suggested in 1973. They emerged from a series of studies in which subjects matched story cards, which contain statements projecting attitudes, to their own personal relationships. In 1990 Texas Tech's Clyde Hendrick, along with wife/colleague Susan Hendrick, Ph.D., produced a Love Attitude Scale to measure all six styles. You may embody more than one of these styles. You are also likely to change style with time and circumstance.

Both men and women prefer demonstrations of love to outright declarations of it.

You may, for example, have spent your freewheeling college years as an Eros lover, passionate and quick to get involved, setting store on physical attraction and sexual satisfaction. Yet today you may find yourself happy as a Storge lover, valuing friendship-based love, preferring a secure, trusting relationship with a partner of like values.

There are Ludus lovers, game-players who like to have several partners at one time. Their partners may be very different from one another, as Ludus does not act on romantic ideals. Mania-type lovers, by contrast, experience great emotional highs and lows. They are very possessive—and often jealous. They spend a lot of their time doubting their partner's sincerity.

Pragma lovers are, well, pragmatic. They get involved only with the "right" guy or gal—someone who fills their needs or meets other specifications. This group is happy to trade drama and excitement for a partner they can build a life with. In contrast, Agape, or altruistic, lovers form relationships because of what they may be able to give to their partner. Even sex is not an urgent concern of theirs. "Agape functions on a more spiritual level," Hendrick says.

The Hendricks have found some gender difference among love styles. In general, men are more ludic, or game-playing. Women tend to be more storgic,

THE COLORS OF LOVE

How do I love thee? At least six are the ways.

There is no one type of love; there are many equally valid ways of loving. Researchers have consistently identified six attitudes or styles of love that, to one degree or another, encompass our conceptions of love and color our romantic relationships. They reflect both fixed personality traits and more malleable attitudes. Your relative standing on these dimensions may vary over time—being in love NOW will intensify your responses in some dimensions. Nevertheless, studies show that for most people, one dimension of love predominates.

Answering the questions below will help you identify your own love style, one of several important factors contributing to the satisfaction you feel in relationships. You may wish to rate yourself on a separate sheet of paper. There are no right or wrong answers, nor is there any scoring system. The test is designed to help you examine your own feelings and to help you understand your own romantic experiences.

After you take the test, if you are currently in a relationship, you may want to ask your partner to take the test and then compare your responses. Better yet, try to predict your partner's love attitudes before giving the test to him or her.

Studies show that most partners are well-correlated in the areas of love passion and intensity (Eros), companionate or friendship love (Storge), dependency (Mania), and all-giving or selfless love (Agape). If you and your partner aren't a perfect match, don't worry. Knowing your styles can help you manage your relationship.

Directions: Listed below are several statements that reflect different attitudes about love. For each statement, fill in the response on an answer sheet that indicates how much you agree or disagree with that statement. The items refer to a specific love relationship. Whenever possible, answer the questions with your current partner in mind. If you are not currently dating anyone, answer the questions with your most recent partner in mind. If you have never been in love, answer in terms of what you think your responses would most likely be.

FOR EACH STATEMENT:
A = Strongly agree with the statement
B = Moderately agree with the statement
C = Neutral, neither agree nor disagree
D = Moderately disagree with the statement
E = Strongly disagree with the statement

Eros
Measures passionate love as well as intimacy and commitment. It is directly and strongly correlated with satisfaction in a relationship, a major ingredient in relationship success. Eros gives fully, intensely, and takes risks in love; it requires substantial ego strength. Probably reflects secure attachment style.

1. My partner and I were attracted to each other immediately after we first met.

2. My partner and I have the right physical "chemistry" between us.

3. Our lovemaking is very intense and satisfying.

4. I feel that my partner and I were meant for each other.

5. My partner and I became emotionally involved rather quickly.

6. My partner and I really understand each other.

7. My partner fits my ideal standards of physical beauty/handsomeness.

Ludus
Measures love as an interaction game to be played out with diverse partners. Relationships do not have great depth of feeling. Ludus is wary of emotional intensity from others, and has a manipulative or cynical quality to it. Ludus is negatively related to satisfaction in relationships. May reflect avoidant attachment style.

8. I try to keep my partner a little uncertain about my commitment to him/her.

9. I believe that what my partner doesn't know about me won't hurt him/her.

10. I have sometimes had to keep my partner from finding out about other partners.

11. I could get over my affair with my partner pretty easily and quickly.

12. My partner would get upset if he/she knew of some of the things I've done with other people.

13. When my partner gets too dependent on me, I want to back off a little.

14. I enjoy playing the "game of love" with my partner and a number of other partners.

Storge
Reflects an inclination to merge love and friendship. Storgic love is solid, down to earth, presumably enduring. It is evolutionary, not revolutionary, and may take time to develop. It is related to satisfaction in long-term relationships.

15. It is hard for me to say exactly when our friendship turned to love.

16. To be genuine, our love first required caring for a while.

17. I expect to always be friends with my partner.

18. Our love is the best kind because it grew out of a long friendship.

19. Our friendship merged gradually into love over time.

20. Our love is really a deep friendship, not a mysterious, mystical emotion.

21. Our love relationship is the most satisfying because it developed from a good friendship.

Pragma
Reflects logical, "shopping list" love, rational calculation with a focus on desired attributes of a lover. Suited to computer-matched dating. Related to satisfaction in long-term relationships.

22. I considered what my partner was going to become in life before I committed myself to him/her.

23. I tried to plan my life carefully before choosing my partner.

24. In choosing my partner, I believed it was best to love someone with a similar background.

25. A main consideration in choosing my partner was how he/she would reflect on my family.

26. An important factor in choosing my partner was whether or not he/she would be a good parent.

27. One consideration in choosing my partner was how he/she would reflect on my career.

28. Before getting very involved with my partner, I tried to figure out how compatible his/her hereditary background would be with mine in case we ever had children.

Mania
Measures possessive, dependent love. Associated with high emotional expressiveness and disclosure, but low self-esteem; reflects uncertainty of self in the relationship. Negatively associated with relationship satisfaction. May reflect anxious/ambivalent attachment style.

29. When things aren't right with my partner and me, my stomach gets upset.

30. If my partner and I break up, I would get so depressed that I would even think of suicide.

31. Sometimes I get so excited about being in love with my partner that I can't sleep.

32. When my partner doesn't pay attention to me, I feel sick all over.

33. Since I've been in love with my partner, I've had trouble concentrating on anything else.

34. I cannot relax if I suspect that my partner is with someone else.

35. If my partner ignores me for a while, I sometimes do stupid things to try to get his/her attention back.

Agape
Reflects all-giving, selfless, nondemanding love. Associated with altruistic, committed, sexually idealistic love. Like Eros, tends to flare up with "being in love now."

36. I try to always help my partner through difficult times.

37. I would rather suffer myself than let my partner suffer.

38. I cannot be happy unless I place my partner's happiness before my own.

39. I am usually willing to sacrifice my own wishes to let my partner achieve his/hers.

40. Whatever I won is my partner's to use as he/she chooses.

41. When my partner gets angry with me, I still love him/her fully and unconditionally.

42. I would endure all things for the sake of my partner.

Adapted from Hendrick, Love Attitudes Scale

(United Nations/John Isaac)

Research has shown that men fall in love faster than women; women are more apt to mix pragmatic concerns with their passion.

more pragmatic—and more manic. However, men and women seem to be equally passionate and altruistic in their relationships. On the whole, say the Hendricks, the sexes are more similar than different in style.

Personality traits, at least one personality trait, is strongly correlated to love style, the Hendricks have discovered. People with high self-esteem are more apt to endorse eros, but less likely to endorse mania than other groups. "This finding fits with the image of a secure, confident eros lover who moves intensely but with mutuality into a new relationship," they maintain.

When they turned their attention to ongoing relationships, the Hendricks' found that couples who stayed together over the course of their months-long study were more passionate and less game-playing than couples who broke up. "A substantial amount of passionate love" and "a low dose of game-playing" love are key to the development of satisfying relationships—at least among the college kids studied.

YOUR MOTHER MADE YOU DO IT

The love style you embrace, how you treat your partner, may reflect the very first human relationship you ever had—probably with Mom. There is growing evidence supporting "attachment theory," which holds that the rhythms of response by a child's primary care giver affect the development of personality and influence later attachment processes, including adult love relationships.

First put forth by British psychiatrist John Bowlby in the 1960s and elaborated by American psychologist Mary Ainsworth, attachment theory is the culmination of years of painstaking observation of infants and their adult caregivers—and those separated from them—in both natural and experimental situations. Essentially it suggests that there are three major patterns of attachment; they develop within the first year of life and stick with us, all the while reflecting the responsiveness of the caregiver to our needs as helpless infants.

Those whose mothers, or caregivers, were unavailable or unresponsive may grow up to be detached and nonresponsive to others. Their behavior is Avoidant in relationships. A second group takes a more Anxious-Ambivalent approach to relationships, a response set in motion by having mothers they may not have been able to count on—sometimes responsive, other times not. The lucky among us are Secure in attachment, trusting and stable in relationships, probably the result of having had consistently responsive care.

While attachment theory is now driving a great deal of research on children's social, emotional, and cognitive development, University of Denver psychologists Cindy Hazan and Philip Shaver set out not long ago to investigate the possible effect of childhood relationships on adult attachments. First, they developed descriptive statements that reflect each of the three attachment styles. Then they asked people in their community, along with college kids, which statements best describe how they relate to others. They asked, for example, about trust and jealousy, about closeness and desire for reciprocation, about emotional extremes.

The distribution of the three attachment styles has proved to be about the same in grown-ups as in infants, the same among collegians as the fully fledged. More than half of adult respondents call themselves Secure; the rest are split between Avoidant and Ambivalent. Further, their adult attachment patterns predictably reflect the relationship they report with their parents. Secure people generally describe their parents as having been warm and supportive. What's more, these adults predictably differ in success at romantic love. Secure people reported happy, long-lasting relationships. Avoidants rarely found love.

Secure adults are more trusting of their romantic partners and more confident of a partner's love, report Australian psychologists Judith Feeney and Patricia Noller of the University of Queensland. The two surveyed nearly 400 college undergraduates with a questionnaire on family background and love relationships, along with items designed to reveal their personality and related traits.

In contrast to the Secure, Avoidants indicated an aversion to intimacy. The Anxious-Ambivalent participants were characterized by dependency and what Feeney and Noller describe as "a hunger" for commitment. Their approach resembles the Mania style of love. Each of the three groups reported differences in early childhood experience that could account for their adult approach to relationships. Avoidants, for example, were most likely to tell of separations from their mother.

It may be, Hazan and Shaver suggest, that the world's greatest love affairs are conducted by the Ambitious-Ambivalents—people desperately searching for a kind of security they never had.

THE MAGIC NEVER DIES

Not quite two decades into the look at love, it appears as though love will not always mystify us. For already we are beginning to define what we think about it, how it makes us feel, and what we do when we are in love. We now know that it is the insecure, rather than the confident, who fall in love more readily. We know that outside stimuli that alter our emotional state can affect our susceptibility to romance; it is not just the person. We now know that to a certain extent your love style is set by the parenting you received. And, oh yes, men are more quickly romantic than women.

The best news may well be that when it comes to love, men and women are more similar than different. In the face of continuing gender wars, it is comforting to think that men and women share an important, and peaceful, spot of turf. It is also clear that no matter how hard we look at love, we will always be amazed and mesmerized by it.

Psychological Disorders

Jay and Harry were two brothers who owned a service station. They were the middle children of four. The other two children were sisters, the oldest of whom had married and moved out of the family home. The service station that these young men operated was once owned by their father, who had retired and turned the business over to his sons.

Harry and Jay had a good working relationship. Harry was the "up-front" man. Taking customer orders, accepting payments, and working with parts distributors, Harry was the individual who dealt most directly with the customers. Jay worked behind the scenes. While Harry made the mechanical diagnoses, Jay was the one who did the corrective work. Some of his friends thought Jay was a mechanical genius.

Preferring to spend time by himself, Jay had always been a little odd. His emotions had been more inappropriate and intense than other people's. Harry was the stalwart in the family. He was the acknowledged leader and decision maker when it came to family finances.

One day Jay did not show up for work on time. When he did, he was dressed in the most garish outfit and was laughing hysterically and talking to himself. Harry at first suspected that his brother had taken some illegal drugs. However, Jay's condition persisted. Out of concern, his family took him to the family physician who immediately sent Jay and his family to a psychiatrist. The diagnosis: schizophrenia. Jay's uncle had also been schizophrenic. The family grimly left the psychiatrist's office. After several more appointments with the psychiatrist, they would travel to the local pharmacy to fill a prescription for antipsychotics, medications Jay would probably take the rest of his life.

What caused Jay's drastic and rather sudden change in mental health? Was Jay destined to be schizophrenic because of his family genes? Did competitiveness with his brother and the feeling that he was less revered than Harry cause Jay's decent into mental disorder? How can psychiatrists and clinical psychologists make accurate diagnoses? Once a diagnosis of mental illness is made, can the individual ever completely recover?

These and other questions are the emphasis in this unit. Mental disorder has fascinated and, on the other hand, terrified us for centuries. At various times in our history those who suffered from these disorders were persecuted as witches, tortured to drive out possessing spirits, punished as sinners, jailed as a danger to society, confined to insane asylums, or hospitalized for simply being too ill to care for themselves.

Today, psychologists propose that the view of mental disorders as "illnesses" has outlived its usefulness. We should think of mental illness as either biochemical disturbances or disorders of learning in which the person develops a maladaptive pattern of behavior that is then maintained by an inappropriate environment. At the same time, we need to recognize that these reactions to stressors in the environment or to the inappropriate learning situations may be genetically preordained; some people may more easily develop the disorders than others.

Serious disorders are serious problems and not just for the individual who is the patient or client. The impact of mental disorders on the family (just as for Jay's family) and friends deserves our full attention, too. Diagnosis, treatment, and the implications of the disorders are addressed in some of the articles in this section. In the following unit, we will explore further the concept of treatment of mental disorders.

Richard Vatz and Lee Weinberg discuss the myth of mental illness in the first unit article. These authors debate the view that mental disturbance may be biologically induced; if so, mental disorders would be less the domain of psychology and more the domain of medicine and biology.

A serious mental disorder is the one Jay was diagnosed with, schizophrenia. Schizophrenia has baffled psychologists for decades. Tony Dajer, in "Divided Selves," introduces us to this mysterious disorder and examines what its causes might be.

Clinical depression, a very intense feeling of despair and hopelessness, is more common than you might think. Depression also causes most of the suicides in our country. As troublesome as depression is, it can be treated. Its

Unit 10

causes and treatments are the focus of "Defeating Depression."

Two other problems of living that are not considered psychological disorders but do cause much turmoil in our lives are discussed next. "Patterns of Abuse" addresses the issue of domestic violence. Millions of women are beaten by their husbands or boyfriends every year. The beatings often remain a secret of the family. Why women are abused, who the victims and abusers are, and what the women can do to find help are detailed in this powerful article. Stress is a very, very common problem for many in our fast-paced, competitive society. The final article in this unit, "The Immune System vs. Stress," examines the causes and effects of stress as well as the types of individuals who are most prone to distress.

Looking Ahead: Challenge Questions

Why do some professionals believe that mental illness is a myth? Do you believe everyone has the potential for developing a mental disorder? What circumstances lead an individual to mental illness? Do you think that mental disorders are biological or psychological? If we discover that most mental disorders are caused by something physiological, do you think they will remain the purview of psychology? Why?

Describe schizophrenia. What do psychologists think causes this disorder? Do you think this disorder is caused by heredity, environment, or some other factor? Defend your answer. What are the treatments currently being used to treat this disorder?

What is depression? How is it different from the everyday blues that many of us experience? What are the various causes of depression? What are the treatments for depression?

What is domestic violence? How common is it? What types of women are victimized by domestic violence? Profile the abuser. How can we break the cycle of violence? How can we assist the victims?

What is stress? What effect does stress have on our physical health? What magnifies the effects of stress? How can we better cope with stress when it occurs?

Is Mental Illness a Myth?

Psychiatrists, physicians, and lawyers are among those arguing over whether deviant, dangerous, or self-destructive behavior has a biological basis.

Richard E. Vatz and Lee S. Weinberg

The authors, Associate Psychology Editors of USA Today, are, respectively, professor of rhetoric and communication, Towson (Md.) State University, and associate professor of administration of justice, University of Pittsburgh (Pa.).

THERE HAS BEEN a running debate over the validity of "mental illness" and its status in the marketplace of ideas. This is to some extent the culmination of many years of criticism of the view that mental illnesses are real illnesses—termed the "medical model"—and more than a decade of efforts in biological psychiatry aimed at demonstrating that they do indeed have a biological basis. The best evidence is that most of the behaviors called mental illnesses are not illnesses and that the skepticism regarding psychiatric claims is increasing, not decreasing.

Psychiatrist Thomas Szasz, whom columnist and former psychiatrist Charles Krauthammer calls "the premier critic of his own profession," has contended for more than 30 years that mental illness is a myth, a point requiring careful explanation. Szasz does not deny that the behaviors labeled mental illness exist. Yet, this remains the most frequent misunderstanding—or

purposeful distortion—of his views. As one typical example, Harvard University law professor Alan Dershowitz said of Szasz's position in an interview, "If you've seen somebody who is . . . [severely] troubled, you can't believe Tom Szasz's argument that there's no such thing as mental illness."

What Szasz maintains, however, is that calling deviant, dangerous, and/or self-destructive behavior mental illness distracts from an understanding of such acts. Moreover, this type of invidious labeling leads to depriving of the freedoms of some innocent people, such as in involuntary psychiatric interventions. In other situations, it allows the unjustified relieving of individuals of responsibility for their actions, even to the point of exculpation of heinous crimes, such as in the case of would-be presidential assassin John Hinckley.

Szasz believes that the great preponderance of what is called mental illness constitutes problems in living and/or deviant behavior. Illness, he argues, is exclusively "a condition of the body. . . . I define illness as the pathologist defines it—as a structural or functional abnormality of cells, tissues, organs, or bodies."

Psychiatrists employ a number of rhetorical devices to promote mental illness as illness, despite there being no such medical evidence for any but a few of the so-called mental disorders. One is to hitch

the general term to a few specific mental illnesses neuropsychiatrists believe have been established as likely authentic brain diseases.

In recent years, biological psychiatrists have concluded that schizophrenia is a disease since structural and chemical abnormalities have been discovered in the brains of some schizophrenics. The notion that certain individuals labeled schizophrenic may have a brain disease is accepted unquestioningly by the public and is conceded by Szasz in his book, *Insanity.*

Having provided some interesting evidence and having won acceptance for the view that one type of mental illness may be a *bona fide* disease, mental health interests try to transfer the credibility of schizophrenia research to imply that *all* mental illness constitutes proven brain disease. The hope apparently is that, if it is accepted that there is an identifiable brain disease at the root of some behaviors labeled schizophrenic, the assumption will be that there also is one at the root of the tremendous range of behaviors that have at times been labeled as mentally ill.

How many people are seen by psychiatry as mentally ill, and how is it determined? As Yale University psychiatry professor Jay Katz conceded several years ago, "If you look at [the diagnostic manual], you can classify all of us under one rubric or another of mental disorder." The National

Institute of Mental Health (NIMH) determined a few years ago through questioning by lay interviewers that 17-23% of adults in America have at least one "psychiatric disorder," and that there is a 29-38% lifetime prevalence. Responding to this "discovery," the *Archives of General Psychiatry* stated that the results indicated that "we need no longer blindly grope about the prevalence of 'psychiatric illness': its prevalence is about that of hypertension."

Does the public think such determinations are legitimate? It probably does, and these views once got little skepticism from the media, few of which ever dispute such "scientific" findings. Speaking with psychiatrists and NIMH representatives on "Nightline" following publication of the survey, Ted Koppel asked only what can be done about this epidemic of mental illness, with no questions about the validity of the survey.

Although they mouth shibboleths like "mental illness is like any other illness" when speaking publicly, many leading psychiatrists and mental health specialists clearly are quite skeptical of their own claims. This can be seen most clearly in psychiatry's *Diagnostic and Statistical Manual of Mental Disorders* (DSM-III-R) and journal articles discussing the upcoming revision, DSM-IV.

The diagnostic manual does not refer to mental illness, only to mental disorders. It almost entirely is a description of behaviors and experiences, a style the American Psychiatric Association (APA) calls "etiologically neutral," meaning it does not deal with the causes. Actually, as a result of this neutrality, there is absolutely no medical validation, much less criteria, for the vast majority of mental disorders. An article discussing "conundrums" facing the Task Force on DSM-IV (authored by several members) in the *Journal of Abnormal Psychology* admits that, "unfortunately, in most instances," biological tests can not be used even as "diagnostic indicators" since they are not specific to particular "mental disorders."

In addition, the article reports that there is heavy lobbying of the Task Force to influence its revisions of DSM-IV ("The zeal . . . is extraordinary"), based on ideological and financial motives. Members of the Task Force wrote in 1990 in the APA's *American Journal of Psychiatry*, "There has been concern that several proposed diagnoses . . . would have adverse effects on women." In the 1991 "conundrums" piece, they stated that "there are those who want some or all mental disorders designated as diseases in order to protect reimbursement and research funding. . . . "

Regarding the concern for diagnostic categories adversely affecting women, they wrote that "it is unclear to what extent the DSM-IV Task Force should be influenced" by such considerations. Regarding reimbursement issues, a frequent topic in diagnostic manual revision articles, they maintain that it "cannot be overly influenced" by them.

One neurologist, who dismisses psychiatry's medical pretensions for all but schizophrenia and certain bipolar disorders (*e.g.*, manic-depression), says of these debates over DSM-IV revisions: "In discussing the biological basis and classification of authentic disease, one would never raise the question of political and economic ramifications. Those issues might have to be addressed in some other forum, but science is science. When you discuss other considerations, you are simply not doing science."

Szasz argues that the mind is not an organ, so there can be no such thing as mental illness. Moreover, not only are the vast majority of mental illnesses not illnesses, if psychiatry were successful in convincing the medical world that they were, it paradoxically would "destroy psychiatry's *raison d'etre* as a medical specialty distinct and separate from neurology." Regardless, how successful is the effort to persuade people to believe that mental illness is like any other illness?

Increased skepticism

There appear to be efforts among many mental health interests to maintain that the battle for the medical model for mental illness is won. Such a claim was made by a psychologist in an article in *Commentary*, as well as in a 1990 book on the homeless, *Madness in the Streets*. The latter blamed "anti-psychiatry" for the homelessness caused by de-institutionalizing those involuntarily committed in psychiatric hospitals. (Szasz opposed both the forced incarcerations and the forced exits.)

In 1987, when Szasz wrote *Insanity*, perhaps his best treatise on what he claims is the myth of mental illness, there was little response, despite a favorable review in the *Journal of the American Medical Association* which conceded that "[Szasz] does an excellent job of answering all of the arguments against his position. . . . "

In 1990 in *Commentary*, Carol Iannone, the embattled nominee to the Advisory Council of the National Endowment for the Humanities, reviewed William Styron's book, *Darkness Visible*, describing his suffering from the "disease" of depression. The review was skeptical of the notion of "depression-as-disease." She wrote that Styron's description of his emergence from depression makes one doubt that it is a disease without choice or a moral dimension. Styron, Iannone notes, states that, while in the throes of being enraptured by Brahms' "Alto Rhapsody," he steeled himself against an act (suicide) which would devastate his loved ones and constitute a "desecration on myself." "What," Ian-

none asked, "were all his neurotransmitters and chemicals and hormones up to?" How, she implied, could a disease be so amenable to the power of thought?

The reaction to Iannone's heresy was swift and vehement. In an article in *The Washington Post*, she says she was asked about her views on mental illness by senators opposed to her nomination to the National Endowment for the Humanities. One psychiatrist at Columbia University asked angrily in a letter to *Commentary*, "How is it possible that, in the year 1990, one can still come across a person of considerable education (and literary erudition) who somehow has not learned that depression (and, most especially, suicidal depression) is a *psychiatric illness*, not primarily a moral dilemma or a mortal sin?"

There is, in fact, evidence that a slowly increasing skepticism is emerging regarding what psychologist Stanton Peele calls "the diseasing of America." Doubts about behavioral addictions abound in the popular press. A column in *U.S. News and World Report* deplored "the it's-not-my-fault syndrome"; Pulitzer Prize-winning feature writer Alice Steinbach derided "The Addiction Addiction" in *The Baltimore Sun;* and a *New York* magazine cover story titled "Don't Blame Me" skeptically examined the exculpatory language of behavioral addiction. Herbert Fingarette's *Heavy Drinking: The Myth of Alcoholism as a Disease* gained substantial attention. Moreover, since the Hinckley verdict, criticisms of the insanity plea have caused the American Psychiatric Association to retreat from its claims to be able to certify whether people can control their commission of criminal actions.

Even within the field of psychiatry, there is doubt about the medical nature of mental illness. Just before his death, Karl Menninger, the dean of American psychiatry, wrote, "[Szasz's] new book, *Insanity*, makes some points that I agree with and have been trying to get across for years." In a published letter to Szasz, Menninger spoke with derisive skepticism about psychiatric diagnosis, prognosis, and treatment, and at one point used the term psychiatric "sickness" in quotation marks. He ended his letter with an implicit admission that much psychiatric treatment might not be the cause of patients' feeling better: "Long ago I noticed that some of our very sick patients surprised us by getting well even without much of our 'treatment.' "

If Menninger came to doubt even partially the major premise of psychiatry—that mental illnesses are authentic illnesses—after a lifetime of accepting and promoting it, the debate over the medical identity of such conditions may be just beginning. That should trigger discussions about a multitude of crucial related matters, ranging from the insanity plea to third-party reimbursements for mental illnesses.

divided selves

To get to the bottom of schizophrenia, two scientific rivals are seeking help from some unusual twins—twins who are identical in all aspects but one.

Tony Dajer

Tony Dajer is assistant director of the emergency room at New York Downtown Hospital.

Fuller Torrey has one goal in life: to prove Irving Gottesman wrong. Gottesman, for his part, is just as determined to nail Torrey. And either would be delighted to see the other win.

Torrey, 55, senior psychiatrist at St. Elizabeths Hospital in Washington, D.C., is a world expert on the viral theory of schizophrenia. Gottesman, 61, Commonwealth Professor of Psychology at the University of Virginia, is one of the best gene sleuths around. The question at hand: whether the baffling illness of schizophrenia springs primarily from an infection or is caused by defective genes. To settle the issue, the friendly archrivals have embarked on an unusual venture designed to leave one of them in the dust. "Irving," says Torrey, "is a lively and honest researcher with whom I can disagree with pleasure."

The whole enterprise hinges on a medical quirk. Schizophrenia is a common disease, affecting over a million people in this country alone. Given such large numbers it's possible to find occasional cases of people with schizophrenia who have an identical twin, a sibling who shares their exact genetic heritage. About half the time the twin is also schizophrenic, but the rest of the time the twin is normal (though some display borderline schizophrenic traits that label them as slightly eccentric). These "discordant" twin pairs—one ill, one well—constitute a potentially powerful means to tease out schizophrenia's secrets.

Despite the mental devastation it creates, schizophrenia leaves maddeningly few traces. You can't point to a definite cause like a virus or a bacterium or a defective gene, as you can with many other brain diseases. Nor can you see glaring damage like holes or scars when you autopsy a schizophrenic's brain. And although researchers have tried scanning the brains of hundreds of schizophrenics and healthy volunteers, they've been unsure if the differences they saw were due to schizophrenia or to individual brain variation.

That's why twins are so inordinately useful for this kind of study. If you could compare a schizophrenic with his or her genetically identical yet normal twin, any differences would very likely be due to the disease process. It would be like superimposing, in the same person, the cardboard cutout for disease on the one for health. If you found discrepancies between the two, you could conclude that that's where schizophrenia probably lurks and search for its cause.

That, in short, was Torrey's reasoning. So in 1986, after seeking out Gottesman's involvement as a "respected counterpoint to my own bias," he assembled a sample of willing twins and a network of psychologists, geneticists, virologists, biochemists, statisticians, and brain scanners to launch an unprecedented assault on the roots of madness.

The first descriptions of what a modern psychiatrist would call schizophrenia were written in 1809, but it wasn't until a century later that Eugen Bleuler, a Swiss psychiatrist, gave the disease a name. Schizophrenia literally means "split mind," but popular myth notwithstanding, it has nothing to do with multiple personalities. Bleuler was referring to an odd ungluing of the mind, to the kind of striking dissociation of reason and emotion that makes patients laugh during funerals or imbue a mundane object or gesture with some spectacularly inappropriate significance. Schizophrenics, who are typically diagnosed when they are adolescents or young adults, become prey to fantastic hallucinations and hear voices conversing in their head. They may develop paranoid or grandiose delusions—a fear that the CIA can control or read their thoughts, for example, or the conviction that their destiny is to fulfill some exalted messianic mission. Yet they can also become intensely withdrawn, apparently unfeeling, or overcome by an apathetic stupor. So profoundly does schizophrenia unhinge the mind that many victims never make their way back to reality.

Torrey vividly remembers his first encounter with the illness. He was 19 and a premed student at the time. "It was the summer before Rhoda, my seventeen-year-old sister, was supposed to start college," he recounts. "She began having delusions that the British redcoats were attacking America. My mother told me she would discuss the Revolutionary War at dinner, the kind of stuff you learn in history class. At first my mother thought Rhoda was kidding. But then one day she found her lying on the front lawn talking to imaginary voices about the British attacks. When I got home from college, my sister looked physically, neurologically sick to me. In just weeks she'd gone from normalcy—the sister I'd grown up with—to full-blown psychosis."

BY THE END of medical school Torrey had decided to specialize in psychiatry. After completing his residency at Stanford Medical School and doing a stint at the National Institute of Mental Health, he was put in charge of a ward at St. Elizabeths. There the young psychiatrist quickly found himself immersed in the mystery of his patients' insanity.

A major influence on him at the time was the physician and virologist Carleton Gajdusek. In 1972 Gajdusek jolted the medical world with his discovery that so-called slow viruses could linger in the brain for 20 years or more before causing symptoms. The classic disease of this kind was kuru, which started as clumsiness and ended as mind-obliterating dementia and which afflicted only tribesmen in the New Guinea highlands who ate the brains of the deceased during their funeral rituals. To contract kuru, Gajdusek found, you had to consume the brain of someone already infected. Gajdusek (who won the 1976 Nobel Prize for medicine) proved his point by injecting infected brain tissue into chimpanzees: not only did they get the disease, but their damaged brains developed the same peculiar Swiss-cheese appearance as those of human kuru victims. "When New Guinea highlanders stopped eating brains," Torrey says, "they stopped getting kuru."

As a psychiatrist, though, Torrey was swimming against the tide of his profession by even considering biological explanations for mental illness. The rise of psychoanalysis at the turn of the century—and a paucity of biological findings—had given psychological explanations like upbringing and bad parenting a stranglehold on the debate over the causes of schizophrenia.

"When I met Gajdusek," he recalls, "the first thing he did was blast me: You psychiatrists have gotten so hung up on Freud, you've forgotten how to be scientists! And he was right; we had stopped treating schizophrenia like a physical, measurable disease." Goaded by Gajdusek, Torrey began acting like a microbiologist. He asked permission from patients to perform spinal taps and an-

alyze their cerebrospinal fluid, the fluid that bathes the brain and spinal cord, to look for the footprints of viral infection. He didn't find much, but back then, no one did. (Gajdusek tried injecting chimps with brain tissue taken from autopsied schizophrenics, but the experiment failed to work.) "When I look back," says Torrey, "I shudder to think how primitive our methods were. In the 1970s viral research was barely in its infancy."

In the meantime, however, the advocates of a biological explanation were getting reinforcements from a very different quarter. Although it was known that schizophrenia can run in families, the blame had usually been ascribed to nurture (the home environment) rather than to nature (the patients' genes). But in the late 1960s and early 1970s studies began to show that genes far outweighed upbringing as a risk factor for schizophrenia. Children of schizophrenics adopted by normal families, for example, had the same risk of developing the illness as children raised by schizophrenic parents. What's more, an identical twin of a schizophrenic was four times as likely to develop the illness as a nonidentical twin.

One of the young researchers who was helping kick the door open for biology was Gottesman. In 1971 he had joined a pioneering team of Danish geneticists that was studying the children of identical twins who were discordant (one ill, one well) for schizophrenia. After following the families for 18 years, Gottesman confirmed the startling finding that the risk of schizophrenia in the children of either twin was exactly the same: 17 percent. That meant that even if "schizogenes" were not activated in one generation, they could be passed on to the next and then make mischief.

But while studies like these showed that schizophrenia had to have a genetic component, they left a thorny question in their wake: If schizophrenia were due only to genes, why didn't 100 percent of the identical twins—not the observed 50 percent—share the disease? "The most likely explanation," ventures Gottesman, "is that the right combination of genes—probably four or five—plus some as yet undefined environmental stressors must be thrown together to trigger schizophrenia. But before we can figure out what activates the genes in the twins who become ill, we must first find the genes themselves. The trick now is to hunt those genes down to their chromosomes and map

them"—a trick that he hopes some of Torrey's twins will help him pull off.

While Gottesman was making a name for himself studying Danish twins, Torrey continued to collect schizophrenics' cerebrospinal fluid and blood in pursuit of a "schizovirus." It was a monumental wild-goose chase, but a number of clues sustained him in his belief.

For example, viral infections of the temporal lobes—notably herpes simplex type I, the common cold-sore virus—can produce hallucinations and bizarre behavior bearing an uncanny resemblance to schizophrenia. In fact, physicians often mistake the one for the other. Moreover, unlike any other mental illness, schizophrenia is more common among those born in winter, when viral infections abound. In a Scandinavian study of children with a strong family history of schizophrenia, an increase of 70 percent in the rate of schizophrenia was found among those whose mothers had contracted influenza during the second trimester of pregnancy.

Yet despite such circumstantial evidence, Torrey's cerebrospinal-fluid and blood analyses failed to turn up solid viral suspects. And even if his schizovirus existed, those tests couldn't tell him where in the brain it might be doing its work. To identify the virus he would have to locate its base of operations.

A possible approach turned up in the 1980s with the introduction of a brain-scanning technique called magnetic resonance imaging (MRI). Compared with existing technologies such as CT scans, the new tool produced dazzling brain pictures with an astonishing amount of anatomical detail. Even so, it wasn't initially all that helpful for schizophrenia. It found variations in schizophrenics' brains—but they were subtle and not peculiar enough to schizophrenia to distinguish it from other brain diseases or even from normal variation. Studies showed, for example, that the ventricles, a pair of fluid-filled structures that curl around the brain's inner pith like ram's horns, were often unusually large in schizophrenics. But enlarged ventricles were also seen in Alzheimer's and Parkinson's patients, and even in normal old people.

By 1986 it was clear to Torrey that only identical twins who were discordant for schizophrenia could show up the small discrepancies he needed to flush out his prey. Through the National Alliance for the Mentally Ill, he gathered twins that fit the bill. So far he has found 30 pairs of

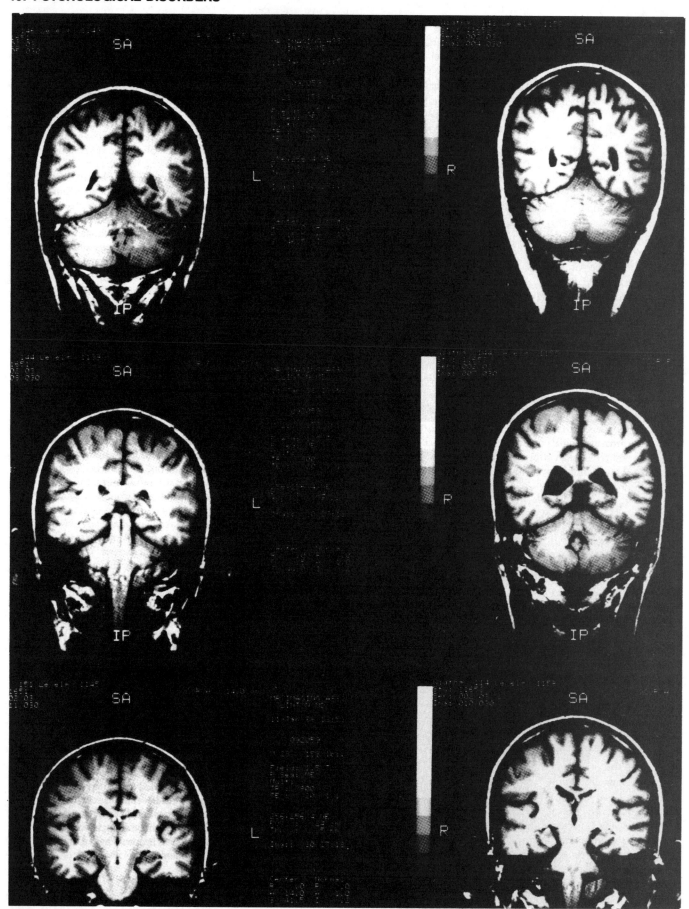

MRI scans show that ventricles at the brain's core are larger in a schizophrenic (center right) than in his normal twin (top left).

clearly discordant twins—and, for comparison, 30 more pairs who are either both schizophrenic, both normal, or somewhere in between (one schizophrenic twin and one ostensibly normal twin with schizophrenic tendencies).

The studies haven't been easy to do, however. MRI scans are obtained by submitting the brain to strong magnetic fields and then measuring the signals from the different tissues inside it. Taking these images requires patients to lie without moving a muscle inside a dark, clanking, tubelike chamber, a process that terrifies even normal patients who have a touch of claustrophobia. For patients whose grip on reality is already fragile, the procedure required immense courage. With one schizophrenic twin, Torrey recalls, "I had to promise to buy her a skirt and blouse if she went through the whole thing. I held her hand the whole time. She was very brave." Altogether, 15 pairs of discordant twins were examined for Torrey's initial MRI study.

The results, published in March 1990 in the *New England Journal of Medicine*, caused quite a stir. Like earlier MRI studies, this one showed that the schizophrenic twins had enlarged ventricles, but it also revealed a striking change in a crucial brain structure called the hippocampus. The hippocampus (the name derives from the Greek for "sea horse," which it's said to resemble) clings to the inner surface of the temporal lobes, which are behind the temples, on either side of the brain. The hippocampus is apparently where input from the senses is hammered into new memories and where the components of old memories are reassembled for recall. And lo and behold, in Torrey's schizophrenics, the hippocampus, especially the left half of the hippocampus, was noticeably smaller than in the normal twins. Indeed, his scanning team thinks that the ventricles may become enlarged in schizophrenics because of a loss of surrounding tissue, including shrinkage of the hippocampus.

That evidence seemed to tie in nicely with autopsy studies begun in the mid-1980s that showed signs of cell loss and disarray in the left hippocampus and its anatomic neighbors in the limbic system. The limbic system controls our emotional response—another function thrown out of whack by schizophrenia. And it fit with another finding: that schizophrenics did poorly on certain memory tests, suggesting that impaired

memory was perhaps a component of schizophrenia.

Classically, schizophrenia was considered a disease of the frontal lobes, the seat of abstract, higher thought. (This idea had unfortunate repercussions: in the 1940s, it served as the rationale for the frontal lobotomies that were performed on thousands of schizophrenics.) But the left hippocampus, linchpin of memory, is part of the left temporal lobe. Could schizophrenia be a problem of the left temporal lobe instead?

ANOTHER NEWER school of thought implicated the entire left side of the brain—the hemisphere that generates language and thus defines the interpretation of words and symbols. One thing that makes the world so terrifying for schizophrenics is the destruction of those defining limits. Thus a misplaced coffee cup can become imbued with peculiar meaning; a stranger's gesture can signal the arrival of the redcoats or the CIA. The result is a paralyzing paranoia.

Torrey, for his part, suspected that the temporal lobe was to blame. But for him the hallmark of schizophrenia is hearing voices. "No other symptom," he argues, "is as specific to schizophrenia: 75 percent of all patients hear voices—voices that command you to kill yourself, voices from outer space, two voices carrying on a conversation, even the voice of God. To us scientists, they seem to be saying, Pay attention, there may be a big clue here."

The temporal lobe, it turns out, is home not only to the hippocampus and other limbic structures but to the nerve fibers that carry input from the ears. If an infection caused the limbic-system damage seen in the autopsy studies, Torrey argues, then maybe it could damage these fibers as well, and one might hear voices. "Autopsies showing cell disarray in these areas," he says, "appear to fit with what we've found on our MRIs."

Still, good as the MRIs have been at locating abnormalities in the brain, they could say nothing about when the damage occurred. That's the question Stefan Bracha, a psychiatrist at the University of Arkansas Medical School in Little Rock, set out to answer. One of schizophrenia's peculiarities is its predictable age of onset: 18 for men, 23 for women, on average. Does that mean that young adults are more susceptible than other age groups to certain viruses or genetic malfunctions? Or is schizophrenia a delayed

reaction to damage that occurred years before? (Kuru, recall, took up to 20 years to manifest itself in New Guinea highlanders who had eaten infected brains.)

Pathological studies of schizophrenic brains have never shown signs of the scarring one would expect from viral infections. However, in the special case of damage caused to a fetus in its mother's womb, the brain doesn't form scar tissue. Instead it ends up with just the kind of cell disorganization described in the autopsies. At the very least, then, these autopsy findings were consistent with the idea that the damage had occurred prenatally. Adding weight to the notion was the Scandinavian study suggesting that influenza infection in the second trimester of pregnancy—months four, five, and six—boosted the risk of schizophrenia.

Bracha knew that the time-tested way of looking for evidence of prenatal infection was dermatoglyphics, the study of fingerprints and finger structure. "But it was old technology, so no one else wanted to do it," he recalls wryly. He also knew that the second trimester of pregnancy is a time of major brain-cell reorganization. If a virus hits at that particular time, it might also affect the hands, which are simultaneously undergoing finishing touches.

UNLIKELY AS IT sounds, it is possible for a virus to infect one identical twin fetus and not the other. So Bracha examined 24 pairs of Torrey's twins for the odd fingerprint whorls and stunted digits that are the "fossilized" evidence, as he puts it, of infections inside the womb. His study, published in November 1991, found that schizophrenics had four times as many abnormalities as their healthy twins, who showed Bracha what the schizophrenics' hands "should have looked like."

These divergent fingerprints suggested that the seeds of schizophrenia are indeed sown very early in life. In the same vein, Torrey has recently completed another study, which uses family interviews and school records to show that the twins start diverging before the age of five. By putting a ceiling on the time of infection, he can focus his search on agents that act in infancy or before.

Meanwhile, back in the geneticists' camp, Gottesman is aware that Torrey has stacked the deck a bit by focusing on clearly discordant twin pairs. This group most likely has a low genetic predisposition to schizophrenia, requiring a big environmental jolt to make the twins so different. But Torrey, remember, has also recruited less clear-cut pairs, where one twin is schizophrenic and the other, apparently healthy one, is only mildly schizoid. From Gottesman's point of view, these twins may prove the most useful of all.

"In these pairs, the healthy twin has some, but not all, of the symptoms of schizophrenia," he says. "So we assume they carry some predisposing genes for the disease, even if they're not fully turned on. Moreover, these healthy twins often display subtle physical signs like abnormal eye tracking or easy distractibility. If we're lucky, these abnormalities may lead us to DNA 'markers,' which are like visible flags inherited along with the actual disease genes. Then we can look for each marker to see if it turns up consistently among families of schizophrenics. If the markers and genes are truly linked—that is, are situated close by on the same stretch

of DNA—we may be able to track down some of the genes we think are involved."

In practice, this approach works well for single-gene diseases such as Huntington's chorea. But when four or five genes are involved, as is thought to be the case with schizophrenia, the task explodes into mind-numbing complexity. Yet if the genes can be found, the rewards will be enormous: researchers will be able to tell very quickly what proteins they make and, eventually, what the proteins do (or fail to do) to cause schizophrenia.

WHILE Gottesman pursues the genes that make the schizophrenic brain malfunction, Torrey is beginning to look at how and where it malfunctions. The procedures he and his colleagues are using can literally see the brain in action. Cerebral blood flow studies and PET (positron emission tomography) scans offer a color-coded glimpse into the brain's workings as eerie

as MRI's sharp dissection of its living anatomy. For the cerebral blood flow studies, xenon gas is inhaled into the lungs to make the patient's blood briefly radioactive; the harder the cells in a particular brain region work, the more blood flow they get and the more detectable radiation they emit. PET uses radioactive glucose or oxygen to similarly light up areas of "hot" metabolic activity in the brain.

Initially Torrey was reluctant to subject his twins to PET scans. "The scans are tough. I take all the tests the patients do, and I found this one uncomfortable. They have to lie in a ring of sensors with their head pinned by a form-fitting mask and IV lines in their arms. And besides, you're asking to read the thoughts of someone who's already paranoid about his thoughts being read." What changed his mind was a study by Susan Resnick, another of his extended network of researchers, at the University of Pennsylvania. PET scans of seven schizophrenics and their normal twins showed a consistent difference in

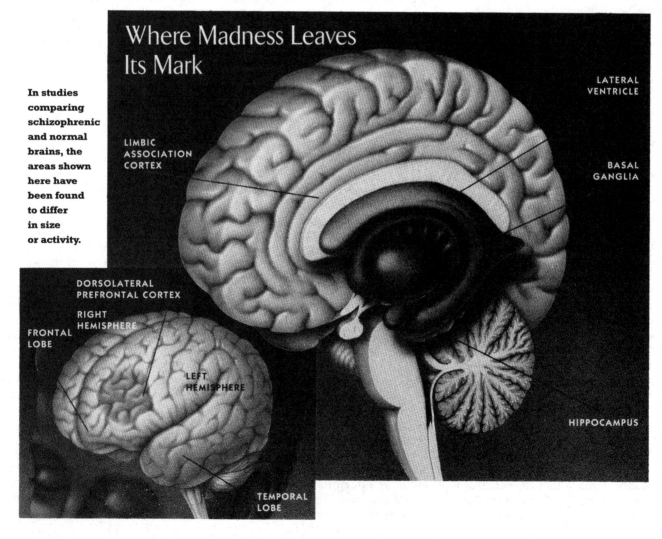

Where Madness Leaves Its Mark

In studies comparing schizophrenic and normal brains, the areas shown here have been found to differ in size or activity.

LIMBIC ASSOCIATION CORTEX

LATERAL VENTRICLE

BASAL GANGLIA

DORSOLATERAL PREFRONTAL CORTEX

RIGHT HEMISPHERE

FRONTAL LOBE

LEFT HEMISPHERE

HIPPOCAMPUS

TEMPORAL LOBE

the basal ganglia, acorn-size cell clusters lying beneath the ventricles at the brain's center. The ganglia are action integrators—if you're a catcher, they help you get the mitt between the fastball and your groin—but in seven out of seven schizophrenics (in contrast to their well twins) the basal ganglia mysteriously "lit up," even when they were resting.

Using such scans, Torrey's Washington team made another intriguing discovery. When they challenged twins to sort playing cards by suit, number, or color, they found that the schizophrenics not only did worse than the normals but also failed to activate a region—technically known as the dorsolateral prefrontal cortex, or DLPFC—within the frontal lobe. This region, says Daniel Weinberger, a psychiatrist collaborating with Torrey, is critical to performing complicated tasks and thinking well-ordered thoughts: "It's highly evolved and serves perhaps more than anything else as a hall-

mark of the human brain." What's more, this year, by comparing the blood-flow scans with MRI data, the team showed that poor DLPFC activation correlated with small hippocampus size. For the first time in the history of schizophrenia research, a functional deficit in one brain area was linked to an anatomical defect in another.

That seems to imply, says Torrey, that schizophrenia is not simply a disorder of particular areas in the brain, but a breakdown—most likely on the brain's left side—in the connections between them. And it so happens that the DLPFC, the hippocampus, the emotion-regulating limbic system, and the basal ganglia are all part of what's known as the brain's dopamine network. Dopamine is a neurotransmitter, and almost all the drugs for treating schizophrenia's symptoms are now known to block dopamine receptors. In the dopamine network, too little activity in one area could lead to overactivity in another. A DLPFC that's too quiet,

Weinberger speculates, "may disinhibit the limbic system and lead to the florid, inappropriate emotionality seen in many schizophrenics." In other words, if the Speaker of the House falls asleep, over-emotional congressmen may soon get out of control.

Of course, that still doesn't settle the question that launched Torrey and Gottesman's original bet: Are genes or a virus the main actor in schizophrenia? Although there's evidence for both, neither researcher is ready to call it a draw. The point is, says Gottesman, to what degree is each important? Could schizophrenia occur without a viral insult? Could there even be nongenetic cases?

"We must each push our theory as far as it will go," Gottesman insists. "If we don't try our darnedest to prove the other wrong, we'll never prove anything right. Is schizophrenia nine-tenths genetic, or one-twentieth? That's what we need to find out."

DEFEATING Depression

An array of new treatments combats the "common cold of mental illness"

Nancy Wartik

Nancy Wartik is a Contributing Editor at AMERICAN HEALTH.

For Charles Kennedy* of Princeton, N.J., the overwhelming sensation was a leaden slowness, as if a heavy weight were bearing down on him. Just beginning a competitive retraining program, the 51-year-old banker needed all his wits about him. Instead Kennedy found it harder and harder to function.

"Usually a challenge triggers my adrenaline," he says. "This time I found it difficult to respond. I couldn't understand the course assignments, much less complete them, which made me feel helpless and hopeless. Everything became very slow." At night Kennedy tossed and turned. He plodded through days in a pall of indifference. "The feeling was, 'Oh yeah, a bus is coming right at me. Should I move or not?' " he says. It was not until a therapist suggested he try an antidepressant drug that Kennedy found relief. "I could sleep better, proceed with initiative," he says. "My indifference disappeared. I became much more of a player again."

Everyone falls into the doldrums at times, or luxuriates in a bit of self-pity or melancholy. But depression is different. A mind-warping, energy-sapping malady, it unbalances the normal rhythms of the body and turns the psychic landscape bleak, robbing a person of vigor and hope. For someone afflicted with clinical (also called unipolar) depression, the sensations of sadness and loss, familiar to everyone on occasion, stretch into weeks or months. Nor does there seem to be an end in sight: Perhaps depression's worst torment is the conviction that things will never change. The depressed feel they will be mired in numbing despair forever.

The trappings of good fortune—wealth, talent or power—confer no immunity. "I am now the most miserable man living," wrote Abraham Lincoln. "If what I feel were equally distributed to the whole human family, there would not be one cheerful face on earth." Sir Winston Churchill, writer Sylvia Plath and actress Jean Seberg were similarly visited with bouts of despair. More recently, TV journalist Mike Wallace, author William Styron and talk show host Dick Cavett went public about their struggles with depression. Last summer, White House aide Vincent Foster committed suicide in the throes of depression apparently triggered by the Capitol Hill pressure cooker. Like Foster, 15% of those suffering from the more severe form of the disorder, which doctors call major depression, will ultimately take their own lives.

Not so long ago, the prevailing belief was that depressed people simply needed to pull themselves together and snap out of it. But an explosion of new research in recent decades has shown depression to be a real disorder that can be diagnosed and successfully treated. "Depression used to be viewed as some sort of moral weakness or personal failure," says Dr. Ewald Horwath, director of the intensive care unit at the New York State Psychiatric Institute in New York City. "Now there's more of a tendency to think of it as a disease, and that's a big improvement."

Most scientists think depression results from an interaction of biochemical, genetic and psychological factors, often, although not always, combined with a change in life circumstances—from the failure of a relationship to the loss of a job. In other words, depression is like many other diseases. "The factors that cause a physical illness such as coronary artery disease include diet, genetics and the way people who have a Type A personality put pressure on themselves," says Horwath. "Cultural factors influence who gets it, how frequent it is in each sex, and how prevalent it is in different epochs. It's the same kind of thing with depression."

Treatments for depression have expanded along with knowledge of its origins. There are now more than 20 antidepressants on the market, many of them "cleaner" drugs with fewer side effects than their predecessors. The most popular is the much-ballyhooed Prozac, already prescribed to more than 5 million Americans. Not that pills are the only antidote to depression: Cognitive psychotherapy, developed specifically to attack the disorder, teaches people how to correct the thought patterns that generate black moods. There's now evidence that regular exercise can alleviate more moderate cases of depression, perhaps because it increases levels of certain brain chemicals that mediate mood,

[*Real names are not used in this article.]

 From *American Health*, December 1993, pp. 38-45, 86. © 1993 by Nancy Wartik. Reprinted by permission.

and has arousing effects on body metabolism and energy. Victims of seasonal affective disorder, whose despondency comes and goes as the seasons change, often benefit from light therapy. And in some extreme cases of depression, electroconvulsive therapy, a much refined and milder form of the "shock therapy" first used here in the 1940s, can help when other treatments fail or would take too long—as when there is a likelihood of suicide. Through one or more of these treatments, the National Institute of Mental Health estimates that 80% to 90% of the depressed can find relief. As researchers sometimes say jokingly, today is the best time in history to feel miserable.

That's fortunate, because huge numbers of Americans do. More than 9 million people endure major depression yearly in this country, and about one in 20 will face the struggle at some point in his or her life. So ubiquitous is depression that researchers now refer to it as the "common cold of mental illness." And millions more are affected by other mood-related disorders. Victims of dysthymia, a recently identified form of chronic, milder depression, may battle gloom for years at a time. People with manic depression (also called bipolar disorder) veer dizzyingly between protracted emotional heights and depths, and cyclothymics go through less intense but more frequent ups and downs (see "Manic Depression: Not for Artists Only").

Many more women than men experience depression. Puberty is the dividing line: Before it, young boys and girls feel gloomy in almost equal numbers, but at adolescence, girls' depression rates begin to soar. At least twice as many women as men will fall prey to the disorder over the course of a lifetime, most studies have shown. Recent research by Johns Hopkins University psychiatrist Alan Romanoski paints an even more alarming picture: Although women and men have a similar risk of major depression, women suffer from more moderate depressions at *10 times* the rate men do. Researchers hotly debating the reason for this disparity have focused on three areas: physiological causes, such as genetic factors or hormonal imbalances; psychological factors, including differences in how men and women learn to deal with emotions; and social issues, from women's greater susceptibility to sexual abuse and battering to their lower economic status.

Sadly, the greatest obstacles to eliminating depression are ignorance and lack of understanding. For all its prevalence, and despite the many therapies available, two-thirds of those who have it don't get the help they need, often because they don't want to admit the problem or don't recognize its signs. "Many people who have major depression wouldn't even call themselves depressed," says psychiatrist A. John Rush of the University of Texas Southwestern Medical Center in Dallas. "If you ask them, 'Do you know you have clinical depression?'—depression serious enough to need treatment—they say, 'I don't know what that is.' " Trying to intervene in more cases, the Department of Health and Human Services (HHS) this year issued guidelines to alert general practitioners and other primary-care physicians to depression's warning signs.

As yet, there's no physical test to pinpoint the disease. Instead doctors look for a constellation of symptoms that persist for longer than two weeks (see "Are You Depressed?"). These include deep sadness or numbing apathy, a lack of interest in things that once brought pleasure—from sex to socializing—and at least four of seven other markers: appetite disturbances, sleep problems, fatigue, difficulty concentrating, undue restlessness or lethargy, feelings of worthlessness, or suicidal thoughts. (Someone mourning a death may have one or more of these symptoms for several months without necessarily being clinically depressed.) Many depressed people are also afflicted with vague physi-

Exercise can alleviate moderate cases.

cal symptoms or complaints. "They come into the doctor's office with stomachaches or joint pain, or they feel blah," says Dr. Rush. "Many of these patients turn out to have major depression." Untreated, the disorder typically lasts for six months or longer.

Researchers now know several risk factors that raise a person's vulnerability to depression, including a family history of the disorder. Research with twins has provided evidence that depression's roots are at least partially inherited. A 1992 study of more than 1,000 pairs of female twins showed that if one identical twin (who shares all of her sister's genes) suffered major depression, the other's risk was 66% higher than that of someone from the general population. If a fraternal twin was depressed, however, her twin (who is no more genetically similar to her than any other sibling) had a risk only 27% higher. While such statistics suggest genetics play a significant role in depression, Medical College of Virginia psychiatrist Kenneth Kendler, who conducted the study, notes that "depression isn't something you inherit 100%, as you do eye color or height. It's probably about 40% influenced by your genes."

Inheritance may also influence certain personality traits that can make a person depression-prone. Some researchers now argue for the existence of a syndrome—at least partially innate—known as depressive personality disorder, which predisposes those who have it to depression problems. People with this disorder, explains psychiatrist Robert Hirschfeld of the University of Texas Medical Branch in Galveston, tend to be pessimistic and brooding, critical of themselves and others. The probability that such individuals will develop clinical depression is correspondingly higher than the average person's.

Genetics or personality structure may prime a person for depression, but life's travails often play a marked role in pushing someone over the brink. Although some people fall into depressions with no apparent cause, the experience of Angela Wolf* is more typical. A vice president at a Manhattan marketing firm, she plunged into paralyzing despair after she discovered that her husband of 16 years was cheating on her. She was unable to work efficiently or sleep soundly; she cried often and paced restlessly. Not until a friend referred her to a cognitive therapist did Wolf realize what was happening to her. "It was a relief when he told me I was depressed," she says. "I could say, 'No wonder! So there's a reason I feel this way.' "

A growing body of research supports the idea that major depressions are often triggered by stressful events of the kind Wolf experienced. A study of 680 pairs of female

Manic Depression: Not for Artists Only

At age 22, Susan Dime-Meenan started her own court reporting company. By 27, she nearly bankrupted it. During one two-month period, she traveled to Los Angeles from Chicago more than 30 times, just for lunch. There was the time she charged $27,000 in clothing purchases on a corporate credit card. Then the 4'10" Dime-Meenan stopped eating and dropped down to 68 pounds. But it wasn't until she told her husband the FBI was trailing her that her family finally took action.

The night they committed her to a psychiatric ward was among the worst of Dime-Meenan's life, but it marked the start of her recovery from an illness that had long gone undiagnosed. "At first I didn't take it very well when they told me I was manic-depressive," says Dime-Meenan, now 38 and executive director of the Chicago-based National Depressive and Manic-Depressive Association. "But the head of the nursing staff showed me a description of manic depression in a medical dictionary, and when I read it, I knew immediately that I was a textbook case."

Some 2 to 3 million Americans, equal numbers of men and women, have the mood disorder known as manic depression, or bipolar illness. The disorder tends to strike early in life: Many manic-depressives first experience symptoms in adolescence. Manic depression manifests itself in different forms: Some patients, like Dime-Meenan, endure manic (high-energy) episodes mostly, others experience mostly depressions, and still others career equally between the two extremes. Many people have symptoms of both mania and depression at the same time.

In a manic state, people feel either intensely irritable or euphoric. They may experience racing thoughts and speech, poor judgment, feelings of grandeur, less need for sleep or a sense of boundless energy; at its extremes, mania can produce hallucinations and delusions. Untreated, mania lasts an average of one to three months, while periods of depression last six to nine months. Cyclothymia resembles a milder form of bipolar disorder, marked by brief, less drastic mood swings over a period of at least two years. A significant number of cyclothymics later become manic-depressives.

While the depressive phase of bipolar illness looks the same as major depression, researchers still don't understand the underlying link between the two. Genetic influences figure much more strongly in manic than in ordinary depression, and an intensive effort is now under way to find the gene responsible for bipolar disorder. The disease clearly runs in families: Like his father, Ernest Hemingway was a manic-depressive (and, like his father, he committed suicide). One of the writer's sons also has the disorder.

That Hemingway's talent coexisted with his illness was probably no coincidence. A number of studies link manic depression to creativity. In her book *Touched With Fire: Manic-Depressive Illness and the Artistic Temperament,* Johns Hopkins psychologist Kay Redfield Jamison estimates that rates of manic depresson and cyclothymia are 10 to 40 times higher among artists than the general public. "People with manic depression have faster, most fluid thinking, high energy levels and a wide range of emotional experience to draw on, from elation to despair," says Dr. Jamison. "Artists have to go where others won't, emotionally speaking, and manic-depressives do that automatically." Writer Virginia Woolf had bipolar illness: "I can't fight [this terrible disease] any longer," she wrote before drowning herself at age 59. Mark Twain, probably a cyclothymic, referred to his "periodical and sudden changes in mood." Jamison adds that there's some evidence bipolar disorders occur at elevated rates among movers and shakers: Broadcasting magnate Ted Turner is among those who've spoken about battling mood disorders.

Today, two-thirds of manic-depressives go untreated, but if ignored, says Jamison, the disease tends to worsen. Many manic-depressives develop substance abuse problems and an estimated 15% to 20% eventually commit suicide. With ongoing treatment—in particular the drug lithium and certain anticonvulsants—up to 80% of those with manic depression significantly improve.

Treatment turned Dime-Meenan's life around: "I've never had a day without medication in 10 years," she says, "and some days are still better than others. Some days the illness wins. But only for a day. The disease isn't controlling my life anymore. I won't let it."

twins, published this year in *The American Journal of Psychiatry,* ranked the importance of nine risk factors for serious depression, including recent upsetting events, genetics, lack of social support, traumas suffered over a lifetime (for example, rape or sexual abuse), and childhood loss of a parent. Of all the variables, recent stress—divorce, illness, legal troubles, bereavement—was the best predictor of a depressive episode. A family history of the disorder ranked second. Similarly, Dr. Romanoski's study, based on data gathered from 800 Baltimore residents, found that 86% of major depressions were precipitated by a real-life event or situation. This research contradicts a prevailing belief that depressions triggered by an identifiable event aren't really illnesses and don't need professional treatment. "Just because we can understand why a person is depressed doesn't mean we shouldn't treat the problem seriously," says psychiatrist Sidney Zisook of the University of California at San Diego. "Depression can develop a life of its own, and once it does, it needs to be addressed, because it's still associated with decreased functioning and suicide."

Painful experiences in early life can also sow the seeds of future gloom. A 1991 Stanford University study attributed up to 35% of the discrepancy between male and female depression rates to sexual abuse of women in childhood. Other research suggests that growing up in the wake of a divorce may also predispose a person to depression. Such trauma may literally be etched into a young brain, some scientists speculate. "Life experiences might create enduring changes in the central nervous system," says Horwath, "and that might alter neurochemistry and place the person at higher risk for depression. The environmental factor ultimately has a biological effect."

Studies have long linked alcoholism and depression, but it's not always clear which is cause and which is effect. Logic would suggest that people in pain drink to ease their sorrow. Yet many studies show that people who are already alcoholic—men in particular—go on to develop major depression, perhaps because high levels of prolonged intoxication eventually unbalance brain chemistry. For women, the cause-and-effect pattern tends to go the other way, although researchers aren't sure why as yet.

No matter what its origins are, the neurochemistry of despair is the same. Imbalances of certain mood-regulating neurotransmitters—chemical messengers that transmit electrochemical signals between brain cells—are thought to underlie depression at its most fundamental level. Among possible scenarios of what goes awry in the brain: Levels of the neurotransmitters that control mood may be abnormally low, or the neural receptors that normally intercept neurotransmitters as they pass from cell to cell may malfunction.

Scientists have so far identified about 100 of the brain's many neurotransmitters. Two of these, norepinephrine and serotonin, appear to be most closely tied to depression. Says psychiatrist Elliott Richelson, director of research at a branch of the Mayo Clinic in Jacksonville, Fla., "It could be that changes in norepinephrine or serotonin levels affect some other neurotransmitter more directly involved in depression. There are probably at least 100 neurotransmitters we haven't even identified yet, so it's highly possible we still have to find the one that's absolutely key in regulating depression."

Antidepressants, which correct brain chemistry imbalances, have been on the market for over 30 years. Some early ones—specifically the tricyclic drugs, such as imipramine—affect neurochemicals other than serotonin and norepinephrine, causing a wide range of potential side effects, including dry mouth, weight gain and drowsiness. Other early antidepressants, the so-called monoamine oxidase (MAO) inhibitors, are inconvenient to take: Patients must avoid cheese, wine and a long list of other foods containing a chemical that reacts with the drug and can send blood pressure soaring. More targeted medications that act solely on mood-regulating neurotransmitters are generally easier on patients' systems. For example, Prozac and another relatively new drug, Zoloft, act only on serotonin. Fewer side effects combined with tales of miracle cures have made these new drugs more popular than the previous generations of antidepressants, which may nonetheless work as well or better in some people.

Researchers estimate that about 75% of those suffering from major depression can benefit from one of these medications. "In the last decade, there's been a shift toward using antidepressants, and I think that's good," says Brown University psychologist Tracie Shea. "They can be extremely helpful when depression has started to affect functioning. Pills don't solve life's problems, but they can put people in a better position to solve the problems themselves. They give people the energy to look at issues going on in their lives, and that gives them more choice and control."

This sort of talk alarms some mental health professionals, who worry that antidepressants are turning into the latest pharmaceutical fad, used in ever milder cases of the blues, rather than for the severe disorders they were developed to treat. "I'm not saying they should never be used," says Dr. Roger Greenberg, a psychologist at the State University of New York Health Science Center in Syracuse, "but I'm concerned at the promise being held out for drugs. I think people should be more cautious about taking them than they have

About 75% can benefit from medication.

been up to now. We want quick and easy solutions for complex and difficult problems—it's a fast-food kind of mentality. Drugs have a natural appeal, they help people say, 'I'm not responsible for my actions, it's my body chemistry.'"

Psychiatrist Peter Kramer, author of the best-selling book *Listening to Prozac,* views drug treatment differently. "There's an idea that there's a moral price to be paid if you're on medication, and that it's better to do things by other means. Is it more comfortable and easier to believe that disorders can be treated through honesty and hard work? Yes. But if you have someone in front of you who's suffering, you have to be realistic about choosing the best way to alleviate their pain."

Patients who've benefited from antidepressants tend to agree with Dr. Kramer. Charlotte Goldberg*, 30, of New York City was plagued by depression after she separated from her husband and switched careers. Yet she had reservations about trying an antidepressant. "I was very hesitant," she recalls. "I was afraid I'd become falsely happy, that it wouldn't really be me. It bothered me to think of being chemically altered." But after she began taking Zoloft, Goldberg changed her mind: "I feel good but not in a stupid, high way," she says. "I can think more clearly, I'm calmer, not as anxious. Being less moody and having more energy has helped me to work through my problems better."

In sum, antidepressants can often restore emotional and physical equilibrium, but they don't make people euphoric or eliminate life stresses. After reviewing more than 400 clinical trials of antidepressants, a panel of distinguished researchers who developed the HHS depression treatment guidelines concluded that "no one antidepressant is clearly more effective than another. No single medication results in remission for all patients." Only 50% to 60% of patients respond to the first drug they try; the rest need to experiment until they find a drug that works for them. Moreover, for reasons researchers still don't understand, it usually takes four to six weeks before patients begin to feel the medication's full effects.

When the HHS guidelines were issued, the American Psychological Association, whose members specialize in talk therapy, issued a press release disassociating the organization from the guidelines on the grounds that they "do not encourage sufficient collaboration with mental health specialists and appear to be biased toward medication." In fact, says Rush of Texas Southwestern Medical Center, who chaired the government panel, 60% of antidepressants are now distributed by primary-care doctors, meaning that many people already take the drugs without accompanying psychotherapy. Some experts see no problem with that. "For the severely depressed patient, I don't think talk therapy is helpful," says the Mayo Clinic's Richelson. "The folks I see are really ill, and they're not going to be helped by the addition of a 50-minute hour."

Still, when the HHS panel compared the efficacy of talk therapy *and* medication with drug treatment alone, they found the combination treatment to be somewhat more ef-

Are You Depressed?

	0-Not at all	1-Somewhat	2-Moderately	3-A lot
Sadness: Have you been feeling sad or down in the dumps?				
Discouragement: Does the future look hopeless?				
Low self-esteem: Do you feel worthless or think of yourself as a failure?				
Inferiority: Do you feel inadequate or inferior to others?				
Guilt: Do you get self-critical and blame yourself for everything?				
Indecisiveness: Do you have trouble making up your mind about things?				
Irritability and frustration: Have you been feeling resentful and angry a good deal of the time?				
Loss of interest in life: Have you lost interest in your career, your hobbies, your family or your friends?				
Loss of motivation: Do you feel overwhelmed and have to push yourself hard to do things?				
Poor self-image: Do you think you're looking old or unattractive?				
Appetite changes: Have you lost your appetite, or do you overeat or binge compulsively?				
Sleep changes: Do you suffer from insomnia and find it hard to get a good night's sleep, or are you excessively tired and sleeping too much?				
Loss of libido: Have you lost your interest in sex?				
Hypochondriasis: Do you worry a great deal about your health?				
Suicidal impulses*: Do you have thoughts that life is not worth living or think you might be better off dead?				

After you have completed the test, add up your total score. It will be somewhere between 0 and 45. Use the key at right to interpret your score.

*Anyone with suicidal urges should seek immediate consultation with a qualified psychiatrist or psychologist.

From *The Feeling Good Handbook,* © 1989 by David D. Burns, M.D. Reprinted by permission of William Morrow.

Total score	Degree of depression
0-4	Minimal or none
5-10	Borderline
11-20	Mild
21-30	Moderate
31-45	Severe

fective. And a number of studies show that in less severe depressions psychotherapy by itself may work just as well as antidepressants. "My hunch is that whatever drugs are doing to brain chemistry, effective therapy can do also," notes Vanderbilt University clinical psychologist Steven Hollon, a specialist in cognitive therapy. "You're changing an attitude and that changes biology—just as biology changes attitude. I think the two are interactive processes."

A 1989 National Institute of Mental Health study of people with mild to moderate depressions found therapy to be as successful as medication in helping patients recover over a 16-week period. Overall, research suggests that some 50% of the depressed can alleviate the symptoms of depression with either cognitive therapy or other types.

Cognitive therapy was developed in the '60s by psychiatrist Aaron Beck, now at the University of Pennsylvania. Its premise is that thoughts create feelings: Change destructive ideas, Beck said, and unhappy emotions will change too. One such destructive pattern is a tendency to blame oneself exclusively when something goes wrong. Explains Dr. Hollon, "Someone who loses his job and says, 'I'm not good enough,' is more likely to get depressed than someone who says, 'It's a lousy economy and Bill Clinton is to blame.' "

The inclination to brood rather than act on difficulties is another pattern believed to be self-defeating and one that might help explain some of the male-female disparity in depression rates. When Stanford University psychologist Susan Nolen-Hoeksema reviewed the literature, she was struck by the fact that "women generally seem to stay with negative emotions, like depression or anxiety, more than men do. It's often talked of as a woman's strength to be able to acknowledge negative emotions, but I started looking at how it works against them."

Dr. Nolen-Hoeksema concluded that people who obsessively ponder a problem and its negative implications can find themselves sucked into a vicious circle of gloom. Those who distract themselves with sports or other enjoyable activities—as many men seem to do instinctively—emerge from unhappy moods faster and in a better state to tackle problems. Why do women tend to be brooders and men doers? "One of our guesses is that young boys aren't allowed to ruminate," says Nolen-Hoeksema. "They're taught to be active from an early age. Research on preschoolers seems to show that one thing parents will not tolerate is emotionality in boys. It's also possible that the things girls worry about actually are harder to deal with than the things boys worry about. Girls think a lot more about interpersonal relationships than boys do, and those are hard to control."

The logic behind cognitive therapy may sound simplistic, but it boasts many enthusiastic converts. Angela Wolf, the woman whose depression was triggered by her husband's infidelities, says cognitive therapy saved her life. " I was assaulted by automatic negative thoughts and my therapist would have me try to prove them to myself, the way you would to a jury. I'd think, 'If I leave this marriage, no man will ever be attracted to me.' Then I'd have to write down why I thought that statement was true, and also why I thought it wasn't. Inevitably, I'd wind up proving it *wasn't* true." Now divorced, Wolf says, "I'm infinitely happier today."

One particularly controversial issue among scientists who debate the merits of psychological vs. drug treatments is recurrence: At least 50% of those who suffer an attack will experience another. "Our whole concept of the disorder is shifting from thinking of it as time-limited to recognizing that it's much more chronic than we thought," says Brown's Dr. Shea. "For many people, depression won't be a one-shot deal." She adds that a few months of treatment with drugs or therapy, until fairly recently considered standard, often aren't enough to keep a patient well: "People shouldn't think of depression as something that can necessarily be cured in 16 weeks."

Therapy proponents argue that patients have a better chance of staying depression-free over time if they learn psychological techniques to help ward off relapses. "Pharmacology [drug therapy] is marvelous," says Hollon, "but it mostly suppresses symptoms. It's like taking aspirin. If you want to take it every day, it will do a very good job of stopping your headache. But if you learn to meditate and you reduce your overall stress level, maybe you won't get headaches to begin with. In that sense, cognitive therapy may be analogous to learning to meditate."

In a recent study published in the *Archives of General Psychiatry,* Hollon and colleague Mark Evans, a University of Minnesota psychologist, found that about 75% of depressed people in each of two groups treated either with medication or cognitive therapy felt well enough to stop treatment after three months. But over the next two years, 50% of those treated with medication relapsed into depressions, while only 20% of those treated with therapy did.

A growing number of doctors, however, are dealing with the threat of recurrence by keeping patients on medication for much longer periods of time—in some instances, many years beyond the six to nine months typically allotted for treating an episode of depression. Some 90% of those who stay on antidepressants remain symptom-free, but it has yet to be seen if prolonged antidepressant use carries undiscovered risks. "I'm a little nervous about the amount of time people are kept on drugs these days," says Hollon. "There probably aren't any really nasty complications lurking out there, but we're mucking around with complex physiology. You always wonder about the risk of side effects."

Clearly, there are complex questions remaining about depression that can only be answered through years of research. One point, however, is clear: Today, no one need stoically endure the lethargy and sense of futility that descend with an episode of depression. "I don't think long-term suffering is very therapeutic," sums up Dr. Zisook of UC-San Diego. "It doesn't help someone become a better person. And it's not something that people need to go through when we have treatments for it."

For more information on mood disorders, contact the following organizations: D/ART (Depression Awareness, Recognition, and Treatment), 800-421-4211; the National Depressive and Manic-Depressive Association, 800-826-3632; and the Depression and Related Affective Disorders Association, 410-955-4647.

Patterns of Abuse

Two million women are beaten every year, one every 16 seconds. Who's at risk, why does violence escalate—and when should a woman fear for her life?

THE STORIES SPILL OUT FROM BEhind bedroom walls and onto the front pages. Back in 1983, before talk shows dissolved into daily confessionals, actor David Soul offered up the stunning admission that he'd abused his wife, Patti. Two years later, John Fedders, the chief regulator of the Securities and Exchange Commission, resigned after he acknowledged that he'd broken his wife's eardrum, wrenched her neck and left her with black eyes and bruises. In 1988, the nation sat mesmerized by Hedda Nussbaum and her testimony about being systematically beaten by her companion, a brooding New York lawyer named Joel Steinberg, who also struck the blows that killed their adopted daughter, Lisa. Now America is riveted again, this time by the accumulating evidence of O. J. Simpson's brutality against his wife, Nicole. Yet, for all the horror, there is a measure of futility in these tales: one moment, they ignite mass outrage; then the topic fades from the screen.

Americans often shrug off domestic violence as if it were no more harmful than Ralph Kramden hoisting a fist and threatening: "One of these days, Alice . . . Pow! Right in the kisser!" But there's nothing funny about it—and the phenomenon of abuse is just as complicated as it is common. About 1,400 women are killed by their husbands, ex-husbands and boyfriends each year and about 2 million are beaten—on average, one every 16 seconds. Although some research shows women are just as likely as men to start a fight, Justice Department figures released last February reveal that women are the victims 11 times more often than men. Battering is also a problem among gay couples: the National Coalition on Domestic Violence estimates that almost one in three same-sex relationships are abusive, seemingly more than among heterosexual couples. But violence against women is so entrenched that in 1992 the U.S. Surgeon General ranked abuse by husbands and partners as the leading cause of injuries to women aged 15 to 44. Despite more hot lines and shelters and heightened awareness, the number of assaults against women has remained about the same over the last decade.

A disturbing double standard also remains. "If O. J. Simpson had assaulted Al Cowlings nine times and if A.C. called the police, O.J. couldn't have told them, 'This is a family matter'," says Mariah Burton Nelson, author of the book "The Stronger Women Get the More Men Love Football." "Hertz and NBC would have dropped him and said, 'This man has a terrible problem.' But family violence is accepted as no big deal." New York University law professor Holly Maguigan says wife-beating was actually once sanctioned by the so-called Rule of Thumb—English common law, first cited in America in an 1824 Mississippi Supreme Court decision, that said a man could physically chastise his wife as long as the stick he used was no wider than his thumb. Even now, Maguigan says, "we're not very far removed from a time when the criminal-justice system saw its task as setting limits on the amount of force a man could use, instead of saying that using force against your wife is a crime."

Changing attitudes is difficult. Although advocacy groups are already claiming that Nicole Simpson's case can do for spousal abuse what Rock Hudson did for AIDS and Anita Hill did for sexual harassment, that may be more rhetoric than reality; there is great ambivalence about family violence. Americans cling to a "zone of privacy"—the unwritten code that a man's home is his castle and what happens inside should stay there. It helps explain why, in some states, a man who strikes his wife is guilty only of a misdemeanor, but if he attacks a stranger, it's a felony. It helps explain why a woman can walk away from a friend who says she got her black eye walking into a door. And it helps explain why men retreat when a buddy dismisses brutality as the ups and downs that "all" marriages go through.

So many look away because they don't know what constitutes domestic violence. Who's a victim? Who's an abuser? Most people believe that, unless a woman looks as pathetic as Hedda Nussbaum did—her nose flattened, her face swollen—she couldn't possibly be a victim. And despite highly publicized cases of abuse, celebrity still bestows credibility. What's more, it's hard for many to comprehend how anything short of daily brutality can be wife-beating. Even Nicole's sister fell into the trap. "My definition of a battered woman is somebody who gets beat up all the time," Denise Brown told The New York Times last week. "I don't want people to think it was like that. I know Nicole. She was a very strong-willed person. If she was beaten up, she wouldn't have stayed with him. That wasn't her." Or was it? The patterns of abuse—who's likely to be at risk, why women take action and when battering turns deadly—can often be surprising, as paradoxical as the fact that love can coexist with violence.

MICHELE INGRASSIA AND MELINDA BECK, WITH REPORTING BY GINNY CARROLL, NINA ARCHER BIDDLE, KAREN SPRINGEN, PATRICK ROGERS, JOHN MCCORMICK, JEANNE GORDON, ALLISON SAMUELS AND MARY HAGER.

WHO IS MOST AT RISK

EXPERTS USED TO THINK THAT BATTERED WOMEN WERE "asking for it"—somehow masochistically provoking abuse from their men. Mercifully, that idea has now been discredited. But researchers do say that women who are less educated, unemployed, young and poor may be more likely to have abusive relationships than others. Pregnant women seem to make particular targets: according to one survey, approximately one in six is abused; another survey cites one in three. There are other common characteristics: "Look for low self-esteem, a background in an abusive family, alcohol and drug abuse, passivity in relationships, dependency, isolation and a high need for approval, attention and affection," says psychologist Robert Geffner, president of the Family Violence and Sexual Assault Institute in Tyler, Texas. "The more risk factors a woman has, the more likely she is to become a candidate."

But not all women fit that profile: statistically, one woman in four will be physically assaulted by a partner or ex-partner during her lifetime, so it's not surprising that abuse cuts across racial, ethnic, religious and socioeconomic lines. "I'm treating physicians, attorneys, a judge and professors who are, or were, battered women," says Geffner. "Intelligent people let this happen, too. What goes on inside the home does not relate to what's outside."

And what's outside is often deceiving. Dazzling blond Nicole Simpson didn't look like someone who could have low self-esteem. But she met O.J. when she was just 18, and devoted herself to being his wife. In her 1992 divorce papers, she claimed that O.J. forced her to quit junior college and be with him all the time. She

Ten Risk Factors

Previous domestic violence is the highest risk factor for future abuse. Homes with two of these others show twice as much violence as those with none. In those with seven or more factors, the violence rate is 40 times higher.

- **Male unemployed**
- **Male uses illicit drugs at least once each year**
- **Male and female have different religious backgrounds**
- **Male saw father hit mother**
- **Male and female cohabit and are not married**
- **Male has blue-collar occupation, if employed**
- **Male did not graduate from high school**
- **Male is between 18 and 30 years of age**
- **Male or female use severe violence toward children in home**
- **Total family income is below the poverty line**

SOURCE: RISK-MARKERS OF MEN WHO BATTER, A 1994 ANALYSIS BY RICHARD J. GELLES, REGINA LACKNER AND GLENN D. WOLFNER

Striking a wife can be a misdemeanor while hitting a stranger is a felony

said she'd do anything to keep him from being angry: "I've always told O.J. what he wants to hear. I've always let him . . . it's hard to explain." For all their jet-setting, she was isolated—and reluctant to discuss what was happening at home, even though some friends say they had known. "She would wear unsuitable clothing to cover the bruises, or sunglasses to hide another shiner," says one. "She was trapped. She didn't have any training to do anything, and he knew that and he used it."

But even feisty women with their own careers can get involved with violent men. Earlier this month, Lisa (Left Eye) Lopes, a singer with the hip-hop group TLC, allegedly burned down the $800,000 home of her boyfriend, Atlanta Falcons' wide receiver Andre Rison. Police say the barely 5-foot, 100-pound Lopes appeared bruised and beaten when they arrived on the scene; friends say it was an open secret that she was abused. (Rison denies the allegations.) Curiously, the lyrics of Lopes's debut album are peppered with references about standing up to men: "I have my own control/I can't be bought or sold/ And I never have to do what I'm told . . ." Was that just a tough act to mask insecurity? Jacquelyn Campbell, a researcher in domestic violence at Johns Hopkins University, concludes that a woman's risk of being battered "has little to do with her and everything to do with who she marries or dates."

WHO BECOMES AN ABUSER

WHAT KIND OF MAN HEAPS PHYSICAL AND EMOTIONAL abuse on his wife? It's only in the last decade that researchers have begun asking. But one thing they agree on is the abuser's need to control. "There is no better way of making people compliant than beating them up on an intermittent basis," says Richard Gelles, director of the Family Violence Research Program at the University of Rhode Island. Although Gelles says men who have less education and are living close to the poverty line are more likely to be abusers, many white-collar men—doctors, lawyers and accountants—also beat their partners.

"Amy," a 50-year-old Colorado woman, spent 23 years married to one of them. Her husband was an attorney, well heeled, well groomed, a pillar of the community. She says he hit her, threw her down the stairs, tried to run her over. "One night in Vail, when he had one of his insane fits, the police came and put him in handcuffs," says Amy, who asked that her real name not be used. "My arms were still red from where he'd trapped them in the car window, but somehow, he talked his way out of it." Lenore Walker, director of the Domestic Violence Institute in Denver, sees the pattern all the time. "It's like Jekyll and Hyde—wonderful one minute, dark and terrifying the next."

Indiana University psychologist Amy Holtzworth-Munroe divides abusers into three behavioral types. The majority of men who hit their wives do so infrequently and their violence doesn't escalate. They look ordinary, and they're most likely to feel remorse after an attack. "When they use violence, it reflects some lack of communication skills, combined with a dependence on the wife," she says.

A second group of men are intensely jealous of their wives and fear abandonment. Most likely, they grew up with psychological and sexual abuse. Like those in the first group, these men's dependence on their wives is as important as their need to control them—if she even talks to another man, "he thinks she's leaving or sleeping around," says Holtzworth-Munroe. The smallest—and most dangerous—group encompasses men with an antisocial personality disorder. Their battering fits into a larger pattern of violence and getting in trouble with the law. Neil S. Jacobson, a marital therapist at the University of Washington, likens such men to serial murderers. Rather than becoming more agitated during an attack, he says, they become calmer, their heart rates drop. "They're like cobras. They're just like criminals who beat up anybody else when they're not getting what they want."

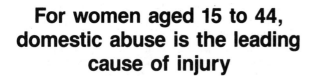

For women aged 15 to 44, domestic abuse is the leading cause of injury

Men who batter share something else: they deny what they've done, minimize their attacks and always blame the victims. Evan Stark, codirector of the Domestic Violence Training Project in New Haven, Conn., was intrigued by Simpson's so-called suicide note. "He never takes responsibility for the abuse. These are just marital squabbles. Then he blames her—'I felt like a battered husband'." Twenty-nine-year-old "Fidel" once felt the same way. When he began getting counseling in Houston's Pivot Project, he blamed everyone else for his violence—especially his new wife, who, he discovered, was pregnant by another man. "When I came here, I couldn't believe I had a problem," he says. "I always thought of myself as a well-mannered person."

Avoiding Abuse

Battered women use a range of desperate methods to discourage partners from injuring them, from running away to fighting back.

STRATEGIES USED BY WOMEN TO END SEVERE SPOUSAL VIOLENCE	
Avoid him or avoid certain topics	69%
Talking him out of it	59
Get him to promise no more violence	57
Threaten to get a divorce	54
Physically fight back	52
Hide or go away	37
Threaten to call the police	36
Leave home for two or more days	32

SOURCE: INTIMATE VIOLENCE, BY RICHARD J. GELLES AND MURRAY A. STRAUS (DATA FROM A 1985 STUDY)

WHY WOMEN STAY

IT LOOKS SO SIMPLE FROM THE OUTSIDE. MANY WOMEN THINK that if a mate ever hit them, they'd pack up and leave immediately. But women who have been in abusive relationships say it isn't that easy. The violence starts slowly, doesn't happen every day and by the time a pattern has emerged there may be children, and financial and emotional bonds that are difficult to break. "I know when I took my marriage vows, I meant 'for better or for worse'," G. L. Bundow, a South Carolina physician, wrote in The Journal of the American Medical Association, describing her own abusive relationship. "But when 'until death do us part' suddenly became a frightening reality, I was faced with some terrifying decisions."

With more women working and greater availability of shelters, financial dependence is less of a factor than it used to be. The emotional dependence is often stronger. "Women are trained to think that we can save these men, that they can change," says Angela Caputi, a professor of American Studies at the University of New Mexico. That mythology, she notes, is on full display in "Beauty and the Beast": the monster smashing furniture will turn into a prince if only the woman he's trapped will love him.

Many abusers *can* be charming—and abused women often fall for their softer side. Denver's Lenore Walker says there are three parts to the abuse cycle that are repeat over and over—a phase where tension is building and the woman tries desperately to keep the man calm; an explosion with acute battering, and then a period where the batterer is loving and contrite. "During this last phase, they listen to the woman, pay attention, buy her flowers—they become the ideal guy," Walker says. Geffner adds that in this part of the relationship, "they make love, the sex is good. And that also keeps them going."

Eventually, however, the repeated cycles wear women down until some are so physically and mentally exhausted that leaving is almost impossible. The man gradually takes control of the woman's psyche and destroys her ability to think clearly. Even the memory of past abuse keeps the woman in fear and in check. "You can't underestimate the terror and brainwashing that takes place in battering relationships," says psychiatrist Elaine Carmen of the Solomon Carter Fuller Mental Health Center in Boston. "She really comes to believe that she deserves the abuse and is incompetent."

WHEN WOMEN TAKE ACTION

THE TURNING POINT MAY COME WHEN A WOMAN CAN NO longer hide the scars and bruises. Or when her own financial resources improve, when the kids grow up—or when she begins to fear for their safety. Sometimes, neighbors hear screaming and call police—or a doctor challenges a woman's made-up story about how she got those broken ribs. "There are different moments of truth," says psychiatrist Carmen. "Acting on them partly depends on how safe it is to get up and leave." Walker says that women decide to get help when the pain of staying in a relationship outweighs the emotional, sexual or financial benefits.

For "Emma," a bank teller, the final straw came the day she returned from work to find that her husband hadn't mowed the lawn as she asked. "You promised me you'd mow the lawn," she said, then dropped the issue. Later they were seated calmly on the couch, when suddenly he was standing on the coffee table, coming down on her with his fists. He beat her into the wall until plaster fell down. "I was dragged through the house by my hair. At some point I began thinking I don't want to live anymore. If it hadn't been for this tiny voice in the background saying, 'Mama, please don't die,' I would have surrendered." Emma finally crawled to the car but couldn't see to drive, so her grandmother took her to the emergency room, where the doctor didn't believe her story about being mugged. "He said, 'You're not fine. You're bleeding internally. You've got a concussion.' He got a mirror and showed me my face. I looked like a monster in a

STOPPING ABUSE: WHAT WORKS

Can a man who batters his partner learn to stop? Can psychotherapy turn an abuser into a respectful companion? Specialized treatment programs have proliferated in recent years, most of them aimed at teaching wife–beaters to manage their anger. But abusive men tend to resist treatment, and there are no proven formulas for reforming them. "We don't have any research that tells us any particular intervention is effective in a particular situation," says Eve Lipchik, a private therapist in Milwaukee. "We have nothing to go on."

Some abusers are less treatable than others. Researchers have identified a hard core, perhaps 10 to 20 percent, who seem beyond the reach of therapy. Experts differ on how best to handle the rest, but they agree that abusers shouldn't be coddled, even if they have grown up as victims themselves. "These men need to be confronted," says New York psychologist Matthew Campbell, who runs a treatment program in Suffolk County. "Giving them TLC just endangers women. The man has to take full responsibility. He has to learn to say, 'I can leave. I can express upset. But I cannot be abusive'."

Some therapists favor counseling abusers and victims as couples, provided the beating has stopped and the relationship has a healthy dimension to build on. But couples therapy is controversial, especially among feminists. In fact, several states have outlawed it. "Couples therapy says to the victim, 'If you change, this won't happen'," says Campbell. "That's dangerous."

To avoid that message, most clinics deal exclusively with abusers, often having them confront each other in groups. During a typical session at Houston's Pivot Project, a private, not-for-profit counseling agency, batterers take turns recounting the past week's conflicts. (As a reminder that women aren't property, the participants must refer to their partners by name. Anyone using the phrase "my wife" has to hold a stuffed donkey.) As each man testifies, his peers offer criticism. Therapist Toby Myers says one client recently boasted that he had avoided punching his wife by ramming his fist through a wall. Instead of praising him, a counselor asked the other participants what message the gesture had sent to the man's wife. A group member's reply: "It says she better be careful or she's next."

There's no question that such exercises can change men's behavior. At the Domestic Abuse Project in Minneapolis, follow-up studies suggest that two out of three clients haven't battered their partners 18 months after finishing treatment. Unfortunately, few abusers get that far: Only half of the men who register at the Abuse Project show up, even though most are under court orders. And only half of those who start treatment see it through.

Drug treatment may someday provide another tool. Preliminary findings suggest that Prozac-style antidepressants, which enhance a brain chemical called serotonin, help curb some men's aggressiveness. Neither counseling nor drug treatment is a cure-all. "We need psychological services," says Campbell, the New York psychologist. "But services mean nothing without sanctions. Men need to know that if they don't change, they'll go to jail."

Not every abuser is sensitive to that threat. Dr. Roland Maiuro, director of the Harborview Anger Management and Domestic Violence Program in Seattle, notes that some men simply become more bitter—and more dangerous—after they're arrested. But until treatment becomes a surer science, keeping those men behind bars may be the best way to keep their victims alive.

GEOFFREY COWLEY *with* GINNY CARROLL *in Houston and bureau reports*

horror movie. It was the first time I recognized how bad things had gotten." For a while, though, life got even harder. "When I arrived in Chicago, I had two children, two suitcases and $1,500 in my pocket to start a new life." She found it running a coalition that provides shelter for more than 700 battered women.

When women do take action, it can run the gamut from calling a hot line, seeking counseling, filing for divorce or seeking a court order of protection. Often those measures soothe the abuser—but only temporarily. "They think he's changed. Then it starts three months later," says Chicago divorce attorney David Mattenson. Some women weaken, too: they may lock the doors, check the shadows—but still let him have the keys to the house. Emma herself briefly returned to her husband when he begged and pleaded. "The same week I went back, he was beating me again."

WHEN COPS AND COURTS STEP IN

BLUNTLY PUT, COPS HATE DOMESTIC CALLS—IN PART BEcause they are so unpredictable. A neighbor may simply report a disturbance and cops have no idea what they will find on the scene. The parties may have cooled down and be sitting in stony silence. Or one may be holding the other hostage, or the kids. Sometimes, warring spouses even turn on cops—which is why many police forces send them in pairs and tell them to maintain eye contact with each other at all times. But dangerous as family combat is, many cops still don't see such calls as real police work, says Jerome Storch, a professor of law and police science at John Jay College of Criminal Justice in New York. "There's this thing in the back of the [cops'] mind that it's a domestic matter, not criminal activity."

Many cities have started training programs to make police take domestic-violence calls more sensitively—and seriously. For several years, the San Diego Police Department has even used details of O. J. Simpson's 1989 arrest for spousal battery as an example to recruits not to be intimidated by a famous name or face. Laws requiring police to make arrests in domestic cases are on the books in 15 states. But compliance is another matter. Since 1979, New York City has had a mandatory-arrest law, which also requires cops to report every domestic call. Yet a 1993 study found that reports were filed in only 30 percent of approximately 200,000 annual domestic-violence calls, and arrests were made in only 7 percent of the cases. Many cops insist they need to be able to use their own judgment. "If there's a minor assault, are you going to make an arrest just because it's 'a domestic crime'?" asks Storch. "Then if you take it to court and the judge says, 'This is minor,' it's dismissed. If you place mandates on the police, you must place them on the courts."

Prosecutors are just as frustrated. Testimony is often his word against hers; defense attorneys scare off victims with repeated delays and many victims decline to cooperate or press charges. "When women call the police, they don't call because they want to prosecute," says Mimi Rose, chief of the Family Violence and Assault Unit at the Philadelphia District Attorney's Office. "They are scared and want the violence to stop. Ten days later when they get the subpoena to appear in court, the situation has changed. The idea of putting someone you live with in jail becomes impossible." Pressing charges is just the first step. The victim is faced with a range of potential legal remedies: orders of protection, criminal prosecution, family-court prosecution, divorce, a child-custody agreement. Each step is complex and time-consuming, requiring frequent court appearances by the victim—and the abuser, if he'll show up.

Courts around the country have made an effort to streamline the procedures; more than 500 bills on domestic violence were introduced in state legislatures last year, and 100 of them became law. In California alone, new bills are pending that would impose mandatory minimum jail sentences and long-term counseling for abusers, set up computer registries for restraining orders, ban abusers from carrying firearms, mandate training for judges—and even raise the "domestic-violence surcharge" on marriage licenses by $4 to be used for shelter services. On the national level, women's groups are pushing for the $1.8 million Violence Against Women act that would set up a national hot line, provide police training, toughen penalties and aid shelters and prevention programs. But those in the field say the question is whether the justice system can solve a highly complex social problem. "We need to rethink what we're doing," says Rose. "Prosecution isn't a panacea. It's like a tourniquet. We put it on when there is an emergency and we keep it on as long as necessary. But the question is, then what?"

WHEN ABUSE TURNS DEADLY

AFTER YEARS OF ABUSE, LEAVING IS OFTEN THE MOST dangerous thing a woman can do. Probably the first thing a battered wife learns in counseling is that orders of protection aren't bulletproof. Severing ties signals the abuser that he's no longer in control, and he often responds in the only way he knows how—by escalating the violence. Husbands threaten to "hunt them down and kill them," says Margaret Byrne, who directs the Illinois Clemency Project for Battered Women. One man, she recalled, told his wife he would find her shelter and burn it down, with her in it. "It's this male sense of entitlement—'If I can't have her, no one can'," says University of Illinois sociologist Pauline Bart. Friends claim O.J. made similar threats to Nicole.

Although conventional wisdom has it that women are most vulnerable in the first two years after they separate, researcher Campbell is suspicious of limiting danger to a particular time. Typically, she says, women report they're harassed for about a year after a breakup, "but we think the really obsessed guys remain that way much longer." In the last 16 years, the rate of homicides in domestic-abuse cases has actually gone down slightly—particularly for black women—according to an analysis of FBI data by James Fox, dean of

■

One third of women in prison for homicide have killed an intimate

the College of Criminal Justice at Northeastern University. Fox is not certain why. "More and more women are apparently getting out of a relationship before it's too late."

Or perhaps women are getting to the family gun first. While studying some 22,000 Chicago murders since 1965, researcher Carolyn Block of the Illinois Criminal Justice Information Authority discovered that among black couples, women were more likely to kill men in domestic-abuse situations than the other way round. In white relationships, by contrast, only about 25 percent of the victims were male. Nationwide, about one third of the women in prison for homicide have killed an intimate, according to the Bureau of Justice Statistics. While judges and juries are increasingly sympathetic to "Burning Bed" tales of longtime abuse, the vast majority don't get off.

Getting Help

These national information and referral centers handle domestic-violence calls from male and female victims as well as abusers, whether gay or straight. Or contact local mental-health organizations.

■ **National Victim Center**
1-800-FYI-CALL

■ **National Coalition Against Domestic Violence**
303-839-1852

Whatever the numbers, men and women kill their partners for very different reasons. For men, it's usually an escalation of violence. For women, killing is often the last resort. "The woman who is feisty and strong would have left," says Geffner. "The one who murders her husband is squashed, terrified by, 'You're never going to get away from me, I'm going to take the kids.' There's nothing left for her. To protect herself or her kids, she ends up killing the batterer."

WHAT HAPPENS TO THE KIDS

THE CHILDREN OF O.J. AND NICOLE SIMPSON WERE REPORTEDLY with their maternal grandparents in Orange County, Calif., last week, riding their bikes and playing with cousins on the beach. Sydney, 9, and Justin, 5, know their mother is dead, but they reportedly have not been told that their father has been charged in her murder. Even if their family unplugs the TV and hides the newspapers, the scars may already be too deep.

"The worst thing that can happen to kids is to grow up in an abusive family," says Gelles. Research has shown that children reared amid violence risk more problems in school and an increased likelihood of drug and alcohol abuse. And, of course, they risk repeating the pattern when they become parents. Former surgeon general C. Everett Koop says domestic violence is often three-generational: in families in which a grandparent is abused, the most likely assailant is the daughter—who's likely to be married to a man who abuses her. Together, they abuse their children. "If you are going to break the chain," Koop says, "you have to break it at the child level."

The effects of violence can play out in many ways. Some boys get angry when they watch their father beat their mother, as Bill Clinton did as a teenager. Other children rebel and withdraw from attachment. All of them, says Northwestern University child psychiatrist David Zinn, suffer by trying to hide their family's dirty little secret. As a result, they feel isolated and unlike other kids. Sadly, it's a good bet the Simpsons' children will never again feel like everyone else. "The worst of all tragedies is to become social orphans—they lost their mother through a horrific crime and now their father has been turned into Mephistopheles," says Gelles. It's difficult enough for any child to overcome the legacy of domestic violence; having it play out on a national stage may make it all but impossible.

THE IMMUNE SYSTEM VS.
STRESS

Psychological distress can suppress the body's defenses to the point of inducing physical illness.

Paul L. DeVito

Dr. DeVito is chairman, Department of Psychology, Saint Joseph's University, Philadelphia, Pa.

A COLLEGE student suffers from a strep throat infection while studying for final exams. A corporate executive loses her voice prior to an important presentation to stockholders. A high school senior wakes up with a horrible headache on the morning of the prom. Both parents come down with the flu after several sleepless nights with their sick child. Virtually everyone has experienced similar reactions.

Who hasn't pondered why illness strikes precisely when it can be afforded least? Often, people wonder if these maladies are real or just "psychological." Consider the following: Johnny may be faking sickness to avoid an exam. Is Melissa unconsciously postponing a date with a popular football star through her asthma attacks because she's scared to death? Is David's drinking prior to a sexual experience with his wife due to uncertainty about his performance—or guilt about an office affair? These situations are complex and require analysis in order to determine the physical and emotional sources. The diagnosis is not always simple and straightforward.

For centuries, physicians, philosophers, and psychologists have noted the apparent relationship among stress, illness, and health. Recently, medical scientists firmly have established causal relationships between them and have shown how our minds and emotions can influence the course of a disease.

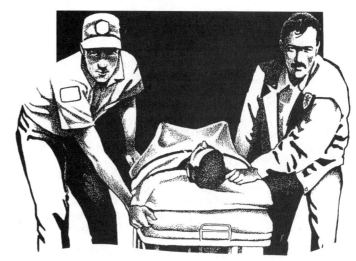

Some historians have traced the word "stress" to the Latin words *strictus* (tight or narrow) and *stingere* (to tighten). Until the 19th century, stress referred more to external forces on physical objects than to internal psychological states; for instance, the stress of extreme weight on a bridge platform, rather than the stress of balancing family and professional pressures. Contemporary use of the term can be traced to 20th-century physiological psychologist Walter Cannon and Canadian physician Hans Seyle. Cannon defined the classic "fight-or-flight" reaction: When faced with stress, the body prepares for the emergency through the sympathetic portion of the autonomic nervous system. Adrenalin, a hormone, is released into the bloodstream through the adrenal glands and generates the energy to cope with the stressors, not unlike an army ready to defend its territory against an invader.

Cannon maintained that this hormonal reaction was a remnant of humans' ancient past, when most stressors could be handled only through radical and robust actions. In order to survive, our ancestors fought prey and fled from predators. Such intense reactions are not required in modern society; in fact, this kind of response potentially could be harmful to one's health and well-being. Consider how inefficient it would be to rely on "fight-or-flight" in order to pay bills, change a flat tire during rush hour, or ask a supervisor for a raise. Burnout may be the result of such overreactions to stress.

Seyle studied stress by identifying those situations in which it occurs. A stressor is an event that places inordinate demands on the body and, in turn, sets off natural adaptive bodily defenses to cope with it. The process that he labeled the General Adaptation Syndrome includes three stages: the alarm reaction, resistance, and exhaustion.

During the alarm reaction, there are increases in hormone levels, strong physical arousal, and severe emotional upheavals. When the alarm reaction is not sufficient to cope, the stressor maintains its attack. Enter resistance. During this stage, when successful, the stressor is tamed and normality returns. If coping is not successful, however, hormonal reserves become depleted, fatigue sets in, and the stage of exhaustion takes over, during which adaptation to the stressor breaks down completely. Depression and anxiety are common. Serious illness, even death, becomes likely.

Illnesses associated with stress once were known as psychosomatic disorders; today, the term psychophysiological more commonly is used. They have been referred to as diseases of adaptation since they are rooted in attempts to adapt physiologically to everyday tensions and problems. Psychophysiological disorders encompass common physical ailments such as asthma, chronic hyperventilation, peptic ulcers, colitis, hypertension, heart attacks, hives, and acne.

Research by the psychologist Marianne Frankenhauser has corroborated Seyles' landmark work. Frankenhauser found that urban commuting, job dissatisfaction, personal conflict, loss of control over individual life decisions, taking exams, noise, anticipation of aversive events, and even boredom are profound stressors.

Psychologists Richard Lazarus and J.B. Cohen have proposed three categories of stressors: cataclysmic, personal, and background. A cataclysmic stressor is one that has a sudden, powerful, and unpredictable impact on a large number of people. Earthquakes in California, hurricanes in Florida, and the ethnic-based warfare in the former state of Yugoslavia are cases in point. Personal stressors also are sudden, powerful, and unpredictable, but affect fewer people, typically limited to an individual. One's personal response to illness, the death of a close associate or relative, or the loss of a job are common examples. Background stressors are chronic, persistent, and repetitive "daily hassles." These include noise, hectic schedules, and neighborhood and family problems. Individually, these events may not pose much harm; collectively, they can be problematic.

Not all stressors are negative. Seyle, in fact, proposed two types of stress—distress and eustress. Distress refers to negative and destructive forms commonly associated with cataclysmic and personal stress—for instance, suffering the loss of a family member or losing one's job. Eustress refers to events that evoke a stress reaction even when good and happy things seem to be

occurring such as celebrating a holiday, enjoying a vacation, or receiving a job promotion or personal recognition. These pleasurable occasions, oddly enough, can be stressful and have been shown to be related to illness.

Personality and health

There are both health- and illness-prone personality types. Neuroticism—a psychological term referring to emotional instability—correlates with a variety of common illnesses and cardiovascular diseases. There is clear evidence that hostility—both withholding it and chronically letting it out—contributes to hypertension and cardiovascular disorders. Introverts, who are shy, quiet, and socially withdrawn, are prone to exaggerated responses to stress. They are likely to become more ill than the average person. Extroverts, who are outgoing, sociable, and more laid back, typically are happier, more energetic, and healthier.

Coronary heart disease (CHD), the leading cause of death in the U.S., long has been associated with stress and anxiety. At the turn of the 20th century, noted physician Sir William Osler wrote that the typical coronary patient is "not the delicate, neurotic person . . . but the robust, the vigorous in mind and body, the keen and ambitious man, the indicator of whose engine is always at full speed ahead." Although more contemporary work has questioned his characterization, Osler's work has fueled valuable research on the relationship between personality factors and CHD. A very notable example was that performed in the 1930s by American psychiatrists Karl, Charles, and William Menninger, who validly associated the trait of aggressiveness with CHD.

During the 1960s, cardiologists Meyer Friedman and Ray Rosenman systematically explored the personality-CHD relationship. They identified the now classic Type-A person who shows hostility, excessive competitiveness, impatience, and pressured speech. An opposite behavior pattern, shown by the Type-B personality, characterizes a more easygoing style of coping. Epidemiological studies conducted over the past two decades have been consistent in showing a strong relationship between Type-A behavior and CHD in both women and men. These psychological factors are as troublesome in this regard as smoking, hypertension, and diabetes.

Through the use of his patient's life charts, physician Adolph Meyer noted in the 1930s that illness clustered at stressful times in a person's life. Researchers Thomas Holmes and Richard Rahe extended this line of thinking in the 1960s by systematically examining the life charts of more than 5,000 patients and identifying those events that appeared at the onset of disease.

They constructed a list of 43 stressful events related to personal, family, community, social, religious, economic, occupational, residential, and vocational aspects of living. Each was given a stress score. For instance, highest on the scale and worth 100 points is the death of a spouse; lowest on the scale and valued at 11 points are minor violations of the law. Other items include divorce (second), a jail term (fourth), pregnancy (12th), outstanding personal achievement (25th), trouble with the boss (30th), and change in sleeping habits (38th). Even vacation and Christmas (41st and 42nd, respectively) made the list.

Knowledge of the immune system and its relationship to illness has grown exponentially over the past few decades. The immune system is akin to a general defense network whose primary responsibility is to protect individuals from foreign agents, known as pathogens, that do not belong in the body and can cause disease. Pathogens normally include bacteria, viruses, and allergens like pollen, but also may include transplanted tissue and abnormal cells growing within the body.

The immune system targets and destroys antigens—any substance or organism that evades the outer defenses of skin tissue and mucous membrane and enters the body. The system contains several types of white blood cells, known as leukocytes, which protect in various ways. Some destroy bacteria; others kill viruses and attack cancer cells; still others produce antibodies that selectively target and then combat particular antigens.

Leukocytes are not perfect. Their actions may backfire; they can overreact and attack a person's own body. When this occurs, the result is a disorder known as autoimmune disease, including such ailments as minor as a common allergy and as serious as arthritis and lupus.

Recent discoveries have demonstrated that the immune system is not as autonomous and independent of other body systems as previously believed. It interacts with both the nervous and endocrine systems; the latter secretes hormones, like adrenaline, directly into the blood stream. This discovery has led to an emergence of a new field of investigation known as psychoneuroimmunology. As implied by its name, psychoneuroimmunology is an interdisciplinary field that studies the relationship between the principles of psychology, neurology, and immunology, as well as the principles of endocrinology and psychiatry. Psychoneuroimmunology is the field that has identified the direct causal relationship between stress and illness, beginning with the work of Robert Ader of the University of Rochester School of Medicine and Dentistry.

Ader, a research scientist who coined the term psychoneuroimmunology, was studying a rapid and potent form of classical conditioning (associated with physiologist Ivan Pavlov and his famous dog experiments) known as taste-aversion learning in animal subjects. In it, the consumption of a distinctively flavored drink—say saccharin water—is paired with the ingestion of some nausea-inducing substance. The result of this experience is that the previously preferred and enthusiastically consumed saccharin water now is avoided permanently. Many people have suffered from the experience of associating a particular food they once enjoyed with another that is upsetting and evokes nausea. This taste-aversion procedure has been used with some success in the treatment of alcoholism. Individuals are given a drug, antabuse, that causes extreme nausea when mixed with alcohol. Subsequently, the alcoholic refrains from drinking when antabuse is ingested.

By chance, Ader used cyclophosphamide (a potent drug commonly used in the treatment of autoimmune disease and transplant surgery to slow the rejection effects of the immune system) as the nausea-inducing substance in his taste-aversion experiment. After pairing it with saccharin water, he unexpectedly found that subjects who subsequently consumed saccharin water had much higher than normal mortality rates than those who did not have saccharin water paired with cyclophosphamide. On the basis of this observation, Ader speculated that the pairing of a neutral taste with an immunosuppressive drug—one whose known result is to weaken the effectiveness of the immune system in defending against pathogens—could result in the conditioning of a weakened immune system.

Further experimentation by Ader and others confirmed this hypothesis and found that the immune system is capable of "learning" to respond to a sweet taste with a drop in immune function. This demonstration of what scientists call conditioned immunosuppression of antibody response to antigens is significant because it demonstrates a direct psychological influence on immunity. The application of this finding to the practice of medicine is equally noteworthy. Studies have shown that the rejection of transplanted tissue may be reduced through this conditioning procedure. It also may be effective in reducing the medication doses required in cancer chemotherapy and arthritis. Dramatically, Ader has shown that the presentation of saccharin water that previously was paired with cyclophosphamide effectively delayed the onset of lupus in rats. Comparable applications to the treatment of lupus in humans currently are being explored.

Psychological distress

Prior to Ader's work, most scientists believed that the brain and immune systems were separate and incapable of influencing each other. Today, scientists are finding many connections of these systems. For instance, nerve endings have been found in tissues that produce, develop, and store immune system cells. The thymus, lymph nodes, spleen, and bone marrow—each intimately involved in immune system functioning—have been shown to respond to signals from the brain. Thus, the field of psychoneuroimmunology is pursuing the relationship between stress and illness with the assumption that psychological distress can suppress the immune system to the point of inducing physical illness.

Psychologists Harry Fowler, Donald Lysle, and others have shown that physical stress and fear are capable of producing immunosuppression. In these studies, animals exposed to physical stressors like footshock (mild electric shock to the foot) were found to be in states of immunosuppression for prolonged periods of time and likely to become ill. They showed almost equivalent reactions when presented with fear-evoking stimuli previously paired with the footshock. That is, a signal—such as a light—that consistently predicted the footshock also induced immunosuppression. Thus, not only does physical stress produce a weakened immune system, but the mere anticipation of a stressful situation triggers a similar effect.

Although direct human experimentation of this nature is not ethically possible, the results of these studies seem clear and applicable to humans. When individuals are stressed, their bodies go into a state of immunosuppression; they become susceptible to those pathogens that typically are adapted to and are likely to become ill. It is not so much that the stress causes the disease as much as it sets the stage for illness. With the elimination of pathogens during stress-induced immunosuppression, it is unlikely that infection-based illness will occur.

A study by psychologist Sheldon Cohen reported comparable effects in people. He gave volunteers injected doses of a known cold virus and then waited to see who came down with a cold. There was a clear relationship between those who did catch a cold and levels of stress experienced during the past year—a striking finding. Additional human research has shown declines in immune system cells in medical students taking final exams, people caring for loved ones with Alzheimer's disease, and women who recently had experienced a nasty divorce.

It currently is believed by many health professionals that some infections, as well as the growth of tumors, may reflect a problem in immunocompetence—the degree to which an antigen is identified and successfully destroyed by leukocytes and other immune system actions. Numerous studies have found evidence for increased tumor growth as a result of stress. This offers a viable explanation for what some psychologists refer to as the Type-C personality—those individuals whose personalities seem especially prone to cancer.

As noted by psychologists Robert Gatchel, Andrew Baum, and David Krantz in their text, *Health Psychology*, the cancer-prone personality has several characteristics: "The first includes a tendency to keep in resentment and anger rather than express it and a 'marked inability to forgive.' In addition, research suggests that cancer victims are ineffective in forming and/or maintaining close, long-term relationships with other people. They are more likely to be loners without extensive social support systems. Third, they engage in more self-pity than what may be considered normal. And these people tend to have poor self-images. Thus the cancer-prone individual 'puts on a happy face' and denies any sense of loss, anger, distress, disappointment, or despair while living an inner life of self-pity, insecurity, and a certain degree of loneliness."

To underscore this notion, one is reminded of a scene from the 1986 movie, "Hannah and Her Sisters." At one point in the film, Woody Allen's character facetiously states: "In my family, we don't cope with hostility and anger . . . we just grow tumors!"

The record seems clear. Chronic stress without adequate coping is damaging to good health, promoting disease and illness through suppression of the immune system. The specific physiological mechanisms have yet to be identified precisely, but the successful modulation of the immune system through conditioning is an encouraging research route.

Studies currently in the pipeline are exciting and promising. For instance, there are ways stress-induced immunosuppression can be inhibited as well as enhanced. This latter effect, known as immunenhancement, ultimately may result in individuals becoming "vaccinated" for the deleterious effects of stress.

To that end, the future seems bright, possibly free of stress. Remember, though, stress does have an important function—it informs people that they are doing the wrong things or just too much. The best advice is to control one's life so as to reduce excessive stress. Heed the call, and learn to relax!

Psychological Treatments

Have you ever had the nightmare that you are trapped in a dark, dismal place? No one will let you out. Your pleas for freedom go unanswered and, in fact, are suppressed or ignored by domineering authority figures around you. You keep begging for mercy, but to no avail. What a nightmare! You are fortunate to awake to your normal bedroom and to the realities of your daily life. For the mentally ill, the nightmare of institutionalization, where individuals can be held against their will in what are sometimes terribly dreary, restrictive surroundings, is the reality. Have you ever wondered what would happen if we took perfectly normal individuals and institutionalized them? In one well-known and remarkable study, that is exactly what happened.

In 1973, eight people, including a pediatrician, a psychiatrist, and some psychologists, presented themselves to psychiatric hospitals. Each claimed that he or she was hearing voices. The voices, they reported, seemed unclear but appeared to be saying "empty" or "thud." Each of these individuals was admitted to a mental hospital, and most were diagnosed as being schizophrenic.

Upon admission, the "pseudopatients" or fake patients gave truthful information and thereafter acted like their usual selves. They no longer said they heard voices. Their hospital stays lasted anywhere from 7 to 52 days. The nurses, doctors, psychologists, and other staff members treated them as if they really were schizophrenic and never saw through their trickery. Some of the real patients in the hospital did recognize, however, that the pseudopatients were perfectly normal. Upon discharge almost all of the pseudopatients received the diagnosis of "schizophrenic in remission," meaning that they were still clearly construed as schizophrenic; they just were not exhibiting any of the symptoms at the time.

What does this study demonstrate about mental illness? Is true mental illness readily detectable? If we can not always detect mental disorders, how can we treat them? What treatments are available, and which work better for various diagnoses?

The treatment of mental disorders is a challenge. The array of available treatments is ever-increasing and can be downright bewildering—and not just to the patient or client! In order to demystify and simplify your understanding of various treatments, we will look at them in this unit.

We commence with two general articles on treatment. In the first, renowned psychologist Martin Seligman discusses what we can hope to accomplish if we attempt reform. Some individuals have successfully shed weight, overcome anxiety and phobias, or quit smoking either by themselves or with professional assistance. Seligman takes a realistic look at what can and cannot be successfully changed.

Not all forms of mental health treatment have side effects. In "Outsmarting Stress," Dava Sobel helps us to understand how we can defeat stress. A multitude of stress-reducing techniques are available that are easy and inexpensive.

As health insurance pays for less and less, the newest thrust in psychology is to help individuals improve their status by means of two other, relatively simple techniques. One technique involves giving social support. Social support is assistance and emotional guidance from friends and family members in times of trouble. Social support, real or imagined, has helped individuals in crises appraise their lives more favorably. Another element critical to psychological improvement is a personal sense of control. Individuals who perceive that they have control over their own fates are more motivated to attempt change and more positive about their success than those who feel helpless or who perceive that they have no control over events in their lives. Research on these two matters is detailed in "Critical Life Events and the Onset of Illness."

Looking Ahead: Challenge Questions

Can people successfully change themselves? When is professional help needed? What can be changed successfully? What problems seem immune to change?

Describe the various methods for reducing stress that are discussed in "Outsmarting Stress." What are the advantages and disadvantages of each? What are other useful techniques that are not showcased in the book?

What is social support? For what modern psychological problems is social support useful? What do psychologists mean by the term sense of control? Why is a sense of control so important to mental health? How do people who perceive that they have personal control over events in their lives differ from those who perceive an external source of control?

What You Can Change & What You Cannot Change

There are things we can change about ourselves and things we cannot. Concentrate your energy on what is possible—too much time has been wasted.

Martin E. P. Seligman, Ph.D.

This is the age of psychotherapy and the age of self-improvement. Millions are struggling to change: We diet, we jog, we meditate. We adopt new modes of thought to counteract our depressions. We practice relaxation to curtail stress. We exercise to expand our memory and to quadruple our reading speed. We adopt draconian regimens to give up smoking. We raise our little boys and girls to androgyny. We come out of the closet or we try to become heterosexual. We seek to lose our taste for alcohol. We seek more meaning in life. We try to extend our life span.

Sometimes it works. But distressingly often, self-improvement and psychotherapy fail. The cost is enormous. We think we are worthless. We feel guilty and ashamed. We believe we have no willpower and that we are failures. We give up trying to change.

On the other hand, this is not only the age of self-improvement and therapy, but also the age of biological psychiatry. The human genome will be nearly mapped before the millennium is over. The brain systems underlying sex, hearing, memory, left-handedness, and sadness are now known. Psychoactive drugs quiet our fears, relieve our blues, bring us bliss, dampen our mania, and dissolve our delusions more effectively than we can on our own.

Our very personality—our intelligence and musical talent, even our religiousness, our conscience (or its absence), our politics, and our exuberance—turns out to be more the product of our genes than almost anyone would have believed a decade ago. The underlying message of the age of biological psychiatry is that our biology frequently makes changing, in spite of all our efforts, impossible.

But the view that all is genetic and biochemical and therefore unchangeable is also very often wrong. Many people surpass their IQs, fail to "respond" to drugs, make sweeping changes in their lives, live on when their cancer is "terminal," or defy the hormones and brain circuitry that "dictate" lust, femininity, or memory loss.

The ideologies of biological psychiatry and self-improvement are obviously colliding. Nevertheless, a resolution is apparent. There are some things about ourselves that can be changed, others that cannot, and some that can be changed only with extreme difficulty.

What can we succeed in changing about ourselves? What can we not? When can we overcome our biology? And when is our biology our destiny?

I want to provide an understanding of what you can and what you can't change about yourself so that you can concentrate your limited time and energy on what is possible. So much time has been wasted. So much needless frustration has been endured. So much of therapy, so much of child rearing, so much of self-improving, and even some of the great social movements in our century have come to nothing because they tried to change the unchangeable. Too often we have wrongly thought we were weak-willed failures, when the changes we wanted to make in ourselves were just not possible. But all this effort was necessary: Because there have been so many failures, we are now able to see the boundaries of the unchangeable; this in turn allows us to see clearly for the first time the boundaries of what *is* changeable.

With this knowledge, we can use our precious time to make the many rewarding changes that are possible. We can live with less self-reproach and less remorse. We can live with greater confidence. This knowledge is a new understanding of who we are and where we are going.

CATASTROPHIC THINKING: PANIC

S. J. Rachman, one of the world's leading clinical researchers and one of the founders of behavior therapy, was on the phone. He was proposing that I be the "discussant" at a conference about panic disorder sponsored by the National Institute of Mental Health (NIMH).

"Why even bother, Jack?" I responded. "Everyone knows that panic is biological and that the only thing that works is drugs."

"Don't refuse so quickly, Marty. There is a breakthrough you haven't yet heard about."

Breakthrough was a word I had never heard Jack use before.

"What's the breakthrough?" I asked.

"If you come, you can find out."

So I went.

I had known about and seen panic patients for many years, and had read the literature with mounting excitement during

From *Psychology Today*, May/June 1994, pp. 34-41, 70, 72-74, 84. Excerpted from *What You Can Change and What You Can't* by Martin E. P. Seligman. © 1993 by Martin E. P. Seligman. Reprinted by permission of Alfred A. Knopf, Inc.

So much child rearing, therapy, and self-improvement have come to nothing.

the 1980s. I knew that panic disorder is a frightening condition that consists of recurrent attacks, each much worse than anything experienced before. Without prior warning, you feel as if you are going to die. Here is a typical case history:

The first time Celia had a panic attack, she was working at McDonald's. It was two days before her 20th birthday. As she was handing a customer a Big Mac, she had the worst experience of her life. The earth seemed to open up beneath her. Her heart began to pound, she felt she was smothering, and she was sure she was going to have a heart attack and die. After about 20 minutes of terror, the panic subsided. Trembling, she got in her car, raced home, and barely left the house for the next three months.

Since then, Celia has had about three attacks a month. She does not know when they are coming. She always thinks she is going to die.

Panic attacks are not subtle, and you need no quiz to find out if you or someone you love has them. As many as five percent of American adults probably do. The defining feature of the disorder is simple: recurrent awful attacks of panic that come out of the blue, last for a few minutes, and then subside. The attacks consist of chest pains, sweating, nausea, dizziness, choking, smothering, or trembling. They are accompanied by feelings of overwhelming dread and thoughts that you are having a heart attack, that you are losing control, or that you are going crazy.

THE BIOLOGY OF PANIC

There are four questions that bear on whether a mental problem is primarily "biological" as opposed to "psychological":

- Can it be induced biologically?
- Is it genetically heritable?
- Are specific brain functions involved?
- Does a drug relieve it?

Inducing panic. Panic attacks can be created by a biological agent. For example, patients who have a history of panic attacks are hooked up to an intravenous line. Sodium lactate, a chemical that nor-mally produces rapid, shallow breathing and heart palpitations, is slowly infused into their bloodstream. Within a few minutes, about 60 to 90 percent of these patients have a panic attack. Normal controls—subjects with no history of panic—rarely have attacks when infused with lactate.

Genetics of panic. There may be some heritability of panic. If one of two identical twins has panic attacks, 31 percent of the cotwins also have them. But if one of two fraternal twins has panic attacks, none of the cotwins are so afflicted.

Panic and the brain. The brains of people with panic disorders look somewhat unusual upon close scrutiny. Their neurochemistry shows abnormalities in the system that turns on, then dampens, fear. In addition, the PET scan (positron-emission tomography), a technique that looks at how much blood and oxygen different parts of the brain use, shows that patients who panic from the infusion of lactate have higher blood flow and oxygen use in relevant parts of their brain than patients who don't panic.

Drugs. Two kinds of drugs relieve panic: tricyclic antidepressants and the antianxiety drug Xanax, and both work better than placebos. Panic attacks are dampened, and sometimes even eliminated. General anxiety and depression also decrease.

Since these four questions had already been answered "yes" when Jack Rachman called, I thought the issue had already been settled. Panic disorder was simply a biological illness, a disease of the body that could be relieved only by drugs.

A few months later I was in Bethesda, Maryland, listening once again to the same four lines of biological evidence. An inconspicuous figure in a brown suit sat hunched over the table. At the first break, Jack introduced me to him—David Clark, a young psychologist from Oxford. Soon after, Clark began his address.

"Consider, if you will, an alternative theory, a cognitive theory." He reminded all of us that almost all panickers believe that they are going to die during an attack. Most commonly, they believe that they are having heart attacks. Perhaps, Clark suggested, this is more than just a mere symptom. Perhaps it is the root cause. Panic may simply be the *catastrophic misinterpretation of bodily sensations.*

For example, when you panic, your heart starts to race. You notice this, and you see it as a possible heart attack. This makes you very anxious, which means

Panic	Curable
Specific Phobias	Almost Curable
Sexual Dysfunctions	Marked Relief
Social Phobia	Moderate Relief
Agoraphobia	Moderate Relief
Depression	Moderate Relief
Sex Role Change	Moderate
Obsessive–Compulsive Disorder	Moderate Mild Relief
Sexual Preferences	Moderate Mild Change
Anger	Mild, Moderate Relief
Everyday Anxiety	Mild Moderate Relief
Alcoholism	Mild Relief
Overweight	Temporary Change
Posttraumatic Stress Disorder (PTSD)	Marginal Relief
Sexual Orientation	Probably Unchangeable
Sexual Identity	Unchangeable

your heart pounds more. You now notice that your heart is *really* pounding. You are now *sure* it's a heart attack. This terrifies you, and you break into a sweat, feel nauseated, short of breath—all symptoms of terror, but for you, they're confirmation of a heart attack. A full-blown panic attack is under way, and at the root of it is your misinterpretation of the symptoms of anxiety as symptoms of impending death.

We are now able to see the boundaries of the unchangeable.

I was listening closely now as Clark argued that an obvious sign of a disorder, easily dismissed as a symptom, is the disorder itself. If he was right, this was a historic occasion. All Clark had done so far, however, was to show that the four lines of evidence for a biological view of panic could fit equally well with a misinterpretation view. But Clark soon told us about a series of experiments he and his colleague Paul Salkovskis had done at Oxford.

First, they compared panic patients with patients who had other anxiety disorders and with normals. All the subjects read the following sentences aloud, but the last word was presented blurred. For example:

dying
If I had palpitations, I could be
excited

choking
If I were breathless, I could be
unfit

When the sentences were about bodily sensations, the panic patients, but no one else, saw the catastrophic endings fastest. This showed that panic patients possess the habit of thinking Clark had postulated.

Next, Clark and his colleagues asked if activating this habit with words would induce panic. All the subjects read a series of word pairs aloud. When panic patients got to "breathlessness-suffocation: and "palpitations-dying," 75 percent suffered a full-blown panic attack right there in the laboratory. No normal people had panic attacks, no recovered panic patients (I'll tell you more in a moment about how they got better) had attacks, and only 17 percent of other anxious patients had attacks.

The final thing Clark told us was the "breakthrough" that Rachman had promised.

"We have developed and tested a rather novel therapy for panic," Clark continued in his understated, disarming way. He explained that if catastrophic misinterpretations of bodily sensation are the cause of a panic attack, then changing the tendency to misinterpret should cure the disorder. His new therapy was straightforward and brief:

Patients are told that panic results when they mistake normal symptoms of mounting anxiety for symptoms of heart attack, going crazy, or dying. Anxiety itself, they are informed, produces shortness of breath, chest pain, and sweating. Once

Issues of the soul can barely be changed by psychotherapy or drugs.

they misinterpret these normal bodily sensations as an imminent heart attack, their symptoms become even more pronounced because the misinterpretation changes their anxiety into terror. A vicious circle culminates in a full-blown panic attack.

Patients are taught to reinterpret the symptoms realistically as mere anxiety symptoms. Then they are given practice right in the office, breathing rapidly into a paper bag. This causes a buildup of carbon dioxide and shortness of breath, mimicking the sensations that provoke a panic

attack. The therapist points out that the symptoms the patient is experiencing—shortness of breath and heart racing—are harmless, simply the result of over-breathing, not a sign of a heart attack. The patient learns to interpret the symptoms correctly.

"This simple therapy appears to be a cure," Clark told us. "Ninety to 100 percent of the patients are panic free at the end of therapy. One year later, only one person had had another panic attack."

This, indeed, was a breakthrough: a simple, brief psychotherapy with no side effects showing a 90-percent cure rate of a disorder that a decade ago was thought to be incurable. In a controlled study of 64 patients comparing cognitive therapy to drugs to relaxation to no treatment, Clark and his colleagues found that cognitive therapy is markedly better than drugs or relaxation, both of which are better than

Self-Analysis Questionnaire
Is your life dominated by anxiety? Read each statement and then mark the appropriate number to indicate *how you generally feel.* There are no right or wrong answers.

1. I am a steady person.

Almost never	Sometimes	Often	Almost always
4	3	2	1

2. I am satisfied with myself.

Almost never	Sometimes	Often	Almost always
4	3	2	1

3. I feel nervous and restless.

Almost never	Sometimes	Often	Almost always
1	2	3	4

4. I wish I could be as happy as others seem to be.

Almost never	Sometimes	Often	Almost always
1	2	3	4

5. I feel like a failure.

Almost never	Sometimes	Often	Almost always
1	2	3	4

6. I get in a state of tension and turmoil as I think over my recent concerns and interests.

Almost never	Sometimes	Often	Almost always
1	2	3	4

7. I feel secure.

Almost never	Sometimes	Often	Almost always
4	3	2	1

nothing. Such a high cure rate is unprecedented.

How does cognitive therapy for panic compare with drugs? It is more effective and less dangerous. Both the antidepressants and Xanax produce marked reduction in panic in most patients, but drugs must be taken forever; once the drug is stopped, panic rebounds to where it was before therapy began for perhaps half the patients. The drugs also sometimes have severe side effects, including drowsiness, lethargy, pregnancy complications, and addictions.

After this bombshell, my own "discussion" was an anticlimax. I did make one point that Clark took to heart. "Creating a cognitive therapy that works, even one that works as well as this apparently does, is not enough to show that the *cause* of panic is cognitive." I was niggling. "The biological theory doesn't deny that some other therapy might work well on panic. It merely claims that panic is caused at the bottom by some biochemical problem."

Two years later, Clark carried out a crucial experiment that tested the biological theory against the cognitive theory. He gave the usual lactate infusion to 10 panic patients, and nine of them panicked. He did the same thing with another 10 patients, but added special instructions to allay the misinterpretation of the sensations. He simply told them: "Lactate is a natural bodily substance that produces sensations similar to exercise or alcohol. It is normal to experience intense sensations during infusion, but these do not indicate an adverse reaction." Only three out of the 10 panicked. This confirmed the theory crucially.

The therapy works every well, as it did for Celia, whose story has a happy ending. She first tried Xanax, which reduced the intensity and the frequency of her panic attacks. But she was too drowsy to work, and she was still having about one attack every six weeks. She was then referred to Audry, a cognitive therapist who explained that Celia was misinterpreting her heart racing and shortness of breath as symptoms of a heart attack, that they were actually just symptoms of mounting anxiety, nothing more harmful. Audrey taught Celia progressive relaxation, and then she demonstrated the harmlessness of Celia's symptoms of overbreathing. Celia then relaxed in the presence of the symptoms and found that they gradually subsided. After several more practice sessions, therapy terminated. Celia has gone two years without another panic attack.

8. I have self-confidence.

Almost never	Sometimes	Often	Almost always
4	3	2	1

9. I feel inadequate.

Almost never	Sometimes	Often	Almost always
1	2	3	4

10. I worry too much over something that does not matter.

Almost never	Sometimes	Often	Almost always
1	2	3	4

To score, simply add up the numbers under your answers. Notice that some of the rows of numbers go up and others go down. The higher your total, the more the trait of anxiety dominates your life. If your score was:

10–11, you are in the lowest 10 percent of anxiety.

13–14, you are in the lowest quarter.

16–17, your anxiety level is about average.

19–20, your anxiety level is around the 75th percentile.

22–24 (and you are male) your anxiety level is around the 90th percentile.

24–26 (and you are female) your anxiety level is around the 90th percentile.

25 (and you are male) your anxiety level is at the 95th percentile.

27 (and you are female) your anxiety level is at the 95th percentile.

Should you try to change your anxiety level? Here are my rules of thumb:

• If your score is at the 90th percentile or above, you can probably improve the quality of your life by lowering your general anxiety level—regardless of paralysis and irrationality.

• If your score is at the 75th percentile or above, and you feel that anxiety is either paralyzing you or that it is unfounded, you should probably try to lower your general anxiety level.

• If your score is 18 or above, and you feel that anxiety is unfounded and paralyzing, you should probably try to lower your general anxiety level.

EVERYDAY ANXIETY

Attend to your tongue—right now. What is it doing? Mine is swishing around near my lower right molars. It has just found a minute fragment of last night's popcorn (debris from *Terminator 2*). Like a dog at a bone, it is worrying the firmly wedged flake.

Attend to your hand—right now. What's it up to? My left hand is boring in on an itch it discovered under my earlobe.

Your tongue and your hands have, for the most part, a life of their own. You can bring them under voluntary control by consciously calling them out of their "default" mode to carry out your commands:

Anxiety scans your life for imperfections. When it finds one, it won't let go.

"Pick up the phone" or "Stop picking that pimple." But most of the time they are on their own. They are seeking out small imperfections. They scan your entire mouth and skin surface, probing for anything going wrong. They are marvelous, nonstop grooming devices. They, not the more fashionable immune system, are your first line of defense against invaders.

Anxiety is your mental tongue. Its default mode is to search for what may be about to go wrong. It continually, and without your conscious consent, scans your life—yes, even when you are asleep, in dreams and nightmares. It reviews your work, your love, your play—until it finds an imperfection. When it finds one, it worries it. It tries to pull it out from its hiding place, where it is wedged inconspicuously under some rock. It will not let go. If the imperfection is threatening enough, anxiety calls your attention to it by making you uncomfortable. If you do not act, it yells more insistently—disturbing your sleep and your appetite.

You can reduce daily, mild anxiety. You can numb it with alcohol, Valium, or marijuana. You can take the edge off with meditation or progressive relaxation. You can beat it down by becoming more conscious of the automatic thoughts of danger that trigger anxiety and then disputing them effectively.

But do not overlook what your anxiety is trying to do for you. In return for the pain it brings, it prevents larger ordeals by making you aware of their possibility and goading you into planning for and forestalling them. It may even help you avoid them altogether. Think of your anxiety as the "low oil" light flashing on the dashboard of your car. Disconnect it and you will be less distracted and more comfortable for a while. But this may cost you a burned-up engine. Our *dysphoria,* or bad feeling, should, some of the time, be tolerated, attended to, even cherished.

Guidelines for When to Try to Change Anxiety

Some of our everyday anxiety, depression, and anger go beyond their useful function. Most adaptive traits fall along a normal spectrum of distribution, and the capacity for internal bad weather for everyone some of the time means that some of us may have terrible weather all of the time. In general, when the hurt is pointless and recurrent—when, for example, anxiety insists we formulate a plan but no plan will work—it is time to take action to relieve the hurt. There are three hallmarks indicating that anxiety has become a burden that wants relieving:

First, is it *irrational?*

We must calibrate our bad weather inside against the real weather outside. Is what you are anxious about out of proportion to the reality of the danger? Here are some examples that may help you answer this question. All of the following are not irrational:

• A fire fighter trying to smother a raging oil well burning in Kuwait repeatedly wakes up at four in the morning because of flaming terror dreams.

• A mother of three smells perfume on her husband's shirts and, consumed by jealousy, broods about his infidelity, reviewing the list of possible women over and over.

• A student who had failed two of his midterm exams finds, as finals approach, that he can't get to sleep for worrying. He has diarrhea most of the time.

The only good thing that can be said about such fears is that they are well-founded.

In contrast, all of the following are irrational, out of proportion to the danger:

• An elderly man, having been in a fender bender, broods about travel and will no longer take cars, trains, or airplanes.

• An eight-year-old child, his parents having been through an ugly divorce, wets his bed at night. He is haunted with visions of his bedroom ceiling collapsing on him.

• A housewife who has an MBA and who accumulated a decade of experience as a financial vice president before her twins were born is sure her job search will be fruitless. She delays preparing her résumés for a month.

The second hallmark of anxiety out of control is *paralysis.* Anxiety intends action: Plan, rehearse, look into shadows for lurking dangers, change your life. When anxiety becomes strong, it is unproductive; no problem-solving occurs. And when anxiety is extreme, it paralyzes you. Has your anxiety crossed this line? Some examples:

• A woman finds herself housebound because she fears that if she goes out, she will be bitten by a cat.

• A salesman broods about the next customer hanging up on him and makes no more cold calls.

• A writer, afraid of the next rejection slip, stops writing.

The final hallmark is *intensity.* Is your life dominated by anxiety? Dr. Charles Spielberger, one of the world's foremost

> 'Dieting below your natural weight is a necessary condition for bulimia. Returning to your natural weight will cure it.'

testers of emotion, has developed well-validated scales for calibrating how severe anxiety is. To find out how anxious *you* are, use the self-analysis questionnaire.

Lowering Your Everyday Anxiety

Everyday anxiety level is not a category to which psychologists have devoted a great deal of attention. Enough research has been done, however, for me to recommend two techniques that quite reliably lower everyday anxiety levels. Both techniques are cumulative, rather than one-shot fixes. They require 20 to 40 minutes a day of your valuable time.

The first is *progressive relaxation,* done once or, better, twice a day for at least 10 minutes. In this technique, you tighten and then turn off each of the major muscle groups of your body until you are wholly flaccid. It is not easy to be highly anxious when your body feels like Jell-O. More formally, relaxation engages a response system that competes with anxious arousal.

The second technique is regular *meditation.* Transcendental meditation ™ is one useful, widely available version of this. You can ignore the cosmology in which it is packaged if you wish, and treat it simply as the beneficial technique it is. Twice a day for 20 minutes, in a quiet setting, you close your eyes and repeat a *mantra* (a syllable whose "sonic properties are known") to yourself. Meditation works by blocking thoughts that produce anxiety. It complements relaxation, which blocks the motor components of anxiety but leaves the anxious thoughts untouched.

Done regularly, meditation usually induces a peaceful state of mind. Anxiety at other times of the day wanes, and hyperarousal from bad events is dampened. Done religiously, TM probably works better than relaxation alone.

There's also a quick fix. The minor tranquilizers—Valium, Dalmane, Librium, and their cousins—relieve everyday anxiety. So does alcohol. The advantage of all these is that they work within minutes and require no discipline to use. Their disadvantages outweigh their advantages, however. The minor tranquilizers make you fuzzy and somewhat uncoordinated as they work (a not uncommon side effect is an automobile accident). Tranquilizers soon lose their effect when taken regularly, and they are habit-forming—probably addictive. Alcohol, in addition, produces gross cognitive and motor disability in lockstep with its anxiety relief. Taken regularly over long periods, deadly damage to liver and brain ensue.

If you crave quick and temporary relief from acute anxiety, either alcohol or minor tranquilizers, taken in small amounts and only occasionally, will do the job. They are, however, a distant second-best to progressive relaxation and meditation, which are each worth trying before you seek out psychotherapy or in conjunction with therapy. Unlike tranquilizers and alcohol, neither of these techniques is likely to do you any harm.

Weigh your everyday anxiety. If it is not intense, or if it is moderate and not irrational or paralyzing, act now to reduce it. In spite of its deep evolutionary roots, intense everyday anxiety is often changeable. Meditation and progressive relaxation practiced regularly can change it forever.

DIETING: A WAIST IS A TERRIBLE THING TO MIND

I have been watching my weight and restricting my intake—except for an occasional binge like this—since I was 20. I weighed about 175 pounds then, maybe 15 pounds over my official "ideal" weight. I weigh 199 pounds now, 30 years later, about 25 pounds over the ideal. I have tried about a dozen regimes—fasting, the Beverly Hills Diet, no carbohydrates, Metrecal for lunch, 1,200 calories a day, low fat, no lunch, no starches, skipping every other dinner. I lost 10 or 15 pounds on each in about a month. The pounds always came back, though, and I have gained a net of about a pound a year—inexorably.

This is the most consistent failure in my life. It's also a failure I can't just put out of mind. I have spent the last few years reading the scientific literature, not the parade of best-selling diet books or the flood of women's magazine articles on the latest way to slim down. The scientific findings look clear to me, but there is not yet a consensus. I am going to go out on a limb, because I see so many signs all pointing in one direction. What I have concluded will, I believe, soon be the consensus of the scientists. The conclusions surprise me. They

will probably surprise you, too, and they may change your life.

Her[e] is what the picture looks like to me:

• Dieting doesn't work.
• Dieting may make overweight worse, not better.
• Dieting may be bad for health.
• Dieting may cause eating disorders— including bulimia and anorexia.

ARE YOU OVERWEIGHT?

Are you above the ideal weight for your sex, height, and age? If so, you are "overweight." What does this really mean? Ideal weight is arrived at simply. Four million people, now dead, who were insured by the major American life-insurance companies, were once weighed and had their height measured. At what weight on average do people of a given height turn out to live longest? That weight is called ideal. Anything wrong with that?

You bet. The real use of a weight table, and the reason your doctor takes it seriously, is that an ideal weight implies that, on average, if you slim down to yours, you will live longer. This is the crucial claim. Lighter people indeed live longer, on average, than heavier people, but how much longer is hotly debated.

But the crucial claim is unsound because weight (at any given height) has a normal distribution, *normal* both in a statistical sense and in the biological sense. In the biological sense, couch potatoes who overeat and never exercise can legitimately be called overweight, but the buxom, "heavy-boned" slow people deemed overweight by the ideal table are at their natural and healthiest weight. If you are a 155-pound woman and 64 inches in height, for example, you are "overweight" by around 15 pounds. This means nothing more than that the average 140-pound, 64-inch-tall woman lives somewhat longer than the average 155-pound woman of your height. It does not follow that if you slim down to 125 pounds, *you* will stand any better chance of living longer.

In spite of the insouciance with which dieting advice is dispensed, no one has properly investigated the question of whether slimming down to "ideal" weight produces longer life. The proper study would compare the longevity of people who are at their ideal weight without dieting to people who achieve their ideal weight by dieting. Without this study the common medical advice to diet down to your ideal weight is simply unfounded.

This is not a quibble; there is evidence

that dieting damages your health and that this damage may shorten your life.

MYTHS OF OVERWEIGHT

The advice to diet down to your ideal weight to live longer is one myth of overweight. Here are some others:

• *Overweight people overeat.* Wrong. Nineteen out of 20 studies show that obese people consume no more calories each day than nonobese people. Telling a fat person that if she would change her eating habits and eat "normally" she would lose weight is a lie. To lose weight and stay there, she will need to eat excruciatingly less than a normal person, probably for the rest of her life.

• *Overweight people have an overweight personality.* Wrong. Extensive research on personality and fatness has proved little. Obese people do not differ in any major personality style from nonobese people.

• *Physical inactivity is a major cause of obesity.* Probably not. Fat people are indeed less active than thin people, but the inactivity is probably caused more by the fatness than the other way around.

• *Overweight shows a lack of willpower.* This is the granddaddy of all the myths. Fatness is seen as shameful because we hold people responsible for their weight. Being overweight equates with being a weak-willed slob. We believe this primarily because we have seen people decide to lose weight and do so in a matter of weeks.

But almost everyone returns to the old weight after shedding pounds. Your body has a natural weight that it defends vigorously against dieting. The more diets tried, the harder the body works to defeat the next diet. Weight is in large part genetic. All this gives the lie to the "weak-willed" interpretations of overweight. More accurately, dieting is the conscious will of the individual against a more vigilant opponent: the species' biological defense against starvation. The body can't tell the difference between self-imposed starvation and actual famine, so it defends its weight by refusing to release fat, by lowering its metabolism, and by demanding food. The harder the creature tries not to eat, the more vigorous the defenses become.

BULIMIA AND NATURAL WEIGHT

A concept that makes sense of your body's vigorous defense against weight loss is *natural weight.* When your body screams "I'm hungry," makes you lethargic, stores fat, craves sweets and renders them more delicious than ever, and makes you obsessed with food, what it is defending is your natural weight. It is signaling that you have dropped into a range it will not accept. Natural weight prevents you from gaining too much weight or losing too much. When you eat too much for too long, the opposite defenses are activated and make long-term weight gain difficult.

There is also a strong genetic contribution to your natural weight. Identical twins reared apart weigh almost the same throughout their lives. When identical twins are overfed, they gain weight and add fat in lockstep and in the same places. The fatness or thinness of adopted children resembles their biological parents—particularly their mother—very closely but does not at all resemble their adoptive parents. This suggests that you have a genetically given natural weight that your body wants to maintain.

The idea of natural weight may help cure the new disorder that is sweeping young America. Hundreds of thousands of young women have contracted it. It consists of bouts of binge eating and purging alternating with days of undereating. These young women are usually normal in weight or a bit on the thin side, but they are terrified of becoming fat. So they diet. They exercise. They take laxatives by the cup. They gorge. Then they vomit and take more laxatives. This malady is called *bulimia nervosa* (bulimia, for short).

Therapists are puzzled by bulimia, its causes, and treatment. Debate rages about whether it is an equivalent of depression, or an expression of a thwarted desire for control, or a symbolic rejection of the feminine role. Almost every psychotherapy has been tried. Antidepressants and other drugs have been administered with some effect but little success has been reported.

I don't think that bulimia is mysterious, and I think that it will be curable. I believe that bulimia is caused by dieting. The bulimic goes on a diet, and her body attempts to defend its natural weight. With repeated dieting, this defense becomes more vigorous. Her body is in massive revolt—insistently demanding food, storing fat, craving sweets, and lowering metabolism. Periodically, these biological defenses will overcome her extraordinary willpower (and extraordinary it must be to even approach an ideal weight, say, 20 pounds lighter than her natural weight). She will then binge. Horrified by what this will do to her figure, she vomits and takes laxatives to purge calories. Thus, bulimia is a natural consequence of self-starvation to lose weight in the midst of abundant food.

The therapist's task is to get the patient to stop dieting and become comfortable with her natural weight. He should first convince the patient that her binge eating is caused by her body's reaction to her diet. Then he must confront her with a question: Which is more important, staying thin or getting rid of bulimia? By stopping the diet, he will tell her, she can get rid of the uncontrollable binge–purge cycle. Her body will now settle at her natural weight, and she need not worry that she will balloon beyond that point. For some patients, therapy will end there because they would rather be bulimic than "loathsomely fat." For these patients, the central issue—ideal weight versus natural weight—can now at least become the focus of therapy. For others, defying the social and sexual pressure to be thin will be possible, dieting will be abandoned, weight will be gained, and bulimia should end quickly.

These are the central moves of the cognitive-behavioral treatment of bulimia. There are more than a dozen outcome studies of this approach, and the results are good. There is about 60 percent reduction in binging and purging (about the same as with antidepressant drugs). But unlike drugs, there is little relapse after treatment. Attitudes toward weight and shape relax, and dieting withers.

Of course, the dieting theory cannot fully explain bulimia. Many people who diet don't become bulimic; some can avoid it because their natural weight is close to their ideal weight, and therefore the diet they adopt does not starve them. In addition, bulimics are often depressed, since binging-purging leads to self-loathing. Depression may worsen bulimia by making it easier to give in to temptation. Further, dieting may just be another symptom of bulimia, not a cause. Other factors aside, I can speculate that dieting below your natural weight is a necessary condition for bulimia, and that returning to your natural weight and accepting that weight will cure bulimia.

OVERWEIGHT VS. DIETING: THE HEALTH DAMAGE

Being heavy carries some health risk. There is no definite answer to how much, because there is a swamp of inconsistent findings. But even if you could just wish pounds away, never to return, it is not certain you should. Being somewhat above your "ideal" weight may actually be your healthiest natural condition, best for your particular constitution and your particular metabolism. Of course you can diet, but

the odds are overwhelming that most of the weight will return, and that you will have to diet again and again. From a health and mortality perspective, should you? *There is, probably, a serious health risk from losing weight and regaining it.*

In one study, more than five thousand men and women from Framingham, Massachusetts, were observed for 32 years. People whose weight fluctuated over the years had 30 to 100 percent greater risk of death from heart disease than people whose weight was stable. When corrected for smoking, exercise, cholesterol level, and blood pressure, the findings became more convincing, suggesting that weight fluctuation (the primary cause of which is presumably dieting) may itself increase the risk of heart disease.

If this result is replicated, and if dieting is shown to be the primary cause of weight cycling, it will convince me that you should not diet to reduce your risk of heart disease.

DEPRESSION AND DIETING

Depression is yet another cost of dieting, because two root causes of depression are failure and helplessness. Dieting sets you up for failure. Because the goal of slimming down to your ideal weight pits your fallible willpower against untiring biological defenses, you will often fail. At first you will lose weight and feel pretty good about it. Any depression you had about your figure will disappear. Ultimately, however, you will probably not reach your goal; and then you will be dismayed as the pounds return. Every time you look in the mirror or vacillate over a white chocolate mousse, you will be reminded of your failure, which in turn brings depression.

On the other hand, if you are one of the fortunate few who can keep the weight from coming back, you will probably have to stay on an unsatisfying low-calorie diet for the rest of your life. A side effect of prolonged malnutrition is depression. Either way, you are more vulnerable to it.

If you scan the list of cultures that have a thin ideal for women, you will be struck by something fascinating. All thin-ideal cultures also have eating disorders. They also have roughly twice as much depression in women as in men. (Women diet twice as much as men. The best estimate is that 13 percent of adult men and 25 percent of adult women are now on a diet.) The cultures without the thin ideal have no eating disorders, and the amount of depression in women and men in these cultures is the same. This suggests that around the world, the thin ideal and dieting not only cause eating disorders, but they may also cause women to be more depressed than men.

The Bottom Line

I have been dieting off and on for 30 years because I want to be more attractive, healthier, and more in control. How do these goals stack up against the facts?

Attractiveness. If your attractiveness is a high-enough priority to convince you to diet, keep three drawbacks in mind. First, the attractiveness you gain will be temporary. All the weight you lose and maybe more will likely come back in a few years. This will depress you. Then you will have to lose it again and it will be harder the second time. Or you will have to resign yourself to being less attractive. Second, when women choose the silhouette figure they want to achieve, it turns out to be thinner than the silhouette that men label most attractive. Third, you may well become bulimic particularly if your natural weight is substantially more than your ideal weight. On balance, if short-term attractiveness is your overriding goal, diet. But be prepared for the costs.

Health. No one has ever shown that losing weight will increase my longevity. On balance, the health goal does not warrant dieting.

Control. For many people, getting to an ideal weight and staying there is just as biologically impossible as going with much less sleep. This fact tells me not to diet, and defuses my feeling of shame. My bottom line is clear: I am not going to diet anymore.

Depth and Change: The Theory

Clearly, we have not yet developed drugs or psychotherapies that can change all the problems, personality types, and patterns of behavior in adult life. But I believe that success and failure stems from something other than inadequate treatment. Rather, it stems from the depth of the problem.

We all have experience of psychological states of different depths. For example, if you ask someone, out of the blue, to answer quickly, "Who are you?" they will usually tell you—roughly in this order—their name, their sex, their profession. whether they have children, and their religion or race. Underlying this is a continuum of depth from surface to soul—with all manner of psychic material in between.

I believe that issues of the soul can barely be changed by psychotherapy or by drugs. Problems and behavior patterns somewhere between soul and surface can be changed somewhat. Surface problems can be changed easily, even cured. What is changeable, by therapy or drugs, I speculate, varies with the depth of the problem.

My theory says that it does not matter *when* problems, habits, and personality are acquired; their depth derives only from their biology, their evidence, and their power. Some childhood traits, for example, are deep and unchangeable but not because they were learned early and therefore have a privileged place.

Rather, those traits that resist change do so either because they are evolutionarily prepared or because they acquire great power by virtue of becoming the framework around which later learning crystallizes. In this way, the theory of depth carries the optimistic message that we are not prisoners of our past.

When you have understood this message, you will never look at your life in the same way again. Right now there are a number of things that you do not like about yourself and that you want to change: your short fuse, your waistline, your shyness, your drinking, your glumness. You have decided to change, but you do not know what you should work on first. Formerly you would have probably selected the one that hurts the most. Now you will also ask yourself which attempt is most likely to repay your efforts and which is most likely to lead to further frustration. Now you know your shyness and your anger are much more likely to change than your drinking, which you now know is more likely to change than your waistline.

Some of what does change is under your control, and some is not. You can best prepare yourself to change by learning as much as you can about what you can change and how to make those changes. Like all true education, learning about change is not easy; harder yet is surrendering some of our hopes. It is certainly not my purpose to destroy your optimism about change. But it is also not my purpose to assure everybody they can change in every way. My purpose is to instill a new, warranted optimism about the parts of your life you can change and so help you focus your limited time, money, and effort on making actual what is truly within your reach.

Life is a long period of change. What you have been able to change and what has resisted your highest resolve might seem chaotic to you: for some of what you are never changes no matter how hard you try, and other aspects change readily. My hope is that this essay has been the beginning of wisdom about the difference.

Outsmarting Stress

The secret of happiness is achieving a balance between the challenges we take on and the skills we develop to meet them.

Dava Sobel

Like a hostage enthralled by her captors, I have come to love my stress. Stress pervades my life, jolts my nervous system at each new crisis and often gives me a positive rush of energy that feels illicit in its power.

I harbor no fantasies of a stress-free existence. It wouldn't suit me at all. What I would like, however, is some assurance that I can live this way without doing myself bodily harm.

Just as alcohol destroys the liver and cigarette smoke rots the lungs, chronic stress, by raising blood pressure and blocking arteries, can generate heart attacks and strokes.

Stress is also behind numerous aches and pains that lower one's quality of life: stomach upset, headaches, backaches and, literally, pains in the neck.

The antidote, as everyone knows, is relaxation—a concept foreign to most professionals. True workaholics and stress junkies don't even understand the meaning of the word.

Is "relaxation" taking a nap? Taking a vacation? Taking work less seriously? How does a person who lives on red alert relax?

Prominent doctors who have studied the health of people leading busy lives agree that it's impossible to avoid stress altogether.

But high-powered types can improve their mental and physical state by actively pursuing specific relaxation strategies that can help eliminate the illness, anger, depression, anxiety and

hostility that accompany stress and give it such a bad name.

Dr. Dean Ornish, the president and director of the Preventive Medicine Research Institute in Sausalito, Calif., teaches his patients how to avoid and even reverse heart disease by using relaxation techniques.

"Busy people think that relaxing means doing nothing—in other words, wasting time," Ornish says.

Instead, he says, practicing simple stress-management techniques on a regular basis—say, a half hour each day—is the real key to helping pressured professionals improve their efficiency and productivity, not to mention the length and quality of their lives.

These techniques include meditation, stretching, deep breathing, visualization and progressive relaxation.

They are not simply relaxing pastimes. They induce a state of physiological relaxation. Thus, they figure importantly in the "Opening Your Heart" program that Ornish developed and describes in his book *Reversing Heart Disease* (Random House, 1990).

Meditation, for example, long associated by corporate leaders with incense and joblessness, is an active process.

As Ornish explains it, "Meditation involves intense concentration on a particular word, phrase or prayer. When you fully develop this ability to pay attention, you find you have a greater capacity to enjoy all things—work, food, music, sex."

Although purists advocate two 20-minute meditation periods per day (at

dawn and dusk), Ornish maintains that taking even a few minutes once a day, sandwiched into a busy schedule, will improve your state of mind, so long as you do it regularly.

Meditation is also the primary means of achieving what Dr. Herbert Benson of Harvard Medical School named "the relaxation response"—a physiological state of profound rest that is more relaxing and restorative then sitting quietly.

With landmark research he began in the 1960s, Benson showed the relaxation response to be the opposite of the inherent "fight or flight" response to stress that keeps the chronically pressured constantly on edge.

Benson's studies showed that eliciting the relaxation response for a mere 10 minutes to 20 minutes once or twice a day could counter the ill effects of life in the fast lane.

The subjects in his studies experienced healthful drops in blood pressure, decreased anxiety, better sleep patterns and heightened immunity to disease.

Benson is now the founding president of the Mind/Body Medical Institute at the New England Deaconess Hospital in Boston.

"The relaxation response is the end product, not a technique," he says. "You can use any one of scores of techniques to achieve the physiological state itself."

These include concentrating on your breathing, repeating over and over a word or phrase (such as the opening of a prayer) or making a sound, such as humming.

From *New Digest*, November 1993, pp. 232-238. First appeared in *Working Woman*, May 1993. © 1993 by Working Woman, Inc. Reprinted by permission of *Working Woman* magazine.

The Wellness Book (Carol Publishing Group, 1991), which Benson co-authored with Eileen Stuart and other members of the institute, offers a quick, four-step plan for relaxing that can be used on a daily or emergency basis, anytime, anywhere:

1. Stop yourself from building up the present situation into the worst-case scenario. 2. Breathe deeply to release the physical tension. 3. Reflect on the cause of your current stress. 4. Choose the way you will deal with the situation. The techniques advocated by Benson and Ornish are similar. Indeed, Ornish credits Benson's research with having helped lay the groundwork for his own studies on relaxation.

As medical doctors, both men prescribe physiological relaxation for its preventive and therapeutic powers.

But another aspect of relaxation's value comes from psychologists who are exploring the way hobbies, pastimes and vacations affect our well-being.

Leisure time is best spent in skilled activities that are structured by rules and goals, says Mihaly Csikszentmihalyi (pronounced "CHICK-sent-me-high"), a professor of psychology at the University of Chicago.

Csikszentmihalyi has spent his professional life studying what makes people happy.

The secret of happiness, he reports, is to achieve a balance between the challenges we take on and the skills we develop to meet them—whether at work or at play.

When we are absorbed in activities that pit our best abilities against a chosen challenge, we lose track of time and our worries, and achieve a state of pure enjoyment he calls "flow," a phenomenon he explores in his book *Flow: The Psychology of Optimal Experience* (HarperCollins, 1990).

Csikszentmihalyi notes that leisure pursuits such as chess, rock climbing, playing music and hobbies that involve arts and crafts provide much more satisfaction than, say, spectator sports or "doing nothing."

Reading for relaxation is a flow-producer, however, because the mind is challenged to concentrate, to create the landscape of the written word, to follow the narrative thread and to make sense of what is being read.

"The best moments in our lives," Csikszentmihalyi says, "come when a person's body or mind is stretched to its limits in the thrill of trying to accomplish something difficult and worthwhile."

This is why television watching, a common form of relaxation, often produces boredom or apathy and rarely the blissful state of flow.

Nevertheless, even the busiest Americans tune in to the tube for as many as 15 hours a week, studies show, because they feel too tired to do anything else when they have free time.

Csikszentmihalyi counters that flow-producing pursuits would give a greater sense of well-being. "They help to make leisure what it is supposed to be—a chance for recreation," he says.

When busy professionals have a big chunk of time earmarked for leisure, many of them plan to relax by taking a vacation. According to the results of a national survey of 500 executives conducted by Hyatt Hotels and Resorts, this works.

Three out of four respondents noted that vacations improve their job performance. Nine out of 10 deemed a vacation a necessity for combating job-related stress.

It's important, though, that travelers make the right vacation choices, says Eileen Simpson, a psychotherapist in private practice in New York.

For example, a beach vacation simply doesn't work for many high-powered professionals. "These people may feel much more refreshed if they travel through a foreign country, where everything is different," Simpson says.

She calls the phenomenon out-of-one's-country-ness and claims that having one's mind actively engaged in an unusual activity is as good as rest for people who thrive on stimulation.

Actual rest, as in napping, is a productive form of relaxation for aficionados of the high-stress life. Rewards to be reaped from napping include improvements in stamina and judgment.

In fact, Paul Naitoh of the Naval Health Research Center in San Diego believes that the enlightened office of the future will encourage napping and employ a "sleep manager" whose job will be to make educated decisions about scheduling rest breaks for the entire work force.

"Napping takes planning and practice," Naitoh says. The secret is timing: Naps should be scheduled before extreme fatigue sets in, as a means to gain refreshment. They should last no less than 20 minutes, lest the sleeper awaken more tired than before, and no longer than 60, so as to ward off the stupor of "sleep inertia."

Many people prefer an exercise break to a nap as a form of relaxation. Even if they are running hard or playing tennis with a vengeance, they find the exertion ultimately rewarding and relaxing.

Medical researchers attribute this effect to the brain's exercise-induced release of feel-good substances called endorphins. The exercise elation known as the runner's high, for example, stems from this internal cascade of chemicals.

Other people prefer to relax by bringing the chemicals in from outside—by drinking a glass of wine or a cocktail after work for a sensation of sweet serenity.

However, recent studies have shown alcohol to exert a variety of effects. Putting aside the gross dangers of alcohol abuse, the effects of a single drink are intriguing.

On the positive side, a substance in red and white wine called resveratrol does help to lower cholesterol.

As a nightcap, however, while alcohol may hasten the onset of sleep, it typically disrupts sleep patterns later in the night, robbing sleep of its restfulness.

Considering the healthy alternatives, I'll take my relaxation straight up, thank you.

CRITICAL LIFE EVENTS AND THE ONSET OF ILLNESS

Blair Justice, PhD

Professor of Psychology University of Texas School of Public Health, Houston, Texas

■ In 1925, when Hans Selye was a medical student at the ancient German University of Prague and observing his first clinical cases, he asked a question that was considered so naive or pointless that his professor dismissed it as unworthy of reply. The question was: What is the "general syndrome of just being sick?"[1] What young Selye—who over the next 50 years became the world's leading authority on stress and disease—wanted to know was, why do all sick people have certain signs and symptoms in common: fatigue, loss of appetite, aches, pains, and other shared features.

After migrating to Canada and joining the biochemistry department at McGill University in Montreal, Selye began the research that eventually answered, at least in part, his original question. People get sick from "diverse noxious agents,"[2] and the resultant stress on the body produces certain nonspecific effects that sick people share in common. Selye learned that these "noxious" influences may come not only from harmful physical agents (such as viruses, bacteria, excessive cholesterol), but from an individual's appraisal of "noxious" or painful stimuli—how one looks at events in life and the meaning one attaches to them.[3]

After many years of studying the physiological effects on the body of stressors of all kinds—from chemical to emotional—Selye formulated a philosophy of life that he considered essential to health and happiness. Since unfavorable events—failures, rejections, losses—occur in everyone's life avoiding such stressors is impossible. What is important physiologically. Selye noted, is not the event but the person's reaction to it. "It's not what happens that counts; it is how you take it,"[4] he was fond of saying.

Although Selye's own work did not establish this finding, other research, both during his time and since, supports his ideas. These studies carefully document that the level and duration of potentially damaging neurochemicals in the body—such as epinephrine, norephrinephrine and cortisol—are a function of how we appraise life events and circumstances.[5,6] If we interpret a "noxious" experience as meaning it is the end of the world, the heart and immune system, as well as the gastrointestinal system, are placed at increased risk of impairment or compromise.[7,8] If, instead, we view an event as being bad, but not something so bad that we "can't stand it," then the body reacts less intensely. Neurochemicals are elevated just enough to prod us into effective action rather than helpless floundering.

How we react to an event—whether it is an illness, a divorce, a nuclear power plant accident, a pregnancy or childbirth—is strongly influenced by our perceived sense of acceptance and affirmation by others, by our interpersonal relationships and by social circumstances. The emerging science of psychoneuroimmunology (PNI) recognizes the association of such psychosocial factors with changes in biological functioning.

Almost a century and a half ago, Rudolph Virchow recognized that our very resistance to disease is affected by social conditions.[9] This perceptive German pathologist and physician char-

*Reprint requests to Blair Justice, PhD, University of Texas School of Public Health, 1200 Herman Pressler, Houston, TX 77030.

From *Comprehensive Therapy*, Vol. 20, No. 4, 1994, pp. 232-238. Reprinted with permission of *Comprehensive Therapy*, published by the American Society of Contemporary Medicine and Surgery.

acterized medicine as a "social science." He knew that physiological processes are affected profoundly by social factors. Investigating a typhus outbreak in Upper Silesia, Virchow reported that people would not have gotten the disease had they lived in a democratic system and enjoyed more favorable social conditions.[10]

A long-term epidemiological view of mortality and life span across populations suggests that people become more vulnerable to disease when they feel little control over their lives and when they lack nurturing communities and supportive families. Leonard Sagan, in *The Health of Nations*,[11] reports a reduction of mortality and extension of life span when two factors materialize—when community and family supports develop, and a sense of control over one's destiny emerges.

Today we can, at least partially, identify the mechanisms by which psychological and social factors impact biological processes, including the cardiovascular and immune systems. When people have little control in their lives, or when conditions interfere with meeting their basic needs for love or attachment, they become more vulnerable to disease and illness.[12,13] Feeling less in control and unsupported, life events are appraised more negatively giving rise to greater arousal over time of both the sympathetic-adrenal medullary system and hypothalamic-pituitary-adrenal cortical system.[14]

HOW SOCIAL SUPPORT WORKS

After two decades of research, a clearer understanding is emerging of the key features of social support that can help protect people from illness or disease and other effects of excessive stress. Sarason,[15] a pioneer in the field, showed that giving social or tangible "provisions" in the form of information, advice, companionship or money can help a stressed person; however, they are not the critical helping features. The core element, he found, is the person's sense of acceptance, a sense of affirmation and affection he or she feels from others. This is an acquired trait. It becomes part of one's personality and is retained no matter where one goes or what life events are encountered. According to Sarason without a sense of acceptance, a person is vulnerable to illness, disease, and lowered performance.

Marital discord and disruption demonstrate the profound impact that social support can have on health. For example, Somers[16] reports that disruption in a marriage can be the single most powerful sociodemographic predictor of physical and emotional illness. Indeed, poorer immune function has been found in divorced men and women who are lonely and continue to feel drawn to their ex-spouses.[17] Similarly, unhappiness in a marriage, as measured by poor marital quality, is associated with lowered immune functioning.[18] Unhappily married individuals report more illness than either

divorced or happily married persons of the same sex, age, and race.[17] These findings suggest that no simple connection can be inferred between an experience, such as being married, and health or illness. Any outcome will be affected by how an individual evaluates his or her experience and reacts to it.

ILLNESS OR DISEASE?

Whether illness or disease emerges from our reaction to life events is an important variable in the new understanding of why—and how—people get sick. Eisenberg,[9] among others, distinguishes between "disease" and "illness." Physicians think in terms of diseases and conceptualize them as abnormalities in the structure and function of individual body organs and tissues. Patients think in terms of how they feel and function as whole human beings, not as separate parts.[19] Eisenberg[9] describes illnesses as "experiences of disvalued changes in states of being and social function." Illness may occur in the absence of disease, just as disease may occur in the absence of illness. The patient is concerned with subjective signs and symptoms that may signal disease. The doctor looks for objective evidence. If none is found, no disease may be present, but an illness may still exist. Nonetheless, disease and illness are equally real to the patient. Whether the evidence is subjective or objective, psychosocial factors influence both the onset and outcome of the problem.

SUPPORT, CONTROL AND HEART ATTACKS

The influence of perceived control and support can be seen in the alternative outcomes of people who experience a heart attack. The critical life event here is myocardial infarction. Both disease and illness are present. The question is: In a group of people with the same tissue pathology receiving equally good treatment, why do some recover much better and faster than others? And, why does illness persist in some patients even when objective measures of pathology show successful treatment of the disease?

One answer involves the patient's opportunity to participate in his or her own treatment. In one study, a group of hospitalized heart attack patients received explanations about the causes, effects and treatment of myocardial infarctions. They learned how they could join in their own treatment.[20] With access to cardiac monitors, they could obtain an EKG tracing whenever they experienced symptoms. They also were taught mild isometric and foot-pedaling exercises which they did under supervision. Compared with a similar group receiving only routine information and no chance to take part in their own recovery, these patients had shorter hospital stays. Whatever greater sense of control and support the first group acquired may have affected how they continued to view their life event. This in turn would impact their cardiovascular system.

Because the cardiovascular system is particularly influenced by strong emotions, which in turn generate stress chemicals, the heart cannot be regarded simply as a mechanical pump if optimal functioning is desired. Payer[10] has observed that "in the United States the heart is viewed as a pump, and the major cause of heart pathology is considered to be due to a physical blockage in the plumbing serving the pump." She adds that "for Germans the heart is not just a pump, but an organ that has a life of its own, one that pulsates in response to a number of stimuli including the emotions."

Research in the United States and elsewhere shows that acute myocardial infarction and angina pectoris—indicating insufficient blood and oxygen supply to the heart muscle—may occur not only because of congested vessels but also because of spasm in coronary arteries, which are not simply inflexible pipes connected to a mechanical pump.[21] Cognitions can give rise to high levels of catecholamines and testosterone. Consequently, they are a key part of the mechanisms underlying arterial spasms and platelet clumping, both of which can lead to myocardial ischemic.[22] Norepinephrine and epinephrine can also stimulate release of thromboxane A2.[23] Both thromboxane A2 and the catecholamines are potent constrictors of smooth arterial muscle and strong stimulators of platelet aggregation.[24]

Given these factors, how well people recover from a heart attack, or whether they ever will ever encounter such a critical event, might therefore depend on their primary care physician's concept of the heart, a pump or an organ with a life of its own, as well as the prescribed treatment or prevention regimen. On patients' part, an increased perception of control and support plays an important role in the effectiveness of both their treatment and prevention programs.

INFLUENCE OF MEANING AND CONFIDING

The effects of trauma, even severe trauma, such as incest or a Holocaust experience, varies according to the meaning ascribed to the event by the survivors and the amount of support they perceive in their lives. Both Frankl[25] and Dimsdale[26] report how survival in concentration camps was deeply affected by whether the prisoner could find meaning in the experience. Even if meaning was expressed in a vow to live in order to seek revenge or to bear testimony, survival was enhanced and a fatal sense of hopelessness and despair averted. The ability to cling to memories of support from loved ones also was a powerful sustaining influence.

More recently, when a Jewish, Russian "refusnik" was released after 10 years of Soviet confinement, he reported that his strength to endure in prison came from knowing that a community of love supported him from the outside.[15] He maintained a strong sense of support even though he was allowed no contact with his family or the outside world for 10 years. As Sarason[15] has indicated, this political prisoner carried in his head a strong feeling that he was accepted, affirmed and loved by those he had left behind. He never doubted that they were thinking of him and working for his release. His sense of support gave him confidence in dealing with his captors. It lowered his anxiety and facilitated positive coping.

Children who recover with the least damage from years of incest or physical abuse are those who find some loving figure in their lives—a teacher, a neighbor or, in adulthood, an understanding spouse—who will listen to them and support them.[27] The most resilient children also perceived some sense of control by turning to God or becoming absorbed in the mastery of a skill.

People who have close ties to others may also benefit from confiding in them during or after a traumatic experience. In a series of recent studies Pennebaker[28] showed that after traumatic events, both psychological and physiological symptoms are relieved by systematically disclosing one's deepest thoughts and feelings either orally or in writing for 15 minutes on each of 4 consecutive days, repeating the cycle as needed. Where there is no one with whom to share painful memories, writing about one's deep feelings can bring significant benefit.[29]

Spiegel et al.[30] found that women with metastatic breast cancer live twice as long if they participate in group therapy, sharing and expressing feelings, and supporting each other in dealing with their disease. Recent studies at UCLA suggest that when people allow themselves to feel and express grief, immune proliferative response increases over time while repression of feelings and depression are associated with a decrease.[31]

PRENATAL INFLUENCES AND CHILDBIRTH

Happy events, as well as traumatic ones, can be critical in one's life. Their effects on health and illness have been well studied. For example, antibody levels are known to fluctuate with mood and happiness, with high mood being associated with high levels and low mood with low levels.[31] Holmes and Rahe,[32] first to demonstrate a correlation between life experiences and illness, argued that adjustment to change, not an event's undesirability, makes an event stressful.[33] Since then, numerous studies have established this. Events that are perceived as undesirable are more strongly correlated with risk of illness than are desirable experiences.[34] Pregnancy and birth are often viewed as happy events, but the mother may not . . . perceive them in this way. Pregnant women who feel that they have little interpersonal support and little control over life's problems may dread having a baby. These women are at higher risk for bearing low-birth weight babies and babies with complications.[35,36,37] Women under equally high stress, measured by the number of changes occurring in their lives, but who have high social support seem to be protected against these problems.[35]

Maternal attitudes toward a pregnancy and having a child have profound effects on the infant, both at birth and later. Studies in the 1970s in Germany, Austria and the United States confirmed that when a baby is unwanted, complications in pregnancy or at birth are more likely to occur.[36,38,39] High levels of catecholamines have been found in the bloodstreams of pregnant women who feel unsupported, without control or are distressed about the prospects of having a baby.[40] Passing the placental barrier, these chemicals impact the embryo and fetus.[41]

This is not the case for women whose pregnancy is welcomed, and who feel supported. What the unborn child reacts to, not only in the mother but in her environment, has increasingly come under investigation. Verny[41] reports that in the 1920s, a German doctor was told by several of his pregnant patients that they felt they should give up going to concerts because their unborn children reacted so stormily to the music. A half century later, research established that from the 25th week on, a fetus will jump in rhythm to the beat of an orchestra drum.[42] Music by both Vivaldi and Mozart seems to calm the unborn, as measured by fetal heart rate and kicking,[43] whereas music by Beethoven and Brahms has the opposite effect. All forms of rock music tend to create internal storms.[43]

SYMPTOMS AFTER NUCLEAR POWER ACCIDENTS

Pregnancy and birth have been the subject of study and speculation since the dawn of humankind. Two new life events equally as profound, however, are so recent that they have become known only in this century—in fact, only in the last decade. One of these new phenomena comes out of today's technology—the creation of nuclear power plants. The other is acquired immune deficiency syndrome (AIDS). The outcomes of people exposed to a nuclear power plant accident or infected with the AIDS virus are influenced by the individual's sense of support and control.

In March 1979 an accident occurred at the Three Mile Island (TMI) nuclear power station near Harrisburg, Pennsylvania. Although the mishap was less disastrous than the later accident at Chernobyl in the former Soviet Union, it took 11 years until the radioactive wreckage was cleared from the site.[44] Damage to the nuclear reactor produced a continued threat of radiation exposure to thousands of people living in the area. Twenty-eight months following the accident, area residents continued to exhibit higher levels of stress than did people in comparison areas who were less affected by the disaster.[45] Psychological, behavioral and biochemical measurements of 103 subjects were taken at intervals of 17 months, 22 months and 28 months after the accident. Residents with the lowest perceived control in their lives experienced the highest somatic distress and depression.[45]

In another study, heightened symptomatology after the accident was associated with a prior history of poorer social support in 312 young mothers living in the TMI area and 161 nuclear power plant workers.[46]

Compared with natural disasters, such as earthquakes, hurricanes or volcanic eruptions, technological disasters seem to have longer-lasting effects on perceived control. The difference, some researchers suggest, may be that technological disasters reflect a *loss* of control while natural disasters are associated with a *lack* of control.[45] People may accept that they lack control over the forces of nature, but believe that they can control technological power. When something goes wrong as in the case of nuclear accidents, the unexpected loss of control can be more profound. In either case, possessing a sense of control and support in one's life generally demonstrates the importance of faith and/or social affirmation for buffering the effects of stress and protecting against illness.[47,48]

PSYCHOSOCIAL EFFECTS, AIDS, AND CANCER

Control and support have an equally significant influence on patients with AIDS, affecting both the onset and course of the disease. Solomon et al. note that "while the prevalent belief among the general public, among persons with AIDS and even the professional community, is that AIDS is invariably fatal, there is a small but growing number of individuals who are alive and well 3, and even 5 years after diagnosis."[49] In Los Angeles, UCLA researchers are studying a group of men who were diagnosed with AIDS as long as 11 years ago.[50] Other investigators are finding that fatalism among those diagnosed with AIDS significantly compromises the immune system and powerfully predicts survival time.[31] Cognitive-behavioral group therapy, in early results, show improvement in immune functioning for HIV-positive persons.[31]

The San Francisco study found that psychological "hardiness" distinguishes long-term AIDS survivors from those who succumb to the disease.[49] "Hardiness" is measured by how much control, commitment and challenge a person reports.[51] Control, on this measure, means the opposite of a helpless-hopeless attitude toward bad events in life. Commitment is the opposite of alienation. People who score high on this dimension find meaning in their work, values and personal relationships. Challenge describes a person's ability to interpret stressful events as changes to be explored and successfully met rather than threats to be dreaded and feared.

Solomon and colleagues also found that one kind of social support seems to distinguish exceptional AIDS survivors who have *Pneumocystitis carinii pneumonia,* a life-threatening complication of AIDS.[49] Those who followed suggestions or took advice from people in their social network lived longer. The San Francisco researchers caution that the number of subjects in their study was small (N=21) and that their results are preliminary. They note, however, that the results are consistent with findings on the effects of control and support in other diseases. For example, Temoshok, Solomon's associate, has reported that a "Type C" coping style is associated with an unfavorable prognosis for cutaneous malignant melanoma.[52] Type C characteristics include being passive, appeasing, helpless and unexpressing of emotion. The San Francisco research group currently is investigating whether Type C in men infected with the AIDS virus is associated with greater risk of developing Kaposi's sarcoma, another serious complication of immune deficiency.

Because the asymptomatic phase of HIV-1 infection can be as long as 10 to 15 years,[53] helping people remain free of symptoms and slowing down the progression of the disease is a matter of top priority. At the Center for the Biopsychosocial Study of AIDS at the University of Miami, researchers report that aerobic exercise training has improved the immunological functioning and psychological health of a group of both HIV-1 seropositive and seronegative men.[54] They note that the exercising not only seems to have direct physiological benefits, but it also results in a greater sense of control. The researchers also are investigating the effects of a program that includes cognitive restructuring, assertiveness training, mental imagery, social support enrichment and progressive muscle relaxation. Preliminary results seem promising, but need further replication.[55]

Similar psychological intervention has been effective in improving affective state and immune function in a group of postsurgical patients with malignant melanoma.[56,57] Thirty-five patients in a 6-week program received stress management, enhancement of problem-solving skills, relaxation training, and group support. Compared to 26 controls, assessment at a 6-month followup showed significant increases in natural killer cells, NK cytotoxic activity, and percent of large granular lymphocytes. The experimental group also showed significantly less depression, fatigue and mood disturbance. They also used significantly more active-behavioral and active-cognitive coping than did the controls.[56,57]

SUMMARY

What can we conclude from these studies? One fact seems certain: there is no simple connection between life events and illness. Whether we get sick from an infection or a negative life experience depends on more than a germ or stress. All disease is multifactorial, and the resources that help protect us have much to do with our sense of support and control over our lives. What happens in our endocrine system and to our immune response is a function of what is going on inside our heads and hearts—the meanings we give to events and the feelings we have about them.

Skeptics have long doubted these tenets.[7,8] However, emerging evidence increasingly dispels these doubts and has replaced them with a biopsychosocial model based on psychoneuroimmunology (PNI). Indeed, Cousins[50] described PNI as "the new science of medicine." To date, more than a dozen academic medical centers in the United States have PNI research programs and the list is growing.

With expanded scientific study of the mind-body connection, people in general will come to recognize that whether they become ill is not always a matter of chance, but to a considerable extent something under their own control.

REFERENCES

1. Selye H: *The Stress of Life.* New York: McGraw-Hill; 1956.
2. Selye H: A syndrome produced by diverse nocuous agents. *Nature* 1936; 138: 32.
3. Selye H: *Selye's Guide to Stress Research.* New York: Van Nostrand Reinhold; 1980.
4. Selye H: *Stress Without Distress.* New York: Signet; 1975.
5. Lazarus RS: *Psychological Stress and the Coping Process.* New York: McGraw-Hill; 1966.
6. Lazarus RS, Launier R: Stress-related transactions between persons and environment. In: Pervin LA & Lewis M ed. *Perspectives in Interactional Psychology.* New York: Plenum; 1978.
7. Justice B: *Who Gets Sick: How Beliefs, Moods and Thoughts Affect Health.* Los Angeles: Tarcher; 1988.
8. Justice B: *Wer Wird Krank?* (A. Pott, trans.). Hamburg, Germany: Goldmann Verlag; 1991.
9. Eisenberg L: Science in medicine: Too much and too limited in scope? In: White KL ed. *The Task of Medicine.* Menlo Park, CA: Henry J. Kaiser Family Foundation; 1988; 290–217.
10. Payer L: *Medicine & culture.* New York: Henry Holt; 1988.
11. Sagan L: *The Health of Nations: True Causes of Sickness and Well-being.* New York: Basic Books; 1987.
12. Leighton AH: *My Name is Legion.* New York: Basic Books; 1959.

13. Leighton AH: Conceptual perspectives. In: Kaplan RN, Wilson AH and Leighton AH ed. *Further Explorations in Social Psychiatry*. New York: Basic Books; 1976.

14. Rodin J: Managing the stress of aging: The role of control and coping. In: Levine B and Holger U ed. *Coping and Health*. New York: Plenum 1979; 171–202.

15. Sarason IG: Sense of social support. Paper presented at the annual meeting of the American Psychological Association, Atlanta, GA; August 1988.

16. Somers AR: Marital Status, Health, and Use of Health Services. *JAMA* 1979; 241: 1818–1822.

17. Kiecolt-Glaser JK, Kennedy S, Malkoff S, Fisher L, Speicher CE, and Glasser R: Marital discord and immunity in males. *Psychosomatic Med* 1988; 50: 213–229.

18. Kiecolt-Glasser JK, Fisher L, Ogrocki P, Stout JC, Speicher EE, and Glaser R: Martial quality, marital disruption, and immune function. *Psychosomatic Med*, 1987; 49: 13–34.

19. Schwartz MA, Wiggins OP: Scientific and humanistic medicine: A theory of clinical methods. In: White KL ed. *The Task of Medicine*. Menlo Park, CA: Henry J. Kaiser Family Foundation; 1988: 137–171.

20. Cromwell RI, Butterfield EC, Brayfield FM, and Curry JJ: *Acute Myocardial Infarction: Reaction and Recovery*. St. Louis: Mosby; 1977.

21. Ornish D: *Stress, Diet and Your Heart*. New York: Signet; 1982.

22. Oliva PB: Pathophysiology of acute infarction. *Annals of Internal Medicine* 1981: 94: 236–250.

23. Hirsch PD, Hillis LD, Campbell WB, Firth BG, and Willerson JT: Release of prostaglandins and thromboxane into the coronary circulation in patients with ischemic heart disease. *NEJM* 1981; 304: 685–691.

24. Moncada S, Vane JR: Arachidonic acid metabolites and the interactions between Platelet and blood vessel walls. *NEJM* 1979; 300: 1142–1149.

25. Frankl VE: *Man's Search for Meaning*. 3rd ed. New York: Simon & Schuster; 1984.

26. Dimsdale JE: The Coping Behavior of Nazi Concentration Camp Survivors. *American Journal of Psychiatry* 1974; 131(7): 792–797.

27. Mrazek FJ, Mrazek DA: Resilience in child maltreatment victims: A conceptual exploration. *Child Abuse & Neglect* 1987; 11: 357–366.

28. Pennebaker J: *Opening Up: The Healing Powers of Confiding*. New York: Morrow; 1990.

29. Pennebaker J: Writing is healing. Presentation at the Hawthorne Training Conference, Houston, TX; March 1990.

30. Spiegel D, Bloom JR, Kraemer HC, Gottheil E: Effect of psychosocial treatment on survival of patients with metastatic breast cancer. *Lancet* 1989; Oct 14: 1888–891.

31. Kemeny M: Mind, emotions and the immune system. Presentation at annual conference of Institute of Noetic Sciences, Arlington, VA; June 1993.

32. Holmes TH, Rahe RH: The social readjustment rating scale. *J of Psychosomatic Res* 1976; 11: 213–218.

33. Holmes TH, Masuda M: Life Change and Illness Susceptibility. In: Dohrenwend BS Dohrewend BF eds. *Stressful Life Events: Their Nature and Effects*. New York: Wiley; 1974: 9–44.

34. Dohrenwend BB, Dohrenwend BP: Life Stress and Illness. In: Dohrenwend BB and Dohrenwend BP eds. *Stressful Life Events and Their Contexts*. New York, Prodist; 1981: 1–27.

35. Nuckolls KB, Cassel J, Kaplan BH: Psychosocial assets, life crisis, and the prognosis of pregnancy. *Am J Epi*, 1972; 95: 431–441.

36. Morris NM, Udry JR, Chase CL: Reduction of low birth weight birth rates by the prevention of unwanted pregnancies. *Am J Public Health* 1973; 3(11): 935–938.

37. Norbeck JS, Tilden VP: Life stress, social support, and emotional disequilibrium in complications of pregnancy: A prospective, multivariate study. *J of Health and Social Behavior* 1983; 24(3) 30–46.

38. Rottman G: Untersuchungen uber Einstellung zur Schwangerschaft und zur fotalen Entwiklung. In: Graber H ed. *Geist und Psyche* Munchen: Kindler Verlag; 1974.

39. Lukesch M: Psychologie Faktoren der Schwangershaft. Unpublished dissertation, University of Salzburg; 1975.

40. Kruse F: Nos souvenirs du corps maternel, *Psychologie Heute* 1978: 56.

41. Verny T, Kelly J: *The Secret Life of the Unborn Child*. New York: Summit Books; 1981.

42. Liley A: The fetus as a personality. *The Australian and New Zealand Journal of Psychiatry* 1972; 6: 99–105.

43. Clements M: Observations on certain aspects of neonatal behavior in response to auditory stimuli. Paper presented at the Fifth International Congress of Psychosomatic Obstetrics and Gynecology, Rome; 1977.

44. Wald M: After the meltdown, lessons from a clean-up. *New York Times* 1990; April 24: B5–B6.

45. Davidson LM, Baum A, Fleming, Gisriel MM: Toxic Exposure and Chronic Stress at Three Mile Island. In Lebovits AH, Baum A, and Singer JE eds. *Advances in Environmental Psychology*. Hillsdale, NJ: Erlbaum, 1986; 6: 35–46.

46. Bromet EV, Schulberg HC: The Three Mile Island Disaster: A Search for high-risk Groups. In Shore JH ed. *Disaster Stress Studies: New Methods and Findings*. Washington, DC: American Psychiatric Press; 1986: 2–19.

47. Levine JS, Schiller PL: Is there a religious factor in health? *J Religion & Health* 1987; 6: 9–36.

48. King DG: Religion and health relationships: A review. *Journal of Religion and Health* 1990; 29(2): 101–112.

49. Solomon GF, Temoshok L, O'Leary A, Zich J: An Intensive Psychoimmunologic study of long-surviving persons with AIDS. *Annals of the New York Academy of Sciences* 1987; 496: 647–655.

50. Cousins N: New dimensions in healing. Presentation at the Tenneco Distinguished Lecture Series, University of Houston, TX; March 1990.

51. Kobasa SCO, Maddi SR, Puccetti and Zola MA: Effectiveness of hardiness, exercise and social support as resources against illness. *J Psychosomatic Res* 1985; 29(5): 525–533.

52. Temoshok L, Heller BW, Sagebiel RW, Blois MS, Sweet DM, DiClemente RJ, and Gold ML: The relations of psychosocial factors to prognostic indicators in cutaneous malignant melanoma. *J Psychosomatic Med* 1985; 29: 139–153.

53. Munoz A, Wang MC, Good R, Detels H, Ginsberg L, Kingsley J, et al.: Estimation of the AIDS-free times after HIV-1 seroconversion. Paper presented at the Fourth Annual Meeting of the International Conference on AIDS, Stockholm, Sweden, June 1988.

54. Antoni MH, Schneiderman N, Fletcher MA, Goldstein DA: Psychoneuroimmunology and HIV-1. *J Consulting and Clinical Psychology* 1990; 58(1): 38–49.

55. Antoni M: Psychosocial stress management and immune functioning in an HIV-1 risk group. Paper presented at the annual meeting of the American Psychological Association, New Orleans, LA; August 1989.

56. Fawzy FW, Cousins N, Fawzy NW, Kemeny ME, Elashoff R, Morton D: A structured psychiatric intervention for cancer patients; I. Changes over time in methods of coping and affective disturbance. *Arch Gen Psychiatry* 1990; 47: 720–725.

57. Fawzy FI, Kemeny ME, Fawzy NW, Elashoff R, Morton D, Cousins N, et al.: A structured psychiatric intervention for cancer patients; II. Changes over time in immunological measures. *Arch Gen Psychiatry* 1990; 47: 729–735.

This glossary of psychology terms is included to provide you with a convenient and ready reference as you encounter general terms in your study of psychology and personal growth and behavior that are unfamiliar or require a review. It is not intended to be comprehensive, but taken together with the many definitions included in the articles themselves, it should prove to be quite useful.

Abnormal Irregular, deviating from the norm or average. Abnormal implies the presence of a mental disorder that leads to behavior that society labels as deviant. There is a continuum between normal and abnormal. These are relative terms in that they imply a social judgment. *See* Normal.

Accommodation Process in cognitive development; involves altering or reorganizing the mental picture to make room for a new experience or idea.

Acetylcholine A neurotransmitter involved in memory.

Achievement Drive The need to attain self-esteem, success, or status. Society's expectations strongly influence the achievement motive.

ACTH (Adrenocorticotropic Hormone) The part of the brain called the hypothalamus activates the release of the hormone ACTH from the pituitary gland when a stressful condition exists. ACTH in turn activates the release of adrenal corticoids from the cortex of the adrenal gland.

Action Therapy A general classification of therapy (as opposed to insight therapy) in which the therapist focuses on symptoms rather than on underlying emotional states. Treatment aims at teaching new behavioral patterns rather than at self-understanding. *See* Insight Therapy.

Actor-Observer Attribution The tendency to attribute the behavior of other people to internal causes and the behavior of yourself to external causes.

Acupuncture The technique for curing certain diseases and anesthetizing by inserting needles at certain points of the body, developed in China and now being studied and applied in the West.

Adaptation The process of responding to changes in the environment by altering one's responses to keep one's behavior appropriate to environmental demands.

Addiction Physical dependence on a drug. When a drug causes biochemical changes that are uncomfortable when the drug is discontinued, when one must take ever larger doses to maintain the intensity of the drug's effects, and when desire to continue the drug is strong, one is said to be addicted.

Adjustment How we react to stress; some change that we make in response to the demands placed upon us.

Adrenal Glands Endocrine glands involved in stress and energy regulation.

Affective Disorder Affect means feeling or emotion. An affective disorder is mental illness marked by a disturbance of mood (e.g., manic depression.)

Afferent Neuron (Sensory) A neuron that carries messages from the sense organs toward the central nervous system.

Aggression Any act that causes pain or suffering to another. Some psychologists believe that aggressive behavior is instinctual to all species, including man, while others believe that it is learned through the processes of observation and imitation.

Alienation Indifference to or loss of personal relationships. An individual may feel estranged from family members, or, on a broader scale, from society.

All-or-None Law The principle that states that a neuron only fires when a stimulus is above a certain minimum strength (threshold), and that when it fires, it does so at full strength.

Altered State of Consciousness (ASC) A mental state qualitatively different from a person's normal, alert, waking consciousness.

Altruism Behavior motivated by a desire to benefit another person. Altruistic behavior is aided by empathy and is usually motivated internally, not by observable threats or rewards.

Amphetamine A psychoactive drug that is a stimulant. Although used in treating mild depressions or, in children, hyperactivity, its medical uses are doubtful, and amphetamines are often abused. *See* Psychoactive Drug.

Anal Stage Psychosexual stage, during which, according to Freud, the child experiences the first restrictions on his impulses.

Animism The quality of believing life exists in inanimate objects. According to Piaget, animism is characteristic of children's thinking until about age two.

Antisocial Personality Disorder Personality disorder in which individuals who engaged in antisocial behavior experience no guilt or anxiety about their actions; sometimes called sociopathy or psychopathy.

Anxiety An important term that has different meanings for different theories (psychoanalysis, behavior theory); a feeling state of apprehension, dread, or uneasiness. The state may be aroused by an objectively dangerous situation or by a situation that is not objectively dangerous. It may be mild or severe.

Anxiety Disorder Fairly long-lasting disruptions of the person's ability to deal with stress; often accompanied by feelings of fear and apprehension.

Applied Psychology The area of psychology that is most immediately concerned with helping to solve practical problems; includes clinical and counseling psychology, and industrial, environmental, and legal psychology.

Aptitude Tests Tests which are designed to predict what can be accomplished by a person in the future with the proper training.

Arousal A measure of responsiveness or activity; a state of excitement or wakefulness ranging from deepest coma to intense excitement.

Aspiration Level The level of achievement a person strives for. Studies suggest that people can use internal or external standards of performance.

Assertiveness Training Training which helps individuals stand up for their rights while not denying rights of other people.

Assimilation Process in cognitive development; occurs when something new is taken into the child's mental picture of the world.

Association Has separate meanings for different branches of psychology. Theory in cognitive psychology suggests that we organize information so that we can find our memories systematically, that one idea will bring another to mind. In psychoanalysis, the patient is asked to free associate (speak aloud all consecutive thoughts until random associations tend of themselves to form a meaningful whole). *See* Cognitive Psychology; Psychoanalysis.

Association Neurons Neurons that connect with other neurons.

Associationism A theory of learning suggesting that once two stimuli are presented together, one of them will remind a person of the other. Ideas are learned by association with sensory experiences and are not innate. Among the principles of associationism are contiguity (stimuli that occur close together are more likely to be associated than stimuli far apart), and repetition (the more frequently stimuli occur together, the more strongly they become associated).

Attachment Process in which the individual shows behaviors that promote the proximity or contact with a specific object or person.

Attention The tendency to focus activity in a particular direction and to select certain stimuli for further analysis while ignoring or possibly storing for further analysis all other inputs.

Attitude An overall tendency to respond positively or negatively to particular people or objects in a way that is learned through experience and that is made up of feelings (affects), thoughts (evaluations), and actions (conation).

Attribution The process of determining the causes of behavior in a given individual.

Autism A personality disorder in which a child does not respond socially to people.

Autonomic Nervous System The part of the nervous system (the other part is the central nervous system) that is for emergency functions and release of large amounts of energy (sympathetic division) and regulating functions such as digestion and sleep (parasympathetic division). *See* Biofeedback.

Aversion Therapy A counterconditioning therapy in which unwanted responses are paired with unpleasant consequences.

Avoidance Conditioning Situation in which a subject learns to avoid an aversive stimulus by responding appropriately before it begins.

Barbiturates Sedative-hypnotic, psychoactive drugs widely used to induce sleep and to reduce tension. Overuse can lead to addiction. *See* Addiction.

Behavior Any observable activity of an organism, including mental processes.

Behavior Therapy The use of conditioning processes to treat mental disorders. Various techniques may be used, including positive reinforcement in which rewards (verbal or tangible) are given to the patient for appropriate behavior, modeling in which patients unlearn fears by watching models exhibit fearlessness, and systematic desensitization in which the patient is taught to relax and visualize anxiety-producing items at the same time. *See* Insight Therapy; Systematic Desensitization.

Behaviorism A school of psychology stressing an objective approach to psychological questions, proposing that psychology be limited to observable behavior and that the subjectiveness of consciousness places it beyond the limits of scientific psychology.

Biofeedback The voluntary control of physiological processes by receiving information about those processes as they occur, through instruments that pick up these changes and display them to the subject in the form of a signal. Blood pressure, skin temperature, etc. can be controlled.

Biological (Primary) Motives Motives that have a physiological basis; include hunger, thirst, body temperature regulation, avoidance of pain, and sex.

Biological Response System System of the body that is particularly important in behavioral responding; includes the senses, endocrines, muscles, and the nervous system.

Biological Therapy Treatment of behavior problems through biological techniques; major biological therapies include drug therapy, psychosurgery, and electronconvulsive therapy.

Bipolar Disorder Affective disorder that is characterized by extreme mood swings from sad depression to joyful mania; sometimes called manic-depression.

Body Language Communication through position and movement of the body.

Brain Mapping A procedure for identifying the function of various areas of the brain; the surgeon gives tiny electrical stimulation to a specific area and notes patient's reaction.

Brain Stimulation The introduction of chemical or electrical stimuli directly into the brain.

Brain Waves Electrical responses produced by brain activity that can be recorded directly from any portion of the brain or from the scalp with special electrodes. Brain waves are measured by an electroencephalograph (EEG). Alpha waves occur during relaxed wakefulness and beta waves during active behavior. Theta waves are associated with drowsiness and vivid visual imagery, delta waves with deep sleep.

Bystander Effect Phenomenon in which a single person is more likely to help in an emergency situation than a group of people.

Cannon-Bard Theory of Emotion Theory of emotion that states that the emotional feeling and the physiological arousal occur at the same time.

Catatonic Schizophrenia A type of schizophrenia that is characterized by periods of complete immobility and the apparent absence of will to move or speak.

Causal Attribution Process of determining whether a person's behavior is due to internal or external motives.

Cautious Shift Research suggests that the decisions of a group will be more conservative than that of the average individual member when dealing with areas for which there are widely held values favoring caution (e.g., physical danger or family responsibility). *See* Risky Shift.

Central Nervous System The part of the human nervous system that interprets and stores messages from the sense organs, decides what behavior to exhibit, and sends appropriate messages to the muscles and glands; includes the brain and spinal cord.

Central Tendency In statistics, measures of central tendency give a number that represents the entire group or sample.

Cerebellum The part of the brain responsible for muscle and movement control and coordination of eye-body movement.

Cerebral Cortex The part of the brain consisting of the outer layer of cerebral cells. The cortex can be divided into specific regions: sensory, motor, and associative.

Chaining Behavior theory suggests that behavior patterns are built up of component parts by stringing together a number of simpler responses.

Character Disorder (or Personality Disorder) A classification of psychological disorders (as distinguished from neurosis or psychosis). The disorder has become part of the individual's personality and does not cause him or her discomfort, making that disorder more difficult to treat psychotherapeutically.

Chromosome *See* Gene.

Chunking The tendency to code memories so that there are fewer bits to store.

Classical Conditioning *See* Pavlovian Conditioning.

Client-Centered Therapy A nondirective form of psychotherapy developed by Carl Rogers in which the counselor attempts to create an atmosphere in which the client can freely explore herself or himself and her or his problems. The client-centered therapist reflects what the client says back to him, usually without interpreting it.

Clinical Psychology The branch of psychology concerned with testing, diagnosing, interviewing, conducting research and treating (often by psychotherapy) mental disorders and personality problems.

Cognitive Appraisal Intellectual evaluation of situations or stimuli. Experiments suggest that emotional arousal is produced not simply by a stimulus but by how one evaluates and interprets the arousal. The appropriate physical response follows this cognitive appraisal.

Cognitive Behavior Therapy A form of behavior therapy that identifies self-defeating attitudes and thoughts in a subject, and then helps the subject to replace these with positive, supportive thoughts.

Cognitive Dissonance People are very uncomfortable if they perceive that their beliefs, feelings, or acts are not consistent with one another, and they will try to reduce the discomfort of this dissonance.

Cognitive Psychology The study of how individuals gain knowledge of their environments. Cognitive psychologists believe that the organism actively participates in constructing the meaningful stimuli that it selectively organizes and to which it selectively responds.

Comparative Psychology The study of similarities and differences in the behavior of different species.

Compulsive Personality Personality disorder in which an individual is preoccupied with details and rules.

Concept Learning The acquisition of the ability to identify and use the qualities that objects or situations have in common. A class concept refers to any quality that breaks objects or situations into separate groupings.

Concrete-Operational Stage A stage in intellectual development, according to Piaget. The child at approximately seven years begins to apply logic. His or her thinking is less egocentric, reversible, and the child develops conservation abilities and the ability to classify. *See* Conservation.

Conditioned Reinforcer Reinforcement that is effective because it has been associated with other reinforcers. Conditioned reinforcers are involved in higher order conditioning.

Conditioned Response (CR) The response or behavior that occurs when the conditioned stimulus is presented (after the conditioned stimulus has been associated with the unconditioned stimulus).

Conditioned Stimulus (CS) An originally neutral stimulus that is associated with an unconditioned stimulus and takes on its capability of eliciting a particular reaction.

Conditioned Taste Aversion (CTA) Learning an aversion to particular tastes by associating them with stomach distress; usually considered a unique form of classical conditioning because of the extremely long interstimulus intervals involved.

Conduction The ability of a neuron to carry a message (an electrical stimulus) along its length.

Conflict Situation that occurs when we experience incompatible demands or desires.

Conformity The tendency of an individual to act like others regardless of personal belief.

Conscience A person's sense of the moral rightness or wrongness of behavior.

Consciousness Awareness of experienced sensations, thoughts, and feelings at any given point in time.

Consensus In causal attribution, the extent to which other people react the same way the subject does in a particular situation.

Conservation Refers to the child's ability to understand laws of length, mass, and volume. Before the development of this ability, a child will not understand that a particular property of an object (e.g., the quantity of water in a glass) does not change even though other perceivable features change.

Consistency In causal attribution, the extent to which the subject always behaves in the same way in a particular situation.

Consolidation The biological neural process of making memories permanent; possibly short-term memory is electrically coded and long-term memory is chemically coded.

Continuum of Preparedness Seligman's proposal that animals are biologically prepared to learn certain responses more readily than others.

Control Group A group used for comparison with an experimental group. All conditions must be identical for each group with the ex-

ception of the one variable (independent) that is manipulated. *See* Experimental Group.

Convergence Binocular depth cue in which we detect distance by interpreting the kinesthetic sensations produced by the muscles of the eyeballs.

Convergent Thinking The kind of thinking that is used to solve problems having only one correct answer. *See* Divergent Thinking.

Conversion Disorder Somatoform disorder in which a person displays obvious disturbance in the nervous system, however, a medical examination reveals no physical basis for the problem; often includes paralysis, loss of sensation, or blindness.

Corpus Callosum Nerve fibers that connect the two halves of the brain in humans. If cut, the halves continue to function although some functions are affected.

Correlation A measurement in which two or more sets of variables are compared and the extent to which they are related is calculated.

Correlation Coefficient The measure, in number form, of how two variables vary together. They extend from -1 (perfect negative correlation) to a $+1$ (perfect positive correlation).

Counterconditioning A behavior therapy in which an unwanted response is replaced by conditioning a new response that is incompatible with it.

Creativity The ability to discover or produce new solutions to problems, new inventions, or new works of art. Creativity is an ability independent of IQ and is opened-ended in that solutions are not predefined in their scope or appropriateness. *See* Problem Solving.

Critical Period A specific stage in an organism's development during which the acquisition of a particular type of behavior depends on exposure to a particular type of stimulation.

Cross-Sectional Study A research technique that focuses on a factor in a group of subjects as they are at one time, as in a study of fantasy play in subjects of three different age groups. *See* Longitudinal Study.

Culture-Bound The idea that a test's usefulness is limited to the culture in which it was written and utilized.

Curiosity Motive Motive that causes the individual to seek out a certain amount of novelty.

Cutaneous Sensitivity The skin senses: touch, pain, pressure and temperature. Skin receptors respond in different ways and with varying degrees of sensitivity.

Decay Theory of forgetting in which sensory impressions leave memory traces that fade away with time.

Defense Mechanism A way of reducing anxiety that does not directly cope with the threat. There are many types, denial, repression, etc., all of which are used in normal function. Only when use is habitual or they impede effective solutions are they considered pathological.

Delusion A false belief that persists despite evidence showing it to be irrational. Delusions are often symptoms of mental illness.

Dependent Variable Those conditions that an experimenter observes and measures. Called "dependent" because they depend on the experimental manipulations.

Depersonalization Disorder Dissociative disorder in which individuals escape from their own personalities by believing that they don't exist or that their environment is not real.

Depression A temporary emotional state that normal individuals experience or a persistent state that may be considered a psychological disorder. Characterized by sadness and low self-esteem. *See* Self-Esteem.

Descriptive Statistics Techniques that help summarize large amounts of data information.

Developmental Norms The average time at which developmental changes occur in the normal individual.

Developmental Psychology The study of changes in behavior and thinking as the organism grows from the prenatal stage to death.

Deviation, Standard and Average Average deviation is determined by measuring the deviation of each score in a distribution from the mean and calculating the average of the deviations. The standard deviation is used to determine how representative the mean of a distribution is. *See* Mean.

Diagnostic and Statistical Manual of Mental Disorders (DSM) DSM-III was published in 1980 by the American Psychiatric Association.

Diffusion of Responsibility As the number of witnesses to a help-requiring situation—and thus the degree of anonymity—increases, the amount of helping decreases and the amount of time before help is offered increases. *See* Bystander Effect.

Discrimination The ability to tell whether stimuli are different when presented together or that one situation is different from a past one.

Disorganized Schizophrenia A type of schizophrenia that is characterized by a severe personality disintegration; the individual often displays bizarre behavior.

Displacement The process by which an emotion originally attached to a particular person, object, or situation is transferred to something else.

Dissociative Disorders Disorders in which individuals forget who they are.

Distal Stimuli Physical events in the environment that affect perception. *See* Proximal Stimuli.

Distinctiveness In causal attribution, the extent to which the subject reacts the same way in other situations.

Divergent Thinking The kind of thinking that characterizes creativity (as contrasted with convergent thinking) and involves the development of novel resolutions of a task or the generation of totally new ideas. *See* Convergent Thinking.

DNA *See* Gene.

Double Bind A situation in which a person is subjected to two conflicting, contradictory demands at the same time.

Down's Syndrome Form of mental retardation caused by having three number 21 chromosomes (trisomy 21).

Dreams The thoughts, images, and emotions that occur during sleep. Dreams occur periodically during the sleep cycle and are usually marked by rapid movements of the eyes (REM sleep). The content of dreams tends to reflect emotions (sexual feelings, according to Freud) and experiences of the previous day. Nightmares are qualitatively different from other dreams, often occurring during deep or Stage 4 sleep.

Drive A need or urge that motivates behavior. Some drives may be explained as responses to bodily needs, such as hunger or sex. Others derive from social pressures and complex forms of learning, for example, competition, curiosity, achievement, *See* Motivation.

Drive Reduction Theory Theory of motivation that states that the individual is pushed by inner forces toward reducing the drive and restoring homeostasis.

Drug Dependence A state of mental or physical dependence on a drug, or both. Psychoactive drugs are capable of creating psychological dependence (anxiety when the drug is unavailable), although the relationship of some, such as marijuana and LSD, to physical dependence or addiction is still under study. *See* Psychoactive Drug; Addiction.

Drug Tolerance A state produced by certain psychoactive drugs in which increasing amounts of the substance are required to produce the desired effect. Some drugs produce tolerance but not withdrawal symptoms, and these drugs are not regarded as physically addicting.

Effectance Motive The striving for effectiveness in dealing with the environment. The effectance motive differs from the need for achievement in that effectance depends on internal feelings of satisfaction while the need for achievement is geared more to meeting others' standards.

Efferent Neuron (Motor) A neuron that carries messages from the central nervous system to the muscles and glands.

Ego A construct to account for the organization in a person's life and for making the person's behavior correspond to physical and social realities. According to Freud, the ego is the "reality principle" that is responsible for holding the id or "pleasure principle" in check. *See* Id.

Egocentrism Seeing things from only one's own point of view; also, the quality of a child's thought that prevents her or him from understanding that different people perceive the world differently. Egocentrism is characteristic of a stage that all children go through.

Electra Complex The libidinal feelings of a child toward a parent of the opposite sex. *See also* Oedipus Complex

Electroshock Therapy A form of therapy used to relieve severe depression. The patient receives electric current across the forehead, loses consciousness, and undergoes a short convulsion. When the patient regains consciousness, his or her mood is lifted.

Emotion A complex feeling-state that involves physiological arousal; a subjective feeling which might involve a cognitive appraisal of the situation and overt behavior in response to a stimulus.

Empathy The ability to appreciate how someone else feels by putting yourself in her or his position and experiencing her or his feelings. Empathy is acquired normally by children during intellectual growth.

Empiricism The view that behavior is learned through experience.

Encounter Groups Groups of individuals who meet to change their personal lives by confronting each other, discussing personal problems, and talking more honestly and openly than in everyday life.

Endocrine Glands Ductless glands that secrete chemicals called hormones into the blood stream.

Equilibration According to Piaget, the child constructs an understanding of the world through equilibration. Equilibration consists of the interaction of two complementary processes, assimilation (taking in input within the existing structures of the mind, e.g., putting it into mental categories that already exist) with accommodation (the changing of mental categories to fit new input that cannot be taken into existing categories) and is the process by which knowing occurs. One's developmental stage affects how one equilibrates.

Ethnocentrism The belief that one's own ethnic or racial group is superior to others.

Experiment Procedures executed under a controlled situation in order to test a hypothesis and discover relationships between independent and dependent variables.

Experimental Control The predetermined conditions, procedures, and checks built into the design of an experiment to ensure scientific control; as opposed to "control" in common usage, which implies manipulation.

Experimental Group In a scientific experiment, the group of subjects that is usually treated specially, as opposed to the control group, in order to isolate just the variable under investigation. *See* Control Group.

Experimental Psychology The branch of psychology concerned with the laboratory study of basic psychological laws and principles as demonstrated in the behavior of animals.

Experimenter Bias How the expectations of the person running an experiment can influence what comes out of the experiment. Experimenter bias can affect the way the experimenter sees the subjects' behavior, causing distortions of fact, and can also affect the way the experimenter reads data, also leading to distortions.

Extinction The elimination of behavior by, in classical conditioning, the withholding of the unconditional stimulus, and in operant conditioning, the withholding of the reinforcement.

Extrasensory Perception (ESP) The range of perceptions that are "paranormal," (such as the ability to predict events, reproduce drawings sealed in envelopes, etc.).

Fixed Interval (FI) Schedule Schedule of reinforcement in which the subject receives reinforcement for the first correct response given after a specified time interval.

Fixed Ratio (FR) Schedule Schedule of reinforcement in which the subject is reinforced after a certain number of responses.

Fixed-Action Pattern Movement that is characteristic of a species and does not have to be learned.

Forgetting The process by which material that once was available is no longer available. Theory exists that forgetting occurs because memories interfere with one another, either retroactively (new memories block old) or proactively (old memories block new); that forgetting occurs when the cues necessary to recall the information are not supplied, or when memories are too unpleasant to remain in consciousness. *See* Repression.

Formal Operational Stage According to Piaget, the stage at which the child develops adult powers of reasoning, abstraction, and symbolizing. The child can grasp scientific, religious, and political concepts and deduce their consequences as well as reason hypothetically ("what if . . ."").

Frequency Theory of Hearing Theory of hearing that states that the frequency of vibrations at the basilar membrane determines the frequency of firing of neurons that carry impulses to the brain.

Frustration A feeling of discomfort or insecurity aroused by a blocking of gratification or by unresolved problems. Several theories hold that frustration arouses aggression. *See* Aggression.

Functionalism An early school of psychology stressing the ways behavior helps one adapt to the environment and the role that learning plays in this adaptive process.

Gene The unit of heredity that determines particular characteristics; a part of a molecule of DNA. DNA (dioxyribonucleic acid) is found mainly in the nucleus of living cells where it occurs in threadlike structures called chromosomes. Within the chromosomes, each DNA molecule is organized into specific units that carry the genetic information necessary for the development of a particular trait. These units are the genes. A gene can reproduce itself exactly, and this is how traits are carried between generations. The genotype is the entire structure of genes that are inherited by an organism from its parents. The environment interacts with this genotype to determine how the genetic potential will develop.

General Adaptation Syndrome (GAS) The way the body responds to stress, as described by Hans Selye. In the first stage, an alarm reaction, a person responds by efforts at self-control and shows signs of nervous depression (defense mechanisms, fear, anger, etc.) followed by a release of ACTH. In stage 2, the subject shows increased resistance to the specific source of stress and less resistance to other sources. Defense mechanisms may become neurotic. With stage 3 comes exhaustion, stupor, even death.

Generalization The process by which learning in one situation is transferred to another, similar situation. It is a key term in behavioral modification and classical conditioning. *See* Classical Conditioning.

Generalized Anxiety Disorder Disorder in which the individual lives in a state of constant severe tension; continuous fear and apprehension experienced by an individual.

Genetics The study of the transfer of the inheritance of characteristics from one generation to another.

Genotype The underlying genetic structure that an individual has inherited and will send on to descendants. The actual appearance of a trait (phenotype) is due to the interaction of the genotype and the environment.

Gestalt Psychology A movement in psychology begun in the 1920s, stressing the wholeness of a person's experience and proposing that perceiving is an active, dynamic process that takes into account the entire pattern of ("gestalt") of the perpetual field. *See* Behaviorism; Associationism.

Glia Cells in the central nervous system that regulate the chemical environment of the nerve cells. RNA is stored in glial cells.

Grammar The set of rules for combining units of a language.

Group Therapy A form of psychotherapy aimed at treating mental disorders in which interaction among group members is the main therapeutic means. Group therapy takes many forms but essentially requires a sense of community, support, increased personal responsibility, and a professionally trained leader.

Growth The normal quantitative changes that occur in the physical and psychological aspects of a healthy child with the passage of time.

Gustation The sense of taste. Theory suggests that the transmission of sense information from tongue to brain occurs through patterns of cell activity and not just the firing of single nerve fibers. Also, it is believed that specific spatial patterns or places on the tongue correspond to taste qualities.

Habit Formation The tendency to make a response to a stimulus less variable, especially if it produced successful adaptation.

Hallucination A sensory impression reported by a person when no external stimulus exists to justify the report. Hallucinations are serious symptoms and may be produced by psychoses. *See* Psychosis.

Hallucinogen A substance that produces hallucinations, such as LSD, mescaline, etc.

Hierarchy of Needs Maslow's list of motives in humans, arranged from the biological to the uniquely human.

Higher Order Conditioning Learning to make associations with stimuli that have been previously learned (CSs).

Hippocampus Part of the cortex of the brain governing memory storage, smell, and visceral functions.

Homeostasis A set of processes maintaining the constancy of the body's internal state, a series of dynamic compensations of the nervous system. Many processes such as appetite, body temperature, water balance, and heart rate are controlled by homeostasis.

Hormones Chemical secretions of the endocrine glands that regulate various body processes (e.g., growth, sexual traits, reproductive processes, etc.).

Humanism Branch of psychology dealing with those qualities distinguishing humans from other animals.

Hypnosis A trancelike state marked by heightened suggestibility and a narrowing of attention that can be induced in a number of ways.

Debate exists over whether hypnosis is a true altered state of consciousness and to what extent strong motivating instructions can duplicate so-called hypnosis.

Hypothalamus A part of the brain that acts as a channel that carries information from the cortex and the thalamus to the spinal cord and ultimately to the motor nerves or to the autonomic nervous system, where it is transmitted to specific target organs. These target organs release into the bloodstream specific hormones that alter bodily functions. *See* Autonomic Nervous System.

Hypothesis A hypothesis can be called an educated guess, similar to a hunch. When a hunch is stated in a way that allows for further testing, it becomes a hypothesis.

Iconic Memory A visual memory. Experiments suggest that in order to be remembered and included in long-term memory, information must pass through a brief sensory stage. Theory further suggests that verbal information is subject to forgetting but that memorized sensory images are relatively permanent.

Id According to Freud, a component of the psyche present at birth that is the storehouse of psychosexual energy called *libido*, and also of primitive urges to fight, dominate, destroy.

Identification The taking on of attributes that one sees in another person. Children tend to identify with their parents or other important adults and thereby take on certain traits that are important to their development.

Illusion A mistaken perception of an actual stimulus.

Imitation The copying of another's behavior; learned through the process of observation. *See* Modeling.

Impression Formation The process of developing an evaluation of another person from your perceptions; first, or initial, impressions are often very important.

Imprinting The rapid, permanent acquisition by an organism of a strong attachment to an object (usually the parent). Imprinting occurs shortly after birth.

Independent Variable The condition in an experiment that is controlled and manipulated by the experimenter; it is a stimulus that will cause a response.

Inferential Statistics Techniques that help researchers make generalizations about a finding based on a limited number of subjects.

Inhibition Restraint of an impulse, desire, activity, or drive. People are taught to inhibit full expression of many drives (for example, aggression or sexuality) and to apply checks either consciously or unconsciously. In Freudian terminology, an inhibition is an unconsciously motivated blocking of sexual energy. In Pavlovian conditioning, inhibition is the theoretical process that operates during extinction, acting to block a conditioned response. *See* Pavlovian Conditioning.

Insight A sudden perception of useful or proper relations among objects necessary to solve the problem.

Insight Therapy A general classification of therapy in which the therapist focuses on the patient's underlying feelings and motivations and devotes most effort to increasing the patient's self-awareness or insight into his or her behavior. The other major class of therapy is action therapy. *See* Action Therapy.

Instinct An inborn pattern of behavior, relatively independent of environmental influence. An instinct may need to be triggered by a particular stimulus in the environment, but then it proceeds in a fixed pattern. The combination of taxis (orienting movement in response to a particular stimulus) and fixed-action pattern (inherited coordination) is the basis for instinctual activity. *See* Fixed-Action Pattern.

Instrumental Learning *See* Operant Conditioning.

Intelligence A capacity for knowledge about the world. This is an enormous and controversial field of study, and there is no agreement on a precise definition. However, intelligence has come to refer to higher-level abstract processes and may be said to comprise the ability to deal effectively with abstract concepts, the ability to learn, and the ability to adapt and deal with new situations. Piaget defines intelligence as the construction of an understanding. Both biological inheritance and environmental factors contribute to general intelligence. Children proceed through a sequence of identifiable stages in the development of conceptual thinking (Piaget). The degree to which factors such as race, sex, and social class affect intelligence is not known.

Intelligence Quotient (IQ) A measurement of intelligence originally based on tests devised by Binet and now widely applied. Genetic inheritance and environment affect IQ, although their relative contributions are not known. IQ can be defined in different ways; classically it is defined as a relation between chronological and mental ages.

Interference Theory of forgetting in which information that was learned before (proactive interference) or after (retroactive interference) the material of interest causes the learner to be unable to remember the material.

Interstimulus Interval The time between the start of the conditioned stimulus and the start of the unconditioned stimulus in Pavlovian conditioning. *See* Pavlovian Conditioning.

Intrauterine Environment The environment in the uterus during pregnancy can affect the physical development of the organism and its behavior after birth. Factors such as the mother's nutrition, emotional, and physical state significantly influence offspring. The mother's diseases, medications, hormones, and stress level all affect the pre- and postnatal development of her young.

Intrinsic Motivation Motivation inside of the individual; we do something because we receive satisfaction from it.

Introspection Reporting one's internal, subjective mental contents for the purpose of further study and analysis. *See* Structuralism.

James-Lange Theory of Emotion Theory of emotion that states that the physiological arousal and behavior come before the subjective experience of an emotion.

Labeling-of-Arousal Experiments suggest that an individual experiencing physical arousal that she or he cannot explain will interpret her or his feelings in terms of the situation she or he is in and will use environmental and contextual cues.

Language A set of abstract symbols used to communicate meaning. Language includes vocalized sounds or semantic units (words, usually) and rules for combining the units (grammar). There is some inborn basis for language acquisition, and there are identifiable stages in its development that are universal.

Language Acquisition Linguists debate how children acquire language. Some believe in environmental shaping, a gradual system of reward and punishment. Others emphasize the unfolding of capacities inborn in the brain that are relatively independent of the environment and its rewards.

Latency Period According to Freud, the psychosexual stage of development during which sexual interest has been repressed and thus is low or "latent" (dormant).

Law of Effect Thorndike's proposal that when a response produces satisfaction, it will be repeated; reinforcement.

Leadership The quality of exerting more influence than other group members. Research suggests that certain characteristics are generally considered essential to leadership: consideration, sensitivity, ability to initiate and structure, and emphasis on production. However, environmental factors may thrust authority on a person without regard to personal characteristics.

Learned Helplessness Theory suggests that living in an environment of uncontrolled stress reduces the ability to cope with future stress that *is* controllable.

Learned Social Motives Motives in the human that are learned, including achievement, affiliation, and autonomy.

Learning The establishment of connections between stimulus and response, resulting from observation, special training, or previous activity. Learning is relatively permanent.

Life Span Span of time from conception to death; in developmental psychology, a life span approach looks at development throughout an individual's life.

Linguistic Relativity Hypothesis Proposal by Whorf that the perception of reality differs according to the language of the observer.

Linguistics The study of language, its nature, structure, and components.

Locus of Control The perceived place from which come determining forces in one's life. A person who feels that he or she has some control over his or her fate and tends to feel more likely to succeed has an internal locus of control. A person with an external locus of control feels that it is outside himself or herself and therefore that his or her attempts to control his or her fate are less assured.

Longitudinal Study A research method that involves following subjects over a considerable period of time (as compared with a cross-sectional approach); as in a study of fantasy play in children observed several times at intervals of two years. *See* Cross-Sectional Study.

Love Affectionate behavior between people, often in combination with interpersonal attraction. The mother-infant love relationship strongly influences the later capacity for developing satisfying love relationships.

Manic-Depressive Reaction A form of mental illness marked by alternations of extreme phases of elation (manic phase) and depression.

Maternalism Refers to the mother's reaction to her young. It is believed that the female is biologically determined to exhibit behavior more favorable to the care and feeding of the young than the male, although in humans maternalism is probably determined as much by cultural factors as by biological predisposition.

Maturation The genetically-controlled process of physical and physiological growth.

Mean The measure of central tendency, or mathematical average, computed by adding all scores in a set and dividing by the number of scores.

Meaning The concept or idea conveyed to the mind, by any method. In reference to memory, meaningful terms are easier to learn than less meaningful, unconnected, or nonsense terms. Meaningfulness is not the same as the word's meaning.

Median In a set of scores, the median is that middle score that divides the set into equal halves.

Memory Involves the encoding, storing of information in the brain, and its retrieval. Several theories exist to explain memory. One proposes that we have both a short-term (STM) and a long-term memory (LTM) and that information must pass briefly through the STM to be stored in the LTM. Also suggested is that verbal information is subject to forgetting,

while memorized sensory images are relatively permanent. Others see memory as a function of association—information processed systematically and the meaningfulness of the items. Debate exists over whether memory retrieval is actually a process of reappearance or reconstruction.

Mental Disorder A mental condition that deviates from what society considers to be normal.

Minnesota Multiphasic Personality Inventory (MMPI) An objective personality test that was originally devised to identify personality disorders.

Mode In a set of scores, the measurement at which the largest number of subjects fall.

Modeling The imitation or copying of another's behavior. As an important process in personality development, modeling may be based on parents. In therapy, the therapist may serve as a model for the patient.

Morality The standards of right and wrong of a society and their adoption by members of that society. Some researchers believe that morality develops in successive stages, with each stage representing a specific level of moral thinking (Kohlberg). Others see morality as the result of experiences in which the child learns through punishment and reward from models such as parents and teachers.

Motivation All factors that cause and regulate behavior that is directed toward achieving goals and satisfying needs. Motivation is what moves an organism to action.

Motor Unit One spinal motoneuron (motor nerve cell) and the muscle fibers it activates. The contraction of a muscle involves the activity of many motoneurons and muscle fibers. Normally we are aware only of our muscles contracting and not of the process producing the contraction, although biofeedback can train people to control individual motor units. *See* Biofeedback.

Narcotic A drug that relieves pain. Heroin, morphine, and opium are narcotics. Narcotics are often addicting.

Naturalistic Observation Research method in which behavior of people or animals in the normal environment is accurately recorded.

Negative Reinforcement Any event that upon termination, strengthens the preceding behavior; taking from subject something bad will increase the probability that the preceding behavior will be repeated. Involves aversive stimulus.

Neuron A nerve cell. There are billions of neurons in the brain and spinal cord. Neurons interact at synapses or points of contact. Information passage between neurons is electrical and biochemical. It takes the activity of many neurons to produce a behavior.

Neurosis Any one of a wide range of psychological difficulties, accompanied by excessive anxiety (as contrasted with psychosis). Psychoanalytic theory states that neurosis is an expression of unresolved conflicts in the form of tension and impaired functioning. Most neurotics are in much closer contact with reality than most psychotics. Term has been largely eliminated from DSM-III.

Nonverbal Behaviors Gestures, facial expressions, and other body movements. They are important because they tend to convey emotion. Debate exists over whether they are inborn or learned.

Norm An empirically set pattern of belief or behavior. Social norm refers to widely accepted social or cultural behavior to which a person tends to or is expected to conform.

Normal Sane, or free from mental disorder. Normal behavior is the behavior typical of most people in a given group, and "normality" implies a social judgment.

Normal Curve When scores of a large number of random cases are plotted on a graph, they

often fall into a bell-shaped curve; there are as many cases above the mean as below on the curve.

Object Permanence According to Piaget, the stage in cognitive development when a child begins to conceive of objects as having an existence even when out of sight or touch and to conceive of space as extending beyond his or her own perception.

Oedipus Complex The conflicts of a child in triangular relationship with his mother and father. According to Freud, a boy must resolve his unconscious sexual desire for his mother and the accompanying wish to kill his father and fear of his father's revenge in order that he proceed in his moral development. The analogous problem for girls is called the Electra complex.

Olfaction The sense of smell. No general agreement exists on how olfaction works, though theories exist to explain it. One suggests that the size and shape of molecules of what is smelled is a crucial cue. The brain processes involved in smell are located in a different and evolutionarily older part of the brain than the other senses.

Operant Conditioning The process of changing, maintaining, or eliminating voluntary behavior through the consequences of that behavior. Operant conditioning uses many of the techniques of Pavlovian conditioning but differs in that it deals with voluntary rather than reflex behaviors. The frequency with which a behavior is emitted can be increased if it is rewarded (reinforced) and decreased if it is not reinforced, or punished. Some psychologists believe that all behavior is learned through conditioning while others believe that intellectual and motivational processes play a crucial role. *See* Pavlovian Conditioning.

Operational Definitions If an event is not directly observable, then the variables must be defined by the operations by which they will be measured. These definitions are called operational definitions.

Organism Any living animal, human or subhuman.

Orienting Response A relatively automatic, "what's that?" response that puts the organism in a better position to attend to and deal with a new stimulus. When a stimulus attracts our attention, our body responds with movements of head and body toward the stimulus, changes in muscle tone, heart rate, blood flow, breathing, and changes in the brain's electrical activity.

Pavlovian Conditioning Also called classical conditioning, Pavlovian conditioning can be demonstrated as follows: In the first step, an *unconditioned stimulus* (UCS) such as food, loud sounds, or pain is paired with a neutral *conditioned stimulus* (CS) that causes no direct effect, such as a click, tone, or a dim light. The response elicited by the UCS is called the *unconditioned response* (UCR) and is a biological reflex of the nervous system (for example, eyeblinks or salivation). The combination of the neutral CS, the response-causing UCS, and the unlearned UCR is usually presented to the subject several times during conditioning. Eventually, the UCS is dropped from the sequence in the second step of the process, and the previously neutral CS comes to elicit a response. When conditioning is complete, presentation of the CS alone will result in a *conditioned response* (CR) similar but not always the same as the UCR.

Perception The field of psychology studying ways in which the experience of objects in the world is based upon stimulation of the sense organs. In psychology, the field of perception studies what determines sensory impressions, such as size, shape, distance, direction, etc.

Physical events in the environment are called distal stimuli while the activity at the sense organ itself is called a proximal stimulus. The study of perceiving tries to determine how an organism knows what distal stimuli are like since proximal stimuli are its only source of information. Perception of objects remains more or less constant despite changes in distal stimuli and is therefore believed to depend on relationships within stimuli (size *and* distance, for example). Perceptual processes are able to adjust and adapt to changes in the perceptual field.

Performance The actual behavior of an individual that is observed. We often infer learning from observing performance.

Peripheral Nervous System The part of the human nervous system that receives messages from the sense organs and carries messages to the muscles and glands; everything outside of the brain and spinal cord.

Persuasion The process of changing a person's attitudes, beliefs, or actions. A person's susceptibility to persuasion depends on the persuader's credibility, subtlety, and whether both sides of an argument are presented.

Phenotype The physical features or behavior patterns by which we recognize an organism. Phenotype is the result of interaction between genotype (total of inherited genes) and environment. *See* Genotype.

Phobia A neurosis consisting of an irrationally intense fear of specific persons, objects, or situations and a wish to avoid them. A phobic person feels intense and incapacitating anxiety. The person may be aware that the fear is irrational, but this knowledge does not help.

Pituitary Gland Is located in of the brain and controls secretion of several hormones: the antidiuretic hormone that maintains water balance, oxytocin that controls blood pressure and milk production, and ACTH that is produced in response to stress, etc. *See* ACTH.

Placebo A substance that in and of itself has no real effect but which may produce an effect in a subject because the subject expects or believes that it will.

Positive Reinforcement Any event that, upon presentation, strengthens the preceding behavior; giving a subject something good will increase the probability that the preceding behavior will be repeated.

Prejudice An attitude in which one holds a negative belief about members of a group to which he or she does not belong. Prejudice is often directed at minority ethnic or racial groups and may be reduced by contact with these perceived "others."

Premack Principle Principle that states that of any two responses, the one that is more likely to occur can be used to reinforce the response that is less likely to occur.

Prenatal Development Development from conception to birth. It includes the physical development of the fetus as well as certain of its intellectual and emotional processes.

Preoperational Stage The development stage at which, according to Piaget, come the start of language, the ability to imitate actions, to symbolize, and to play make-believe games. Thinking is egocentric in that a child cannot understand that others perceive things differently.

Primary Reinforcement Reinforcement that is effective without having been associated with other reinforcers; sometimes called unconditioned reinforcement.

Probability (p) In inferential statistics, the likelihood that the difference between the experimental and control groups is due to the independent variable.

Problem Solving A self-directed activity in which an individual uses information to develop answers to problems, to generate new problems, and sometimes to transform the process by creating a unique, new system. Problem solving involves learning, insight and creativity.

Projective Test A type of test in which people respond to ambiguous, loosely structured stimuli. It is assumed that people will reveal themselves by putting themselves into the stimuli they see. The validity of these tests for diagnosis and personality assessment is still at issue.

Propaganda Information deliberately spread to aid a cause. Propaganda's main function is persuasion.

Prosocial Behavior Behavior that is directed toward helping others.

Proximal Stimulus Activity at the sense organ.

Psychoactive Drug A substance that affects mental activities, perceptions, consciousness, or mood. This type of drug has its effects through strictly physical effects and through expectations.

Psychoanalysis There are two meanings to this word: it is a theory of personality development based on Freud and a method of treatment also based on Freud. Psychoanalytic therapy uses techniques of free association, dream analysis, and analysis of the patient's relationship (the "transference") to the analyst. Psychoanalytic theory maintains that the personality develops through a series of psychosexual stages and that the personality consists of specific components energized by the life and death instincts.

Psychogenic Pain Disorder Somatoform disorder in which the person complains of severe, long-lasting pain for which there is no organic cause.

Psycholinguistics The study of the process of language acquisition as part of psychological development and of language as an aspect of behavior. Thinking may obviously depend on language, but their precise relationship still puzzles psycholinguists, and several different views exist.

Psychological Dependence Situation when a person craves a drug even though it is not biologically necessary for his or her body.

Psychophysiological Disorders Real medical problems (such as ulcers, migraine headaches, and high blood pressure) that are caused or aggravated by psychological stress.

Psychosexual Stages According to Freud, an individual's personality develops through several stages. Each stage is associated with a particular bodily source of gratification (pleasure). First comes the oral stage when most pleasures come from the mouth. Then comes the anal stage when the infant derives pleasure from holding and releasing while learning bowel control. The phallic stage brings pleasure from the genitals, and a crisis (Oedipal) occurs in which the child gradually suppresses sexual desire for the opposite-sex parent, identifies with the same-sex parent and begins to be interested in the outside world. This latency period lasts until puberty, after which the genital stage begins and mature sexual relationships develop. There is no strict timetable, but, according to Freudians, the stages do come in a definite order. Conflicts experienced and not adequately dealt with remain with the individual.

Psychosis The most severe of mental disorders, distinguished by a person being seriously out of touch with objective reality. Psychoses may result from physical factors (organic) or may have no known physical cause (functional). Psychoses take many forms, of which the most common are schizophrenia and psychotic depressive reactions, but all are marked by personality disorganization and a severely reduced ability to perceive reality. Both biological and environmental factors are believed to influence the development of psychosis, although the precise effect of each is not presently known. *See* Neurosis.

Psychosomatic Disorders A variety of body reactions that are closely related to psychological events. Stress, for example, brings on many physical changes and can result in illness or even death if prolonged and severe. Psychosomatic disorders can affect any part of the body.

Psychotherapy Treatment involving interpersonal contacts between a trained therapist and a patient in which the therapist tries to produce beneficial changes in the patient's emotional state, attitudes, and behavior.

Punishment Any event that decreases the probability of the preceding behavior being repeated. You can give something bad (positive punishment) to decrease the preceding behavior.

Rational-Emotive Therapy A cognitive behavior modification technique in which a person is taught to identify irrational, self-defeating beliefs and then to overcome them.

Rationalization Defense mechanism in which individuals make up logical excuses to justify their behavior rather than exposing their true motives.

Reaction Formation Defense mechanism in which a person masks an unconsciously distressing or unacceptable trait by assuming an opposite attitude or behavior pattern.

Reactive Schizophrenia A type of schizophrenia in which the disorder appears as a reaction to some major trauma or terribly stressful encounter; sometimes called acute schizophrenia.

Reality Therapy A form of treatment of mental disorders pioneered by William Glasser in which the origins of the patient's problems are considered irrelevant and emphasis is on a close, judgmental bond between patient and therapist aimed to improve the patient's present and future life.

Reflex An automatic movement that occurs in direct response to a stimulus.

Rehearsal The repeating of an item to oneself and the means by which information is stored in the short-term memory (STM). Theory suggests that rehearsal is necessary for remembering and storage in the long-term memory (LTM).

Reinforcement The process of affecting the frequency with which a behavior is emitted. A reinforcer can reward and thus increase the behavior or punish and thus decrease its frequency. Reinforcers can also be primary, satisfying basic needs such as hunger or thirst, or secondary, satisfying learned and indirect values, such as money.

Reliability Consistency of measurement. A test is reliable if it repeatedly gives the same results. A person should get nearly the same score if the test is taken on two different occasions.

REM (Rapid-Eye Movement) Type of sleep in which the eyes are rapidly moving around; dreaming occurs in REM sleep.

Repression A defense mechanism in which a person forgets or pushes into the unconscious something that arouses anxiety. *See* Defense Mechanism; Anxiety.

Reticular Formation A system of nerve fibers leading from the spinal column to the cerebral cortex that functions to arouse, alert, and make an organism sensitive to changes in the environment. *See* Cerebral Cortex.

Retina The inside coating of the eye, containing two kinds of cells that react to light: the rods that are sensitive only to dim light and the cones that are sensitive to color and form in brighter light. There are three kinds of cones, each responsive to particular colors in the visible spectrum (range of colors).

Risky Shift Research suggests that decisions made by groups will involve considerably more risk than individuals in the group would be willing to take. This shift in group decision depends heavily on cultural values. *See* Cautious Shift.

Rod Part of the retina involved in seeing in dim light. *See* Retina.

RNA (Ribonucleic Acid) A chemical substance that occurs in chromosomes and that functions in genetic coding. During task-learning, RNA changes occur in the brain.

Role Playing Adopting the role of another person and experiencing the world in a way one is not accustomed to.

Role Taking The ability to imagine oneself in another's place or to understand the consequences of one's actions for another person.

Schachter-Singer Theory of Emotion Theory of emotion that states that we interpret our arousal according to our environment and label our emotions accordingly.

Schizoid Personality Personality disorder characterized by having great trouble developing social relationships.

Schizophrenia The most common and serious form of psychosis in which there exists an imbalance between emotional reactions and the thoughts associated with these feelings. It may be a disorder of the process of thinking. *See* Psychosis.

Scientific Method The process used by psychologists to determine principles of behavior that exist independently of individual experience and that are untouched by unconscious bias. It is based on a prearranged agreement that criteria, external to the individual and communicable to others, must be established for each set of observations referred to as fact.

Secondary Reinforcement Reinforcement that is only effective after it has been associated with a primary reinforcer.

Self-Actualization A term used by humanistic psychologists to describe what they see as a basic human motivation: the development of all aspects of an individual into productive harmony.

Self-Esteem A person's evaluation of oneself. If someone has confidence and satisfaction in oneself, self-esteem is considered high.

Self-Fulfilling Prophecy A preconceived expectation or belief about a situation that evokes behavior resulting in a situation consistent with the preconception.

Senses An organism's physical means of receiving and detecting physical changes in the environment. Sensing is analyzed in terms of reception of the physical stimulus by specialized nerve cells in the sense organs, transduction or converting the stimulus' energy into nerve impulses that the brain can interpret, and transmission of those nerve impulses from the sense organ to the part of the brain that can interpret the information they convey.

Sensitivity Training Aims at helping people to function more effectively in their jobs by increasing their awareness of their own and others' feelings and exchanging "feedback" about styles of interacting. Sensitivity groups are unlike therapy groups in that they are meant to enrich the participants' lives. Participants are not considered patients or ill. Also called T-groups.

Sensorimotor Stage According to Piaget, the stage of development beginning at birth during which perceptions are tied to objects that the child manipulates. Gradually the child learns that objects have permanence even if they are out of sight or touch.

Sensory Adaptation Tendency of the sense organs to adjust to continuous, unchanging stimulation by reducing their functioning; a stimulus that once caused sensation no longer does.

Sensory Deprivation The blocking out of all outside stimulation for a period of time. As studied experimentally, it can produce hallucinations, psychological disturbances, and temporary disorders of the nervous system of the subject.

Sex Role The attitudes, activities, and expectations considered specific to being male or female, determined by both biological and cultural factors.

Shaping A technique of behavior shaping in which behavior is acquired through the reinforcement of successive approximations of the desired behavior.

Sleep A periodic state of consciousness marked by four brain-wave patterns. Dreams occur during REM sleep. Sleep is a basic need without which one may suffer physical or psychological distress. *See* Brain Waves; Dreams.

Sleeper Effect The delayed impact of persuasive information. People tend to forget the context in which they first heard the information, but they eventually remember the content of the message sufficiently to feel its impact.

Social Comparison Theory proposed by Festinger that states that we have a tendency to compare our behavior to others to ensure that we are conforming.

Social Facilitation Phenomenon in which the presence of others increases dominant behavior patterns in an individual; Zajonc's theory of social facilitation states that the presence of others enhances the emission of the dominant response of the individual.

Social Influence The process by which people form and change the attitudes, opinions, and behavior of others.

Social Learning Learning acquired through observation and imitation of others.

Social Psychology The study of individuals as affected by others and of the interaction of individuals in groups.

Socialization A process by which a child learns the various patterns of behavior expected and accepted by society. Parents are the chief agents of a child's socialization. Many factors have a bearing on the socialization process, such as the child's sex, religion, social class, and parental attitudes.

Sociobiology The study of the genetic basis of social behavior.

Sociophobias Excessive irrational fears and embarrassment when interacting with other people.

Somatic Nervous System The part of the peripheral nervous system that carries messages from the sense organs and relays information that directs the voluntary movements of the skeletal muscles.

Somatoform Disorders Disorders characterized by physical symptoms for which there are no obvious physical causes.

Somesthetic Senses Skin senses; includes pressure, pain, cold, and warmth.

Species-Typical Behavior Behavior patterns common to members of a species. Ethologists state that each species inherits some patterns of behavior (e.g., birdsongs).

Stanford-Binet Intelligence Scale Tests that measure intelligence from two years of age through adult level. The tests determine one's intelligence quotient by establishing one's chronological and mental ages. *See* Intelligence Quotient.

State-Dependent Learning Situation in which what is learned in one state can only be remembered when the person is in that state.

Statistically Significant In inferential statistics, a finding that the independent variable did influence greatly the outcome of the experimental and control group.

Stereotype The assignment of characteristics to a person mainly on the basis of the group, class, or category to which he or she belongs. The tendency to categorize and generalize is a basic human way of organizing information. Stereotyping, however, can reinforce misinformation and prejudice. *See* Prejudice.

Stimulus A unit of the environment that causes a response in an individual; more specifically, a physical or chemical agent acting on an appropriate sense receptor.

Stimulus Discrimination Limiting responses to relevant stimuli.

Stimulus Generalization Responses to stimuli similar to the stimulus that had caused the response.

Stress Pressure that puts unusual demands on an organism. Stress may be caused by physical conditions but eventually will involve both. Stimuli that cause stress are called stressors, and an organism's response is the stress reaction. A three-stage general adaptation syndrome is hypothesized involving both emotional and physical changes. *See* General Adaptation Syndrome.

Structuralism An early school of psychology that stressed the importance of conscious experience as the subject matter of psychology and maintained that experience should be analyzed into its component parts by use of introspection. *See* Introspection.

Sublimation Defense mechanism in which a person redirects his socially undesirable urges into socially acceptable behavior.

Subliminal Stimuli Stimuli that do not receive conscious attention because they are below sensory thresholds. They may influence behavior, but research is not conclusive on this matter.

Substance-Induced Organic Mental Disorders Organic mental disorders caused by exposure to harmful environmental substances.

Suggestibility The extent to which a person responds to persuasion. Hypnotic susceptibility refers to the degree of suggestibility observed after an attempt to induce hypnosis has been made. *See* Persuasion; Hypnosis.

Superego According to Freud, the superego corresponds roughly to conscience. The superego places restrictions on both ego and id and represents the internalized restrictions and ideals that the child learns from parents and culture. *See* Conscience; Ego; Id.

Sympathetic Nervous System The branch of the autonomic nervous system that is more active in emergencies; it causes a general arousal, increasing breathing, heart rate, and blood pressure.

Synapse A "gap" where individual nerve cells (neurons) come together and across which chemical information is passed.

Syndrome A group of symptoms that occur together and mark a particular abnormal pattern.

Systematic Desensitization A technique used in behavior therapy to eliminate a phobia. The symptoms of the phobia are seen as conditioned responses of fear, and the procedure attempts to decondition the fearful response until the patient gradually is able to face the feared situation. *See* Phobia.

TAT (Thematic Apperception Test) Personality and motivation test that requires the subject to devise stories about pictures.

Taxis An orienting movement in response to particular stimuli in the environment. A frog, for example, always turns so its snout points directly at its prey before it flicks its tongue. *See* Orienting Response.

Theory A very general statement that is more useful in generating hypotheses than in generating research. *See* Hypothesis.

Therapeutic Community The organization of a hospital setting so that patients have to take responsibility for helping one another in an attempt to prevent patients from getting worse by being in the hospital.

Token Economy A system for organizing a treatment setting according to behavioristic principles. Patients are encouraged to take greater responsibility for their adjustment by receiving tokens for acceptable behavior and fines for unacceptable behavior. The theory of token economy grew out of operant conditioning techniques. *See* Operant Conditioning.

Traits Distinctive and stable attributes that can be found in all people.

Tranquilizers Psychoactive drugs that reduce anxiety. *See* Psychoactive Drug.

Trial and Error Learning Trying various behaviors in a situation until the solution is hit upon; past experiences lead us to try different responses until we are successful.

Unconditioned Response (UR) An automatic reaction elicited by a stimulus.

Unconditioned Stimulus (US) Any stimulus that elicits an automatic or reflexive reaction in an individual; it does not have to be learned in the present situation.

Unconscious In Freudian terminology, a concept (not a place) of the mind. The unconscious encompasses certain inborn impulses that never rise into consciousness (awareness) as well as memories and wishes that have been repressed. The chief aim of psychoanalytic therapy is to free repressed material from the unconscious in order to make it susceptible to conscious thought and direction. Behaviorists describe the unconscious as an inability to verbalize. *See* Repression.

Undifferentiated Schizophrenia Type of schizophrenia that does not fit into any particular category, or fits into more than one category.

Validity The extent to which a test actually measures what it is designed to measure.

Variability In statistics, measures of variability communicate how spread out the scores are; the tendency to vary the response to a stimulus, particularly if the response fails to help in adaptation.

Variable Any property of a person, object, or event that can change or take on more than one mathematical value.

Weber's Law States that the difference threshold depends on the ratio of the intensity of one stimulus to another rather than an absolute difference.

Wechsler Adult Intelligence Scale (WAIS) An individually administered test designed to measure adults' intelligence, devised by David Wechsler. The WAIS consists of eleven subtests, of which six measure verbal and five measure performance aspects of intelligence. *See* Wechsler Intelligence Scale for Children.

Wechsler Intelligence Scale for Children (WISC) Similar to the Wechsler Adult Intelligence Scale, except that it is designed for people under fifteen. Wechsler tests can determine strong and weak areas of overall intelligence. *See* Wechsler Adult Intelligence Scale (WAIS).

Whorfian Hypothesis The linguistic relativity hypothesis of Benjamin Whorf; states that language influences thought.

Withdrawal Social or emotional detachment; the removal of oneself from a painful or frustrating situation.

Yerkes-Dodson Law Prediction that the optimum motivation level decreases as the difficulty level of a task increases.

Source for the Glossary:

The majority of terms in this glossary are reprinted from *The Study of Psychology,* Joseph Rubinstein. © by The Dushkin Publishing Group, Inc., Guilford, CT 06437.

The remaining terms were developed by the Annual Editions staff.

Credits/ Acknowledgments

Cover design by Charles Vitelli

1. The Science of Psychology
Facing overview—Photo by Harvard University Press.

2. Biological Bases of Behavior
Facing overview—WHO photo. 31—© 1994 by Bob Sacha. 34—Photo courtesy of E. Fuller Torrey, M.D. and Daniel R. Weinberger, M.D., National Institute of Mental Health Neuroscience Center, Washington, DC. 35—Photo courtesy of Nick Kelsh. 36—Photo by the American Philosophical Society. 43—Illustration by Carol Donner. 45—Illustration by Tomo Narashima. 53—Patricia J. Wynne; courtesy of Clement Fox, Wayne State University. © Williams & Wilkins Company.

3. Perceptual Processes
Facing overview—Photo by EPA-Documerica. 74—Illustration by John Karapelou. © 1993 by the Walt Disney Company.

4. Learning and Remembering
Facing overview—United Nations photo by O. Monsen. 89—United Nations photo by John Isaac. 93-94, 96-97—Photos by Ross Cheit.

5. Cognitive Processes
Facing overview—Photo by The Dushkin Publishing Group, Inc. 104-105—Photos by Jonathan D. Cohen, Carnegie Mellon University. 106-108—Photos by Marcus E. Raichle. 109—Illustration by Guilbert Gates. 110—Photo courtesy of Rodolfo R. Llinas, New York University Medical Center.

6. Emotion and Motivation
Facing overview—United Nations photo by John Isaac. 127—Models by Central Casting. 130—Drawings by Riviere from *The Expression of Emotions in Man and Animals* by Charles Darwin.

7. Development
Facing overview—Photo courtesy of Louis P. Raucci Jr.

8. Personality Processes
Facing overview—Photo by Digital Stock.

9. Social Processes
Facing overview—Dushkin Publishing Group, Inc., photo by Pamela Carley. 203-204—Graphics by Jared Schneidman Design.

10. Psychological Disorders
Facing overview—Photo by Digital Stock. 228—Photo by Max Aquilera-Hellweg. © 1992 by the Walt Disney Company. 230—Illustration by John Karapelou. © 1992 by the Walt Disney Company.

11. Psychological Treatments
Facing overview—United Nations photo by G. Palmer.

ANNUAL EDITIONS ARTICLE REVIEW FORM

■ NAME: _____ DATE: _____

■ TITLE AND NUMBER OF ARTICLE: _____

■ BRIEFLY STATE THE MAIN IDEA OF THIS ARTICLE: _____

_____

_____

_____

_____

■ LIST THREE IMPORTANT FACTS THAT THE AUTHOR USES TO SUPPORT THE MAIN IDEA:

_____

_____

_____

_____

_____

■ WHAT INFORMATION OR IDEAS DISCUSSED IN THIS ARTICLE ARE ALSO DISCUSSED IN YOUR TEXTBOOK OR OTHER READING YOU HAVE DONE? LIST THE TEXTBOOK CHAPTERS AND PAGE NUMBERS:

_____

_____

_____

_____

_____

_____

■ LIST ANY EXAMPLES OF BIAS OR FAULTY REASONING THAT YOU FOUND IN THE ARTICLE:

_____

_____

_____

_____

■ LIST ANY NEW TERMS/CONCEPTS THAT WERE DISCUSSED IN THE ARTICLE AND WRITE A SHORT DEFINITION:

_____

_____

_____

_____

*Your instructor may require you to use this Annual Editions Article Review Form in any number of ways: for articles that are assigned, for extra credit, as a tool to assist in developing assigned papers, or simply for your own reference. Even if it is not required, we encourage you to photocopy and use this page; you'll find that reflecting on the articles will greatly enhance the information from your text.

We Want Your Advice

ANNUAL EDITIONS:
PSYCHOLOGY 95/96
Article Rating Form

Here is an opportunity for you to have direct input into the next revision of this volume. We would like you to rate each of the 47 articles listed below, using the following scale:

1. **Excellent: should definitely be retained**
2. **Above average: should probably be retained**
3. **Below average: should probably be deleted**
4. **Poor: should definitely be deleted**

Your ratings will play a vital part in the next revision. So please mail this prepaid form to us just as soon as you complete it.
Thanks for your help!

Annual Editions revisions depend on two major opinion sources: one is our Advisory Board, listed in the front of this volume, which works with us in scanning the thousands of articles published in the public press each year; the other is you—the person actually using the book. Please help us and the users of the next edition by completing the prepaid article rating form on this page and returning it to us. Thank you.

Rating	Article	Rating	Article
	1. Scientific and Professional Psychology		27. How Kids Benefit from Child Care
	2. Has Psychology a Future?		28. Child Injury and Abuse-Neglect: Common Etiologies, Challenges, and Courses Toward Prevention
	3. Pollsters Enlist Psychologists in Quest for Unbiased Results		29. Why Schools Must Tell Girls: 'You're Smart, You Can Do It'
	4. Nature or Nurture? Old Chestnut, New Thoughts		30. Teaching Young Children to Resist Bias: What Parents Can Do
	5. Born Gay?		31. Current Perspectives on Dual-Career Families
	6. Eugenics Revisited		
	7. The Human Mind: Touching the Intangible		32. Midlife Myths
	8. Mind and Brain		33. The Assault on Freud
	9. The Vision Thing: Mainly in the Brain		34. Piecing Together Personality
	10. Good Vibrations		35. On the Power of Positive Thinking: The Benefits of Being Optimistic
	11. The Sniff of Legend		
	12. Touching the Phantom		36. Is Hostility Killing You?
	13. Does ESP Exist?		37. The Dynamics of Social Dilemmas
	14. Measured Learning		38. Media, Violence, Youth, and Society
	15. How Kids Learn		39. The Lessons of Love
	16. Memories Lost and Found		40. Is Mental Illness a Myth?
	17. A Child's Theory of Mind		41. Divided Selves
	18. Visualizing the Mind		42. Defeating Depression
	19. Rethinking the Mind		43. Patterns of Abuse
	20. The Return of Phineas Gage: Clues about the Brain from the Skull of a Famous Patient		44. The Immune System vs. Stress
			45. What You Can Change and What You Cannot Change
	21. Silence, Signs, and Wonder		
	22. Where Emotions Come From		46. Outsmarting Stress
	23. A Doubtful Device		47. Critical Life Events and the Onset of Illness
	24. How to Master Your Moods		
	25. Chemistry and Craving		
	26. How Competitive Are You?		

(Continued on next page)

ABOUT YOU

Name_____ Date_____

Are you a teacher? ☐ Or student? ☐

Your School Name _____

Department _____

Address _____

City_____ State _____ Zip _____

School Telephone # _____

YOUR COMMENTS ARE IMPORTANT TO US!

Please fill in the following information:

For which course did you use this book? _____

Did you use a text with this Annual Edition? ☐ yes ☐ no

The title of the text? _____

What are your general reactions to the Annual Editions concept?

Have you read any particular articles recently that you think should be included in the next edition?

Are there any articles you feel should be replaced in the next edition? Why?

Are there other areas that you feel would utilize an Annual Edition?

May we contact you for editorial input?

May we quote you from above?

ANNUAL EDITIONS: PSYCHOLOGY 95/96

BUSINESS REPLY MAIL

First Class   Permit No. 84   Guilford, CT

Postage will be paid by addressee

D **The Dushkin Publishing Group, Inc.**
Sluice Dock
DPG **Guilford, Connecticut 06437**

No Postage
Necessary
if Mailed
in the
United States